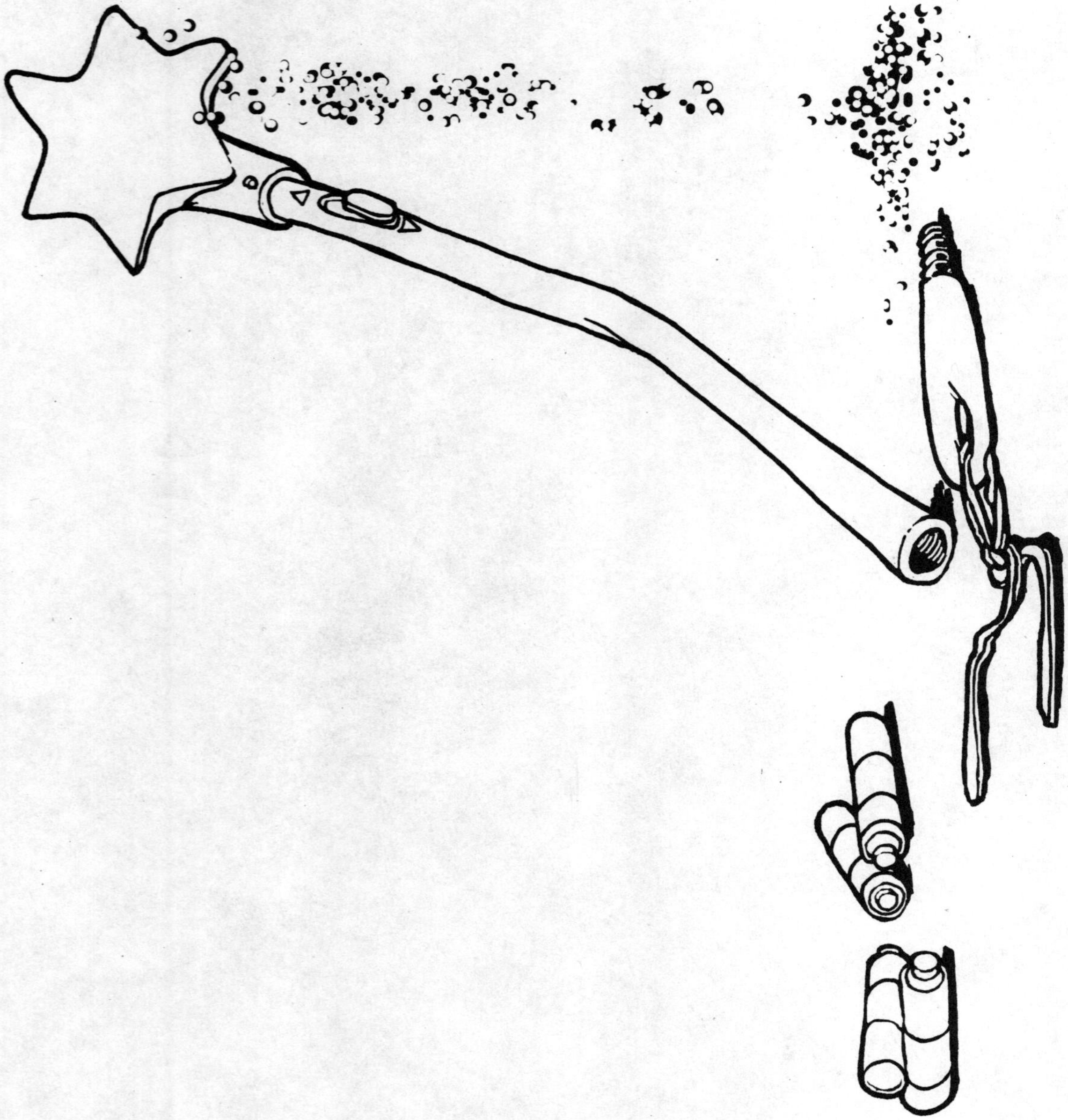

THERE IS NO SEX FAIRY

TO PROTECT OUR CHILDREN FROM BECOMING SEXUAL ABUSERS

featuring:
The Ten Commandments of Raising Sexually Respectful Children

By Jan Hindman
Illustrated by Tom Novak

ISBN 0-9611034-7-7

Library of Congress Control Number: 2006908751

Published 2006 by: AlexAndria Associates
PO Box 816
Lincoln City, OR 97367

www.janhindman.com

Printed in the United States of America, 2006

First Edition

Designed and Illustrated by Tom Novak, Novak Studios, Baker City, Oregon

Layout Consultant & Computer Guru: Kevin Bradford, Haines, Oregon

Specific information in each chapter's vignette is fictional although often representing real life situations. Case examples throughout this publication however, relate to actual professional experiences of the author although names, dates, times and other exact information has been changed to protect the privacy of those involved.

DEDICATION

To Katie, her daughters, and the P. Fairy

TABLE OF CONTENTS

THE JOURNEY—
KATIE, THE *P* FAIRY, AND ME

KATIE

In 1983, Katie died. In a drunken stupor driving at 100 miles per hour, she challenged the icy, busy, six-lane road. Losing the contest, she won her mission, which was ending her life with *consistency*. Her self-abusive lifestyle mirrored the sexual abuse she suffered from her father throughout childhood and it ended just the same. In adolescence, a pattern of alcohol and drugs, sexual promiscuity and unwanted pregnancies localized her pain in a *consistency of chaos*. Through self-destruction, Katie avoided feeling the psychological pain of family betrayal from a childhood robbed and lost. But as time ticked on, and as the unmentionable trauma of sexual abuse tiptoed viciously on her shoulder, demanding attention, Katie's need to control her pain through self-abuse intensified, thus her screaming and screeching death.

But the tragedy of Katie's destruction did not end with her automobile crash. With cruel reality, and long after ambulances, funerals and family tears, the tragedy of unresolved sexual abuse smoldered, as did the fires from her raging and spectacular demise. Tragically, with Katie's death, her two orphaned baby girls, who had never known their fathers, were now systematically returned to Katie's parents, and *Grandpa*, Katie's childhood abuser. The calamity unfolded as the deadly cycle of generational secrecy treaded forward, allowing Katie's baby girls no option but to be placed with the person who indirectly caused their mother's death.

AND ME

Katie's death and the fate that awaited her innocent daughters tearfully forced me back to a previous decade. She was the first sexual victim I had encountered in my career, dating back to her chronological adolescence in 1973 and my adolescence as a newly graduated *professional*—or so I thought. Naïve, enthusiastic, and with a master's degree that almost said I could cure the world of emotionally disturbed adolescents, I listened intently to the principal of the large inner-city high school where I had just been hired, fresh out of my graduate program.

"You will have a very special class to teach," he explained and clarified.

Continuing the dialogue, I asked, "How will it be special?"

A special waiting list to get in your class floated quietly in the air before the content of this special list was explained by the pontificating administrator.

"Once a student has three expulsions or six unexcused absences, or nine unexcused tardies, they will be placed on the special waiting list for your class," was his answer. As the reality of that answer hovered, he went on.

"But the most special thing about your special class is that you won't have hallway duty or cafeteria duty like the other teachers," he furthered, and when I weakly inquired about how I could avoid those pesky tasks dreaded by most of the faculty, he continued:

"You are going to be off-campus" was his sheepish reply, hoping for my naïve excitement to his proposal. And off-campus it was, about thirty blocks from the main high school in an old bus garage converted into a classroom—still smelling of diesel, but nonetheless with the concrete floor painted a very attractive Army green. The principal also pointed out that in this not-so-luxurious facility there were no hallways and there was no cafeteria—thus no unsavory, dreaded faculty duties. At least, I thought.

Was there anything else that was special about my job? I wearily inquired of my new, but intended-on-being-separated boss, and his answer was affirmative. My job description was not complicated, he explained, having only two primary duties. With pen in hand, I prepared to take notes on those two obligations that pertained to my life-long goal of single-handedly changing the world for troubled teenagers.

"Just keep the little *peckers* in school," was the first sentence I wrote on my tablet, noting in the margin to search my college files for the course I must have taken on *pecker* education strategies. Further explanation from the principal included something about basic school support money lost to the district when the *peckers* didn't attend. And he also mentioned that allowing them (the *peckers*) to smoke in class would help the financial portion of the *peckers-in-attendance* project, thus the coffee cans he proudly presented while explaining that they could be used for ashtrays. *Why*, the entire faculty had helped with the coffee can collection as a contribution to the cause, he eagerly reminded me.

As he ventured toward the door of the soon-to-be-smelling-of-smoke facility, he reminded me that my job only had one other requirement beyond keeping the *peckers* in attendance. I listened intently to the second item in my non-complicated job description, hearing him pronounce:

"Just make sure they pass all competency-based, state required tests at the end of the school year, because our school support funding is also based on test scores."

There it was; my job, with only two requirements. All I had to do was just make sure they attended every day, and that they (the *peckers)* passed all the magic tests at the end of the school year. Any two-point job description seemed manageable to me, but I still didn't understand about the *peckers* and the money business. In my recently completed graduate program, I never studied anything about funding, but in the weeks ahead I would become educated about the history of the *pecker problem* and why a special off-campus program was needed to keep them in school, and keep them smart enough to pass all the government tests at the end.

Eventually, I learned that the *peckers* were the children labeled by the educators as *anti-social, bothersome, delinquent*, or *misfit,* usually subject to rejection, suspension and expulsion. Those labels came after lots of rude gossip in the faculty lounge from folks who were fed up with these troublesome teens. These kiddos were just a problem—thus the term, *peckers.* In the past, it had been easy for the faculty and administration to just get rid of the pesky kids and their *pecker* problems, but timing was everything in the business of big bucks from the government.

I learned that my two-part job description existed because the old ways of relating to the *peckers* was about to end. In the good old days, all students (even the *peckers)* were tallied on the school attendance books at the beginning of the year or semester, and those numbers were used to determine basic school support money allotted to the school district from the government. So after the *bean counters* for the district determined the total number of students, the checks from the government would roll in. And with the troubling nature of the *pecker* kids, not much mattered to the school district after they were counted and paid for by the government's big bucks. In the past, suspensions, expulsions, and dropouts were the nicely rationalized plan for the *pecker* problem once the bean counters for the school district had them on the tally books.

But then things began to change. In the 1970s, the federal government, under pressure from folks who cared about kiddos, revisited the constitutional right of education *for all children*. Eventually the Feds said *yes,* it is true that many children have special needs, such as being deaf or needing a wheelchair, and *yes,* they understood it would be quite a burden for school districts to teach those kiddos who had limitations. But *no,* the government opined, regardless of what handicap children may have, they were all guaranteed an education. And *yes,* the heavy-hitter government folks told school districts all over the country that they would financially help with this task, but the bean-counting process about the tally business was about to change. And change it did.

The government has always excelled at bean counting and when this problem of education for *all children* caused a fuss, the bean-counting business tightened up everywhere. The school bean counters were told by the Feds that discarding the *peckers* just because they had problems was no longer an option, but they also had more bad news. From one group of bean counters to another, the government explained that the school district couldn't just count all those special need kids once at the beginning of the year, semester or quarter, in order to earn the big beans for the big problem kids—*peckers*, actually. Shocking as it was, the Feds said there would be no beans counted for the troubled kids unless they were actually in school, being educated, every day and, in fact, *in every class of every day*. Those Fed checks of basic school support money would be based on daily or hourly attendance, which explained half of my job description and the allowance for smoking-in-class. Just *keep the little peckers in school*, I remembered him saying, and now I understood it was all about the beans.

I also learned that in order to get the big bucks from the Feds, the school folks needed titles and labels for these troublesome kiddos. Ideas were floated around such as *handicapped, special needs kids*, or *challenged*. But for the *peckers*, without wheelchairs or missing limbs, it was difficult to find just the right terms. Finally, the school bean counters came up with the fancy handle of *Emotionally Disturbed*. The title seemed magnificent and quite prestigious, clearing the way for the big bucks from the government but doing nothing to change the way the educator folks felt about teaching the *peckers*. That job would be left to a wide-eyed, naive teacher with only two items on her new job description in a far away bus garage-turned-teaching-facility. The *peckers* had to attend, they had to pass the competency-based tests at the end of the year, and they had to be managed by someone who understood all the bean-counting business. But there was more.

There were other details about the *peckers* in the program that also became clear to me within a very short period of time. First, there were forty-five of them, ranging in age from 14 to 21, giving a new meaning to lunch hour complications when one of the students can buy beer for the rest of them. The *peckers* were all considered failures in school, yet I quickly learned their intelligence level often exceeded mine and the rest of the staff, also confined to the not-so-luxurious, off-campus *pecker* program. These kiddos were victims of abuse, neglected, abandoned, throwaway children who, as angry adolescents, found it difficult to garner sympathy from anyone. The majority of them had hair-trigger tempers prone to explosion, or they seemed psychologically beaten into submission, silenced by sadness. There was nothing they wouldn't try, at least once, and as youth have it—they believed themselves immortal in the long run and bulletproof in the moment. But never mind all of that, my boss non-verbally suggested. Now they had a tidy label of *Emotionally Disturbed*. Yet in reality, they were simply *emotionally disturbing* to everyone on the main campus from where they had been conveniently exiled. And most importantly, all forty-five of them deserved more dignity than being called *peckers*.

Katie was there at the beginning, stunningly beautiful, a fire in her eyes and enough sexual intensity in her soul to take on the entire varsity football team—from the main campus where the off-campus *peckers* were not allowed. Never mind that restriction, I figured, Katie could eventually find a way.

She was highly intelligent, but when I began teaching her, I became aware she had never earned a single high school credit, even though she was fifteen and had been in high school (counted as a *pecker*) for several years. Katie had boyfriends—lots of them, lots of times—changing them about as often as she changed her socks. The same was true for her girlfriends that she organized into a revolving door. First, demonstratively taking custody of them with great passion, then quickly discarding them, moving to a new one, lest she have any reason for closeness or trust.

After the first few weeks, I noticed Katie was often tardy for school. Having my own flair for bean counting, I worried that too many tardies reported back to the district office could result in her suspension and eventual expulsion. But that wasn't all. Katie's tardy reports to the school bean counters also suggested that I wasn't doing so well in the *pecker* attendance obligation so I needed to take action. One morning when Katie stormed into class 30 minutes late, I gently inquired about her tardiness, using the advanced communication skills I learned in graduate school. With a cigarette in her mouth and vengeance in her heart, she stung,

"If your father screwed you every morning, you might be late too!"

There it was, hanging in the air—*sexual abuse of a child.* And even though later I would find out that 90 percent of the *peckers* suffered from sexual abuse, never once had I heard that term in my entire graduate program—the same program designed to prepare me to work with emotionally disturbed adolescents.

But at that moment, Katie was the issue. Off I went to the principal, asking for *special* consideration regarding her tardies and impending suspension. After all, he had assured me, I had a *special* job with *special* children. I pleaded. He purported:

"Our absentee protocol indicates that three unexcused tardies equals last year's suspension rate to the third power, minus the student's grade point average of the last quarter added to the total of absences for the preceding year..."

As he mumbled on, I realized that the importance of his pontificated protocol paled in comparison to Katie's rage at the ritual of her morning rapes.

"And if we don't stand for our protocol, what do we stand for?" was his final question, bringing me back to the reality of his office and the futility of Katie's situation. And what we stood for, I didn't really know, but I knew in spite of his disregard, I would stand for Katie.

And stand for her, I did. No matter what, I said to myself, someone would stand for this child! But over the weeks, month and years, that promise was extremely difficult with her *emotionally disturbing* efforts at self-destruction. Katie thrived on chaos—not because she was bad, but because the chaos kept her from feeling the pain of sexual abuse. Katie could be persuaded by wagering teenagers to fight another girl in the parking lot if Hostess Twinkies were the prize and if she had forgotten her lunch. Torn clothing, bloody noses, screams of profanity and tangled/ripped underwear just didn't matter to her. In other instances of consistent chaos, Katie would offer oral sex to boys in exchange for a ride home from school—if it rained. And in Portland, Oregon, it rained a lot. In *standing for* Katie, I took her to pregnancy tests, venereal disease tests, and tried to help her pass her academic tests at the end of the year. I stood for her through all of this, picking up the pieces, but only ever so carefully.

I quickly learned that Katie, in her self-destructive lifestyle, required distances from anyone or anything where trust was on the menu. Any effort on my part to show her support or caring on a personal level, would suffer the calamity of her running away from home, temporarily dropping out of school or creatively causing a turmoil that in a cloud of chaos destroyed any hope for something positive. And then, when she was sure she had ruined everything, she would feel safe enough to tiptoe back. I really didn't know how to help her, but in my mind I was steadfast in just being there to *pick up the pieces* and, of course, *stand for her*, whatever that meant. As time went on, the pieces she threw to be picked up were quite disturbing, just like her fancy diagnosis.

The years treaded on and after three of them, Katie graduated from high school. Marching into the huge auditorium in the middle of the opening prayer, she handed me her first baby girl. Having a husband or a designated father for this two-month-old child would have been to Katie about as sensible as being on time for her graduation. She had done it (graduate, that is), and she was working very hard to pretend she wasn't proud. As I held her infant, I wondered if the child's *Grandpa*, Katie's sexual abuser, was in the audience watching her defiantly flaunt across the stage. I also pondered if Katie trusted anyone except her teacher to hold this little one. I will always ponder that question because, of course, to ask Katie something so personal would have been a disaster.

With her academic success affirmed by a diploma she thought she would never obtain, Katie faded away from my constant watch, although she would occasionally visit the *pecker* program, proudly touting a new tattoo, a new hair color, a new boyfriend, or the fact the she was about to have a new baby. And she did, and again the baby didn't—have a father that is, at least not one that was acknowledged. After Katie's second daughter was born and after I left the *pecker* program, she kept in touch, but even as a mother of two she needed to keep moving, keep destroying, and keep things off-balance lest she be forced in the quiet and calm to feel the pain of her sexual abuse. In our infrequent contacts, I always noticed that she seemed to put her daughters between us, suggesting I needed to care for her kiddos because, of course, she needed nothing from me.

Then in 1983, hearing of her death and of the plight of her baby girls, I was crushed beyond repair. Questions were profound. *What could I have done differently to protect Katie and her future daughters? What could any of us have done to prevent the tragedy of not only Katie's abuse and death, but what cruelly awaited her daughters with Grandpa? How could I have failed so significantly, smugly thinking that for years I stood for her when my standing for her was really nothing of value? Could I ever forgive myself for not doing something else to save her?*

I looked in the mirror and proceeded with the painful process of introspection, wondering whether or not to stop working in this futile field and instead, sell shoes for a living.

With tears in my eyes and Katie in my heart, I had to choose. I could give up in despair and guilt, or I could try to do something to end the deadly cycle her daughters would face. Shoe selling seemed particularly repulsive, so I ventured out to my deck and tried to write about my rage—toward what, I wasn't sure. I had furious fantasies of sending messages to Katie's daughters—screaming to *watch out for Grandpa.* I had visions of my wheelbarrow piled high with printed warnings, ceremoniously dumped in the front yard of Katie's childhood home. I imagined piles of brightly colored signs for the little girls, making a grand scene of remonstration even though neither child could read and one of them probably couldn't walk. *But never mind,* I said, as I made notes on my papers for planning a protest parade surrounding the block of the abuser's home, complete with a marching band and waving placards touting that Grandpa was being watched.

Then, as usual, my fantasies took a rude reality turn. I also imagined police cars, sirens and being taken away in handcuffs for disturbing the peace and littering. Then, with more reality setting in, I knew there was probably nothing a wheelbarrow full of scribbled pages, thrown hysterically on a browning lawn in February, could do to help a toddler and a preschooler living under the control of a powerful sex offender. My rage was grand but useless, and I pondered if there was another, perhaps more rational, way to channel my grief and guilt.

In all the clutter and mess of my papers, I noticed that even though the written ideas were couched in anger and pain, they were still pretty good. The positive message to children about sexual abuse was unmistakable in the tatters. It wasn't about the wheelbarrow dumping warning signs, but about trying to prevent sexual abuse *before it happened.* I began to think that perhaps I could contribute to Katie's daughters through a prevention approach that could help other vulnerable children and, of course, keep me out of jail.

So a book began to loom in my thoughts—not a novel, not a best seller, not a volume set, just something small and simple for vulnerable children and perhaps something to help me with my sorrow. And I couldn't extinguish the ever-so-slight hope that just somehow, someday, one single copy just might make its way to those little girls that Katie tried so desperately to love.

Writing *A Very Touching Book* in 1983 was easy, since I just used the terms and language from my ghostwriters, who were children in my therapy program. In the years after leaving the pecker program, many abused children taught me what was working and what was not working in understanding sexual abuse tragedies. But the illustrations for the book were much more complicated. Miraculously, I met an also-tender-*touched* man, Tom Novak, who created child-friendly and grownup-grumping illustrations for the book. His images were grand, capturing the precious nature of childhood just as I had hoped. Soon the book was finished and just a few copies were privately printed to heal my wounds of guilt, and to perhaps help a handful of children who might stumble onto a copy.

Expectations of book sales were low, but a quiet little contribution to the cause of helping a quiet little bunch of sexually abused children was not the result of *A Very Touching Book*. Soon the word was out—and to many, the word was not pretty. As sales soared, so did the volume of hate mail, primarily because the prevention approach of the book was positive and quite in conflict with the preferred *stranger danger* or the *evil-around-the-corner* focus touted by most. The book suggested children should be taught that their sexuality, and their right to make sexual decisions in the future was as important as their bicycles. *Positive indeed*, some of the cranky hate mail writers screamed with their bright purple faces and baskets of outrage. But I tried to listen to the fussing—that skill taught to me by another courageous child.

LISTEN LOUDER

Years before, a tattered four-year-old sat on my lap, smelling badly, hair rumpled with electricity, and her shirt turned inside out and backwards. She was a picture of neglect and abuse, just as her file history confirmed. I was choked with sadness as she explained a rather normal day in her abusive family. I searched my mind for something positive just to break the silence of sorrow. I asked, "Sweetie, what do you do best in your family?" hoping the question might bring her some bragging rights.

"I ***listen louder*** than anyone else in my whole family," she exuded with sunshine pride. And I thought to myself, what a life plan—to *listen louder* than anyone else. And so listening louder to the hate mail I tried to do.

First, I recognized the *doing the don't dance* was the preferred method for most parents concerning sexuality, and that resulted in *don't talk to strangers, don't have sex before marriage,* and most importantly, *don't ask me anything about anything pertaining to that area between your belly button and your knees.* For sure, there was nothing positive in these traditional efforts of sex education, *just don't do it*. But there was something else I noticed when I *listened louder* to the hate mail and fussing about the positive approach to *A Very Touching Book.*

DO AND DON'T DANCING

The opposition didn't come from parents who shied away from the *do dance* in other areas of education and protection of their children. It was from grumpy folks who actively taught their children: *do* become a Baptist, *do* tell the truth, *do* look both ways before crossing the streets, and *do* be nice to your sister even though she smells funny. These complaining parents seemed to control their children's education in every other area without waiting or withholding.

Remembering my little listening louder friend, I tried to determine the difference between the *don'ts* and the *do's* for these outraged parents and the conclusion was interesting, if not a bit delusional. The ranting was profuse. *Why tell children they have penises and vaginas?* with the subtle suggestion that maybe the kidlets didn't already know they had them. And further, *Why give children names of their body parts*? suggesting that the *poo-poos, pee-pees, pussies,* and *potties,* commonly used in most families, were more respectful and therefore would be easily protected from sexual abuse. It was absurd. And there was more.

KIDDO COCOONS?

The resistance was founded on a belief that unless a child accidentally stumbled onto *A Very Touching Book* or some other catastrophic event occurred, such as the son and a wayward friend finding Dad's raunchy magazines under the mattress, children were completely isolated and insulated from sexual information, living in a magical world of innocence. Childhood was a cocoon—safe and secure from sexual influence—these Moms and Dads hoped. The hate mail authors wanted no part of anything that interrupted their perceived status quo of sexual innocence for their ignorant children, which they believe existed.

The madness continued as these same folks anticipated (hoped) that their children would marry and perhaps provide them with grandchildren, which unfortunately has that pesky little requirement of sex. *Yes,* parents had plans that their children would someday be sexual and for sure they wanted the kiddos sexually respectful. But how that was to happen seemed incomprehensible and not part of any parenting plan. So with this foolishness and folly, all I could do was turn to magic, because it seemed these parents believed that somehow the kiddos would *magically* become sexually respectful people, without any guidance or teaching, perhaps with just a poof and a puff.

With that absurdity in mind, I began to imagine that maybe there was a Fairy Godmother of sex—that would magically take childhood innocence and turn it into adult sexual respect. It was preposterous to think of a fairy in charge of sex, but it was fun and it was fitting for the nonsense I noticed when I listened louder to the hate mail about *A Very Touching Book.* I remembered my own childhood Fairy Godmother who magically exchanged my bloody baby teeth for shiny quarters under my pillow, or who magically turned pumpkins into princess carriages in my storybooks. And for these parents to believe that somehow their children would have healthy sexual attitudes without any help from them was just as silly—and fairy-like. So I further fantasized that there must be a *Sex Fairy* that would ceremoniously zap the *previously sexually innocent* children in the crotch when they walked down the aisle to get married, solving the missing-in-action-sexual knowledge problem. It was madness, but it fit the magic and the myth of a Sex Fairy, and it was so much fun.

A FAIRY IN CHARGE OF SEX?

So the myth, the madness and my love of fairies and fun moved me to thinking about a new book, a companion to *A Very Touching Book,* that would travel hand-in-hand with parents down a humorous and playful path toward respectful sex education that would prevent sexual abuse. I began to think about a rip-roaring book, filled with laughter and absurdity known only to fairies and fantasies. I imagined a Sex Fairy, poofing and puffing parents along the way to examining the madness of their thinking and helping them understand that they must take control of their children's sex education in order to protect them from sexual abuse. So, a new book, with the title *THERE IS NO SEX FAIRY–To Protect Our Children From Sexual Abuse* began to materialize in my mind.

TOM AND PROMISES

With my fun fairy fantasies, I began to talk with Tom Novak about illustrating our magical friend—a fairy in charge of sex. We began to laugh, plot and plan as nothing seemed more outrageous that combining Tom Novak, a Sex Fairy, and purple-faced parents who needed to be rounded up in a reality rodeo for the task of protecting their children from sexual abuse. Great plans were made for this perfectly preposterous publication, with the Sex Fairy designated for outlandish and outrageous outfits, clashing orange (tangerine, actually) hair, a slightly bent fairy wand, and her must-have-purple-panty-hose-for-teaching-purple-faced-parents skills in talking to their children about sexual abuse.

It was grand, imagining this new publication to piggyback *A Very Touching Book.* Katie had been gone for about a year and there was still time to protect her daughters from sexual abuse, or so I thought. But *not so fast,* I should have said, because no matter how deep my commitment to writing a Sex Fairy book in Katie's honor, and no matter how much sorrow I felt for what I hadn't done for her, I was headed for more of the same.

MORE MIRRORS

Even though I wanted to mirror the outrageous way parents sexually educate children with an outrageous Sex Fairy, sadly and shamefully, over the next twenty years I became a mirror of society. My intentions were good when I promised Katie's daughters I would be different for them than I had been for their Mother—just like society promises to protect children. But in reality, I became seduced into the familiar and reactive *something had to be done*, as I trotted off on one project or another, always finding a fire to put out, a project to complete, a letter to write or a contract to secure. Katie had broken my heart but over the next two decades, I broke my promise to be proactive.

Whether it was studying sexual abuse trauma, conducting research, developing investigation protocols, attending conferences, writing books or providing national trainings, I always tried to justify why *something had to be done* with the problem in front of me, which was just a fancy way for me to procrastinate writing the proactive Sex Fairy book. As Katie's daughters got older, and as I began to tire of my own rationalizations, an impeding fear seemed to envelop me that I wouldn't be in time to help them.

SULLEN SEX FAIRY

On airplanes and in hotel lobbies, lecturing throughout the United States, I fantasized conversations with my mythical Sex Fairy friend, who gradually became sullen with waiting. I pretended that with the finesse only known by fairies, she would whisper, "*Write the book about me to help parents protect their children from sexual abuse.*" And in these magical conversations, I would relieve my guilt by explaining that I was too busy with too many honorable missions, hoping I could make myself feel better. Besides, I would lament in our magic conversations; I was still standing for Katie and her children, wasn't I?

As the years went on, the fear that was previously soft and subtle became stone-cold obvious as deep inside I knew things for Katie's daughters were, in reality, on the proverbial back burner. To handle the impending fear, I just instigated more flamboyant changes to appear, on the surface, that I was really doing something. I assumed in my fairy fantasy that my dreams of prevention for Katie's daughters would eventually come to fruition (perhaps, even fairy fruition) with just another project around the corner, just another diversion, contract, lecture or book. And as these diversions trudged on, Katie's daughters were heading for junior high.

FAKE FOCUS

In spite of the looming fear, the more I procrastinated, the more I promised myself that I wasn't. Hearing the whispers of my imaginary Sex Fairy chatting with Tom Novak about his creative ideas for her book spurred me on to a flamboyant, but fake focus, to make it seem as though I was really getting somewhere. I would announce to my staff that I needed to sequester myself in a fancy hotel without telephones or interruptions just to concentrate and finally write the book. It was grand, making the reservations and taking long trips to these faraway places to finally *get to it.* During these times, off by myself, I would work very, very, hard unloading boxes, filing resources, stacking articles, and making use of 3 by 5 note cards just as I had learned in eighth grade English class. And although the hotel maids were probably impressed with the volumes of information stacked carefully throughout my room, I knew, in reality, the grandiose piles of disconnected pieces of information only represented I was too afraid to truly organize the book, in fear it wouldn't be perfect and that after all, considering that Katie's daughters were heading for high school, maybe it was too late.

As the fear continued to strangle, I created more pomp and circumstance about my hollow efforts. I began to make slides of the book title *THERE IS NO SEX FAIRY–To Protect Our Children From Sexual Abuse* for my lectures, announcing to thousands, my promises for a publication protecting children from sexual abuse. There were times when television cameras caught the announcements of my grand Sex Fairy plans and lady talk show hosts, with long, red fingernails and perfectly coiffed hairdos, marveled at the clever idea of a Sex Fairy book to protect children from sexual abuse. I relished at the compliments and encouragement from those throughout the professional community who also said it was a great idea. And with the new slides, new announcements and new enthusiasm, came old, hardcore fear that in reality it wasn't getting done.

PRETEND PREPARATIONS

But that wasn't all to my pretend preparations. Computers and other machines allowed me to rationalize that maybe with electronic assistance I could really get going. *What Web site*, I asked, would be complete without the grand announcement of a new publication suggesting that soon I would single-handedly protect children from sexual abuse? Somehow I felt that if I just advertised the book enough or if I just promised the book enough, then I would be shamed into really getting the

Sex Fairy book finished. But I was only right about the shame part—because fear of not being proactive and again letting Katie down, froze me into failure.

But I continued with my pretending. I collected complicated research articles, I studied charts and graphs, and organized indecipherable tables for each chapter. Pertinent newspaper articles were ceremoniously clipped with enthusiasm. When things would slow down and the reality of what I wasn't really getting done for Katie's daughters would nag, I would whirl myself into a grandiose shopping spree, purchasing new file folders (much better than the previous seven sets), new 3 by 5 cards (better colors and coordinated now with the file folders) and, of course, a *smart* (smarter than the last four) carrying case for each of the vigorously prepared chapters, filled with bits and pieces of important *stuff,* but also reeking of fear. And the more I promised and pretended the book was moving along, the tighter the fear became, freezing me into silent submission.

POSTPONING PROCRASTINATION POTIONS

Miraculously (fairy-like perhaps), it all suddenly ended. One day, standing in a lecture hall far away from home, my eyes followed over a familiar slide I had used many times about my latest *something had to be done* project—juvenile sex offenders. But rather than just accepting the slide's cue and trudging forward with an explanation, a strange sensation prohibited my thoughts from moving along the predicted path, tackling the next lecture point. Although my words continued for the audience, my mind lingered at the on-screen message.

OUR AMERICAN SOCIETY—

Are We Raising a Generation of Sexual Thieves?

The words were familiar to me, but the interest in this old slide was not. *Our society raising sexual thieves* echoed loudly, lingering ever so pervasive in my mind, the words holding me captive. Minutes later, another old slide seemed to zap (fairy-like, perhaps) with additional new interest.

IF WE TEACH OUR CHILDREN NOT TO BE RAPED, ARE WE TEACHING THEM NOT TO BECOME RAPISTS?

My mind flashed at the revelation or the novel idea of *sex offender prevention.* I pondered it. The thought of preventing children from becoming sex offenders raced through my mind, but it wasn't the old, worn, *something has to be done feeling.* It felt different. The idea did not ignite that familiar urge to trot off in a swirl of energy, furiously writing a position paper or a letter to the editor, frantically calling the Governor with urgent pleas for action, or purchasing a new *something* for office reorganization to accommodate the new *something has to be done* project. I felt deeply pensive and I felt a strong urge for quiet introspection.

After the lecture, and departing for home, I thought of Katie and my honorable promise to her daughters who now probably had daughters of their own. In the airplane window I saw my reflection. I still stood for Katie, I still cared about her children, but twenty years of procrastination had passed. In those two decades I had become smarter about many aspects of the sexual abuse tragedy, but was I really wiser about the proactive prevention I promised her innocent little girls? What had the fear meant and what was the meaning of the procrastination?

My continued introspection confirmed that my postponing wasn't because of a lack of energy or drive. *Why,* I had accomplished many things, never afraid to tackle a challenge that eventually contributed to a rather chubby Curriculum Vitae. *Why*, I had lectured in every state, fearlessly accepting speaking engagements that would terrorize the weak-kneed. *Why*, I had conquered professional criticism that always seemed to follow my cutting edge (*or she's gone off the edge*) work. Why, I had endured legal/ethical challenges always submitted by those ever-familiar *pissy professional people.* But why didn't my no-fear abilities help me take on the task I promised to Katie's daughters? What made her project my frozen-in-fear nemesis?

There must be a reason the honorable commitment of writing Katie's book had taken a sabbatical, I decided. And there must be a reason that the message on those slides startled me so. The image of sex offender prevention was first curious, then followed by a strange feeling of resolve. I couldn't find where anyone was doing anything to stop sexual offending at the source—children who were raised to become sexual abusers!

For the first time in twenty years, I felt serenely purposeful and ready to write. And even before I crawled into bed, home at last, a new title for the long-awaited Sex Fairy book was fondly formulated—***THERE IS NO SEX FAIRY—To Protect Our Children From Becoming Sexual Abusers.*** There was no hesitation; there was no fear. I knew this was the book that needed to be written. After twenty years of procrastination, the real writing had begun.

MAGIC, NOT MADNESS

The next few weeks seemed magic, but tranquil. The purging began. Those charts, graphs and complicated research papers (that I didn't understand and screamed of the fear *I won't get it right)* were ceremoniously sentenced to the incinerator. The pastel 3 by 5 note cards that would have been so appreciated by my English teacher, and the color-coordinated files and labels so carefully categorized by hue and shade (lest the fear of disorganization set in) were gleefully scattered into disarray. And the hundreds of electronic tidbits and snippets of information on four different computers, so obsessively prepared with the fear I might forget an idea or thought, were dutifully introduced to the DELETE button. Because without the fear that had frozen me for so long, I finally accepted that the answer to protecting children from becoming sexually disrespectful was simply within me. I also knew that the most honorable thing to do for Katie was to protect children from becoming sexual abusers.

TWO COPIES

With all this resolve, however, I recognized that the novel idea of preventing children from becoming sexual abusers would be rudely rejected by a reluctant world. Understanding that if parents were already hesitant to talking to children about sex, I imagined Godzilla-sized resistance for talking to children about becoming sex offenders. What parent, I asked myself, would have the courage to buy a book, if that purchase suggested their child was at risk for becoming a sex offender?

But even with this stark reality, still there was no fear. And *yes*, I knew I would probably only sell two copies of my book—one to both of my sisters—but *no,* even that publishing disaster didn't seem frightening. In fact, I felt an old, familiar, internal strength replacing the fear that had disabled me for so long. Even though twenty years previous, I knew *A Very Touching Book* would cause a purple-pucker stir, I was not afraid and that courage seemed with me again, and like an old loving friend, I welcomed back my bravery. Finally, after twenty years of frozen fear, I was free. And with this new book and a new purpose imagined, the feeling was *really* right and I knew my two sisters would *really* appreciate their copies.

THE LADIES

Not only did I have a refreshed and invigorated attitude about my once-lost-now-found book, but my attraction to fairies and magic was also rekindled. I enjoyed contemplating that perhaps there had been some fairy-fussing that guided me through the past twenty years toward publication postponing. I imagined a *Fairy in Charge of Procrastination,* just as I had gleefully imagined a *Fairy in Charge of Sex.* And I delighted in imagining the two ladies (The Sex Fairy and the Procrastination Fairy) over tea and twinkles, fairy-fluttering and fussing about my situation.

Maybe the sullen Sex Fairy pouted and complained about all the years of weary waiting—about all my procrastinating and pretending that her book would be written. Maybe she fussed and fumed with her fairy sister, retrieving a Kleenex from her brassiere, sniffing sweetly, dabbing away tears of frustration. In this fantasy of the two fairies, I pondered that one was just like me, fluttering, flitting and flying around in circles of endless energy, while the other was patient, slow and sedate, with the purpose of postponing. I imagined the P. Fairy, never looking at her watch, checking her planner or glancing for a calendar (since those in the business of waiting never need to do those things), soothing her fairy sister about the wisdom of waiting. I imagined the P. Fairy, deliberately dawdling as she encouraged the Sex Fairy into understanding that sometimes waiting can be a good thing. And perhaps together, over tea and twinkles with all the fairy finesse possible, they joined their wands together for the honorable mission of protecting children from becoming sexual abusers.

AND FINALLY

My Dear Katie,

In the past twenty years I have remembered you, but in my remembering I became frightened. Katie, I am *so sorry* that I didn't know how to help you when you were a teenager and I know now that my *so sorry* was honorable—but disabling. In my misery, I became frozen with fear, unable to be proactive and work on prevention. Just as a mirror of society, I have been *picking up the pieces*—just like I did so long ago.

But now Katie, all that procrastination is over. Finally, I have told your story and I have written the book in your honor—even though you will share that dedication with the Procrastination Fairy, and your two daughters.

Katie, this book is the ultimate prevention of sexual abuse—guiding parents to teach sexual respect. The purpose is to prevent children from growing up to be like your father, and thus prevent children from your suffering. It is an honorable mission, but it will be controversial, it will be a source of fussing and fuming, but together, with you in my mind, it can be done. Katie, I am back, with enthusiasm, with dedication, with love and most importantly, without fear.

Katie, this book will start with this tribute—a journey I have taken that has finally brought me to a resolve of what I need to do for you. Your story needed to be told, even though it is somewhat tardy—just as you were tardy so long ago in high school. THE JOURNEY is also a special tribute to your daughters whereever they may be—hopefully with their own daughters safe and secure.

After the story of our journey, with rip-roaring, ridiculous laughter, the First Chapter will feature the outrageous and outlandish ***Sex Fairy Myth***—where good, well-intentioned parents turn the sex education of their children over to a frumpy fairy who will fly in after the wedding reception and with a few poofs and puffs, create sexual respect. The nonsense of this mythology, in actually believing that a fairy in charge of sex will help their children learn sexual respect, will be hooted and howled with ludicrous laughter—hopefully encouraging a better idea through the rest of the book.

Our Second Chapter will honor the plight of sexual victims just like you, asking Moms and Dads to think about a *Victim Wall Of Honor*. This chapter will challenge the belief that families will be spared the ugliness of sexual abuse if they just do everything perfect but leave out understanding that sexual abuse can happen anywhere. All the myths and misconceptions about sexual abuse trauma that would have helped me know how to rescue you, will fill the pages of this Second Chapter, offering knowledge to help loving parents so they don't make the same mistake.

The Pied Piper of Perversion in the Third Chapter will describe the outrage of how Americans lead children down the path to sexual disrespect through a provocative and salacious sexual society but, at the same time, with great pomp and prudery, withhold healthy sexual information. And then, with pretend and posturing, that same society becomes reactive, punitive and retaliatory—punishing those kiddos who took the path of sexual disrespect.

And then Katie, we will present *The Ten Commandments of Raising Sexually Respectful Children,* providing the blueprint for parents who really care about their kidlets. These chapters each begin with a vignette, hilariously poking fun at everyone—talk show hosts, mental health types, sex therapists, sex educators, religious pundits, entertainers, feminists, sexists, counselors, researchers, teachers, cops, pastors, and befuddled, purple-faced parents. These vignettes will be just as outrageous as the way in which most parents handle the issue of sexual respect education and no person, nor any group will be spared from taking a trip to the mirror and examining the great pretend of society—that everyone cares about protecting children from sexual disrespect but that nothing is done to teach it.

And Katie, as we poke fun with our sarcasm, silliness and slang, we must be prepared for the naysayers and complainers. All kinds of folks will be upset about a word, a phrase, an idea or a potshot we launch—probably sending volumes of mail in protest. They will fume and fuss about details—finding the big-picture of neglect difficult to envision.

We will honor their narrow focus of fussing and their complaints, but then, with great respect, we will gently turn them from their pissy posturing, to the kiddos they love, urging them to talk and teach their children, regardless of how they feel about our book or our potshots. Remember Katie, if we just get their attention, and eventually they take on the task of teaching their children sexual respect, then we will be successful. And besides, we can always get bigger mailboxes.

Our book will be funny, rip-roaring and irreverent—something I can do now with my fear under control. I intend it to be brash, rude and raucous—purposely trying to get folks to examine the foolish posturing that Americans are a sexually moral society without ever teaching anything positive about sexual respect. The language will be flip and hopefully funny, primarily to challenge the tight-lipped, glum-faced, teeth-clenched approach so commonly used by adults trying to educate children about sex.

No, there won't be complicated research, heavy-duty dissertations or complicated theories. Those things were all lost to the incinerator the day I found my courage. Scholars with calculators, searching for correlation coefficients before they see a need to talk to children about sexual respect, will be disappointed. And as some frantically search for research citations, we will encourage them to have faith in themselves to teach the children they love. Katie, the answer in raising sexually respectful children is a great deal of common sense, mixed with courage, and all the helpful hints from the Sex Fairy Clipboard at the end of each of the Ten Commandments.

And just to maintain the cheeky mood in the book, alliteration will be our flippant mantra, hoping that as parents cry about the seriousness of the message, at the same time they can laugh at the *awful alliterations*, representing a stuttering and stammering fairy in charge of sex.

You see, Katie, the Sex Fairy does exist in the book in a ridiculous regard, leaving her fairy droppings of ludicrous language throughout— just to remind folks about how they are placing their children's sexual future in the hands of a Sex Fairy who stutters and stammers when it comes to sex.

But the ultimate spoof of our book is that the Sex Fairy will be a centerfold in the middle —a Playboy/Penthouse magazine image, in all her tackiness, taking a stab at glamour. Her image as a magazine foldout is meant to poke fun at the ridiculous pretend of our society that morality is assured until the kiddos walk down the aisle to get married and the Sex Fairy shows up at the honeymoon hotel. Her image as a sex symbol is just as silly as the myth surrounding her and maybe folks will get the point that they need to get serious in teaching sexual respect in this very sexually disrespectful society.

And Katie, as I believe I tried to stand for you, however fruitless it was, now I need you to stand for me. Considering all my distractions over the last twenty years, it is clear that working on prevention is lonely. There are no immediate rewards or payback for *stopping* something from happening. In my other *picking up the pieces* projects over the last two decades, I have garnered support, accolades and honors. The compensation for my efforts has been clear and immediate reinforcement. But now, you and I will be working on preventing children from becoming sexual offenders, and we will get nothing in return because our successes will be elusive. That is why we need to stand together; just remembering it is the right thing to do.

You and I will never know if children who may benefit from our book, and don't become offenders, will grow up and become good Mommies or good mechanics, good lawyers or good layers of pipe, good nurses or those who grow good nasturtiums. We will never know if, because of our book, children become good Daddies, good dancers, good dairymen or those who dig good ditches. Each time one parent puts forth effort to raise a sexually respectful child, and they are successful, that triumph will quietly tiptoe away, never giving us a single *thank you,* never honoring a single contribution from our righteous effort. And so, my dear Katie, we must stand together and we must write this book, but not for immediate rewards, national recognition or television talk shows invitations. It must be done, not only because it is the right thing to do, but because it is long overdue.

Jan Hindman & the Sex Fairy

Chapter 1
The Myth & the Madness

CHAPTER 1: THE MYTH & THE MADNESS

The audience was a buzz, albeit a respectable buzz, in anticipation of HER arrival. Generalized anxiety related to EAT wasn't one bit connected to the menu at the reception sit-down dinner, rumored to have taken a big bite out of Ernie's savings account. Instead, EAT was related to HER *Expected Arrival Time*. Tension permeated the air, rivaling the competency of an international airport during a snowstorm. *When will it be?* they all wondered.

Finally, Aunt Verna, Uncle Allen, and Cousin Dennis arrived, much to the relief of the already settled wedding guests. Grandma Effie, the oldest and most respected member of the bride's family, was worried her oldest son, living 100 miles away in Hootersville, wouldn't make the wedding of her youngest son's daughter, Emmilou, at least on time. So a sigh of contentment infused the front pews as Aunt Verna settled her not-so-slim posterior in between her husband, Allen, and cousin Annabelle. And of course the Kettlemen family, with all their noisy children, were organizing themselves into the third pew as everyone remembered their nickname, *A Kettle of Kids*. But even the noisy kettle kids wondered about when SHE would show up.

Concentration on HER arrival was so intense that some diverted their attention to less anxiety producing topics, such as the wedding color scheme. And Emmilou's choices weren't easy. Edward, the groom, had trouble making a commitment regarding the complicated coloring business for the wedding. *Yes*, he liked his bride's narrowed down colors of rich raspberry, perfect peach and mock mustard, but *no*, Emmilou could not squeeze a commitment from him about his absolute preference. And when in a huff she insolently quipped, "Well, maybe I'll just use all of them," Edward, in his usually agreeable, and totally smitten-with-whatever-his-bride-wanted demeanor, followed with, "That would be fine, sweetie." Grandma Gertrude, not knowing a thing about this conversation, thought the rich raspberry had a pleasant and not-too-fancy touch for the wedding of her favorite granddaughter.

Everything seemed perfectly choreographed with the cut dahlias, day lilies and dianthus all matching the real raspberries picked and frozen into submission in Emma's kitchen in preparation for adorning the reception punch. Raspberry bows, perfectly perched on each church pew, also adorned the aisle that SHE would eventually grace, or so it was hoped.

The wedding programs, predictably with rich raspberry ink, printed of course, on *purity* white paper (signaling SHE hadn't arrived yet) announced who would do what and when. But HER arrival time wasn't listed in the program even though everyone predicted she would arrive with the same certainty that Reverend Ricardo would wear an obnoxious tie that would probably sport any color other than the sweet and subtle rich raspberry.

And there were other predictions. The wedding-waiting folks began to ponder the reception punch, predicting that Uncle Nathan would probably spike the concoction with a bottle of Old Crow. And for some, there was pondering about whether the rich raspberry bridesmaid dress would fit Cousin Camille, whose secret pregnancy status was anything but secret. And some wondered if the dainty china Emmilou picked out at the Big Rip department store would really be used for Edward's tacky store-bought breakfast burritos. And, most of the younger wedding-waiting folks pondered how to handle the snippy wedding planner who forbade them from even considering bringing their ice chests of cold beer into the reception.

Emma rested for a moment in her designated spot in the front pew after being ceremoniously deposited by one of the ushers. As the mother of the bride, she contemplated that her aerobics classes over the past two months had really paid off. In fact, now Emma pondered the wisdom of the princess-waist style dress, so cleverly schemed by Doris at the dress shop to hide what she called, Emma's *tons of tummy*. At the time it seemed sensible, but now Emma questioned whether all the huffing and puffing around the gym would have allowed her to risk a more revealing waistline at the wedding of her precious daughter. In her princess-waist pondering, Emma couldn't help but think that Erma, the groom's mother, probably never had to consider a dress style disguise since she always remained so petite, apparently with absolutely no *tons of tummy* problems. A slight pang of jealousy was quickly dashed when Emma remembered the wedding planner's advice, suggesting that the mother of the bride *should be a showcase of poise and polish* in the way of weddings. The troublesome task of holding in a tummy would certainly distract from that honorable mission Emma figured. She was just fine in her princess-waist dress, she comforted herself, also remembering she didn't want petty thoughts of dieting to spoil her last moments with her princess Emmilou—that is before SHE arrived and changed that princess status.

Now Ernie, Emma's husband and Emmilou's father, had his own contemplations waiting for HER arrival and not one of his thoughts had anything to do with his waistline. Why, to Ernie, his *tons of tummy* suited him just fine and in fact, when Emma wasn't around or when Ernie was bowling with his buddies, he would joke that his tummy was actually a *tool shed*, protecting his *tools* underneath. This raucous joking about tools and tool sheds was perfectly fine for Budweisers and bowling, but not for today, Ernie winced to himself. For Dad Ernie, telling rude stories about tools under the tummy was not one bit comfortable for this wedding situation. As he pondered, the thought of his little princess Emmilou even being in the same hotel room with his soon-to-be-son-in-law's tools was absolutely unbearable. But then SHE was supposed to make all of that manageable, Ernie remembered, feeling somewhat better.

Yes, the hotel room after the wedding scene was just too much for Ernie, so he forced his mind to other, more comfortable things, such as his stretched, and now rather thin, wallet. *No*, he didn't really understand why there had to be a sit-down dinner at the reception instead of a help-yourself buffet he so enjoyed at the Elk's club. But *yes*, Ernie was secretly happy to spend the extra money for the sit-down dinner since the choice postponed the wedding and HER arrival by several months. *No*, Ernie eventually thought, the sit-down dinner was a must, which really meant the bride and groom had to wait for an opening at the community center, the only reasonable accommodation for such an affair. And *no,* Ernie didn't really understand why a honeymoon in Hawaii was necessary since the weather for a June wedding would be plenty warm, and after all, there was a swimming pool at the hotel in Hootersville. But again, Ernie was glad to spend the extra Hawaii money knowing that his daughter and her groom couldn't leave for their honeymoon until after the wedding reception, of course suspending things a little longer. And Ernie knew that flying from Hootersville to Hawaii would take a very, very long time, again postponing what Ernie didn't want to think about.

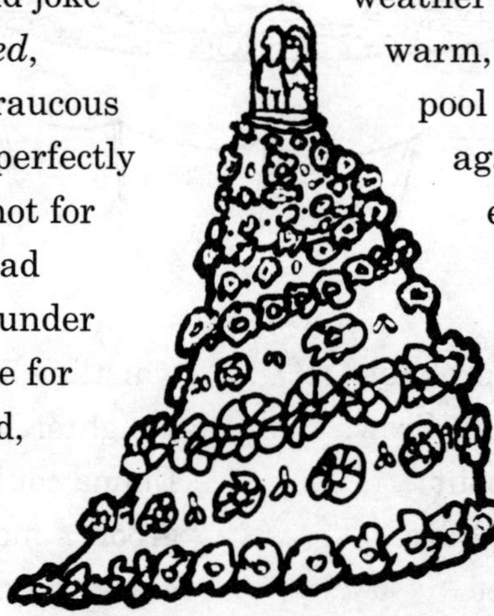

With a smile, Ernie sheepishly remembered his ploys and tricks nearly a year ago when Edward and Emmilou suggested a fall wedding and Ernie had secretly feigned a money shortage just to stall things until June. Although he remembered his sensible and almost cheap wedding to his beloved bride Emma, so long ago, for his little princess Emmilou, he suggested *extravagance.* Not because Ernie really believed that wedding-of-the-year was the natural designation for his daughter and her groom. But Ernie was smart enough to know that extravagance took time and of course, those fancy plans would require the hiring of a wedding planner, taking tons and tons of time, which is really what Ernie wanted.

Now the whole concept of a hired wedding planner was something that most folks in town had never considered, so many wondered whether it was necessary. *Why*, when Ernie was the Exalted Ruler of the Elks club, Emma, with the help of the *Elkettes* (wives of the real Elks), pulled off the Barbecue & Baseball picnic without a single problem. Surely she and Emmilou could handle this wedding, close friends and family had implored to an awkward Ernie. *No,* Ernie explained, nothing was too good for his little princess and a wedding planner it would be.

Of course, hiring a really competent wedding planner could also stall things, Ernie secretly surmised. And after Ernie fussed as much as he could about hiring just the right person, for just the right attention to detail, he was finally squeezed into settling for a rather stern and somber woman who was a stickler for tradition. She was also quite *stuck up*, some thought, especially when she made it clear that being on a first name basis smacked too much of informality and *W.P.* for *wedding planner* was just fine with her. Ernie privately laughed about her initials of W.P., suggesting to his friends that he had spent a lot of money on a wedding planner to WHIP everyone in shape, but secretly Ernie wanted the wedding planner to take as long as possible in that *whipping.* And for him, postponing the fall wedding until late, late, late spring, was a smart thing to do for a dad who wanted HER arrival to take as long as possible. Money was no object if for Ernie, it bought him more princess time with Emmilou before SHE arrived and it was over.

Across the aisle from the princess-style waistline and the please-keep-her-princess-as-long-as-possible contingency of Emmilou's parents, sat the family of Edward. Strategically, the hired wedding planner insisted that the ushers be firm in their opposite-sides-of-the-church ushering.

"Bride's family on the left and the groom's family on the right," was her stern proclamation.

In fact, during rehearsal the night before, W.P. made the four ushers practice their strict partitioning of the families, but it didn't go very well. When Edward's cousin, who W.P. suspected had a few Budweisers in his belly, impishly challenged her authority by suggesting it really didn't matter where people sat, she was forced to respond to his insolence with a short dissertation on wedding tradition.

"The families are separated before the ceremony," she reminded the rehearsing crowd, "symbolizing the need for a union of both families at the reception following the wedding," she finalized. *Union indeed,* smirked several in attendance followed by an immediate feeling of embarrassment about that inevitable merger of bride and groom that no one really wanted to say out loud. But the feeling about the disgusting unionizing was soothed, remembering SHE would make everything okay—after all, that was her job.

Back at the wedding and on the groom's side of the aisle, the parents of Edward were also deep in thought, but unlike the bride's parents, there was not a trace of *princess* in their pondering. Yes, they cared for Emmilou and in fact, they loved her like a daughter—perhaps the daughter they never had. But no, they had been quite happy having what they called a *batch of boys*. And that is probably why Erma never had to concern herself with princess waistlines, because rather than tons of tummy that Emma worried about, Erma had batches of boy activities to keep her hopping AND slim. Why, Edward and his brothers even considered Erma one of the boys, which was perfectly fine with her.

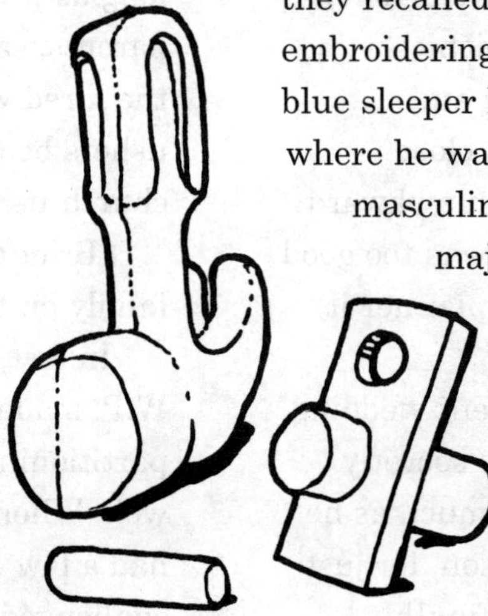

After the first two boys were born, Edwin and Erma wondered about having a baby girl, especially considering that they might run out of "E" names for their male units. Even though they liked the names of Evelyn, Edwinna and Edna, after they thought about it, being in the boy business was just fine, especially considering what they knew about the differences in male and female children. To Edwin and Erma, boys were easy—blunt, straightforward and strong—weakened only by that pesky and inevitable attraction to females. Female units were so different they thought, and more complicated. *Batches of boys* would just work out best for them, that is until SHE arrived for the boys and changed everything.

While Edwin and Erma waited, sitting properly ununionized from the bride's side of the aisle, their pride in Edward loomed. Fondly, they recalled their delight in his boyness—embroidering a rather masculine toolbox on the blue sleeper he wore home from the hospital where he was born. But it didn't stop there—his masculinity that is. Edward was wearing major league baseball caps before he walked and he had a real toolbox (not embroidered) before he started first grade. And as the batch of boys grew, so did the batch of boy training centered on sports, strength and stifling of sniveling. *No room in this family for whining or weakness* the parents taught and the batch of boys confirmed.

Edwin and Erma knew they placed a lot of responsibility on their eldest son Edward, often encouraging him to be a role model for the younger boys in the batch. And serious he was, practically parenting his younger brothers, somberly concentrating on sports and having little time or patience for members of the opposite, and to Edward, weaker sex. *Yes*, he went to the senior prom all right, but the fuss about a matching corsage, the wearing of an uncomfortable tuxedo and an expensive dinner of some fancy chicken wrapped in what Edward thought was raw bacon, was just not his idea of a good time. *No*, he didn't want to see the cheeky pictures of himself and his date before leaving for the dreaded dance and *no*, he wouldn't be calling her again, Edward announced to his well-intentioned parents. Secretly, Erma and Edwin were happy that their oldest and most responsible son was more interested in sports, fishing and, of course, his *tools*, rather than female units. That was until Emmilou came along.

Within just a few weeks, Edward's parents watched their strong and silent son morph into a weak-kneed, tongue-wagging mess when it came to Emmilou. And speaking of wagging, when Emmilou just walked into the room, Edward seemed to wag his tail, something his parents wished they never knew he had. It was more than smitten; Edward seemed *engulfed* by Emmilou and her princess preparations. *Yes,* Erma had a small makeup case that she kept secreted away, only for dressing up for church on Sunday. But *no,* there were no other female trappings in either of their two household bathrooms just so the batch of boys could be comfortable with their masculine things. *No fuss, no muss* was the prevailing theme for the mostly male household. But now, Edward was mysteriously weakened by all of that feminine stuff. He showed a sudden interest in color-coordinating his wardrobe when previously he chose his clothing according to which baseball team was leading the league. Usually a young man of few words, Edward suddenly displayed disappointment if he and Emmilou only talked for two hours on the telephone. A once no-frills kind of guy, Edward now agonized over which scent to consider when choosing the best air freshener for his pickup that had once been comfortably cluttered and which now begged for white-glove inspection. Erma and Edwin worried, *what had happened to their son?*

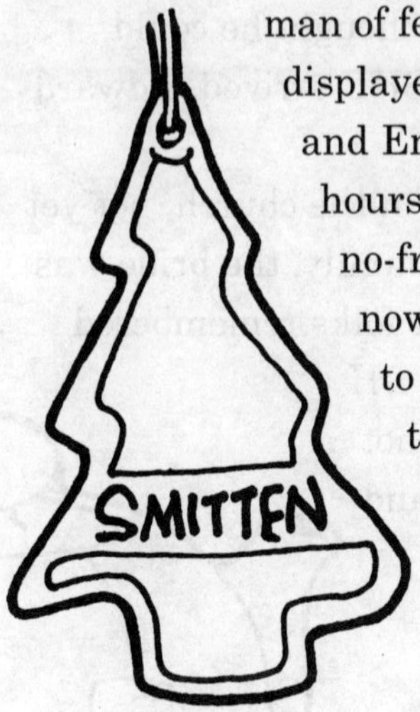

Everything about Emmilou seemed important to Edward, from how she curled her eyelashes to the shade of her lipstick that, she secretly explained to him, sometimes matched her underwear. With Emmilou around, Edward forgot things, dropped things and probably fantasized about things Erma and Edwin never wanted to think about. And it wasn't that Erma and Edwin didn't like Emmilou, they just wondered what happened to their strong and self-assured son. They also somehow knew in the back of their minds that following the wedding,

Edward's weakness for Emmilou would only grow stronger, which is very hard for parents of male children to think about. And even though Erma and Edwin had never heard Ernie's jokes about *tools* and his *tons of tummy tool shed,* they knew their son would be involved with a new *tool implementation* neither of them had talked to him about, but who both thought he could figure out. Of course when SHE arrived, Edward would be fine, they hoped.

Back on Emmilou's side of the church, not yet unionized with the groom's family, the bride was pondered. Some of the older folks remembered sweet Emmilou, taking her 4-H hot pads to the fair, selling hot dogs at the church bazaar, and fixing hot tea for Grandma Effie when she had the flu. Some of the family folks were misty-eyed thinking about how all the sweetness they loved about Emmilou would be gone after SHE arrived. No one would talk about it, but they all knew after SHE arrived, their Emmilou princess would be drastically changed and that is why all the feminine princess preparations were needed for the grand finale of her princess status. It was somewhat sad, but also sweet and certainly part of the tradition.

The bride's quarters were down the hallway decorated by Mr. Peabody's Sunday school class with finger-painted world peace pictures. Now that Emma, in her rich raspberry, princess-waistline dress had been ushered away to her proper designation on the not-yet-unionized-with-the-other-family side of the church, the bride and bridesmaids began their tittering about secret stuff. Sure, Emma had hosted the usual bridal shower at her home where traditional toasters were the gift of choice, but she was not invited to the special bridal shower where Emmilou and her bridesmaids traveled to Hootersville and stayed overnight at the Motel 6. *No,* Emma really didn't want to know if the rumors about the girls going to a strip club were true, mostly because when SHE arrived and the wedding was over, Emma knew her sweet little princess wouldn't be interested in such things. *No need to worry now,* she remembered, only for a second wondering what anyone saw in a strip club since every person on earth could look at a naked body in the bathroom mirror after their morning shower.

With Emma gone, the girl giggling erupted. Even though Emmilou had already adorned her white wedding dress in her mother's tearful presence, she now unzipped the satin-sheen garb, pulling it down around her hips to show her hysterical friends the also white and satin sheen camisole that was breathtakingly sheer and clearly princess-like. Gasping followed the giggles as the girls swooned. *No,* Edward hadn't seen it, Emmilou assured, but she had described it to him in whispers three nights ago while they were visiting Grandma Effie who was pontificating about her rather simple wedding to Grandpa Elmer, sixty years ago.

"There was no need for frills in those days," Effie had explained, as a distracted Emmilou was whispering about her camisole to Edward. "We just went huckleberry picking the day after the wedding," Effie reminded Edward and Emmilou who really weren't paying attention.

While the bride and groom whispered to each other, Grandma Effie remembered that she had picked huckleberries her entire life before her marriage to Elmer, but in her memory, picking huckleberries *that day* seemed different to her, probably because SHE had arrived the previous night at Effie and Elmer's honeymoon hotel—changing everything forever.

But back in the bride's quarters it was clear that the dresses weren't the only thing causing a fuss, as the girls blushed and swooned looking at Emmilou's negligee—white of course, since Emmilou would model it for Edward before SHE really arrived, changing the symbolism of the colors. They giggled about the gag gifts (unauthorized by Emma) given to Emmilou at the Motel 6 secret bridal shower, which she packed in her *going away* suitcase. The secret items included *Luscious Lips Lipstick,* "guaranteed to last until the morning" the package directions dictated. There was *Incredible Edible Underwear*, "guaranteed to be completely organic and harmless," the package assured. And, there was the contraption needing two double AA batteries guaranteed to "pinch-hit if the groom grounds out," promised the baseball terminology on the package. Even though Emmilou knew Edward liked baseball, she guaranteed her friends he wouldn't like the message on this battery-operated tool. Emmilou may have been Ernie's sweet little princess, but she was savvy enough to know that jokes about *tool failure* were just for her friends and not for her groom. Some things were just off-limits, she knew.

In the front of the church near Reverend Ricardo's office, the groom and his brood were also being a little ripe with their raucous joking and it had nothing to do with rich raspberries. The center of their teasing was about the shades of raspberry Edward turned during the previous night's bachelor party when the *sort-of stripper* had danced very close to Edward's *tools.* Wanting to be a good sport to his partying friends, Edward had been slightly shy and only privately reluctant about the stripper business to his younger brother, who was not only the best man, but who was also in charge of the bachelor party entertainment. Evan had encouraged Edward to just hang in there with the tradition of the stripper since after all, he explained, it symbolized Edward's last night as a free man. Free of what, Edward and Evan weren't sure, but they were sure the hooting and hollering about the stripper was acceptable just prior to HER arrival. They also knew, once SHE got there, all of those shenanigans would be over for Edward.

But regardless of the differences in the talking, tittering bride group and the ribbing, raucous groomsmen, the two family factions would eventually be unionized. W.P. had a serious job in the way of weddings, bringing together, first the bride and groom, then the families, then the gifts and even Mr. and Mrs. Salt and Pepper Shaker at

the sit-down dinner. Everyone knew it, expected it, anticipated it, but no one talked about it—even as the final process began.

First, with a shift in the organ music, signaling the unionizing was about to happen and that the waiting was almost over, Edward and Edwin stoically walked down the aisle together, heading for the front of the church, joining a smiling Reverend Ricardo. But there were no smiles gracing the father and son procession, only strength and seriousness, just the way it was supposed to be. Then, with precision but sweetness, Emmilou's bridesmaids were escorted down the aisle in their rich raspberry dresses, color-coordinated with the rich raspberry cummerbunds of the groomsmen with whom they signified the first unionizing of the divisions, as they moved to the music, arm-in-arm.

Of course Erma and Emma were not only sitting strategically in the front on obviously opposite sides of the aisle, but they provided the final smiles to the choreographed couples before they split up again—joining opposing teams of the bride and groom's party in the front of the church, still not yet unionized. Then, as tradition has it, and as W.P. had carefully planned it, all eyes turned to the back of the church for her entrance—Emmilou that is—not yet time for HER arrival.

The familiar tune signified the bride was coming and as the door opened, she and her father did just that. Down the aisle came Ernie with his only-for-a-short-time-left princess, Emmilou. Her white dress, signifying princess purity, was stunning as was her rich raspberry bouquet and her smile underneath the veil. The lightly lacy veil carefully camouflaged Emmilou's blushing cheeks, which everyone hoped were actually blushing (suggesting SHE hadn't arrived yet). Ernie had informed W.P. that he really liked the veil idea and had actually advocated for a bigger, perhaps thicker veil, regardless of the cost. That was because he recognized that the veil, however thin, was the last separation between his princess and Edward. But W.P. would have none of it and she convinced the nervous dad that the light and lacy veil was best. Ernie remembered losing the argument long ago as he now furthered down the aisle with his thinly veiled princess.

As the procession continued, everyone was smiling except Ernie, as he bit his lip a bit, attempting to divert his attention from the lump forming in his throat and the tears forming in his eyes. With his soon-to-not-be princess on his arm, Ernie made his way down the aisle where in a moment he would recite his wedding line of only four words—"Her mother and I." His contribution would happen only when Reverend Ricardo asked about who was giving Emmilou away.

In the way of weddings, there is a big difference in who *giveth* and who *taketh*, even though W.P. didn't describe it in those terms. No one gave Edward away and that automatically placed him in the *taketh* department. But Ernie, in his "Her mother and I" script, moved into the *giveth* category, symbolizing the giving up of Emmilou to Edward and in the way of weddings, this was also a giving up of Emmilou's princess status. Tradition makes it clear there is a difference in the *accounts payable* and *accounts receivable* departments in the *givething* and the *takething*, which was the way SHE demanded it to be.

After Ernie finished his *givething* and Edward did his *takething*, the bride and groom did some fancy promising in front of everyone in the church. Emmilou, in her sweet little voice and with her blushing cheeks (still covered by her lightly lacy veil) told everyone (in fancier words) she planned to hang in there with Edward whether he was feeling good enough to play City League Men's Softball or if his head was hanging over the toilet with the flu. Either way, Emmilou promised, it would be all right with her. And Edward, in his fancy promising, made sure everyone knew he planned on sticking it out with Emmilou regardless if they had the big bucks from his job at the tractor dealership to buy new carpet, or if they didn't even have enough money for the frosted kind of Pop Tarts and they had to settle for the generic ones. Yes, the big promising was finalized by the ring exchange, which Reverend Ricardo explained was circular, symbolizing more moving toward that pesky unionizing and coming together that everyone knew was inevitable, but which no one really wanted to talk about. Of course, the ring business was one of W.P.'s favorite parts because it was so formal and so final.

Then Emmilou and Edward got even closer to the unionizing when, after all the promising and ring rigmarole, the reverend announced that Edward was allowed to take things one step further by kissing Emmilou in front of everyone. He didn't suggest that this *kiss permissioning* was up to Emmilou, but since Edward did the *takething*, it was his job to *taketh* a kiss from his bride. The lightly lacy veil previously covering Ernie's precious princess was now lifted by a palm-sweating Edward and then the kiss was calculated and contemplated by everyone, knowing that HER arrival was getting even closer.

The way of weddings suggested the now sanctioned kiss wasn't before-sanctioned. No, previous to the *givething* and *takething,* as well as promising procedures, Emmilou and Edward waited of course, at least that is what the wedding mystic would hope. But the wedding kiss did mean the unionizing process was officially heating up and even though everyone really wondered if Edward and Emmilou might have had some heat control problems of their passions during courtship, now, because of the way of weddings, everything was okay. And until

the reverend said they could kiss, the real unionizing hadn't had the official *tip off*, or so it was pretended. But more was to come.

The wedding planner was quite strategic in the sit-down dinner place-tags, making it sternly clear that each table needed to *hitch up* the families of both Emmilou and Edward, encouraging more *unionizing* for the whole affair. She did her best to *tie the knot* between the families with her designated place-tags, but she knew there was some place-tag-switching by those who either didn't understand the way of weddings and the need for unionizing, or by someone who had been nipping out of Uncle Nathan's Old Crow bottle. She was quite miffed about the place-tag switching, but she was used to it from all the weddings and receptions she had planned. Some folks, she understood, just didn't *get it*—the unionizing she meant.

As the evening *heated up,* the bride and groom set a good example for more of the *hooking up* as they romantically danced the first dance and snuck an occasional, and of course now-sanctioned, kiss. There were toasts of champagne, complete with winks and nods about how tying of the proverbial knot would be honorable with HER help. But that wasn't all that had changed. Because things were different now, Edward would be able to traverse up Emmilou's previously not-subject-to-traversing leg (honorable now because of all the promising) to retrieve the *something blue* garter she had been wearing. Then W.P. would guide, if not push, Edward into throwing the *something blue* garter into a throng of single, and too-much-champagne-in-their-bellies, men. The retriever of the garter would be designated as next in line for HER visit.

And even though the bridal bouquet was perfect rich raspberry and would have lasted the entire flight to Hawaii, in the way of weddings, Emmilou couldn't keep it. W.P., looking sternly over her half-glasses, arranged all the single women into another throng to see which female would also be next in line for HER visit. But the bouquet toss would not be without conflict, as cousin Camille, in spite of the her secret-but-everyone-knows-pregnant status, got in the front of the line for not only catching the bouquet, but in hopes of catching the father of her baby.

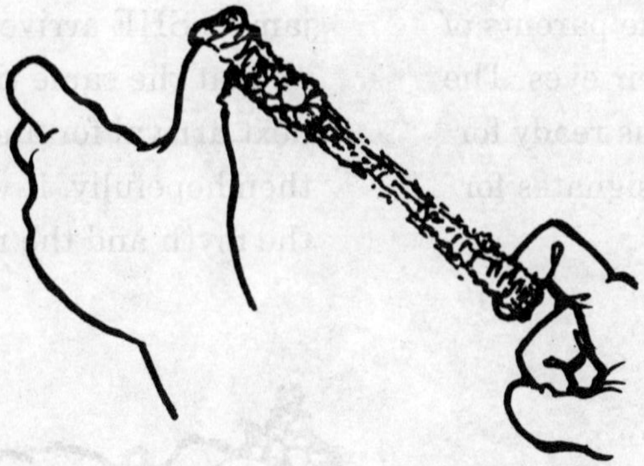

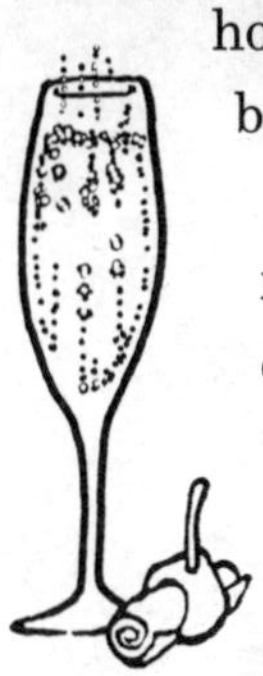

And that is why Camille was messing things up for W.P. who was obsessed with tradition, especially since the wedding winding down was picking up speed. As she tolerated the giggling about Camille and fumed about the disregard for tradition, she also remembered the previous conflict when Emmilou and Edward opted to omit the *obey* part of their promising vows. W.P.'s pontificating about tradition didn't faze the cooing lovebirds. They thought the ***obey*** was a bit bossy and not only that, they explained to the exasperated W.P., but they wanted birdseed instead of rice thrown when they made their exit. Apparently, Emmilou had gotten the birdseed idea from one of those disgusting bride magazines that W.P. so resented, suggesting birdseed was more environmentally friendly than rice. W.P. had suspected Emmilou was one of those *tree-hugger* types, so she admonished her about the break in tradition by suggesting Reverend Ricardo might be upset with the secondary effect of too many birds feasting on the church sidewalk, but that reasoning was to no avail. But since W.P. had won the battle of true traditional trappings of *something old, something new, something borrowed* and *something blue,* she felt that overall, things had tipped in her favor. So as Cousin Camille shoved herself (rudely, W.P. thought) into the front of the single-women-throng, W.P. wished she had broken her working vow of not a single sip of wine until the bride and groom were riced (or birdseeded) away.

But for now, after all the pomp and circumstance in the wedding-winding-down finality, things must be in proper position—and they seemed to be. The sit-down dinner was in the tummies of most everyone as was the spiked punch or the red wine (almost matching rich raspberry, W.P. had assured Emmilou). Wedding guests had the ready-to-throw birdseed in their hands and the parents of the bride and groom had tears in their eyes. The gifts had been collected, and W.P. was ready for wine. Most importantly, the next designates for HER next stop-off (after Emmilou and Edward) had the something blue garter and the rich raspberry bouquet captured. Everything had fallen into perfect and choreographed precision just like all the other traditional trappings. The only remaining problem was the potential traffic jam as SHE arrived for Emmilou and Edward, and, at the same time, was designated for HER next arrival for another couple. But then,hopefully, it will all work out--because of the myth and the madness.

THE MYTH AND THE MADNESS-AND SEXUAL SANCTIONING

And what is the HER—connected to the EAT in the wedding of Edward and Emmilou? And what is the myth in the tradition? What is the absurdity?

Actually, the EAT is the *expected arrival time* and HER is none other than the Sex Fairy—the big time star of the silliness that, in spite of all the other meticulous planning for the wedding, sexual preparation is omitted. And that lesson's absenteeism isn't because Ernie's wallet couldn't afford it, nor is it because sexual issues aren't part of the whole wedding way. It is just because that although sexual sanctioning is a silent focus of everything else parents do at weddings, sexual guidance (however important) is usually a no-show. And this chapter is about that missing-in-action component of sexual teaching in the way parents raise their children. The absurdity surrounds the idea that in weddings, where a big piece of the whole rigmarole has to do with the glorified and glamorized sexual sanctioning, no one does anything to teach sexual respect. That omission leads to the conclusion that since sex is so very important, but so very silent, it all must be handled by the magic of a Sex Fairy.

And silly it is, putting a fairy in charge of something so important as sex. Even beyond the issue of religion, the idea of the wedding ceremony giving the green light to sex between the couple is pretty obvious. Yet in comparison to the other wedding planning and preparation, the flowers, the programs, and the color schemes, there was rarely even so much as one birdseed throw of effort for how that really, really important sexual stuff would unfold for Edward and Emmilou. And since the missing-in-action sexual guidance is typical for most families, with mostly good parents, it must be assumed that somehow they believe it will all work out somehow, perhaps magically. And that is the Sex Fairy myth.

THE MYTH

Of course we love our children—we do everything for them. We raise them to be Baptists, Catholics or Mormons. We teach them how to do Little League and how to make a good omelet. But when it comes to sex—we believe in the magic of a Sex Fairy. As parents, we resist teaching about sex, just so nothing gets spoiled or ruined. We just hope that the Sex Fairy will somehow zap our children in the crotch when they walk down the aisle to get married, or when they walk down the honeymoon hotel hallway. And with that single zap, they will turn into happy, healthy, and respectful sexual human beings without any effort on our part. Yes, it will be magic, this fairy in charge of sex.

And silly it is—putting a fairy in charge of something so important as sex.

THE MADNESS

And that is the myth—that doing nothing about sex will guarantee the kiddos have a respectful sexual future. This thinking is so absurd that only a fairy could handle it. Considering the stretching of Ernie's wallet to everything else, it is amazing the dedicated Dad would think only a bit of poofing and puffing from a fairy would help his little princess navigate safely in the hotel honeymoon suite. How could these loving and caring parents do something so irresponsible? And for sure, this neglect couldn't be found in other areas of being the parents of Emmilou and Edward.

NO LIMITS

There were no limits to what Edward endured in the education department from his parents when growing up. Erma and Edwin taught their oldest son tie-dying, fly-fishing, and theories of fuel injection. Edward learned from his parents how to play soccer and he learned about stock investments. As a little guy, they taught him how to be an all-star catcher, and as a teenager they taught him what to do if he caught a cold. Edward was taught common sense as well, always remembering to keep a flashlight, a flare and a flask of water in his pickup for emergencies.

"You can't be too careful," Edwin schooled his oldest son about a good sense of direction when they went hunting, and a good sense of bargain when they went grocery shopping for their hunting trips.

Further down the perfect parent package, Edward was taught how to balance his checking account and he learned how to balance the tires on his pickup. Edwin and Erma made sure Edward learned patriotism and the Christian thing to do if a panhandler approached him on a street in downtown Hootersville. But in spite of all the parental effort, in spite of all the education, in spite of all the love they had for their son, not a word was taught to Edward about sex—not a word. And that is why Erma and Edwin, two good parents in every other way, must believe the Sex Fairy will take care of everything.

MORE PERFECT PARENT PACKAGE

Emmilou had the same deliberate and detailed dedication from her parents, but also the same neglect in the high-priced commodity of sex, even though her parents probably had big hopes for her honeymoon hotel adventure. Ernie and Emma taught their oldest daughter about weaving, how to make a good waffle, how to become a Brownie, how to make brownies, and eventually she learned how to get brown coffee stains out of the white carpet in the family room. In swimming, Emmilou learned how to do the backstroke, and in shopping she learned how to take back the bad smelling chicken without being rude. Emmilou was taught to drive and how to use a screwdriver—although not very well.

Ernie was proud to teach his daughter to shift the gears in the tractor, and Emma was proud to teach Emmilou how to expertly sift the ingredients for her father's favorite buttermilk biscuits. Her parents diligently taught Emmilou to sit quietly in church, she was taught to be honest, and she was taught to feel sad about the Holocaust. But probably few words were ever taught to Emmilou about sex. And that is why the madness suggests Emma and Ernie also had to count on the Sex Fairy who, with just a few poofs and puffs, would make everything all right in the sexual department for their beloved daughter.

SEX FAIRY FAITH?

A Sex Fairy indeed would be the resistance from the parents of Edward and Emmilou if it were suggested they believed a fairy would take care of something as important as sex for their children. They would be outraged at the idea. And if encouraged to defend what appears to be *Sex Fairy faith,* they would probably rely on tradition, tucked somewhere away with all the other scripting they learned from their parents.

Our parents didn't do things any differently might be their rationalization. And, it does appear that generations have had Sex Fairy faith, most of the time taking care of lots of things, but nonetheless sending their kidlets off to the honeymoon hotel without so much as a single Kotex pamphlet. But things seem to be different from the times Mom and Dad might have worked up a sweat, bobby-socking it after getting a glimpse of the risqué nature of seeing the twin beds of the seemingly asexual partners on *I Love Lucy* television. In contemporary society, sexual disrespect is loud and clear, no matter how much faith there is in the Sex Fairy. And the reality is that sex, respectful or disrespectful, is very, very powerful.

COMMODITY, CURRENCY AND COST

If Ernie thinks the cost of Emmilou's wedding will stretch his wallet for many years after the wedding planner sternly accepts her final check, he and the rest of the well-intentioned-but-caught-up-in-the-myth Moms and Dads should think about the commodity and cost of sex in general. Sex is one of the most powerful currencies among the human race. From the boardroom to the bedroom, fortunes have been made or lost because of that three-letter word. Sex can be the reason huge empires are built and sex is sometimes the reason for the construction of huge prisons. Sex may be why important people spend fortunes or ordinary people spend the family paycheck on fashion. Because of sex, people often divorce or teenagers often dally long after their curfew.

Absence of sex often signifies purity of Grand Pooh Bahs in important positions such as nuns, priests and monks, while in other situations the absence of sex may result in suspicions about someone's sexual orientation or an automatic career in library science. Sex can be why people

Generations of parents have had *Sex Fairy Faith*—taking care of everything else but sending their kids off to the honeymoon hotel without so much as a single Kotex pamphlet.

get elected and why people get rejected. Sex is the reason some people get married, sometimes not too wisely, and sex is sometimes the reason people get unmarried, especially if the puffing and poofing by the Sex Fairy doesn't measure up as advertised. And speaking of advertising, sex sells anything from fashion, fun, and fudge to fingernail polish. Sex sells soap, sandwiches and ceiling tiles. Sex is the *best of the best* and the *worst of the worst* in society. Why then, with all of this power and influence, is this high-priced commodity of sex omitted from the educational clipboard and basically turned over to a fairy?

TOOLS, TRAPS, TRADITION & FAIRY FRAYS

Not only is sex a powerful commodity, becoming the currency toward ruin or royalty, but the preparation for how to use the tools to make it all work is pretty pitiful. With all that power and currency, it would seem that the bride and groom would be a little more prepared, yet both Edward and Emmilou are sent into the trap, with no map, only madness.

After all the pomp and circumstance of the wedding, Edward and Emmilou are trotted off to the hotel honeymoon suite with different tools and traps, strengths and weaknesses, with only a *fairy hope* that things will work out. One of them enters the fairy fray being pure and princess-like, as well as being in the *accounts payable* (*giveth away*) department. And, of course, in this madness, that is Ernie's princess, Emmilou. The other partner in the traditional fairy fray, enters the trap strong, competent and in the *accounts receivable* (*takething*) department. But that is not all. The tradition of the trapping has it that Edward is not only in charge of the *takething,* but the tools and proper tool use is also in his job description.

This tool competency is very different than the tool training Edward received from his parents about crescent wrenches, pipe wrenches, box wrenches and torque wrenches. No, in the myth of the traditional trap, Edward needs to be in charge of the kind of tools protected by Ernie's *tons of tummy tool shed,* although he has had not one moment of this kind of tool training from his loving parents.

Emmilou doesn't have tools in the mythical madness of the Sex Fairy fray—exactly, that is. But there is princess pressure on Emmilou to have enough *princess power* to guarantee that Edward's tool implementation is effective. The whole thing is a pretense and it is precarious. In the myth, no one apparently thinks it will take more than a poof or a puff for everything between the bride and groom to be just *fine.* No one wonders if the Sex Fairy will lose her way or get caught in a traffic jam, but everyone expects everything will not only be *fine*, but the expectation is that the *fine* should last a lifetime. And probably no one thinks about the price Emmilou and Edward may pay if the ***fine*** isn't so ***fine.***

SEX FAIRY FAITHFUL OMISSION

Beyond the silliness of Sex Fairy faith and the total inadequacies of preparing children for the Sex Fairy fray, questions could be raised about why—that is beyond the tradition handed down from generations of tight-lipped, red-faced parents. No doubt sex is a high-priced commodity, so why would good folks omit sexual respect training and leave it up to a fairy? The answer lies in the smug safety of omission.

"We aren't like those drug-using parents who shack up before marriage and who use swear words at soccer, so no need for all that nastiness," is a cry from the Sex Fairy faithful.

"There is no evidence of sexual stuff in our family," Mom smugly surmises, convincing herself childhood is a time of sweetness and interest in such things as Sweet Tarts, certainly not sex. And it doesn't take much for Mom to further rationalize, "Sammy is showing no signs of cross-dressing or premature ejaculation, so *no need for nuthin'* now."

And if Mom, even for a moment, notices that something ever-so-subtle might give Sammy one iota of information about the *birds and bees*, she just might make a mental note to solve the problem by deciding to let Sammy have two hamsters instead of one, just in case there was a need for a small introduction into this pesky sex stuff. Thus, the myth is fortified by the Sex Fairy faithful through omission, since *no need for nuthin'* suggests the Sex Fairy will handle things just fine later on.

NO NEED NONSENSE

But if parents who are counting on the *no need for nuthin'* approach really take a look at the sex stuff around them, it is clear why only the magic of a Sex Fairy could provide the rationalization for the omission. Even small children learn about wiggling hips, smacking lips, and teenagers taking skinny dips while Mom and Dad are pretending there is *no need for nuthin'* until after the wedding reception.

Children may not know the intricacies of simultaneous orgasms or teen pregnancy, but they recognize the omission of sexual information from their parents, while the sexual world tutors them very differently. Children like Emmilou and Edward grow up observing their parents handle piano lessons, pottery making and a perfect understanding of punctuation, but they aren't fools in figuring out the excitement of the stuff Mom and Dad left out. Just like the adventurers or discoverers their parents taught them to be, they learned about sex and they learned about their parent's failure—clear symptoms of Sex Fairy faithfulness.

OH! OH! OMISSION

It was a large bookstore, a chain in fact, with a national reputation, and the bigger part of an entire block occupied in a busy and upscale shopping mall. The bookstore in Las Vegas, Nevada had huge aisles with huge varieties of books, periodicals, newspapers, games, and many other brightly decorated offerings. The

No doubt sex is a high-priced commodity, so why would good folks omit sexual respect training and leave it up to a fairy? The answer lies in the smug safety of omission.

Even small children learn about wiggling hips, smacking lips, and teenagers taking skinny dips while Mom and Dad are pretending there is *no need for nuthin'* until after the wedding reception.

No one wonders if the Sex Fairy will lose her way or get caught in a traffic jam, but everyone expects that with her fairy poofing, everything will not only be fine, but that the *fine* will last a lifetime.

choices were endless and the children's section was also quite impressive, featuring everything possible to stimulate the little ones before they could sit up in their cribs, to train their ears toward classical music before they could use the toilet, and to increase appreciation for their baby sister before sibling homicide is considered by the four-year-old. There are sets and volumes of books to teach children not to bully, tattle, steal, cheat or snoop. There were resources on how to help children avoid being greedy, forgetful, rude, lazy and selfish. There was material for parents on how to keep children from throwing tantrums or throwing the newborn puppies. Material was available for children to learn how to pick up their toys and the importance of not picking their noses. But what about materials for teaching sexual respect?

The curious customer examines each department in the children's section, searching for information on teaching sexual respect. Finally she locates a beaming sales clerk who is obviously eager to help, just as her friendly name badge suggests.

"Do you have a children's sexual health section?" is the question posed in the air that seems to drip with breathlessness, rivaling Reverend Ricardo's command for kissing at the wedding.

Gone is the smile of the clerk, replaced by a strong chin and clenched teeth. A stern takeover of the clerk's previously-comfortable-and-helpful posture occurs and the answer "follow me," is the only sound breaking the silence. Down she goes through the sections, shelves and tiny stools to an out-of-the-way corner where high on the shelf she severely points to about 1.5 inches of seven tiny books squeezed between her fingers. "There," was all she said, quickly retreating to find other customers with perhaps less upsetting requests. Sadly, a quick perusal of the material determines that the tiny collection only focuses on how fast sperm can swim in the fallopian tubes or the proper adjustment of Kotex pads.

That's it in the nature of children's sexual health—about 1.5 inches of material and a few words about the biological result of when the honeymoon hotel trap tools work. But not one word is there about sexual respect—sexual loving or sexual caring. As the customer leaves, she passes through books, records, periodicals, videos, and magazines, all clearly sporting the sexual disrespect side of things. It is everywhere, in every package. And just outside in what some call *Sin City*, there is a whole lot more for children to learn about sexual disrespect. Billboards, magazines, music, television, and newspapers all scream messages about the prevalence of sexual disrespect, suggesting it may border on the ***norm***. But the tiny children's sexual health section (or so it is pretended) of this bookstore would support any parent wanting to rationalize *no need for nuthin'*.

"Surely there would be books about it if it was important," might be the resistance to thinking differently, without considering that the bookmakers probably also belong to the Sex Fairy faithful.

HONEYMOON HAZARDS

It is easy to subscribe to either the *no need for nuthin'* or the *but this is the way it has always been* ideas when parents consider that something else might need to be done for their children in the sexual department. But a more realistic issue is whether parents would be motivated to do something different if they understood the hazards of believing in the Sex Fairy myth. After all, the parents of Emmilou and Edward professed to care a lot about their kidlets. So perhaps protecting children from everything that can go wrong in that honeymoon hotel may provide the motivation to cancel the Sex Fairy subscription.

GRAND GUILT

In the myth, it is assumed (even though it may be a ridiculous assumption) that folks like Emmilou and Edward are clean slates, wandering into the Sex Fairy zapping process of the honeymoon hotel suite, totally innocent. Much of the pomp and circumstance of the wedding is about the purity (white dress and all), especially for Emmilou. So the big, big pressure is on the *nuthin' has happened yet* myth, which might be perfectly fine, if it were true. But with the national statistics suggesting that more than half of the kiddos in America are having intercourse by age 14, and 90% of marriages are not virginal, then the chances of the honeymoon hotel clean slate are pretty weak. But there will be no weakness of the pretend in the wedding planning that everything is quite pure and sweet which may just open the door to some bride and groom guilt.

What if Emmilou practiced her princess power a little too much before the wedding, maybe with someone other than Edward before she swept him off his stumbling feet? With all the purity princess pressure on her for the wedding, will she feel guilty and disappointed in herself or in the whole princess plan—starting out a supposedly lifetime marriage with a failing grade?

Or what if Edward powered up his power tools a few times, just for practice, before he carried Emmilou over the threshold of the hotel room in Hootersville? Will Edward feel as though he messed up the clean slate image and begin his marriage with feelings of failure? While their parents were omitting sex and believing that the Sex Fairy would take care of things later, maybe Emmilou and Edward wandered a bit, forcing them to begin their life together feeling like C-minuses, or worse? And if so, was all that guilt really necessary and what their good parents wanted?

That's it in the nature of children's sexual health—about 1.5 inches of material and a few words about the biological result of when the honeymoon hotel trap tools work. Not one word is there about sexual respect—loving or caring.

And what if, in all that pressure and anxiety, the couple needed more than Emmilou's menstruation movie in the fifth grade or Edward's condom talk with Dad?

ARE WE THERE YET?

Switching potential honeymoon hazard possibilities, what if just like the myth and the magic suggests, neither bride nor groom did any practicing before the wedding and this really was the very first time for Emmilou to use her princess power and for Edward to power up his tools. Maybe they waited and with unbelievable crescendo building, they entered the honeymoon hotel with the prescribed purity, and with tremendous expectation for not only bells and whistles, but also imagining that somehow the Mormon tabernacle choir would sing from the hotel balcony at the precise moment the sex stuff happened. And what if, in all that pressure and anxiety, the couple needed more than Emmilou's menstruation movie in the fifth grade or Edward's condom talk with Dad? What if things don't turn out so well and in fact, the whole thing is a big fat disappointment—questioning *is that all there is?* Is it acceptable to let two young people drown in their ignorance about sex just so the purple faces of the parents can be protected in the Sex Fairy myth?

SAD SEX

But there are more hazards in sending brides and grooms to the honeymoon hotel without a flight plan and with a Sex Fairy in charge of everything. What if someone sexually abused Emmilou and Edward long ago when they were younger? What if the sadness of sexual abuse happened when neither of them understood about sex, but when they both recognized that their parents didn't talk about sex stuff? What if secrecy about the *sad sex* for little Emmilou and Edward was rationalized with the solution of, "When I finally get married to the right person, all these bad feelings about bodies and sexual touching will be gone?" And sadly, what if those bad feelings aren't gone, no matter how carefully the wedding planner prepared everything in Hootersville? What happens if sexual abuse trauma isn't fixed just because everything matched the rich raspberry color scheme? What happens when the Sex Fairy's faithful efforts aren't enough to solve the secrecy and shame of childhood sexual abuse?

HONEYMOON HANKY-PANKY

But the potential hazards for the honeymoon hotel room could be worse if the puffing and poofing from the Sex Fairy isn't enough. What if Emmilou or Edward, heavily influenced by the *screaming sexual subtleties* all around them, and getting *no need for nuthin'* parental guidance about sex, decided to adventure out on their own with a little misguided hanky-panky? What if getting naked at the slumber party went a little too far and with the adventuresome spirit taught to them by their parents in other areas, they trudged forward with their own sexuality—maybe taking advantage of younger, more vulnerable kiddos, however innocent at the time.

Later, when the wedding planning is just about finished and the honeymoon waits, how do the formerly engaged-in-slumber-party-hanky-panky bride and groom handle the now sanctioned sexual fanfare? What happens when they realize that with all the pristine purity preparation, the rules about sexual sanctity have already been broken and they are the guilty party? Will their marriage, with such a strong sexual component, limp into the future because teaching about sex was ignored and omitted with the smug safety idea of *no need for nuthin'*, since in the myth, the Sex Fairy will take care of everything. At risk for parents believing in the Sex Fairy are children's futures, marriages, and, of course, potential grandchildren. Yet, in reality, parents seem more content with counting on the Sex Fairy and rolling the sexual dice in a risk-based *crapshoot*. And ironically, Sex Fairies are not known to do well at gambling and in fact, they may struggle even saying the word *crap*.

DENIAL DANCE TEACHERS

With all the myth and madness, the solution isn't in calling the sheriff to arrest Ernie, Emma, Erma and Edwin for child neglect in sending their children into the precarious situation of sanctioned sex, chaperoned only by a Sex Fairy. *Nope,* in a society saturated with sexual disrespect, but nothing on how to teach sexual respect, Edward and Emmilou's parents can't be blamed, because they are in good company. Doing the dance of denial about sexual disrespect is easy for most parents, because there are some very good teachers to follow.

THE TRIUMVIRATE

In the big picture of denial there appears to be a threesome—three levels of *doing the dance of denial* at the peril and risk of children loved as much as Emmilou and Edward. First comes society leading the heavy-hitter charge of *no need for nuthin'* using loud legislation and other official fussing against sexual disrespect—of course to cover up society's neglect in the sexual respect department. Society's broad brush of posturing about laws and punishment starts the denial dance, making way for the Sex Fairy faithful.

Then, after being quite impressed with society's slapping down of sexual badness comes local communities, easily catching the beat of the denial dance. With a variety of well-intentioned and quite misguided (but nonetheless grand) efforts, communities get really fired up about the badness. When communities do the pretend protests at the schools, libraries or coffee klatches, making big splashes about maintaining morality in the swimming pool dressing rooms or the halls of the elementary school, everyone feels a whole lot better. Relief is right around the corner because the community attacks the disrespectful sex stuff of adult bookstores, raunchy movies or a sex education program in school, making it easier to believe in, and follow, a Sex Fairy.

At risk for parents believing in the Sex Fairy are children's futures, marriages, and, of course, potential grandchildren. Yet, in reality, parents seem more content with counting on the Sex Fairy and rolling the sexual dice in a risk-based *crapshoot.*

But the powerful three-ring circus of denial gives justification for the madness of believing that if disrespectful sex is the focus of outrage, respectful sex will automatically follow, especially with a Sex Fairy in charge.

Third in line of the triumvirate of denial dancers is the *family,* with a great pretend that just because drug use is prohibited and a screen keeps smut from the computers, sexual respect is almost guaranteed within the confines of the abode. And in the family denial, there are rationalizations about waiting to take the sexual respect plunge until the wedding, especially since the family folks believe that the community and society have handled the disrespectful dirt bags through laws and rules, taking care of everything. By the time the family joins the dance, waiting for the Sex Fairy is an easy beat to follow.

In reality, members of the triumvirate are all one, since society is made up of communities and families. But the powerful three-ring circus of denial gives justification for the madness of believing that if disrespectful sex is the focus of outrage, respectful sex will follow, especially with a Sex Fairy in charge.

WAGING WAR ON THE WICKED

Right out of the chute, society gets busy in the business of sexual disrespect, but the interest doesn't seem to be in the positive part of helping Emmilou and Edward begin their marriage with sexual respect. Contrarily, getting fired up about the bad part of sex seems just the dance society prefers. With great fanfare, war is waged on the wicked, and society seems to have a couple of weapons in the battle.

First, there is always a demand to take the lead in protecting society because safety is right at the top of society's dance card, as it should be. Probably with the increase in mass (and rapid) communication has come the reality of the sexual disrespect problem, previously more secretive without such communication miracles as the Internet. *Yes*, the sexually disrespectful get lots and lots of attention in society's media, especially the electronic form. So, from society's perspective, something has to be done about waging war on the wicked because the battle seems so close. And it has to be done now. So the first weapon in the combat is punishment, and, besides, talking about what to do with the sexually disrespectful who look bad and smell bad is much easier than figuring out how to talk about being a sexually respectful four-year-old engaged in tree fort hanky panky.

BUT IT'S FOR THE CHILDREN

When society begins the dance of waging war on the wicked, it is usually with the mantra of *protecting the children*—society's most vulnerable. It is done in their name and with the hope it works. And it seems the only weapon in helping the wee ones is to punish the bad ones—those who hurt the precious kiddos. That is an honorable mission, and it is for ALL the children, but sometimes this war waging effort is for specific kiddos.

FOR JACOB

In 1989, on a Sunday afternoon in Saint Joseph, Minnesota, eleven-year-old Jacob Wetterling was cruelly abducted as he rode bicycles with his pals. Immediately a search was organized, but eventually abandoned because Jacob was never found. Most appalling for the grieving family came later when they learned some of those first on the scene to help search for their beloved child were sex offenders! *Yes,* those really disrespectful folks, often known by police but not known by those who were most vulnerable, joined a family searching for a missing and loved child, undetected and unforgiven. The *how could this happen?* screamed loudly. How could the most vile, boast a passport of audacity and permeate the sanctity of searches for an innocent child? Something had to be done—and it was. Eventually, through the Jacob Wetterling Act, the right to know (not the ability, but the right) about the bad folks became law. *Sex Offender Registration,* in Jacob's honor (honorably), became the national effort allowing any concerned citizen to keep track of the wicked.

AND POLLY

But then there was Polly. Petaluma, California had never experienced anything like this. Here it was—a slumber party in an upscale neighborhood where an innocent child was abducted in the middle of the night while her two pals watched in horror, similar to Jacob's friends. The Polly Klass Foundation was immediately organized and right away good things began to happen. Money poured in to help search for Polly and for one of the first times ever, society started a new idea in dealing with missing kidlets by disseminating their picture everywhere. This was long before pictures of missing children could be found on milk cartons so the idea of sending Polly's picture throughout the world was quite clever. Everyone figured out this was a new way to search for children and it was considered brilliant. But in spite of these efforts, soon and sadly, Polly's body was discovered, raped and murdered by Richard Allen Davis.

The indignant screamed, "How could this happen?"

Eventually, a sore and sorrowful community learned that Mr. Davis was pretty practiced in the *being bad* business and in fact, he had a criminal history longer than the train on Emmilou's radiant wedding gown. Over and over, and over, Mr. Davis had been released from the safety of incarceration, just to apparently do more disrespectful things. The big picture pundits said, *enough was enough,* and with society's sweeping hand of punishment, things changed. The revolving door for the bad guys ended with the *Three Strikes and You Are Out* legislation that was not only passed, but welcomed as a solution. Whether it was pandering, pick pocketing or stealing a pizza, as long as there were three of them, you were out,

How could the most vile, boast a passport of audacity and permeate the sanctity of searches for an innocent child?

Whether it was pandering, pick pocketing or stealing a pizza, as long as there were three of them, you were out, gone, finished.

gone, finished. *The three bells of three strikes* rang clearly, first in California, then throughout the country, making most of the good folks feel better and again reminding them there was really *no need for nuthin'* in the form of teaching sexual respect since the disrespectful were just batted out.

AND MEGAN

But the cocoon of smugness society tends to feel with a broad-brush-punishment approach to sexual disrespect in cases such as Jacob's or Polly's, just didn't seem to work since more bad news unfolded, year after year. When a sweet little girl named Megan Kanka was abducted, raped and murdered in her New Jersey neighborhood, naiveté' about safety was shattered when it was learned that Megan's sex offender was comfortably living within the vicinity of trust. And for those believing that sexual respect was automatic in nice neighborhoods like Megan's, the outrage was profound.

"Why did this happen, and why didn't we know?" was the heartbreaking question.

Soon, outrage was the posture and action was the outcome. First federal, then state laws, fighting back for Megan, were implemented to guarantee that everyone would *now know* about the disrespectful folks in the form of Sex Offender Notification laws. *No more gullibility in neighborhoods* was the plan, allowing the good folks to know about the bad folks. And as they began to know, they were again reminded *nuthin'* needs to be done with teaching sexual respect to children since the sexual disrespecters would be known to everyone.

A PEEK AT PERVERSION

If we know what they look like, if we can identify them, chart them, graph them, and, of course, profile them, things will be okay, easily becomes the effort by society in the hope for enhancing sexual respect. But in reality, it is all aimed at knowing about the disrespectful. The power of just knowing about them (perhaps mug shots on pervert posters) was society's courageous step, resulting in Sex Offender Registration, Sex Offender Notification, and getting the umpires to count the strikes until the disrespectful people struck out.

BUSHES BOB

But, there is another side of society's effort at dealing with the disrespectful. Jacob, Polly and Megan helped everyone think about what to do once the bad guys were caught, but society's sex police weren't finished. Lots of folks decided that figuring out how to spot them *before* they hurt kiddos might be a good thing to do, so *profiling the perverts* became the next step. Whether formally or informally, *typical* sex offenders were imagined, and of course, everyone liked what they saw in the image.

The profile picture of who to watch for (before it was time to keep track of them) was a *Bushes Bob* fella—male, of course, since it just couldn't be perceived that the Emmilou types could ever get into the sexual disrespect business. In society's pervert image, Bushes Bob was a kind of guy in the public park, lurking behind bushes, holding a sack of stale candy in his hands that sported dirty fingernails. In the imagined profile, Bob was considered unmarried, perhaps living in a renovated apartment, never having children of his own and easily spotted lurking in the shadows of park shrubbery. Society encouraged this kind of thinking and the solution was to just focus on the park bushes and parks rather than focusing on the idea of teaching children sexual respect. And society's heavy hitters, who passed the laws and planted the ideas of the park-pervert posters, probably never, ever thought that perhaps with these tough punishments and the stigma of the profile, maybe they should go home and talk to their own children about staying on the sexual respect side of things.

HAVOC AND HEAVY-HITTING

In the fifteen years since Jacob Wetterling brought society to its knees about sex offenders moving through society and causing havoc, the solutions waged by a society with weapons, but no plan to educate children, finds even more problems requiring more heavy hitting.

In 2005, when precious Jessica Lunsford in Florida met the same fate as Jacob, Polly and Megan more than a decade previous, the answer was more punishment, even though the heavy hitters should have done some heavy checking to recognize this tactic didn't seem to be working. Obviously the *striking out* and *figuring out* who is behind the bushes wasn't stopping the sexual disrespect, but never mind. With Jessica Lunsford's tragic death, the heavy hitters got heavier with their punishment. The Florida folks got quite busy and passed the Lunsford act, really setting things straight—or so they hoped.

The Lunsford Act overwhelmingly passed by the Florida legislature demands a twenty-five year prison sentence for those who act sexually disrespectful. But that doesn't end the heavy hitting. Even when those bad folks finish their twenty-five year prison sentence, the fussy Florida folks plan to keep track of them for life, making sure that none of them ever hurt another child like Jessica. Why, the law even requires GPS, the fancy Global Positioning System that allows satellite surveillance of sex offenders, which is a whole lot more sophisticated than checking the park bushes. But the one question that might be poignant to the legislators with tears in their eyes about Jessica is, how much funding will be allotted to help teach sexual respect to Florida families?

If we know what they look like, if we can identify them, chart them, graph them, and profile them, things will be okay.

But the one question that might be poignant to the legislators with tears in their eyes about Jessica is, *how much funding will be allotted to help teach sexual respect to Florida families?*

OH, OHIO

As other kiddos are hurt, the in-charge folks of society continue their well-intentioned efforts to deal with the disrespecters rather than teaching sexual respect to the Emmilous and Edwards. They did just that in 2005, when Ohio folks heard what the fuming Florida folks were doing. Not to be outdone in the *meanness methods,* Ohio thought of another idea to keep track of the bad folks. Yes, pink license plates were suggested for the sex offenders, just so people could tell when the bad folks were driving to the parks to find bushes. A fine idea it was, and again it suggested there was *no need for nuthin'* in the teaching sexual respect department as long as in Ohio, the disrespectful people could be spotted. The pink-license-plate process eventually petered out but similar ideas will continue to be bantered around in society's war waging. And again the question was whether any of those heavy-hitter folks in Ohio took the time to sit down and talk to their own kidlets not only about sexual respect, but also about what the great State of Ohio planned to do if they wandered off the respectful path.

MARRIAGE MESSES

But beyond the pervert posters and the punishment pomp, society does other things to stamp out sexual disrespect. At first blush (and for some it is worth blushing about), lots of folks worry about what needs to be done with the marriage mess. The sad reality is that for the opposite sex folks like Edward and Emmilou, things aren't exactly doing too well in the success department. More than half of the Ernies in society will eventually see the sadness of their princesses turn from Mrs. Edward to single-mom-of-Ernie's-grandkids without one bit of princess left in her. *No*, the heterosexual folks aren't exactly batting with any degree of competency in the marriage department, but in society's effort to right the disrespect ship, they decided that the sanctity of marriage needed protecting. With the nagging worry about marriage messes, and with the best of intentions, the fussing and fuming focused on legislation and loud protests to make sure that no two people with the same set of tools would be allowed to *tie the knot* or *get hitched*, two terms abhorred by most wedding planners.

TITILLATING TELETUBBIES

Beyond the officialdom of television talk shows or legislative action to stamp out gay marriage, society's slaps sometimes come in a more humorous, but not necessarily harmless, way. First it was the Teletubbies—a television program for toddlers, featuring cartoon cuties sporting only rudimentary lessons in language. Pretty harmless it was thought to be until society's slappers noticed something of concern, right there on toddler television. One of the cartoon characters, Tinky-Winky, was dressed in a dreadfully-suggestive-of-gayness purple outfit and with none other than a triangle (the symbol known to all two-year-olds as signifying homosexuality) on his tubby little head. And besides that, Tinky had a purple purse, color-coordinated however, likely pleasing the likes of most wedding planners but causing great havoc for society's sexual police.

Screaming, the sanctity-of-marriage folks raged forward with their efforts to get this *Teletubby titillation* stopped. It was important, they thought, to ban the purple Teletubby; so poor Tinky-Winky was denounced, lest he lead innocent toddlers down the homosexual path. Some heavy hitters seriously and strenuously vowed to never wear purple again and some pondered how triangles might someday be banned from geometry textbooks for high schoolers just to make sure the marriage mess gets tidy.

ANOTHER BOB

But the Teletubbies were only the beginning of society's attempts to clean up toddler television and prevent the little ones from cuddling up with their same-set-of-tools friends. Soon, a different Bob was brought into the sexual disrespect foray, but not a Bob from behind the park bushes. SpongeBob SquarePants, an underwater cartoon character who was delightful to preschool children, also made society's hit list. After some poking around in SpongeBob's underwear, the society slappers got suspicious AND busy. *Yes*, it was pretty clear to those who wanted to protect marriage that SpongeBob was probably gay. To support their snippiness, they pointed out Bob was unusually sensitive, flamboyant, gregarious and sometimes breaking out in song with an also-suspicious and muscular female friend, Sandy the Squirrel. How else could those things be explained, some of society's slappers wondered? But most concerning, they opined, was that sometimes SpongeBob held hands with his friend Patrick (who is, by the way, a starfish with no signs of underwear) and worst of all, they said S.B. always seems to have a sunny and cheerful disposition, probably knowing nothing about power tools and hotel suites. Pointing out the possible perversion of SpongeBob SquarePants was well intentioned and with the clear promise of saving morality for American preschoolers.

But SpongeBob and Tinky-Winky were in good company with all the fussing and fuming about what was, or was not, in their underwear. Society slapping has been going on for a long time against anything that looks to bring down the *sanctity of marriage* idea even though the bean counters suggest it really doesn't exist. There were also suspicions about Peppermint Patty of Peanuts, Velma of Scooby Do and Bert and Ernie of Sesame Street. Society's sexual police fussed about whether or not Patty, Velma, or Bert and Ernie were concentrating on same-set-tool tendencies in spite of the very big reality that these characters—the subject of so much controversy, were just that—characters. They weren't real. And while all the fuss emerged

Pretty harmless it was thought to be until society's slappers noticed something of concern, right there on toddler television.

And while all the fuss emerged about whether or not the triangled Teletubby or SpongeBob was or was not homosexual, every child in America that these well-intentioned folks wanted to protect from a homosexual influence, learned even more about the subject.

about whether or not the triangled Teletubby or SpongeBob was or was not homosexual, every child in America that these well-intentioned folks wanted to protect from a homosexual influence, learned even more about the subject. But everyone probably felt better, especially since after chasing down the Teletubby smut and checking out SpongeBob's underwear, it was thought the Sex Fairy would take care of all the Edwards and Emmilous in the honeymoon hotel.

COMMUNITY CLASHING

With great dance teachers from society, communities can pick up the beat and *beating* they do in the quest to take care of the sexual disrespectful stuff on a local level. Watching the attacks on Teletubbies or scruffy characters in the park, various community folks get together to do their own version of chasing down anything that smacks of sexual disrespect. It might happen with a get-together at the library—bringing everyone's attention to possible smut among the pages of books that might just come under the scrutiny of the kiddos. Very old books like *Catcher In The Rye* bring very new complaints year after year. And whether it is *Heather Has Two Mommies* or poor *Harry Potter,* the idea is that beating down the sexual disrespect in the community will guarantee the infusion of sexual respect for all the kiddos, unless of course, they need just a little boost of help from the Sex Fairy later on.

LOCAL WICKED WARS

Other community clashes get to be pretty exciting with Moms and Dads doing such things as organizing big protests when the adult bookstore gets a permit to set up shop. *There will be no pornography in our town,* scream those from the sexual respect community army, trying to make sure that the disrespectful smut doesn't reach anyone's shopping bag. In one community-clashing effort that made the nightly news, a concerned Dad thought he had the answer. Not surprisingly, when the adult bookstore took up residence on the road where he drove his daughters to school, there was no sacrifice too great. *Why,* he even explained to the perky Channel 3 news lady with the really big jewelry, that he took time off work for the protest and was considering quitting his job to become a full-time *smut fighter*. With pride, he demonstrated for the six-o'clock news crowd how he had set up a video camera to capture any purple-faced fool who attempted to purchase the smut. Dad was quite convinced his sex surveillance was just the right thing to do and he was very excited about getting even more outraged community folks to join in his smut fighting. And it could be wondered if this Dad ever returns to driving his *for-sure-innocent* daughters to school again. Will he ever take any time to teach them the sexual respect side of things, or will he just be content with fighting the smut and simply renew his subscription to the Sex Fairy faithful fan club?

SNUFFING OF THE SMUT

Sometimes the smut slinging starts with the littlest of folks just to make sure the smut gets stuffed early. Sometimes this happens throughout American schools as everyone feels a great sense of relief when a six-year-old first grader is suspended for *sexual harassment,* which certainly ranks high in the disrespect department. In one 2006 example that hit the nightly news, the culprit (first grader actually) teased a female classmate and during story time, he apparently gave her a kiss on the cheek—but only after his first grade male friend made the suggestion. *Well, this just won't do in a community that takes pride in keeping track of sexual disrespect,* they all opined as the first grader was sent away in a police car. Sure, he will get back into school but will anyone talk to him about sexual respect and it's key to the whole sexual harassment issue? Probably not—but what will happen is most of the slappers will feel a lot better that the snuffing of the smut begins early in their community.

Other ways in which communities get fired up about sexual disrespect includes such smut smashing as fighting the sex education program in school. *No talk about Kotex pads for our kids* becomes the mantra for this righteous outrage, making everyone feel totally in control of saving morality. More community clashing may include demands to remove the condom machine from the Guzzle Gas Station that is close to the school where lots of teenagers purchase their after-school sodas, or organizing parade and protests banning the sale of Playboy magazine from the Smoke Shop even though no one under 18 is allowed in the cigarette-selling place. Or some parents may tackle sexual disrespect by firing up a petition to force the cheerleaders to lengthen their skirts and cut back on the wiggling of hips at varsity basketball games. And it is all done to fight sexual disrespect, believing (usually honorably) that these community efforts will create sexual respect, which of course affirms the *no need for nuthin'* in actively teaching sexual respect.

AND FAMILY DENIAL

Taking the dance cue, first from society, then from the communities, families join the denial dance. Supported by the rage and war from society and community efforts, families turn to the *wells,* the *waits* and the *whens* to avoid teaching sexual respect, which really results in *nothing needing to be done* and therefore, leaving everything to the Sex Fairy. And families are so good at finding reasons not to do the sexual respect teaching.

And it could be wondered if the smut-fighting dad will take time to teach his children about sexual respect or will he just renew his subscription to the Sex Fairy faithful fan club?

THE WONDERFUL WELLS—THE PAUSE THAT REFRESHES

✓ Well, my kids need to be protected from sexual information. They are too innocent.

✓ Well, I am prepared with the Kotex pamphlet my mother gave me and I did just fine.

✓ Well, my children just aren't capable of understanding the complicated concept of sperm/egg fertilization or ovulation prediction cycles. It is just far beyond their comprehension.

✓ Well, I live in a good neighborhood and I have the best kept home in the cul-de-sac. My kids have a current set of encyclopedias and they are eating from the seven basic food groups every day. What more do they need?

✓ Well, I am a good parent, and therefore my kids will be good. Influencing their minds with the nastiness of sex will only cause problems.

✓ Well, my children are growing up on a farm and they have a clear understanding of the way things work, especially concerning "the birds and the bees." That is all they need.

✓ Well, we don't subscribe to cable television and we have pornography protection on our Internet. There shouldn't be a problem keeping our children sexually innocent.

✓ Well, our kids have extremely high self-esteem. Even though they don't know about sex, they will make good sexual decisions in the future if they just feel good about themselves.

✓ Well, my children don't need sex education because they have access to many other things to stimulate their minds. Our home is filled with video games, books, educational movies, etc. Our family philosophy is just to keep their little minds busy and sex won't be an issue.

THE WAITING AND THE WHEN GAMES

The *wells* seem to provide a handy avoidance for parents, especially for the cute little ones who don't even notice when Mr. and Mrs. Hamster get a little frisky in the cage. But as children get older and seem to pay attention to the teacher arrested for sexual abuse or the bashing of a Teletubby's sexual preference, a few pangs of worry tiptoe forward, causing a concern that the *no need for nuthin'* might be over. This is especially true for good parents, like those of Edward and Emmilou, who take care of everything else in the education department. But eventually a good Mom and Dad (once the *wells* seem to be wearing out) are soothed by a new avoidance of sex education, the *waits.*

✓ I will wait until she starts her period, then I will talk with her about sex.

✓ I will wait until he becomes interested in girls, but now he wants nothing to do with the opposite sex.

✓ I will wait until they are more mature. Right now they don't even understand the concept of the Virgin Mary, so how could they understand sex?

✓ I will wait until they have sexual questions.

✓ I will wait until Fluffy has kittens and then they will understand.

RUDE RATIONALIZATIONS

The *wells* and the *waits* feel good and safe to families in denial. After all, they have society slapping the bad folks and communities also dancing the tune of just being against the bad stuff, since it is hoped with all that bad slapping, the kids will automatically become good folks. But what if the same denials were used in other areas so important to parents, like the Ernie, Emma, Edwin, and Erma contingencies? Would these same parents use the *wells* and the *waits* concerning being Catholic, being polite, or showing respect for the Star Spangled Banner? Would good parents wait until their daughter got her first job before they taught her to be honest? And when fairies in charge of these critically important issues (like a fairy seems to be in charge of sex) are considered, absurdity abounds.

✓ Well, I am waiting for the Personality Fairy to show up to teach him how to be sensitive to others.

✓ Well, I am waiting for the Be Nice Fairy to teach manners.

✓ Well, I am waiting for the Baptist Fairy before I take them to Sunday school.

And if lie detectors were established in the parental confessional booth, it would probably be easier for good parents if their child was a *victim* of sexual abuse rather than a *sexual offender*. It is the darkest denial of all.

THE DARKEST DENIAL

So the denials have it—society, communities and families, determining that protecting marriage and the sanctity of sex requires just *punishing the perverts* who obviously seem to be upsetting the pretend perfect way things should unfold in the honeymoon hotel room. There is nothing positive about this well-intentioned but miserably failing approach, but it certainly feels better. Strengthening the noose around the neck of the bad folks feels better and feels safer than trying to figure out how to prevent someone from growing up to be a rapist, a murderer, or abductor of precious children like Jacob, Polly, Megan and Jessica.

But folded carefully into the dynamics of denial is the darkest secret for parents-something no one really talks about. If sexual offenders are the ultimate in sexual disrespect, and if the slapping society really means business about punishing, then why wouldn't parents talk to their children about the punishment business so their children could at least go to the honeymoon hotel before they go to prison?

Usually parents are good at the negative in such things as, *don't get venereal disease, don't get pregnant, don't have premarital sex,* so why not, *don't become a sex offender?* More than likely, the consideration of a child becoming a sexual offender is so shameful, most parents couldn't even muster up the strength to weakly climb aboard that ***don't*** bandwagon. And if lie detectors were established in the parental confessional booth, it would probably be easier for good parents if their child was a *victim* of sexual abuse, rather than for their child to be *a sexual abuser*. The darkest denial it is—*that my child could ever become a sex offender.*

WE CREATE WHAT WE FEAR

Yet children do become offenders, sometimes easily, as they drown in a society of constant subtle seduction, encouraging sexual acting out. And this is juxtapositioned to a society entrenched in deep denial, but nonetheless ready to slap anyone who steps outside the lines that no one in that same society, community, or family really wants to draw. Many innocent children, because of sexual education neglect, are led down the path to sexual disrespect by a world too ashamed to even prevent what they so abhor. So as the sexual offending problem continues to blossom, society continues to scream loudly and parents, in the darkest denial about parental shame, withhold sexual information, actually preferring their children to be victims rather than offenders. And in doing so, what is feared is created, sadly and surely.

THE CHALLENGE

Absolutely absurd it is—creating what is feared most, and it is absolutely marvelous if Emmilou and Edward, in the precarious nature of that honeymoon hotel room, make everything work out. But a better (and safer) plan for parents would be to put lots of the money, time, effort, and love (long before they even met each other) into teaching sexual respect. But that hardly ever happens and good parents just hope it turns out okay, which means they must believe a silly fairy will make everything work out. And this absurdity happens even though the *sanctity of marriage* isn't really doing too well, no matter how many Teletubbies or Sponge Bobs lose their jobs.

So the challenge is to stop the absurdity—stop the madness and with that, give up the myth that SHE will take care of this very, very important thing of sexual respect. But that is a tough order, especially with society so sure that denial is the way to go, and that punishment of those who are sexually disrespectful is the chosen avenue in creating a sexually respectful society. This book challenges not only the Sex Fairy myth, but also the ease with which SHE is followed.

IF THERE AIN'T ONE, WHY IS SHE HERE?

But SHE does exist in this book—however precarious and poignant for parents.

Perhaps the Sex Fairy exists as a humorous reminder of the absurdity in the parental belief (hope, actually) that the children they love, nurture and teach in every other way, will learn sexual respect if they just turn everything over to the magic of a Sex Fairy.

Perhaps the Sex Fairy exists as an *illusion*—sprinkling fairy finesse to help parents understand that believing in a fairy in charge of sex is just that—an illusion.

Perhaps the Sex Fairy represents the parental *silliness* in smugly believing they are really in control of their children's sexual education and that not until they give the green light and decide to open the previously-thought-to-be-shut-gate, will kiddos ever learn anything about sex.

Perhaps the Sex Fairy in all her silly trappings, represents the farce about the sexually provocative society in which most kids live, reminding parents of the absurdity in thinking that the kiddos are sexually innocent until they show up at the honeymoon hotel.

Perhaps the Sex Fairy exists with all her fairy paraphernalia representing all the sexual *stuff* permeating children's lives, every day, in every way—hopefully encouraging parents to get busy teaching and guiding rather than counting on the poofing and puffing of a Sex Fairy.

Perhaps the Sex Fairy exists to lighten up the potentially boring data and research that sometimes must be used to mobilize good Moms and Dads into action.

Perhaps the Sex Fairy needs to use her wand to point out to parents the absurdity of fighting the sexual disrespect battle with the wrong weapons, such as just punishing disrespect without providing sexually respectful guidelines.

Perhaps the Sex Fairy exists for a little fun and fantasy—fluffing parents into true protection and love for their kidlets.

Perhaps the Sex Fairy exists for a little fun and fantasy, fluffing parents into laughing at the absurdity of their thinking.

Perhaps the Sex Fairy with all her fussing about appearance needs to provide a mirror to those who care about children—helping them see that perhaps in their own reflections, they can find sweet sexual respect, and then teach it to children they love.

ENTER HER MAJESTY

The Sex Fairy has bright orange hair that makes pumpkins pale, but that doesn't always match her rich raspberry nail polish so adored by the wedding planner and Emmilou.

The Sex Fairy is female, really female, perhaps teaching the preposterous nature of sexism that suggests only females should be in charge of the sexual teaching.

The Sex Fairy has a wonderful wand that sometimes wanders, not always on target, sometimes erecting things that simply need directing.

The Sex Fairy has a hurt heart when adults abandon their children concerning sexuality, which forces her to carry Kleenex in her brassiere for the tears that need to be shed about this neglect.

The Sex Fairy has majestic morality, which is honorable, but which also causes her to pucker purple when sexual slang is used, which is quite precarious for the fairy in charge of sex.

The Sex Fairy has way-too-heavy princess slippers which make her feel taller, but which sometimes cause her wings to wilt with weight, as she flies only slightly above the ground.

The Sex Fairy is less-than-mobile, finding flying a bit cumbersome since she has spent much of her time worrying about sexually abused children, and because she is clearly anti-aerobic.

The Sex Fairy wears a bit too much blush, suggesting that natural blush on the fairy in charge of sex would certainly challenge her authority to sexually educate children.

The Sex Fairy reads slasher books at night to go to sleep. In this way she can keep up with sex offenders and keep her mind on precious children who are abandoned by their parents in teaching sexual respect.

The Sex Fairy studies and studies and studies about sexual offenders and sexual deviancy. She knows a lot about sexual disrespect, but in that vast knowledge, she just flutters and falters, never really being able to take care of children for which parents put her in charge.

The Sex Fairy is a bit dysfunctional and she has a stammering, stuttering speech, making her prone to *awful alliteration* that, in turn, makes her tongue-tied, providing a great example for the absurdity of adults leaving sex education to a stammering Sex Fairy.

The Sex Fairy has researched extensively about who is likely to become a sex offender. She is smart, but because her heart is broken about abandoned kiddos, the research just piles and piles. She, like most parents, has wonderful intentions to take care of things, but she just can't get the job done.

And the Sex Fairy adorns the glossy foldout in the middle, a spoof on Playboy and Penthouse magazines—the symbols of tawdry titillation. She wants everyone to laugh at the pin-up image so that the ridiculous nature of a fairy in charge of sex can be realized. Clearly, she is too tacky, too absurd, and too incompetent to protect children from society's sexual saturation, suggesting that after all the laughing and crying, it is a tragedy and a travesty to hand over the task of teaching sexual respect to a fairy so incompetent. But what she does really well in all her silliness, is handing the task and her wand back to us. For it is only through education and our direct effort that we can raise sexually respectful children and help them to avoid becoming sex offenders.

The Sex Fairy has majestic morality, which is honorable, but which also causes her to pucker purple when sexual slang is used, which is quite precarious for the fairy in charge of sex.

Chapter 2
Voices of Victims

CHAPTER 2: VOICES OF VICTIMS

He was perfect at birth just like they had imagined he would be so long ago. Many years earlier, when Mom and Dad first met at Lucky's Laundromat, they somehow knew there was *family* in the future and *he* was the focus of that fantasy. As they sorted their underwear—Mom with her lilac Victoria's Secret panties and Dad with his rather boring boxers—it seemed to be love at first sight and suds.

Following underwear mingling at Lucky's, there was dating, but it didn't seem to take long for both of them to know this was *the big one.* Sure, they had each dated before, but Mom easily tired of *boy bravado* so typical of her previous dating experiences, and Dad found his past female dates to be *boring bimbos* and quite tedious. This time seemed different. Dad had always looked for a solid girl, who would help him with his lifetime dream of becoming a dentist and, of course, *a Dad.* And Mom was also seeking solid; someone who would not only help her become a teacher, but someone who would share her passion for *Mommyhood.*

And passion it was for the two of them. Although both were practical—wanting to do things right—their love (and lust) hurried things along. First came the secret promises in the back seat of the Chevrolet, then the engagement ring, followed by a silly picture in the local newspaper with an ocean sunset in the background, announcing wedding plans to a community inhabited by only a small percentage of folk who had ever even seen the ocean. Then came the showers, the bachelor party, the wedding, and too many toasters. But no matter how complicated the wedding plans tended to be, deciding between the potential seventeen ring bearers and flower girls in their large families, Mom and Dad were really interested in becoming just that—a Mom and a Dad. But before those dreams could be realized, obstacles were to be overcome.

At the beginning of the marriage, things were tight, except of course, concerning their big budget dreams for a family. Dad's college was balanced with his work as a veterinarian assistant in the office of Dr. Barklot. Night school was tough, and studying late into the night often resulted in Dad falling asleep on the one-missing-cushion-couch, and Mom sleeping alone in the lumpy bed purchased with pride at the Goodwill Store. But that didn't matter. Even with long days of too much coffee and aspirin, Dad could still remember the reason for all the work, and that was to someday have a *perfect family*.

For Mom, her job at Traditional Trust Bank didn't begin until 2 p.m. for a couple of reasons. First, the bank manager, Mr. Dollarhide, was a *bean counter,* Mom said, and he only wanted her to work the rush hour, which began at 3 p.m., following the shift change at the nearby fertilizer factory. The second reason Mom didn't go to work until the afternoon was that her classes at the teacher's college were scheduled in the morning. *Yes*, Mom wanted to be a teacher. And even though she was busy learning the art of lesson planning and how to make the pilgrims perfect for second graders, she was constantly fantasizing about her own Thanksgiving dinners far into the future with her own kiddo pilgrims decorating the table in her fantasy house with her fantasy (and perfect) family.

But before all that could happen, coupons needed to be clipped for groceries, an oil filter needed to be purchased for the thirteen-year-old Volvo, and the Christmas Club savings account needed to be cashed out in June if they were going to fly home for the Fourth of July family reunion. The almost-matching dish set and their small studio apartment was just fine for them because they had plans for later on. Sometimes on Saturday night when they splurged on banana splits at the Corn Husker Drive-In, they would cuddle up and remember the reason for all their hard work. And later, on the couch that was missing one cushion, they would fall asleep in weariness, forgetting about the prerequisite for making that family. But then, on Sunday morning, their only sleep-in day, their faith and memory was renewed. They remembered that after Dad was finished with dental school and after all their other perfect plans were realized, they could actually plan for *his* (or her) arrival.

And they did, and here he was. The first child always seems to have a special place, and rightly so. Not only had they worked and waited until things were perfect for their family starting, but now *he* was here and *he* seemed perfect. He had the perfect number of elbows, toes, and teeth, with only a slight adjustment imagined from an orthodontist. The family fan club for first-born Son only enhanced the perfection status as Grandmas, Grandpas, Aunts and Uncles all doted on Son as well.

As time went on, the perfect family fantasies about Son abounded. Maybe law school at a prestigious university they wondered, while cleaning up the Fruit Loops he had smashed into the carpet. Or perhaps medical school was in his future allowing Son—who had just poured his milk down the furnace vent—to cure the world of a raging disease. Or could it be, they pondered, that their perfect son could fulfill the most honorable vocation of all—becoming a good dad? It didn't matter. For now, he was just perfect.

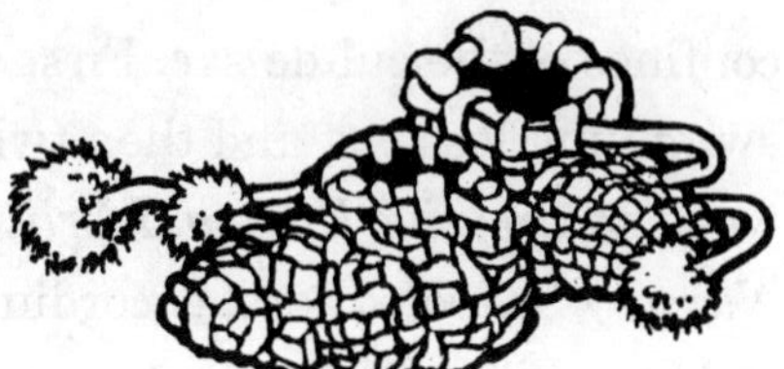

What was important now was that things seemed *perfect* just as Mom and Dad had planned long ago in the backseat of that now-gone-to-the-car-graveyard Chevy. Their studio apartment that once had been perfectly fine was replaced by a five-bedroom home in an upscale gated community, complete with tennis court and swimming pool. Their cushion-missing couch had long ago been carted off to the dump, replaced by all new furniture, this time, matching perfectly. A Mercedes replaced the limping Volvo for Dad, and a leather-seated SUV was designated to Mom, who fantasized every time she started the engine about the time when she might be driving Son to his various kiddo activities in a Mommy car pool.

And that time came when Son not only demonstrated his competency with Play Dough and Sneaky Snakes at home, but his perfection ventured outside the confines of the cul-de-sac. First, it was swimming lessons, and then twice a week at *Creative Kids and Critters Nursery School* where, according to Mom, his artistic talents would be stimulated with finger painting for four-year-olds. And Dad could hardly wait for the weekend when he and Son would take what Dad called *learning laps,* visiting museums or the library. And even though Son seemed a little bored at age five with the study of corn germination, Dad felt sure that someday he would further his brilliance with Tinker Toys toward some kind of scientific inquiry.

Every morning when Dad left for work at the dental office, he and Son would recite the alphabet and count to twenty, just to make sure Son started first grade with a slight advantage. *All that finger painting had paid off,* Mom thought to herself. Why, when she attended parent meetings at the school or when she had coffee klatches with the neighbor ladies, it was clear that Son already had a reputation. Everyone seemed to know that just as Son had entered the world perfect, he entered school (however private and expensive) the same way—perfect.

Although Mom and Dad had considered public school for Son because most of the children in the gated community attended Star Bright Elementary, they eventually nixed that idea in favor of the prestigious private school across town. It would be a lot of driving for Mom, but they both felt Son had a potential that might not be developed at Star Bright, sharing one teacher among twenty-four, six-year-olds. *Small classes, individual attention, and high school preparation begins in first grade,* was the promise of Mr. Noright, the private school's administrator. Mom and Dad were convinced and Son was enrolled.

Mom's day began focusing on Son's education endeavors, involving a forty-five- minute, one-way drive to deliver still-perfect Son to school and ending her day with the rotation of Son's absolutely perfect pictures of pilgrims on the refrigerator.

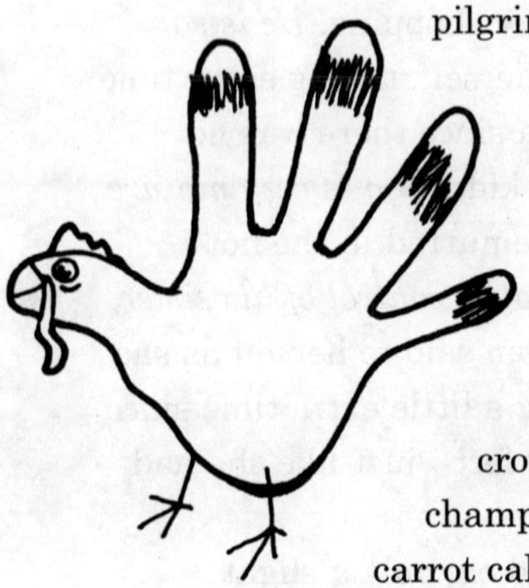

The evening meal ritual often involved Mom giving math problems to Dad and Son, Dad pretending to error, and then Son being crowned the math champion right before the carrot cake. *Yes*, the whole family revolved around Son, and rightfully so. He was perfect—perfect in Little League, as well as math, reading, and swimming, and Dad still had hope for Son's someday interest in corn germination. Son looked perfect too, straight teeth (no need for Dad's dental assistance), naturally curly hair, and a smile that could melt even the most hardened of hearts.

When Sister was born, she also had her own dose of perfection. Unlike Son, with his dark wavy hair, Sister was *perfectly* bald. Unlike Son, who slept blissfully in Dad's arms in the birthing wing of the hospital, Sister was *perfectly* loud with her blood-curdling screams of indignation with the entire birth process. Unlike Son, who slept through the night after two weeks, Sister was *perfect* in keeping Mom and Dad from sleeping more than two hours at a time. And when Son inquired about his perfectly peaceful world now-turned-upside-down, Mom and Dad explained to him that Sister was too little to know that Son had an important Little League game in the morning. They consoled him, helping him understand that Sister was too little to know all the things Son knew. But never mind, they were a three-member team dealing with Sister's differences and with this camaraderie, the perfect family plan would be just that—perfect.

There wasn't time to get Sister into *Creative Kids and Critters* with all the driving Son to and from private school, as well as attending his sporting and other competitive pursuits. Perched perfectly in her car seat, Sister became part of the projects in helping Son excel. And after all the driving to and from Son's soccer games, karate lessons, and usually a sleepover or two with friends from the Outdoor Adventure group, it was just as well that Sister liked tagging along with Mom, following and admiring Son. The two of them were an all-girl tag-team. They giggled together, and both Mom and Dad knew someday Sister would understand the differences. It wasn't that they loved her less, but she was just different—sweet, but different. Dad was clearly

smitten with Sister, bursting with pride when he called her his little *Precious Pie.* For Dad, it was a different feeling than when he called Son his *little man.* Sister was his pet and his pride; Son was his future.

Mom loved Sister too, especially when she was so cute clapping for her brother as he hit the ball over the fence in the Little League championship game. She was sweet on her own, but it was even sweeter when Son carried Sister into the dugout to give his friends a highly coveted, high-five handslap with Precious Pie Sister. Son was an image of Dad in his Precious Pie admiration, doting on his sister, but also being very much in charge of her. They all seemed to have mutual little fan clubs for one another. Sister was perfect in cheering for Son, perfect in knowing when it was time to pick up Son from school, and perfect in knowing that in this family, Son was perfect.

And Son's perfection also included Sister stuff.

"You teach Sister how to tie her shoes," Dad instructed Son, taking deep pride in how well Sister minded and respected her brother.

Mom was proud when Son eagerly complied (in such an adult way) by taking Sister to the church basement restroom while Mom and Dad were busy with adult prayer meetings. Mom and Dad were proud of Son who volunteered for an afternoon in Sister's bedroom, trying to teach her the alphabet before she started first grade at Star Bright Elementary School. And yes, at the young age of twelve, Son could be trusted to baby-sit his six-year-old sister while Mom did aerobics and went grocery shopping. *He is so responsible,* she said to herself, taking extra time in the locker room sauna since there was no need to worry about the kids. *Son is very mature for his age,* Mom later demurred in the hot shower, and *he has complete control of his sister, since she adores him,* Mom said to herself as she finished sudsing—taking a little extra time since her family seemed so perfect—just like she had planned.

As time tiptoed on, only a slight hairline fracture in the perfect family picture emerged. In academics, it seemed Sister shuffled while Son sprinted.

"Well, Sister is going to make some young man very happy," Mom consoled as she shared Sister's barely-passing-grade report card with Dad as he cleaned the backyard swimming pool in preparation for Son's fifteen-year-old birthday party.

"She doesn't have to be a Rhodes scholar to be my little Precious Pie," Dad reminded Mom.

As time trudged on, not only did Sister shuffle in school, but a certain sullenness seemed to creep into the perfect family picture about the time she refused to have a party for her tenth birthday. *No way,* she told Mom, did she want girls coming to her house. Yes, Sister was slipping in the social department, as well as in school. And soon the shuffles turned to sullen, which turned to sarcastic, which eventually turned to scary for Mom and Dad.

"I just don't know what has gotten into her," Mom worried to Dad as they packed for a weekend jaunt to a nearby city where Son was the quarterback (as a sophomore, no less) for the high school football team.

"She always liked to watch his sporting events in the past," Dad pondered.

"Why doesn't she want to go with us?" Mom queried packing the ice chest with sports drinks and energy bars to ensure Son had every edge possible in the contest. "She said she just wants to be alone. She doesn't have any friends to invite over and she doesn't want to stay with anyone else. She seems so isolated. I don't worry about her getting into trouble, I just worry about why she is sullen and sarcastic."

What to do, Mom and Dad wondered as they remembered the perfect plans for the perfect family were now slightly slipping because of Sister.

"Maybe Son can help," suggested Mom, feeling slight relief with the idea.

"He just has a way with her," cooed Dad, as they both confirmed that since he was pretty perfect in almost every way, he was the likely solution to the now sarcastic-sullen-scary sister not wanting to join the family outing. And he did. Only about forty-five minutes alone with Sister in the bedroom and the problem seemed solved. Sullenness and sarcasm remained but the *I'm-not-going-with-you-anywhere* was absent. Reluctantly she would go. Oh, Mom and Dad were thrilled and once again filled with the wonderment of Son's talents.

True, he excelled in sports, academia, and social climbing, but Son's perfection also included the *not-to-do* list. He only dated girls for the important things like proms or formal dances even though plenty of teenage girls called the house, giggling and gaggling with a hope for more from him. But he wasn't impressed and he wasn't interested in all those raging hormone outlets so common to many of his male friends.

"He has his priorities right," Dad opined to Mom as he remembered his teenage struggles with sexual desire being overcome by his desire to have a perfect courtship, perfect engagement, perfect wedding, and perfect family. Although Son was only an *idea* during those long ago days of Dad's sexual self-restraint, it seemed to Dad that Son was somehow cut from the same mold.

As for Son's apparent restraint in the female department, Dad was proud.

But as Son excelled in nearly every category, Sister seemed perfect at failing. But in spite of her struggles, the *Precious Pie* part of Sister was still there for Dad, at least for a time. When Sister started to menstruate, the challenge loomed. Not only were *Precious Pie periods* difficult for Dad to fathom, but with the onset of puberty, Precious Pie seemed to get worse with her sullenness and sarcasm. And as she struggled, Son seemed to get more perfect as he ended high school and began more perfect plans for college.

At the same time, in Sister's adolescence, things really deteriorated for the youngest in the nearly-perfect-except-for-her family. Sister seemed more interested in staying out after curfew and choosing the perfect color of purple for her hair and her not-authorized tattoo. The only thing Sister seemed to accomplish was making Mom and Dad, and of course Son, worry. *Yes*, Son routinely joined his parents in pondering what was wrong with Sister. She made them all so uncomfortable, coming home in the wee hours of the morning, beer on her breath, and seemingly hatred in her heart. Hatred for what, they didn't know. But what they did know was that Sister was in trouble and actually, she was quite *troubling* to the family perfection plans.

As Son left for Doctor college, Sister left high school finding herself *Precious Pie pregnant* by a twenty-one-year-old auto mechanic. For a fleeting moment of *girl talk*, Sister convinced Mom that marriage would help her settle down.

"Mom, I just know I will be happy once I'm married. I know you don't like him, but he's perfect (good words for Mom) for me. It will be fine," the formerly-known-as-Precious Pie, very pregnant, fifteen-year-old urged. A quick wedding by a Justice of the Peace dashed any hopes Dad may have had for a white wedding like the one he had with Mom so many years ago.

As the baby arrived, Mom and Dad tried to be proud, but it was difficult. The marriage between Sister and hubby was already showing signs of wear as evidenced by an absent birth father—one who thought being in the delivery room was far less enticing than celebrating his baby's entrance into the world with Budweisers and friends at a pub located near the hospital.

In a few months, the marriage seemed as uneventful as the baby's birth had been. The tiny studio apartment shared by Sister and her now-mostly-absent husband reminded Mom and Dad only briefly of their earlier days when the perfect family plans were only a hope and a dream. Now, as they maneuvered their donated baby bottles in competition with the Budweiser bottles for space in the small, only-now-and-then-working refrigerator, they silently wondered what had gone wrong with Dad's Precious Pie.

But at least Son was still fine, they consoled themselves. While Sister took Precious Pie #2 to daycare in order to work at the mechanic shop where her husband-now-run-off-with-the-Burger King-cashier used to work, Mom and Dad relished Son's acceptance into a prestigious medical school. *No,* Sister refused to move home when she was left stranded, even though the offer was clearly honorable from Mom and Dad. *Too many memories*, Sister explained, crying in a phone booth after departure of hubby-on-the-highway was discovered. *They would always be there for her, no matter what she needed,* was their tearful response as they later wondered at what point in that promise Sister had hung up the telephone.

Mom and Dad doted as much as they could on Sister and Precious Pie #2, but it was hard. They never knew exactly what they would find visiting in the studio apartment with a walking, talking three-year-old who was sometimes the center of Sister's attention, yet sometimes the center of her wrath. She seemed so conflicted about being a Mom, and they noticed that confusion even in the hospital when Precious Pie #2 was brought into the world. The confusion seemed profound, as Sister seemed to both coo and curse at the newborn. And then, three years later, the same conflicts within the struggling Mom were just as evident.

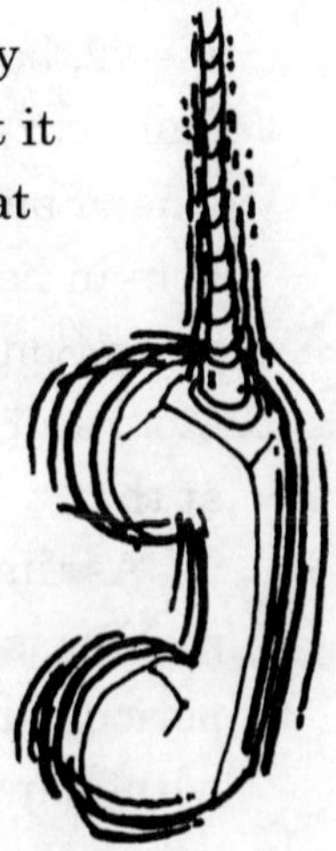

Sister also seemed conflicted about those perfect family get-togethers at all the perfect family times, back in the gated community—a stark contrast to Sister's rundown studio apartment. *Yes*, she would often attend and participate in the glorification of perfect Son's accomplishments that always occurred sitting around the Thanksgiving dinner table or sitting around the picnic table at the Memorial Day camp site. But the glaring discrepancies between Sister and Son seemed so obvious that those family events were eventually avoided by Sister with excuses about needing to work a second shift at the café, needing to earn extra money for gas or needing to find a babysitter for Precious

Pie #2, because she just didn't want the now four-year-old to spend the night at Grandma's when Son was visiting from college. She was firm in her *no overnight stays* for the little one when Son was home. It didn't make sense to Mom and Dad but Sister had always been *perfect* at that.

As time tiptoed forward, Sister continued to shuffle as she had done since the Precious Pie periods arrived. Mom and Dad tried to help her with many offers of education, moving home, counseling, and of course, money. When Sister had a chance to be rescued by Mom and Dad's efforts, she seemed to resist, not with rage or fussiness, but with an overwhelming sadness neither of them understood. Sobbing uncontrollably, she would often tell them *no, she didn't want any help*. Mom and Dad were reminded of their old days of clipped coupons and a high frequency of frozen burrito breakfasts as they tried to offer financial support. She would have none of it. It was sad because they had so much to give and Sister had so many reasons to refuse.

Son always asked about Sister while away at medical school, and he often sent her little gifts and sweet cards of support. Just as they had always done, Mom, Dad and Son formed the worry group, wondering what was wrong with Sister. Dad continued dentistry, Mom continued volunteering for honorable causes, and Son continued to shine. In his final year of doctor practicing, Son called home with good—no, *perfect* news. *Yes*, he had a fiancée and *yes,* he wanted to bring her home to do the proverbial *meet the parents*. And he did.

Of course, this was the next step in the perfect family picture, so Mom and Dad were thrilled. Sister was invited—no *urged*—to join the celebration, to which she reluctantly agreed, with now five-year-old Precious Pie #2 in tow. Everything was perfect for the weekend visit, with Son's fiancée and his plans for courtship, engagement, and wedding falling into perfectly timed choreography. Mom and Dad were so proud as Son announced that the wedding would happen in about a year with plenty of time to prepare. Restraint had always been easy for Son, they remembered. By the time they were to be married, Son would be a real doctor. Such perfect planning it was. And when Mom and Dad cuddled on the couch after the wonderful weekend, they remembered what it was like to be in love so many years ago. Their eyes glistened when they thought about their pride in Son, but their eyes *teared* when they thought about Sister who seemed so listless and lifeless. There didn't seem to be a piece of any *Precious Pie* left in her. So sad, they lamented.

When the wedding finally arrived, Mom and Dad were almost disappointed because the year of planning, organizing, and arranging had been so exciting. They tried to include Sister in the fanfare, but she usually had an excuse to avoid the festivities. Mom and Dad really wanted her to be part of the fun so they called on Son to help engage Sister in the celebration. Son and his soon-to-be-bride even asked Sister to be one of the bridesmaids, which was a highly-coveted position in the soon-to-be-wedding-of-the-year. But *no,* she explained, reminding them of her embarrassment with the extra hundred pounds she seemed to have gained after giving birth to Precious Pie #2. But when they asked if Precious Pie #2 could be the flower girl in the wedding, Sister, between sobs, sadly agreed.

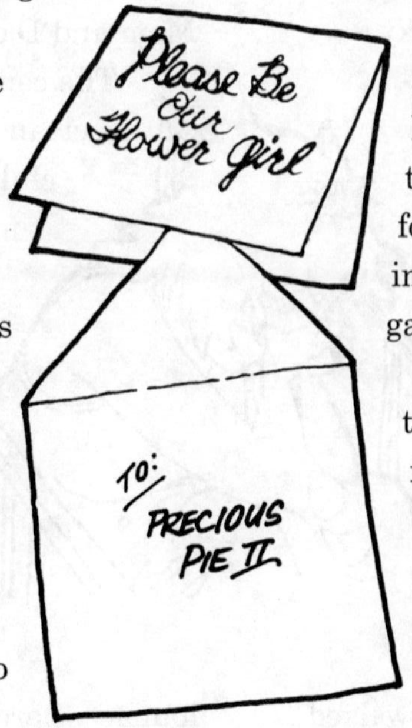

It might be good for her to dress up in something fancy, different from the Salvation Army attire she usually wore, was the secret conversation of everyone in the family about the flower girl invitation. It wasn't that Mom and Dad didn't shower Precious Pie #2 with lots of new clothing—some of it the very best—just like Sister had worn in childhood. But they had noticed the strange dispatch of those presents with fancy brand name labels. Sister seemed only somewhat grateful when the expensive outfits were gifted to Precious Pie #2, but strangely, Mom and Dad would eventually find those items of clothing never worn, mostly left in their original packaging, collecting dust in the missing-knobs-chest-of-drawers often far past the time when Precious Pie #2 had outgrown them. Strange, they always thought, but never mind. Now they looked forward to dressing their granddaughter in a real Precious Pie/bride outfit for the gala event of Son's wedding.

Then, the night before the wedding and three hours before the groom's fancy rehearsal dinner, the wedding practice took place in the church. Everyone tried to ignore it but Sister's abrupt and tearful departures every now and then was just too obvious, especially while Mom and her soon-to-be-co-grandma dressed the flower girl and the five-year-old ring bearer who was grandson of the bride's mother. As Precious Pie #2 adorned her miniature-wedding gown and the little boy dressed in his grown-up tuxedo, Sister made her final, tearful escape. Later she was found crying uncontrollably on the church steps. They all wondered again, *what went wrong?*

Dad was called out of the wedding rehearsal and urged a promise from Sister, lest the perfect wedding plans be ruined with her outbursts. Dad was tender, but he tried desperately to inspire the love he knew Sister felt for Son so long ago. And in Dad's campaign for holding back the tears until after the wedding, it seemed Sister got worse. *No,* she didn't want to talk about it. *Yes,* she would guarantee that Precious Pie #2 would participate in the wedding. But *no*, she couldn't stay and attend the rehearsal dinner. With that shaky promise, Dad walked Sister and her wide-eyed five-year-old to the old, needing-a-new-muffler Volvo. The two of them departed with Sister still in tears, but guaranteeing Dad she would not mess things up for Son and his perfect wedding.

The next day, and before the wedding began, even Son's attempts to console sad Sister were not successful. Although Precious Pie #2 looked very *Precious Pie-like* in her baby bride dress, Sister sobbed out loud when the miniature bride and groom (now flower girl and ring bearer), walked sweetly down the aisle, signaling that the wedding was about to begin. And when it did begin, Sister ended, leaving the church and her daughter for a destination unknown.

The wedding went on with Sister's abrupt departure only providing a small hairline fracture in the perfect plan. Many noticed Sister's absence, just as her uncontrollable sobs had been noticed during the first few steps of Precious Pie #2's trip down the aisle. Mom and Dad were immediately saddened by their youngest's departure, but they were also well seasoned to Sister's sadness, so it was easy for them to go on with the joy and celebration of Son's wedding and reception.

But what wasn't so easy was the later-in-the-evening visit of two police officers at the country club wedding reception who quietly informed Mom and Dad that Sister was in the hospital. The cops knew Mom and Dad, from teeth cleaning and shared carpools for all their children, so it was a precarious moment. Questions about what happened to Sister were followed by sensitive suggestions from the cops. Gently, they informed Mom and Dad that it appeared to be a *deliberate* car wreck, preceded by too many *tiddilies*, as the officers referenced double shots of whiskey at the Holiday Inn lounge where Sister worked *in housekeeping* as Mom called it, which really meant she was a motel maid.

"She's physically okay," the cops encouraged. "But since it was a suicide attempt, the EMTs took her to lockdown at the psyche unit."

The word *suicide* terrorized Mom and Dad to the core, but reassuringly, the cops explained there was nothing they could do right then.

"You folks go back in there and enjoy your son's wedding," they implored, remembering how they had hoped for an invitation to *wedding of the year*. They further suggested Mom and Dad wait to visit Sister until the following day.

"She'll need some time to wear off those *tiddilies,*" was their final advice.

At that precarious moment, with the cops politely departing from the side entrance of the country club, Mom and Dad were faced with the predicament of how to finish the reception gracefully—without anyone knowing—and how (and whether or not) to tell Son about Sister's situation before he departed for a Hong Kong honeymoon.

"We've always been so honest with him," Mom cried to Dad as she wiped away her running mascara with his handkerchief.

"I know," Dad consoled, "but this is his night. He has always been so good to her. It's not fair that we ruin his special day."

There. It was decided and done. Mom and Dad forged on *pretending perfect* for the rest of the reception and Son left with his perfect bride for the perfect honeymoon. But the *perfect* was about to be plundered and pillaged in the perfect family.

The next morning, the shattering began. At first, Mom and Dad were shattered when neither Sister nor the therapists at the hospital would talk to them. *No*, they were advised not to send flowers or cards as Sister was not only being transferred to the Psychiatric Institute for severe mental disorders, but gifts were not allowed in *lockdown* or for those on *suicide watch*. The words *lockdown* and *suicide watch* shattered the senses of Mom and Dad.

And *no,* as parents, they had absolutely no right to know about Sister's problems or her treatment. *No right*? they questioned in horror. And the final NO in the nailed coffin was *no*, Sister had not agreed for Precious Pie #2 to stay with Mom and Dad.

"Foster care is her choice," the tight-lipped, Birkenstock-wearing social worker huffed as she led a tearful Precious Pie #2 from the perfect home of Mom and Dad. *Foster care instead of our home* was just about the most painful thing Mom and Dad had ever heard, but this was only the beginning of more pain than they ever realized possible when cuddling up on that missing-one-cushion couch, so long ago.

The questions they had in the unanswered column, continued the shattering. "What happened to her? Why has she shunned us? What did we do wrong?" were the pondered points of Mom and Dad as they sadly looked at Son's perfect wedding pictures nearly ten days after the gala event. They kept their covenant to Son, leaving him out of the shattering. After all, he was a newlywed and newly established doctor.

But the shattering wasn't over. Eventually, Sister's therapists requested (finally) a meeting. It was a *family intervention* session they called it. Relief with this news was replaced by anger, which was eventually replaced by fear, as Mom and Dad ventured into the sprawling mental hospital with an atmosphere they only imagined would have served the Spanish Inquisition centuries past. *No,* Sister didn't want them to hug her at the beginning of the session, even though it had been almost a month since the wedding mess. *No,* the therapists didn't shake hands or even pretend Mom and Dad had anything to offer except to be *intervened upon*.

The tight-lipped therapists seemed similar to the Birkenstock Babe who took Precious Pie #2 into foster care in spite of all the tears. And *no*, Mom and Dad didn't (just couldn't) believe it when sobbing Sister tried to tell the final, shattering secret. ***Sister was a victim of sexual abuse***, the therapists said, as it became clear Sister couldn't stop her crying long enough to provide the shattering news herself. *Shocking* it was at first, and then *who* it was came second. The question hung in the air, at first unanswered.

In the seconds that the announcement of *sexual abuse* levitated in the air, Mom and Dad searched their internal databases about the subject. Well, Mom remembered a brief mention of the topic in her teacher training, and also, Mom remembered two cases of sexual abuse in the school where long ago she taught fourth grade, putting Dad through dental school. For Dad, he remembered reading about sexual abuse cases every now and then in the morning newspaper, and he also remembered his feelings of disgust as he wondered *how some pervert in the park could do that to a child*. Mom had the same type of reflection about the two cases in her elementary school, postulating with other teachers in the faculty lounge that those were *bad* families, from *bad* parts of town with *bad* behaviors, like using drugs and alcohol. *Smoking, too,* she and her teacher colleagues concluded about *those families* where incest or sexual abuse occurred. Yes, a leering, sneering *Snidely Whiplash* kind of man, smelling badly from behind park bushes was the conjured image for both Mom and Dad with the words "relating to *sexual abuse*." So, when Sister finally said it was *Son*, nothing computed.

There it was for Sister, and there it *wasn't* for Mom and Dad. No way. Son was perfect. *It just couldn't be,* was their only thought, no matter how much the therapists tried to explain. The thoughts of Son being one of those park perverts was beyond their comprehension, even though the therapists said (while Sister sobbed) that Son had sexually abused her from age of five through age twelve. As Mom and Dad were *intervened upon* by the glum-faced therapists, they were told the sexual abuse was frequent, but Sister didn't know how many times. Further *intervening* informed Mom and Dad that there were lots of sexual behaviors and lots of quiet coercion. The therapists went on with their *interventioning,* using words such as *sensuous, sucking, seductive,* and *secret,* which made absolutely no sense, it was so disgusting. For Mom and Dad, there was no comprehension or conclusion—trying to somehow equate the park pervert image with their Son. *It just couldn't be,* was their only conclusion.

With all the sobbing and shattering, it was a miserable scene. The therapists went on and on, and Mom and Dad went deeper and deeper into their own denial. It was just unbelievable. But remembering they were good parents, they finally asked Sister what they could do for her because, of course, they still loved their Precious Pie #1. But she asked the most impossible thing of her loving parents—*"Believe me."* Sadly, they couldn't and Sister knew it.

On the way home, Mom and Dad contemplated the situation. Why, Son was no pervert, he was perfect. In fact, Dad reminded, "Son wasn't even interested in sex during high school. Remember all the times when girls called and he showed no interest?"

Dad questioned Mom as they pulled into the gated community they once believed a testimonial to their perfect family plans. Mom remembered all right, not only how Son demonstrated sexual restraint, but also she remembered the opposite for Sister. Memories of Sister's promiscuity, her sexually provocative nature, and her unwanted teen pregnancy provided some relief to Mom in the comparative calculation of Son and Sister.

And then, of course, veracity (truthfulness) in the *kid-comparisons* also loomed. They sadly agreed that between the two of them, Son seemed to have the honesty advantage. His Boy Scout Merit Badges were compared to Sister's cutting classes and forging parental permission slips. His work ethic, beginning with his paper routes in grade school, was compared to Sister's various low-paying jobs and mysterious firings from fast food restaurants where she feasted obsessively on the free food. Son's church confirmation classes were compared to Sister's refusal to attend Sunday school, often sneaking out to play on the church playground or sneaking a smoke with her friends at the mall. And even though, as parents, they tried never to compare their two children, it was impossible not to be pulled into the kid-comparing with all of this shattering. Somehow, they had to understand this incredible conflict of who did what to whom. They loved them both, but now they were forced to choose which kidlet was the most believable. In considering the intervening and the challenging from the tight-lipped therapists, as well as Sister's pleas, they had to do some decision-making in the kid comparisons, because a resolution to the mess was, for sure, required.

Finally, and with the best of intentions, Mom and Dad concluded that what the therapists were suggesting just couldn't be. Sister had to be mistaken. *Maybe because of her emotional problems, her mental health issues, and her bizarre behavior, she had just gotten mixed up?* they hoped. And then, ever-so-slowly, they began to feel relief with their conclusions. *No,* Dad explained, they couldn't believe Sister about her crazy accusations of Son. *Yes,* they had been methodical, careful, and fair in their analysis, Mom confirmed. They were intellectual people. They had searched the Internet for basic sexual abuse information, but most important in honoring their conclusions about the kid-comparison was that they loved ***both*** children. Just as they had done in those early years so long ago, they buckled down to hard work. They wanted to be good parents for both of their children, and they resolved to be.

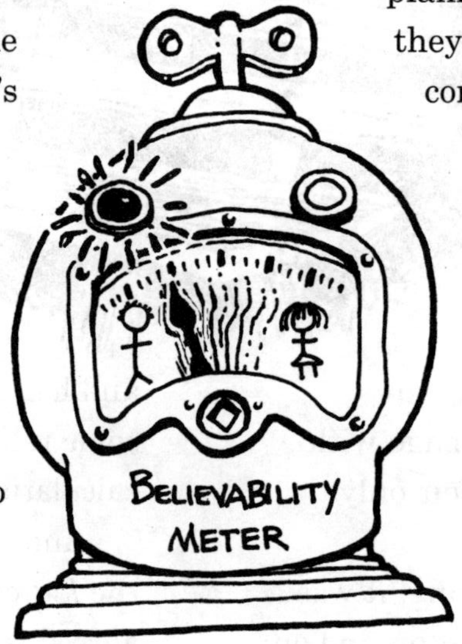

Quickly, Mom and Dad became excited about what they were going to do to help their mistaken and confused, youngest child. They planned, planned, and planned. *No,* they weren't going to call Son, as they concluded Sister was just mistaken. There was no need to bring him into the past triumvirate of worrying and wondering about Sister as they had always done. But *yes,* they were going to do everything possible for her. *No sacrifice will be too small,* Mom remembered out loud. *She will be our top priority,* both of them confirmed over a simple bowl of soup, the first meal either had been able to eat since the *intervention* nightmare.

Dad explained they were going to get Sister the very best care, perhaps finding a new hospital to help her with her delusions.

"I don't care what it costs," said Dad, a now-getting-some-relief protector of his youngest child and his former Precious Pie.

And Mom began to make lists of what Sister really needed to help her feel better. Her contemplations included a membership to the country club for weight loss training, perhaps a new wardrobe from the fancy Factory Outlet Mall, and of course, Mom would do everything to get custody of Precious Pie #2 rather than that terrible situation of foster care so mysteriously instigated by Sister and seemingly relished by the Birkenstock Babe from social services. The plans were intense and energizing.

And since Mom and Dad were finally organized and actually refueled after a week of deadly kid contemplations, they decided to write a letter to Sister and her therapists.

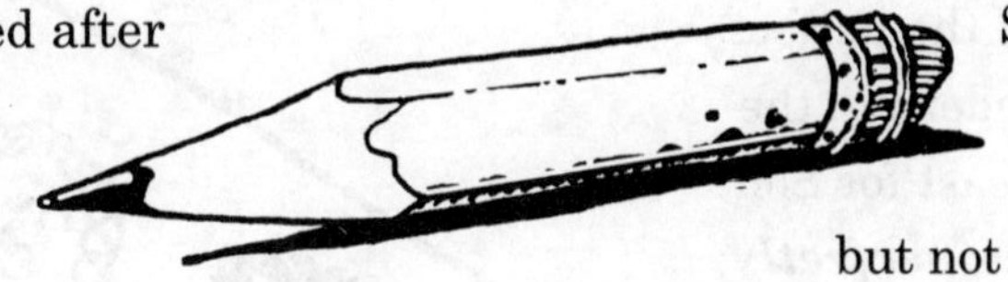

"It just seemed so hard for them to listen to us," was Dad's plea to Mom in attempting to solicit her agreement to put a message to Sister *in writing.*

They contemplated that by sharing a written *task-driven* list of what they planned to do to help their beloved (and that's how Dad said to sign the letter) daughter, things would get better and she would know for sure that they loved her. Yes, a letter would be better than another *therapy* session where Mom and Dad didn't feel anyone listened at all, only *intervened* upon them.

And so, the well-intentioned letter of assistance for Sister was prepared, critiqued and finalized on quite attractive and clearly expensive stationary. As it was mailed, they included a cute picture of Precious Pie #2 in her flower-girl-pretend-bride outfit—just to really cheer up Sister. And to make sure everything coordinated harmoniously, Mom and Dad left a message with the therapists telling them help for Sister was in the mail. *No*, they didn't want to visit her until she read the letter, Mom and Dad explained, but they also encouraged the therapists to be enthused because the written words would help Sister turn everything around. And *yes*, Mom and Dad asked the therapists to call them with the good news when Sister read their helpful correspondence.

And the therapists did call, but not about Sister's glee over Mom and Dad's letter, nor about her excitement with the country club membership. They called to say Sister had *suicided.* That was a fancy mental health word for Sister taking her own life after receiving the letter and after secreting away enough medication to do the *suiciding.* Not only was the term *suicided* confusing to Mom who took the call, but the fact that their help *hadn't helped,* was beyond confusing. Words couldn't describe the devastation of Mom and Dad. Their baby was gone, their Precious Pie had perished, and so had their perfect family plan that went with her. There was no finger pointing or blaming—just overwhelming and engulfing sadness.

After the funeral, Mom and Dad could only conclude that perhaps their letter had arrived too late, even though the therapists confirmed she had read it. Probably, they proposed, Sister just felt too guilty about making the false accusations against Son? Well, maybe. Perhaps she just felt there was no way out of telling a falsehood, Mom and Dad tearfully contemplated.

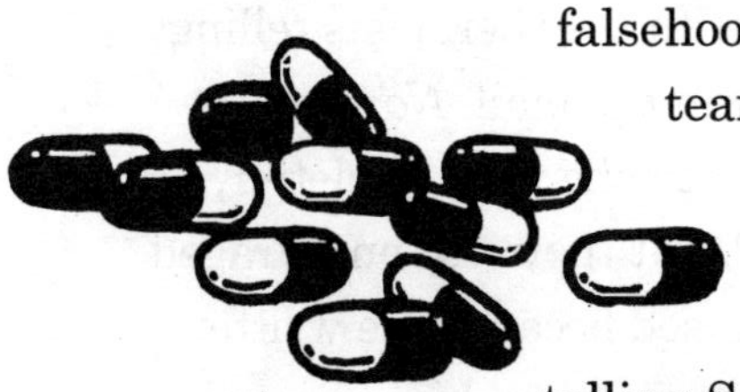

And speaking of telling, Mom and Dad decided that telling Son would only cause him unnecessary misery. There was no need. They would bear the burden quietly, always wondering what went wrong with the perfect family picture. And with this wondering, the only relief they felt was that, at least for Son, they had done pretty well—in fact, ***perfectly***.

VOICES OF VICTIMS

From Katie, from Sister and from countless other innocent victims, robbed of sexual safety and security, comes the *Voices of Victims*, resounding loudly but sadly, often to the deaf ears of society, community and families. And why can't those voices be heard? Are Mom and Dad just ignorant about sexual abuse suffering and that is the reason for excluding sexual abuse prevention from their perfect parenting plan? Or are Mom and Dad caught up in the same dance of denial of Ernie, Emma, Edwin and Erma—in their adherence to the philosophy *no need for nuthin*? Surely the deepest, darkest denial is the shame parents might feel if their child was a sexual abuser. But what shame, however secondary, comes to the family where a child is the sexual victim? And, of course, the deepest, darkest most deadly disgrace for parents is when they raise *both the victim and the sexual offender?*

THE SUFFERING OF SEVERAL

From the time Mom and Dad met at Lucky's Laundromat, they had a perfect plan for their family. Then, at the apex of their adult children's lives, things shattered. Who is to blame and who are the sufferers? First in line for the suffering is obviously Sister, not only sexually abused by her brother, but also abandoned (however justified and rather normal) by her well-intentioned-but-nonetheless-ignorant parents. In the gated-community, with the late model sedans in the triple-car garage and with the false sense of security that *those cases* of sexual abuse happen somewhere else in bad families, Sister is, and will always be, the primary victim. Her voice, just as the voice of Katie, must always be first in the honor line of suffering—something her parents couldn't give her.

GROWN-UP VICTIM?

Did Mom and Dad abandon Sister out of ignorance, simply not having the tools to know about victim suffering, or did they discard her because of their shame? The answer is unreliable but what can be guaranteed is that Mom and Dad are also a *kind of victim* in the perfect-family-plan failure. Probably they didn't learn about sexual respect from their parents and because they were reinforced by the dances of denial in society, Mom and Dad joined the beat of *no need for nuthin'* in the sexual respect department thinking sexual disrespect happened in those *other* families or behind the park bushes. But the sad reality is that they lost a child, and maybe a grandchild because of that omission. And they certainly lost their chance to live their lives relishing their perfect family plan. Potential pride will forever ring the bell of guilt for two well-intentioned but nonetheless neglectful parents. So in the suffering from not hearing the voice of victims, Mom and Dad are victims as well.

And of course, the deepest, darkest most deadly disgrace for parents is when they raise both the victim and the sexual offender.

True, few folks have empathy for sexual abusers. But are those children who step into sexual disrespect also victims of parental neglect, suffering long into their futures—and robbed of sexual contentment?

VICTIM VOTING?

What about Son and the voting for *who is* and *who isn't* victimized because of parental neglect in teaching sexual respect? Without education about the touching rules, and without any information about possible sexual trauma for Sister, Son takes sexual advantage. It was probably innocent at first, but then things changed. Once Son may have figured out it was wrong, he wasn't likely to admit to his encouraging-perfect parents that in fact—he wasn't.

Mom and Dad openly encouraged Son's resistance to the pitfalls of peer sex but didn't tell him anything about what to do with his sexual feelings. So with sexual arousal a reality that Mom and Dad didn't want to think about, Sister was available. Could the victim votes be tallied to suggest in addition to Sister, as well as Mom and Dad—that Son will also suffer as a result of being a sexual offender? True, few folks have empathy for sexual abusers. But aren't those children who step into sexual disrespect also victims of parental neglect, often suffering long into their futures—robbed of sexual contentment as adults?

As time goes on, will Son be filled with grief about his actions beyond healing— skewing his headed-for-perfect life toward disaster and depression as he slowly begins to contemplate that he may have been responsible for Sister's demise? Or, will Son be like many sexual offenders, self-centered and prone to bask in his own perfection so much so that Sister's ruination only affirms for him that his needs will always come first and society's rules only apply to others, less perfect than he? Will Sister's abuse and his unscathed reputation teach him to break other rules, being prone to overcharge his patients for medical procedures or becoming the kind of person who cheats on his taxes?

Will Son's unbridled self-esteem that may have contributed to his offending take him into adult life having affairs, being dissatisfied with his partner and becoming a *sexual thief* of sorts? And who will know whether Son's own children will be at risk, so typical of other offenders who cross over from childhood offending into being an adult sexual abuser of children? Those questions are perplexing, but what is not confusing is that, regardless of which road perfect Son takes, he too, is a victim of parental neglect in teaching sexual respect because even his plight may have been avoided..

SOCIETY AND SUFFERING

So Sister, Mom, Dad, and in his own way, Son, are all victims of sorts, as sexual abuse education was omitted from the perfect family plan. But there is more suffering as a result of Mom and Dad's neglect. Society in general suffers if a single victim is sexually abused or if a single child becomes an offender. The cost of sexual abuse is staggering, whether it is in the investigation, prosecution, conviction and incarceration of the bad people, or if it involves picking up the pieces for all the innocent people like Sister, who desperately need services. All the SpongeBob bashing in the world will fail to heal a single survivor of sexual disrespect and even though society doesn't want to think about it—society will pick up the tab for victims' suffering one way or another. So, especially in the pocketbook, society also becomes a victim of sorts when parents don't educate their children about sexual respect.

BUT THE MOST TRAGIC

And just as Katie and her daughters needed honoring, so does Precious Pie #2, perhaps the most tragic in the *Several Suffering* perspective. In her first five years she was robbed of the opportunity to have a contented mother, and deprived forever of her only true parent. Precious Pie #2 will suffer endlessly with questions of "Why Mommy, why?"--never receiving an answer from two silenced grandparents and a *pretend ignorant* Uncle Son. If the Birkenstock Babe has her way, maybe there will be a long custody battle between the Mom and Dad faction, fighting for grandparent rights against the state child protection faction, who claim; *No way. You didn't protect your daughter, how can you protect your granddaughter?* And if this custody combat occurs, Precious Pie #2 will likely be the weapon in the battle, losing the sanctity of childhood no matter what the outcome. So, in the suffering hierarchy, Precious Pie #2 comes out ahead, at least in the tragic delineation of heart-breaking suffering that didn't need to happen.

HEARING THE VOICES

It isn't that people don't care about victims of sexual abuse. Nothing can inspire a rally or urge legislation easier than tearful stories about victim tragedy, especially children. Pictures of a ten-month-old sweetie pie, with a yellow ribbon scotchtaped to her bald head can urge multitudes into sympathy AND action. But sadly, the effort usually seems to result in grand punishment of offenders rather than understanding trauma to victims. And if the darkest parental denial of *my child could never become a sex offender* is so great that parents couldn't be persuaded to teach sexual respect, then perhaps they could be persuaded by hearing the voices of suffering victims.

TUNING IN TO TIME

If only things could be different. What if in the Fairy Godmothering of parenting, Mom and Dad could have a rerun—being allowed to do things over—not only in the way they handled Sister, but the way they organized their perfect family plan? And if they could start over, what would they need to do differently? To truly hear the voices of suffering victims in order for Mom and Dad to have a better shot at their perfect plan, they needed several basic areas of understanding.

And if the darkest parental denial of *my child could never become a sex offender* is so great that parents couldn't be persuaded to teach sexual respect, then perhaps they could be persuaded by hearing the voices of suffering victims.

The way in which Sister remembered the abuse was troublesome to Mom and Dad in their CSI (Crime Scene Investigation) hats, and Sister's convoluted memory was one of the reasons she was so traumatized.

First, the *moving changing memory* over time is what Sister needed them to understand because as she developed and her brain changed, her memory moved and readjusted. But like most folks, Mom and Dad probably watched too much television about court witnesses and detective cop types who thrive on absolute accuracy. The way in which Sister remembered the abuse was troubling to Mom and Dad in their CSI (Crime Scene Investigation) hats, and Sister's convoluted memory was one of the reasons she was so traumatized.

Secondly, understanding the *Ages and Stages* of child development could have helped Mom and Dad accept what happened so long ago, rather than thinking about Sister's current problems of gaining weight or losing a loser husband. Yes, time was the developmental problem that made it impossible for Mom and Dad to understand enough to reach out to help the daughter they truly loved.

But there is more in hearing the voices of victims in order to better rescue Sister. If Mom and Dad had known about *Potholes in the Road to Trauma* that predictably tripped Sister, things would have made more sense to them. When Precious Pie #2 walked down the aisle as a miniature bride, at the same age as when Sister's sexual abuse began, she was triggered into the final pothole. It was just *too much to take,* after she had plodded through the previous potholes in the road to trauma, sadly steering her toward suicide.

TRUE TRAUMA?

But that wouldn't be all Mom and Dad needed to know if they were given the Fairy Godmother chance at rewind, and to do things differently. When the secret was *out,* Mom and Dad pulled *out* what they thought they knew about trauma, and in doing so, things fell *out* the rescue window. Like most folks who make it their business to *not know* about sexual abuse, when someone like the stuffy therapists make them *know,* Mom and Dad pretend to do just that—*know*. Somewhere from either the evening news, from prison movies, or from legislative dalliances in Congress, folks believe they know what sexual victims need. Unfortunately, the wrong tools are often used, actually increasing victim trauma and suffering.

The Big Four and The Big Trouble were Mom and Dad's guidebook in trying to figure out if Sister was abused and those were the wrong tools. Challenging those commonly held myths and misconceptions about victim suffering would have helped Mom and Dad because they would have rejected the myths and understood *True Trauma Factors,* opening the door for Sister's rescue.

FATHER TIME

Mom and Dad were so confused as the ugly secret was rudely dropped upon them and one of the reasons for their ineptitude had to do with a *time problem*, so familiar in the failures to hearing the voices of victims. Just like jet lag sufferers, Mom and Dad suffered from a time warp in understanding. Ironically, they were no strangers to the miracle of timed milestones in their children's lives, as Mom carefully kept track of all the stages of development for her kidlets, recording their first steps, their first day at school and their first sleepover. When the sexual abuse secret was out, those developmental stages and the precious nature of what being a child was all about escaped them with the same ease as the therapists escaped from giving Mom and Dad any credit for their parenting efforts.

True, Son began his abuse when Sister was five years old and then stopped (typically) when puberty set in and the *Precious Pie pads* were required. But when the stuffy therapists told Mom and Dad that Sister was sexually abused so long ago, it was difficult for them to go back in time and think of their five-year-old Precious Pie being sexually intimidated and abused by their twelve-year-old son. The true picture with correct chronology was deleted from their calculations, and the childhood scrapbooks Mom had carefully prepared were in psychological storage. Instead, they had in front of them a troubled, sullen, sarcastic, problem-ridden, not-so-good-mother of their only granddaughter, who seemed to always cause a cloud over any family event. What they didn't have was the ability to go back in time when the abuse started and remember how it was for Sister when the sexual abuse began. Her innocence was lost to Son as her offender, but her innocence was also lost on her parents with her voice of suffering silenced because they couldn't remember the way it was so long ago.

THE UNAWARE

In understanding the ages and stages of sexual development, it is clear that children in the preschool period—under the age of seven or eight—usually have no idea about sexual things or about sexual abuse. Right or wrong, most parents want their kiddos being *unaware* and this ignorance fits nicely. Sure, toddlers often know they shouldn't strip naked in the car wash, and they also know parents panic purple concerning anything between their belly buttons and their knees. But in spite of that rudimentary awareness, in this first stage of sexual development, Sister was completely UNAWARE of the significance of Son's sexual touching and thus, the stage was set for disaster as time trudged on.

But there is more bad news about Sister's UNAWARE stage of development. For victims like her, especially considering an offender like Son, cooperation in the sexual behaviors is very common, especially those sneaky and secretly exciting behaviors that provide sexual pleasure. And because kiddos in this stage are ignorant,

Somewhere from the evening news, from prison movies, or from legislative dalliances in Congress, folks believe they know what sexual victims need. Unfortunately, the wrong tools are often used, actually increasing victim trauma and suffering.

Her innocence was lost to Son as her offender, but her innocence was also lost on her parents as her voice of suffering was silenced.

From a behavioral perspective, they are consenting, but from a developmental perspective they know absolutely nothing about what they are doing. And for sex offenders, this is a terrific time to sexually abuse.

they not only cooperate, but they often encourage or initiate the sexual involvement. From a behavioral perspective, they are *consenting*, but from a developmental perspective they know absolutely nothing about what they are doing. And for sex offenders, this is a terrific time to sexually abuse.

CONSENT, CONCERNS, AND THE POST OFFICE

Each state, in its wisdom, decides when children are no longer UNAWARE through their *Age of Consent* laws that vary across borders, rivers, and state lines, really suggesting that children are victims of sexual abuse according to their post office zip codes. As an example, the age of consent in the sunny State of Hawaii is fourteen, since the lawmakers in hula skirts (unisex, of course) believe that when children turn fourteen, they have the developmental capacity to make a sexually consenting decision, which really means they are no longer UNAWARE. It's just a birthday *poof*, and the *Awareness Fairy* zaps kidlets into a magnificent and immediate sexual understanding. Anything before that magic time designated by the lawmakers, means the kiddos didn't know enough about sex (actually UNAWARE) to consent and, therefore, to involve a child in sexual activity (even if they behaviorally cooperate) is a very large crime.

But flying across the Pacific Ocean from the sandy beaches of Hawaii, things change dramatically on the mainland. If a fourteen-year-old girl, one day after her birthday *poof*, flies east with her boyfriend, and her airplane lands in the State of Washington; *whoops*, she will need to wait two more years before legally being allowed to sexually *fool around* with her partner sleeping next to her on the airplane, because he is tired from too much *legal sex* the night before on the Hawaii beach. The age of consent in that much cooler State of Washington is sixteen, perhaps because they don't wear as many swimming suits as children do in Hawaii.

But if, for some reason, the Seattle, Washington airport is fogged in and she is forced to land slightly south, in Portland, Oregon, she and her hanky-panky partner will have to wait *four more years*, since the age of consent in that state is eighteen. In contemplating the wisdom of a child needing to wait extra years in these colder states to engage in the same behavior that would have been perfectly fine in a Honolulu hotel may be a futile exercise in logic, but nonetheless interesting to zip code enthusiasts and map makers. But, in spite of this folly of birthday *poofings*, the reality is that all the lawmakers agree that young children (like Sister), at least below the age of fourteen or so, cannot consent to sex, and the foundation for that belief is that they *just don't get it*. They are not aware and, therefore, they fit the diagnostic category of the UNAWARE victim.

For Sister, this means that as a child, she didn't know one thing about what her brother was doing, but that ignorance of long ago is lost on Mom and Dad as they are sternly confronted by the crabby social workers. But Sister did know some things in this UNAWARE stage. She knew how much she loved her brother. She knew he commanded a great deal of respect in the family. She knew that he often took on a parental role, and she knew his special, loving attention in those secret bedroom scenes was wonderful. And so, with her precious (pie not included) innocent mind, she not only cooperated with the abuse, but she cooperated in keeping the secret.

THE UNFORTUNATE

Moving forward in sexual development, Sister approached the UNFORTUNATE stage, which was also lost to Mom and Dad as they tried desperately to understand things like *how could this happen and why didn't you tell.* As children leave the cuddling comforts of total reliance on Mommy and Daddy (and the UNAWARE stage), they begin to notice more of the world, developing a keener interest in sexual snippets and tidbits but also realizing something about their parents.

It didn't take much for Sister to figure out that Mom and Dad did everything for their kidlets in educational efforts. The books and educational games stacked high in their rooms, their papers of academic accomplishment posted on the refrigerator, the fact that even Fruit Loops or corn germination could become a teaching moment, told Sister that *Mom and Dad teach everything—well, almost everything.* The omission of information about sexual stuff was obvious, even to an innocent twelve-year-old, and that started her shame.

In the UNFORTUNATE stage of development Sister also entered puberty, resulting in a bombardment of disgusting feelings, only adding to the shame component. Maybe Mom did the proverbial *Kotex pamphlet* presentation or maybe Sister got a sixth grade reproduction lesson from a purple-faced, teacher. But the whole idea of her body developing was awful (UNFORTUNATE). With new knowledge about sex, however repulsive to her, she was also (with her more sophisticated memory machine) rethinking those events that began when she was UNAWARE. Rather than feeling outrage at Son's sexual abuse, and running to Mom and Dad with shrieks of, *how could he do that to me*?, she recoiled in sullen sarcasm with new memories, saying to herself, *how could I have done that*? And of course, since Son continued to shine, Sister began her shuffling into adolescence with the troublesome partner of shame and self-degradation as companions.

So the message was, *Mom and Dad teach everything—well, almost everything.* The omission of sexual teaching was obvious, even to an innocent twelve-year-old.

And of course, since Son continued to shine, Sister begins her shuffling into adolescence with the troublesome partners of shame and self-degradation as companions.

THE UNCOMFORTABLE

The UNCOMFORTABLE stage of sexual development occurs in adolescence—those terrible teenage years when sexuality seems so important. Even though Son stopped the sexual abuse when Sister entered puberty (probably worrying about those Precious Pie Kotex pads), Sister's brain raced forward, learning more about sex and loathing herself even more with the moving memories. And just like Katie, the rage Sister felt turned inward.

As Sister tried to socialize with high school girls, she recognized her peer incompatibility. When girls in the cafeteria were giggling about whether or not they might kiss their boyfriends at the movies on Saturday night, Sister wondered what they would think if they knew she had already performed oral sex on her brother before she entered fourth grade. When her sort-of friends wrote seductive notes about whether sex at the dance was as exciting as they read about in the smut magazines they had discovered in one of their father's underwear drawers, Sister recognized that she had experienced her first orgasm in the third grade with her brother. She just didn't assimilate or fit in with other teenagers in this UNCOMFORTABLE stage of sexual development, bringing on the shuffling and the sullen sarcasm.

And when finally, Mom signed the yes-to-sex-education-program permission slip for Sister's health class, and Sister learned about such topics as teen pregnancy, date rape, and sexual assault, she finally recognized what had happened to her. But in this recognition and in this UNCOMFORTABLE stage of sexual development, deadly deliberations tiptoed forward in Sister's mind, moving the memory again. Finally, Sister's brain was capable of understanding the truth of her abuse, but there was another message cozying up to Sister. She knew the reality of what Son did to her and in deciding whether to give up the secret, Sister did some kid comparing.

Precious Pie #1 pondered disclosure and immediately saw herself losing the battle in the kid comparing. First, she wondered who would believe her, since Son was so perfect and he certainly didn't look anything like the park perverts Dad sometimes talked about when reading the evening paper. And the most difficult side of the kid comparing for Sister had to do with what she saw in her mirror. She had nothing but problems, she was failing in school, she didn't have any friends, and in the perfect family plan, she was anything but. So Sister didn't report, in spite of her adolescent anger. She did what many teenage victims in this UNCOMFORTABLE stage do—she raged inward, excelling at internal chaos. She outclasses everyone with her uniqueness in not fitting in the family and with her perfect self-loathing. There is no doubt that Sister excelled in this effort. She was the very best at perplexing her parents. She was the best at promiscuity. She was the best at risk-taking. The rage she wanted to turn toward her abuse was stifled with constant reminders that with the kid comparisons, she loses and Son is the big winner. And in this self-destruction, Sister makes everyone UNCOMFORTABLE.

THE UNRESOLVED

The breathless nature of Sister's internal rage in adolescence took her into adulthood, perhaps sooner than she wanted. With the untimely arrival of Precious Pie #2, Sister was flung into adulthood rudely—no celebration, no rites of passage, no ability to feel accomplishments of anything except going against the perfect family plan. The result was a stifled shuffle forward, in a dull pretend silence, trying to put the abuse behind her (or so she thought), failing to realize that the pain made her backside posterior extremely vulnerable to *trigger bites* as she traveled down the road of trauma.

So when Mom and Dad, sitting in their own time warp, were forced into the present with so many *how could this have happened?* questions in their minds, they forgot Father Time and the way it used to be for their children. They couldn't fathom the different stages of sexual development in which Sister had passed, and all they could consider was the present, which was disastrous for Sister—robbing her from the rescue she deserved.

POTHOLES IN THE ROAD TO TRAUMA

Back to the Fairy Godmother parental rerun, it would have been helpful to Mom and Dad, in trying to understand what had happened to their children, if they would have known that Sister was tripped up (falling into potholes) in certain times of her life, especially heading into adulthood. Many of Sister's behaviors, thought so strange to Mom and Dad, could have made sense if they only understood how trauma predictably erupts with certain life milestones. Sexual abuse suffering is not static; it changes, it moves, and there are cracks and crevices along the road to trauma. The *pothole* perspective of Sister's travels provides understanding to her path and plight, leading to Sister's eventual demise by suicide, but leaving Mom and Dad confused and shattered.

PUBERTY POTHOLE

Sister's predicament with the onset of puberty signified her first recollections of knowing the reality of what her brother had done to her, but that memory also portrayed herself as a cooperative partner, often enjoying and even initiating the sexual contact. So clearly, the puberty pothole was a difficult one, sealing Sister into re-examining what happened to her and encouraging her absolute disgust with her developing body.

And the most difficult side of the kid comparing for Sister had to do with what she saw in her mirror.

Sexual abuse suffering is not static; it changes, it moves, and there are crooks and crevices along the road to trauma.

PRECEDING POTHOLE—FIRST TIME

The second pothole in the road to trauma seems to occur when victims first engage in sexual (and of course, arousing) situations on their own. Perhaps Sister, in the back seat of the car, after guzzling too many wine coolers, took the first step toward her own sexuality—*her first actual choice.* Although memories of Son's abuse may have cornered her thoughts (especially since that first rude pothole of puberty), Sister began to believe sex would be different if she was only in control. She was hopeful, and she was sexually on her own. Oh, the freedom she felt, taking off her blouse, listening to her also-too-many-wine coolers partner's love professions and sensing her *very own* sensuous pleasure for the first time.

But then, as her body responded, she was psychologically driven back, crashing into the pothole of what occurred in her pink Precious Pie bedroom so long ago. As her arousal and sexual response grew in the backseat, she fell into the pothole of seeing Son's face, his touch, and his tenderness. She couldn't connect her own arousal to the *here and now* in the back seat. Right there connected to her arousal, resides Son; ever present, ever perfect, and ever controlling. As she realized that her body is trained to connect sexual arousal to Son, she attempts to solve the problem of Son's back seat sexual invasion with hope (however hazardous) for the future. Although Sister is disgusted with her arousal to Son, she begins to rationalize that maybe things will be better if she just finds something to fix it.

HAZARDOUS HOPE POTHOLE

As Dad commented proudly on Son's sexual restraint, Sister found her uniqueness in having none of it. The coping mechanism for the dreadful presence of Son in her backseat sexual experiences was a hazardous hope connected to better times ahead. The *if onlys* pervaded her everyday thoughts. "*If only* I were married; *if only* I meet the right man," or most powerful was the "*if only* I could become a Mom and protect my child, just like I needed to be protected." Her hazardous hope is that something in the future could erase Son's sexual presence in her own sexual experiences. So with those hopes she felt it was okay to practice sex, even if it was connected to her brother. *Someday it will be better, so for now, this is it.* And practice she did.

When Sister faced her pregnancy and her potential/possible marriage, those prevalent *if only* hopes shone the light of promise. She faced what could have been (in her mind) a relief. Just perhaps if she married, moved out, settled down, *everything would be okay.* And her pleas to Mom to honor the marriage and help her renew her faith were honorable. And Mom agreed. However, it wasn't long before the next pothole loomed again in Sister's path down the trauma road.

AND BABY MAKES THREE

In the few short months between Sister's Justice of the Peace wedding with a short lilac wedding dress and flowers from Wal-Mart, she felt unbelievable joy. Finally it might be over—the suffering of Son's sexual abuse. Here she was, house of her own, a new husband (who was quite tolerant when his bride sexually struggled in the bedroom), and a perfectly working toaster Mom had saved from her wedding days. And *yes*, Mom and Dad did their best to support Sister in her enthusiasm. *Yes*, they loved her no matter what. *No*, they weren't going to judge her. And *yes*, she should know that Son loves her too and sends his best from college.

But then, when Precious Pie #2 comes into the world, the original Precious Pie #1 answers with ambivalence. As she holds this baby girl close to her, the manifestations of the *Baby Makes Three Pothole* are profound. Part of Sister rages at her abuser, who was so convincing so long ago, that *she was the baby seductress.* Conflicts abound as she tries to sort out her anger at herself for being a *sexual child,* as she gazes at her innocent and completely vulnerable newborn.

Those years of blaming herself for what perfect Son had done were now challenged. And the result was both wanting to scoop up her daughter and run to a faraway paradise protecting her Precious Pie #2, coupled with strange and strong desires to push her six-hour-old infant away in the same disgust she felt for herself for so many years. In this contemplation of loving and/or hating her baby, she remembered that Son just couldn't be bad, so she had to be bad—just as it had always been.

HAPPY BIRTHDAY POTHOLE

But never mind, Sister eventually said to herself, deciding to dull herself since the hazardous hope for healing proved to be just that—*hazardous.* She trudged forward in dreariness, accepting her marriage failure, her job problems and her horrific weight gain. She sunk inside herself, careful not to take advantage of any opportunity offered by Mom and Dad, lest she get hopeful again. *Better things just stay the same,* Sister said to herself, thus no fancy clothes for Precious #2, no job changes even though she worked with her now-gone-and-not-supportive hubby, and for sure, no hoping for anymore wine cooler backseat relationships. There was safety in avoiding hope, Sister convinces herself, thus her hopeless lifestyle, so misunderstood by Mom and Dad.

But with the *happy birthday* of Precious Pie #2 turning age five, Sister gets even more conflicted about her own innocence or seductress status when she was the same age and Son began the abusive shame. Just as when she was born, Precious Pie #2 brings old memories and confusion to her mother. But things really clash and quarrel with Sister's sanity when Precious Pie #2 walked down the aisle in the church as a *mini-bride*, and in Sister's convoluted mind, as a

The *if onlys* pervaded her everyday thoughts. "*If only* I were married; *if only* I meet the right man," or most powerful was the "*if only* I could become a mom and protect my child, just like I needed to be protected."

***Yes*, they loved her no matter what. *No*, they weren't going to judge her. And *yes*, she should know that Son loves her too and sends his best from college.**

grown-up-sort-of-about-to-be-sexual-after-the-wedding image. Those conflicted feelings of her *innocent or seductress* status from the past, rage for Sister. All the years of confusion about either seeing herself as a blameless victim, or blaming herself as a childhood Lolita, surface in the image of Precious #2 in her mini-bride outfit. And it is just too much.

So much in the *family intervention session* would have made sense to Mom and Dad if they had only known about these potholes. They could have better understood how in the middle of all the wedding festivities, Sister perished. But they didn't understand, and when faced with the embarrassed cops at the reception, they ignorantly began their contribution to Sister's ruination.

THE BIG FOUR AND THE BIG TROUBLE

With the long-awaited-and-absolutely-unwelcome disclosure of Sister's sexual abuse by Son so long ago, Mom and Dad began doing the *dance of discounting.* The music to the dance is in traditional myths and misconceptions about what factors cause trauma and what factors actually reduce trauma. Even though Mom and Dad don't know a lot about sexual abuse, they nonetheless set upon a course of understanding (misunderstanding, actually), just like society tends to do without any justified information—only gut reactions. And these snippets of erroneous sexual trauma information resulted in another big-time loss for Sister.

THE BIG FOUR AND BIG TROUBLE

Folks who postulate knowing about the wounds of sexual abuse tend to believe that certain factors (four, actually) raise the bar of trauma. Those four commonly used tools are *The Big Four* of violence, frequency, penetration, and age of the child. The thinking is, in one form or another:

- ✓ *Violent sexual acts are much more damaging than those sexual behaviors that are soft, subtle, or non-aggressive.*
- ✓ *The smaller number of times that sexual abuse happens will always be less traumatic than when sexual abuse happens numerous times.*
- ✓ *Real sex (penetration) is always more traumatic than such things as fondling.*
- ✓ *Younger children are much more damaged than older children who are sexually abused.*

This thinking honors the Big Four (violence, frequency, penetration and age) and with the best of intentions these assumption are used in an effort to understand how victims suffer. And, in the dance of discounting, the absence of those four factors is thought to reduce the suffering. It is all very tidy, but very misguided.

GOOSES AND GANDERS

But from where did this wisdom come about the suffering of sexual victims? Was it based on detailed, comprehensive trauma studies, or was the Big Four really (and rudely) taken from sex offender-sentencing laws? Were the *gooses and ganders* (victims and their offenders) mixed up without truly knowing whether or not they were really correlated? The answer to the question explains why Mom and Dad (like society) find it so easy to do the dance of discounting.

Actually, each state in its wisdom, uses the BIG FOUR (violence, age, frequency and penetration) in not only sex offender sentencing, but in the partnering effort of determining sex offender risk. *Who are the bad guys and what should we do with them?* is the question, and the answer comes from those four sentencing and risk-based factors. Whether it is Idaho, Ohio or Oregon, the punishment is more severe if the offender uses the Big Four as tools in sexual abuse. If violence is part of the assault, if the offender penetrates the victim (real sex), if the victim is younger rather than older, and if there are several incidents, the calculations begin and it isn't good news for the bad folks when that happens.

But those Big Four factors were developed in an effort by each state to figure out what to do with those who abuse, and the thinking was that those four things make some of the bad folks even ***badder,*** which eventually relates to the sex offender risk. And speaking of bad, those four factors aren't bad in actually predicting risk for sex offenders, but the question is if those *really bad* offenders cause *really bad* trauma for victims.

WHOOPS

The same tearful folks who are trying to figure out how to heal sexual victims automatically adopted the same four factors in their thinking about what makes or breaks victim trauma. For *gooses and ganders* (victims and offenders), the same blueprint was used. Perhaps without truly wondering or researching whether or not high-risk sex offenders automatically cause high trauma in sexual victims, the marriage was made. *Those dirty, rotten sex offenders; wielding knives, raging with violence, who prey on young children and who penetrate them (numerous times, of course) automatically cause more trauma,* was the thinking. And the opposite of that thinking partnered up as well. When older children were abused, perhaps only one time, with sort-of-soft, sensual touching (not real sex), in a relationship with the offender rather than a weapon, those victims were discounted, just as with Sister. And things really get messy in the *discounting dance* for sisters who don't have things done *to them,* but instead are seduced (softly and sweetly) into performing oral sex on their perfect brothers?

All the years of confusion about either seeing herself as a blameless victim, or blaming herself as a childhood Lolita, surface in the image of Precious #2 in her mini-bride outfit. And it is just too much.

But from where did this wisdom come about the suffering of sexual victims? Was it based on detailed, comprehensive trauma studies or was the Big Four really (and rudely) taken from sex offender-sentencing laws?

DISCOUNTING DANCE

When the therapists gave Mom and Dad the dreary details, with Sister sobbing in the corner, the BIG FOUR permeated the discussion and guided their *discounting dance,* although neither Mom nor Dad had ever heard the term BIG FOUR. From society's snippets of information about sexual abuse, the Big Four nuzzled nameless in the discussion. *No,* the therapists assured, there was no penetration of Son to Sister, but there were years of fondling, examining, and Sister's touching of Son, using whatever happened to be handy, such as her hands or her mouth. Of course, *no penetration* made Mom and Dad feel a lot better. And *no,* there was *no violence,* they were relieved to hear from the stuffy therapists. Son loved Sister, the therapists explained, and the *touching* (no longer sexual abuse, but *touching*) was first game playing, followed by mutual (*yes,* Sister did it and liked it) consent. *Yes,* there were lots of cuddling and special secrets, certainly nothing like violence and force (or real sex), they explained. The fact that he wasn't accused of violence made Mom and Dad feel much, much better about Son, but it made them feel a little puny about Sister and her ever-crumbling victim status.

And when questions were raised about *how many times and when,* the picture that emerged wasn't pretty. Sister couldn't really remember when it started, but she had clear memories of things beginning around age five, the stuffy therapists enlightened. But disappointing to Mom and Dad's detective minds, Sister had trouble remembering times and dates, failing to provide the CSI (Crime Scene Investigation) details so familiar and important to the cop shows on television where the absolute truth is resolved in test tubes or in cotton swabs. So, as the therapists provide the snapshot of what Sister said Son had done, Mom and Dad went home for a little picture developing of their own with, unfortunately, the Big Four as their guideline.

KID COMPARISON AND THE BIG FOUR

When Mom and Dad tried to make sense of Sister's scary accusations, the first step was, *did it really happen?* Using the tools of the *Big Four,* things got easier. And when Mom and Dad embarked on a kid-comparison—a solution seemed inevitable, at least for them.

"Well, she just seems so confused and well, her story is all over the place without any consistency," confides Dad, who has always had an analytical mind and actually thought about becoming a *forensic scientist* before he settled on dentistry.

"The facts just don't seem to line up," confirmed Mom, really wondering about her own mothering, since part of the perfect family picture put her in charge of household happenings. "You know, it's not like they were unsupervised or left with babysitters," she opined. "I was always around; he was so busy and I don't have any idea *how* or *when* this could have happened."

And Dad chimes in, "He was always so good with her, and for sure, he was her hero as well." *No,* the violent dirt bag behind the designated-for-park-perverts image that Mom and Dad know from their perceived knowledge with the *Big Four* just doesn't fit Son, and most importantly, the tools of the Big Four discount what happened, *if it really did happen.*

In their need to solve the problem, Mom and Dad partner-up discounting *that it didn't happen* with discounting *that even if it did happen, there wasn't much of a foul.*

"Well, she said it wasn't real sex," was the first step in The Big Four tool use. And then, "It doesn't sound like there was any screaming or fighting, or even an attempt to tell us something was wrong," Dad confirmed out loud to Mom who, in her own use of the Big Four tools suggested, "And I tell you, she never hesitated to tell on him if he was bothering her. Why, if this happened, wouldn't she have told us a long time ago?"

And the final nail in Sister's kid-comparison-coffin focused on her responsibility, or lack thereof. "You know, they said it was mutual and that she did things to him," began the first of Mom's nailing.

"But, you know," Dad reminds, "she has been so dishonest about so many things in her life—staying out late, drinking, never keeping a job for very long, and all of those other problems, maybe she just needed to have a reason to explain her mess-of-a-life."

Nailing completed. The Big Four guides the kid comparison and the *discount dance* with the conclusion being that it must not have happened (Son certainly isn't a violent rapist in the park) and even if it did happen (big risk for the perfect parent plan), it wasn't a very big deal because Sister can't remember the so-important CSI details. Case closed, coffin nailed in the kid comparison, guided by the myths and misconceptions of the Big Four.

From society's snippets of information about sexual abuse, the Big Four nuzzled nameless in the discussion.

TRUE TRAUMA FACTOR FINDINGS

But what have true trauma studies revealed about why some sexual victims endure horrific sexual assault and seem to walk away unscathed, while others with a single touch in a single incident are shackled with a lifetime of suffering. What do the studies say about why three children abused at the same daycare, by the same offender, in the same way, take three different paths down the road to trauma with some joining Sister as she falls into potholes, while others seem to miraculously dodge those trauma traps.

The fact that he wasn't accused of violence made Mom and Dad feel much, much better about Son, but it made them feel a little puny about Sister and her ever-crumbling victim status.

Case closed, coffin nailed in the kid comparison and the *discount dancing,* guided by the myths and misconceptions of the Big Four.

SHOULD HAVE, WOULD HAVE, COULD HAVE

If the Fairy Godmother of parental rerun was possible and Mom and Dad could go back and throw out the Big Four and society's snippet-based belief about Sister's suffering, *true trauma studies* should have guided them into a better response. When Sister said those hopeful words of *believe me*, she was indirectly asking her parents to understand how she had suffered and why her trauma prevented her from behaving in ways that would have pleased Big Four enthusiasts. But it didn't happen, and it *should have* happened, and if it *would have* happened, the therapists *could have* told Mom and Dad about eight research-based trauma studies making everything turn out a lot better for Sister and for their honorable plans for a perfect family.

#1 SENSUOUS STUFF—SEXUAL RESPONSE

Mom and Dad would have felt more comfortable with a violent, vile kind of sexual abuse scene, complete with weapons, screaming and blood/guts images—similar to television shows where law and order eventually prevail. That kind of sexual abuse scene usually has nothing to do with the victim's participation and arousal since those situations conjure an image of a pounce and a pounding, making everyone feel a lot better about *who did what to whom.*

But when sexual abuse happens with a loved one, and when the sexual abuse is soft, slow, and sensuous, things really fall apart in the Sister-rescue department—for not only victims like her, but for parents like Mom and Dad. When the therapists told Mom and Dad that there was no violence, and that in fact, Sister seemed to cooperate and seemed to sexually respond, they were pinpointing the problem and revealing high levels of trauma that occurred without a single park bush. But that information wasn't available to Mom and Dad in the rude intervening.

But Mom and Dad, with their smelly, pervert-in-the-park image, couldn't allow the *Sister liked it* to compute in their minds. And the reason Sister fell into so many potholes as her memory moved and changed over time was that she didn't so much remember him abusing her, but she had the deadly memory of how *she sexually responded.* The guilt was overwhelming and the arousal of Sister was just too much for Mom and Dad.

But for Son—nothing could have been more perfect in keeping the secret since while she was UNAWARE, he touched her sensuously and her body responded, recognizing that later on, she could never tell on herself when she figured everything out. For Son offender, this was such a better plan than wielding a wicked weapon, hurting or bruising Sister's body. So the bean counters about victim trauma understand that violence in sexual abuse becomes a *badge of innocence*—often healing many victims. To Sister, Son was anything but violent; he was seductive and sensuous, robbing Sister of any opportunity to ever wear that coveted badge of innocence.

#2 TERROR AND TIME

Another trauma factor that could have helped Mom and Dad rescue Sister has to do with *how* the abuse occurs, especially concerning the issue of terror, which must be separated from the concept of violence. Different than violence with smashing and smacking, terror has a process of *anticipation*, which is deadly for sexual victims—especially those who live with their offenders. When the sexual predator jumps from the park shrubbery and attacks an unsuspecting victim, there is surprise and the process of anticipation is a no-show. But when children experience a *pattern of abuse,* when they know it is going to happen, the waiting and the agony of anticipation adds to the suffering, often long after the sexual abuse has stopped.

For Sister, she knew the drill, even from a very early age. In the pattern, Son would sexually abuse her just before she went to sleep. Of course Mom and Dad, in their prideful efforts to have Son join in the *helping Sister* process, felt satisfied knowing that Son would give hard-to-get-to-sleep Sister the comfort she needed for sweet snoozing—or so they thought. Reading her a bedtime story was a perfect pattern of sexual abuse opportunity for Son, because according to Sister's five-year-old thinking—it was all sanctioned by Mom and Dad. And the schedule of anticipation, with Sister *expecting it to happen,* made his work easier—without complications of surprise or resistance.

But for Sister, there was terror in that waiting and anticipation. As the evening hours ticked on, trauma tumbled forward for her—knowing it was going to happen, knowing she couldn't stop it, and knowing she couldn't tell or escape. And when those periods of panic through anticipation were followed by pretend-perfect family plans, giving her hope something might be different the next day, she was constantly disappointed each time it happened again. When the sexual abuse stopped and when Sister was no longer anticipating—the neurological damage from a childhood of terror wreaked havoc on her overall approach to life. What if the therapists could have helped Mom and Dad understand that Sister's tendencies toward being lethargic, being dull, being prone to *not being* anything, may have been her way to cope after years of intense anticipation and terror?

#3 & #4
WHO IS GUILTY? WHO IS INNOCENT?

The relationship between the offender and the victim is a significant contributor in making or breaking sexual abuse suffering. The formula for trauma seems to be; *The Greater the Expectation For Someone, the Greater the Trauma Through Betrayal.* A Snidely Whiplash

But what have trauma studies revealed about why some sexual victims endure horrific sexual assault and seem to walk away unscathed, while others, with a single touch in a single incident, are shackled with a lifetime of suffering?

To Sister, Son was anything but violent; he was seductive and sensuous, robbing her of any opportunity to ever wear the badge of innocence.

kind of guy has no relationship with an unsuspecting victim walking by his coveted park bushes, and, therefore, relationship betrayal is absent in those abusive scenarios. So that means in relationships—especially in relationships between offenders and victims who care for each other—the trauma factor of *who is guilty* and *who is innocent,* unfolds.

When Mom and Dad contemplate the kid comparisons, they become a mirror of society, which assumes that a *good guy* (like Son) would never abuse, and a *bad girl* (like Sister) would probably lie about sexual abuse. Nothing could be further from the truth, but when those lines about *who is guilty and who is innocent* become blurred, victims are unable to exonerate themselves by claiming their innocence, and trauma unfolds. But there is more in the victim/offender identity process.

The therapists should have been able to explain to Mom and Dad that when victims clearly designate their perpetrator as the guilty party, as totally responsible, they will be on the road to rehabilitation. But that didn't happen because the manipulation Son used against Sister was his positive relationship status with the family, with the extended family, with the community, and most importantly, with Sister. *How could the perfect Son be guilty of anything*? was the challenge. And besides, *he adored Sister* they all thought and Sister confirmed. Contrarily, Sister had problems, and no claim to innocence in the minds of most as well as in Sister's own mirror, when she had the courage to look. And what might have happened if the therapists could have told Mom and Dad that *yes*, their Son was perfect in many ways, and *yes,* Sister had her difficulties? What if they would have explained that the perfection of Son and the imperfection of Sister did nothing to determine *if* it happened, but that those issues really increase Sister's level of trauma? If they just could have discussed the precarious identification of *who is criminal* and *who is innocent* between the two children, maybe Mom and Dad could have responded differently and maybe Sister would still be a member of the not-so-perfect-but-still-trying family. But they didn't and the results were the killer-of-the-kid comparisons.

#5 FOOTPRINTS—Memory Messes & Consistency Chaos

Memory Messes

Child development experts and good Moms and Dads know that children try to make *sense out of nonsense* as they move through learning milestones. When something happens to a child they don't understand, they *fix it* in their brain, making it understandable, at least to them. A good question Sister's therapists should have asked her would have been, "*As you walked away from your brother's sexual abuse, what did your brain tell you?*" That question would provide guidelines in helping Mom and Dad understand why Sister couldn't tell them about the sexual abuse by Son. And that question would have addressed the FOOTPRINTS that are so powerful in understanding how victims suffer from childhood sexual abuse long into their futures.

Two common FOOTPRINTS or coping skills (making sense out of nonsense) appear in those victims that tend to be most traumatized. The first coping skill is one of memory restructuring or blurring. When the moving memory fades in and out as the victim moves through various developmental stages and potholes, sometimes it is just too much for the child. *Can't take it* is often the cry from the victim. As the memory fades in an out, forcing the child to think about the abuse, then blurring that memory provides some sort of relief. This Band-Aid coping skill skews the memory—readjusts it, purposely smudging and smearing it, at least for immediate relief.

But the problem with this coping skill is that later on, when the victim is in therapy or when the victim really wants clarity, the smudged and smeared recall raises doubt and raises the trauma level. Mom and Dad wanted a videotape of the sexual abuse to ease their challenging minds, and Sister, because she coped by clouding her memory, just couldn't deliver and that made her rescue unreachable. And of course, the facts needed to be smudged and smeared for Sister to survive so long ago, and now the facts can't be retrieved for her parents with their clipboards of reality.

Consistency Chaos

The second kind of coping skill so frequently used by the most traumatized sexual victims, matches the *badness* of the sexual abuse with the victim's *badness,* urging the victim to seek a *consistency of chaos.* Certainly, when Sister didn't know better, she loved her brother, loved his perfect persona, she cooperated with the secret game, and she actually felt as though her parents approved of Son's guidance in such things. The touching was pleasurable and the special time with the coveted Son was a treat. But when the memory began to move and change, the reality of what had happened fell into Sister's new awareness, and it all felt *bad.* Son was *good,* and yet the touching was *bad.* There was no match.

So Sister did what many sexual victims do to cope; she sought consistency. If the sexual abuse was bad and Son was good, she could fix everything in her mind by *being bad.* Thus, Sister did just that; she became bad. The consistency of her acting out, behaving badly, and going against the perfect family plan (chaos) allowed her some safety in the resolution. It all made sense and it all matched. But when the kid comparisons were calculated, when Mom and Dad matched the goodness of Son with the badness of Sister, the winner and loser of the competition only added to her trauma and eventual demise.

The formula for trauma seems to be— *The Greater the Expectation For Someone, the Greater the Trauma Through Betrayal.*

If they just could have discussed the precarious identification of *who is criminal* and *who is innocent* between the two children, maybe Mom and Dad could have responded differently and maybe Sister would still be a member of the not-so-perfect-but-still-trying family.

#6 TRAUMA BONDING

In the studies of true trauma factors, the issue of *trauma bonding* emerges, raising its ugly head, especially in families like Son and Sister's. The trick in understanding trauma bonding has to do with a *hook*; a return back to those triggers of trauma, and the word *bond* may say it all. If Snidely Whiplash sexually assaults a child and is trotted off to prison, there won't be too many demands upon the victim to think about Snidely, to wonder how he is doing or if Snidely should get copies of the family Fourth of July parade pictures while incarcerated. There is no bond.

But when victims are sexually abused by someone they will be connected to forever, or when victims have contact with people who continue relationships with the abuser, the trauma bonds tighten, holding the victim hostage from any kind of rescue.

In her deadly contemplations about taking her own life, Sister must have thought about the future, and Son's hook or bond with the family. *How would the future family Thanksgiving dinners be ten years into the future if the turkey was overcooked because everyone was visiting Son in prison? How will Christmas be joyful for the grandchildren if everyone is thinking about sexual abuse instead of Santa Claus?* Sister may have contemplated about how she could ever visit with Mom and Dad knowing their hearts were broken because she informed them that their perfect family plan was actually shattered. The bottom line in trauma bonding is that for folks not abused by Snidely Whiplash, the *hook,* the connection, the rerunning and rehashing of relationships with people who are all connected to the abuser is a deadly sentence for the future. And Sister was in a trauma bond with her brother, she knew the connection was tight, and she said to herself, "I'm just too tired to break the bond."

#7 TELLING TRAUMA

The questions or shrieks from Mom and Dad, "Why didn't you tell us?" pervaded the controversy about whether Sister should be rescued or reprimanded. For this research-based issue, the trauma seems to be in the telling or the not telling, or for sure, when did the telling happen?

Mom and Dad, in their perfect family picture, assumed that their children would talk to them about anything, making them pretty raw in the telling business when Sister tells them why she didn't speak up. She kept the secret at first because she didn't know it was wrong. Then, after she saw herself as involved (sexual arousal and such), she couldn't tell them *how bad she had been.* And besides, what words would she use to do the telling since Mom and Dad left out that educational effort. Then, when she finally took the big step and told, Mom and Dad's response was a kinder, gentler version of, "Why now, why not then?"

When it is clear to everyone in the *therapizing* that Sister didn't tell in childhood, the burden of carrying the secret for her entire childhood should have stirred up feelings of sadness and empathy for poor Sister. If Mom and Dad knew about the *not telling* trauma factor, her rescue would have been imminent, swift and safe. But instead, the fact that Sister kept the secret only made Mom and Dad doubt her and defend their perfect family plan. *Why, there were no secrets with our children* was their stand as they tried to shield responsibility. Rather than Sister's *not telling* helping everyone know how to rescue her, the *not telling* became the battleground and, in the war, Sister lost.

#8 REPORT AND RESPONSE

When Mom and Dad finally asked what they could do for Sister (true testimony of their love) and her answer was *believe me*, it was just too much for them. All the years of waiting in secrecy now were over, and Sister had taken the precarious path toward even more vulnerability by finally giving up her secret. The therapists had encouraged her to tell Mom and Dad, probably because that is what the therapy books suggested—*identify the problem and resolve it.* But the therapy books probably never mentioned the dilemma facing Mom and Dad and their need to deny any cracks in the perfect family plan. The therapists probably thought Sister's disclosure would fix everything and she would be rescued—after of course Mom and Dad did the *believing*. But they didn't. And just like other highly traumatized sexual victims, the response to the disclosure is often more traumatic than the sexual abuse.

In the big picture of traumatic events that happen to humans, responses from others differ. Sometimes a horrific event can be devastating to one person yet the same event can be a character-building experience for someone else. The difference seems to lie in how others respond to the victim. If a child falls down a well in Texas, and for days rescuers attempt her recovery, good folks may send prayers and teddy bears. When she is finally rescued and adorns the cover of *national magazines* as an American hero, she has all the ingredients to not only recover but to actually *do better*, because of her traumatic event. Jessica McClure, one such little girl in Texas, still enjoys parades on her birthday as people relish her victim status as honorable. She is an easy victim to love and respect—making everyone feel better about her tragedy.

Not so with Sister. Society tends to admire and respect certain victims and for those, the rescue is immediate, grand and having birthday parade possibilities. But in general, sexual victims seem to come in last in the *who is who* in victimology popularity contests, with sexual victimization making everyone feel sleazy and slimy. The only exception in society's rejection of sexual victims is that *the dead ones* tend to have a fan club. Children who are raped and

And of course, the facts needed to be smudged and smeared for Sister to survive so long ago, and now the facts can't be retrieved for her parents with their clipboards of reality.

How would the future family Thanksgiving dinner be ten years into the future if the turkey was overcooked because everyone was visiting Son in prison?

But in general, sexual victims seem to come in last in the *who is who* in victimology popularity contests because sexual victimization makes everyone feel sleazy and slimy. The only exception in society's rejection of sexual victims is that the dead ones tend to have a fan club.

murdered garner great support, but the live ones, like Sister, tend to make folks like Mom and Dad feel ashamed, robbing those victims of a chance of recovery.

Sadly, Sister's disclosure could have been different. With accurate knowledge about true trauma factors, Mom and Dad could have responded in a way that would have helped her. But they didn't, and when Sister, who desperately needed a *Jessica McClure* kind of response to her report, was met with *how could this be,* her victim voice was stifled. Her hope of *believe me* was impossible for Mom and Dad who really wanted to help but who didn't have the right tools.

NO UNRINGING

The deadly *not knowing* about what happened will plague the tried-to-be-perfect family forever. With Sister's suicide, the problem may appear to be over, but unanswered questions will tiptoe heavily on Mom and Dad's memory for the rest of their lives. The bell can never be *unrung.* All of the potential opportunities for future family pride and joy will be slightly smudged with Sister's accusations rudely hovering over every family event. *No,* they didn't really believe her; and *no,* they didn't want Son to be told about the accusations, so nothing will ever be said. But in old age, sitting on their porch rocking chairs, Mom and Dad will never be able to remember anything about their parenting days without a soft whisper of shame, wondering if it really did happen, and if so, what went wrong.

An agonizing lifetime sentence is their plight, and sadly it all could have been prevented if Mom and Dad had the courage to take that step toward sexual abuse prevention, which contributes to sexual respect. Decades in the past, as Mom and Dad cuddled on the missing-one-cushion couch and planned for their family, they did what many families do. They rationalized that because they will do everything for their children, because they will be perfect in their parenting, the problem of sexual abuse need not be addressed. And because of that omission, Sister's childhood was marred and miserable, a granddaughter was robbed of her mother, and Mom and Dad are sentenced to a lifetime of secret shame.

Had Mom and Dad taught Sister and Son about sexual respect, then maybe Sister would have been savvy about Son's suggestions—resisting or at least telling. Maybe if the sexual respect lessons had been as important as corn germination studies, Son might not have stepped across that sexual disrespect line. What if Mom and Dad taught their children to respect their bodies with the same vigor as they taught Sister and Son to protect their bicycles? How long would Sister have kept the secret if someone had stolen her bicycle?

IF ONLY

Mom and Dad, standing by Sister's grave, choking back tears, not only for her, but for their perceived failures, probably said the *if onlys. If only things had been different. If only we would have had the courage to say to ourselves that sexual abuse can happen in any family and we owe our children the best of education. If only, in our family planning, we would have promised each other that we must not only protect our children from sexual abuse, we must, in the perfect family plan, protect our children from becoming sexual abusers. If only we had heard the voices of victims.*

The bell can never be unrung. All of the potential opportunities for future family pride and joy will be slightly smudged with Sister's accusations rudely hovering over every family event.

If only things had been different. If only we would have had the courage to say to ourselves, sexual abuse can happen in any family and we owe our children the best of education.

Chapter 3

The Pied Piper of Perversion

CHAPTER 3: THE PIED PIPER OF PERVERSION

For Kameron, things were tough, as they'd always been since his birth twelve years ago. He came into the world with the deck of cards stacked against him and it was a rather puny package of cards, at that. A true father, excitedly waiting in the delivery room, wasn't a reality. In fact, his mother didn't invite any of the four possible sperm donors to the not-so-happy occasion. *Too much to decide and too messy,* Mom thought, and after all, there was the same confusion about male parentage at the birth of Kameron's two older brothers and they turned out okay. *No need for fathers; we are a family just fine, thank you,* was an old cliché for Kameron's Mom, by then a mother of three.

Now, at age 12, Kameron found himself feeling alone in the tiny, crowded and chaotic rental house, with two older brothers and two younger sisters. Things were hectic and about the only organization under Mom's control was the names of the children—all beginning with "K"—*Kenneth, Kevin, Kameron, Kathy, and Katie.* Mom loved the sounds of the *K's,* and perhaps she liked the names of her children better than she liked to mother them in a traditional sense. Basically, Mom was a kind soul, but she lived for the moment—loving whichever *K-kid* was in front of her, often forgetting about those pesky parent details such as parent/teacher conferences, the need to pay the light bill, or the idea that the *K-kids* should brush their teeth every now and then. The big picture of being a Mom easily faded as she

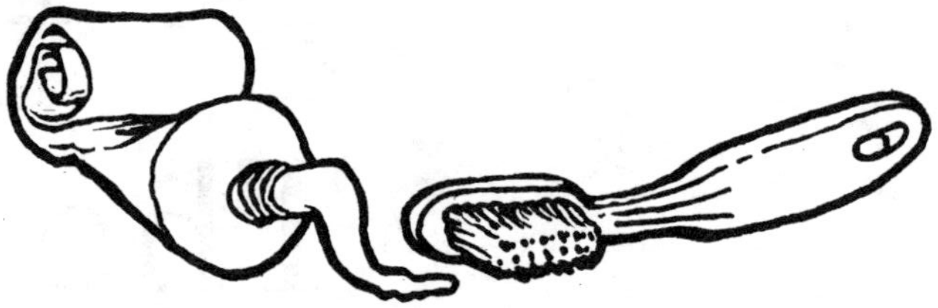

waited tables at the truck stop, pouring coffee and advice to the lonely truckers who, in turn, poured their hearts out to her and often found themselves on her couch after a long Saturday night celebration of a meager paycheck. Proudly, Mom sacrificed for her *K-kids,* giving one of the two bedrooms in the rental to *the boys* and the other to *the girls.* The couch was just fine for her she decided, in her perceived posture of unselfishness.

Mom worked hard, but she could hardly keep up with all the demands of her five *K-kids* without a single dad to help. However, that was the way she wanted it. Proud of her independence and *not needing those troublesome fathers who can cause all kinds of other problems,* Mom was content. Long hours at the truck stop helped rationalize her role as being a *good Mom.* When she did make it home from the truck stop, she would make a stab at parenthood, enthusiastically sharing her tip money tally with the *K-kiddos* and igniting excitement for the next day's trip to the Baskin-Robbins ice cream store, which was way out of Mom's budget, but something she told herself was worth the sacrifice. Never mind the rent was due and the milk designated for the morning Cheerios had soured. Mom found her spot in the *Good Mother* tally by a frenzied splurge of expensive ice cream, never worrying too much about long-term goals.

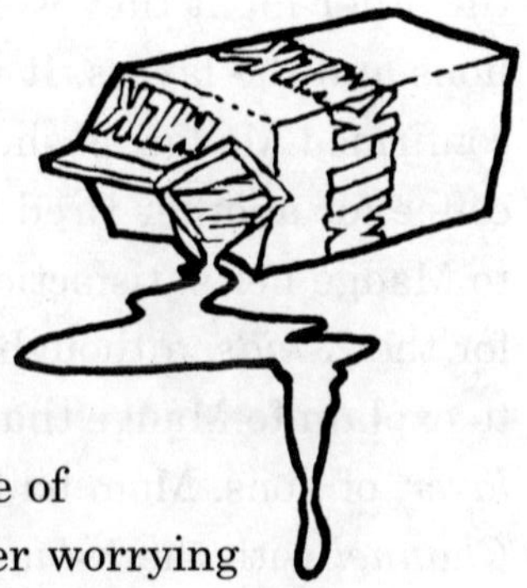

Most importantly, Mom took pride in her vanity license plate, even though it was expensive. ***KKDSMOM*** was the ultimate way she relished her status as a good mom, even if about half the time the 1989 Volvo didn't start in the morning and the prideful license plate only adorned the parked car in front of the rundown rental.

One day, Kenneth, the oldest child, fell nicely into Mom's tendency of immediate gratification by suggesting that he could contribute best to the family by quitting high school and taking a job at the *Big Block Movies* video store two blocks from home. Kenneth's campaign to Mom was the lure of contributing to the *family* (her most vulnerable topic), and the final nail in Kenneth's high-school-degree-coffin was reminding Mom that with his employment at *Big Block Movies*, the *K-kids* would have free and unlimited rental of the store's entire video stock. *Of course the videos would only be used for educational pursuits,* Kenneth explained, knowing full well that Mom loved hearing proposals about how something would help her *K-Kids' family*.

"Think how much these videos will help Kevin when he has to watch the *babies* while I am at work," implored Kenneth in his efforts to convince Mom to sanction his newly-acquired-but-not-yet-known-to-Mom, high school dropout status.

Fine, Mom concluded, as she completed her final makeup process, which included lilac eye shadow, perfectly matching her acrylic and lilac fingernails, also matching her lilac tattoo honoring her family name of *King*. But she wasn't finished with her lecture. "But Kenneth, you will still have to help around the house with *the babies*, especially with *Katie-Kid* (the family nickname for the youngest *K-kid*) when Kathy and Kameron are in school. I will not have that *baby* going to daycare" she fumed. "You know how I feel about those mothers," Mom reminded him. And *yes,* Kenneth knew how his mother felt about such examples of bad mothering. Mom continued, "I want those babies taken care of, Kenneth, because we are a *family* and we stick together," she scolded, content that her good mothering skills were always reinforced when she referred to Kameron, age 12; Kathy, age 9; and Katie, age 5, as her *babies*.

Kenneth won the challenge of quitting high school (even though he had already been expelled) by focusing on Mom's vulnerability, which was her mothering of the *sticking-together-family.* Since Kenneth reinforced what would be best for the *babies* if he were to take on a more adult role, Mom trotted into acquiescence. Victory concluded, Mom went to work; Kenneth went to *Big Block Movies* to visit his friends who also worked there; Kevin went to the telephone to call his girlfriend with news of Kenneth's victory; and Kameron, Kathy, and Katie-Kid went to the television.

Long ago, Mom made a financial decision that the *K-kids* could do without $200 Nike shoes or fancy furniture from the Goodwill store (Mom's very own shopping mall). But paying for cable television was a must, especially for *the babies.*

"You just have to make some sacrifices for your kids," Mom told her friend, Madge, who shared Mom's night shift at the truck stop. "Those babies are comforted when I am at work. They just feel safer with cable TV, and there are some really good shows for them to watch," Mom murmured and Madge agreed.

"My kids like the *History Channel* or *Discovery.* It teaches them all kinds of things, like birds, baboons, and bowling. Just the other night they were watching a show on lions and the layers. It was so interesting," confirmed Madge as she poured another cup of coffee for another tired trucker. Mom furthered to Madge her satisfaction with cable television for the *K-kids,* although she made a mental note to explain to Madge that it was a *lair,* not a *layer,* of lions. Mom had seen the same *Discovery Channel* with the *K-kids* on a Sunday afternoon, resting on the couch after too many truck stop tequilas the night before.

Back at home, *Discovery* it was for *the babies.* Kameron, Kathy, and Katie-Kid gathered around their familiar spots directly in front of the television. Since the quarters in Mom's 800-square-foot rental house were tight, watching television placed *the babies* on the couch only five feet from the screen. And *discover* they did, not on the *Discovery Channel* learning about the lair (not layer) of lions, but *discovery* that was all about sex. The youngest *K-kids* did their discovery of sex while watching MTV or a country music channel where sexual overtones of arousal and sexual conquests were common audio and visual themes. They *discovered* sex through talk shows where guests talked about changing their sex or changing their sexual partners. They discovered Beavis and Butthead and South Park cartoons where

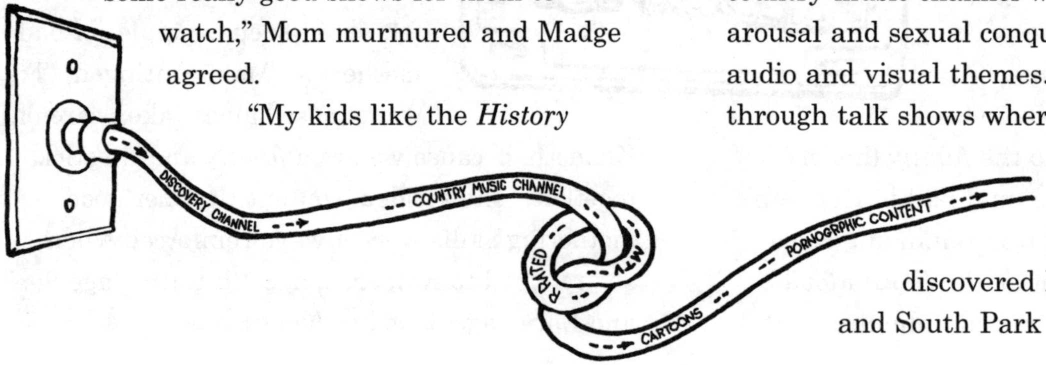

masturbation and other bodily functions were not only discussed, but also demonstrated with full sound effects. Yes, they were *discovering* all right, but not about Madge's ideas of birds, baboons, bowling, or lion layers.

The youngest *K-kids* usually controlled the remote (officiated by Kameron, the oldest of *the babies*) until the older *K-kids* (Kenneth and Kevin) were present. Then, not only did the bigger boys dominate the television, but the girlfriends of the brothers also spread out on the couch for kissing and other

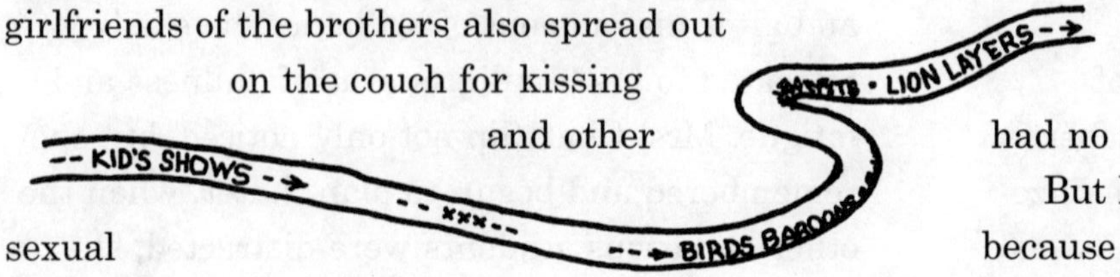

sexual mimicking of what they saw on the tube. The discovery about sex was enhanced with the television R-rated sex shows, but also with Kenneth's new job at *Big Block Movies*, where X, XX, and triple-X movies were easily discovered in the *K-kids*' home. And of course, with all the sexual stuff, plus raging hormones, minus adult supervision, *the babies* also *discovered* firsthand how all the sexual stuff really looked, smelled, and sounded, as their brothers attempted privacy for *hands on sexual discovery* in the tiny house. Yes, sex was discovered on a daily basis, that is of course until Mom returned (which was not often), and then it was back to the real *Discovery Channel* and lessons of lions and their layers/lairs.

As time went on, Kameron found himself squeezed in the middle of the family. He didn't fit in with Kenneth and Kevin as they had girlfriends and their sexual discovery seemed to be a full-time job. Kenneth worked nights requiring a great deal of daytime sleep even though he was the designated caretaker of *the babies*. Kevin, *K-kid* #2, worked all day at skipping school to eventually justify his upcoming plea to Mom for achieving the same *working* status as his older brother. Clearly, Kenneth and Kevin had no time for little brother.

But Kameron was also lost in the middle because he didn't seem to fit in with the younger *K-kids* either. The female girlfriends of Kenneth and Kevin doted on Kathy, as they tried to make points with their boyfriends by braiding her hair and teaching the nine-year-old makeup techniques. Katie-Kid also held a special spot in the *K-kid* pecking order, since the two older boys tried to make points with the girlfriends by doting on the youngest *K-kid*.

"Girls like the father type, so pay attention to Katie-Kid when they are here," was Kenneth's advice to his younger brother Kevin, as they discussed tips and techniques for female sexual conquest.

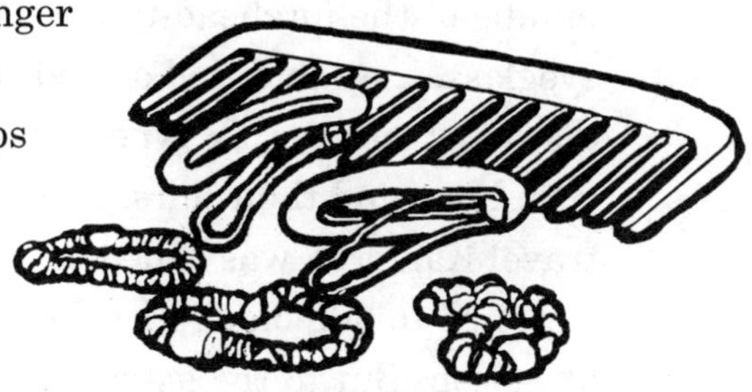

Everyone had a role in the sexual *discovery* business except Kameron, who, in more ways than one, was stuck in the middle and directionless.

But things were worse for Kameron at school. The genetic cards stacked against him resulted in struggles with poor eyesight, small stature, and flaming red hair. The gene pool from which Kameron emerged was deep and at age twelve, he seemed to be drowning. Although bright, Kameron's academic environment was a battleground as he was often the subject of classmate teasing, peer rejection, and teacher impatience. Kameron couldn't seem to organize himself. He often forgot his homework, if it was ever completed, and even though he most often knew the answer to the teacher's questions, his overall fatigue (too much *discovery*) dulled his reaction time to hand raising, and his brilliance usually went unnoticed.

But then, one afternoon, Mrs. Chartflip, a perceptive teacher, saw through Kameron's dirty *Beavis and Butthead* T-shirt, his cluttered desk, and his middle-of-the-forehead-taped eyeglasses, and noticed a hidden spark of *discovery,* not the TV type nor anything to do with lions and their lairs. During a lesson on air travel Kameron was called on, and as usual, she expected to admonish him for not paying attention. But to the astonishment of everyone, Kameron not only gave the correct answer, but an answer that was far beyond the other children's comprehension. Amazing it was, compared to Kameron's usual daydreaming that allowed the *cool* sixth graders even more ammunition with which to tease him. In fact, the absence of booing and hissing when Kameron gave an answer even surprised Mrs. Chartflip as she joined the class in their shock at his knowledge. The quiet was loud with amazement.

But Kameron wasn't fazed by the attention and after his moment of brilliance, he easily retreated to his familiar status of dullness and fatigue. Mrs. Chartflip not only noticed, but she remembered and began to plan. Later, when the other obnoxious students were distracted, she inquired of Kameron about his special interest in airplanes. Alone, away from the shyness needed to survive the teasing and taunting, Kameron became a floodstream of knowledge, explaining his disconnected, but nonetheless brilliant, understanding of aeronautics.

Kameron knew about the first airplane built by the Wright brothers. He knew about planes that flew into the World Trade Center on September 11, and he knew why birds, bats, and paper airplanes (folded quickly when Mrs. Chartflip was in the restroom) could fly. He knew the difference between jet engines and those flying machines with propellers. Not only was his knowledge astute (however scattered), but his understanding also seemed to ignite energy behind the eyes of this usually tired and listless child. It was amazing!

Mrs. Chartflip decided to encourage the newfound interest of Kameron and proposed that during reading class he could work on the library computer, and perhaps research the Internet for aeronautical information and make a special report on airplanes? The idea floated in the air. Kameron contemplated and then agreed. Teacher and student had a plan, and both were enthused about new possibilities for the usual stagnation of Kameron's academic endeavors.

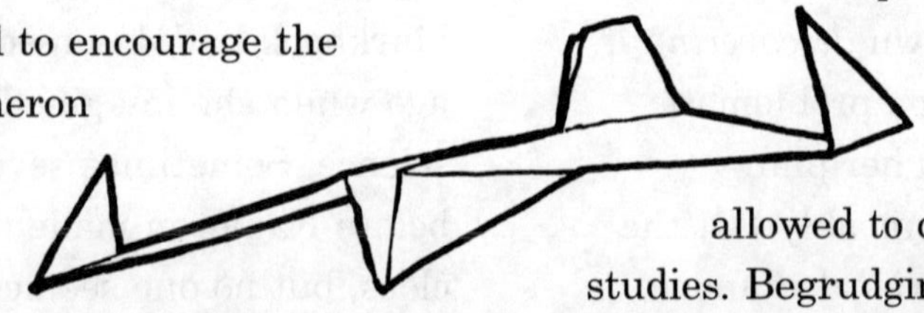

With the best of intentions, Mrs.Chartflip took her often-listless student to the library with the hope of kindling an interest in airplanes, or just an interest in anything academic. She began her project by introducing Kameron to Mrs. Markbook, who sternly glanced over her half glasses expecting, of course, another rowdy child who was disturbing a classroom and sent to the quiet sanctuary of *her library*. She had been in this position before and her attitude toward teachers who couldn't control their students was less-than-positive. Her body language made it clear to Mrs. Chartflip that she would not, even for one minute, accept the idea that Kameron was a well-behaved student who needed further educational stimulation. She knew about children and their *stimulation* behind the library bookshelves, and she wanted none of it. Mrs. Chartflip tried to soothe things with the librarian, explaining that Kameron would be *on probation* for a week and that after that time, a conference would be held to determine if Kameron would be allowed to continue his independent studies. Begrudgingly, Mrs. Markbook acquiesced and after the departure of Mrs. Chartflip, she parked Kameron in his *cubby*.

Mrs. Markbook had worked hard to convince the school board that creating *cubbies* for students in the library was the right thing to do if she was to maintain order in her sanctuary. She campaigned on the grounds that the cubby project would enhance better learning, create a healthy academic environment, and, of course, increase test scores. But she secretly wanted the cubbies to prevent the children from library *stimulation* that had nothing to do with education. That dreadful pinching, poking, and who knows what else that happened between the unseparated children had to be stopped, Mrs. Markbook believed. She also hated their talking, their passing notes, and their throwing spit wads. But to the school board, she only emphasized *test scores* when they considered the cubby expense. Eventually, the school board felt Mrs. M. just couldn't be denied. She was proud of her victory as she planted

Kameron in her favorite cubby—one that kept the child far enough away so that asking her questions was difficult, but also a cubby that was close enough for her to do her own *discovering* if Kameron began to paddle down a problematic path. She felt quite confident in her plan, expecting Kameron would not probably last the week in this isolated spot that was also under her careful scrutiny.

After a brief explanation of computers and the Internet, Mrs. Markbook found several Web sites about airplanes and told Kameron to just read the information, expecting for him to tire easily, bringing on complaints of boredom as happened with most children. But he didn't; he wanted more. When Mrs. Markbook suspected he hadn't really read the material as he claimed, she gave him an on-the-spot quiz. But he surprised her with his knowledge and his eagerness to write about what he had learned. She was shocked but moved into action, giving Kameron further lessons on using computers for word processing to enhance his report writing. And he excelled at that as well. She couldn't believe it.

Mrs. Markbook was so pleased (and shocked) with Kameron, she gave him lessons on how to improve his Internet searches for information about airplanes, and the result was that his cubby became quieter than ever. When Mrs. Markbook checked with Mrs. Chartflip, they both agreed that Kameron-in-the-cubby was a win/win situation for everyone. He came every day and he worked quietly, just like Mrs. Markbook had dreamed students would do long ago when she imagined a career in library science. Sometimes several hours would pass before Kameron made it back to his regular class, but no one seemed to miss him. And when he did return, he could still pass all the math and reading tests that were a struggle for some of the other sixth graders who had been part of the daily lessons. Kameron just seemed to find safety in his cubby and in the world that opened up to him through the Internet, far beyond the cruelty of his classroom and the close, chaotic confines of the *K-kids'* house.

Kameron continued working in the quiet cubby, proudly showing Mrs. Chartflip his papers on airplanes, as well as his now well-established collection of paper flying machines. And at home, when he came home, Kameron seemed to cooperate with the chaos, either quietly joining the television viewing on the couch, watching violent or sexual television, or playing games in the bedroom with Kathy and Katie-Kid. Why, the older *K-kids* were quite pleased that Kameron wasn't complaining about missing his kid shows, and to Kenneth and Kevin, Kameron seemed to be enjoying the pornography they passed about. And the older boys were also pleased with Kameron, since he

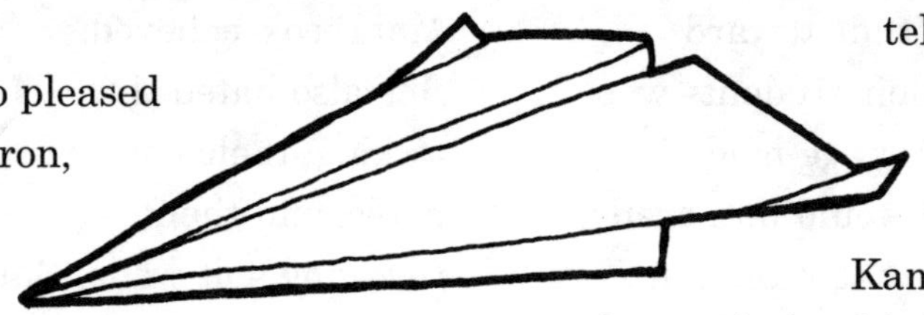

was often late coming home for dinner, making the madhouse in the *K-kid* kitchen a little easier. *Yes,* from the classroom, to his cubby, to the closet, to the *K-kid* kitchen, things seemed to be going well for Kameron.

That is until two FBI agents knocked on the *K-kids'* door. Kenneth was nervous with their unexpected arrival because some of the videos he borrowed from *Big Block Movies* had clear labels forbidding use for anyone under the age of 21. Although Kenneth had never been very good at math, he could figure out the age/chronology problem. Kevin was also nervous with the FBI guys arriving because of the pungent aroma of his marijuana joint, smoked a hour before.

The *K-kids* female units were also in a fret with the cop types showing up. Kathy and Katie-Kid were huddled in the bedroom with the girlfriends, who were worried about being in trouble for cutting P.E. class in order to get an early start on after-school discovery at the *K-kids'* house without chaperones. *But would those infractions be reason to have a visit from the FBI* they pondered?

After several tense moments, the FBI agents learned of Mom's job and got the truck stop telephone number from Kevin and Kenneth. The Feds excused themselves, after giving their business cards to Kenneth, with instructions for Mom to call them should they be unable to speak with her between the ham and cheese omelets at the truck stop.

As the FBI maneuvered out the driveway in a black car with darkly tinted windows, Kenneth, feeling as though he had dodged a bullet, quickly implemented his authority and called a *K-kid* summit, somewhere between the cluttered kitchen table and the portable dishwasher that hadn't worked for years.

Panic was profound, duties were divided, and the videos vanished, as did the girlfriends. And in the chaos, Kenneth noticed Kameron was absent. The "where's Kam?" question prompted the *K-kids* to remember that the pattern of Kameron not coming home until long after dinner had become routine, but not to the point of anyone's concern—at least, not until now. Although none of them minded Kameron missing dinner, since it meant more Spaghetti-O's or Hot Pockets for the rest of them, they now remarked in unison, "Where is Kam?" They worried in unison as well, not because they necessarily cared about Kameron, but because his absence might make

Mom even more suspicious than the FBI characters who changed everything in the *K-kids'* harmony house only an hour or so ago. In fact, Mom's being suspicious was very concerning as Kenneth yelled, "Kathy, don't clean the dishes too good. Mom always knows something is up if it's too tidy. Back off a little." And when Mom got home, it was clear Kenneth was right. Mom was definitely suspicious.

The FBI missed Mom at the truck stop and she, with a surprise of ice cream bars for the *K-Kids,* was very, very suspicious when she returned home to find her house spic and span, her four *K-kids* sitting properly on the couch, and the television turned to a *Discovery Channel* program about lions. Right away, she knew something was wrong. With the ice cream bars melting on the clean kitchen counter, Mom instigated her interrogation. But just as two minor confessions about not taking the garbage out and a few unbrushed teeth were solicited from the *K-kids*, the FBI knocked again.

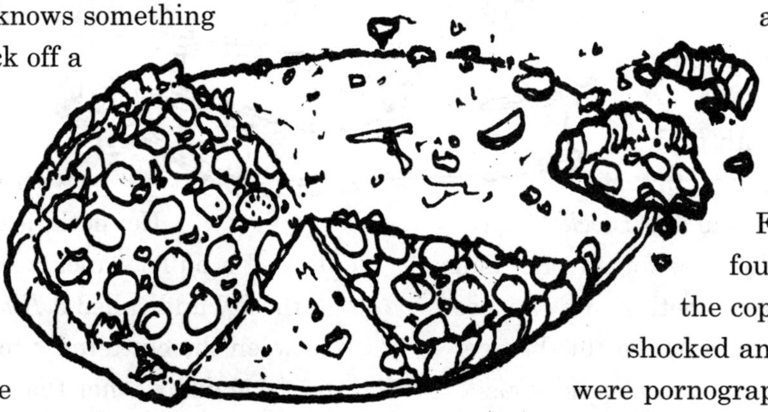

Kameron, Mom learned, was in custody of Social Services after being apprehended in the apartment of a pedophile that had been under FBI surveillance for many months. When the door of the pedophile's apartment burst open, the Feds explained, Kameron was found comfortably lounging on the couch in his Spider-Man underwear where before him lay an impressive array of pepperoni pizza, Dunkin Donuts, and lemon twist Pepsi—his favorite. Video games, Lincoln Logs (organized, not like at home), race cars, and a huge collection of toy airplanes decorated the living room, the FBI explained. Also found in the apartment, the cop types reported to a shocked and stupefied Mom, were pornographic pictures of Kameron and Mr. Pedophile, engaging in sexual acts. But that wasn't all, they said. Other pictures suggested that Mr. P. had been very busy with numerous other children, and it appeared that Kameron had access to all those child-porn pictures. The discovery (not the TV type) was amazing, the FBI suggested to a somewhere-between-shocked-and-enraged Mom. Yes, Kameron was in custody they said and he was a witness—a very important witness needed to punish Mr. P. and send him away to prison for a very long time.

At first, questioning of Kameron by the FBI folks was difficult, since he was devastated by witnessing his beloved Mr. P. being taken away in both tears and handcuffs. All the cop's meanness toward Mr. P. was very confusing to Kameron, who found so much safety and love with his special friend. Although the FBI agents attempted to comfort Kameron by telling him everything was okay, he felt things were anything but okay since he was clad only in his Spider-Man underpants. And he was also uncomfortable when the FBI agents looked at pictures of Kameron without even those.

They told Kameron he was not in trouble, but to Kameron it felt as though he was, especially when they took him to the police station and with their badges and really mean faces they questioned him for hours before Mom finally arrived. And once she did, Kameron was even more confused about whether or not he was in trouble.

Like the FBI agents, Mom said she wasn't mad, but it seemed like she was, especially when she kept yelling at Kameron, "Why didn't you tell me?" Mom was also very loud when she shrieked, "How dare you sneak around behind my back and not come home? You know how I feel about you kids being late for dinner."

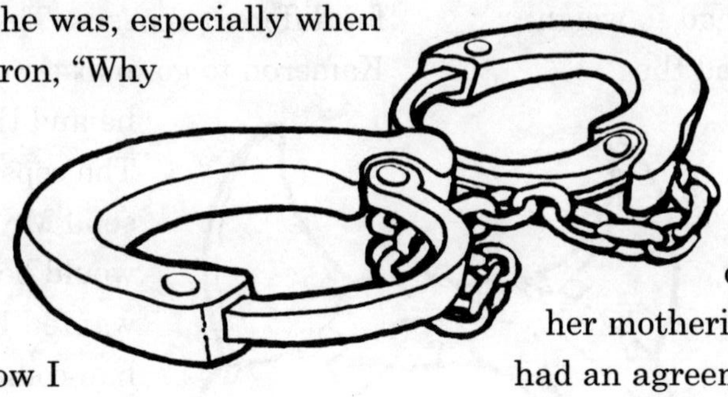

This really confused Kameron, because Mom was never home for dinner. Mom also yelled over and over. "I told you kids to stay away from strangers, now didn't I?" glancing at the cops and social workers each time she said it, which was so mixed up for Kameron, since Mr. P. wasn't a stranger at all. Kameron and Mr. P. had been visiting for months—first on the Internet, then at McDonald's, then at the Toy Tower, and finally at Mr. P's apartment they fondly referred to as the *Paradise Play Palace.* Mr. P. wasn't a stranger, no matter what the FBI folks said. He was Kameron's friend, and frankly, Kameron felt much safer with Mr. P. than he did in school or at the *K-kids'* home. *Stranger indeed,* Kameron thought to himself.

And it went on, this confusion for Kameron. Soon, many people were interviewing him, asking him questions and appearing to be mad. The social workers said Kameron's safety was their main concern as they wondered whether he should be placed in foster care or whether Mom could stop her yelling long enough to care for her *K-kids*, including Kameron. *Yes,* the social workers needed to talk to all the *K-kids* to figure things out; it was part of the rules and it was part of Mom's frustration.

Mom didn't want any questions, especially those about her mothering. After all, the *K-kids* and Mom had an agreement that they were a *family* and that no one was allowed to ask questions without Mom being in charge. Mom was beside herself with anger at any suggestions that the *K-kid* family might need the stupid *state assistance* that the social workers seemed to feel was just what every mother would desire. Kameron didn't know who to believe when they were all yelling and urging him to understand he wasn't in any trouble.

The law enforcement folks were concerned about their case against Mr. P. because Mom wanted Kameron to come home with her and prove there was no foul, at least in the mothering department. The cop types worried Mom might mess things up, since she kept saying things like, "Oh, boys will be boys. This is just a little hanky-panky. Didn't you boys (meaning the FBI guys) ever get a little frisky when you were kids?" Mom asked the red-faced cops. "I'll just take him home and we can forget all about it," Mom insisted, making the legal folks very frightened about their case. Kameron forgetting about it was just what the cops didn't want to happen because they needed him for their case against Mr. P.

And then the school folks also had to weigh in on what to do about Kameron and the Paradise Play Palace hookup from the library. The school heavy hitters were nervous since Mr. P. had solicited Kameron from his cubby in the library. Mrs. Chartflip and Mrs. Markbook fretted that they might be in trouble, since it appeared that Kameron found an open invitation to the Paradise Play Palace on their watch. So in defending themselves, they reminded everyone that they were also victims (kind of), since they had never given Kameron permission to *chat* on the Internet and it must have been his own deviousness that made everything turn so messy. With their jockeying and their justification, they explained to authorities that it was Kameron who went against the rules and that, in fact, they had *followed all the rules.* Mom, of course, would have none of their rationalizations about blame, she was firm on that. And even though she never attended any of the scheduled parent-teacher conferences, she did some shrieking at Mrs. Markbook and Mrs. Chartflip for not *immediately* notifying her of any problems. She implied that if she had just known, things would have been different, but the school ladies weren't convinced.

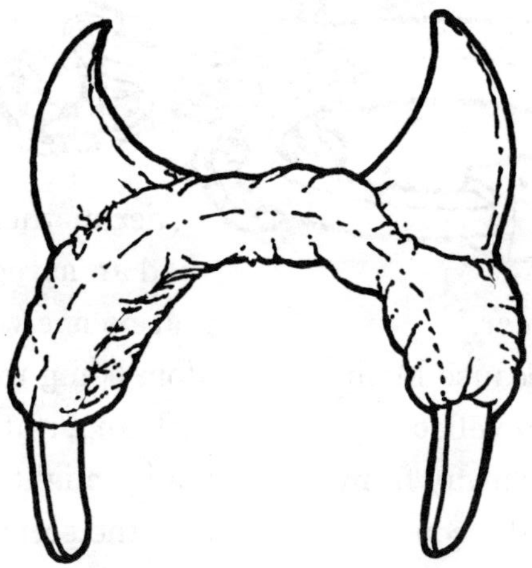

Yes, everyone wanted a piece of Kameron, but for different reasons. The social workers wanted Kameron to go to foster care so they could know he and the other *K-kids* were safe. The cops wanted Kameron to send Mr. P. to prison so their case would be successful. The teachers wanted Kameron to prove they had committed no foul so they wouldn't be in trouble. And Mom wanted Kameron to prove she was, as she always knew, a good mom—after all, her license plate said so.

And they all got what they wanted in the next few months. That is, everyone except Kameron. The cops got Kameron to testify against Mr. P., who was trotted off to prison for a very long time. *Good enough*, they said. The teachers were exonerated after the trial as everyone learned how really deviant Mr. P. was, and the whole school district openly fussed about the perils of the Internet and the deviousness of children like Kameron.

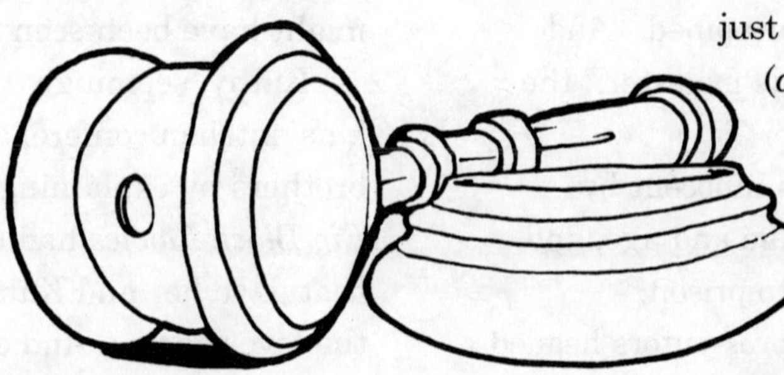

And Mom got to maintain her status as a good Mom, because her son's status as a sexual victim (smelling slightly of bad mothering) suddenly switched. Instead of being under suspicion for not being a good Mom, she became Kameron's *victim*. He broke the family rules, she explained, again and again to anyone who would listen. He went against the *K-kids'* code by keeping secrets from the family clan, Mom told the rest of the slightly-now-subdued *K-kids. Yes, it was Kameron's fault things got messed up,* as Mom reminded everyone of her license plate once again. Everything switched and turned upside-down with Kameron at the bottom of the pile.

But there was more. What the cops, the prosecutor, the FBI, the social workers, and the child protection folks had learned from their own *discovery* was that ever since Kenneth started bringing home Big Block Movies *discovery*, Kameron and Kathy had been playing *lover games* in the closet. Easily and innocently, Kameron told everyone, what they did in the closet. After all, everyone in all the offices told him he wasn't in trouble and they said he should tell them every single thing that happened. Without any hesitation, he described how he and Kathy would suck on each other's private parts, just like they had learned *(discovered)* from cable TV, from Kenneth's free videos, and from what they saw in the far-too-small house between their brothers and their girlfriends.

Kameron also admitted he and Kathy, when playing house in the closet, would do the *humping game*. Just like he had been encouraged to do in court, Kameron told the investigators everything. And when Kathy confirmed the lover and humping games, the calculations began.

By virtue of state laws where Kameron resided, he was clearly a victim of sexual abuse by Mr. P. In fact, at age twelve it would be four more years before Kameron, at sixteen, would have the ability to consent to sex, the lawmakers determined. He didn't have the developmental capacity to understand sex enough to be able to consent to sex with Mr. P. It just couldn't happen, the court confirmed. When Mr. P.'s defense attorney pointed out that Kameron willingly went to the Paradise Play Palace and he willingly participated in the sexual games, the prosecutor convinced the jury it didn't matter.

"Kameron is an innocent young man," he purported. "He is only 12 years old and he can't consent. His cooperation with this child abuser doesn't mean anything since Kameron doesn't understand sex," the prosecutor opined. "And that's why you must convict this molester," the prosecutor urged the jury.

There it was. Kameron was innocent by virtue of his developmental stage and age, and Mr. P. was guilty and sent off to prison.

But while the FBI and the prosecutors headed to the pub to celebrate Mr. P.'s conviction with a glass of champagne, Kameron was headed off to juvenile detention because of what happened with Kathy. With calculations continuing, it was determined that in Kameron's state, the *age differential* between children in order for *sexual criminal conduct* to exist was three years, the usual national average. And certainly there was three years between Kameron and sister Kathy. And with this calculation, Kameron was then switched from a sexual victim to being *a sexual offender*.

Mom, of course, like the good Mom she was, rushed to rescue Kathy, giving clear permission, and *yes*, justification, for Kameron to be charged with a crime and incarcerated for his bad deeds. With great drama, Mom lined up the *K-kids* in the kitchen to get to the bottom of things. And bottoms emerged. Kenneth and Kevin admitted that, *yes*, they had girlfriends in the house, and *yes*, there had been times when some sexual things (only minor, of course, they assured) might have been seen by *the babies*. Mom fumed.

Kathy, seemingly the most upset at the *K-kids'* kitchen conference, tattled on her older brothers by explaining to Mom about the videos *Big Block Movies* had donated (officially or not) that gave her and Kameron ideas on how to play the lover games. And although Katie-Kid was too little and too frightened to offer much (with all of Mom's fuming), she did relate that what she saw Kameron and Kathy doing in the closet was no different than what she saw her older brothers doing with their girlfriends in the two tiny bedrooms. For Kathy and Katie-Kid, it all seemed ***normal***. Mom really fumed with this *discovery*.

So on it went. Discovery, discovery, and nothing was discovered about birds, baboons, or bowling. Mom not only got the picture (and it wasn't pretty) of what had been happening, but she also got a glimpse of her good Mom status being threatened, especially with those snoopy social workers poking around. But the precarious nature of her good Mom position didn't last for long. After all, the *K-kids* were a family and they stuck together. So, Mom started the sticking.

"Haven't I taught you kids better than this?" Mom queried. And the *K-kids* confirmed, much to Mom's contentment. "And didn't your brother know better than this?" she sternly questioned. And again, confirmation from the *K-kids* was unquestionable about Kameron *knowing better*. The question only momentarily hung in the air, as Mom's mother status and Kameron's innocent status were in conflict. *Who was really to blame?* they pondered. Then, in unison, consensus of the *K-kids* provided clarity.

Mom had taught them better, and *yes*, they agreed, Kameron *knew better*. The solution loomed. Mom was a good mom. She had taught them better and even if there had been a little hanky-panky going on in the *K-kids*' house, Kameron still *knew better*. Kathy, in her confusion, challenged the triumvirate of Mom, Kenneth, and Kevin. She was bewildered about her role in the *knowing*, since she actually felt like one of the lovers in the game. "I did it too, Mom," Kathy pleaded. But she was quickly hushed and reminded that Kameron was older, and besides, they all reminded, Kameron *knew better*. As it ended, Kenneth and Kevin were exonerated of their sexual discovering because Kameron *knew better*. Mom was vindicated of any suggestion of bad mothering, since Kameron *knew better*. Kathy and Katie-Kid remained confused about how Kameron *knew better*, but Mom promised someday they would understand.

No one wants to accept blame because the problem of sex among the kiddos is utterly unspeakable. And that may be where the problem lies—about what is spoken and what is not.

THE PIED PIPER OF PERVERSION—LEADING CHILDREN DOWN THE PATH WE PROHIBIT

The tragedy of Kameron's plight personifies this society's response to sexual activity among children, and it is happening every day and in every corner of the country. For sure, *children molesting children* is a disgusting problem warranting disgusting consequences, but in consideration of what is done and not done in teaching about sexual respect—are children really sexual criminals at the same time that they are considered sexual victims? The answer to that question has to do with *the knowing*. In attempts to dodge the responsibility bullet, the big question becomes *who knew what, when, and where; who should have known, who might have known, who didn't know, and who knew for sure?* No one wants to accept blame because the problem of sex among the kiddos is utterly unspeakable. And that may be where the problem lies—about what is spoken and what is not.

Children, by nature of their inequality to adults, depend on the grown-up folks for guidance about which path to take. Usually adults try to do as much path preparation as possible toward the preferred route. If children are taught not to steal, but they still make a heist from the local 7-11 Market, there is no problem regarding path navigation pondering. The grownup folks can easily determine the petty thieves knew the proper path, but in favor of three Baby Ruth candy bars, they took a detour. They knew it was wrong because they had been taught. Without so much as a slight sweat, the punishment is administered and deserved for the junior burglars. But when it comes to path navigation about sex, when so much about this topic is unspeakable and unspoken, things aren't so clear for the kiddos. But what is clear is that when sex among the kiddos happens, the grown-ups want to pass the responsibility bullet and say, *they knew better.*

MR. PIPER PLEASE

Oh, it was awful! Squeaking and squawking, hurrying and scurrying, the vermin had overrun the town of Hamelin. Rats were in the vats and even found their way into the ladies' hats. Rats were everywhere, ruining the peaceful life of Hamelin Corporation. Worries and woes about the rat infestation plagued the city council folks until one day a strange fellow, "thin and tall, and with a coat of yellow and red," made an offer to the rat-frustrated folks of Hamelin in the very old fairy tale *The Pied Piper. Yes,* for a mere thousand guilders he would rid the rats, he promised. But the mayor of the corporation was so pleased with the Piper's offer, he flamboyantly promised *fifty-thousand guilders* if truly the rats would run. "No, no," affirmed the Pied Piper. "I only need the promise of one thousand guilders for my task."

But *never mind* said the anxious city council folks. *Anything,* they promised—one thousand or fifty-thousand guilders—it just didn't matter if the vermin really vacated. And with that verbal commitment and promise of integrity, the Piper began piping.

With his mysterious pipe, the even-more-mysterious Piper went out into the streets and began to play. Unable to resist, the rats began to romp after him. With secret charm, the rats were rendered helpless and they haplessly followed the Piper, eventually tumbling over the cliff to their ocean demise. *Mission accomplished*, the town folks said, as they rang the bells in celebration of their now-rat-free town of Hamelin. The celebration was stupendous, smacking of the utmost glee but also a certain failure to remember the previous Piper promise.

"Where are my thousand guilders?" queried the Pied Piper amid the merriment for his work.

But with shortened integrity and rude rationalizations, they refused, claiming their past promise of payment was only a joke. *No,* they pretended, *we weren't serious about payment—it was just a joke.* After all, they secretly pondered, the rats were gone, the problem was solved, and the Piper was a rather frivolous fellow and seemingly *without his own counsel or power,* or so they thought.

But the Pied Piper remembered the integrity of the promise and he was not to be short-changed. *A deal is a deal,* he probably thought to himself as he began to pipe again, but this time with a different tune. Out into the street again he went, playing strange sounds with even stranger responses. Running from homes, schools, and churches came the Hamelin children, unable to resist the compelling sound, seemingly forgetting their parents and the safety of their homes. They were dancing and smiling and celebrating, following the strange music, ignoring the pleas from the panicked parents.

And soon, as the children followed the music, the Piper mysteriously opened the mountainside, providing a continued path for their gleeful dancing. Into the mountain the children skipped and at the last minute the Pied Piper followed them, carefully closing the mountainside and shutting out tearful parents—their children gone forever. The town's precious youth and the strange Piper were gone, except for one child, left as a rude reminder of integrity lost.

Hamelin's citizens gazed aghast upon the only youth left behind. There in the dust was a small lame child, too weak to follow the others. As he limped back to the devastated parents, the lesson was clear. In his crippled condition, he was left behind to remind the astonished parents what happens when they fail to keep their promises of youth protection. *No,* the loss of the children wasn't the fault of the strange Pied Piper. *Yes,* the town of Hamelin was to blame for

But the Pied Piper remembered the integrity of the promise and he was not to be short-changed. *A deal is a deal,* he probably thought to himself as he began to pipe again, but this time with a different tune.

the loss of the children. They failed the children and forever they would suffer the consequence of looking at the one lame child, a constant reminder of the punishment when promised integrity is lost.

They failed the children and forever they would suffer the consequence of looking at the one lame child—a constant reminder of the punishment when promised integrity is lost.

THE PATH TO PERVERSION

The Pied Piper story is a reminder of what this society does to children like Kameron. The problem of sexual abuse in America needs fixing, just as the rats needed ridding in Hamelin. So, like the mayor and the city council folks, society makes a promise about protecting children from sexual abuse. They pass laws and they posture about punishment. But just as the Piper was tricked, American society also tricks its own children. Society's unspoken path to perversion is there for youth to follow as they learn about sex from the most provocative and promiscuous sources. And just like the music from the Piper was so irresistible, children in America follow the sexual path.

But then, when the withholding-of-respectful-sexual-information adults find out the children have acted out sexually, the promise of protection is broken as kiddos like Kameron are punished. And just like the promise to the yellow-and-red-dressed Piper, integrity and responsibility are somehow forgotten and blame will be laid on the perverted ones—the children—rather than society accepting any responsibility to leading children down that path. The joke really is: *We were just kidding when we said we would protect you. And we were just kidding when we indirectly, subtly and softly seduced you to become sexual. And we were just kidding when we said we would give you the tools to navigate the path.* The result of the broken promise is that just like the lame child left behind, children in this society become lame with the consequences given to them for sexually acting out, even though society does little to protect them from going down the prohibited path.

Kameron was seductively led down the path toward perversion by his environment and his circumstances. The television (not Discovery), the videos, the sexual escapades of his brothers, the lack of supervision, and the absence of any helpful socialization, easily laid the path toward the Paradise Play Palace and toward the lover games in the closet with Kathy. But when Kameron *normally* responded as a result of his environment—everyone pretended as though he was *abnormal.* The playing of the pipe goes on, as does society's deep denial about any responsibility for the path. And the result is lame children, limping along in life, branded as sex offenders, sentenced to lifetimes of shame, because protection was really a pretend promise—just a joke.

ONE CHILD, ONE BRAIN?

But there is more to the facade and dodging of the responsibility bullet when children like Kameron are considered two things at the same time, even though they have only one level of functioning—only one brain. How did the heavy-hitters in Kameron's situation make two different decisions about Kameron concerning what he knew and what he didn't know?

When the FBI discovered Mr. P. and his hanky-panky with Kameron at the Paradise Play Palace, there were no questions about Kameron *not knowing*. Every state has laws to protect children from sexual abuse, as indicated by Age of Consent statutes, which means that before the age designated by the state, the kiddos can't say *yes* to anything sexual. Good enough, the cop types determined. Kameron was a victim because he couldn't consent. He didn't have the developmental skills at age twelve to make an informed decision about his own hanky-panky with Mr. P., making Kameron a clear victim of sexual abuse. There was no question about it and the responsibility bullet belonged to Mr. P.

But wait. Once Mr. P. trotted off to prison there was a new mess to clean up, and it started in the *K-kid's* closet. Finding out about Kameron and Kathy's hanky-panky made everyone uncomfortable and the responsibility bullet needed dodging. Primarily because Kameron was older and male, and because none of the adults wanted to look in the neglect mirror, it was decided that Kameron was the culprit, and the same brain that only a few days previous was unable to consent to Mr. P. suddenly became fully culpable and criminal. But how could Kameron's brain be both an innocent victim and a junior Mr. Pervert, at the same time? The answer to how this could happen lies in the great pretend of society—the great integrity deficit. No teaching, no education, no guidance about the nasty subject of sex happens everyday in everyway—just so society can maintain it's pretend purity. And the deadly outcome is adults basking in the bullet blame dodge— convinced children like Kameron *knew better*.

How could the brain be both an innocent victim and a junior Mr. Pervert, at the same time?

MORE PRETENDING

A pretty good Mom is making a purchase for the emergency school board meeting, where she will strongly vote against the proposed sex education program. Believing high-minded liberals who are likely homosexual and card-carrying members of the American Civil Liberties Union probably sponsored the sex education program, Mom wants no part of it for her sweet and innocent kiddos. While she buys the doughnuts to help everyone sustain lots of energy, for lots of arguing in the meeting, Suzie, her fifth grade daughter, is Mom's partner on the shopping trip. In the checkout line, while Mom visits with her friend, Marilyn, who feels the same outrage about this sex stuff in school, Suzie practices her phonics skills as she reads:

And just like the city council in Hamelin, Mom is counting on her integrity to protect her children, yet in reality, it is just a joke.

Mom thinks she is prohibiting the smut, yet sex is sneaking around every corner, softly encouraging Suzie and her friends to do exactly what Mom is fighting.

Sexual Tips to Keep Him Satisfied

The Parts of His Body He Doesn't Want to Talk About

47 Ways To Make a Difference in the Bedroom

How to Tell Him How You Want to Be Touched

Seven Secrets to Dressing Sexy

Men On The Chase—How to Catch Them With Sex

451 Ways to Look Sexier for Summer

Clinton Tells All—His Favorite Lesbian Fantasy

Erotic Sexual Secrets of Teen Idols

Everything Men Wish Women Knew About Their Bodies

Just like Kameron's Mom and her pretend protection of *the babies*, Suzie's Mom will do some pretend protecting of her own kiddos by fighting the liberals in the PTA meeting. *No way* will her sweet and innocent Suzie be exposed to the hanky-panky business of menstrual cycles or swimming sperm. And when driving to the meeting where her daughter's sexual purity will be maintained if Mom has her way, at the traffic stop Suzie reads a bus advertisement for *hot wings* and *hot girls* at Joe's Jock Joint—complete with hot girl photos on the bus posters.. But it doesn't matter in Mom's mind. She doesn't notice the connection of sexual information Suzie is already receiving and she doesn't consider the path to perversion that is enticing her daughter to dance along—just like the Pied Piper and his music.

BEAUTY/BOOBY SHOP

Only haphazardly does Mom note her awareness that during the school board meeting, while she is fighting the dreaded liberals from teaching about sex gymnasium, limited supervision is provided for the children of the sexual purity crusaders playing in the library corridor. Not really considered by Mom is that Suzie and her female friends might play games that on the surface seem harmless, but are nonetheless sexual. The *Beauty Shop* game, glorifying glamour of fingernail painting and eye-shadow application, might be a nonchalant choice for the female units. The male children of the smut fighters may also engage in seemingly harmless sexual role games, hooting and howling outside the door, giggling mimics of *Booby Shop* rather than *Beauty shop* to their female counterparts. Although the kiddos know nothing about the sexual rules of the game playing, they participate just the same, tiptoeing ever so close to engagement. Sure, there will be no exchange of bodily fluids with the flirting, but these are the practice sessions for treading down the sexual path. Mom thinks she is prohibiting the smut, yet sex is sneaking around every corner, softly encouraging Suzie and her friends to do exactly what Mom is fighting. And just like the city council in Hamelin, Mom is counting on her integrity to protect her children, yet in reality, it is just a joke.

THAT WE PROHIBIT

But what will Suzie's mom, just like Kameron's Mom, Mrs. Chartflip, Mrs. Markbook, the prosecutor, the cops, and the social workers do if the *Beauty Shop* girls and the *Booby Shop* boys should ever engage in a little boob business of their own (all while the parents are preventing any educational presentation of egg/sperm get-togethers)? If the responsibility bullet is dodged, the hammer will fall, especially on the boys of the *Booby Shop*. If the kids do a little fooling around—the outrage will be clear and the song will be familiar. *They knew better*. Even though it is likely that the beauty/booby shop kiddos slowly got the message and encouragement for sexual acting out from the society of their parents, the punishment for taking that path will likely be swift while the adults shun any responsibility for leading them down that same path.

WHO KNOWS?

But in some situations, knowing is not always enough—or is it? As Frances drives home from work, she notices those pesky blue and red lights flashing behind her. She knows to pull over, and she does. She knows she must show her driver's license and her automobile registration to the stern-looking officer, and she does. When Frances is told that she will be ticketed ($150 worth of ticket) for traveling at a speed of 90 miles an hour in a 65-mile-an-hour speed zone, it all has to do with *the knowing*. If the responsibility bullet veers near, she won't likely get very far pleading to Officer Poo Poo, "I didn't *know* the speed limit was 65."

Sorry Frances. The claim of not knowing is a *no go*. It is Frances' responsibility, when she pulls out on that highway, to know the speed limit. It just comes with the responsibility and privilege of having a driver's license. Frances had criminal intent; she was culpable and she *knew*—and if she didn't really know (perhaps putting on her makeup when she drove by the speed sign), she *should have known*. And by not knowing, that will be a $150 *not knowing* boo-boo for Frances.

What responsibility do the punishers of the rules have to post the rules to those who may wander down the prohibited path?

But if Kameron really knew enough to be responsible for the huge legal consequence he will face for the rest of his life, why aren't children Kameron's age allowed to serve on his jury?

SIGN OBLIGATION?

But what would happen to Frances and her *knowing* dilemma if the State Highway Department didn't post speed limit signs? What responsibility do the punishers of the rules have to post the rules to those who may wander down the prohibited path? Could airplane passengers be punished (federal offense) for smoking if the flight attendants didn't make those clever announcements to the passengers about all the miserable things awaiting the poor fool who disarms a smoke detector in the airplane lavatory? Could parking tickets be issued without the annoying signs forbidding it, or could fines be issued for errant campfires if there were no directions on where Dad could cook the wieners without getting thrown in jail? Of course not, some might say, suggesting there is some responsibility on the rule regulators to post the signs about the rules.

REALITY AND RULE WATCHING

In reality, however, Frances is still in trouble, in spite of how good it sounds to put the pressure on the punishers to post the signs. True, the troopers are much happier when their bosses (state government folks) post speed limit signs, because those signs make things a lot safer on the highway. But technically, when Frances signs underneath her rather somber mug shot on her driver's license, she officially accepts responsibility to know the speed limit. Even without the signs and even though the signs make things better, the bullet can't be dodged by Frances. Even though posting the signs makes things run smoother, society demands the *knowing* of its age-of-majority consent folks like Frances.

And the *age of majority/consent* may be the operative words that make what happened to Kameron so egregious. Frances had to be a certain age to get that driver's license, as she had to be in order to vote or do other cool things like register for the military or carry a handgun. And Frances was also protected from someone doing sexual things to her until a certain age when the government folks figured she would *know* whether to say yes or no (consent, actually). But when she reached those magical birthdays designated by *State Whatever*, the buck stopped there and Frances became responsible.

JUGGLING JURIES

But in Kameron's situation (the lame child left behind), everyone said he should have known not to fire up the hankies and pankies with Kathy even though he didn't know about Mr. P.'s hanky-panky. And the irony is that a very, very serious legal punishment awaits Kameron, now designated and branded as a *sexual offender*. But if Kameron really knew enough to be responsible for the huge legal consequence he will face for the rest of his life, why aren't children Kameron's age allowed to serve on his jury? The friendly United States

Constitution promises that everyone has a right *to be judged by their peers* so why not judge Kameron with twelve-year-old jurors? *No way* would be the fuss from grownups facing such a challenge. They would probably claim that kiddos Kameron's age aren't capable of making those scary legal decisions, so they shouldn't serve on juries. But if that is true—that children can't make those important decisions, how did the legal bean counters figure Kameron could?

NO MURDERING

Further consideration of the bullet-dodging done by adults and their responsibility to children, relates to the posted signs along the proverbial path. Clearly, there are some behaviors inherently forbidden by society without so much as a single sign. Rarely do public places sport written announcements or warnings such as *No Murdering, No Stealing,* or *No Jack Hammering On Heads.* Those behaviors are universally forbidden and no one needs to put up signs. But the difference seems to be that the prohibitions of these behaviors, such as murder, are usually taught to children through one method or another. Suzie's mom wouldn't be outraged at a program advocating *NO MURDERING*, but she might object to money spent on such nonsense, since that lesson is already on her parent curriculum clipboard. Most societies have taboos against such things as taking a life or stealing another's possessions (jack hammering heads also), and in good families those taboos are actively taught, usually negating the need for the signs. It is expected that *everyone know*, but it is also expected that everyone will be taught.

SIGN SHORTAGE

But where are the signs for children, like Kameron, who sexually act out? And if the defense of sign shortage is that *everyone knows*, where is the education and teaching for children so that they will know not to sexually act out with other children. But wait! Children *not knowing* about sex seems to be exactly what parents want even though when the ignorant kiddos sexually act out, everyone pretends as if *they knew,* and therefore, had criminal intent. And at the same time, when children *don't know* and stumble into sexual activities indirectly taught by the seductive society, they are punished with the arrogance of Kameron's disciplinarians, smugly suggesting, of course, *he knew better.*

But wait! Children *not knowing* about sex seems to be exactly what parents want even though when the ignorant kiddos sexually act out, everyone pretends as if *they knew* and had criminal intent.

HELP US, MR. HINCKLEY

It was on a street in Washington D.C., and there were lots of cop types around with the purpose of protecting the President of the United States. Everything was just fine with President Ronald Reagan until John Hinckley Jr. moved unexpectedly from the crowd. And before the really scared Secret Service officers could subdue him, Mr. Hinckley shot President Reagan as well as others in the entourage. Not

Not only is sex everywhere—encouraging children to engage in friskiness whenever possible, but criminal sexual conduct is almost normalized in society with only faint whispers of the punishment part—that is until the hammers are ready to fall.

only was it shocking, but millions witnessed the savagery on live television. There was no doubt about who did what to whom. But when the trial of Mr. Hinckley got underway, many questions emerged about the *knowing* nonsense.

John Hinckley, it seemed, had a bit of a problem, his attorney suggested. And those problems related to his mental illness. Why, Mr. Hinckley, they pleaded, could not tell the difference between right and wrong because he was mentally impaired. He just didn't understand (*know*, actually) the nature of his actions and he couldn't, therefore, form the ability to have criminal intent, his attorneys said. And of course the jury, hating passionately what Mr. Hinckley had done to their beloved President, nonetheless had to make allowances for Mr. Hinckley's *not knowing*. They reluctantly concluded that Mr. Hinckley couldn't be guilty of attempted murder because he just *didn't get it*—(not knowing in its original form). Not so for poor Kameron, who wasn't afforded a single consideration for his inability to tell right from wrong.

Most states have laws to accommodate for diminished mental capacity, which are fancy words for *just doesn't get it*. Good enough. And it makes sense, because the law requires something called "criminal intent" in order for someone to be truly guilty of a crime. So, special laws and special circumstances try to separate an impaired person, such as Mr. Hinckley, from the frustrated Frances, who *should have known* how fast to drive on the highway. These special considerations of *knowing* seem to be a good thing, since knowledge of the punishment for a crime (rules posted on the path) should occur in a fair world, which would pertain to Frances, but would exclude Mr. Hinckley, who couldn't know.

KNOWING BETTER BALANCE

In the *knowing better* business, it is sadly clear that things are out of balance for American children struggling with the path of perversion that seems so enticing—especially since no one is really talking to them about sex. Encased in the whole business of catching a break, like John Hinckley, is the issue of knowing about the *punishment* for the pesky problems that get everyone upset. It isn't enough to know that something is wrong—the legal punishment must also be understood in order to form *legal consent.* Because of the not-so-friendly signs sprinkled around everywhere, someone can know it is wrong to let Fido do his business on the perfectly coiffed lawn of the gas station picnic area. The signs are clear. And if it is also known there is a legal punishment awaiting whoever is on the other end of Fido's leash, then everything should be okay when the really fat fine is handed out. Not only was the behavior wrong AND ILLEGAL, but there is a legal punishment, making those two issues the key to true culpability—*knowing* actually.

MISSING PUNISHMENT PART

But for children, trying to navigate the path of perversion, the signs pertaining to sex and punishment are out of balance. Not only is sex everywhere—encouraging children to engage in friskiness whenever possible, but criminal sexual conduct is almost normalized in society with only faint whispers of the punishment part—that is until the hammers are ready to fall on children like Kameron. During the sensational trial of the Jeffrey Dahmer case, even grade school children joked about Dahmer cookbooks, since, unfortunately, this despicable killer engaged in cannibalism of many of his victims. Many children knew he raped, murdered, and ate (in some cases) more than seventeen young, helpless men. But the nasty side is probably all children learned. It is doubtful that the kidlets cracking jokes about the culinary skills of Mr. Dahmer ever saw the punishment side of this tragedy, beyond perhaps just knowing Mr. D went to prison.

Beyond the titillating headlines of the Dahmer case, children were not likely to learn about the death threats Mr. Dahmer's innocent family received from hate-filled citizens screaming for not only the death penalty, but those punishment suggestions were also leveled against Mr. and Mrs. Dahmer. Vicious responses were relentless in the Dahmer case, but generally on the backside of newspapers not usually perused by fifth graders after gym class. Children were not likely to learn about how Mr. Dahmer, while in prison, was brutally beaten to death by another inmate who obviously had nothing left to lose. *No*, the Dahmer case was out of balance, understood by children in only snippets and tidbits—all about the lurid details of his crime. The joking children learned nothing about the tragedy and punishment of Mr. Dahmer or any of the long-term consequences. And if really *knowing better* requires signs on the path to perversion about the punishment of sexual misconduct, most children will be prone to miss the turnoff.

And if *knowing better* requires signs on the path to perversion about the punishment of sexual misconduct, most children will be prone to miss the turnoff.

PRESIDENTIAL PERVERSION

In considering the out-of-balance fund of information available to children about whether *they knew* or *didn't know*, the sexual escapades of former President Bill Clinton was also one-sided. The term *oral sex* became somewhat of a household word for American families during the Clinton scandal involving the White House intern, Monica Lewinsky. *Yes*, poor Bill seemed to get himself into trouble in the White House with a little hanky-panky involving oral sex. And as the scandal unfolded, children giggled at purple-faced newscasters trying to use complicated words to describe the sexual trysts of the commander-in-chief. It was delicate.

"I had to explain to my son about oral sex," one father complained on national television.

The titillating tidbits of unauthorized White House friskiness filled the airwaves of national television. Lurid descriptions of everything from

In Kameron's *normal* life, sexual promiscuity, sexual taking, and sexual acting out was clearly the *norm*.

dress stains and the sexual possibilities of wrapped cigars gave everyone red-faced information, whether they wanted it or not. But the scoop about the presidential punishment was only a soft whisper from political pundits, and not likely to impact the average child catching tidbits of news information while finishing a peanut butter sandwich before catching a ride to the skateboard park.

But William Jefferson Clinton did get in a lot of trouble during the impeachment hearings that followed his scandal. Many of his critics were crabby and cranky for years after. However, national television coverage of the impeachment hearings was probably lost to most kiddos, and the shame and humiliation that became the tune of his presidency did not usually register for the giggling children. But years later, when President Clinton was chosen by President George W. Bush to be a spokesman for a Tsunami relief fund in 2005, the message to children may have been, *a little presidential perversion goes unpunished,* and years later, an honorable position awaits. How then can children really know (be culpable) if no one teaches the punishment part of the path?

NORMING OF THE NORMS

So in the big scheme of things, how does the issue of *normal* evolve in a society that saturates the powerful prevalence of sexual disrespect, yet does little to expose children to the punishment for going against society's rules? Most of the time, society establishes laws prohibiting certain behaviors, depending upon the issue of *normal.* Whether it is primitive countries in jungles, or high-tech advanced societies, laws and rules are established to maintain order based upon whatever that society considers as the norm. In fact, the definition of normal is *what is most accepted by the majority of society's members.* If, for some reason, a society decided that purple hair for men and shaved heads for women were just the things to do (and everybody did it), those traditions would be considered *normal.*

Kameron's world seems to be a mirror of American society. In his family, sexual acting out seemed to be the *norm* rather than the exception. Mom didn't talk to Kameron about respecting the private parts of Kathy and Katie-Kid; in fact, she would have none of that nasty talk for her *babies.* In comparison, the private parts of the girlfriends of Kenneth and Kevin, as well as the private parts of the men and women on the *Big Block Movies* videos, were hanging out all over everywhere, with no apparent respect, but with lots and lots of action. And when Mom screamed, "How could you do that?" the answer Kameron probably wanted to give if he had the language understanding was, "Because I thought it was *normal."*

No one was talking to Kameron about sexual morality and the importance of making appropriate sexual decisions in his future. In fact, the only sexual decisions made in the *K-kids'* household seems to be whether to watch a pornographic video from *Big Block Movies* (since they have to be returned the next day) or simply turn on the *Playboy Channel* and not be bothered with the cumbersome task of getting the aged VCR to function properly. Other sexual decisions, Kameron observed, pertained to whether it was Kenneth or Kevin's turn to have the privacy of the biggest bedroom for girlfriend hanky-panky. In Kameron's *normal* life, sexual promiscuity, sexual taking, and sexual acting out were clearly the *norm.*

And the same seems true for much of American society. When Kameron is punished and sent off to junior prison for his crime, the legal folks in their wisdom, decided that it was *not normal* for children like Kameron and Kathy (three years apart) to be sexual. But considering the slant of sexual information available in American society, is that really the *norm*? Without taking any responsibility for the lack of healthy information available to children, a punishing society smugly purports that children *know what is normal* and, therefore, it is acceptable to punish them for going against society's norms. Suzie's Mom probably convinced herself that the kids don't need the liberal/hippies program, because *normally* they are innocent. And yet in reality, what adults really want for children—sexual tenderness, sexual appreciation, and sexual respect—would not appear to be the norm, at least considering the signs that are posted along the path.

THE DEADLY DILEMMA—CHILDREN WHO SEXUALLY ACT

Society's report card on educating children about what that same society plans to do with them if they fall outside the norm is pretty pitiful. When children sexually act out, they can suffer lifetime consequences while adults smugly turn away. And although probably not too many folks across the nation really cared about Kameron, the consequences for society about this lost integrity are potent and powerful—not only ruining the lives of children and families—but wrecking havoc in the plans for safety.

Society's report card on educating children about what that same society plans to do to with them if they fall outside the norm is pretty pitiful.

SIDE ONE

On one side of the what-to-do with sexually acting children dilemma is the *no action* response. Just like Kameron's Mom initially wanted to approach the Paradise Play Palace problem by asking the red-faced cops about their past hankies and pankies, families and society often try the same justification when the kiddos are found in the closet. This side of the dilemma justifies *boys will be boys, this is just a little funny business, this was just playing doctor*, or *this child was sexually abused in the past and so what else did we expect*? Side One of the dilemma suggests *no foul, no action,* and lots of rationalization for the behavior so nothing needs to be done.

The bean counter researchers about the cycle of sexual disrespect know that the *no-foul, no-action* response usually contributes to the continued cycle with sexually acting children often becoming adult sex offenders.

But sadly, research suggests that the majority of adult sex offenders were *sexually abusing* in childhood and nothing happened—except, of course, some well-meaning adult's rationalizations. The bean counter researchers, about the cycle of sexual disrespect, know that the *no-foul, no-action* response usually contributes to the continued cycle with sexual acting children becoming adult sex offenders.

Perhaps those adult sex offenders who began sexually acting out as children could have been deterred if a better solution or intervention occurred when they were first discovered naked in the tree fort. So Side One of the dilemma suggests that ignoring children when they are *truly offending* brings another lifetime sentence with the likelihood that they will continue sexually abusing into adulthood—further contributing to a disrespectful society.

SIDE TWO

But what about the other side of the dilemma where children like Kameron are unfairly or inappropriately considered to be sexual offenders, even when they are not? What is the result of labeling a child as a sexual offender and treating that child as a junior Jeffrey Dahmer when they were innocent and, for them, acting quite normally? The answer has the same result as Side One of the dilemma. An innocent sexual stumble for a child can assure a response that the child *knew better*, the child had *criminal intent* and is therefore a *sex offender*. And that sex offender designation is often for a lifetime, with no wiggle room for consideration of society's neglectful teaching. And if the child wasn't an offender before this harsh response, the prophesy will eventually be fulfilled.

WANDA/CHARLENE

She really was a good sister and a good babysitter. She loved her four-year-old brother and his two same-age male cousins. At age twelve, Charlene felt quite important taking care of the *little ones* while her Mother and two aunts worked together in the family-owned restaurant. It was a family affair, with everyone pitching in to help, and now that she was in charge as the babysitter, Charlene was finally considered *one of the grown-ups*. It took her twelve years to get to this elevated position, and she was very proud of herself.

After lunch, naps, and the afternoon snack, their favorite television show was finally on channel 5. It was wrestling. And even though neither Charlene's Mom nor her aunts particularly liked the wrestling show, their silence gave non-verbal permission for the kiddos to watch it. All four children gleefully sang the opening song, *The Bitch is Back*, as they welcomed the purple-haired wrestling pro, *Wicked Wanda,* onto the television stage and their pretend stage of the coffee table. Oh, it was fun, wild with fanfare, screaming, touching and posturing—right there in the double wide trailer's living room, with the three little boys pretending to be Wanda/Charlene's entourage.

And just as they saw on the wrestling show, the boys grabbed Wanda/Charlene between her legs for a body slam onto the avocado shag carpet of the trailer house living room. And she, (Wanda/Charlene) reciprocated by grabbing the boys between their legs, doing the *Grab Crotching* (as the TV announcers had called it) as she slammed, ever so carefully, the little boys onto the avocado couch. And yes, Wanda/ Charlene's breasts were grabbed in the mimicry of what the real Wanda on the wrestling show called *Boob Bouncing*. The *Grab Crotching* and the *Boob Bouncing* occurred on the outside of the clothing in the avocado adorned double wide, but it nonetheless happened. It was all very exciting; both on television and in the living room, until a small accident occurred and brother got bumped on the coffee table with the matching avocado ashtray. Tears ended the game, and Mom's arrival made everyone feel better.

Through her inquiry about the bumped noggin, Mom learns about the *Boob Bouncing* and the *Grab Crotching* among the children. Being a good Mom, and in the spirit of a supportive family, Mom calls her sister in a faraway state who works as a social worker in the child abuse section of that state's Human Resources Department. *Sister will know what to do,* Mom is sure. Sister's advice, of course, is to seek assistance from the local child protection agency which Mom does. And the action begins, not as exciting as the Wanda/Charlene action, but a much more powerful action.

The investigator, with her *Sexual Abuse of Children* state training manual open on her desk, interviews the four children, who all admit to similar stories, suggesting no level of secrecy about the boob business and the crotch grabbing. The twelve-year-old Wanda/Charlene does not understand the significance of her behavior, so she openly admits to not only touching the boys and their sexual parts, but *yes,* she admits it was her idea to get the boys to touch her sexual parts. No secrets here. Mom had taught Wanda/ Charlene to always tell the truth and like Kameron, she did.

Well now, the social worker contemplates and calculates. Two criteria exist in her state training manual to determine if a sexual crime has been committed, and this right-out-of-state-training employee knows she has both elements of a sexual crime in the Wanda/Charlene dilemma. According to the manual and her supervisors, the ***age differential*** (more than three years in this state) is the first consideration and, yup, way more than three years exists between Wanda/Charlene and the younger boys. But secondly, the manual says the ***type of behavior*** must be a primary consideration, which is a fancy way of simply referring to adult state laws already in existence. So, with careful calculation, the investigator determines she has *Sexual Abuse in the First Degree,* three counts, of course, since the age difference is a whopping eight years, and the fondling (coercion too) is clearly defined by

She triumphantly writes in the file FOUNDED SEXUAL ABUSE. There it is—sexual criminal conduct with lifetime consequences for a 12-year-old.

the state statute. She triumphantly writes in the file *FOUNDED SEXUAL ABUSE.* There it is—sexual criminal conduct for Wanda/Charlene and lifetime consequences forever.

Though charges may not be filed against her, unless Wanda/Charlene's Mom hires a dream-team of lawyers, this twelve-year-old will be subjected to sex offender notification, which will happen immediately due to society's screams for public safety. With manual in hand turned to the *Notification Section*, the social worker/investigator (by law) has the right and the obligation to contact Wanda/Charlene's school and notify the grade school principal of the charges against her. And in the spirit of safety, he of course, passes the information on to not only Wanda/Charlene's sixth grade teacher, but to the entire faculty as well. This all happens because just like the promise to the Piper, everyone pretends this is best for kiddos in general—but certainly not for Wanda/Charlene. And because everyone in her family was cooperative and looking for help, the hammer will fall easily. Ever so innocently, Wanda/Charlene has joined the world of sex offending and her future will be forever impacted, as everyone in the town of 1,400 *now knows* she is a sexual offender who *knew better* all along.

HEAVY HAMMERS FOR THE PATH NAVIGATION

In many states, sex offenders—regardless of age—at a minimum, face sex offender registration. In other situations, they face sex offender notification, as in the case of Wanda/Charlene. No matter where she goes or what she may attempt to accomplish many years into the future, Wanda/Charlene could be required to inform law enforcement of her address, her whereabouts, and of course, her lifetime status as a sex offender. In some states, Wanda/Charlene may be placed on a sex offender registry through cyberspace, where anyone who checks their local neighborhood for perverts could learn that sex offender Wanda/Charlene resides among them.

Critics might cry foul, suggesting *that kind of punishment never happens in real life for children.* But even though it shouldn't happen, it does, often with the same quietness that the Hamelin city counsel told the Piper their promise was just a joke. As every corner of the country reels from the panic and fear about the magnitude of the sexual abuse problem, the *something has to be done* urgency almost always focuses on punishment rather than prevention. But rather than being responsible for putting up the signs to help children avoid becoming offenders, the responsibility bullet is again dodged with the comfy conclusion that Wanda/Charlene, like Kameron, *knew better*.

As every corner of the country reels from the panic and fear about the magnitude of the sexual abuse problem, the *something has to be done* urgency almost always focuses on punishment rather than prevention.

FIXATION, FANTASY, AND THE FUTURE

Somewhere in the middle are those who suggest that in an effort to prevent sexual abuse, tough measures are necessary. And besides, they claim, the juvenile justice system is founded on rehabilitation, not punishment. The justification for serious, lifetime consequences for both Kameron and Wanda/Charlene is that the offending kiddos will be in *treatment*. Any hints of suggestion that these harsh punishments are wrong are comforted with the pretend solution of ***therapy.***

As Kameron and Wanda/Charlene are trotted off to treatment, everyone who sent them on their way feels better. After all, this is the *help* they needed to become *normal* after their *abnormal* behavior was discovered. But careful consideration of what that really means may be a little less comfy, especially for those who want to look at the big picture of the really big problem of sexual offending.

Usually, treatment methods for offending kiddos will happen in residential care where they will share bathrooms, bedrooms and breakfast with other *abnormal* kiddos, often those who are also labeled (some rightly so) as sex offenders. Usually, the therapy involves sitting children in a circle with other kiddo sex offenders and sometimes spending years talking about their past hanky panky in the closets, tree forts, and secret tents. The Kamerons and the Wanda/Charlenes getting this thought-to-be-helpful ***help*** will spend lots of time talking about their deviancy, their crimes, the trauma they caused and everything else negative about what they did as a *sex offender* to their *innocent victims*. This concentration on all the bad stuff will be detailed, ongoing, and usually for a very long time.

The therapists of these deviant children will hustle off to national conferences where they will learn how to take adult sex offender treatment techniques and apply those methods to children, of course with little regard for the developmental differences between adults and children. Rather than thinking about the sexual development of these children and the idea of *sexual fixation* occurring with treatment's constant concentration on deviancy, the therapists will (with a flavor of retaliation driving the effort) focus (and fixate) on the sexually negative. And even if the staff and the therapists take pride in being strong supporters of the kidlets in treatment, the critical years of concentration on deviancy may be the most damaging. And if there was any doubt about Kameron or Wanda/Charlene truly being sex offenders in the beginning, after two years in a treatment program of focusing on their *deviancy*, there will be no doubt about that status when all this therapy *help* is finished.

Usually, the therapy involves sitting children in a circle with other kiddo sex offenders and sometimes spending years talking about their past hanky-panky in the closets, tree forts, and secret tents.

With tears and fears about sexual abuse, the heavy hammer for those who sexually offend is hoped to bring honor to victims.

FROM MILITARY TO MEDICAL SCHOOL

Not only will Kameron and Wanda/Charlene focus on deviancy in treatment without much on building healthy sexual arousal, but when they are released, they will face other serious consequences. Sex offender registration and sex offender notification usually await both children, and many important doors, not usually considered by the investigators and court types who sent them there, will be closed. If Kameron and Wanda/Charlene live in states where juvenile sexual records can never be expunged, their offending records will follow them forever, limiting many options. Medical school and the military are examples of those who will say *no* to sex offenders. Neither child will ever be able to become a teacher or work in areas such as law enforcement. Employment applications will usually inquire about past criminal behavior, and when Kameron and Wanda/Charlene answer honestly, they will be rudely rejected in many employment situations where employers, like Suzie's mom, want no part of that messy stuff. So, two children will be punished for a lifetime by a society that takes no responsibility for failing to post the signs or help them navigate the path to perversion. Integrity is lost, and promises to American's youth about protection is rendered only a joke.

THE GREAT FALSE HOPE

Perhaps it was an honorable hope—this favored approach of lifetime punishment—even for kiddo sex offenders. With tears and fears about sexual abuse, the heavy hammer for those who sexually offend is hoped to bring honor to victims. But questions could be raised about whether Kameron's sister Kathy will be honored or horrified by heavy hitting responses to her brother. What about the brothers and cousins of Wanda/Charlene? Is there a risk that they could be traumatized by her punishment?

VICTIM JUSTICE?

At times, she felt like the Maytag repairman, sitting around without a lot of prosecuting to do. Measure 11 had passed in the State of Oregon, and the number of cases she could prosecute were limited since the defense attorneys were telling all their clients to plead "not guilty" and head for a trial. No one was going to admit guilt if they were facing a 100-month prison term with no other options for the sentencing judge. At first, the prosecutor thought Measure 11 was perfect because she really hated what sex offenders did and she really cared for sexual victims as well, often being brought to tears when she read police reports or watched the videos of victim interviews.

But recently it had become clear that Measure 11 hadn't seemed to unfold as she had hoped—actually making prosecution that much tougher. But for now, she might have some work. A new case file is opened on her far-too-tidy desk. Checking the legal charts, the first *yes* is recorded. Yep, the alleged defendant is age sixteen, and certainly fits the over-age-fifteen criteria for Measure 11. And *yes*, the alleged victim is age twelve. Careful calendar-counting however, told her that in only nine days there would have been less than the three years age difference between the alleged offender and victim. But considering the single incident, she had before her, the nine days didn't matter.

Checking further, she learned that the sexual stuff alleged included penetration, but it was *digital,* which always made her feel a lot better to say in a report rather than the other crude descriptions for the poking and prodding of body parts. And her final tally was that *yep*, there was enough fooling around to constitute those felony crimes pertinent for Measure 11. *Good enough,* she says to herself, especially when all the reports confirm that the sixteen-year-old confessed and no one, at this point, had hired a pesky defense attorney to slow everything down. And as she filed the charges against the juvenile and collected her coat, she said a little promise to the victim in the case, guaranteeing that she, the prosecutor, would make sure justice was served.

VICTIM VOICES?

She was devastated, and hadn't been to school for days. She felt so guilty about everything. It was only two weeks ago when she was on the top of the world, bragging to her best friend about her new boyfriend. She and Marissa had giggled at lunch remembering the slumber party the previous weekend. Telling Marissa about how romantic it was to fool around with her friend's big brother was so exciting. She trusted her best friend and she just couldn't keep the secret. Together they hoped he would call her again, even though he was older and she was two years behind him in school.

Well, now everything was miserable and it felt as thought her life was over. Everything started to fall apart when the cops showed up after Marissa's mother had called them. Marissa had tried to apologize, explaining she didn't know her Mom had to tell the cops because she was a school counselor who had to report child abuse. The term *child abuse* just didn't make any sense to her. But now, she hated Marissa, she hated Marissa's Mom, and she hated herself.

She had tried to explain to the cops that she was the one who went into his bedroom. Crying through tears, she explained that it wasn't his idea to even get undressed, at least at first. When the cops started talking about *sex crimes*, she just couldn't believe what she heard. When his parents starting asking whether she would *press charges,* she didn't know what to think. Pressing charges didn't make any more sense to her than

No one was going to admit guilt if they were facing a 100-month prison term with no other options for the sentencing judge.

And at age thirteen she feels hopeless and helpless—hating herself and others who with the best of intentions hoped punishing her boyfriend would bring her honor.

child abuse. She was devastated when boys at school started talking about how she was a slut for telling on him, sending her notes and yelling at her in the hallway. When the child advocacy center counselor started talking about how she was supposed to feel better since he would go to prison for eight years, she couldn't stop crying. But when her parents started talking about moving her to a private school where she could live with her grandparents, she began to feel somewhat better, although the loss of her friends, her family and her life as she knew it would never be replaced. And at age thirteen, she felt hopeless and helpless—hating herself and others who, with the best of intentions, hoped punishing her boyfriend would bring her honor.

THE BACKFIRE

Not surprisingly, the well-meaning efforts of punishing *sexual offending* children often backfire for victims. This madness does not take into account how many children, seduced down the path of perversion, take the sexual plunge *together* and even though there is often an age differential, the cooperation or consensual differential may have been nonexistent. When only one of the children is punished, the other, often believing *I was consenting too*, may be sentenced to a lifetime of guilt, long after the offender child is released from whatever punishment is imposed by the do-gooders, who really believed their heavy hitting and hammering was in honor of victims.

THE TERRIBLE TWO STEPS

Along with revisiting the plight of Frances with her $150 ticket for *not knowing*, John Hinckley and his big break of *not knowing* because of mental illness, and Kameron's punishment suggesting that he *knew better*, comes the word: culpability. Two criteria must exist for culpability to be assured and those are *knowing the behavior is wrong* and *knowing there is a punishment for the behavior*. This is the time-honored way to determine culpability or criminal intent. This two-step is really just a fancy way to give legal meaning to the *knowing better*.

But there is more two-stepping in the critical decision-making process about sexually acting children and the lifetime sentences that are hammered down. Just like Wanda/Charlene's investigator tallied, the age differential between the kidlets and the adult statutes of sexual misconduct are needed to charge kiddos with crimes. Considering the unique nature of children and considering the lack of posted signs on the paths toward perversion, questions could be asked about the wisdom of this two-stepping using only adult laws and the age differential between the sexually acting kiddos.

TWO CRITERIA, TWO FAMILIES

Two families, and those two criteria, can be a miserable, although a time-honored way, to respond to sexually acting children. The Smith house and the Jones house provide an interesting hypothetical demonstration of the madness. If the national average age differential of three years is used in conjunction with the common adult legal charge of *Penetration With a Foreign Object,* an interesting theoretical situation unfolds to point out the madness of only using two tools to punish children for a lifetime.

Mrs. Smith has taken her children to the family physician for school physicals. Their bodies are prodded and probed during the process, much to their discomfort. The sensitive doctor uses various instruments in his examination, which includes wooden tongue depressors to probe the children's rectums, throats, noses, and ears, hopefully not in that order. Following the grueling, but necessary examination, the children leave the doctor's office a bit grumpy. Mrs. Smith is a Mom sensitive to her children's discomfort and their bravery with the poking and prodding. As consolation, she stops by the local convenience store, awarding her kiddos with Popsicles to soothe their wounded pride.

Later, as Mom parks in the family driveway, she sees Popsicle juices dripping from the elbows of her now-contented children, and at the same time, she remembers her newly waxed, white kitchen floor. She quickly suggests that the children go to the creek behind the house to wash, play, and finish their dripping Popsicles. The kidlets, in better spirits, scamper down to the creek. As they play, familiar ideas set the plan. The Popsicle sticks are inserted into the rectums of the younger children by the older children who mimic the doctor's examination they have just endured. If one of the Smith children is three years older than another Smith child, the legal consequences should automatically render a sexual felony conviction, subject to lifetime consequences, for the older child. If those two criteria are the only measures used for consideration, just like the hot-on-the-prowl investigator type that handled Wanda/ Charlene, the older Smith kid will be a sex offender for a lifetime.

But on the opposite side of town, in the hypothetical Jones house, someone like Jeffrey Dahmer, a clearly psychopathic sex offender, could be sexually acting out against others in his childhood residence. A brutal, intimidating, and vicious *putting the sticks in butts* could occur in the Jones house, and if there were three years age difference, the same crime would be charged as for the Smith house kiddo, even though many other things would play into the scenario. But if adults, in their hopes of across-the-board-simple-to-decide-two-step process only use the narrow confines of the law, then a psychopathic sex offender would receive the same sentence as the Popsicle-stick-poking kid.

But if adults, in their hopes of across-the-board-simple-to-decide-two-step process only use the narrow confines of the law, then a psychopathic sex offender would receive the same sentence as the Popsicle-stick-poking kid.

CONCLUDING THE CULPABILITY QUAGMIRE

Society leads children down the path to perversion, avoiding sex education and avoiding responsibility for their lack of education for children. And yet, when children follow the path of perversion, society responds with a vengeance, fueled by false hopes that in punishing children for taking the path, society will be safe and sexual victims will be honored. And as Kameron's plight suggests, the issue of what children *really know* (forming criminal intent and having true culpability) is rarely examined, even though it would seem to be society's responsibility to help children know, or at least post the proverbial signs to help them *know*. The quagmire of culpability allows a neglectful society to consider children victims of sexual abuse because they weren't culpable (didn't *know better*), yet in other circumstances, smugly suggesting a lifetime sentence of punishment is acceptable to the same children because they were culpable and *knew better*.

SOMETHING ABOUT ALL THE LEFT LAME CHILDREN

In the spirit of *There is No Sex Fairy to Protect Our Children From Becoming Sexual Abusers*, parents and society need to accept responsibility to help children *know better*. It can't be assumed that they really knew, especially considering the scarcity of respectful sexual information and the abundance of disrespectful sexual information in this society. The pretend posturing of folks who want children to be sexually respectful, but who don't want to teach them—is just that—a great pretend and a farce. Just like the joking folks in Hamelin lied to the Pied Piper, Americans are lying to children about protecting them. And as children are sentenced to a lifetime consequence, all of society will be sentenced to the reality of limping lame children left behind to remind them of their neglect. That is, unless they change and take on the task of teaching sexual respect. Thus, THE TEN COMMANDMENTS OF RAISING SEXUALLY RESPECTFUL CHILDREN.

Chapter 4

First Commandment
Thou Shalt Begin at the Beginning

CHAPTER 4:
FIRST COMMANDMENT THOU SHALT BEGIN AT THE BEGINNING

The morning recess usually characterized by the dodging of dodge balls, the jumping of jump ropes, and the chasing of children who want to be chased, today is somber and with none of it—no dodging, jumping and chasing, that is. Inside, coveted *Parental Permission Slips* are the focus of an informal faculty meeting of five—stiffly standing outside the library as they separate the *Now* group from the *Not Now* group as the slips dictate. Predictably, the five faculty folks were also divided into the *Nows* and the *Not Nows* just as they had been at the special PTA meeting in the junior high gym three weeks ago. So now, with the counting competency of a Florida presidential election, the *Parental Permission Slips* are stacked into the opposing groups, each tally resulting in a small (but silent) victory for whatever side they supported.

The forming of the combatants hadn't been easy when the parents and teachers had previously gathered for the heated debate, so things were still smarting a bit. Sure, it had all started out friendly at the special evening conclave, but when the big-glasses big-guy from the health department showed up early and placed a pamphlet on everyone's chair before they even arrived, things were tense from the very beginning. Some embarrassed and clearly in the *Not Now* group just sat on them, not even wanting to touch the darn things. They figured some silly pamphlet wasn't going to change their minds and they secretly hoped the school janitor would have a big mess cleaning up all the unused pamphlets when the meeting was over—making their position of *Not Now* seem even more powerful. Many also felt that the *planted* pamphlets sort of set the meeting off-balance from the beginning, since some in the *Not Now* group wanted the chance to decide if there would even be a discussion about the drawings on the pamphlets that, to many, looked like the Big Horned Sheep mounted in Principal Pudge's office. With the pamphlets already in position and some of the *horns* haphazardly showing, the *Not Nows* were feeling defensive, thus the sit-down-on-them silent protests.

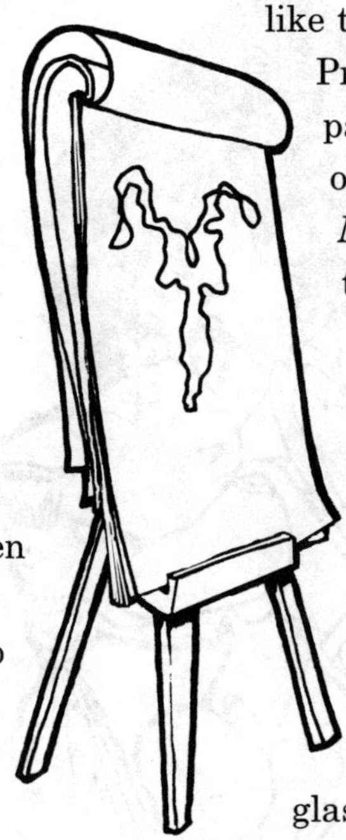

Now the big-glasses guy was from the satellite office and since the school district had reported to the Health Department that the two groups were so divided (and, at times, rude) with their *Now* and *Not-Now* debates, he had agreed to make the 57-mile trip to speak directly with the pondering parents. Not only were he and his glasses rather large, but the thickness of his spectacles made it very hard for the worried and suspicious parents to see if he was shifty-eyed, so typical many thought of folks from the city. And the missing buttons on his trying-to-be-white dress shirt that allowed his rotund tummy to protrude, didn't help him one bit in the credibility department. So when he stuttered and stammered a bit, telling everyone he was much more comfortable talking about mumps or measles, his purple-faced attitude was even more troubling to the worried parents. *Here he was,* some whispered, Director of the Health Department, *and he didn't look one bit healthy* or one bit comfortable trying to help the parents decide whether they were *Nows* or *Not Nows.* Reassuring, he was not, but in charge, he was.

Glasses Guy (G.G. as they started calling him) began the meeting with *getting one thing right on the table,* which everyone knew came from people who attend lots of government meetings. He told everyone that he had no opinion one way or another, and that he didn't want anyone to try and *pin him down* about the decision, which made everyone consider that pinning him down on anything would be very hard considering his size. G.G. showed them his perfect government attitude of being neutral—*just some facts* and, of course, the darn pamphlets were all he had to offer. And the facts were demanded, especially from the *Not Nows.*

"What are the reasons the health department thinks children in the fifth grade need to be taught some of those things *now?*" was the question that hung in the air in many different forms. And so, he gave them reasons.

He was pretty fancy with his facts and his reasons, using a stand-up flip chart, an aged projector, and a lighted pointer, making everything about the facts seem quite official. The sad numbers (***stats*** he called them, trying to be informal as best he could) were about rises in teen pregnancy, about the increased dangers of venereal diseases and, of course, date rape. The ***stats*** were uncomfortable and foreboding for both groups of fretting folks.

"Some schools just make the decision to teach children early, trying to stop problems that could develop," he said awkwardly.

And, of course, the *developing* business was what many in both groups worried about, since they all knew the fifth graders seemed to be *developing* much sooner than everyone hoped. So there were more questions and, naturally, G.G. had more facts.

"Originally, this program was designed for sixth graders," he explained, "but as some of you know, times and children have changed, so many schools are choosing the fifth grade to get an early start."

His comment just hung in the air as each parent had horrible thoughts about their children *developing* behind their backs. And when G.G. seemed to get nervous with the silence, or some thought he just might have been hungry and worrying about a missed dinner, more facts were requested.

"Don't you think parents are the best ones to handle this *in the home* rather than in a school program?" asked one member of the leaning-to-the-*Not Now* group.

G.G. answered in perfect *government lingo*, being non-committal, and answering affirmatively that home-schooling was a good choice for some folks, but, of course, mentioning that other parents wanted *academic assistance*, which most of them understood was another fancy government term.

"But if the fifth graders are ready, why not have the program available?" asked a Dad clearly in the *Now* group and secretly recognizing that having membership in this faction would relieve him of the dreaded duty later on.

"*Yes*, many children will benefit from the lessons now," G.G. reminded, with an additional reminder to the parents of the ticking time clock of *developing* AND his 57 mile drive home. But the biggest question in the late hour from both groups had to do with *who* would do the thing if, of course, it was going to happen.

G.G. had no problem explaining about the *WHO* from his beloved Health Department, which considering his weight problems, many knew he obviously appreciated from an employment situation, but not from a dietary lifestyle perspective.

"A very well- trained, seasoned, and no-nonsense woman, who has been with our department for years will make the presentation," G.G. explained to the pondering parents with his own professional satisfaction in her resume, since after all, he had trained her.

"She has two master's degrees—one in public health and one in public administration, not to be confused with *menstruation*," G.G. tried to joke, which didn't go over very well and which made some of the parents sit even harder on the Big Horn Sheep pamphlets. He went on about her presentation organization, her presentation precision, and her perfunctory presentation skills—"never ever wavering into any kind of value judgment for the children—she just gives the facts," he assured.

The image G.G. gave of this SHE, highlighting *no-nonsense* and *no-values* was especially comforting to the *Nows*, but also, enticing to some of the on-the-fence *Not Nows*.

As the meeting went on, there was fussing, blaming, criticizing and even some snoozing from one of the Dads in the back who worked the night shift at the gas station. And with all the posturing from the *Now* and the *Not Now* groups, resolution seemed impossible until G.G. pulled out his trump card: the coveted *Parental Permission Slips* (finally), making everyone feel relieved. Just as the prudish questions had hung in the air earlier, now resolution occupied that space.

There it was—the answer. With the permission slips they could all decide if the time was *Now* or *Not Now*, without a single one of them having to pick up a single copy of the Big Horned Sheep drawings on the planted parent pamphlets.

So now, ten days later, the small faculty-of-five enclave in the hallway had the tally and, of course, Mrs. Numbersnot, the math teacher, had it all figured out with parental percentages.

"About two-thirds of the fifth graders will be in the permitted group," she mathematically murmured, really referring to the *Nows*, although she didn't say that out loud to her faculty colleagues, since she was secretly in that group.

The librarian, Mrs. Wormbook would have to deal with the remaining third—the kiddos from the families of the *Not Nows*, which was perfectly fine with her since she was a card-carrying member of that group. Ever since her Library Science graduate work she had always been more interested in what *wasn't* happening, especially in the library milieu of not talking, not giggling, and not getting into trouble. So, slips counted, the percentages partitioned and for two-thirds of the fifth graders it was going to happen, and happen *now*.

Back outside for the morning recessers, balls barely bounce, children hardly chatter, and the anticipation is agonizing. Then, they hear it. A lone automobile on an even lonelier country road slowly approaches. In its final descent into the dusty parking lot, the engine emits its final grunts and groans as the ignition key is extracted and lights automatically turn off. Glum-mouthed children watch as *Nurse Ratchet* (known in other circles as the county health nurse) slowly lumbers her buxom body from the now cooling and slightly dusty 1996 Ford Taurus. In she walks, as the stoic children note her foreboding boxes and briefcases, likely laden with her tools of torture for *the BEGINNING*. Without direct commands, children obediently file inside, tiptoeing with trepidation about what lies ahead. Most of them have heard the home battles about

Now or *Not Now* decisions and they know it is time, at least for some of them.

N.R. (Nurse Ratchet) lumbers into the hallway outside the fifth grade classroom, which will soon become known to slightly over 66 percent as *the dungeon*. Being clearly task-oriented as her boss G.G. always taught, she begins meticulously, overseeing Mrs. Numbersnot's calculations, but only briefly. N.R. always recognized the no-nonsense tendencies of math teachers, so with satisfaction that there will be accuracy in the tally, she turns to her next task, which, of course, is segregation.

N.R. has been solicited to this rural grade school to begin SEX EDUCATION, and although scientific research suggests sex involves both genders, that diversity will not occur on N.R.'s watch. Two-thirds of the girls are about to receive instruction on their sexuality, which will focus on menstruation—complete with a *pad* presentation and a twenty-minute video involving swimming sperm (imagined fully clothed) doing the backstroke through the fallopian tubes that are represented by the horns of the sheep. But first, the segregation, and there are two of them.

Hushed hallways provide the environment for sorting: males to the library and, at first, ALL females to the fifth grade dungeon of instruction. Then Mrs. Wormbook, with the coveted permission slips turned over by Mrs. Numbersnot, extracted those female fifth graders of the *Not-Now* group, trotting them out to join the boys in the library. And certainly under Mrs. Wormbook's watch, there will be additional gender separation in the confines of her librarian reign. The male units titter with excitement on their segregated side of the library and begin planning some type of rebellion, against what they aren't sure. Sternly, N.R., who is overseeing the library separation process, gives the boys a clear, nonverbal notification that she, as G.G. suggested, is a *no nonsense* kind of person. The boys pull back with her powerful admonition, knowing she will soon be gone with the rest of her prisoners. The girls paroled from the fifth grade dungeon, and obviously offspring of the *Not Now* parents, settle in on the other side of the segregated library with several resources picked out by Mrs. Wormbook to ease their feelings of isolation.

The children of the *Now* group feel the sense of being in prison as the door of the fifth grade classroom is stealthily closed by N.R., so they obediently and quietly take their seats. As N.R. is satisfied with the segregation arrangements, she notes her final, uncompleted task. With the expertise of the Gestapo, N.R. whips out a well-worn paper grocery bag from her satchel and tapes it over the door window, masking the only viewpoint in or escape out. The brown bag over the window closes the final outlet of the dungeon, lest some young man peek into the secret summit of the *Now* children and N.R.'s foreboding lesson.

With the door masked and shut, N.R. *masks* her emotion (which has always been easy to do in her work as a health nurse) and provides a short, initial instruction to the stone-faced girls. *Quiet now* was all she spoke with the seriousness of a Supreme Court Judge, as she unpacked her instruction tools. Out came two strategically placed flip charts. A videocassette is placed in the VCR positioned for frontal view above her presenter's position, which, in reality, was a makeshift podium of two stacked file boxes. Her 3 by 5 cards are strategically placed near the lectern, and a wall-sized reproduction drawing replicating the Big Horn Sheep in Mr. Pudge's office (fallopian tubes, actually) is tacked to the center wall. The horned drawings from the parental pamphlets, long ago stuffed into the janitor's garbage, would only be demonstrated to the girls in a quick visual overview.

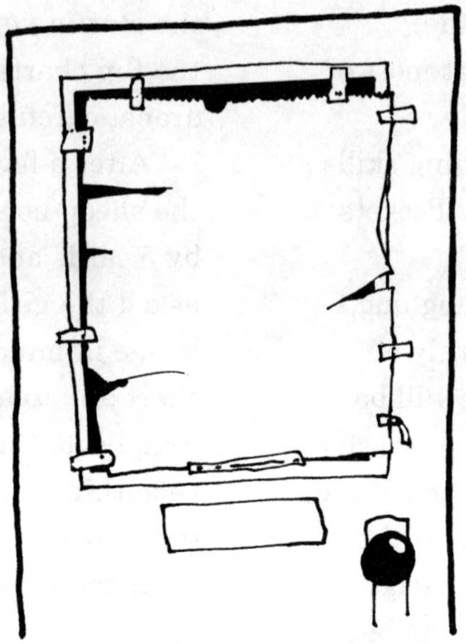

"They didn't need to actually *touch* the pamphlets," N.R. and G.G. had concluded long ago in their presentation planning meetings.

Everything was unpacked precisely and with precision—carefully positioned for the perfect presentation, perfectly choreographed and of course, *perfectly timed.* Signaling she was ready for *it* to begin, N.R. straightened her gray, tailored business suit, perfectly matching her smart and sensible gray shoes. She also straightened her broach, perched perfectly on her high neckline blouse and her throat that she loudly cleared before giving her second set of instructions.

"Ladies, here are the rules," she announced, preferring to call her inmates *ladies*, since for them, now is the time for that crossover into *ladyhood.* N.R. didn't need to reference her notes for her stern admonitions about the rules since she knew them by heart. The strict *rules of conduct* made the promises of G.G. concerning *no-nonsense* and *no-values* fall right into place. ***Just the facts*** rang true for N.R. and she didn't want any wavering into those pesky values as a result of an errant procedure or an embarrassing question.

In a war-room-like manner, N.R. dictates her strategy and her planned maneuvering to the mouth-gaping girls.

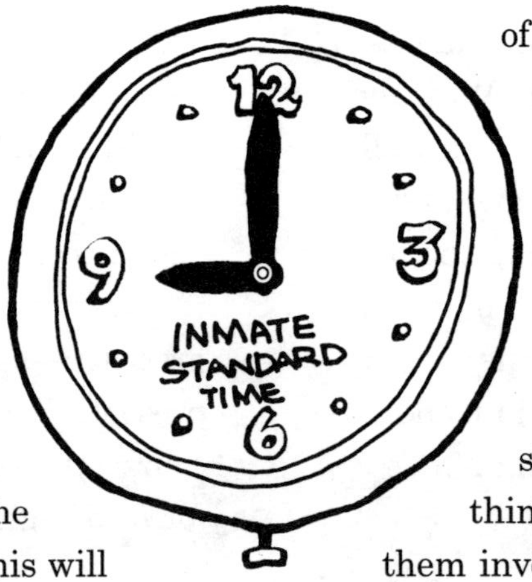

"We only have a short period of time," she announced, going on to explain that the information she is about to impart will impact their lives *forever*. N.R. always paused after the forever part—seeking strong emphasis just to make sure the girls knew this was serious stuff. "This will affect you for a lifetime, as mothers," she warned, being apparently unaware that most of her female-unit inmates were currently preoccupied with mastering hop-scotching skills or creating strategies for playing Polly Pockets at recess.

"And there will be no talking, no laughing, and no questions," N.R. furthered, sternly of course, as the silence was stifling. "We will be finished in forty-five minutes, closing up exactly on time when our video is finished." Each of the girls glanced longingly at the clock and at the masked window where the brown paper bag seemed to move ever-so-slightly. Then she began their *beginning*.

Using her pointer, she directed attention to the Big Horned Sheep replication of female reproduction on the wall-size chart, stating in so many words to the in-wonderment girls that they had this tube/horn contraption somewhere in their lap area. Some of the girls glanced down to check, but without a single recognition of even one horn, most of them quickly refocused their eyes on N.R. as she continued. Now came the complicated part. N.R. explained that some kind of clock inside each one of them would go off—not ring like their Snoopy alarm clock many of them imagined—but she assured that at some point, things would *start up* for each one of them involving their lap contraptions. Now the *starting up* stuff needed to be explained from the flip charts on each side of her presentation arena, carefully segregated, of course.

After a few words about the jumpstart with the sheep-horn-in-the-laps, N.R. checked her 3 by 5 cards and went on with the lecture. She asked the girls to keep the Big Horned Sheep image in mind as she focused on the left-side flip chart and to a barrage of complicated information about such things as eggs, fallopian tubes, ovaries, linings, fertilization, monthly cycles and, of course, cramps. She tried her best to be positive, but the big news to the girls was that all of this stuff was going to *start up* inside their bodies, suggesting to the fifth grade scholars

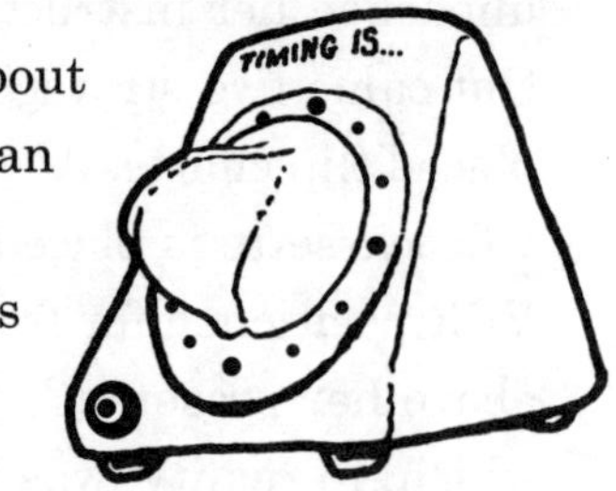

there was absolutely no escape from the clutches of femininity. With more technical language representing the onset of menstruation, the girls basically learned about the *Red Fairy*, with her flight plan of zapping the female inmates in their crotches, approximately every 28 days, bringing on the dreaded PADS.

And, right there in the fifth grade dungeon, she brought them on. Moving from the left-side flip chart with *Red Fairy* trappings, N.R. removed from her well-worn satchel an actual one—a Kotex pad. Although it was probably the most sanitary item within twenty miles of the classroom, and even though she clearly designated it as a *sanitary* pad, even N.R. seemed repulsed by the thing. She doesn't really explain where the pad gets perched, but she talked about things such as *discharge* and waste, much to the discomfort of the prisoners who would rather think about pads used for gymnastic exercises or the heating pads Mom uses when they sprain their ankle ice skating. N.R. and G.G. had concluded in their solemnizing that it was important to be honest with the girls about what awaits them in the feminine future. Therefore, the graphic nature of *discharging* and *wasting* was just necessary, however disgusting.

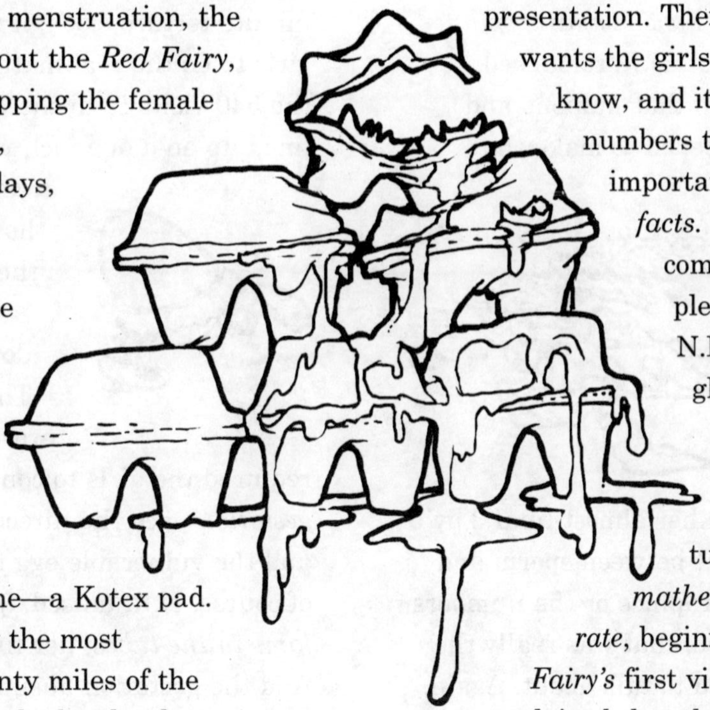

But N.R. isn't finished with the pad presentation. There are some numbers she wants the girls (ladies, actually) to know, and it seemed it was the numbers that helped N.R. keep the important promises of *just the facts.* With mathematical competency that would have pleased Mrs. Numbersnot, N.R. explained to the eyes-glazed-over girls that their eggs will be released into the horned sheep's horn/tubes and disintegrate at a *mathematically cumulative rate*, beginning with the *Red Fairy's* first visit. Doing the math, she explained that the girls have hundreds of thousands of egg targets, but with the calculative mathematics and the disintegration process, she explained they would only end up with two or three eggs left by the time they were grandmothers. Numbed to the numbers, the girls were also assured that in their calculated *lady lifetime*, the *Red Fairy* would do her crotch-kicking about 540 times, resulting in pad use for those same 540 months before things slow down.

But then, the most difficult part of the presentation was upon N.R.—that is before she turned everything over to the helpful video, moving everything in perfect timing right up to the 45-minute mark. Approaching the right-side flip chart, N.R. exposed a single sperm with *his* tail or, as N.R. preferred, *his swimming spinner*. But *single* wasn't exactly it, N.R. remarked, enlightening her prisoners that millions and millions of sperm were needed to make the mothering possible, compared to the truly *single* egg. That was the closest she and G.G. really wanted to get in explaining things.

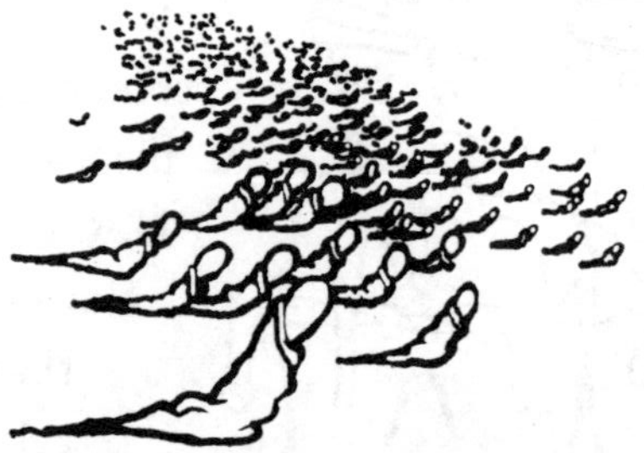

Yes, she clarified from her almost-final 3 by 5 card, things were different between sperm and eggs, especially in demographics or the numbers department, and, of course, that was really the only difference she wanted to talk about. Again, with a mathematical presentation for which Mrs. Numbersnot would be proud, N. R. asked the girls to think about 300 million sperm trying to chase down one of the 540 vulnerable eggs that each month will innocently stroll down those Big Horned Sheep's horn/tubes. *A traffic jam in the tubes* was how she phrased it, showing her first jest at humor to the not-laughing girls. And just to emphasize the math part (helpfully deflecting any inadvertent thoughts about ***how*** the sperm/ egg get-togethers happen), N.R. told the almost-ladies that the sperm were so small that if 500 of them were lined up in a row, the sperm parade would only be one inch long! Watching the 45-minute torture clock, it was just too much for the girls to do the real math of trying to calculate the 540 visits from the *Red Fairy*, the 500 sperm lined up on a one-inch ruler, and, of course, the dreaded pad count for each of those monthly attacks until they were grandmothers.

But N.R. wasn't quite done with the numbers. The final math presentation from N.R. required the girls to consider 266 days of *gestation* once the directionless swimming sperm and the vulnerable egg finally hooked up. That is of course, N.R. mused, *if there were no traffic jams in the tubes,* her final attempt at levity. And the gestation business made no sense to any of them (as N.R. had probably planned) since no pathways, traffic separators, turnpikes or highways were explained that cause the gestation, just that it would take 266 days for them to be mothers.

And then, at last, came the video with more about swimming sperm, feminine hygiene, and the complications of conception. The video had funeral-like music in the background and really white-teethed, not-so-friendly looking folks in white-starched jackets, speaking solemnly about such things as pads and *menstrual cramps* in what appeared to be an obviously *sanitary* environment of a hospital. But the biggest difference between the video and N.R.'s presentation was the electronically induced *ARROWS*. How the sperm actually make their way into the fallopian tubes (both horns of the poor stuffed creature in Mr. Pudge's office) isn't exactly explained, but sperm travel plans represented by the arrows demonstrated their eventual attack on the innocently-strolling-down-the-horned-path egg. The arrows showed it all moving along at traffic speed and indirectly (and only quickly) suggesting some kind of sperm/egg mixing. The girls gazed at the indecipherable video that reviewed and reemphasized much of what N.R. had pontificated in the same indecipherable way. The stern white-jacketed nurse type narrating the video was pretty impressive to some of the girls, but in reality, they didn't think she would have answered any of their questions either. Some even thought there was a slight resemblance between the video moderator and N.R. since neither of them smiled, but they both used the same language that would take the now-girls-soon-to-be-ladies years to decode.

As the video ended in the fifth grade classroom/dungeon, closing up was next. N.R.'s briefcase, video canister, and flip charts were precisely stacked in front of the dazed girls who all wondered if there was any possible chance of changing their gender and bailing out of this whole lady business. The presented *pad* was quickly slipped into the file and secreted away in N.R.'s briefcase, to the relief of everyone. The clicking and snapping of N.R.'s boxes and cases give finality to the session with great reprieve to the girls who were afraid about what to do next.

N.R. had no such hesitation as she lumbered out, not wanting to talk to anyone, but for sure wanting to give a second stern, glaring admonition to the peeking boys who were snickering in the hallway, somehow escaping the confines of Mrs. Wormbook's library surveillance. Even though they were momentarily successful at peeping behind the brown paper bag masking the window, it had been difficult for them to decipher the whole PAD business, and for sure, they knew nothing about the seemingly swimming arrows. Not wanting to appear ignorant, the giggling boys continued with their levity as the female inmates departed the dungeon of discussion, glum-faced and desperately wanting to sneak off to the bathroom and make one final check about the possibility that the horned sheep was somewhere in their crotches. No one except the fifth grade prisoners knew for sure what had actually happened as N.R. left, but everyone seemed to know it had *begun* and thank goodness, it was over.

THE TEN COMMANDMENTS FOR RAISING SEXUALLY RESPECTFUL CHILDREN

There are Ten Commandments for raising sexually respectful children, each designed to provide parents with a road map for the precarious, and often purple-faced process. For sure, the most obvious goal in taking on such a task is to prevent children from becoming a disrespectful person, which is a sexual offender. That is a ***don't*** goal.

But the ***do*** goal of the mission goes beyond making sure the kiddos don't end up either behind a park bush or on a post office pervert poster. Teaching sexual respect to children contributes to a bigger and more honorable goal. Sexual respect leads the path toward shared intimacy with a loving partner which, in this highly disrespectful society, is a gift and perhaps a blueprint for other areas of living that could use a little respect booster-shot.

So the *Ten Commandments of Raising Sexually Respectful Children* provides parents with the companionship and encouragement to turn in their traditional trappings of believing a Sex Fairy will take care of things, and then march forward with a Sex Fairy as a cheerleader in teaching sexual respect.

Some of the Ten Commandments involve dispelling myths and changing thinking in order to muster the motivation to take on the usually-uncomfortable task.

Some commandments provide specific examples and prescriptions of exactly how to handle things, while other commandments explain exactly how to stop handling things.

Some of the information in the Ten Commandments is sad, some is silly, and some is downright scary. Most importantly, the Ten Commandments are a continuum, building from one to the other, making the foundation more solid with each step, and hopefully guiding parents *in guiding* children toward sexual respect.

PAST & PRESENT PERVERSION

Sex is a tough subject and the resistance to talking about sex will be overwhelming to most parents. Few positive role models for parents exist since most likely no one talked to them about sexual respect. Moms and Dads will be seduced toward doing nothing, by a *morality police society* that suggests throwing rocks at the sexually disrespectful will automatically create sexual respect. *Just stop talking about it* will be society's encouraged path to those parents who attempt using the Ten Commandments as the clipboard curriculum of sexual respect.

Because it is not an easy task to go against past scripting and the contemporary grain of society, each commandment will be sprinkled with laughter, with irreverent humor, and with everything a Sex Fairy could fluff and puff, hopefully making the path toward sexual respect easier.

Sexual respect leads the path toward shared intimacy with a loved partner which, in this highly disrespectful society, is a gift and perhaps a blueprint for other areas of living that could use a little respect booster-shot.

But in reality, the ridiculous *ready* debate about when to begin sex education may really be about the readiness of Mom and Dad, costumed behind their bright purple faces.

In this fantasy, childhood is considered a carefree time, and FREE from thoughts about sex—unless of course the kidlets may have inadvertently watched Fluffy have her kittens, which should only cause minor disruptions in the childhood innocence paradigm.

And so, the First Commandment begins with *the beginning,* not only for children, but for enlightened and courageous parents who have taken on the honorable task of teaching sexual respect to the children they love.

THE FIRST COMMANDMENT—Thou Shalt Begin At The Beginning

READY OR NOT—*NOW* OR *NOT NOW?*

Right at the top of the resistance in talking to children about sex is the *ready* business. *When are they ready?* is the question many well-intentioned folks ponder. But in reality, the ridiculous ***ready*** debate about when to begin sex education may really be about the readiness of Mom and Dad, costumed behind their bright purple faces. And since most parents aren't ready themselves, focusing on the kids not being ready is a whole lot easier. And the longer and stronger the debate takes, about who is ready and who is not ready, the easier it is to just put everything on the proverbial back burner. But there is more to the *ready* ruminations.

AND THEN THERE WAS NONE

In debating about when to begin sex education, both the *Nows* and the *Not Nows* had to make an initial assumption about the *beginning* business. That platform postulated (or hoped) nothing had yet begun, since the fuss about when to begin would be meaningless if everything had already started up. This critical decision about the beginning had to mean both groups thought it hadn't—begun that is. Partnering with that convenient assumption was the idea that children innocently dance through an idealized childhood with their primary interest focusing on socks, sand, and Silly Putty, leaving the decision about *the beginning* up to the parents. In this fantasy, childhood is considered a carefree time, and FREE from thoughts about sex—unless, of course, the kidlets may have inadvertently watched Fluffy have her kittens, which should only cause minor disruptions in the childhood innocence paradigm.

But both groups assuming that nothing was happening before they made their decision about being a *Now* or *Not Now* was the last time of any unity between the two groups. The parting of the paths began with the expertise of G.G. followed by the brilliant presentation of N.R., making the *Now* folks satisfied they took the plunge of *beginning,* ultimately taking care of everything in the sex department for their children, that is until Sex Fairy time, following the wedding reception. The *Nows* decided it was time for the fifth grade girls to learn about the Big Horned Sheep somewhere in their lap area, and they smugly smiled about the discomfort of those cowardly *Not Now* folks who had to deal with the beginning, on their own.

NOT NOWS AT HOME

In making their decision about being a *Now* or a *Not Now,* both groups of parents were spurred to action by the time-honored ticking of the sex clock, which usually relates to the onset of puberty. It is the same clock analogy that N.R. mentioned about the *starting up* that would someday bring the *Red Fairy* to her female inmates. The *Now* folks believed that the fifth grade girls were developing and close to stepping into the puddles of puberty. Therefore, they felt N.R. needed to show up with her Big Horned Sheep drawings about the tube traffic jams of sperms (all 300 million of them) chasing after that one victim-like egg. For the *Not Nows* at home, they need a starting point as well, and the puberty puddle usually becomes the familiar alarm clock about when to begin the *beginning*.

THE KOTEX QUANDARY

For female children of the *Not Nows,* the arrival of the *Red Fairy* (referring to N.R.'s humorous stab at telling the fifth graders when they will begin menstruation) usually spurs a *Not Now* Mom into action. Although she wanted no part of N.R. and her presentation, Mom now has to do some presenting of her own to developing daughter captured in the bathroom with her first Red Fairy visit. This carefully choreographed event is the ritual presentation from Mother to daughter of the infamous *Kotex pamphlet*. In this *beginning,* the Kotex pamphlet to be ceremoniously presented to daughter is not a crumpled piece of paper inadvertently thrown under the bathroom sink somewhere between the Pine Sol and the Panty Puffs. *No,* this is the *heirloom* Kotex pamphlet, ceremoniously stored in the family safety deposit box after being handed to Mom, many years previous, by her own purple-faced Mother, who was probably a board-certified member of the *Not Nows*. It is time.

This carefully choreographed event is the ritual presentation from Mother to daughter of the infamous *Kotex pamphlet.*

Mustering up the confidence and expertise of N.R., Mom corners daughter in the bathroom and gives her the pamphlet, feeling so good that the drawing only shows a side view of the horned sheep contraption in her daughter's lap rather than the embarrassing full view of both horns found on the planted parent pamphlets. But Mom isn't done with the Kotex pamphlet presentation. She also hands daughter her very own box of pads and with a reassuring pat on both Daughter and the pad box, Mom smiles and exits the bathroom, wondering why N.R. would have needed forty-five minutes to explain everything. So, with the presentation of the Kotex pamphlet and the pads, sex education begins (and usually ends) for female units of the *Not Now* parents who said they would handle it themselves.

THE WET DREAM WAND

For boys, there is also a *beginning* milestone of sex education in the minds of the *Not Now* parents, usually related to something totally different than the *Red Fairy*. N.R. separated the

The Scooby-Doo sheets that once so comfortably cuddled her precious little pooper in Pokemon pajamas, now reveals clear and irrefutable evidence that his body is changing, the sperm are in action, and there isn't a single Big Horned Sheep pamphlet to be found.

genders before her presentation and she also *masked* the door, prohibiting any male eyes from glancing even once at the Big Horned Sheep imitation. Thinking about boys and horns was way out of N.R.'s league, even though on one of the perfectly separated flip charts, she did give the girls a sperm count, relating to the mathematical equation of one egg and 300 million sperm. But the math was as far as N.R. wanted to go with male references, even though she knew that eventually boy units had at least something to do with the whole not-so-pretty sexual picture.

But when the *Not Now* parents were suddenly forced into some sperm counting of their own, things changed and things were forced into action for the tiptoeing-into-puberty male children. This action of *beginning* usually occurs after some event such as Mom discovering evidence of her son having a *wet dream,* or in a more N.R. type of indecipherable term, *a nocturnal emission*. The Scooby-Doo sheets that once so comfortably cuddled her precious little pooper in Pokemon pajamas, now reveals clear and irrefutable evidence that his body is changing, the sperm are in action, and there isn't a single Big Horned Sheep pamphlet to be found.

Quick on her *sex-education-beginning* feet, Mom searches the yellow pages for a sex therapist specializing in eleven-year-olds. None are available, so she does the next best thing by telling Dad to take son hunting. Very little conversation transpires between Mom and Dad about the hunting mission, except both remember pronouncing proudly to G.G. that when it was time, they would handle it. But now, *it is time*. Dad, of course, is thrilled that he doesn't have to paint the deck, so he and his formerly little pooper spend a delightful weekend hunting. The reason for the postponed deck painting is easily forgotten in favor of smoky campfires, eating baked beans from the can, and absolutely no bathing. But on the way home, Dad suddenly remembers why he didn't have to paint the deck.

With white knuckles *unwrenchable* on the Jeep steering wheel, Dad stammers, "Ah, er, ah, son, your mother wanted us to talk," obviously attempting by proxy to slide Mom into the Jeep discussion so she can take the blame for any of Dad's failures in this important *beginning* of sex education.

"What about, Dad?" past pooper queries.

"Well, er, ah, about, you know, son, the birds and the bees," Dad stumbles, embarrassed. The silence is deafening, but only for a moment or two. Then the son brings calm to Dad and a clear indication that all is well in his *beginning* of sex education.

"Well, Dad, I pretty much know everything," the recently-waving-his-wet-dream-wand son comforts.

With a clear resolve that his son's sex education has truly begun, Dad proudly closes the book on the project by announcing, "Your mother will be so glad we had this talk!"

And on the way home from successfully avoiding deck painting and doing what Mom and Dad in the *Not Now* group didn't want anyone else to do, Dad figuratively pats himself on the back with his triumph as he remembers his own *beginning* of sex education.

A very long time ago, when Dad himself was a little pooper, he also took a mysterious ride with his purple-faced father. He remembered how confusing his father's curriculum had been. Although, in this memory it was hard for Dad to remember exactly when his own wet dreams began, he did recall when his father decided *it was time.* And that was all Dad's father said in organizing the capturing of his son in the car—"Son, it's time."

Dad remembered that at the time of the curious ride, he had been experiencing strange things with his penis, and he and his friends had been talking about strange things they thought girls did in the bathroom. Dad thought this secret stuff was probably somewhere in the car capturing effort, especially considering his father's stern face. All that Dad could remember in his *beginning* of sex education with his own tight-lipped, profusely sweating father were just a few words.

"Son, you have always had a weapon—***now*** your weapon is loaded." And that was it—the beginning and the end so long ago. As Dad pulled into his own driveway after deck-painting avoidance, he thought about how long it took him as a child to figure out what his father was trying to explain about loaded weapons. But now, he smugly concluded that his camping trip curriculum with past-pooper-now-sexual-son seemed a much better *beginning.*

All that Dad could remember in his *beginning* of sex education with his own tight-lipped, profusely sweating father were just a few words.

CHAPTER ONE COMPLETED—THE BODIES WORK

So both the *Nows* and *Not Nows* choose their own way to begin the sex education of their children, usually connected with a milestone of puberty and the changing of bodies into working mode. Thus ends the first chapter in the well-intentioned but dreadfully misguided saga of providing sex education to children. Using N.R. or forging on their own was the only question in the first installment for the *Nows* and *Not Nows.* But what about the second chapter after the puberty puddles have been navigated?

Different than the pamphlet, the Scooby Doo sheets prompting a hunting trip, or a car capture resulting in advanced ammunition studies, the second chapter in the two-part sex education system forces parents to consider that the working body parts will eventually need to get connected. Yes, N.R. carefully avoided any explanation of conception (body parts hooking up) except that the result of the sperm/egg get-togethers (babies, actually) would take a whole lot of days—266 of them. But that was as far as

N.R. and G.G. wanted (or could) go about the second chapter involving the body parts partnering up. And sooner or later, parents of both the Nows and the *Not Nows* groups have to take that next step, no matter how well they might want to mask the windows.

With panic and puckers, parents are faced with a horrifying mind-flash of their children involved in sperm/egg hookups in the *tube traffic jam.*

FORD FONDLING

With panic and puckers, parents are faced with a horrifying mind-flash of their children involved in sperm/egg hookups in the *tube traffic jam*. In the flash, parents conjure an image of sex beginning with two frantic teenagers in the cramped back seat of the family Ford the boy has borrowed from Dad. In the flash, and in horror, the teenagers are imagined to have sheer determination and sweating desire, not for sexual fulfillment, but to simply avoid the unsavory questions from their friends, "You haven't even done it yet?" But the image of the Ford fumbling is usually too uncomfortable for pondering parents in either the *Now* or the *Not Now* group. To replace the anxiety of the groping teenagers, a more sedated and anesthetized image brings comfort about a better *beginning* to sex in the second chapter.

A BETTER BEGINNING?

Better than Ford fumbling, the parental fantasy focuses on an idealized courtship, somewhat similar to the prelude of Edward and Emmilou making their big announcement. In this second-chapter-sex-education-installment, it is imagined that boy meets girl and eventually feelings are sparked between the couple beyond what parents believe might have happened in the back seat of the Ford or at the junior/senior prom. As the parental fantasy continues, an image of the young couple gazing into each other's eyes, obviously separated by a checkered tablecloth in a not-so-fine Italian restaurant, is conjured. The restaurant is dimly lit, but garlic smelling. In the parental fantasy, the young man nervously proposes marriage in a shy and stumbling manner, to the also shy and demurring female. The couple participates in a halting, but serious, conversation about a marital commitment having nothing to do with sex, but everything to do with mortgages, furniture payments, and 2.3 children.

In this second chapter of parental fantasy, in the not-so-fine Italian restaurant, discussion of marriage is initiated, of course, by the male and met with a fluttering eyelash twitter from the female, who also makes a non-verbal promise to faithfully iron his underwear into eternity. After consuming 1.4 glasses of wine each, a joint decision is made for a matrimonial commitment. This happens in the fantasy only if the father of the bride will be accepting of the proposal, or so the fantasy goes. And the Sex Fairy in this parental fantasy about the second beginning of the couple's sexual future does not have wine herself, but instead begins to sharpen her wand and mix her magic potions for the upcoming wedding, where SHE, just like with Edward and

Emmilou, will make the final installment of sexuality with just a few poofs and puffs in the hotel honeymoon hallway following the wedding reception.

THE AP*PARENT* INSTALLMENT PLAN

So parents seem to have an installment plan for educating their children about sex, with the first step being puberty—involving something related to Nurse Ratchet, the *Red Fairy*, the Wet Dream Wand, hunting trips and loaded weapons. Secondly comes the installment based on the rude reality that at some time in the future those tube traffic jams are going to take place, which will include a visit from the Sex Fairy in the honeymoon hotel after the wedding reception. There it is, mission accomplished and sex education supposedly installed. But what about sexual respect?

BEGIN WITH THE END

The question is whether this is a wise direction for parents who truly wish to raise sexually respectful children, or is this installment plan of beginning with wet dreams and menstruation pads, and a little hope of wedding reception fairy poofing, the way to go in teaching sexual respect? Perhaps a better plan would have a different *beginning,* focusing on the end, at *the beginning.* And if parents don't understand the end product at the beginning, then the educational goal may need some curriculum redesign, not likely organized by N.R. or G.G.

BY COMPARISON

Interestingly, the end product of other parenting projects doesn't seem to be aloof or confusing. If good Moms and Dads hope their child will become an architect, they probably begin early with fantasies of coffee table books featuring Son's massive building designs of world renown. If parents fantasize about their daughter becoming a lawyer, they imagine national conferences where legal beagles from throughout the world will flock to hear words of wisdom as she saves the innocent from the death penalty. If parents just have modest hopes for their kidlets, they may simply imagine a ranch-style home in an upscale cul-de-sac, two late-model sedans in the driveway, and grandchildren who don't use drugs or squabble over Scrabble when they visit Grandma and Grandpa. But what do parents hope and dream for the end product of their children's sexually respectful futures?

Rather than fantasies about fairy poofing or garlic smelling restaurants, parents should create an image of their children being role models of sexual health, respect and love. And if, at the beginning, parents began with this positive end product, the first question would be whether or not *Red Fairies*, pads, a now-loaded guns, or tube traffic jams resulting in an egg capture by swimming sperm, have anything to do with sexual respect? Is Nurse Ratchet with her pursed lips, stern demeanor and her masking tape, a good representation of sexual

Rather than thinking about loaded guns or Italian restaurant promises, parents need to imagine the end product of sexual respect.

intimacy and sexual respect, fulfilling the dreams of parents regarding their children's sexual futures? And in reality, what does reproduction or swimming sperm have to do with sexual respect?

IF NOT, THEN WHAT?

Well, if that isn't it, what is the sexual respect image? Wouldn't the perfect image of sexual respect education include a hope that children would become adults who treasure privacy and respect sexual intimacy? Aren't commitment and the promise to place a sexual partner as the most respected and honored person from all others, really more important than a wedding color scheme, promises to iron underwear, or a complete understanding of sperm navigation into sheep-horned fallopian tubes?

Isn't seeing Grandpa, at 74 years of age, kissing Grandma tenderly in church, smiling into her eyes and sparking still-familiar feelings of honeymoon hotel memories, the real end-product that should be postulated by parents from the very beginning? Wouldn't it make more sense to teach sons to honor and appreciate that sperm/egg traffic jam to the point that they cry and cuddle their sexual partner in the hospital delivery room and have no fears of showing vulnerability about the miracle of birth, without even a single thought of pads or *Red Fairies*?

Isn't the sexual respect end product for children ideally imagined with a sweet 45-year-old Mom still wanting to hold hands in the supermarket with hubby? Isn't sexual respect about preparation for life's relationship challenges, where couples remember, with misty eyes, the sexual commitment they made at the wedding, using that promise to neutralize any silly conflict about checkbook balancing or the overdue mortgage payment?

Do parents ever contemplate that when they return home from the wedding of their adult children, they will have the same sexual sweetness and respect in their own bed that the wedding couple will have in the honeymoon hotel suite? Isn't the real end-product wish for parents who wish to raise sexually respectful children connected to a lifetime of sexual appreciation and commitment rather than about pads or pervert posters in the park? And if not, then why not?

THE FUTURE IS NOW

So right out of the chute parents make the mistake of not concentrating on the end-product of sexual respect at the beginning, but also they err in really believing that they have some kind of choice about beginning sex education at puberty or the dreaded, but sometimes sanctioned, arrival of the Sex Fairy following the wedding. But in reality, *the future is now* and kiddos are learning about sex—and learning very early. So the First Commandment suggests starting with very young (yes, very young) children, which requires an honest and realistic understanding of childhood—not so comfortable for parents like the *Not Nows* who think waiting is a good idea, or even a choice.

READY SET EQUIPMENT

The beginning process for raising sexually respectful children requires giving up the idea that Sex Fairy dust sprinkled on testicles and vaginas will make them work properly, somewhere around the time of puberty, or in the back seat of the Ford. Sexual equipment doesn't fly in on Sex Fairy wings just previous to Dad organizing his hunting trip curriculum. Although uncomfortable for most parents, the reality is that children already have the *equipment* for sexual pleasure and sexual arousal, even before they are born. Children fondle themselves in the womb, confirming that not only does sexual equipment arrive early, but studies show that even a fetus seems to know that genitalia touching feels different and a whole lot more pleasurable than touching an elbow. The toddler may not understand how Mr. Sperm meets Ms. Egg in the tube traffic jam, but toddlers are sensuous human beings and they know that touching the sensuous equipment between their legs (even during Mom's Tupperware party) is actually quite interesting and pleasurable. Son's unauthorized Tupperware touching will really begin his sex education, especially if Mom, at the same time she serves fondue for her guests, gives him a clear and powerful *no, no.* Even her nonverbal sternness begins the learning about his strange, between-the-leg fondling. Even though she may be contemplating sex education for her son long into the future, she fails to realize that his equipment is working just fine long before she considers encouraging his father to teach the little pooper about his loaded weapon.

CRIB CUDDLING

But there is more concerning the jumpstart in sex education for the really little kiddos. Not only do the wee ones have the equipment for frisky feelings, even in the crib, but the little, little kiddos get lots of sensuous touching from grownups who are contemplating when to begin. Parents who smugly think they can postpone sex education until puberty, nonetheless admit to hugging, kissing, holding and caressing the crib kiddos, beginning life with a very sensuous jumpstart.

Sadly, as children grow older, Mom and Dad begin to pull away from this wonderful, sensuous (and sexual) beginning they actually *began* for their little poopers, cutting back on the holding, kissing, and caressing in direct proportion to their children's development. With the decline, they begin the nonsense belief that nothing else sexual will happen until they talk to their children about sex with a Kotex curriculum or

Aren't commitment and the promise to place a sexual partner as the most respected and honored person from all others, really more important than a wedding color scheme, promises to iron underwear, or a complete understanding of sperm navigation into sheep-horned fallopian tubes?

Although uncomfortable for most parents, the reality is that children already have the *equipment* for sexual pleasure and sexual arousal, even before they are born.

wait for another *beginning* after the wedding reception. The thought is that somehow they can cut off all that sexual (yes, sexual) touching and the kiddos won't miss it. Later, the Sex Fairy will zap back the sensuousness as needed.

THE POWER OF CHILDHOOD

But there is more in this misunderstanding about the true beginning of sexuality in children. Contrary to parental fantasies of believing and hoping for an asexual childhood, the brains of young children are not on autopilot until parents organize the hunting trip or order a visit from Nurse Ratchet. In fact, in areas outside the realm of sexual development, the early developing brains of children are respected for having a significant impact on how the child will venture into adulthood. Scientists are pretty sure that influences on a child's brain in the early years of life last a lifetime and seem to be *hard-wired.* When very young children are exposed to high levels of stress, physical abuse, or any type of behavior that causes frontal lobe damage or corrosion of the cortex brain covering, the result is earmarked for some of society's most violent or troublesome citizens. There is little resistance from those who study child development in accepting the hard reality that the brains of children are a breeding ground for negative influence. But what about the other side of a child's formative years connected to the positive or sexually respectful?

SPONGING SENSUOUSNESS

Since childhood is a time when children sponge powerful information about many different things, why wouldn't the same be true for sexual information? In reality, by the time adults are ready with reservations at the Italian restaurant, children may have already completed most of their sex education, leaving parents behind in the proverbial Sex Fairy dust of neglect as their child's sensuousness sponge, so rich at the beginning but pretty full when N.R. gets the call.

MAKING SENSE OUT OF NONSENSE

But there is more to the *power of childhood* and the collection (sponging) of sexual information. In addition to absorbing information about lots of things, children have the uncanny ability to make sense out of *nonsense,* and since parents tend to avoid sexual teaching directly, the kiddos are indirectly tying it all together. Parents who truly wish to raise sexually respectful children need to understand that just because they aren't at the sex education lectern with color-coordinated flip charts, their kiddos forge ahead—making sense of their sexual world.

MANAGING THE MATCHING

Instructive parents who feel schooled in technique usually teach children to match things in non-sexual subjects. A tutoring Aunt Tilda may say to her nephew, "See? The sky is blue and so is your shirt," hoping Antonio will learn to match his colors. Kiddos are taught to match their socks and match the same-colored birdies in their pre-kindergarten science lesson. And most of the time children are unclear about why they have to match things, but there is no confusion about the importance of hitching up previously unhitched things. And even without guidelines, the kidlets continue the matching. It is a child's way of making sense of things, even if nonsense is the result.

GOD'S BEAUTY COLLEGE

The trauma begins every Sunday morning. They must match. Even though to the seven-year-old, the entire outlay of the bedroom and bathroom seems to contain thousands of barrettes, it appears to the panicked child that none of them are quite the same on Sunday—thus no matching. Matching barrettes before church is an age-old tradition in this family and, for the child, this contributes to Sunday morning mayhem. With secret sleuthing, she attempts to slip by her Mother (considered by the youngster to be the *barrette police*) wearing a red one and a blue one. Busted! Mom sternly drags her back and there is no reprieve.

"They must match on Sunday," Mom reminds.

In frustration, the seven-year-old imprudently asks, "Why?" challenging the tradition of the Sunday morning barrette-matching madness.

Mom is not fazed nor lacking confidence as she promptly announces to her precocious child, "Because God wants them to match!"

MORE MATCHING

Mother, who thinks she is in charge of the Sunday school respect curriculum, demands matching barrettes in an attempt to teach honor for church, hoping the seven-year-old will learn that what happens in the sanctuary of Sister of Grace Church is different than preparing for a field trip to the mink farm or visiting Aunt Alta's beach house. Usually in this typical-of-most-families' educational effort, Mom doesn't exactly verbalize the sanctity of religion lecture, but she nonetheless believes she is teaching her daughter respect for religion by the matching barrettes routine. *Good effort* and *good enough*, Mom believes.

The child, however, with incomplete information about Mom's barrette-matching purpose, may do her own matching of God attending beauty school with her older sister who is also attending a beautician program. The ***Sister*** of Grace Church certainly starts this hookup or matching of understanding. And there may be more in the sister-saga-with-a-beauty-school-God as the seven-year-old knows Sissy spends hours in the bathroom putting barrettes in her hair and spending lots of money buying matching barrettes at the Pick & Pack Drug Store. The mixing and matching of God, Sister Grace's church, sister in the bathroom with

Sadly, as children grow older, Mom and Dad begin to pull away from this wonderful, sensuous beginning for their little poopers, cutting back on the holding, kissing, and caressing in direct proportion to their children's development.

In addition to sponging up information about lots of things, children have the uncanny ability make sense out of *nonsense* and since parents tend to avoid sexual teaching directly, the kiddos are indirectly tying it all together.

barrettes, and beauty school, all get hooked up whether Mom wants it to happen or not. If Mom knew that the result of the barrette-matching business on Sunday morning resulted in her daughter conjuring an image of God mixing hair dye solutions or learning the art of applying acrylic nails, she might want to change her lesson plan. And that is usually what Mom will do in other areas related to God studies if her daughter gets her mixing and matching tangled.

GOOD GOD

Just as the seven-year-old doesn't really know why she has to match her barrettes, she nonetheless makes an attempt to understand the disjointed information, and in her mind, God ends up in beauty school. In other areas related to God, children also put things together with religious mix and match most often because good parents want the religious training, but they aren't savvy about those tiny little brains doing the information shuffle, sponging up and spitting out how they matched everything together.

As an example, children were asked to write letters to God in a Catholic school classroom. The adult goal of the assignment was probably to help the kidlets remember God's presence just in case they had some un-God-like ideas about what to do when the teacher's back was turned. So the kids wrote and it was cute, but it was also really clear that the kids were mixing and matching things about their everyday lives with what was being taught on Sunday mornings. From *catholic-pages.com* come the delightful remarks made from children making sense out of nonsense.

LETTERS TO GOD

Dear God:
Send me a pony. I never asked for anything before. You can look it up.
Bruce

Dear God:
If we come back as something, please don't let me be Jennifer Horton because I hate her.
Denise

Dear God:
I want to be just like my daddy when I get big, but not with so much hair all over.
Sam

Dear God:
I think the stapler is one of your greatest inventions.
Ruth

Dear God:
Are you really invisible or is it just a trick?
Lucy

Dear God:
Instead of letting people die and having to make new ones, why don't you just keep the ones you have now?
Jane

Dear God:
Maybe Cain and Abel would not kill each other so much if they had their own rooms. It works with my brother.
Larry

Dear God:
My brother told me about being born but it doesn't sound right. They're just kidding, aren't they?
Marsha

Dear God:
Did you mean for the giraffe to look like that or was it an accident?
Norma

Dear God:
Who draws the lines around the countries?
Nan

Delightful! The knowledge is there, in mixed-up pieces, matched ever so haphazardly. Children are routinely rounded up and taken (barrettes matching or not) to Baptist, Catholic, Presbyterian, or Jewish places of worship, beginning their religious education very, very early. There seems to be no fighting among the *Nows* or *Not Nows* about when to begin the God lessons. Children are taken to sunrise Easter services even though during the chilly morning fanfare they are more likely to think about their Easter baskets rather than some idea of resurrection or eternal life. Parents force their children to participate in Christmas plays or attend Bar Mitzvahs without any guarantee that they will truly understand every bit of it. The kiddos don't always know what is going on, but most parents want the ongoing exposure to the God business, with the hope that someday they will figure it all out and become good Methodists, Mormons, or Muslims.

Unlike the Sex Fairy myth, there is no rabbi waiting in the wings with a satchel full of Jewish teachings that will be sprinkled at a specific time and provide a single lesson in scripture appreciation. There is no N.R. or G.G. to help parents ponder the parental permission slips for when to tell their children that being a Baptist is the best way to go.

Why not have the same beginning with teaching sexual respect since every day in a child's life *sense is made of nonsense,* conclusions are drawn, things are connected to things that may be totally unrelated, and piles of information continues to stack. And like it or not, this includes sexual learning.

The mixing and matching of God, Sister Grace's church, sister in the bathroom with barrettes, and beauty school, all get hooked up whether Mom wants it to happen or not.

OUTSIDE THE GOD BOX

Beyond God, morality in areas other than sex is taught to children without hesitation, long before plans are made for hunting trips or pamphlet presentations. This early education happens when children don't *get it* right, just like with God mix-ups. Children might be punished if they take candy from their brother, or if they are rude to Uncle Ralph even though, as the children explain, "He has buzzard breath." Morality and sincere empathy toward others may not be truly possible for really young kidlets, but nonetheless, they are required to ***practice*** morality long before they understand the true concepts of being honest or respectful to a smelly Uncle. Why not begin the same sexual teachings for children, long before they truly understand the intricacies of cucumber condom application in eleventh grade Health class?

MOM ASLEEP AT THE WHEEL

In a classic example, the ongoing sexual learning that occurs for children, independent of their parent's affiliation with the *Nows* or *Not Now* groups, is unveiled in an accidental conversation between an almost-sexual-learning child and a stranger in a public restroom. A woman in a large hotel lavatory absent-mindedly makes her way out of the privacy stall, eventually traversing to the restroom exit door. Unnoticed until now, a five-year-old child who has completed her bathroom stall duties abruptly converges with the stranger as both are departing the facility. The child immediately stops the exiting process by holding her hands in front of the woman, blocking her exit, and demanding, "Wait!"

Without hesitation, the child turns and waddles to the bathroom sink while the curious woman follows her, finally asking, "Why do we wait?"

The precocious child answers, "I have to wash my hands," as she begins sudsing her small upper extremities.

The woman, always interested in the power of childhood and the reasoning of a child, inquires further, "Why do you wash them?"

With a smirk, the child confidently announces, "Because you are in here," as she flips her now-drenched paper towel into the waste can.

The woman is amazed at the little girl's thinking, so she furthers the discussion, asking, "Do you wash them if no one is in here?"

Even though the question momentarily hangs in the air, the child is clear in her answer because she has figured out the hand-washing process by watching her unknowing mother.

"Nope," is her quick response. "If someone else is in the bathroom, you have to wash your hands. If no one else is in the bathroom, my Mother doesn't have to."

And there it is, perfect logic for daughter of a Mom who failed to realize what she was indirectly teaching her daughter about sex. She has observed her Mother washing her hands properly when someone else was in the restroom—perhaps at a basketball game of the older brother, in the restroom of a busy airport, or in a not-so-fancy hotel lobby following the rally squad conference of the older sister. Without Mom noticing, her youngest child has learned when hand washing is necessary and when it is not, depending on restroom roll call. It is a five-year-old who used the power of childhood to put things together, and whether or not her Mother consented to the curriculum, the student learned something about privacy, modesty, and body functions, which are an important part of sexuality.

THE QUARTER QUANDARY

Three little boys walking down the street find an errant quarter, and they are in a quandary. A decision must be made among them about what will be purchased with their single financial stockpile. The first young man attempts diplomacy, suggesting, "Let's get something for all of us, like maybe bubble gum."

The second child, also wishing for a corporate compromise, provides another suggestion for their purchase. "Bubble gum isn't big enough. How about if we buy popcorn? Then we could each have a lot."

The third child, who has listened to both purchase propositions about the quarter quandary, scratches his head and makes a different proposal. "No. Let's take our quarter and buy a Tampon!"

The other boys chime in with questions. "What would we do with a Tampon?"

"I don't know," says the third child, "but I know if we have a Tampon, we can go horseback riding and swimming," which to all three of them sounds much more tantalizing than gum chewing or popcorn munching.

Obviously, the third financial wizard of the triumvirate has ventured out on his own, learning about Tampons and something about his sister's dilemma when she starts her period but she still wants to go horseback riding and swimming. He didn't peek through the brown paper bag and witness Nurse Ratchet's presentation about the *Red Fairy*, and at age eight, he is not likely getting a head start on becoming a gynecologist. He has probably heard or observed family fussing about females, who may have been in tears because the Tampon supply was depleted, thus hampering plans for picnic events that might include horseback riding or swimming. This wise child has begun his sex education whether his parents are ready or not.

WHAT IS AND ISN'T SEX?

A group of first graders, who had only been attending public school for approximately one month, learned from their purple-faced parents that some kind of sex education would be delivered on Tuesday and today was it—Tuesday. In this rural and isolated community, the school board granted permission for the local

The kiddos don't always know exactly what is going on, but most parents want the ongoing exposure to the God business, with the hope that someday in the future they will truly figure it all out and become good Methodists, Mormons, or Muslims.

mental health program to provide basic sex education to the youngsters—not to teach them about the *birds and the bees*, but simply prepare them for several years later when Nurse Ratchet's sister might show up. It was an old rendition of *Just the Facts*.

As a glum-faced teacher and her aide exited the first grade classroom, the children huddled underneath their desks, giggling out of control with the excitement about the upcoming event. They don't exactly know what is going to happen, but after making the usual connections and matching, they know that this *sex stuff* is very perplexing to their parents and teachers. They remember several weeks ago when Mrs. Firespit, the fifth grade teacher, had a temper tantrum about the proposal, making Principal Pulverize very nervous. They didn't know exactly why their beloved principal was in a panic, but they just knew he was.

They have also heard their parents argue about the event and they know there is some connection to what is about to happen with the foreign lady and the trouble they got into at home when they were caught looking at Grandma's girdle. They have bits and pieces of information in their confusion, but there is no confusion about how exciting everything is, compared to the scheduled lesson about the rumored wooden teeth of the very old President George Washington.

The mental health professional notices the giggling and twittering from the raucous class and calmly asks the first graders to explain their laughter. With her inquiry, one child answered, "We are laughing because you are the sex lady. Our mom told us you were coming."

The giggling erupts even louder with those comments from a brave first grader. Rather than make the assumption that the children really understood the term *sex lady,* she saw the window of opportunity open and asked the most obvious question related to her newly appointed title--sex lady.

"What is sex?" was the question, which only made the children escalate their giggling and writhing underneath their study desks. "Tell me what sex is, if I'm supposed to be the sex lady," was an additional level of investigation from the only adult in the room. And with that question, the children provided their definition of the powerful three-letter-word SEX, again demonstrating the convoluted piles of knowledge they already have about sex and relating to the myth that parents are really in charge about when to begin.

- ♦ Sex is..."Seeing my parents take a bath when they think I'm asleep."
- ♦ Sex is..."Putting two hairy things together."
- ♦ Sex is..."When your sister gets a boyfriend."

- Sex is... "Underneath my dad's pickup seat; that's where he keeps his magazines."
- Sex is... "Screwing something like a tire."
- Sex is... "Birds and the bugs."
- Sex is... "When your mom looks pretty."
- Sex is... "When my dad gets drunk."
- Sex is... "Splashing on the waterbed."
- Sex is... "When your parents get mad at your questions."
- Sex is... "Fruits."
- Sex is... "A halter top."
- Sex is... "A book my mom read me that I don't understand."
- Sex is... "Parents taking showers together and laughing."
- Sex is... "Queer."
- Sex is... "A weenie and a weenie roast."
- Sex is... "Like something creepy is crawling on you, like you know, when you get goose bumps."
- Sex is... "Humping and other camels."
- Sex is... "Dicks and Jane."
- Sex is... "Seeing pretty faces in underwear."
- Sex is... "Mom and Dad sleeping in the same pajamas."
- Sex is... "Cigarettes."

Describing sex as being "cigarettes" was curious to the presenter. "What does sex have to do with cigarettes?" she asked.

With her hands on her indignant hips and with the confidence of a Rhodes scholar, the child stated, "You know, sex is cigarettes because of the butts!"

There it was—cigarette *butts,* jokes about big *butts*, and Mom's admonition that Sister's hip-hugger jeans showed too much *butt*—all somehow mixed and matched for first grade wisdom determining that sex is all about the cigarettes.

"I don't know," says the third young man, "but I know if we have a Tampon, we can go horseback riding and swimming."

KIDDO COLLECTION

While parents wait, the kiddos collect. They have managed and matched information about under-the-seat magazines, Mom and Dad sleeping in the same pajamas, and sex being about Sister getting a boyfriend. Not only have these first graders begun to form sexual conclusions, but their conclusions are less than positive (with the exception of parents taking showers together and laughing). What these children already know about sex is likely to be the opposite of what parents have in mind for the future sexual fantasy for their children. The source of information for the kiddos' collection is not found in Nurse Ratchet's satchel, but in the every day events of children with their brilliant little minds making sense out of nonsense and stacking the facts—however disjointed and disrespectful.

They have also heard their parents argue about the event and they know there is some connection to what is about to happen with the foreign lady and the trouble they got into at home when they were caught looking at Grandma's girdle.

PERCEPTION OF PERVERSION

But just as important as it is for parents to *begin with the end* in imagining sexual respect for their children, perhaps they should also *begin with the end* in understanding about what they don't want from their children in the sexuality department. If sexual respect is the goal, then perhaps sexual disrespect should be understood and become the anti-curriculum focus. What, for the purpose of this First Commandment about when to *begin,* could be said about the makeup of sex offenders to encourage parents to rethink waiting for sex education until periods are started or ejaculations are squeezed out between the Scooby-Doo sheets?

TAKERS OR THE TENDERHEARTED

Right or wrong, most parents believe they know about the disrespectful folks, and those perceptions of the perverted have no resemblance to their little poopers coming in from a 4-H club meeting or returning from a Brownie camp excursion. In actuality, becoming a sex offender or a sexually disrespectful person has more to do with how children grow up to be either *takers* or the *tenderhearted,* and most parents know that kind of learning begins very, very, early. Becoming a sex offender is more about the basic concepts of *people issues* than it is about something sexual, and for most parents those teachings begin early. Sexual respect is related to sharing, caring, and being aware of *following the rules;* ironically, that's something parents begin teaching in their children very early in life.

RECIPE FOR DISRESPECT

Leading experts on psychopathology and anti-social personality traits do a lot of fancy thinking outside the people-box, focusing on those *not-so-nice* folks who tend to go against the grains of a *nice* society. Those traits don't always describe a violent fiend, frothing at the mouth, cursing wildly, and with bloodshot eyes, shifting glances toward innocent victims on a lonely road. In fact, according to the experts, many psychopathic traits are related to such simple family issues as cheating, breaking rules, and being *not nice.*

Psychopaths don't always become serial rapists, but can be dishonest doctors, unprincipled politicians, stock swindlers, cheating journalists, unethical lawyers or wealthy CEO's who, without conscience, trick good folks out of their life savings without even batting a financial eye. The importance of recognizing these negative traits and teaching against them are described in the Eighth and Ninth Commandments. But in this First Commandment about when to begin, the question is about *waiting* before parents would teach these basic human skills of honesty, kindness or being fair, since these traits provide the recipe for sexual respect and the lack of these people skills is the recipe for becoming a sex offender.

WAITING WAILING

Parents don't wait until their son has his first job before teaching him about honesty, and good parents don't wait until their daughter has been assigned her first college roommate before teaching her about sharing. These *people skills,* or the lack of them, are a key ingredient in becoming a sexually respectful or disrespectful person and parents usually don't wait to teach those honorable traits. There are no Parental Permission Slips concerning when it is time to teach *Spaghetti O* sharing with a sister or the importance of taking off muddy boots before tracking dirt across Grandma's kitchen floor. Yet, these things pertain to becoming a sexually disrespectful person and should be part of the curriculum, early on, for teaching sexual respect.

THE FADING CREDIBILITY THEORY

A final reason why the *Thou Shalt Begin at the Beginning* Commandment is so important for parents pertains to *The Fading Credibility Theory*. As parents wait to provide sex education, they fail to realize that a normal process of development instills independence in children, which in turn threatens parent credibility. Each day in a child's life contributes to the erosion of Mom and Dad's brilliance. At birth, children are completely dependent on parents for nourishment, safety, emotional strength and of course, Pampers. But as time goes on, children become more independent, first from a physical perspective, and then from an intellectual level, leaving their parents in the proverbial dust. And most parents actually encourage children to become independent, honoring the milestone of becoming *big boys* and *big girls* or doing things *all by yourself*. Good enough—at least for most parental processes.

Even though this natural resistance to parent reliance begins at the moment of birth, it seems more pronounced when children enter puberty, which just happens to coincide with the time that parents and Nurse Ratchet are ready with their permissions slips and their podiums. When postponing parents are ready with sexual wisdom, children have usually spent the previous ten to thirteen years charting the fading credibility of their parents.

While parents are waiting for their ceremonious entrance to the front of the lecture hall of sexual wisdom and maturity, in the minds of their children, Mom and Dad have become less brilliant and in fact, sometimes reaching the proverbial position of knowing absolutely nothing. As Mom is readying her presentation of the Kotex pamphlet, her daughter is likely pulling away, feeling the natural and normal tug of *no need for Mommy anymore.* Sadly, when the big moment arrives and parents are ready, children may have danced through the developmental stages of needing nothing.

In actuality, becoming a sex offender or a sexually disrespectful person has more to do with how children grow up to be either *takers* or the *tenderhearted,* and most parents know that kind of learning begins very, very, early.

Parents don't wait until their son has his first job before teaching him about honesty, and good parents don't wait until their daughter has been assigned her first college roommate before teaching her about sharing.

TERMINALLY STUPID

Beyond puberty and pad presentation time, adolescence seems to be a time when parents have become *terminally stupid*—at least in the mind of their teenagers. To paraphrase the old theory, the point is illustrated.

"When my son was seven, he thought I knew everything. When he was fourteen, to him I knew nothing. But when he turned twenty-one, he was amazed at how much smarter I had become in the previous seven years."

The stupidity of parents in the eyes of adolescents will not actually be terminal, usually becoming cured in young adulthood, but long after the sexual seeds have been sowed for the child to be sexually respectful or a sexual offender. By waiting to begin sex education, parental wisdom fades and the kidlets, who already have piles of collected and connected information about sex, usually want no part of their parents' stupid lectures by the time Mom and Dad are ready to begin.

Sex Fairy Clipboard

- Stop the belief or hope that "innocence equals ignorance." Reject the contention that children are not sexual and the longer they are ignorant, the greater their level of *innocence*.

- Remember, puberty does not bring children to a sudden interest in talking about sex with their parents. It is important to accept the fact that puberty usually brings to children the clarity that their parents are really, really stupid about sexual matters.

- Consider the sexual "package" of human beings. Remember that Mr. Sperm meeting with Ms. Egg is only a small fraction of the human sexuality package. Consider how little menstruation and wet dreams have to do with sexual respect, and actively, early, and intensely, teach sexual respect.

- Don't wait! Consider your children sexual beings by the way they touch, respect, and honor each other. Sexually respectful people gained these tools very early in life and focused on how they love or detach from others.

- Accept and acknowledge the fading credibility theory. Don't count on children believing their parents are reliable sources of information about sex. This requires teaching about sex when Mom and Dad are still really smart in the minds of their children.

- Abandon the idea that beginning sex education with children during the preschool period will produce both syphilis and grandchildren before the fifth grade.

- Make a commitment to control sex education—making sure that doesn't mean withholding sex education.. Honor the unfortunate reality that there is no choice about if kidlets will receive sex education. The only choice for parents is how, and under what conditions, children will learn about sex.

- Accept the fact that children already have the ingredients for becoming a sex offender. Wail and weep about this uncomfortable fact and then get busy.

Chapter 5

Second Commandment
Thou Shalt
Communicate

CHAPTER 5 – SECOND COMMANDMENT THOU SHALT COMMUNICATE

They were perfectly prepared, just as he demanded. Pens were poised on writing pads that were also positioned perfectly. Laptops were booted and latte containers languished in garbage receptacles, as required before he graced their presence. They eagerly awaited his arrival, ready to organize the next week. Then it happened. Just as millions of others did each day, his staff greeted him with admiration and a stand-up applause. And just as he did for his week-long worshippers, the good doctor reciprocated with warmth and welcome to those he so depended upon for selling *the product.*

Dr. Fillemup's mission was clear to all who worked for him, and they admired his ability to sell what they were all about. It was a *marketing magic medium*—ingrained in all of them since the beginning. Every so often, each of them remembered being hired and the pressure put upon them to remember *the product* and the importance of selling it. It was what they were all about, this Monday morning, with their beloved Dr. Fillemup.

When the applause faded, the staff knew two things. First, they were keenly aware they had to propose various options for the next five-day week and secondly, they knew that *the product* would be the measure of everything they were about to do, or about to *undo,* as the doctor considered their proposals. Some of their efforts would fail and some would be successful, but they all knew as long as *the product* was the barometer for decision-making, everything would be fine and Dr. Fillemup's demand for *product adherence* would be met.

Nancy was nervous, not only because she was new to the staff and *product* selling, but because she would be presenting first regarding day Number One of next week. The pressure was clear. She would not only present the patients (families, actually) for Dr. Fillemup to diagnose, but because there were too many of them for one show she would also have to present enough options so that elimination by the doctor could occur. The need for *the product,* Nancy knew, would determine which families were accepted and which ones would get the proverbial axe.

Nancy knew she shouldn't, but having favoritism toward the Nutsqeeze family was unavoidable. It wasn't that she liked them better; she just knew they had that special *product sensitivity* so important to the doctor. But Nancy also knew that the doctor wanted her to be fair so she needed to demonstrate balance among all the potential families, which really meant she needed to nuke the Nutsqueezes from the top of her priority list by concentrating on her other four options.

The Frugalers were also right up there at the top of her list, as were the Stingiers, and who could forget the Downclamps or the Wadtights? Nancy felt good about her final selection of five families out of more than one hundred who responded to the titillating title of *Penny Wise or Family Foolish?* At first, Nancy tried using the title of *Charting the Checkbook* or *Money Matters,* but Dr. Fillemup sent her a memo encouraging the title combination of penny-pinching and family dysfunction, since focusing on hurting families with big problems would provide the *spin* he wanted, eventually bringing about the best use of *the product. Yes,* these five families were sure to give the doctor plenty of material to decide who would most benefit from *the product,* and, in turn, Nancy's efforts could sell his *product* to the millions of folks who had similar family fussing about penny-wisdom.

Her first point of presentation required Dr. F. to know that it was Mr. Downclamp who intricately separated the two-ply toilet paper to make it last twice as long. She mused about his

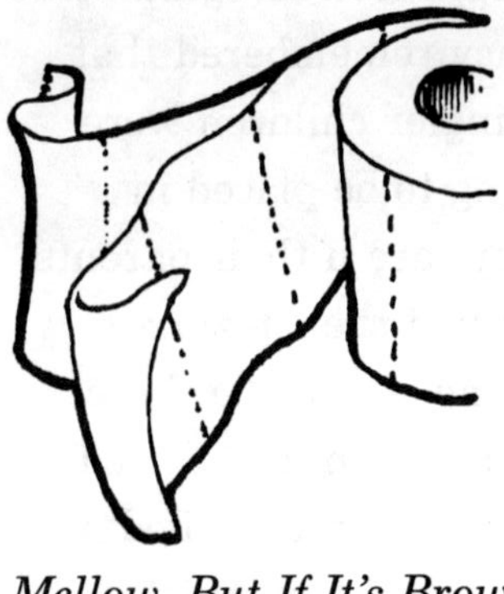

other penny-pinching bathroom behavior that involved forcing the Downclamp kiddos to only flush occasionally, saving water, of course, and singing the refrain: *If It's Yellow, Let It Mellow, But If It's Brown, Flush It Down.* Mrs. Downclamp told Nancy that she was disgusted and ready to leave Mr. D. if things didn't loosen up—so to speak. Nancy knew *the product* would be very important to this family since the Downclamps reported getting along in nearly every other marriage department except the bathroom penny-pinching. Yes, the Downclamps definitely needed some *product,* Nancy noted.

Then she thought of the Frugaler family. Unfortunately, they were only a bit enticing for *product* use, but she would still report on them, letting Dr. Fillemup decide. Sure, Mr. Frugaler was a bit strange, having milk bottles in the refrigerator labeled *Shredded Wheat, Coco Puffs* and *Fruit Loops,* since he made the Frugaler kids recycle their cereal milk, over and over just to save a few pennies.

But it seemed to be Mrs. Frugaler who was the *cheapskate champion* in the family, as she demanded everyone use and reuse the same piece of dental floss for at least a month, cleverly hanging the strands on a special clothesline apparatus perched over the commode. And Nancy was assured Mrs. Frugaler was really the tightwad since, after the studio interview where she told Nancy of her pride in saving money, she was observed on the discreet video using an available Kleenex and without even so much as a pause, putting the dirty tissue back in the box and, ever so carefully, positioning it for use with the next unsuspecting guest. These penny-pinching tendencies were certainly interesting, but as Nancy thought of the Frugalers, it was clear they were *together* in their penny-pinching. They both loved being *Frugal Freaks* (as they proudly called themselves) and since they didn't have a problem in their penny-pinching relationship, she suspected the doctor would not rate them high for *product* need.

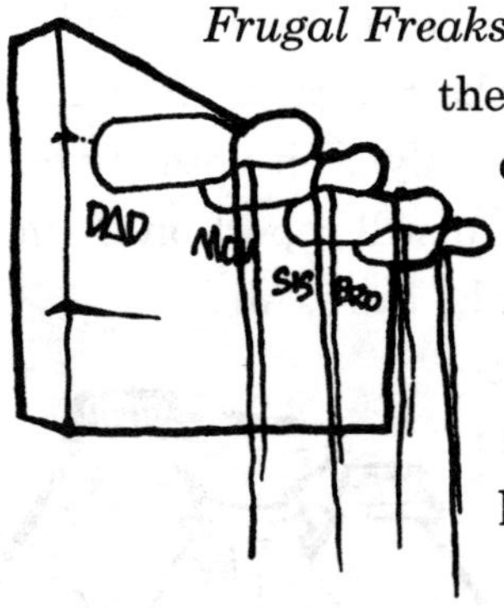

Down her list Nancy pondered the third family, the Stingiers, and their complete preoccupation with saving money. The most interesting focus of their possible *product* use was that their penny-pinching preoccupations bordered on criminal conduct, which she knew would be very interesting to Dr. Fillemup. The Stingiers talked at length about the joys of stocking their kitchen with heisted condiments from fast food restaurants, Starbucks coffee houses, and any other public place that might have items for thievery. Mr. and Mrs. Stingier's eyes seemed to glaze over with thrill as they discussed making their own paper towel rolls from pilfered napkins pinched from the deli at the grocery store, as well as

their prize collection of stolen ballpoint pens heisted from unsuspecting grocery checkers. Mr. Stingier took pride in the fact that he made his own Q-Tips with dryer lint and toothpicks, but what really excited him was stealing free stuff with Mrs. Stingier. *Why*, they told Nancy, they would take empty Starbucks' Styrofoam cups into the coffee shop to fill with *Half and Half* when no one was looking. Sugar was pilfered as well, and they were so proud as they displayed their gallons of *Half and Half* in their refrigerator, as well as canisters full of pinched sugar packets.

But again, Nancy worried that just like the Frugalers, the Stingiers loved their heisted cache, they loved working as a thievery team and they weren't about to change. Without a desire for rerouting their robbery tendencies, Nancy thought their *product* use appeared marginal. But then, Nancy remembered that the Stingier children were asking to be placed in foster care if their parents continued their bizarre snatching, so maybe there was some parent/child need for *the product*. She smiled as she remembered how much Dr. Fillemup loved using *the product* to help innocent kidlets.

Before Nancy returned to her proclivity toward the Nutsqueeze family, she thought about how she would present the Wadtights, who in reality, were Nancy's second favorite family and certainly they had high needs for *the product.* Oh, she was excited about their

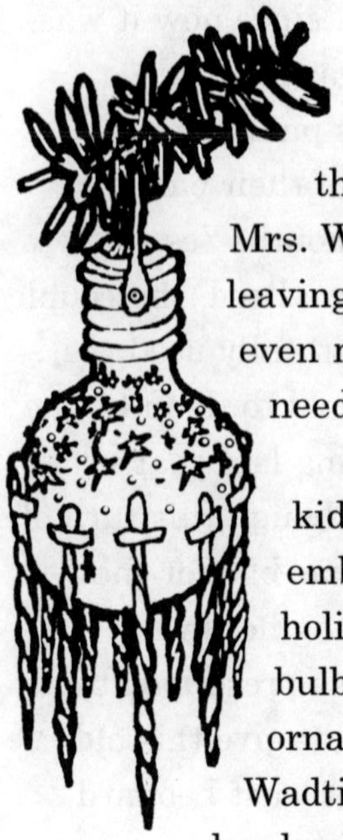

conflicts, since everything was in an uproar with the kids threatening to leave their parents. And Mr. and Mrs. Wadtight were at the point of leaving each other, which suggested even more potential for *product* need.

Not only did the Wadtight kiddos complain about their embarrassment during the holidays, since burned out light bulbs were used for Christmas ornaments on the tree, but Mrs. Wadtight said she was fed up with her husband's demand for wrapping presents, both Christmas and birthday gifts, in newspaper or used aluminum foil. She said she had also reached her breaking point when Mr. Wadtight made the children use two-inch pencils for school as well as discarded three-ring binders he heisted from the panty hose company where he worked. He thought it was perfectly fine for his *Ho Ho Hosiery* logo binders to be used in school by the kiddos, including his second grade son.

Mrs. Wadtight told Nancy that she was contemplating divorce if her hubby didn't loosen up a bit. She was tearful when she called Mr. Wadtight a *humbug,* and she was sick to death of having to wash the cat litter instead of buying new. She also said she wanted to leave the marriage, but Mr. Wadtight only allowed her to carry a single quarter in cash, so she was without the financial means to escape with the also-fed-up kidlets. Oh yes, the Wadtights desperately needed *the product* and Nancy was pretty sure she wouldn't have to do much selling to the doctor about their need.

And finally, Nancy challenged herself about the Nutsqueeze family. She thought that more than any other family they needed *the product,* but she didn't want Dr. Fillemup to think she had jumped to conclusions. It all fell on Mrs. Nutsqueeze, who balanced her anger with tears as she told Nancy all the terrible things her husband did to save money. She wept as she described her penny-pinching husband lining up the three Nutsqueeze children in the bathroom for the morning teeth brushing money saver. Sure, she reported, they were each allowed to have their own toothbrush, but Mr. Nutsqueeze made the oldest brush first, spitting his used paste onto the middle one's toothbrush, who when finished, would do the same to the youngest Nutsqueeze kiddos, making one portion of toothpaste last for all three children. *It was just too much,* Mrs. N. said,

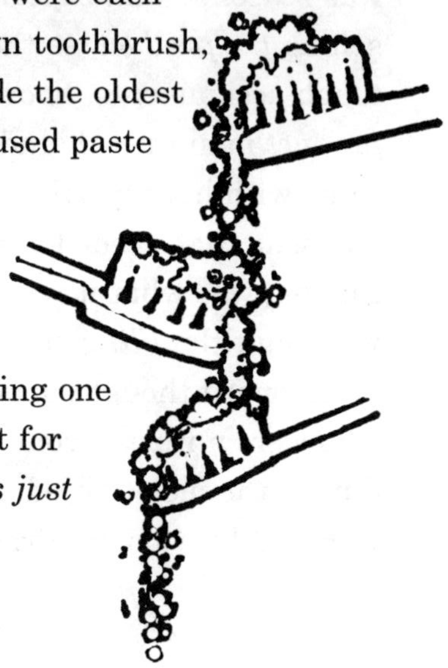

dabbing away tears and breaking Nancy's heart. But for Nancy, her biggest decision was whether or not to actually state how Mrs. Nutsqueeze, in a tearful rage, described her husband's tightness. She pondered whether she should tell Dr. Fillemup that Mrs. Nutsqueeze said, "He's so tight, he probably farts through a rag to save the grease."

Nancy couldn't decide if the fart statement was just too rude for the staff meeting, or maybe if she did tell them, she should say *flagellate* rather than *fart*. There was so much to think about. Either way, she knew the doctor would know the Nutsqueezes really, really needed *the product.*

At the same time Nancy perused her notes, Leonard made his own contemplations for day Number Two of the next week. He wasn't new to the staff, and perhaps that was the problem. He was seasoned and experienced, especially about selling *the product,* so they always gave him the tough assignments, knowing he was a pure *product* man in each and every way. But what came with his expertise was an assignment of an old issue that needed a new fling. And, of course, flinging was what it was all about—thus his working title, *Fling or Forever?*

Leonard thought about Bert and Ernestine who were a repeat from more than a year ago during the melee titled, *Aren't Those My Panties?* Previously, Ernestine had been terribly distressed with Bert's wandering wardrobe problems, because she often found her panties in his lunch pail. But a year later, it seemed things were changing in the panty problem department, since now it was Bert who was finding Ernestine's panties in the back seat of their pastor's 1999 Plymouth. Yes, Leonard realized, the couple hadn't faithfully used *the product* sold to them by the doctor during last year's program. Although this turn of events (and panty problems) was bad for the couple with Ernestine now doing her own flinging, the lack of *product* use prescribed by the doctor over a year ago might give this old topic a new fling of its own—at least Leonard hoped.

Leonard then thought about the Coatturns who provided only marginal *product* interest. Each year, Marvin and Mabel continued to struggle with his flinging escapades at the rubber glove convention in Wichita, and Mabel's special and continual flinging with a chocolate cream pie two or three times a day just to spite Marvin, since he was so critical about what he called *chubby chicks.* The Coatturns really needed *the product,* but Leonard realized they were a bit lethargic with rubber glove concerns and who knows what else that might have involved another latex product. But the doctor would know the measure of need, so Leonard just went on thinking about the other *Flingers or Forever* folks on his list.

Right there at the top were the Reckerhomes, Randal and Ruthie. Now they just might pump some life into this well-worn topic of marital indiscretions with *flinging,* since they had both done some *pumping,* it seemed. Who knows when it really all started, Ruthie had mused to Leonard. But for sure she knew about Randal's fling with her maid of honor in the church broom closet right before bridesmaids' dresses were adorned for Ruthie's wedding to Randal. And of course, Ruthie explained she was not to be outdone in the flinging, so later she retaliated with a little closet action of her own in the janitor's closet at Mercy Medical Hospital with Randal's sister's husband, while sister-in-law was delivering her third child. Over the years, The Reckerhomes' flinging had continued with neighbors and nannies in the family room, or co-workers and co-pilots in the airplane lavatory. But what was tantalizing for Leonard, and his consideration for their *product* use, was that Randal and Ruth had also done some flinging with each other, producing five little Reckerhomes that certainly called for stopping the flinging and thinking more about the forever part. Leonard knew the doctor just might be able to push *the product* on this trying-to-be-formerly-flinging couple.

Mona was somewhere in the experience index between the seasoned Leonard and the newly-hired Nancy. With her slightly familiar topic of *Mother-In-Law Madness,* she was feeling pretty confident that she could present the good doctor with families who were ripe for *product* use. Mona was in charge of day Number Three, so she could learn a little from Nancy and Leonard's presentation before her turn rolled around. Dr. Fillemup, in previous conversations on Mother-in-law issues, always talked about how most of these problems were based on good intentions from the Moms, and he usually believed that with just a little *product,* things should be okay—even with the pesky idea of meddling mothers.

Mona thought about Mrs. Buttinsky who, according to her frustrated daughter-in-law, claimed to have mysteriously won a trip to Hawaii in a not-talked-about contest at the local fish cannery where she worked—coincidentally coinciding with her son's honeymoon in Hawaii. *Yes,* the new Mrs. B. was quite perturbed and suspicious about her mom-in-law showing up at the same honeymoon hotel and calling the newlyweds with various requests, such as borrowing hangers and a handkerchief she couldn't do without on the honeymoon night. Daughter-in-law told Mona that the final straw was when Mrs. Buttinsky asked to sleep in the newlywed's room on the third night of the honeymoon since she was afraid of an island thunderstorm. Right there on the couch, she had spent the night, with her tight-lipped son Bertram, seemingly helpless in getting Mommy under control. Apparently, Bertram and the new Mrs. B. tried many solutions, but nothing seemed to work with the clever and cunning ways of Mother-in-law Buttinsky. It was pathetic, their lack of *product use*, but that was the good news. Mona knew Dr. Fillemup would clearly see this family as needing piles of *the product* since there was obviously such a lack of it.

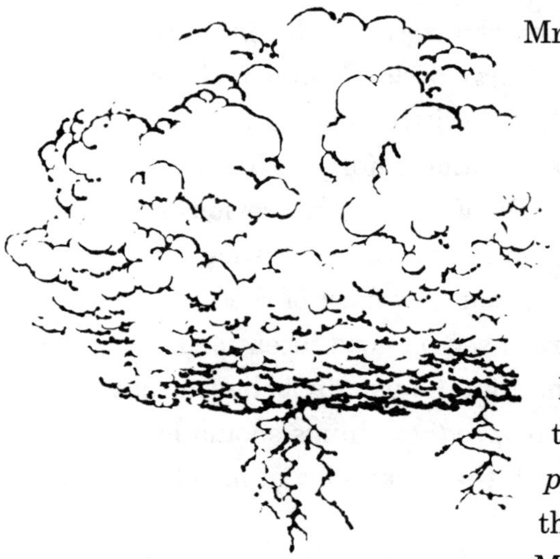

Mona also planned to present the Meddlers, knowing full well the doctor would have a preference for this family and *product use*, since some things were a little different in this family, bringing a fresh slant to this old problem of *Mother-in-law Madness*. Different than Mrs. Buttinsky, mother of Bertram, Mrs. Meddler was the mother of the wife, and her Mother-in-law meddling was against her very own daughter, who she fondly called, *Pumpkin*.

It seems Mother-in-law Meddler didn't have any confidence that Pumpkin was capable of anything, especially cleaning. Priscilla (Pumpkin, actually) found evidence of wandering Windex on the windows after venturing out of the house for her job at the Dollar Store. Mona learned that it would not be uncommon for Priscilla Pumpkin to return home and find her furniture rearranged (more appropriately, of course), her floors mopped spic and span, and the fish in the aquarium burping to death from too much cleaning. If Priscilla Pumpkin planned a meal, Mrs. Meddler would often arrive with a completely different array of not only dinner contributions, but usually something the children preferred to Pumpkin's whole-wheat pasta and vegetable tray. Her meddling was maddening, and Mona knew the doctor would be salivating to push *the product* on Pumpkin and her very frustrated hubby.

And finally, Mona checked her notes about Mrs. Snooperuski, who just couldn't keep out of the business of her son's marriage. Oh, there were a wide range of complaints from daughter-in-law Snooperuski, who was strongly considering either divorce or a very, very long vacation in a faraway place unknown to her husband's meddling mother. With tears, she told Mona about her mother-in-law's insistence on ironing her son's boxer shorts and her claims of being unable to go to sleep at night unless her son (*Sonny Boy*, as she called him) locked her apartment door from the outside.

Sonny Boy's wife just didn't think she could survive the mother-in-law madness, since no matter if they planned a weekend jaunt to the beach or a family picnic, Mrs. Snooperuski seemed to ruin everything. Apparently, she either showed up to the family outing uninvited (accidentally, of course), or she concocted some illness or problem that demanded Sonny Boy's immediate attention, taking him away from his family. These mother-in-law distractions often left the family stranded in the emergency room parking lot with the fried chicken and the should-be-cold-potato salad at about the same temperature in the back seat of the car while inside, technicians worked feverishly on Mrs. Snooperuski's problem with something hysterical, such as impacted blanket fuzz in her right nostril. When Mona interviewed the culprit, senior Mrs. Snooperuski, she noted that Mom-culprit was also tearful as she talked about how much Sonny Boy meant to her, which really suggested that *the product* was desperately needed in order for daughter-in-law to fire her divorce lawyer or cancel her airline faraway trip tickets.

After Nancy, Leonard and Mona, came the fourth day's presentation from Harley with his chosen title of *Hanging Tough or Hanging On.* Dr. Fillemup had consulted with Harley about the importance of bringing together those folks who just dangled with divorce decisions, making any final solution impossible. Of course, since the doctor cared so much for children, this topic was very important because, as he always said, the little ones suffered the most in these divorce danglings without use of *the product.* Harley had been sifting through what seemed like hundreds of options, coming up with three couples that the doctor could consider for *product* use.

Harley thought about the Brawlers who had some vicious things to say about each other as they attempted to wind down their divorce. But without *product* use, they just kept dangling. Ironically, everything about custody of the two Brawler children and the three-bedroom house on Tuckered Street was settled, as well as child support arrangements. But the divorce danglers just couldn't give up on a couple of things, which was very stressing to the Brawler children. Mrs. B. was being quite stubborn about the spotted owl ashtray given to her by her Grandpa Heckle so many years ago. She thought Mr. Brawler was just being spiteful, refusing to relinquish custody of the thing, but he had a completely different story. Mr. Brawler told Harley he was holding onto the owl ashtray because his almost-ex-wife just couldn't seem to find his Elk's Club plaque honoring his year of service as the Exalted Ruler for 1999. With a quivering voice, he shared with Harley that Mrs. Brawler, in a spiteful rage, said that he was nothing but an *exhausted rooster* (rather than an Exalted Ruler) during that year at the club, which really hurt his feelings and made him hang onto the owl ashtray in the divorce dangling. Harley knew Dr. Fillemup would think this couple was just perfect for *the product.*

In addition to the Brawlers, Harley thought about the Scraplots in his presentation of the dangling divorce couples. The Scraplots were such a mess, Harley wondered if the doctor would think *the product* would even make a difference with this warring couple. The Scraplots had most things settled in their divorce except for a few pesky, but nonetheless important, items that were causing everything to dangle and dangle. Also like the Brawlers, the Scraplots were hanging onto just a couple of items that embroiled them in a three-year divorce dangle. Mrs. Scraplot wanted her soon-to-be-ex-husband to pay for the removal of a tattoo he had encouraged her to get during their courtship seven years previous. With tears, she told Harley that she just couldn't go on until the three-inch (and purple) *Only Oliver's* tattoo was removed from her right breast cleavage that was visible in just about anything she wore. When Harley inquired about why she thought Oliver resisted, she was demure, shy and non-committal, which was confusing, but a clear signal for *product* need. Using a little *product* himself, Harley talked to Oliver, who tearfully explained that he was holding out on tattoo removal payments until Mrs. Scraplot returned the pool table that he so treasured. When Harley asked Mrs. Scraplot why she refused to relinquish custody of the pool table, she could only quip that Oliver had played enough *pocket pool* during their marriage that he shouldn't need the real kind. Oh, Harley could see this tattoo/pool playing conflict was vicious and not likely settled without good use of *the product*.

Finally, Harley thought about the Hardblows who were also in great conflict with their divorce dangling and hanging onto the silliest of things. The Hardblow children were a mess as they watched their parents care little about them, but care a lot about custody *and visitation* of the family pets. There were arguments about the three kitties; Tyrone, Tucker and Tallulah. Since there were two Hardblow parents and three felines, the third leg of the pet/divorce decision seemed at an impasse. But it got worse when it came to Tiddily, Diddily and Doody, the three Schnauzers. There were accusations of pooch abuse from both Hardblows, as well as suspicions of withholding Friskies during visitation. There were also claims by Mrs. Hardblow of purposefully induced bowel problems for Doody that resulted in rush trips to the veterinarian right after Mr. Hardblow brought the canines back from camping. It was a clear *critter clash* with no solution in sight.

Harley noted that the Hardblow children felt totally left out as their parents filed complaints in divorce court about how the precious pets were to be divided, so much so that the divorce had been dangling for two and one-half years. And since Doody was aging rapidly and needing insulin several times a week, a settlement was urgent. Harley was convinced the doctor could use *the product* to rescue everything before the Hardblow children were grown, and before Doody's demise. Yes, the Brawlers, the Scraplots and the Hardblows were in desperate need of Dr. Fillemup's *product,* especially concerning trauma to the children in their parents' divorce danglings.

Blanch had the fifth slot for the last day of next week's calendar and she knew that it was likely she wouldn't have much time for her presentation to the doctor, just because of the way the staff meeting unfolded. But being the most experienced and elderly member of the team, she knew she wouldn't need much—time that is. About once a year, Dr. Fillemup reminded Blanch about *the Birds and the Bees Business*, as he put it, and Blanch always knew what to do. It was just about the easiest assignment for her all year long. Even though the process was routine and the audience response was usually overwhelming, *the product,* so important to Dr. Fillemup in every other topic, was just a *side dish* in this *Bird and Bee Business.* But Blanch remembered that the doctor was unequivocal in his belief that even though *the product* wasn't all that important in this topic, "our responsibilities to the families" was the driving force for this show at least once a year.

Blanch knew the drill and only had to briefly check her notes. She thought Dr. Fillemup would be proud of her for snagging a very important celebrity, actually a somewhat-competitor to the doctor in *product* selling, who wanted to come on the show and ask about when it was *time* for her daughter. Even though in private meetings the doctor sometimes called her a fake flake, Blanch knew the doctor would consider her a draw for the topic, jazzing up the other somewhat mediocre parents scheduled for the *Birds and Bees Business* show.

As she contemplated her presentation, Blanch thought about the Mom who felt so embarrassed about getting the job done, she wanted to hire a therapist to take care of things with her two children. And she told Blanch she was willing to spend lots of money just to get it all accomplished and to avoid taking on the pesky task herself.

Blanch also remembered the couple who home-schooled their kids and wanted the doctor's guidance on the B and B business, worrying that the state curriculum required the lesson but there were no guidelines on the how-to-do-it, which was perplexing to the home-schooling parents. They thought surely the doctor could help them plan for the big event around the kitchen table classroom.

But the favorite bunch for Blanch were two families on two different ends of the spectrum, which was always very interesting and attractive to Dr. Fillemup. He was like that—always wanting opposing sides and second opinions in order to sell his *product.*

One set of these end-of-the-spectrum parents wanted to be guaranteed that their kids would be protected from anyone outside the family trying to "do the dirty" as the father had explained to Blanch in a telephone interview. He wanted total control of the B and B business, and his screaming about it bothered Blanch. But she knew the doctor would find this Dad's ranting and raving challenging for the dull topic.

On the other end of the spectrum, Blanch found parents who seemed to have gone way, way overboard in the other direction. Blanch would explain to the doctor that these parents wanted help in teaching their children about such off-the-wall stuff as condom application on cucumbers or interpersonal skills in negotiating with a prostitute. Why, they wanted help with stuff that was way beyond the traditional curriculum of *Birds and Bees Business,* which Blanch found troubling, but she also knew would be very interesting to Dr. Fillemup.

Each year when Blanch was given this assignment, her immediate thought was always one of futility about how she could spice up the topic since it always seemed so simple AND BORING. Although according to Dr. Fillemup, this topic was a responsibility, there was never much use for *product* since it was always just a one-time thing. But looking over some of her parents and their extremes in thinking, Blanch had a renewed sense of excitement that maybe there might be a little action for the show, but as usual, very little *product* need. Although the screaming Dad, clever celebrity, and cucumber-condom folks sounded somewhat exciting, Blanch knew this kind of topic tended to be counterproductive to *the product* use philosophy of everything else that Dr. Fillemup did, all year long, in each and every other problem.

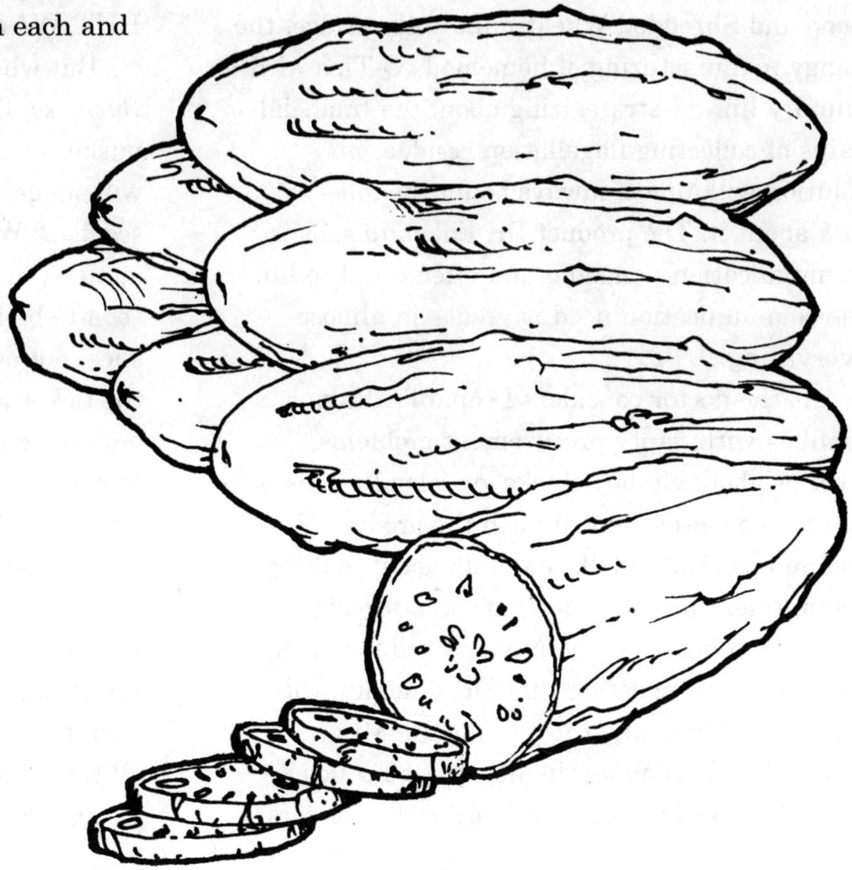

Yes, in the *Birds and Bees Business*, this talk pusher will strategize with the frantic parents about where to have *the talk*, how to make eye contact during *the talk*, and how to be very careful not to talk about something the kiddos don't already know—during *the talk*.

THE SECOND COMMANDMENT

The Second Commandment, *Thou Shalt Communicate,* is about *the talk* issue, so important to parents in the *Now* and the *Not Now* groups of the First Commandment, and also important to the good Dr. Fillemup—the king of *talk*. The talk show host, the pusher of *the product* of communication, suggests that the solution to nearly every single ailment of almost every single problem is communication or talk—and not once, but over and over. Whether Dr. Fillemup is dealing with the penny-pinching of passing the used toothpaste, the reusing Fruit Loop and Shredded Wheat milk in the fridge, the stingy manufacturing of homemade Q-Tips with laundry lint, or strategizing about the financial gains of collecting flagellation residue, his solution will almost always be for the folks to *talk* about it. The product Dr. Fillemup sells is communication—ongoing and often—and to him the communication need is great—in almost everything.

As the doctor considers Leonard's flinging families with panty procurement problems, worries about chubby chicks, or sexual romps in the broom closet, he will push the product of communication, so folks can talk about making a commitment for the more pro-social *forever,* or if they will continue their *flinging*. And it will only be with communication that Dr. Fillemup will work with Mona and the problems of Mrs. Buttinsky sleeping on the honeymoon couch, Mrs. Meddler lurking with Lysol spray, or Mrs. Snooperuski ironing Sonny Boy's underwear. It won't stop there either, as Harley's families will need to talk out their problems of dangling divorces, fighting over owl ashtrays, smirking about exhausted roosters, and being in tears about tattoo removal or rumors of pocket pool. Why, even when it comes to Tiddily, Diddily and Doody, or Tyrone, Tucker and Tallulah, the solution can be found in communication, and that is not only the solution to the problem, but communication (talk, actually) is the solution (reason) for Dr. Fillemup's success.

BUT WAIT

But when it comes to Blanch's *Bird and Bees Business*, Dr. Fillemup, the king of talk and the pusher of communication for every other issue, will suggest for the kiddo's sex talk, *just one segment.* With hand-wringing, fussing, and anxiety, he will suggest to the nervous, and soon-to-be-having-a-talk parent, that a single slice, not ongoing communication, will be just the ticket when sister begins to ask about why boys have boobs or how her baby brother got in Mommy's tummy. Yes, in the *Birds and Bees Business*, this talk pusher will strategize with the frantic parents about where to have *the talk*, how to make eye contact during *the talk*, and how to be very careful not to talk about something the kiddos don't already know—during *the talk*. Different than his solutions for all the other problems where he will recommend communication (yes, lots of it, lots of times); for sex education, just once ought to do it. And what a farce that singular talk suggestion is, when considering how ongoing communication is the *product* the good doctor pushes with so much vigor and, by the way, with so much success.

TALK THE TALK

Dr. Fillemup and other talk peddlers will orchestrate talk shows about *Sexual Confidence, Sexual Aggression,* and *Sexual Swinging.* They will have shows about *Female Orgasms* and the faking of them. And for more sexual titillation, they will feature shows about *Sexual Slumps, Sexual Gymnastics, Sexual Styles, Sexual Games, Sex For the Aging,* and *Sex For the Sagging*. There will be shows about those who want to give up sex and those who want to fire up sex. Show after show, month after month, year after year, sex will sell in the talk business. In fact, the topic of sex for most radio and television talk shows becomes the playing field of competition as they try to outdo each other in selling the sensational, and therefore the most profitable, programming. The talk business sells, because sex sells.

TRAGEDY IN THE TRAVESTY

But there is a travesty in the sex talk selling when it comes to children and sex, suggesting that in spite of the fact that every other problem is solved with talking, only ***one talk*** for kiddos about the birds and the bees will be A-okay. The tragedy in this travesty is that there is no shyness for using the topic of sexual disrespect as an underpinning for most talk shows, and, in fact, the really, really bad part about sex really, really sells. Whether it is rape, child sexual abuse, sexual assault, date rape, incest, or other sexual weirdness, these sexually disrespectful issues fill the airwaves and bring in the big bucks. It is everywhere, this sex stuff (mostly the bad side), yet those same purveyors of smut who make their living pushing the product of communication, still suggest that for children, the strategy to teaching them about sex is one *talk.*

The tragedy in this travesty is that there is no shyness for using the topic of sexual disrespect as an underpinning for most talk shows and, in fact, the really, really bad part about sex really, really sells.

MORE TRAVESTY

The travesty is furthered when someone like Dr. Fillemup suggests a single effort at sex education and bird/bee business for the kidlets will do just fine juxtaposed against what the kiddos might see if they watched *his* television show. The thinking is akin to the Sex Fairy myth—suggesting the kiddos don't pay attention to what is on the television and, therefore, Mommy and Daddy can choose when to impart knowledge to the kiddos in a single talk because, after all, crotch zapping after the wedding will take care of everything. It is a Sex Fairy kind of belief that children are kept in cardboard boxes in the backyard, waiting to be retrieved for either a visit from Nurse Ratchet, or for the one big talk strategized and planned by the white-knuckled parent who watched Dr. Fillemup's *Birds and Bees Business* show. And of course, when the king of talk teaches parents that one talk ought to do it, he must assume that not a single kiddo ever watches any of his sexually disrespectful shows, which is probably accurate since what parent would allow electricity or a television hookup for the backyard cardboard boxes. It is a farce, a tragedy, and a travesty, and Dr. F. is not the only peddler of talk in the madness.

NO CARDBOARD BOXES, NO CHOICES

In reality, children are receiving sexual information from a steady stream of sources with the subtlety of a Mack Truck. If children were oblivious to sexual stuff and protected from the mainstream of family, school, and community life, then perhaps Mom and Dad could actually choose when to talk to their children about the miracle of swimming sperm in the fallopian tubes. But putting kiddos in backyard cardboard boxes, or sending them to the monastery may not be the best choice for parents who wish to raise sexually respectful children. And *choice* is the operative word.

But putting kiddos in backyard cardboard boxes, or sending them to the monastery may not be the best choice for parents who wish to raise sexually respectful children. And *choice* is the operative word.

As the parents tussled with the big-glasses government-guy, G.G., in the school board meeting of the First Commandment, fussing about when to begin sex education, they magically thought not much was going on in the risqué department. Therefore, they believed they were in the sexual driver's seat about when to begin. But if there were a dose of reality for the *Nows* and the *Not Nows* or for Dr. Fillemup, the choices about sex education are starkly limited. Since the cardboard boxes in the backyard are rarely an option, a more realistic assumption should be that they are already getting it (sex education, that is), and the only real choice for parents is how, and under what conditions children receive the sex education desired by the parents. Sexual information is the tapestry of much of this society's message and medium, and therefore the choice for parents isn't *if*, or *when,* but *how.* And that takes a basic understanding of the ongoing information flow already happening for children and then, just as the good doctor purports, learning to weave communication about sex into that already existing sexual maze.

Sexual information is the tapestry of much of this society's message and medium, and therefore the choice for parents isn't *if*, or *when,* but *how.*

TAKING CHARGE—THE TWO STEP

So, for those folks who really wish to take charge of the sex education of children, and who are not particularly fond of watering and feeding kiddos in the cardboard box routine, action is the name of the game. And there are two steps to taking charge. The first step involves taking inventory of what kind of sexual information is already being communicated to the kidlets. This means examining what is being heard, felt, learned and digested by the children about sex, often from the most insignificant sources. And those communicated messages to children about sex, however helpful, horrifying or haunting, need to become the fodder for the parental clipboard of lesson planning.

SECOND STEPPING

Secondly, parents who really want to control sex education and raise sexually respectful children will watch for those tidbits and snippets of sexual learning and turn them into *windows of opportunity* to teach, guide, and nurture the sexual ideas parents wish to impart. These windows of opportunity are the natural, unrehearsed, and often unintended situations where children learn about sex, actually quite by accident. Take-charge parents will be ready, with the tool of communication, to convey their ideas as normally and naturally as they might in other areas of raising children. These windows will provide the opportunity, and it will be communication, not a podium in the fifth grade class or one *teeth-sweating* parent with a planted pamphlet, that will teach sexual respect.

And these windows of opportunity are the natural, unrehearsed and often unintended situations where children learn about sex, actually quite by accident.

TREE FORT FRISKY

She was stressed and the stern social worker wasn't helping the tension level in the interview room of the State Child Protection agency. As the government gal peeked over her perched half-glasses, she appeared to Mom as having the congeniality skills of an FBI agent. The social worker was investigating claims of some hanky-panky going on with Mom's kiddos in the neighbor's tree fort where several of the four-and five-year-olds were discovering the fun of getting naked. Tight-lipped parents of all the kiddos had been marched into the agency office in order to get to the proverbial *bottom* of things. But with the social work types, there was always a concern about where the kidlets could possibly have learned about sex (the cardboard box mentality) with the obvious worry about those nasty issues such as porn channels on the television or the possibility that one of the children's father had dirty magazines hidden in a secret toolbox. Worse yet, the FBI-friendly type remembered the state training manual requirements about probing the possibility of seedier things in the families of the no-longer-naked children, such as sexual abuse. So the government gal's questions to Mom related to *what* her children knew about this sex stuff and, of course, *how* they knew it. The inquisitor's questions were sharp and pointed, but Mom was ready.

With the confidence of an also-not-so-friendly CIA agent, Mom explained the philosophy of sex education in her household, employed by herself and her husband.

"We have always been very straightforward with our children about sex, the oldest ones could tell you. We wanted to be very open and we made a commitment that if they ever had any sexual questions, we would be honest. We have always been there for them if they had questions or concerns about sex."

And there it was; smug, secure and sure. If the kids had any sexual questions, they would be answered. So, problem solved.

When a child writes a letter to God, thanking him for inventing the stapler, Mom and Dad smile, but they probably make a mental note to correct the idea about God being in the office supply business.

THE LUTHERAN HOUR

But could this same mother have the same strategy of communication and education for other important learning issues, such as wanting her kids to be Lutheran?

Would it make sense for an intending-on-being Lutheran parent to say, "I didn't take them to the Lutheran church, I didn't read them any Lutheran books, I never talked to them about being a Lutheran, but by golly if they had any questions about being a Lutheran, I was always there for them and I always gave them straight answers?"

This strategy may give a new meaning to the idea of the *Lutheran Hour,* which is about all it would take in this sexual scheme of things to become Lutheran. And surely an hour (Lutheran type) would be fifteen minutes more than Nurse Ratchet needed for her 45-minute swimming sperm lesson, which made all the *Now* parents quite happy. The new *Lutheran Hour* idea is absurd to Lutheran Moms and Dads, and they would shudder with the thought of their children only learning about being Lutheran if they had questions.

LUTHERAN TWO-STEP

How do good Lutheran parents do their teaching? Well, the answer to family Lutheran education may provide a good blueprint for sex education and a review of the two-step process of communication. The first step for Mom and Dad Lutheran, who are probably taking their kids to the Lutheran church on a weekly basis, is to discover what the kiddos are already learning about being Lutheran; and secondly, make a commitment to watch for the windows of opportunity to intervene and communicate about Lutheran business. If the goal was to create little Lutherans, Mom and Dad would adopt a posture of vigilance just to make sure that everything goes okay as the kiddos tiptoe down the Lutheran path. And if anything happened along the way, if the kids started to get things wrong, Mom and Dad would step in with a Lutheran clipboard.

Remembering the *Letters to God* written by children in a Catholic school is a classic example of doing the *two-step of communication* in educating children. The letters were sweet and precious, but clear evidence of children getting things sort of right, but mostly wrong, about God—Lutheran or Catholic. And good parents would seize upon those stumblings to re-route the kidlets who got God wrong.

OH GOD OFFICE SUPPLY

When a child writes a letter to God, thanking him for inventing the stapler, Mom and Dad smile, but they probably make a mental note to correct the idea about God being in the office supply business. With quick observation of the first step (knowing what they know), it is easy to understand that after Sunday school and learning about Lutheran miracles, the kids might have gone with Dad to the Staples store and inadvertently learned about the miracle of a stapler. The connection with two types of miracles is cute, but for good parents, it is over. Lutheran-teaching parents make note of what their child is already learning about God, miracles, and staplers; they see the confusion as sweet but needing an adjustment. They will use communication to make the correction, re-routing the child along the correct path toward getting God back in heaven and out of the office supply business.

PREACHING PODIUMS

In a sex education comparison, it would be rare that upon hearing their child believes God invented the stapler or that God's geography committee drew the lines around the countries, that parents would first panic, then move two podiums into the family room and with the Gestapo attitude of Nurse Ratchet (complete with flip charts and pointers), give a one-time, 45-minute lecture on the Lutheran God. Quite the opposite usually happens with something so important as parents teaching spirituality.

The Lutheran lesson is usually nurtured by communication (slow and easy) in the child's language, and with parental love and patience. And it won't be once, but over and over, pulling Lutheran teaching into daily life, far beyond the one-hour Sunday school class. Why wouldn't that same blueprint for Lutheran education (no podiums, please) be adopted in efforts to teach children sexual respect?

STEP ONE—WHOOPS WINDOWS

So the first step in the Second Commandment focusing on *Thou Shalt Communicate* is to be alert to the tiny, appearing insignificant, unintentional, and usually *whoops* type of communication that already occurs in the lives of children. And often this kind of accidental communication occurs through omission, especially when adults are trying to protect children from sexual information and the whole thing backfires as another message is actually communicated to the thought-to-be-innocent kiddos.

GRANDMA KNOWS NOSES

Through omission, even little kiddos learn early—*you can show Grandma your nose, you can show Grandma your eyes, you can show Grandma your ears, but you do not show Grandma your pee-pee if you want her to live through Thanksgiving.* With proud delight, children show off their anatomy knowledge to Grandma. But through omission, even toddlers know that to show the same competency in naming body parts between their legs would likely send the old girl into diabetic lift-off. They don't know why, they just know not to do it. This omission is not mean-spirited on the part of parents, and it is usually founded on a belief or hope that keeping Grandma from *knowing* that the little folks *know* they have sexual body parts (even though she already *knows* it) will result in some kind of morality for the children, which is

It would be rare that upon hearing their child believes God invented the stapler or that God's geography committee drew the lines around the countries, that parents would first panic, then move two podiums into the family room and with the Gestapo attitude of Nurse Ratchet (complete with flip charts and pointers), give a one-time, 45-minute lecture on the Lutheran God.

just another tragedy and travesty. But omitting those body parts from the showing-off-to-Grandma routine communicates a powerful message to children—one that is usually the opposite of what parents wanted them to learn.

He learns the same message from his G.I. Joes as he does from protecting Grandma from a coronary by not giving names for what is between his five-year-old legs. The omission teaches.

NOTICING NOTHING

Children also learn from omission when dolls are used to represent people, but some things are clearly missing from the play pretend people. As Jason dresses his Ken doll, who is preparing for a date with Barbie (operated by Jason's sister), he is keenly aware of his own set of testicles and his perfectly functioning penis, quite different from Ken who is in the *nowhere* department between his legs. Additionally, Jason notices that other details of his jet set doll and his G.I. Joe action figure are accurately copied from real people, even to the finest details of fingernails and eyelashes. But when it comes to the doll's crotch, Jason calculates the vacancy. He learns the same message from his G.I. Joe as he does in protecting Grandma from a coronary by not giving names for what is between his five-year-old legs. The omission teaches. Children like Jason *notice the nothing* and for sure, they learn from the missing parts.

Katie finds the same mystery of omission with her prized Polly Pockets dolls. Polly, just like G.I. Joe and the Ken doll, is equipped with everything imaginable in the body department. She not only has hair, but she has various hairstyles and various hair equipment such as barrettes, hair clips, fake hair buns, and hair flips. She has bras, panty hose, and actual panties of every color and cut, including thongs. She has breasts (no nipples, however) and she has all kinds of breast equipment such as halter-tops, tight-fitting tube tops, and tank tops. And Polly also has a lot of body sexual equipment with her nicely shaped legs, perfectly curved buttocks and splendidly sensuous breasts. But just like G.I. Joe, she is in the *nowhere* department between her legs and on the protruding parts of her breasts. And for sure, Katie notices the nothingness, and she learns.

The message, or the intended communication from the doll makers (who were guided by the parents) was probably honorable, hoping the missing-in-action body parts on the Ken doll and Barbie would curb sexual influences on the innocent children until Mom and Dad decide the time is right for Nurse Ratchet, or when Dr. Fillemup gives parents the go-ahead for the one big talk. It is an out-of-sight-out-of-mind mentality that hopes everything precious and moral will be ensured with the omission. But the intended goal of dolly-body-parts-omission to create some sort of sexual purity is just like the travesty of Dr. Fillemup using every aspect of sex to sell talk television, but then pretend like the kids won't know anything until the purple-faced parents corner them on the patio for *the talk*.

Children playing with these genitalia-omitted dolls are actually learning a lot about sex, and not necessarily the purity idea. Even though G.I. Joe is missing a penis, the boys playing with the army characters are certainly learning about male sex role modeling in fighting, being strong, and of course, male preoccupation with weaponry. And whether it is Polly Pockets or Barbie, being *sexy* is the important message communicated to girls, even though the real sexual stuff between the legs or at the very end of the coveted Barbie breasts is missing. The absence of the sexual parts communicates a two-level message to the playing children: First, *grown-ups can't talk about this stuff if they can't even look at it or tolerate it.* And secondly, *wow-- this missing stuff is really exciting and forbidden.*

FORBIDDEN FONDNESS

Most folks have it, but sex offenders seem to have more of it. The issue is an attraction toward the forbidden. Whether it is the six-year-old's creative genius in heisting the cookie Mom said he couldn't have (even though others were available), or whether Mom has an obsession with being the first one of her Bunko group to have an avocado-colored refrigerator. The attraction toward the uncommon, the unobtainable, or *the forbidden* seems to thrive among humans. It can be relied upon in fashion that nothing is really reliable or static. Just when Dad is finally convinced to buy a powder-blue leisure suit, the whole concept goes out of style and he is the laughingstock of those attending the stockholder's meeting. Bell-bottom pants are in, that is until everyone has them, and then the attraction will shift to circulation-stopping, ankle-grabber pants. For those with tons of money, seeking out what no one else has often takes creativity, such as the famous and, of course, rich basketball star that just thought his life wasn't complete until he had a bedspread made from wolf muzzles. It seems what folks can't have is what they want in their attraction toward the forbidden.

Most folks have it, but sex offenders seem to have more of it and the issue is an attraction toward the forbidden.

Most people shuffle along in life and make it just fine in this love affair with what they can't have. But with sex offenders, the attraction toward the forbidden seems way out of control. Before research became a reality in the sex offender business, the good folks who took on the task of trying to understand the bad folks, just couldn't—understand, that is. It was just too much, they said, to comprehend sexual arousal toward, as an example, *an infant*. Yet sadly, sexual abuse of the really little ones became a frightening reality in the early 1990s and the pondering was pitiful.

***How could an infant be sexually arousing to anyone,* they all asked?**

Was it her pink gingham bow, Scotch taped to her bald little head that rendered the sex offender completely out of control with sexual desire? Or was it her baggy, saggy thighs that her older sister said looked a lot like Grandma's thighs, that were the focus of arousal? *How could a baby be sexually arousing to anyone,* they all asked?

And when omission of sexual information makes children attracted to what is left out, the omission should be considered a breeding ground for learning sexual disrespect.

MORE PITIFUL PONDERING

But there was more confusion. With the sexual history taking of sex offenders as a normal part of treatment and study, sexual assault of the elderly, or the infirmed, became another sad reality. *What could possibly be arousing about an 82-year-old comatose patient?* was the difficult question. But when the smart people really took a look at sex offender arousal patterns, a wide range of perversion seemed to be a common theme. The same sex offender who replaced his infant son's bottle with his own penis, and who had intercourse with an elderly woman in a nursing home where he worked as a respiratory therapist, also had affairs with adult neighbors and did everything he could to convince his wife that Saturday night sex would be greatly enhanced if certain vegetables could be considered sex toys. The theme was clear. The interest was in the *forbidden,* not the sexual attractiveness of the partner/victims. And when omission of sexual information makes children attracted to what is left out, the omission should be considered a breeding ground for learning sexual disrespect.

BACKFIRE

So it would seem that the omission of sexual parts on dolls and toys, intended to create disinterest in sex at the least, and encourage purity or morality at the best, probably backfired and for good reason. While Jason is learning how to be a real man with his penisless Power Rangers, he is nonetheless sitting right on top of his very own penis that he holds in his hand about six or seven times a day when he urinates. And of course, Katie also knows what is nestled between her legs while in her play she gets her sexless Barbies and Pollys very *sexy, sexy, sexy.* This sober absurdity that the kids won't compare the reality of what they are sitting on to the missing-in-action dolly body parts may have the opposite impact of creating arousal toward the forbidden, which is deadly for parents who want to protect their kids from becoming sex offenders.

STEP ONE SOLUTION?

So if step one in the *Thou Shalt Communicate* commandment is to understand what sexual message is already being communicated, then the omission stuff is very important for the overall curriculum. The answer is not to forbid G.I. Joes and Barbies from the home, nor do parents who want to raise sexually respectful children need to go into the doll-making business or solicit the services of a seamstress who will attach the pesky appendages to create reality. No. The answer is to take the first step in this Second Commandment and figure out that the children notice the nothingness in body part roll call. Then in the second step, there must be communication about the omission of body parts, using the logic of the Third Commandment as the lesson plan.

MORE OMISSIONS—TEACHING & TUNES

There are other sexual messages being communicated to children by well-intended omissions that are founded on the hope of a morality message. However, when children do their dot-connecting, the message is something other than morality. What does the fresh-out-of-Sunday-school-class kiddo, who has just learned that Jesus' mother was a virgin, think when her fourteen-year-old sister hums along to the car radio with Madonna's popular song, *Like A Virgin*? On the way home from church, the older sister joins the rock star in the familiar refrains of "touched for the very first time," or "you feel so good inside," while the little sister ponders how the whole thing worked out if Joseph and Mary were both virgins. The intended religious message might have been honorable for parents teaching the sanctity of birth for the Christian's Son of God, but the message for children will not only be convoluted and confusing, but the omission screams a louder communication in the virgin comparison department.

VYING VIRGINS

Even for the little sister, it won't take rocket science for her to figure out the real story about who is vying for being in charge of the virgin competition, especially since Mom and Dad probably just assigned virgin titles to some of the church characters and omitted any other explanation. Thinking, of course, the kiddos don't really need to know about virginity for a very, very long time. But in vying for power in the minds of the kids, Madonna and her music will end up being a whole lot more powerful than the statue of the virgin lady in church who doesn't look to be having very much fun at all—at least to the singing sisters.

Through Madonna's popular music, the girls will learn about the cool times that can be had by giving away their virginity, long before they ever even know what it is. It will be obvious to them that Madonna concerts bring in a whole lot more action that the yearly church Christmas play where the Virgin Mary gets played by the girl who is least likely to giggle when she somberly holds the pretend baby Jesus, which is actually a wrapped up railroad flashlight. And compared to Madonna's ongoing performances, albums, and notoriety, the Sunday school-quick overview of just announcing that Jesus' Mother was a virgin (omission complete) will be rather boring, making Madonna the big winner. And that kind of omission is also a travesty and tragedy since if asked, most parents would eagerly admit that virginity is immensely important to them, and a huge hope for their children. But in spite of that virgin value—true communication about it is routinely omitted from the sexual respect clipboard.

There are other sexual messages being communicated to children by well-intended omissions that are founded on the hope of a morality message. However, when children do their dot-connecting, the message is something other than morality.

Parents fail to recognize that children know they don't go to the circus to learn math, they don't go to the pizza parlor to buy shoes, and they don't talk to someone about sex who doesn't do it—sex that is.

CONCEIVING CONCEPTION OMISSION

But there is more learning through omission that messes with the quest of raising sexually respectful children. When honest sex education from parents is postponed or omitted, the kids still plod along with their learning. Not only is there a serious danger in becoming attracted to what is omitted and/or forbidden, but there is another kind of communication happening that is deadly. The credibility of parents in the sex department is often shattered by the time they are ready for Nurse Ratchet or *the talk* orchestrated by Dr. Fillemup. It is the fading credibility theory personified and out-of-control.

Just as Madonna wins the popularity contest with Virginity 101 lessons, the kiddos are in the winning fast lane, scooping up tons of sexual information, while their waiting and withholding parents are left in the dust. Subtle exposure to kissing, touching, being sexual, selling sex, crying for sex, dying for sex, or getting sex, is constantly observed by children who make an easy conclusion that this sex stuff has nothing to do with their own parents. Without thinking about the *power of omission,* parents hide their own sexuality from their children even though they wanted to be in total charge of their children's sex education. But the bad news is that being in charge of the sex stuff, in the minds of the kidlets, requires Moms and Dads to know something about it in the first place. Parents fail to recognize that children know they don't go to the circus to learn math, they don't go to the pizza parlor to buy shoes, and they don't talk to someone about sex who doesn't do it—sex that is. Sure, there might be hints and whispers by children about Mommy and Daddy locking the bedroom door on Sunday morning, but if the reality of parents really being sexual ever hits the kids, it can be terrifying.

KIDS COUNTING

Two sisters, about age seven and ten, watch in horror while Miss Emily, their beloved family cat, hisses and claws in the shrubbery with Mooner, the neighbor's tomcat. Fur flies and the screeching is deafening in the mating madness. While the felines do their ruckusing, three of Mom's prized azaleas are sent flying off the patio deck. The scene is disgusting and horrifying, especially to the youngest of the shocked sisters. The oldest, and only slightly wiser sister, notices a window of opportunity for sibling harassment. She smugly suggests to the younger one, "Guess what Sissy? Our parents did exactly the same thing."

The seven-year-old is at once horrified with the image of her Mother and Father hissing and clawing, as well as knocking over azaleas in their effort to *cat hump.* It was just too much and her panic became evident to the almost-harassing sister. The older one, who was initially confident in her announcement, quickly notices her little sister's horror and reroutes her rudeness. She soothingly assures her sister,

"Don't worry Sissy, they only did it twice, once for you and once for me."

There. The asexuality of Mom and Dad is restored and maintained, with just two little slips in the image of purity, resulting in the birth of both daughters.

In reality, few adults could easily conjure an image of their own conception. Focusing on a pictured scene of the morning, evening or lunch hour they were conceived is, for most, impossible if not horrifying. *My parents, huffing and puffing—no way,* might be a familiar response to the image request. On some cognitive level most children, at some point, learn they are the product of Daddy's swimming sperm arresting Mommy's ovulation cycle. But to really imagine Mommy, who makes a creative peanut butter sandwich, or Daddy, who takes out the garbage without complaining, running their tongues over each other's teeth, or in unison, watching the erection of Mom's nipple from Daddy's tender touching (like they see on television or in the movies) is just too much.

THE CHECK-OFF

So as children learn about sex from their day-to-day world, they separate the factions. They have a sexual world with tidbits of exciting, secret, forbidden stuff, prone to giggles and jiggles, while they also see the other world of their parents, which is quite different and actually quite boring. An image of their parents humping in the azaleas is usually unavailable to children. Instead, they imagine their parents as a wasteland of knowledge and experience with the excitement or energy level of Nurse Ratchet. The message is loud and clear. Check off parents, both on the reliability and credibility scales. And more important, when it comes to sex, children learn their parents can't be trusted.

BACK TO BODIES

Not only is there a whole lot of nothing going on in the crotches of their dollies, but children also learn something about the whole lot of nothing from their parents in the naming of those non-existent parts. Kiddos can't seem to figure out much consistency in *pee-pees, wee-wees, poo-poos, bums* and *boo-boos,* and of course, the ever-popular *tweedles, deedles* and *dums.* They know their friends have even more names for those exciting body parts, and they also learned the opposite from their parents for other body parts, suggesting there is only one way to describe their elbows—Mom and Dad are firm on that. But that is not the way it is with the *cocks, dicks, pussies* and *poops* of language given to them by should-be-reliable adults when describing those sexual body parts. The cutesy little words are tolerated and sometimes encouraged by parents with the hope that the omission of the proper names will postpone sex education at best and at *really best,* they hope the omission maintains their children's sexual innocence. But this thinking fails to take into consideration what children learn from the omission of *credible and reliable* body part language.

In reality, few adults could easily conjure an image of their own conception.

They can't seem to figure out much consistency in *pee-pees, wee-wees, poo-poos, bums* and *boo-boos,* and of course, the ever-popular *tweedles, deedles* and *dums.*

Mom took the two-step brilliantly, by first being alert to what her little Z-Man was learning, then she turned it into a window of opportunity for communication—zooming her credibility into first-place with the first born son.

OPPOSITE OF OMISSION

First grader Zachary doesn't yet appreciate the gift he has received from his honest and proactive parents as he arrives home from his fourth day of school being quite perturbed. After rudely dropping his backpack in the entryway, he heads toward the kitchen with the subtlety of an Amtrak train. With indignation, he announces, "Mother, they are calling it a *cock*, a *dick* or a *doo-doo*! No one in my entire first grade has ever heard the word *penis*. What is going on?"

Even though Zachary is in immediate panic as he tries to sort through first grade genitalia terminology, there is good news. He is about to learn that his parents *are* reliable compared to the parents of his slang-slinging friends. Zachary's mother not only taught him the proper terminology at the same time he was learning the difference between elbows and ears, but in her wisdom she is ready to do the second step of opening the window of opportunity for further communication with Zachary, really strengthening her credibility with first-born son.

"Honey, I'm so proud of you for coming to me about your friends and their silly words. The reason Daddy and I told you the right words is that we wanted no tricks about things as important as penises. Some Moms and Dads don't tell their kids the right things and the kids learn silly words like *cocks* and *dicks*. Just remember Z-Man, we will always give you the straight scoop about everything, whether it is about penises or presidents. And speaking of scoops, would you like one or two scoops of Peanut Butter Brickle ice cream for your after-school treat?" Mom took the two-step brilliantly, by first being alert to what her little Z-Man was learning, then she turned it into a window of opportunity for communication—zooming her credibility into first place with the first-born son.

MORE OPPOSITE

And the opposite of Zachary's situation is even more startling and dangerous for not only children, but for parents who really did want to control their child's sex education. If Zachary, with his reliable information about the names for body parts, confronts his friends about their misinformation, it is not likely the slang-slingers will drop their backpacks in their own entryway, head for the kitchen conference table and pronounce: "Mother, after consultation with my friends, I have detected you are in error concerning your vernacular pertaining human genitalia terminology, and, as your first-born son, I demand clarification. Today some nerd kid suggested that what I determined to be my *cock,* my *dick,* or my *doo-doo,* was actually a *penis.* This kid named Zachary deemed my rotating terminology to be slang. What is going on?"

Unfortunately, the scenario of the slang-slinging child challenging Mom's lack of credibility about *cocks, dicks*, or *doo-doos* is not likely to occur. No, the kiddo who didn't get the right information will just do the parental check-off. His contemplations will be something along the lines of, *My parents are unreliable—so never, never, never count on them for this sex stuff.* And since the nerd kid (Zachary, actually) had only one rather boring word, *penis,* the other kids not only learned the stupidity of their parents, but they learned how much more exciting and powerful their *cocks, dicks,* and *doo-doos* tended to be. Arousal, excitement and *interest in the forbidden* are the communicated messages for the cocks and dicks kiddos, heading to the path of sexual disrespect, while Zachary may actually find his Peanut Butter Brickle ice cream more exciting than the word *penis.* Ironically, getting disinterested in the sexual body parts is probably what the slang-slinging parents wanted, but didn't understand. And Z-Man's Mom with her honesty and her resistance to omission, won the battle on the path to sexual respect.

BATTLE OF BODY FUNCTIONS

If children are learning about sex by omitted body parts on dollies, by silly-slanged body parts from the incompetence of their parents, they also learn about sex from household hummings of body part functioning. Contrary to parental hope that sex education is related to swimming sperm doing the backstroke in fallopian tubes, real sex involves (no, *requires)* bodies to *function.* According to general authority on such things, sex does not occur with two bodies lying side-by-side with the Sex Fairy flying in with her slightly bent wand, mixing things up. Sex requires bodies to work, and how children learn about body functions in their homes provides a plethora of curriculum regarding sexual respect or disrespect that demands the two-step of communication implementation.

NOISES AND SEXUAL COMMUNICATION

The way in which privacy and modesty are handled within a family isn't always healthy, and is often absurd. One man laments about his shock the first time he heard his new wife urinate through the honeymoon hotel bathroom door. *She tinkled!* He had grown up in a household common to many American families where the female-gendered folks were directly or indirectly taught to vigorously run tap water when their urination noises were in jeopardy of being heard by others. While the females in his family took the dainty route in pretending their bodies didn't actually work, this man/boy learned that female folks urinate with the ferocity of water buffaloes.

He was horrified when his bride (who grew up in an abnormal, but honest-about-body-functions family) actually *tinkled* in the bathroom. So with the pretending of his home, he learned that women really, really pee, but indirectly he learned that whatever happens in the bathroom business is very different between the male and female sexes. From bathroom noises, he learned one gender's body functions

His contemplations will be something along the lines of, *My parents are unreliable—so never, never, never count on them for this sex stuff.*

Contrary to parental hope that sex education is related to swimming sperm doing the backstroke in fallopian tubes, real sex involves (no, *requires)* bodies to *function.*

And when issues such as shame and embarrassment are communicated about body function, the connection with sexual disrespect is clear.

And that probably happens because of so many female water buffaloes hanging around American bathrooms with the great pretending that female bodies don't work.

are more respectful and the other gender's body workings are more embarrassing. And when issues such as shame and embarrassment are communicated about body function, the connection with sexual disrespect is clear.

BOY BATHROOM BUSINESS?

It seems that the functioning of bodies in most families appears much more acceptable for boys than for girls even when normal regular things happen in normal, regular households. There is no real need for girls to pee quietly or to sound like hydropower plants every time they urinate but somehow that message is communicated to the female gender. The result is that it just seems more acceptable for boys to have body functions such as passing gas, yet many a teenage boy would strongly protest to someone suggesting the same body function for the opposite sex, proudly proclaiming, "girls just don't fart." And that probably happens because of so many female water buffaloes hanging around American bathrooms with the great pretending that female bodies don't work. So in this commandment's two-step, what does this pretend-our-bodies-don't-work message communicate to children, and what is the window of opportunity when it opens for those parents who want to teach sexual respect?

DREAD AND DREAM

Most parents dread the thought of an unwanted pregnancy for their children, yet most parents also dream about having grandchildren. Yet this very important project of fulfilling dreams of wanted and timed grandchildren is unfortunately not actively taught. Rather, it seems that most parents believe or hope that FORTY-FIVE minutes with Nurse Ratchet will help their daughters make responsible decisions about giving even one single sperm, one swimming chance, at even one of her eggs. But there's more. Most parents fail to see the messages that are being communicated to their daughters in body-function-household-hummings that screams that their dread will come before their dream.

SHAME GAME

In order for daughter to make responsible sexual decisions about her reproductive system that may bring the dreams, she must value her body and her body's functioning. And the valuing is not about having the best boobs on the rally squad. It is about respecting sexual decision-making and sexual reproduction. For sure, the one thing old Nurse Ratchet was right about has to do with the importance of those dreaded pads, since the gateway to the dreaming, or the dreading, about pregnancy has to do with menstruation. When girls are taught directly or indirectly that menstruation is shameful, the respectful part is usually lost. Phrases such as *the curse, she's on the rag, or the Red Fairy has kicked her in the crotch* are powerful forms of communication to girls about their body functions that actually should (in a sexually respectful context) be coveted and celebrated. Sometimes daughters simply learn menstruation shame as a result of the Kotex being secreted away, forbidden from the more comfortable spot in the bathroom next to the toothpaste. And many times it is the male units in the family who do the communicating about this shame, which takes up a huge space on the sexual respect clipboard.

SUPER SHAME

Mom has the flu and Dad is reluctantly in charge of securing her menstruation supplies and getting the kids out of the house so she can catch a much-needed nap. In the Super Saver store, even though he has only one item on his list, Dad nervously fills his cart with unnecessary items in preparation for concealing his eventual procurement of ***Super Tampax***. In his cart goes several camouflage purchases, much to the confusion of the children, who only add to Dad's panic when they question the need for two very tall sacks of barbecue briquettes in the middle of a January snow blizzard. After some fussing, the briquettes are returned to the shelf as Dad replaces them with also-very-tall packages of paper towels that will serve as substituted masquerade materials.

The girls watch as Dad strategically darts in and out of various aisles with what seems like an unplanned, but nonetheless frantic, mission. They watch his frenzied sleuthing in and out of shopping areas seemingly searching for something in the potted plants, pot scrubbers, and deli potato salad, but looking for what, they aren't sure. Finally Dad, after bobbing in and out of one section or another, for what seemed like hours, finds the perfect moment and zips into the dreaded *feminine hygiene* section, finally making his heist. With great expertise, and at precisely the time when no one else is in the section, Dad swipes up the needed package of Tampax Supers. Into the camouflage system they go, carefully hidden between the super-size paper towels and the briquettes that Dad had secreted back into the cart when the children weren't looking.

All is well for stage one of the burglary, except as Dad begins his sleuthing to find the best checkout section, his four-year-old sitting in the shopping cart seat begins to fondle the Super Tampax box, much to Dad's horror. Quick on his feet, Dad distracts her with a promise of candy treats, which both the seven-year-old and the nine-year-old know Mom would never allow them to have before lunch. They also notice that not only do they get forbidden treats if they just keep their hands off the mysterious item, but Dad seems obsessed with choosing VERY LARGE boxes of candy that provide more

And many times it is the male units in the family who do the communicating about this shame, which takes up a huge space on the sexual respect clipboard.

Dad chooses her specifically as she appears to be the kind of person who would not be fazed if her panties fell off in the fruit section of the Super Saver grocery store. Good choice!

camouflage for his tiny, but extremely powerful ***Supers***—secreted away, underneath the piles.

They are confused about some things, but for sure they know that Dad's sweating brow is just as remarkable as his promises of forbidden treats. The thinking wheels are turning for the female children, and the wheels of Dad's cart are also turning toward the most difficult part of the Super-Saver-Super-Tampax mission, which is the dreaded checkout.

Dad didn't choose his checkout line haphazardly, settling on a middle-aged woman, rough in appearance, and seeming to be methodically enduring her day in the most far away checkout line, commonly used for those with garden purchases six months previous. Dad chooses her specifically as she appears to be the kind of person who would not be fazed if her panties fell off in the fruit section of the Super Saver grocery store. Good choice! Dad approaches this no-nonsense appearing woman and begins to carefully place his checkout items on the conveyor belt, hoping against all hope that Mom's Supers can slip by, unnoticed by the checker who Dad fantasizes has a name something like *Brunhilda.*

In the checkout process the children try to help as they usually do with Mom, but as they attempt to shuffle the purchased items onto the conveyor belt, they are roughly pushed aside by brow-sweating Dad, who takes over and takes great care in placing the Tampax between the paper towels, the charcoal briquettes and the VERY LARGE packages of forbidden candy treats. The children notice Dad's trembling fingers compared to Brunhilda's methodical shuffle through the checkout process. They don't exactly know what is happening to their usually-calm-collected-Dad but they know to pay attention because this whole Dad-terrorized thing seems to be a very big deal. They watch as things go reasonably well until, to Dad's panic, Brunhilda experiences difficulty with the scanner and the Supers. In excruciating embarrassment, Dad watches as she runs the Tampax box across the uncooperative scanner, one, two, three, four, five, and six times. Without looking at Dad's bright purple face, Brunhilda grabs the loud speaker and blurts out to all the Super Saver shoppers: "Price check on Tampax, SUPER SIZE, 48 count!"

In Dad's moment of unbelievable anxiety, he is quite convinced that there are likely no less than 7,000 shoppers peering upon his purchase of feminine hygiene products. Flashing before Dad's mind is the horror of Pastor Pickings lurking around the corner and seeing Dad's shameful procurement. Images of his favorite Aunt Bessie or his Boy Scout Troop, also peering upon his purchases, tip-toe through his panicked mind. The wait is excruciatingly painful as Brunhilda continues to wait for the price check and the children continue to watch Dad's terror. In the price-check wait it seems to Dad that Brunhilda's chewing on her toothpick speeds up, ever-so-subtly.

Finally, from far back in the store, a question for Brunhilda booms back from the loud speaker in response to the quest for a price to satisfy her waiting scanner. The question was impregnating: "Do you want the push-in or the pound-in type?" It came from the store employee who has obviously mistaken the word *Tampax* for *thumbtacks,* and it is devastating to Dad. The anxiety was just too much. He is unable to continue with his carefully chosen Brunhilda, and he is unable to survive her response to the thinking-it-was-thumbtacks store employee. Dad scoops up the horrified children and runs hysterically from the Super Saver, leaving Brunhilda with the *Tampax/thumbtacks* finally ready for Mr. Scanner.

Now if Dad wears his rational hat instead of his purple face of embarrassment about female body functions, he must concede that half of the world's human population menstruate, and without Mom's ovulation cycle working perfectly, the three kiddos that Dad dearly loves wouldn't be a reality. But for Dad to have purchased the products that make the whole business of menstruation function is unbearable for him, especially if those Super Tampax get mixed up with thumbtacks. But the important thing concerning the Second Commandment of communication is that with the Super Saver debacle, the teaching sexual respect moment arrived and Dad should have recognized it as an opportunity (step one) and then used the Super Saver shopping as a window of opportunity to communicate (step two). That is, of course, unless Dad really wants his *dreads* rather than his *dreams* about grandchildren.

TWO-STEPPING TAMPAX

Following this Second Commandment of communication, Dad needs the two-step in his thinking and in his actions when the Super Saver window of opportunity opened. First, Dad needs to understand what the kiddos might learn from his sweating brow and planted, unnecessary winter briquettes. He has to figure out that his daughters are learning a lot about female body functions with his frenzy. So how could Dad rewind, check the sexual information level of his astonished daughters, open the window of opportunity and then teach?

THE DREAM WINDOW

It is probably too much to ask Dad to change careers and plan to become a gynecologist, but with a little Second Commandment reminder, he could remember how much he wants his daughters to make sexually respectful decisions in order to assure him the dream of planned grandchildren. He must also recognize that the menstruation situation unfolding between the Briquettes and not-allowed Baby Ruth candy bars is a beautiful window of opportunity for teaching sexual respect. Dad isn't likely to whip out a podium in the Super Saver parking lot and give a motivational speech on the *Joys of Tampax Selection.* But if Dad and Mom wanted

The question was impregnating: "Do you want the push-in or the pound-in type?"

Now if Dad wears his rational hat instead of his purple face of embarrassment about female body functions, he must concede that half of the world's human population menstruate, and without Mom's ovulation cycle working perfectly, the three kiddos that Dad dearly loves wouldn't be a reality.

If parents don't seize the window, then the daughters will learn a lot about Dad's sweating brow with the Super Tam/Thumb/pax debacle, sadly figuring out that the menstruation process is shameful and therefore, why should they treasure it, protect it, or make sexually respectful decisions about it?

Why not give it away if it is so disgusting? **is the sad thinking for many girls.**

to do better, and instill a sense of pride for respectful sexual decisions, the answer is communication. The solution and drive toward the dream is to talk to children, not once, but often—even at the Super Saver. If parents don't seize the window, then the daughters will learn a lot about Dad's sweating brow with the Super Tam/Thumb/pax debacle, sadly figuring out that the menstruation process is shameful and therefore, why should they treasure it, protect it, or make sexually respectful decisions about it?

BUFFALOES AND BRUNHILDA

In reality, there isn't much difference in the deadly nature of Dad's embarrassment with sneaking through the checkout line of Brunhilda and the amazed man who grew up with peeing female water buffaloes. The female who can't let anyone know she urinates and who can't imagine Dad surviving the purchase of Mom's Supers will devalue her own sexuality in the back seat of the Chevrolet, providing more chance of dreads than dreams for her parents. *Why not give it away if it is so disgusting?* becomes the sad thinking for many girls. But there is more negative learning among the sexes. If Dad's seven and nine-year-old females see their male role model (Dad) unable to even acknowledge menstruation, then in choosing their male partners, body function appreciation (respect, actually) will not be a priority either. In reality, Dad probably dreams of his daughters choosing a partner that will value and respect their bodies and all their body workings, yet he is demonstrating the exact opposite through his Super Saver embarrassment which results in a missed window of opportunity for teaching respect.

MENSTRUATION MILESTONE

But if Dad was the opposite, carefully planning for his *dreams* to avoid his *dreads,* he would use the shopping trip to communicate to his daughters that someday they would need *Supers* and that he would be in charge of the celebration honoring that menstruation milestone. He would have seen the shopping mission as an opportunity to teach. Mom had the flu, Dad had a list, and the girls had an opportunity to learn something, which completes Step One of the communication commandment—figuring out what they are already learning. Then, in Step Two, the Super Saver window opened and could have been used to communicate his dream for their sexually respectful futures.

PLAYING THE PERCENTAGES

To make the communication commandment effective, the first step of trying to figure out what is already being communicated requires a peek at the percentages between verbal and non-verbal information children already receive about sex. Whether it is the glum-faced fifth graders listening to Nurse Ratchet or the curious kiddos of Dad listening to him explain why extravagant piles of candy are necessary to build a fortress around Mom's tiny package of Super Tam/Thumbtax. It is the non-verbal messages from adults to children that scream the loudest—providing most of the communication.

Timmie, while chomping on his after-school-oatmeal-cookie-snack, distractedly asks Mom, "Where did I come from?" For Mom, the moment of sexual communication has arrived, since she and her husband had always believed *if they have any questions, we will be there.* Scouring the sink and chopping the walnuts is easily forgotten as Mom marches Timmie into Daddy's den for the answering. There she retrieves two items, the *Encyclopedia Britannica* letters *RST*—carefully marked in the "R" section (highlighting *reproduction),* and secondly, her carefully cataloged notes from Dr. Fillemup's *Birds and Bees Business* talk show.

Before Mom opens the book to her own version of fallopian-tube-Big-Horned-Sheep drawing, she checks her notes from Dr. Fillemup about making eye contact, sitting comfortably across from the child/victim and avoiding disruptions. She quickly calculates that Timmie's sister won't be home from soccer practice for at least thirty minutes and that she can position herself across the desk from Timmie to guarantee everything else on the one-big-talk instruction note from her beloved talk show host. So all is set.

With the expertise of a college professor, the no-nonsense demeanor of Nurse Ratchet, and tips and technique from Dr. Fillemup, she trudges ahead with a Reproduction 101 lecture. She doesn't have a podium or separate flip charts, but she has a pointer of sorts, inadvertently using the *Heaven Help Us* pen she accidently heisted from the local Christian bookstore. And after a breathless, but nonetheless brilliant, twenty-minute reproduction presentation from Mom, Timmie walks away muttering to himself, "That's funny, Kevin came from Kansas!"

And as Mom puts away her lecture materials, she feels smug and she should, at least as far as her words were concerned. But in playing the percentages, Mom is the big loser. What Timmie learned from professor Mom was about 80 percent non-verbal and the lesson wasn't pretty. He learned that unless he wants a lecture, a sweating-brow mother, or being cornered in Daddy's den with a funny-looking moose drawing, he better not ask Mom any questions. Mom's desire to be in charge of Timmie's sex education went out the window because she didn't recognize the window that opened for communication with Timmie, and she didn't understand the percentages of power between her words and her non-verbal and *very loud* messages.

It is the non-verbal messages from adults to children that scream the loudest—providing most of the communication.

DYNAMICS OF DIALOGUE

Mom's reproduction lecture is no more helpful than Nurse Ratchet's stiff-lipped dissertation. Her words were basically lost, while her body language and demeanor provided

With the expertise of a college professor, the no nonsense demeanor of Nurse Ratchet, and tips and technique from Dr. Fillemup, she trudges ahead with a Reproduction 101 lecture.

He learned that unless he wants a lecture, a sweating-brow mother, or being cornered in Daddy's den with a funny-looking moose drawing, he better not ask Mom any questions.

the message. Timmie really wanted to know where he came from because his new friend at school just moved from Kansas. If Mom would have seen his question as an open window and then used a dialogue, things might have been different. And lectures are very different than a dialogue.

Kobe Bryant, a popular national basketball player and hero to many basketball-bound boys, was arrested and charged with sexual assault in Colorado, even though he resided in California, home to his team, the Los Angeles Lakers. Media coverage was profound, as were opinions about his guilt or innocence, with most sports fans leaning toward "not guilty" because *he was such a good basketball player*. This thinking inadvertently suggested that real rapists probably play basketball with the grace of walruses, nothing like the three-point shooter, Mr. Bryant. With the media attention, sports fans everywhere became experts on sex offender typology.

One father interviewed on a national sports talk show lamented the Kobe Bryant situation as it pertained to his task of being in charge of his twelve-year-old son's sex education. Dad was sad, whining to the talk show host about the whole mess. Was he upset that either a young woman had been raped or that a young man had been unjustly accused of rape? No. He was upset because his twelve-year-old son, a fan of Kobe Bryant, had been exposed to information about sex and, of course, Dad wanted to be *the first to talk with his son* about such matters. Dad lamented that his chance to be the first to communicate with his child was thwarted because of the case. Of course, Dad didn't take into account that if his son watches basketball on television, he is already learning about babes and Budweisers, as well as what to do with a 36-hour erection if the Viagra dose gets a little out of whack.

WANDERING WINDOW?

Beyond the absurdity that Son doesn't know anything about sex and that he will be thrilled for Professor Dad to enlighten him, there is something else about wandering windows for talking to children about sex. The Kobe Bryant case should have been considered a window of opportunity for every Dad in America who wanted to raise a sexually respectful son. But with the open window from the Kobe Bryant case, Dad doesn't flip charts or with white knuckles, clasp his pointer. He needs a *dialogue* and in line with the first step of the communication commandment, he needs to first figure out what is already being communicated to his son about the Kobe Bryant debacle.

With dialogue in hand, the question is, "Son, what do you know about sexual assault? Son, what does rape mean?" Because it is with a question that a dialogue begins, and professors Mom and Dad's lecture with their pointer and podium presentations, ends. And for the basketball enthusiasts, what better chance to open a dialogue than talking about sexual disrespect accusation with a sports hero?

RULES FOR KITCHEN COMMUNICATION

In the kitchen, Mom serves oatmeal cookies and milk to her daughter Jessica who has recently returned from an ordinary day in third grade.

"How was your day?" Mom asks as daughter smacks away at the tasty morsels.

"Great Mom," she mumbles. "It was great."

Mom, a master of two-stepping communication with her children, automatically continues the discussion, even though she is somewhat distracted as she puts away four packages of on-sale macaroni and cheese.

"What were some of the great things that happened, Sweetie?" Mom inquires.

Jessica replies, "Well, we poked a hole in the boys' bathroom wall and we were watching them pee!" There it was, hanging in the air like a pregnant balloon—sexual disrespect.

Mom's first thought is to rip the lips off her daughter or shriek, "Oh, my God, how could you do that?" forgetting the podium and pointers, jumping into a not-so-well-planned tirade about the sins of sexual deviancy through voyeurism. Another Mother would have given Jessica a harsh admonition, perhaps followed by a severe punishment, after Mom and Dad have a late night marathon discussion about canceling Jessica's college fund, enrolling her in an all-girls Catholic school, and grounding her until her 39th birthday. But not for Jessica's mom, the diva of dialogue.

For this card-carrying-communicating Mom, no matter how horrified she is at Jessica's peeping, she sees the window of opportunity open and it is time for her to step in with a conversation—which requires an equal dialogue. She says to herself, *The most important thing is that Jessica told me about the hole. I can handle everything about patching up the hole and stopping the peeping later, but for now, I want to talk. So I must remember the Two-Sentence rule.*

TWO SENTENCE RULE

Mom wants a dialogue about peeping on the boys, but beyond that, she wants Jessica to come back to her with the next sexual escapade that is common among children but usually unknown to parents. And the only way Mom will really be in charge of Jessica's sex education is to remember—COMMUNICATION is more important than naked boys or patching plaster holes. Too often parents respond to the sexual behavior of children, bringing on the lecture and in doing so, slam shut the window of opportunity.

But not this proactive Mom. She is not happy with Jessica's peeping prank, but she thinks beyond the bathroom wall hole into the next opportunity for sexual communication. So her first sentence in the dialogue with Jessica is to honor the next communication opportunity. She bites her truth tongue and says, "I'm glad you told me, honey." And with that courageous statement, the window stays open regardless of Jessica's errant ways of peeping on the unsuspecting boys.

Was he upset that either a young woman had been raped or that a young man had been unjustly accused of rape? No.

The Kobe Bryant case should have been considered a window of opportunity for every Dad in America who wanted to raise a sexually respectful son.

And the only way Mom will really be in charge of Jessica's sex education is to remember—the COMMUNICATION is more important than naked boys or patching plaster holes.

So after thanking Jessica for the window, Mom only has one more sentence if she follows the two-sentence rule. In order to keep the conversation going, that second sentence must be a question so that Jessica can join the dialogue dance. But the question from Mom shouldn't be "Why on earth are you doing that nasty stuff?" or "Do you have any idea what this will do to my chance of being PTA president?" Those questions will communicate to Jessica that Mommy is mad and she best do whatever she can to get out of this problem, starting with ending the discussion. Instead, the wise mother finds a question that will further the dialogue, such as, "How big is the hole, honey?" And with her two-sentence rule in hand, once Jessica answers, Mom only has two new ones—a statement to continue the dialogue and then a question. That is the art of communication with children—especially about sex.

OH NO NONSENSE

Unless children grow up in cardboard boxes in the backyard, they will, in the normal world, try out sexual things. Usually these pesky behaviors are less about sexual deviancy and more about putting tidbits of sexual information together as explained in the First Commandment. And when children exhibit these embarrassing and sometimes upsetting behaviors, it is a dialogue—an avenue of communication that is most important for parents who want to be in charge of their children's sexual education. In the 80/20 percent split, with non verbal messages being the most powerful, it is clear that parents who communicate rather than *panic and pucker* will really be in charge of the ongoing sexuality of the kiddos. And morality doesn't have to be sacrificed for parents who focus on the communication factor rather than the ***Oh, No*** types of sexual behavior of children.

Jessica needs to earn the money to buy the plaster for patching the hole, she needs to apologize to the principal for her behavior, and for sure, she needs to suffer a little indignation. But most importantly, she needs parents who will talk to her, guide her, and help her reroute her curiosity. And that can only happen with a dialogue through communication that is balanced and organized by parents who are willing to give up their need to be powerful and, of course, brilliant when it comes to talking about sex.

PURPLE PERCENTAGES/ABANDON BRILLIANCE

If the percentages suggest children learn more from the non-verbal messages in sex education than they do from the words, what do parents do with their purple faces of embarrassment? Well, the answer lies with the same two-step process of the Second Commandment. The first step is to figure out that kids observe and learn from their parent's purple faces, so smart parents will use their kiddo's observations as a focus for dialogue. But this takes courage for parents to abandon their brilliance, especially when it comes to sex.

Normally, parents want to consider themselves smarter than their children and rightly so. There is pressure on Moms and Dads to know everything and to impart that wisdom to the wee ones with grand parental power. But as children get older, good parents will not be afraid to relinquish their so-sought-after brilliance and recognize that the kids quickly catch up and sometimes pass adults in various categories of knowledge. So parents who want to appreciate and use the Second Commandment steps of communication should view their purple face of embarrassment, or their incompetence in being comfortable in sexual discussions, as a breeding ground for success in raising sexually respectful children.

BRILLIANT IGNORANCE

Dad is armed with every skill possible in following the Second Commandment of *Thou Shalt Communicate*. At the top of his checklist are the TWOS—two steps and two sentences. In his two steps, he first recognizes that his Son, Aaron, is learning a great deal from Dad's embarrassment about sexual matters and in taking the second step, Dad sees his purple face as an open window of opportunity for educating Aaron—not in spite of Dad's anxiety, but *because* of it. Of course Dad knows he must have a dialogue with Aaron, never getting more than two sentences ahead of his Son in this sexual discussion. And finally, especially since Aaron is a teenager, Dad knows that by abandoning his own brilliance, giving up his position of authority, feigning ignorance on how to do things right, the communication door will open even wider for adolescent Aaron, giving him a free pass down the path to sexual respect.

With his ego in his back pocket, Dad approaches Aaron and says, "You know Aaron, your little Sister just doesn't understand the proper words for her private body parts. I don't know how to talk with her and it is embarrassing for me and your Mother (*notice how Dad wants to include Mom in abandoning brilliance*) to talk with her, so I hope you could help with some of this. She needs to have a lot of respect for her private body. She needs to learn the word *vagina* for her inside private parts. And, of course, she needs to respect the word *vulva* for the outside private parts. I want your little Sister to make important decisions about her privacy, and so she needs to begin learning this respectful stuff right away. I wonder if you could help me teach her the rules, you know, in a positive way."

Now even if Aaron doesn't talk to his Sister about her vagina, that wasn't the point. It is Aaron who received a respectful (and powerful) message from Dad in his *unpowerful* (and purple-faced) approach to his son. And in the best of family situations, older brothers would be in a position to teach and protect the privacy of

And with her two-sentence rule in hand, once Jessica answers, Mom only has two new ones—a statement to continue the dialogue and then a question. That is the art of communication with children—especially about sex.

Dad knows that by abandoning his own brilliance, giving up his position of authority, feigning ignorance on how to do things right, the communication door will open even wider for adolescent Aaron, giving him a free pass down the path to sexual respect.

their younger sisters. In sexually healthy families, EVERYONE works for the same goal of pride and privacy, and helping older children become the *family touching teachers* only furthers this honorable goal of sexual respect.

PREVENTION PODIUM

And speaking of safety, a significant category in the *don't* basket of typical (and negative) sex education for children pertains to preventing sexual abuse. It is an honorable mission, but most prevention program efforts discount the issue of communication and wholeheartedly support the lecture-with-podium business.

Beyond lessons about swimming sperm, many parents, in concert with school districts, opt for a sex education program involving sexual abuse prevention. It seems easier to teach children about what might happen *to them* rather than thinking about what they *might do* on their own. And of course, the negative in the *don't dance* is really, really important in preventing the pouncing of perverts from behind the park bushes. Or so most adults hope. But in appreciation of the first step in the communication commandment, which is to figure out what children are already learning from sexual information, careful consideration must be made for the way prevention programs are implemented and what is really communicated to the kidlets in these prevention efforts.

Rarely are school faculty given guidance or the go-ahead for doing sexual abuse prevention on their own—*it is just too messy, all that smut,* most school folks decide. So they believe a better plan is to bring in a *foreigner* from far away to talk to the kids about this tough stuff of sexual abuse. The message they want to communicate is that sexual abuse is *out there somewhere else,* so a call is often made to the local child abuse center for securing the services of an expert to deliver the yearly talk about the Snidely Whiplash guys in the park shrubbery. The administration wants to do the right thing (usually) to keep the kiddos from being preyed upon by predators, but they also have that pesky child abuse reporting requirement that could be messy if the kiddos start telling their teachers at the drinking fountain line about what Uncle Bert did at the family Easter egg hunt.

But the message to children when a foreign person comes to the school to provide sexual abuse prevention education, is something else and it is loud and clear—at least to people doing the two-step in the second commandment about communication. The real message to the kiddos is that *once a year the communication door opens, and when the good touch, bad touch, teaching hour ends—it is over—that is, until next year.*

In a small rural school district, the prevention specialist from the urban area finally arrived. It was her tenth year of providing some type of sexual abuse education to the first through eighth grades. She was familiar with the school, with the faculty, and with the children—many of whom had heard her lesson for each year since their first grade enrollment. For each classroom, she made a presentation about prevention, simple of course for the little ones, getting more sophisticated as she moved to the higher grades. The children knew her and the experience had been generally positive for the previous nine years.

But in this tenth year, something unusual happened in the fifth grade filled with children who had already heard her yearly message on four previous occasions. As she walked into the familiar classroom, a blonde-haired girl handed her a note written in flaring aqua-felt-tipped pen.

"What is sex? If it is putting the boy's thing in the girl's thing, isn't it the biggest, baddest sin of all?"

Quick on her feet, the prevention specialist recognized the note as a cry for help and after the session ended, the girl was asked careful questions about the possibility of sexual abuse. Sure enough, she reported being sexually abused in her home by both her father and her grandfather. Authorities were contacted and the case was passed on to the legal folks. The next morning, the prevention specialist attempted closure with the child, so after retrieving a Gatorade from the hallway vending machine, they chatted.

"You did a good job of helping me understand what kind of touching trouble was happening to you at home. What made you decide to give up your secret today?" asked the specialist, hoping her comments and conversation would help in the child's healing. But the answer was shocking and pertinent to understanding the true message communicated to children with a once-a-year presentation from the "foreigner."

The child answered honestly, saying, "I had to tell today, because I didn't know if I could wait a whole *nuther* year for you to come back."

There it is—the message. *Once a year, someone is here for you. Once a year the out-of-town foreigner will visit so you will have someone who can talk to you about sex. But during the rest of the year, you are on your own.* The tragedy and travesty of communication is revisited.

In sexually healthy families, EVERYONE works for the same goal of pride and privacy, and helping older children become the *family touching teachers* only furthers this honorable goal of sexual respect.

RUDE REALITY FROM SEX OFFENDERS

And speaking of prevention, it is the barometer of communication between children and their parents that just may be the answer to the ultimate prevention of sexual abuse. Sex offenders are wise and competent people who know how to pick certain children to offend. Their choices are neither random nor haphazard. Rarely are children offended in a

"What is sex? If it is putting boy's thing in the girl's thing, isn't it the biggest, baddest sin of all?"

There it is—the message. *Once a year, someone is here for you. Once a year the out-of-town foreigner will visit so you will have someone who can talk to you about sex. But during the rest of the year, you are on your own.* The tragedy and travesty of communication is revisited.

single incident when someone attacks from a park bush. Most children are molested more than once by someone in the life circle of the victim, which requires secrecy in order for offenders to be successful. With confidence, sex offenders carefully choose children, and the best target is a child who has no one to talk to, who has no avenues of communication with protective adults.

One sex offender pontificated to his therapist, "You know, there are two kinds of children to pick for sex. First, you can choose the kids who are struggling, the kids who don't have people caring for them, because they won't have anyone to talk to about what is happening. Those kids are good victims because even if they do tell, most people won't believe them because they have so many problems. But also, even if adults do believe these messed up kids, they just won't care because the children are so troubled." But this savvy offender had more to say.

"But the best kind of kid to molest are the ones who come from the perfect families, where the parents are so perfect, that nothing about sex is ever, or could ever, be mentioned. Kids from the uppity families, where no one talks about sex, are the best victims, because these kids couldn't possibly talk to their parents about this nasty stuff. It doesn't take much effort to get these kids to keep it all a secret, because they would never disappoint their parents by bringing up stuff that the kids know the parents couldn't talk about."

But that wasn't all he had to say about the vulnerability of children. He went on.

"For myself, as a teacher, I always voted against the sex education program efforts. I did everything I could to keep anyone from suggesting that sex should be talked about. The more closed the communication, the easier it is to engage these kids and keep everything a secret. And that is the truth."

Sex Fairy Clipboard

- Remember that children learn about sex every day, in many ways. The idea of one big talk is just about as smart as considering raising children in cardboard boxes in the backyard to protect them from sexual information.

- Remember that to teach morality and sexual respect is a good thing, but that doesn't happen by omitting things. It happens by communication, by talking, by guiding—just as earnestly as raising a child to be Methodist, Mormon or Muslim.

- Remember to consider what is already being communicated to children about such things as missing body parts on dolls or giving them silly names for their genitalia. Taking control means using communication—ongoing and all the time about everything connected to sexual respect.

- Remember that to be successful in controlling children's sexual information, the two-step must occur. First, figure out what the kiddos are already learning, then use the opportunity or situation for communicating and teaching.

- Remember that children live in a very sexual world and they will learn from omissions. They will learn to get excited about the forbidden, which is a key to being a sexually disrespectful person.

- Remember, children learn a great deal about sexual respect or disrespect by the way body functions are handled within families. And one of the most important things in preventing unwanted pregnancies is to avoid the shame of body functions and to celebrate the milestones of puberty. And that respectful body function communication should involve both boys and girls—both Moms and Dads.

- Remember, about eighty percent of what children learn from their parents' typical attempts to talk to them about sex is non-verbal. And that is why the dialogue—using the two-sentence rule—is the key to success in raising sexually respectful children.

Kids from the uppity families, where no one talks about sex, are the best victims, because these kids couldn't possibly talk to their parents about this nasty stuff.

Chapter 6

Third Commandment
Thou Shalt
Teach Logic

CHAPTER 6 - THIRD COMMANDMENT THOU SHALT TEACH LOGIC

As usual, they shuffled into the auditorium for the dreaded, but necessary district meeting. It was irritating for the high school teachers when so many elementary school folks migrated to the coveted front seats, suggesting they planned to take over. And they had a right to be miffed. After all, this meeting would determine the curriculum for *only* grades 9 through 12 and the secondary staff wasn't so sure the teachers for the little ones should put their two cents into the *hot topic* decision-making process.

"What do they know about challenges facing high school kids?" some of them griped as they settled for fifth and sixth row seats.

The mood was cranky and rightly so, considering the disastrous curriculum planning meeting they had only recently attended.

It had been about three weeks since the secondary staff tried to finalize the school district's sex education curriculum, but things got so heated that nothing was settled and for sure, nothing had cooled down. They had gotten off to a rough start when the superintendent, Mr. Bickersly, gave them the bad news about how many of the high school students were, as he so delicately put it, *doing it*. And speaking of *doing*—that was the task for the curriculum meeting—to figure out *what to do about the doing*. So right away the lines were drawn and the warring factions just about came to blows as the conflict and combat ended up being pretty nasty. Heading up one side was the ABSTINENCE-ONLY group that was eventually dubbed the OATs—*Only Abstinence Teaching,* by several in the meeting. Actually they liked the sound of the title, since it had such a wholesome sound—***OATs***. These folks had a narrow agenda with only one goal for the high schoolers—*don't do it*.

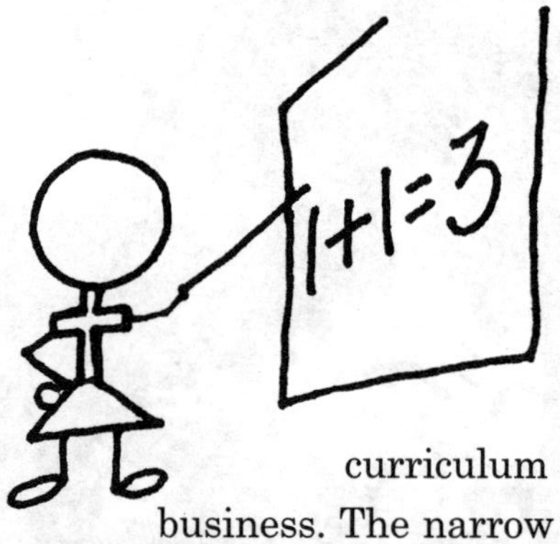

On the opposite side from the wholesome-sounding OATS was the *comprehensive sex education* group who wanted a smorgasbord of curriculum about the *doing it* business. The narrow focus of ABSTINENCE-ONLY was just too pinched and rigid they thought, so they adopted the name of NATs—*No Abstinence Teaching*. Their agenda was basically, *if they are already doing it, we must get the doing safe*. So just a few weeks ago the OATs and the NATs were going at it, fuming and fussing about what to do about *the doing* of the high school kiddos.

The OATs, of course, had the extra weapon in the war from the Federal Government, which was certainly attractive to the district's bean counters as they were all about the big bucks. The government, it seemed, really, really liked the ABSTINENCE-ONLY focus, and for the last five years they had handed out more than 600 million dollars to other school districts who would go along with the OAT philosophy. Whether or not those in the accounting office really liked the narrow focus of ***just don't*** didn't seem to matter, because the ABSTINENCE-ONLY approach just made sense when they looked at the black and red columns in the district budgeting business. Being an OAT cheerleader was right there in the number-crunching for the district bean counters.

But the OAT focus was narrow, and the big bucks from the Feds weren't without strings attached. The government had their eight education points (must ***do's,*** actually), which formulated the bible for the OAT program, and which absolutely, positively had to be taught with *no going outside the lines*. So, the OAT approach was attractive for those with a flair for the rigid and for bean counting, giving the OAT contingency a lot of support with few questions asked.

But on the other side of the battle were the NATs, who were against the ABSTINENCE-ONLY approach and they didn't give one rip about the big bucks offered by the government, especially if only eight points made up the curriculum. Some of the OATs called the NATs (secretly, of course) liberal hippie types who were stuck back in the 1960s in the days of free love and really cheap sex. There were rumors that some of the NATs were *flower children* who attended the famous Woodstock concert long ago, but usually those were just the snide comments made by a few in the more-rigid OAT group. Regardless of what they did in their youths, the NATs were very worried about the kids who they thought needed more than eight silly points put together by a bunch of tight-lipped government policy pundits.

The NATs also fussed that the ABSTINENCE- ONLY approach was way, way, too narrow and they wanted a comprehensive program teaching lots of different things to the *doing it* kids. Their curriculum choice was all about giving the high school kids more tools to get things that were out of control, back in control. But the OATs thought just the opposite, suggesting that if the kids had more information, they would be *doing* their *doing* a whole lot more, which was pretty frightening to them. The NATs and the OATs were very upset with each other and the battle had raged all day, at times getting pretty nasty.

But there was one thing that the OATs and the NATs were together on and that was the seriousness of the situation. Neither side questioned that for sure, the high school poopers were *doing it*, there was no mistake about that.

And even though most district folks had great pride in much of what the schools had to offer in the academics, sports and cultural exposure, in the sex department it seemed things for the teenagers were on the fast and dangerous track. Both groups knew they had to come up with a curriculum that would get all the *doing* stopped, but it was in the *how* to slow things down that the OATs and NATs so furiously battled with no resolution in sight as the last hour of the several-weeks-ago meeting had approached.

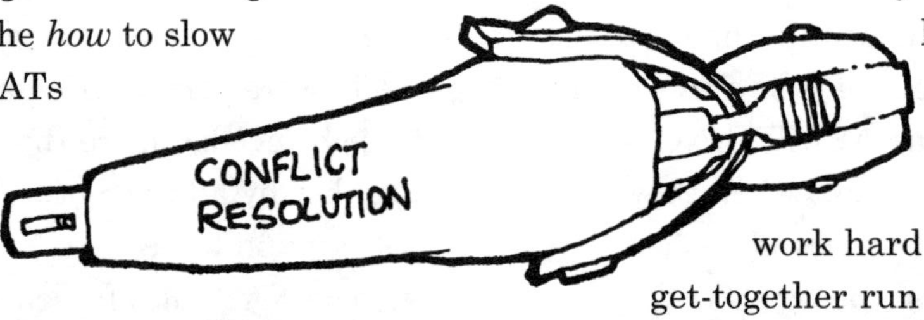

Typical of teacher types, the superintendent, Mr. Bickersly, chose a process to cool things down by using that old trick of scheduling another meeting. That made everyone feel a little better, especially when he suggested a closure group activity to prepare for the next get-together. First, he split the raging OATs and NATs in two groups, actually removing them from within speaking range of each other. He'd learned this technique in his *Conflict Resolution* class many years ago and he thought it just might work in cooling things down. He sent the OATs to the home economics room and he sent the NATs to the shop class area with both groups having a three-part assignment. First, they were each to choose a spokesperson to make a presentation representing their group's views at the next meeting. Secondly, they were to use a flip chart to list the main points about why their (OAT or NAT) approach was the only way to go. And thirdly, they were to use the same flip chart to list the reasons why the opposing side should be nixed. Mr. Bickersly gave them each forty-five minutes to complete the three step assignment, hoping they would be anxious to go home and therefore hurry with the process. But he knew in his government heart that things would heat back up at the next meeting, so he had to work hard to make the next district get-together run a little smoother.

And that is why they were all there in the auditorium now. The memo had been quite clear that this was a *district-wide* meeting about the sex education curriculum for the high school. He was proud in his problem-solving approach of bringing in everyone—just to diffuse the raging battles between the high school contingencies of OATs and NATs. He had actually contacted his college professor who had taught the Conflict Resolution class years ago and asked her advice. She told Mr. B. to "widen his base of options and avoid the two-party posturing."

Yes, he remembered the rule about how levelheaded minds are more likely to prevail if there is more on the table than just a black or white decision. So his agenda for the district-wide meeting was to have different departments or schools of study give their ideas about a sex education curriculum—just to increase the options. Even though he secretly knew it would probably come down to choosing between the OATs or the NATs, he believed more choices on the table were just the ticket to solving the *doing it* problem and getting him an early start on his weekend rafting trip with his golf buddies.

Mr. Bickersly began the meeting with what he called "housekeeping," telling everyone how long the meeting would last, reminding them to turn off their cell phones, and explaining to those unfamiliar with the high school where they could find the restrooms. Then he had what he called a *motivational moment,* and as they listened to the *Fighting Falcons* school song, he reminded them that in spite of the differences, everyone in the room really cared about the district's kids. And it was a particularly nice *motivational moment* when Mr. Bickersly playfully reminded everyone that none of them could possibly be in the educational business for the *big bucks,* so they must do the work because they cared about children. It was sweet, but it was also time.

With everyone feeling a little camaraderie, he jumped right to the touchy topic at hand, explaining that there were three points he wanted to make with the first requiring everyone to understand the statistics, which really meant accepting the sad facts that more than half of the high school kids were *doing it*—plain and simple. Refusing to entertain those who wished to fuss about the numbers, he plowed on to the second point, which required everyone to understand that there would be no discussion about IF a sex education program would be implemented for grades 9-12. The board of education was firm on that and it was a *done deal,* he said.

And the third issue he pontificated, was about how they would determine the goal or approach of the sex education curriculum. He explained it was not a three-ring circus as some in the audience had quipped, but a three-point plan. With his one, two and three-pronged outline smartly shown on a PowerPoint slide, but smelling of rigidity, the mood in the auditorium changed slightly to one of resistant crabbiness. Then, Mr. B. explained that he was confident bringing the district teachers together would solve the problem, because they were so bright and cared so much for children. These compliments seemed to tone down the cranky mood and with everyone feeling somewhat perky, he pushed forward.

Going over his notes from his old professor's advice and flipping to his next PowerPoint slide, he revealed to everyone his structured agenda for the meeting. First there would be presentations from several different departments, each with ideas for a sex education curriculum. He made it clear every school of study had something to offer and that during secret meetings during the last week he had heard the various presentations and he had been impressed with the possibilities. After pumping up anticipation for all the other options for curriculum choice, he just slipped in his comments that the OATs and NATs would also present the material they already prepared some time ago. Everyone tittered with this announcement, remembering how the last meeting ended. Then he announced that after all the presentations, there would be a paper and pencil vote as they left the meeting. He reminded everyone that no one would be allowed to leave early, but he assured them the meeting would adjourn promptly at 3:50 sharp, giving them plenty of time to fill out their ballots and vote on a curriculum before dismissal at 4 p.m.

Oh, he was so proud of himself, scheduling this meeting on a Friday, knowing everyone would be in a hurry to leave and hopefully discouraging anyone from wanting to hang around to argue. Mr. B. asked everyone to be considerate of the speakers who would only be allotted eight minutes for their presentations—not allowing any time for questions. Remembering how everything had been so tedious and contentious in the last meeting, he tried a little humor by showing them his timer whistle, borrowed from the P.E. teacher, Mr. Lotsweat, just to keep everyone on schedule. And then it began.

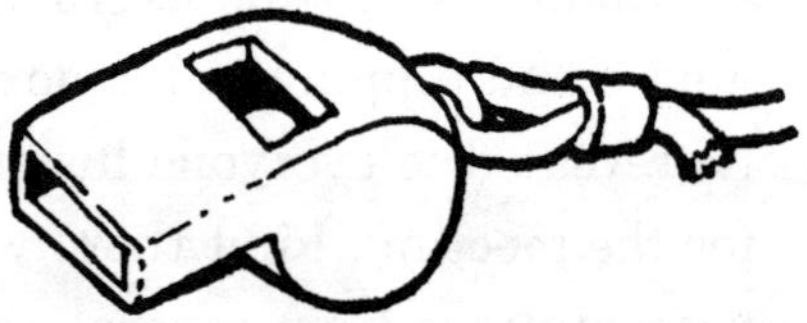

Mrs. Boxpill, the school nurse, and the science teacher, Mr. Tubetest, were together in their medical/science contribution to the curriculum debate. They teamed up for a somber, and at times disgusting presentation about the medical reasons the kids shouldn't *do it*. Of course the OATs, and their love affair with the nasty part of *doing it,* loved the *blood and guts* overheads. Mrs. Boxpill and Mr. Tubetest showed colorful pictures of weeping skin lesions as a result from Gonorrhea, dying AIDs patients in African hospitals, and the highly fertile nature of teenage girls presenting fallopian tubes as Welcome Wagon hostesses for traveling sperm. But, the NATs also liked the medical scientific stuff, supporting their contention that the kids needed lots of information about how to avoid these messy medical problems.

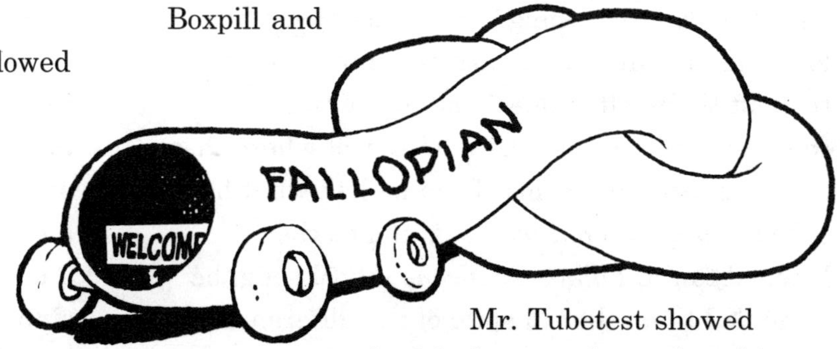

Halfway through the eight minutes, Mrs. Boxpill and Mr. Tubetest showed more graphic and in-color overheads that were fancy, but in reality, just a sophisticated version of the Nurse Ratchet lesson about the Big Horned Sheep. The two medical science folks were rather glum as they made the point that the fifth grade sex education presentation about swimming sperm obviously hadn't been successful if half of the high school students were now *doing it*. Although their eight minutes were up, Mrs. Boxpill just threw in the mix that better understanding of the ovulation cycle and how *fertile* those fallopian tubes tended to be just might help the girls put a damper on *doing it*. But, both she and Mr. Tubetest found no reason to include the boys in this type of curriculum. Their presentation ended on a disappointing note.

Next came Mrs. Fraud who reminded everyone that in about two more terms of night school she would be Dr. Fraud, and as a Ph.D. psychologist, there was an old and familiar ring to her name, which made her very proud. Many were familiar with her *deep-dish* psychological ideas that figuring out how the kids lined up in the cafeteria or what color of pen they used on a math test could bring the answer to any question. To Mrs. Fraud, there was always a deeper and hidden psychological meaning to everything and some faculty found her ideas tedious. *What on earth could she offer from a psychological perspective for a high school sex education curriculum?* they wondered.

She began with a poignant plea to consider the emotional side of the kids *doing it*. Almost-to-be-Dr. Fraud explained that diagnosing why so many teenagers are *doing it* would be a start, and then she suggested that psychological surveys be conducted on when and how they *do it*, just to gather a larger database. Eyebrows raised as she dramatically purported the need for group therapy for the fifty percent of kids who were feeling left out because they were not *doing it*, which was a new and interesting suggestion. She threw out terms like Transactional Analysis, finding the Inner Child, inducing hypnotic trances of not wanting to *do it*, and, of course, suggestions for positive peer culture groups implementing group discussion, feedback strategies, and rebirthing exercises for those kids who had already *done it* and wanted to start over. She spoke so fast that some of her ideas were lost to the confused and not-so-inclined-to-deep-dish-thinking folks. As she sat down, others thought the idea of putting sexually active kids in a group circle encouraging sexual disclosure and a group hug was just too much.

For the next presentation, Mrs. Skullnumb from the math department began her eight minutes. She had her flash cards of data and although she knew others might think it was a long shot to develop a sex education curriculum through the math department, she thought she could find a way. She began by explaining that perhaps other programs had failed because the approach was so *feeling*-based—messy, she thought, with such varying human responses of emotion and mood. Not so with math, she proudly explained. Using numbers avoided guesswork and fuss, she urged. *The mathematical answer to things never changed,* which she suggested was just what these kids might need. She really went out on a limb when she actually said that maybe the kiddos had received so much emotional nonsense about sex that they couldn't figure out (in a mathematical way) what to do. She wanted everyone to consider that with math's no-nonsense calculations, the kiddos might be motivated out of *doing it*. Then she really fired things up, turning to her fancy PowerPoint presentation with all the numbers.

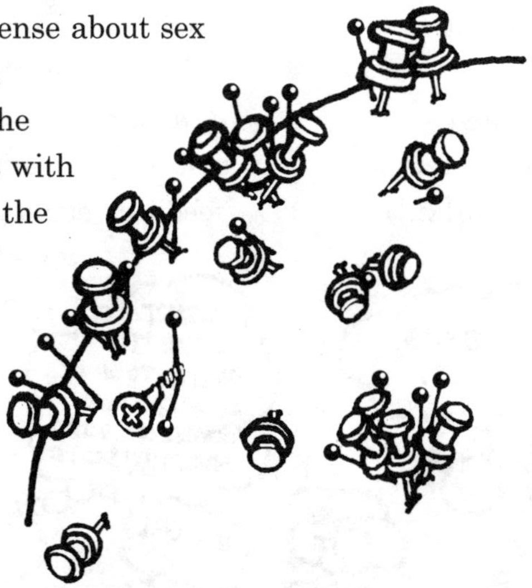

"Two Thirds (or as she preferred, 66 percent) **of High School Students Will Have Intercourse Before Their Junior Year,"** read the first slide—hanging in the air obtusely for those who had hoped it was only half. Mrs. Skullnumb was excited when the next slide was shown, reading, **"9.1 Million 15-20 Year Olds Had a Life Threatening STD Last Year."** As an ordered and highly mathematical person, she preferred the abbreviated STD to the longer term of *Sexually Transmitted Disease*, but she nonetheless showed some sensitivity as she asked if everyone knew what she was talking about. The silence made everyone nervous but no one commented. She went on with more attractive slides, touting clever charts and graphs, highlighting the unsettling equation that there were 822,000 pregnancies for unmarried teens between the ages of 15-19 during the last year. That was really a lot of high school kids *doing it,* some whispered.

Knowing that the math approach was resulting in some eyes-glazing-over, she ended with her most powerful mathematical point that she knew would get everyone stirred up. *Yes*, her trump card was the fancy fact that pertained to the failure rates of condoms. She knew this was a big hit in the last meeting, so she showed her mathematical expertise by throwing out such concepts as retrograde analysis, random selection of different brands, and reviewer subjectivity on the part of those who had to ask the pesky questions about why there was a latex letdown. But her summation was what brought everyone back to reality. Mrs. Skullnumb made it clear that in math, better than all the fluffy guesswork of other curriculums, there were answers for how to get the *doing it* stopped.

As the math proposal ended, Mr. Globemeiser, the geography teacher, was met at the podium by Mr. Pastproof, the history teacher and right away they made everyone groan with a request for two, eight-minute sessions rather than splitting one time slot. No, Mr. Bickersly affirmed, they would just have to share the time because of the tight schedule. So they did. Mr. Globemeiser began by showing a beautiful map of the United States that he had painstakingly color-coded, accentuating the highest numbers of teen pregnancy (blue markers), the areas prone to non-AIDS sexually transmitted diseases (red markers), and then the map designating the highest concentration in the country of infected AIDs patients (in purple). Several sensitive folks wanted a political discussion about Mr. Globemeiser's color choice for the various sexual problems, but Mr. Bickersly wouldn't allow it. Mr. G. also had a geographical map, color-coded in green, representing where most abortions were performed in the country, which didn't help anyone feel better because one of the biggest green areas on the map was no more than a half day's drive from the school district, even in bad weather. He concluded by suggesting a geographical approach might give the kids the global tools to help them cut down on their *doing it*.

His partner, Mr. Pastproof, was very excited to make his presentation, but frustrated with his four-minute limitation. He quickly went into *beginning at the beginning*, which is a favorite approach for historians, suggesting the kids might strive for virginity if they knew the history of it, of course beginning in biblical times. Since the OATs were really interested in virginity, they found themselves on the edge of their auditorium seats. Mr. Pastproof assured everyone that he knew about the separation of church and state, but if history was used for the curriculum, everything would be "kosher," immediately regretting his choice of words if he was trying to get away from the church business. He went on.

He proposed that by teaching about sexual history and how attitudes have changed over time, the kids might "loosen up," which was another very poor choice of words, especially for the OATs who wanted the *abstinence only* approach to get things even tighter. He discussed teaching the kids about wars that had been fought over sexual trysts, Queen Victoria's round-up of sexual sin, and the scary sexual habits of King Henry the VIII that he thought would be so frightening to high school kids that none of them would even consider *doing it.* Sticking to the curriculum high points of every other presentation focusing on STDs, pregnancy,

abortion, etc., he just suggested that the kids would pay more attention if a historical perspective to those pesky problems was provided. As he finished, many wondered if studying the old days would get the kids to stop what they were doing in the new days, but nonetheless, it was a nice presentation by both Mr. Globemeiser and Mr. Pastproof.

Time was ticking away as Mr. Grouper from the social studies department took the podium microphone and informed everyone he only had seven minutes, but since he was a *group person* (social studies and all), he would cooperate with Mr. Bickersly's timing whistle schedule. This concession from Mr. Grouper set a nice tone for his not-so-nice focus on sex education from a social studies perspective. He began with the ACLU and right out of the chute told everyone (much to the OATs' chagrin) that the American Civil Liberties Union had filed lawsuits over federal funding of *abstinence-only* programs, claiming they discriminated against any hanky-panky going on that was outside a legally married man and woman. Some in the audience moaned about the pesky issue of non-traditional relationships coming up in the curriculum-choosing meeting, as it didn't seem to anyone that the traditional stuff was even under control. *Shouldn't they take care of the normal lifestyle problems before tackling the alternative lifestyle problems?* many wondered.

But without letting anyone even try to complain, Mr. Grouper jumped right into the problems facing teens about gender confusion, homosexuality and lesbianism. The terms were so shocking that no one was about to interrupt him. But he had more bad news as he talked about using a social studies viewpoint to teach the kids, bringing up the awfulness of date rape, child sexual abuse and sexual assault. He furthered his social studies perspective presentation right up to the last thirty seconds, discussing the importance of sex offender registration and sex offender notification, concluding that if the kids could learn about the social implications of *doing it,* things just might settle down in the *doing it* department. The confusing terms of *social conscience, social norms* and *social strata* all blurred together for the audience as Mr. Grouper sat down after finishing his nine-minute presentation.

Now it was time for the heavy-hitter presentations that had caused such a fuss at the last meeting between the OATs and the NATs. After a contentious coin toss to determine who was first, the *abstinence-only* folks started. Right out of the chute came the OATs with the platform of ***Just Say No,*** which was just a kid-friendly way of saying *abstinence only*. They used their allotted eight minutes to pontificate about how their program would, for sure, make the government folks feel better, since the curriculum would follow their tidy eight points.

With their flip charts and their PowerPoint slides, they did a fine job of making sure everybody knew the *No, No* approach was the only way to go, and they emphasized the dreadful part if any other path was taken by handing out charts and graphs (colored of course) showing increases in diseases, unwanted pregnancy and associated mental health problems from *the doing.* Oh, they had a pretty juicy list of the bad stuff, even bringing up really disgusting news in the sexual stampede about sterility and even suicide, which made everyone pretty jumpy. The OATs not only wanted the curriculum to focus on monogamous marriage, but they also made it clear there would be lots of teaching about the pitfalls and problems with same-sex friskiness. And their final trump card was, of course, the money business. The head OAT made it clear it was *their way or the highway,* unless the district was willing to put up the big bucks offered by the federal government.

As the OAT's eight-minute presentation closed, the speaker cleverly said he anticipated questions and complaints about whether there was anything positive in the scare-tactic OAT approach, so he jumped right into an answer to the not-allowed-to-be-asked question. *Yes,* there were lots of positive parts of the OAT's curriculum, he suggested, beginning with showing a picture of the very nice, peach-colored pledge card the students would receive if they promised to follow the OAT philosophy—saving everything for their heterosexual marriage. And *yes,* he reported, the kids who filled out the pledge card and made the promise in an out-loud oath at the end of class, would get to wear a special *OAT Graduate* necklace that he featured in his next slide for everyone to see. But *no,* he didn't see anything wrong with just being positive about the lesson of, *if you don't do it, these bad things won't happen.* And there it was, he explained, the positive nature of what the kids would avoid if the abstinence-only was the curriculum.

When it was time for the final eight-minute presentation of the NAT program, some of the OAT folks tried to walk out, pretending that they all had an uncontrollable urge to use the rest room. That was quite perplexing for Mr. Bickersly who wanted to forbid the obvious protest, but he also knew there were state guidelines about employee rights to toilets and such. But after a little cajoling and shaming, they all trotted back to their seats and listened to the head NAT summarize the less rigid and more comprehensive approach to sex education designed to get the kids who were *doing it,* to be more careful.

Right at the top of the NATs platform were the *doing it* numbers for the high school kids, suggesting to their counterpart OATs that teaching *abstinence-only* and making a big deal out of the badness of premarital sex would be damaging to half the student body who were, according to the stats, already *doing it*. In frustration, the speaker claimed that it was nonsense to teach ***Just Say No*** when more than half of the teenagers had already said ***yes***. The NAT plea was to give the kiddos tools, lots and lots of them, to avoid all the pesky problems cited by the OATs and categorized as teen pregnancy, sexually transmitted diseases, and emotional problems from *too-early-doing-it*. Giving kiddos the tools seemed like a pretty rational thread and some of the OATs began to wonder if maybe the strict inflexibility of the *abstinence-only* approach might not be the answer. A sweet smell of compromise filtered ever so slightly in the air, but only for a moment.

Thinking that things were going to work out came to a grinding halt when the spokesperson for the NATs went way overboard and began to talk about a great teaching film demonstrating female self-breast exams and the theory of effective condom application, practicing on zucchini squash. Immediately, the whole place fell into an uproar and there was nothing Mr. Bickersly could do to stop the mass potty breaks of the OATs, which was silly since basically the presentations were over and it was time to vote.

Anxiety hung in the air, as did feelings of anger and frustration from all sides. But just like Mr. Bickersly had planned, everyone was also tired and hungry, ready to start their weekends. He cautioned against talking or trying to leave, quietly handing out his special ballots, allowing everyone to simply vote for one program philosophy with an X or to use the twelve lines on the ballot for a written comment. Obviously, some of the only-X markers were first to leave, handing in the ballots to Mr.

Bickersly's secretary as they huffed out the door. Some stayed a little longer, using the time to write out an opinion on the tiny twelve lines. Those who stayed the longest were obviously upset without a forum for discussion, but with Mr. Bickersly purposely making himself scarce backstage, leaving only his secretary to collect the ballots, most just grumped out of the auditorium fearing that whatever curriculum was chosen, the chances were the high school kids would just keep *doing it.* Most everyone knew the battle would continue, just like the *doing it* of the teenagers would also roll on.

The idea is to make sex really disgusting so the kids won't *do it.*

Don't touch yourself— it's dirty down there—save it for someone you love.

THE THIRD COMMANDMENT — Thou Shalt Teach Logic

Whether an OAT or a NAT; whether from the Math, Geography, Psychology, Science, Medicine or Social Studies departments; whether Catholic, Lutheran, Baptist, Muslim, Mormon, Jewish or Buddhist; whether from differing political parties, religious traditions, ethnicities, customs, communities or families; a consistent thread (however secret and not talked-about) truly exists regarding dreams for raising sexually respectful children. Unfortunately, that dependable message is hardly ever part of the sex education curriculum anywhere, usually ousted by the more comfortable blood and guts material of *just don't do it or these bad things will happen* approach. The idea is to make sex really disgusting so the kids won't *do it.* But sadly, that lesson has not a shred of connection to what most parents want and, for sure, it not only lacks logic but it ignores what the OATs or the NATs lessons really teach..

BAD EQUALS GOOD LOGIC?

Most adults want children to have healthy and respectful sexual futures, that is for sure. But how will the kiddos get to the good stuff if the bad stuff is the only approved curriculum? Both sides of the curriculum question are guilty of having nothing positive to teach, since the OATs in their *abstinence-only* approach use the negative to scare the kiddos into hopefully not *doing it* until marriage, and their opposing NATs adopt a more refined negative approach, which is teaching the *doing it* kids how to *do it* to avoid those terrible problems. But if sexual respect is the goal, what is the specific curriculum and what is the logic?

THE LOGIC

Just as outlined in the Second Commandment—*Thou Shalt Communicate,* the first step is to take note of what the kiddos are already learning from the madness of the OAT and NAT approaches to sex education. Changing the logic can't be successful if the current logic lesson isn't understood. No matter how it plays out in school or the family room, no matter who is in charge of the program curriculum or who gets the government big bucks, from a perspective of logic, this is the message children traditionally receive from both of Mr. Bickersly's warring factions;

Don't get pregnant, don't get diseases, and don't have sex. Don't touch yourself—it's dirty down there—save it for someone you love.

The madness of this logic is clear but avoided by most good folks who think they have a better way. Most caring adults want children to experience love, have sexual respect for their partners, and grow into adulthood appreciating the beauty of intimacy.

But with the existing logic, children learn that sex is absolutely the most disgusting and horrible thing in the entire world—*while they are children.* But then, there is also hope that this nasty, ghastly thing will somehow be deeply respected and cherished later on—*saving it for someone they love!* The dichotomy is outrageous! This illogical thinking must be founded on the hope that the Sex Fairy comes in with her magic wand and straightens everything out in the honeymoon hotel. There are four really wrong things with this logic, or lack thereof.

REALLY WRONG ONE—THE NASTY NEGATIVES

First, *the don't do it because really bad things will happen* approach doesn't work all that well for a population of adolescents that tend to consider themselves bulletproof and immortal. Teens strive for being cool and brave, believing that nothing bad could ever happen to them. *Those* miserable problems, or *those* people dying from AIDs in a remote country are to them, just *those other people,* and nothing like the beautiful, sexy people they see at the keg party or the homecoming dance. And, in fact, the naysaying and negative approach focusing on the dangers of sex may turn out to be downright attractive for the bullet proof-thinking teenagers. Being independent from adults, having the courage to be bold and fearless, tends to be much more attractive than a classroom presentation from a purple-faced health teacher discussing the virility of sperm chasing down an unfertilized egg in the fallopian tube traffic jam.

REALLY WRONG TWO

As the OATs and the NATs argue about how bloody to make the classroom curriculum, the kids are figuring out that sex can't be all that bad because it sure is important, especially in selling stuff. The illogical nature of fussing about the silly curriculum usually means adults aren't paying much attention to the fact that children are recognizing that *sex is everywhere, sex is really important, everyone is doing it, and the consequences (contrary to the curriculum) don't look all that bad.*

If as much energy was spent on really checking out what the kids are learning about sex as was spent on their battle ballots, the whole school district curriculum contingencies would figure out how impotent their message of *don't do it or bad things will happen* really tends to be for most teenagers. Children, teens and even toddlers are exposed to a constant stream of influences about the consequences of *doing it,* and in reality, the message they receive isn't anything about the nasty stuff the grownups try to teach. Looking at the world, children see a logic that *sex really works*. They constantly witness their heroes, their sexual role models (which usually have nothing to do with their parents or teachers), *doing it* all the time and not only do these beautiful people avoid bad things, but it seems that really good things come to the folks who are hopping in and out of the sack with a whole bunch of other beautiful folks.

Sex is everywhere, sex is really important, everyone is doing it, and the consequences (contrary to the curriculum) don't look all that bad.

The only consequence most children notice for sexually acting out seems to be that their heroes become popular, rich and more beautiful. So the *bad things will happen if you do it* just isn't logical for most children.

And the logic comes from folks who probably had the first three commandments on their parenting clipboard long before the OATs and the NATs had even unpacked their flip charts.

Young children who peek at Mommy's soap operas see Julia, John and Josephine doing the sack-hop with a variety of partners in a variety of bedroom scenes, seemingly unscathed by having sex lots and lots of times, over and over again. In music, movies, and television not only do the heroes of children seem unfazed by their sexual indiscretions, but these heroes show up again and again, in other songs, in other television shows or other movies, even more beautiful, more powerful, and for sure, more rich. In the minds of children, nothing seems to harm the beautiful people who have a new partner on the next edition of the same sitcom, or the same actor, in a different movie, with a different leading partner from the last movie or television show. The only consequence most children notice for sexually acting out seems to be that the heroes become popular, rich and more beautiful. So the *bad things will happen if you do it* just isn't logical for most children.

REALLY WRONG THREE

More study about what logic really shakes out with the *abstinence only* philosophy further points to what is really wrong with this approach. The calculations begin and they aren't pretty. If half of the teenagers are already *doing it*, and the program is to place *abstinence-only* on a pedestal with no wiggle room for any (not any) other choices, it may be that with the pressures of ***just don't do it***, some kids just give up and say to themselves *it is over and I am ruined.* And then, with this fatalistic attitude to which teenagers are so easily prone, *they just give up* rather than *just say no.*

And the giving up doesn't relate to going to the monastery or becoming a celibate spinster. It usually means giving up the hope for the honor touted by the ABSTINENCE-ONLY rigidity, and instead just having lots of sex since the abstinence only education makes it real clear that only with waiting, will good things come. Since waiting went out the window for at least half the *doing it* kids, there is no hope. Thus is the formula for lots of disrespectful sex. The perky necklace and the peach-colored pledge cards will look pretty pathetic when kids who might have responded better to a different learning logic, *just give up.*

REALLY WRONG FOUR

And finally, what is really wrong with this *don't do it or else* approach for teenagers has to do with time and child development. As the First Commandment implies, the *Fading Credibility Theory* suggests that as a normal part of growing up, teenagers must turn away from adult guidance. Adolescence is a time when everyone over the age of 21 has become terminally stupid in the minds of most teenagers. So waiting to teach children about sexual respect until their teenage years is dreadfully wrong. It won't work and, in fact, it may backfire and make things worse since it is rare that a parent or a teacher will suddenly spike in I.Q. score to the point that the teens will demand Mom and Dad turn the family room into a lecture hall.

So neither the OATs nor the NATs were right in their approaches, and if they had just taken a look at the first three commandments—things might have been different. In review of the first two commandments, the idea is to begin early when children still respect adults *(#1 Thou Shalt Begin At The Beginning*), and secondly, it is important to communicate, not lecture *(#2 Thou Shalt Communicate).* Then comes the Third Commandment, *Thou Shalt Teach Logic,* which requires a plan that makes more sense than ***don't touch yourself—it's dirty down there—save it for someone you love.***

RERUNNING THE LOGIC

Rather than the pontificating from the curriculum planners about whether to use the historical, geographical, sociological, medical, psychological or mathematical curriculum guide, a simpler but powerful logic is purported from those who may not have the *hoity-toity* degrees, but for sure, have wisdom. A return to the closure of Mr. Bickersly's meeting may reel in the logic that touts the common thread of what most good parents want but find difficult to reach. And the logic comes from folks who probably had the first three commandments on their parenting clipboard long before the OATs and the NATs had even unpacked their flip charts from the district supply cabinet.

LESSONS LEARNED

After the contentious meeting of all the smart folks in the district, some not-so-educated-but-understanding-of-children folks had a little chat about the discussion that had just taken place. Mr. Lesspot and his janitorial staff were cleaning up the auditorium with the help of the food service folks who were pitching in just to hurry up the building-closing-up process so that all of them could begin their weekend. And in their simple conversation, an uncomplicated but powerful logic emerges as a mirror or blueprint for teaching sexual respect.

Matillda speaks first, trying a little sarcastic humor, as she lights her unauthorized cigarette and stacks the used Styrofoam cups.

"Listening to all that *hootin'* and *hollerin'* makes me know for sure that those fancy-dancy college degrees don't mean nothin' in the common sense department. *Good God, Gertie!* Seems to me that the more learnin' you get, the easier it is to get your panties in a knot. Did you hear all the moanin' and groanin' about this and that?" she lamented. "Lord, you could have piled up their pissiness. I don't know why they don't just teach the kids when they are little that sex is just a really big deal and that they better take care of it. Seems simple to me," she declared, taking a final puff before dousing the Marlboro in a paper cup of leftover lemonade.

I don't know why they don't just teach the kids when they are little that sex is just a really big deal and that they better take care of it.

"Seems like a good way to do it, if you ask me. Don't take no college degree to know we should get kids excited about sex, at least the good part."

Madeline, Matillda's food service partner, chimed in with the same simplistic but powerful thought—and she did it without lighting up anything except ideas.

"Well, when my kids were really little, I started teaching them about the bicycles they would have someday. Why, before they could even think about riding one, I got them excited about it. Years before they were even old enough to get a bike, I helped them start saving their money. When the big day came and they finally got their bikes, they thought it was so cool, even though they were second-hand bikes from their cousins."

The cleaning crew all smiled and mumbled approval without words. She went on.

"They were proud as punch once they finally got their bikes, just cause we made them get so pumped up about 'em. And I'll tell you what. Those guys took care of their bikes too—just cause they spent so much time hanging around waitin' for em. And that ain't all," Madeline opined, sneaking one cupcake left of a Hostess Cupcake package in her apron.

"I see my oldest married son doing exactly the same with his boy, already getting them fussing about their bikes. Why all those smart people don't just do the same teaching about sex is beyond me. Too many brains don't mean you have even a thimbleful of smarts," Madeline finished.

Larry, the assistant to Mr. Lesspot, also contributed to the logic.

"When my kiddos were really, really little, I used to tell'em stories about their Mother. From the time they were little farts, I would tell 'em how I picked her out of all the other girls at Fruitdale School. They knew I went to that two-room school, so they loved the stories when we would drive by," Larry explained as he put out his cigarette in the cuff of his Levis.

"At first, they were just thrilled to hear stories about when their Mom and I were kids cause they mostly thought we had always been old—sort of born old," Larry chuckled. "But later when they got a little older, I told them that if they worked really hard on picking out the right person, like I picked their Mom, it would be so cool. Of course the boys just loved their Mother to death, so instead of fussing about the birds and bees, or diseases, I just told them to work really hard at picking someone just like her, which they figured out would be terrific, especially considering how much they liked her cooking," he explained as he fondly fondled his tummy, which he always told everyone was clear evidence that his wife really was a good cook. But he wasn't quite finished with his wisdom.

"My wife did the same for the little girls, which didn't scare 'em, but instead got them excited about getting a hubby like their good old Daddy-O, which I thought was pretty cool. Seems like a good way to do it, if you ask me. Don't take no college degree to know we should get kids excited about sex, at least the good part."

And there it was. These common-sense folks suggested a sex education logic that focuses on the positive—getting children to look forward to respectful sex. Rather than waiting until high school (after the bean counters have figured out they are *doing it*), these Mom and Dad teachers know to start talking about it early with the little ones, teaching them that not only are sexual decisions important (bicycle-like important), but also teaching them the positive stuff about sex. These wise folks know there is no need for color-coded maps of abortion clinic locations or studies of Henry the VIII's sexual hanky pankies. *No,* they just know that getting kids excited about sex (respectful sex) is the needed logic.

RUDE RESISTANCE

Of course, the resistance to a positive logic or a *get-kids-excited-about-sex* approach is that *if we tell them it is great, it will just make them do it more.* But that result has never been proven, and in fact, the naysaying negative or the be-really-scared-about-sex approaches of the OATs and the NATs does not seem to be working, according to the government folks with the big bucks and their counted beans. And when the dichotomy of the logic, "Don't touch yourself—it's dirty down there—save it for someone you love," is examined, it certainly doesn't make sense that children will grow up with good sexual attitudes, or with protective and respectful attitudes about something portrayed as so despicable for so many years. That is, of course, unless there is a Sex Fairy who will switch all the nastiness around after the wedding reception.

BUMBLING, BEERS AND BIG DEALS

As the teenagers consume two Budweisers each, their inhibitions lower, the tight-lipped talk provided previously by either the OATs or NATs (complete with podiums, pointers and pathetic problems about *too-soon sex*) fades for both of them, and the door of romance beckons. Without really ever making a decision to *do it,* these two teenagers are now in possession of the ingredients for such action—lowered inhibitions and a bonfire burning in the most remote and powerful parts of their bodies.

In the unchaperoned home of a friend whose trusting parents have made an overnight trip to the Salt Lake City airport to pick up Grandma, the teenagers are not really intoxicated, but feeling frisky. They find themselves in a spare bedroom and they begin to fumble, bumble, and paw, with each believing that the other one has the roadmap to success. The young man has never engaged in sexual intercourse and barely understands the mechanics, but the one thing he has learned from television and music is that he is *supposed to know*, or pretend to know how it all works. The female is also unsure about exactly how to do this important thing that her parents don't talk about, but that her friends constantly talk about. But what she does know is that she doesn't really have to know

Now these two teenagers have a pregnancy. Regardless if an abortion occurs, an adoption takes place, or a baby is brought into this world with *babies* for parents, the result is a lifelong impact on the lives of three humans because of this one hurried, bumbling, beer-driven moment of indiscretion.

And of course, since Dad understood the importance of logic as a tool, his Son not only really, really paid attention to the lessons when they finally came, but in using respectful tools, Dad's credibility with Son topped the charts.

everything—firm in the belief that her bumbling Budweiser partner knows everything, or so she hopes. So in spite of all the *not knowing*, in the next seventeen minutes the bumbling, *Budweisered,* and formerly-innocent teens will embark on something so significant that their lives could be changed forever.

With the grace of two bathing walruses, slight penetration of a penis, almost in a vagina, occurs with a hurried and actually *anti-climatic* climax for the young man. The female seemed to miss everything as it happened so quickly. In spite of the differing responses and navigation needs, the couple was in sync with their silent wondering, *was that all there was to it?* But regardless of their disappointment, the emotional rush of the last seventeen minutes resulted in one swimming sperm capturing one single egg, and just as nature intended for the cavemen and cavewomen who needed more babies to preserve the tribe, conception occurs.

Now these two teenagers have a pregnancy. Regardless if an abortion occurs, an adoption takes place, or a baby is brought into this world with *babies* for parents, the result is a lifelong impact on the lives of three humans because of this one hurried, bumbling, beer-driven moment of indiscretion. The bell cannot be *unrung,* and now three lives will forever be changed.

Yet, who prepared these teens to make these critical decisions, and who provided the roadmap for the life-threatening journey three must now take? The OATs and the NATs were both right in suggesting this awful outcome is why someone needs to talk to the kids about sex. But is the only logic that smart people can purport is to just scare the pants off the kids with the hope they won't—take their pants off, that is? And is that foreboding logic the preferred curriculum for preparing children for other precarious and possibly life-altering experiences?

OTHER DIRECTIONS

When children are preparing to do other important things such as hunting with a gun, a different approach is taken rather than the nasty negatives of unwanted pregnancy, horrible diseases and all kinds of emotional problems/trauma for *doing it* too soon. No, if a child is going to use a gun, the first thing Dad probably does is get Son excited about going hunting really, really early (First Commandment). Through lots and lots of positive conversation (Second Commandment), Son is taught that it is really cool to emulate his hunting father and maybe even as a little guy he will help Mom cook the grub to be carefully packed for Dad and his friend's coveted week of elk hunting. Then, just to further enhance the excitement long before Son hunts, Mom and Dad begin to plan for his twelfth year when he will ***finally*** earn the privilege to go on the hunting trip with Dad—just to hang out with the boys—not, of course, touching any guns, just yet.

But before that coveted twelfth year, Son would be encouraged to get excited about Dad coming back from the trip and telling thrilling stories to the future hunter. What Dad knows is that when he finally gets to the real *how to do it* of gun use, he wants his son motivated to learn gun respect. So the excitement is critical for the respect—otherwise the whole gun safety lesson would be boring or resisted, kind of like the excitement and enthusiasm of studying Big Horned Sheep drawings or having a spelling test on the different kinds of sexually transmitted diseases. But there is more to gun safety and Dad's wisdom.

Not only does Dad start young (First Commandment), and not only does Dad do lots and lots of talking (Second Commandment) about the excitement of using a gun, but Dad also has a set of tools to make everything work, especially in the gun respect department. The first tool will be a hunter safety course, and then Dad will do his own safety course in the home, in the car and finally around the campfire that Son has been dreaming about for a very long time. And since Dad understood the importance of logic as a tool, his son not only really, really paid attention to the lessons when they finally came, but in using respectful tools, Dad's credibility with Son topped the charts. For the wise father with the tool of logic in his hip pocket, gun respect and gun safety will all work out. Yet this same approach is hardly ever used for sex education.

NURSE RATCHET & THE N.R.A.

Now, if the teaching-son-about-guns Dad followed the sex educator's approach of Nurse Ratchet, things would be absurd. In this ridiculous comparison, Dad would insist that the sister of Nurse Ratchet from the National Rifle Association (glum and cranky, of course) lecture to fifth grade boys. Her somber presentation to the male units (after the females were trudged off to the library for segregation) would be about how guns work even though none of them would have had any previous knowledge or interest in using guns. With confusion and fear, they would listen to a convoluted and incomprehensible forty-five minute lesson on cartridge identification, gunpowder composition and bullet trajectory rates. But the hysterical and hypothetical comparison goes on.

After N.R.'s sister sternly departed the wide-eyed boys, nothing else would be mentioned about guns until the teenage years, even though there would be lots of temptations for the kids to use them. Then, without any warning, the high school gun curriculum would focus on the nasty negatives, featuring all the bad things that happen with gun boo-boos. The curriculum would feature pictures of mangled limbs and mutilated body parts from gunshot wounds. There would be full-colored overheads of dead bodies resembling hamburger substances because of shotgun accidents, and the highlight of the lessons would be videotaped interviews of family members who have lost a loved one

Everyone would assume that if the nasty negatives of guns were taught, then the kiddos would stay away from them until they get an overt invitation for a spot around the campfire and then the Gun Fairy would zap everything, helping the young man know exactly what to do with his firearm.

So in consideration of how parents teach other important things, compared to the way they teach about sex, it is no wonder so many teenagers are *doing it*, and *doing it* without much respect.

because of errant gunfire. It would be really, really bloody and awful, just like the negative sex education curriculum. Everyone would assume that if the nasty negatives of guns were taught, then the kiddos would stay away from them until one day they get an invitation for a spot around the campfire and then the Gun Fairy would zap everything, helping the young man know exactly what to do with his firearm. And the thinking behind this approach would ignore that just like with sex, children constantly see guns as symbols of status and actually being quite handy in the everyday lives of their beautiful and powerful heroes. Just like with sex, gun safety taught in this manner, without anything positive and without logic, would do nothing but turn children away from parents, making them particularly vulnerable to irresponsible gun use.

SENSE AND NONSENSE

The same nonsense in teaching such behaviors as playing with matches, crossing the street, or driving a car make the need for logic even more clear. Mothers who want the kids to be safe in the home or on the street wouldn't choose the nasty negatives teaching method of showing children burned down houses or charred patients in the hospital burn unit. The lacking logic method of showing black and white crime photos of deceased hit-and-run victims or pictures of mashed kittens on the road would be absurd. No, smart parents teaching safety would get the kiddos excited about earning the privilege of walking to school or being chosen to light the candles at church. They would get excited about finally being old enough and safe enough to light the campfire at the Boy Scout barbecue. And there would be rewards when the kiddos found a book of misplaced matches and turned them in to Dad. And there would be big celebrations when the older sister carefully helped her brother across the busy street. Mom and Dad might even take pictures for Son's scrapbook when he became a crossing guard at school just to make sure everyone in the family really appreciated street safety. This learning with logic about safety would be powerful and positive.

STEERING SENSE

The same First, Second and Third Commandment use could also be connected to preparing children for driving a car. Good parents would start young, they would do lots of communicating about driving and they would use logic. First would come the excitement and motivation to learn the great stuff about cars and driving when the kiddos were really, really little and when, in the minds of the kids, the parents were really, really smart. Later, the kiddos would ride with Dad as he explains about gear shifts, brakes and seat belt safety with great excitement and fanfare, all the while Mom and Dad are thinking ahead to the days when the six-year-old will actually be a sixteen-year-old, standing in the Motor Vehicle driving test line. When the actual tools for safe driving are implemented and include a perky manual and actual driving test, most of the work in teaching vehicle/driving respect has already occurred. And there would be absolutely no need to show the kids brutal pictures of fiery auto crashes with mangled and dangled bodies strewn on Second Street. So, in consideration of how parents teach other important things, compared to the way they teach about sex, it is no wonder so many teenagers are *doing it*, and *doing it* without much respect.

THE LOGIC LAMENTED

Most adults don't want to begin sex education early for fear that the kiddos will be having intercourse on their foam rubber mats during preschool nap time. Parents lament that although loathsome to think about, they begrudgingly admit that the kids might need something about sex—but not now, while they are sweet and innocent. And for sure, the OATs lament that the kids would do more of their *doing it* if the sex program strays from the nice and tidy eight points dictated by the government big buck curriculum of ***Just Say No.*** And the NATs lament that the kids need tools to *do it* more safely. But few lament that the lack of logic is a problem. And in failing to lament the lack of logic, the OATs and NATs are in good company, especially with the prevention folks who believe their job is to prevent sexual disrespect.

THE TOUCHING TRAP—LACKING LOGIC

Not only do the sex educators really get excited about the *scared straight* or *rotting-body-parts-if-you-do-it* approaches, but sexual abuse prevention experts use the same nasty negatives, forgetting that the kids are doing their own search for understanding and logic. *Good Touches* versus *Bad Touches* or *Red Light Touches* versus *Green Light Touches* are the favored approaches in sexual abuse prevention with the grand goal of helping the kiddos know what to do with the bad guys behind the bushes in the park. The theme is "don't let anyone touch the private parts of your body and for sure, never touch yourself." *Good enough,* the prevention folks suggest, just make the sexual touching really ugly in the effort to protect the kidlets from sexual abuse without a single thought about the real logic lesson.

DOCTOR DOES IT?

Mom, who may have brought the cookies to the prevention program for the fourth grade class, might be quite pleased when the *bad touch* and *don't-let-anyone-touch-you* curriculum scared the kiddos to the bone about all that nasty stuff she reads about in the newspapers concerning sexual abuse. Smug with thoughts of success in protecting her children from the park weirdos, that same Mom doesn't make a single calculation about logic as she loads the kidlets in the car and takes them to the doctor for a school physical. As

Does Mom really think her children can sift through the double-jeopardy logic of forcing her kids to cooperate with the doctor's touching of their private parts, but expect them to resist a sex offender who might also want to touch their private parts?

the doctor conducts a normal examination, and in doing so touches the forbidden private parts, how do the children sort out the logic? To them, Mom is non-verbally condoning sexual abuse or *bad touching,* at least according to the lesson they learned from the foreign, tight-lipped prevention expert just hours before. Does Mom really think her children can sift through the double-jeopardy logic of forcing her kids to cooperate with the doctor's touching of their private parts, but expect them to resist a sex offender who might also want to touch their private parts? How can Mom have faith in the prevention teaching when there is no logic, no understanding, only the all-too-familiar-and comfortable *nasty negatives.*

But if everything is sorted out from a logical perspective, it is not the *sex* that is wrong with the sexual abuse of children—it is the *lack of consent.*

DADDY DOES IT?

The same confusion might occur on the home front for a fresh-out-of-nasty-negative prevention program child. In the classroom, the kiddos learn about bad touching and that they should call the cops if it ever happens. Good enough. But how do they sort out that logic when they come home from the doctor's office (where to them, sexual abuse just happened) and they watch Dad change baby Sister's poopy diapers because Mom's errant spaghetti is running all over the kitchen? When these fresh-out-of-bad-touch-teaching kids watch their father touch the forbidden private parts of their 13-month-old sister (considering the logic recently handed to them,), they will observe their second sexual offense of the day. But there is more.

AND GRAMPS?

And if later that day one of those kiddos is fishing with Grandpa, and when he finds his britches have become a collection site for frogs, pollywogs and one cubic foot of mud, he needs some help with his shower before dinner. If Grandson and Grandpa shower together and there is help with bathing that requires normal touching of genitalia by Grandpa to Grandson, then using the logic of bad touch or *don't let anyone touch you,* the kiddo has no choice but to consider old Gramps his third observed sex offender in one day! It is likely that a very large cop won't be called and neither will the doctor, Dad or Gramps end up on a post office pervert poster. But without logic, children learn that nothing coming from grownups about touching or sex really makes sense, so they turn away, feeling confused and betrayed by the missing-logic parents who wanted to protect them.

THE SEX FAIRY & PREVENTION

At best, children who participate in these negative prevention approaches will feel betrayal and recognize the stupidity of their parents telling them not to let anyone touch them, but then touching them or condoning other people touching them. But at worst, how will children ever grow up and feel positive about a sexual commitment (respect, actually) if in prevention programs, private part touching is viewed as *bad touching?* The logic to this kind of teaching is no different than showing the *doing it* teenagers pictures of AIDs patients dying from open sores since it suggests that sex and sexual body part touching is bad—really, really bad. In fact, some prevention efforts make sure the people who do the touching are portrayed as also really, really bad, making a broad brush of the nasty negatives.

NO SEX!

But if everything is sorted out from a logical perspective, it is not the *sex* that is wrong with the sexual abuse of children—it is the *lack of consent.* Most adults, in some capacity, figure out that sex is pretty nice, but not for kids and the big difference has to do with children being unable to consent. Every state in the country makes laws just so everyone is clear that the little ones don't know enough about sex to consent. So, it is the lack of consent that makes sexual abuse of children so wrong.

Yet most prevention programs fail to teach that logic and instead focus on the handy-dandy nasty negatives, forgetting what that approach does to the sexual futures of children. The logic that children are supposed to learn is:

This kind of private-body-part touching is really, really bad. In fact, it is disgusting and criminal. But don't worry kiddos, you will have a good time doing this kind of touching when you are twenty-five.

That is as absurd as thinking Nurse Ratchet is a positive role model for respectful sexual decision-making. So the only way adults can resolve the absurdity of what they are teaching children is just to hope the Sex Fairy flies in after the wedding, and with a little magic, takes twenty-five years of negative learning about sex and *poofs* it into something wonderful AND respectful.

So the only way adults can resolve the absurdity of what they are teaching children is just to hope the Sex Fairy flies in after the wedding, and with a little magic, take twenty-five years of negative learning about sex and *poof* it into something wonderful AND respectful.

THE LOGIC LEARNED

She was familiar to the children after traveling to the school for many years providing sexual abuse prevention, just as the school board had directed her. As she had done in the past, she talked in a positive way about the different kinds of touching and warned about someone wanting to secretly touch the private parts of the kiddos in a park or during the refreshment break at Bonanza Bingo. But because the sixth graders were familiar with her and she had always created a positive atmosphere in the classroom, they felt no resistance to posing the question, "WHY?"

The question about why the touching of private parts should be forbidden floated through her brain with a remembrance that first, they were children and needed a child development-sensitive answer; and secondly, these kiddos would know if she tried any magic or *foo-foo logic* in her explanation. They knew her and they couldn't be fooled with a nonsense explanation. Also remembering that she always wanted to be positive and not rely on the *don'ts* of sex education, she began her positive explanation.

And again, she asked herself, *Why do we only share those parts of our bodies with one person?* And yet thinking of her personal life and her own sexual partner, the truthful answer just floated.

"Well kids, remember those parts of our body on our chests and between our legs are very, very special, and so we treat them very, very differently than we do, say, our elbows."

To her, the answer was pretty good, until she heard their response, which was a simple and in-unison, "Why?"

Attempting to regroup her thoughts, but to keep the message positive, the prevention specialist continued.

"Well, we treat those body parts with lots and lots of respect. You know, like when the hottest day of the year comes around and we take off lots of clothes? Well, we usually keep those body parts on our chest and between our legs private and special, not like our knees or our foreheads."

And again, they asked "Why?"

She contemplated a conversation with herself to find the truth and, therefore, the answer for the children. *Why do we cover those sexual parts?* she pondered as she prepared her answer.

"Well, you see, we treat those body parts differently because when we grow up (gulp!), we share those parts of our body with a very, very special person that we have picked out of all the other people in the world. And once we pick that person, we don't share those parts with anyone else."

Feeling pretty confident that she had told the truth, remained positive and given them the answer, she was shocked when they again asked, "Why?"

And again, she asked herself, *Why do we only share those parts of our bodies with one person?* And yet thinking of her personal life and her own sexual partner, the truthful answer just floated.

"Well, the reason we only share those private parts with the one special person we have picked out of all the others is that if we shared them with everyone else, the sharing wouldn't be a really, really big deal for that one really, really special person we picked."

And to her comfort, the sixth grader's response was a resounding, "Oh."

LOGIC LEARNED

Right there it was, a logic that would have pleased the OATs and probably would have been just fine for the NATs. ***Choosing someone to share your body with when you grow up and picking the most special person in the world*** is a wonderful and positive logic that should be the cornerstone for all teaching of sex education. This logic is in respect of the First Commandment of beginning early, and the Second Commandment of communicating. And for every single incident when the window of opportunity opens and children learn something about sex, the logic is there. Or at least it should be.

RULES, ROBBERY AND RESCUE

Expanding the concepts of the *picking part* (which is really about teaching children to make responsible sexual decisions) and emphasizing the needed logic, an organized format of *Rules, Robbery and Rescue* emerges with beautiful simplicity, but also power. The Three R's would be quite palatable to both the OATs and the NATs, as well as the wisdom-thinking janitor and food service folks cleaning up after Mr. Bickersly's bickering teachers.

It is easy for children to understand that there are rules about touching and picking (choosing someone as a sexual partner), because rules make a lot of sense and rule-teaching is a tried-and-true technique of parenting. A simplistic view of the Three R's approach emphasizes that the rules demand little people have the chance to protect the private parts of their bodies (and for a great reason) and that bigger people need to be following that rule and, therefore, touching the children is prohibited. But that isn't enough—to just stop the touching.

This rule exists in the logic, not because those body parts are smelly, nasty or dirty parts that make Grandma pucker, but these body parts need protection because something terrific happens when children grow up. The whole logic depends upon teaching children that after they grow up and do some checking, they will pick someone with whom to share those body parts and it will be terrific—(excitement personified). Of course, these rules also demand that the kids understand there is to be no ***picking*** until they grow up, since the decision is so important and while they are children, their picking should only be about things like television shows, the color of socks, and which ice cream cone sounds the best after skate boarding.

The whole logic depends upon teaching children that after they grow up and do some checking, they will pick someone with whom to share those body parts and it will be terrific—(excitement personified).

THE RULES REIGN

The issue of RULES is extremely important in raising sexually respectful children and in preventing sexual abuse, but the focus must be positive, avoiding the nasty negatives. Families that begin talking about the rules early, not only make it difficult for someone outside the family to sexually abuse children, but the rules make it clear for older children that engaging in sexual behaviors with younger children is a big ***no-no*** and a clear violation of the family code of honor (rules, actually).

The story of Kameron reflects the tragedy in many families where nothing about the rules is taught, and when the kiddos get in the closet for the lover games, everyone gets quite upset. The rule police, like Kameron's Mom, the teachers, the social workers, and the cops made quite a fuss that Kameron broke the rules confirming that he *knew better*—and making them feel better about giving him a lifetime sentence through his label as a sex offender. But sadly, those same rule police never taught Kameron the rules, which was their responsibility. When trying to raise sexually respectful children, the rules need to be taught to not only protect children from Kameron's fate but also to teach the positive aspect of adult sexuality.

If Son has inadvertently used Sister's bra for a blindfold in the hide-and-seek-game, or if Mom catches the kids giggling about catching Grandma changing her girdle, the rule explanation is always the same—positive logic and a focus on privacy violation.

Sexual respect will never be achieved with shame or embarrassment, nor will it be instilled with discussions of rotting body parts from diseases or abortion survivor group therapy tragedies.

PRIDE AND PRIVACY

Finally, the touching rules have the ability to teach a very important part of respectful sexuality which relates to privacy. Usually unenlightened parents teach privacy, but in a negative way, adopting such responses as, "Don't be nasty, and close the bathroom door," or "Don't be naughty and touch your sister's underwear." This privacy teaching is usually without logic and just another category of the nasty negatives. But actually, the rules about privacy can also be taught in a very respectful way without sacrificing morality, but instead, encouraging it—that is, if logic is used.

PRIVACY PLEASE

Explaining to children that those body parts (with proper names, of course) aren't shared on the school bus, in church, or at Mom's beauty parlor is a great start. Pointing out that vaginas, breasts, testicles and penises are in need of very safekeeping, instigates the healthy approach to privacy. And when Larry, Matillda and Madeline were opining about the needed logic (bicycles or sex), that was it. When the common sense folks spoke about getting kids excited about sex, they were talking about following the rules to privacy, because something great happens through privacy protection. Yes, using logic about sexual decision-making is the right answer, but *getting kids excited about sex* can make the strongest of parents weak-kneed. That is, of course, unless the teaching is tuned in to that overall goal of raising sexually respectful children.

PRIVACY AND PERVERSION

When events occur in a child's life and the window of opportunity opens for communication about sex (as the Second Commandment suggests), then teaching the *beauty of privacy*, not the *shame of privacy,* is the answer. The normal happenings in families that first seem like perversion should always be approached with a positive frame of privacy. If Son has inadvertently used Sister's bra for a blindfold in the hide-and-seek-game, or if Mom catches the kids giggling about catching Grandma changing her girdle, the rule explanation is always the same—positive logic and a focus on privacy violation. These typical childlike behaviors aren't about the potential *perversion of cross-dressing* with sister's bra nor are they about the kids ending up in prison as *Peeping Toms* with a deep-dish voyeurism diagnosis. These are windows of opportunity to communicate the positive logic that those parts of the body (underneath Sister's bra and underneath Grandma's girdle) need protection and they need respect.

THE ROBBERY

Of course the robbery in the Three R's of logic has to do with the possibility that the rules might be broken, and this logic has a strong foundation in the overall effort to raise sexually respectful children. Sexual respect will never be achieved with shame or embarrassment, nor will it be instilled with discussions of rotting body parts from diseases or abortion survivor group therapy. In fact, the best way a young person can make a respectful decision, long before an invitation to jump in the back seat of the Ford, is to have the *I word* of *indignation* deep within the sexual soul. Indignation comes when something rude happens or is taken away—robbed, actually. So teaching sexual respect requires children to appreciate the product in order to protect it.

The lesson should be that if the wonderful picking-someone-when-you-grow-up rules are broken, an outrage (indignation) should be the response. Protecting something of value (such as the right to pick someone to share your body with when you are older) is easy for teenagers if those ideas were instilled, in a positive way, from the time the kiddos could tell Grandma about their noses. Children do not feel indignation about something like rotting body flesh or the shame of not having a peach-colored pledge card. But if as little ones, they were taught to protect those parts of their bodies for a positive reason, they would feel pride in privacy as well as indignation if someone invited them to engage in tree fort friskiness as young children or a little hanky-panky in the back seat of the Ford when they are teenagers. It is all in the positive nature of the logic.

THE RESCUE

Sadly, the OAT approach and many of the NAT ideas for curriculum, foster rigidity and indirectly suggest that if kids ever waver or wander from the exact blueprint of *don't do it*, or *if you must do it, do it carefully*, there is no hope and no rescue. There were no questions allowed from the girls in Nurse Ratchet's presentation, and usually children understand that when only *foreigners* are brought in to deliver the prevention message, no one in the family or in the school is capable of talking to them. There seems no sanctuary or rescue for children if things are confusing. And for most kiddos, as they watch their teeth-sweating parents try to deliver a white-knuckled lecture about reproduction in the driveway, the message is the same about their closed-door-not-open-to-rescue parents.

To add to the rescue fadeout, children usually grow up doubting that their parents are even sexual, let alone capable of talking to them, since it seems like they *pucker purple* when anything between belly buttons and knees is ever mentioned. But, if in the logic there was a clear message about the open-door-to-any-discussion policy of Mom and Dad—then the rescue in the *Three R's* is a message that no matter what, Mom and Dad not only have the answers, but they have the ability and desire to help with anything sexual—even sexual mistakes.

But if as little ones, they were taught to protect those parts of their bodies for a positive reason, they would feel pride in privacy as well as indignation if someone invited them to engage in tree fort friskiness as young children or a little hanky-panky in the back seat of the Ford when they are teenagers.

"We treat these body parts differently and we make sure they are very, very private. We don't do this because they are dirty or nasty or silly. We keep them private because something terrific happens to those parts of your body when you grow up."

THE PERFECT PARENT PACKAGE

Dad begins his teaching about the logic of the touching rules, about the robbery that could happen if the rules are not followed, and he is teaching about the rescue that could occur if the rules are broken.

"Now, let's see if we can remember the touching rules. You kids have very special parts of your bodies that need a lot of protection. The private parts of your body are between your legs and on your chest. You girls have breasts on your chest and between your legs you have a vagina on the inside and a vulva on the outside. That vulva takes very, very good care of the vagina so they are both important parts, working together. You boys have penises and testicles, which are also terrific just like the breasts, vulvas and vaginas for girls are great.

"Remember, the rules say we keep those parts of our bodies private, special and different from how we handle, say our elbows or our ears. We treat these body parts differently and we make sure they are very, very private. We don't do this because they are dirty or nasty or silly. We keep them private because something terrific happens to those parts of your body when you grow up."

Dad continues with confidence that only slightly falters when he thinks about his weapon-now-loaded talk from his father so very long ago.

"Someday, you kids will grow up and pick someone to share your body with, just like I picked your Mother out of all the ladies in the whole world. Your Mom is the only person I share the private parts of my body with, and it is terrific for your Mother and I, especially since she also picked me out of all the people in the world. Before that picking, we met lots of people, we thought about it over and over again, and finally, from everyone we knew, we picked each other. We don't share those parts of our body with anybody else, and that's what makes sharing them with each other such a terrific thing."

Dad breathes, and then speaks again.

"When you are a kid, you should be picking puppies, ice cream, or what you want to watch on TV. Kids can't pick someone to share their body with because that is too big of a decision, even for super kids. The rules say that kids can't pick—flat-out no! Choosing someone to share the private body parts with is very important and should only be done by grownups."

Dad continues on, gaining more confidence.

"But kids have a very important job about the private parts of their bodies. No matter how little they are, they have to work as hard as they can to take very good care of the private parts of their bodies. Now, I know your little brother sometimes runs through the house with his penis blowing in the breeze, but he is little and we are all trying to teach him that someday he will learn more about privacy and picking. Right now, he is just our little pooper and we should all try to help him with privacy as best we can, of course, without making him afraid or nervous. Just like when you kids were also little poopers, we had to teach you about privacy and that is what your brother needs now. Together, as a family, I think we can help him get it right so that he can learn all the great things about privacy."

Taking a breath, Dad continues in his logical education.

"So those are the rules, kids. But now I want to tell you about how sometimes the rules are broken and there is a robbery. Sometimes people break the touching rules, which is just awful, because following the rules makes kids and grownups happy. Just like there are rules in the forest about raccoons and rabbits, people have rules about touching the private parts of their bodies. Just like sometimes there is a rotten raccoon, people sometimes break the touching rules, too. When the rules are broken and an older or bigger person tries to touch a child's private parts, they are breaking the rules, and kids always need to tell someone, especially safe people like your Mom or me. The older or bigger person doing the rude rule-breaking robs kids of the right to grow up and pick someone to share their body with (all on their own), just like I picked your Mother. And that is a really big robbery of a kid's rights and it is awful. It is really wrong to try to take that right away from kids, so something needs to be done when it happens. I want you kids to know that we will always help or *rescue you* if rule-breaking should ever happen, or if you just have any questions about protecting your private parts. When kids have this kind of *touching trouble,* they need to get some help from someone who follows the rules like your Mom or me. Rule breakers need to be stopped and kids need to be rescued from the rule-breaking so they can grow up happy about their privacy."

The children listen as Dad continues.

"But, I don't want you kids to be afraid. See, the rules about bodies are not just a good idea; the rules have to do with the law. It is true that privacy and being able to pick someone all on your own when you grow up is a great idea, but it isn't just the rules in our family. It has to do with laws for everyone. If the touching rules are broken, people can get into trouble because lots of people get crabby if the rules aren't followed.

"But even if someone older touches you, we will rescue you and help you, no matter who it is or how crabby we feel about the broken rules. And the best part of the rescue is that if someone breaks the rules and touches you, it really doesn't count for your picks in the future. All of your picks, when you grow up, will still be terrific, just like it is terrific your Mom and I picked each other a very, very long time ago."

Whew! Dad has done it—a beautiful lesson with logic.

"All of your picks, when you grow up, will still be terrific, just like it is terrific your Mom and I picked each other a very, very long time ago." Whew! Dad has done it—a beautiful lesson with logic.

Rather than the *DON'Ts*, this is a positive approach emphasizing the beauty of human sexuality.

But honoring, teaching and encouraging healthy affection and touching in families is not only a good thing for the logic end of things, but when there is lots of healthy touching at the breakfast table, touching that is openly talked about, children are less desperate teenagers in the back seat of the Ford.

CAR SEAT BACK SEAT

When Dad makes this positive, logic-driven presentation to his children, he is not only explaining how they should handle sexual abuse, but he is honoring all their future sexual decisions. He is preparing for better decisions in the back seat of the Ford before his children are out of their car seats in the Chevrolet. Dad is also doing everything possible to have his children respect their bodies, respect their sexual future, and respect the entire concept of sexual decision-making. If someone has touched the children, they will learn it is not their fault and that they can be rescued. If children are contemplating touching another child, they may be deterred because of Dad's rules explanation. And through this teaching, Dad becomes a reliable source of information, starting while they are young and while he still has credibility.

LOGIC LANGUAGE

In this tender logic, the language is important to send the little ones on their way to indignation about sexual disrespect. Children will feel betrayed if they are told, "Don't let anyone touch you!" and then are taken to the doctor, or allowed to watch Dad change the baby's diaper, or challenged to jump in the shower with Grandpa. In explaining the touching rules, language is important to not only describe the different kinds of touching, but to also preserve the positive logic outlined in the *Rules, Robbery, and Rescue* curriculum of Dad's rules.

TOUCHING TRIUMVIRATE

Taking into account the first two commandments about beginning early and communicating, three different kinds of touching should be the language in the curriculum for the Third Commandment—*Thou Shalt Teach Logic.* First, in providing the best logic for children, the term *good touching* should be used to describe affection. As the Tenth Commandment teaches, society adapts a touching prohibition because of fear of sex. But honoring, teaching and encouraging healthy affection and touching in families is not only good for the logic end of things, but when there is lots of healthy touching at the breakfast table, touching that is openly talked about, children are less desperate teenagers in the back seat of the Ford. So the term *good touching* should be encouraged, practiced and discussed.

Secondly, the logic of language should include the term *bad touching,* but not for the traditional nasty negatives of the OATs and NATs. In raising sexually respectful children, the term *bad touching* should be used to define violence, aggression and any other type of physical hostility, having nothing to do with sexual behavior that is reserved for the *positive picking partner part.* The logic in raising sexually respectful children should always include a negative concept of *bad touch*ing referring to the violation of another person's right to physical safety.

The third term in the logic of language is *secret touching,* referring to sexual contact, but also working to protect the reverence for sexual respect. Remembering that it is not the sex that is wrong in sexual abuse, the term *secret touching* focuses on the motivation of the offending person (rules, actually). And with the term *secret touching,* the what-to-do about three family perverts observed by the fresh-out-of-prevention-kiddo in a single day, is easily solved since it helps the kiddos sort everything out in their logic-driven heads.

If family teachers explain to children that no one should ever touch the private parts of their bodies *in a secret way,* then the trip to the doctor, a peek at Dad changing diaper or the shower with Grandpa will be understood as falling within the realm of normal, genital touching ***because it wasn't secret***. With this logic and language, children can easily understand that Mom knows about the doctor touching—(no secret there), everyone watches Dad cleaning up sister's surprise in her pants—(still no secret), and Grandma will know about the extra help from Grandpa in the shower, rendering all of these situations outside the realm of secrecy. Sex offenders rely on secrecy and using the term *secret touching* makes a direct contribution to the safety of children, but it also preserves the respectful part of sex when children reach adulthood and treasure their rights for sexual decision-making.

THE LOGIC IN ACTION (INACTION, REACTION OR PROACTION)

Mom is standing in the checkout line of Safeway (the local grocery store) on the night before Thanksgiving. It seems to her there are seven hundred people ahead of her in line and, at the same time, she feels as though seven hundred people are coming to her house for Thanksgiving dinner. As she re-examines her grocery list, hoping she didn't forget something as important as olives or cheese spread, she observes her three-year-old son standing in the cart. She notices with terror that he has his penis out, his penis is erect, he is touching his penis, and he has a smile on his face that would bring the sun up at midnight!

She notices with terror that he has his penis out, his penis is erect, he is touching his penis, and he has a smile on his face that would bring the sun up at midnight!

Within the next few moments, Mom faces a decision tree of being inactive, reactive or proactive in how she handles the son-with-a-penis-in-hand situation. First, right there in the grocery checkout line, she can be inactive, negative, cruel, and abusive, but nonetheless someone the OATs would have put at the head of the squadron. She can scream at her son, "Don't touch yourself! Hair will grow on your hands and you will need glasses when you grow up!"

But Mom has other choices as well, which are far beyond the inactive, negative response. She may want to be more reactive, and do what some of the well-thought-of-talk-show-host guests have suggested on the issue of masturbation. With teeth-clenched into a plastic smile, she may give instructions for her little

"Now, how are you going to keep those parts of your body private and special, saved for someone you pick, if you are hanging them out here next to the cranberries?"

pooper to put his penis away temporarily, with granted permission for trotting off to his room for the task of *self-stimulation* just as soon as they unpack the Pistachio ice cream at home. She stops the Safeway stimulation and gives him permission to continue at home in the privacy of his room. This is the reactive response she learned from parenting magazines that suggested she give kiddo permission to touch himself.

"Remember, that kind of touching is not okay in Safeway. You can wait until you get home and you are in your own room before you touch yourself, okay honey?"

Mom would be proud of herself for taking this approach without resorting to hysterics, without punishing her son, but with the knowledge that she will likely have nightmares for several weeks contemplating what her little *pooper* might be doing when his Snoopy decorated bedroom door is closed.

Mom's reactive response is not traumatizing to her son, but it ignores the window of opportunity that just opened to explain the rules of sexual respect.

Her third option is the proactive response—thinking about her son's sexual future, as the first three commandments suggest.

Mom chooses for her Safeway clipboard the logic that will not only prevent further embarrassment in Safeway, but will contribute to her Son's sexually respectful future.

Mom remembers the First Commandment that beginning early is a good thing, she remembers the Second Commandment that she must watch for windows and communication, AND she grasps the Third Commandment of logic and responds with a proactive lesson.

"You have a very nice penis and two wonderful testicles," she explains, wiping the sweat from her brow and hoping Barbara Backdrop in the checkout line in front of her doesn't hear. "You need to keep them very private and special because remember, someday you will grow up and share them with someone you have picked out of all the people in the whole world. It will be terrific to share those private parts of your body when you grow up, ***IF*** you keep them private when you are a kid. Now, how are you going to keep those parts of your body private and special, saved for someone you pick, if you are hanging them out here next to the cranberries?"

Silence prevailed for a few awkward seconds as Mom's little pooper tried to make sense out of his Mother's statement. Then he remembered briefly about the keeping of those parts private. He remembered something about privacy and that the parts of his body between his legs are different from his elbow. The rest of the lesson slips him, but it doesn't really matter. Partially, it made sense, and he tucks away his three-year-old penis and in his three-year-old reasoning, he believes he will save it for another day.

This proactive Mother saw the window of opportunity open. She remembered the rules about touching and she took her son to his future sexual decision-making process with logic. This Mom didn't have to tell him about centimeters of penile penetration needed to achieve maximal opportunity for conception, nor did she need to explain the legal punishments in her state for crimes such as indecent exposure. There was no need for a podium or a hunting trip with Dad. All this mom needed to do was remember that her son is little, and while she is still a reliable source of information in his mind, she can teach him about the touching rules. She is protecting the positive aspect of sexuality by providing logic that children can understand, and that logic is founded on the rules of respect.

LOGIC FOR THE LONG HAUL

Returning to the scenarios of the Second Commandment where parents try to figure out what the kids were already learning and then use those educational moments as *windows of opportunity* to communicate, it is clear that logic is the answer. For those teeth-sweating moments for parents, the positive logic should be woven into the everyday lives of children as they are learning sexual respect. A rerun of some of those Second Commandment scenarios can be a logic reminder and an exercise in familiarity and comfort, so important for teaching sexual respect.

IF ONLY THEY HAVE QUESTIONS MOM

When Mom, who eventually ended up being interviewed by the not-so-friendly CIA caseworker, found her kids getting naked in the tree fort, the logic should have been there, loud and clear. *Yes,* the kiddos should have been marched into their respective time-outs, and yes, that should have only occurred after they had adorned their missing-in-action clothes. But *no,* the message should not have been negative, frightening or lacking in logic. Just like Mom in Safeway, the logic should have taken the really-liking-to-get-naked kids into their sexual futures with a lesson on sexual respect and a punishment for not following the rules about something terrific. And when Mom had to explain things to the tight-lipped investigator at the social service agency, rather than the illogical, "we were always there for them if they had questions," Mom should have explained her logic in teaching sexual respect.

"We have always told the children that they need to keep those parts of their bodies private and special, because someday they will choose someone with whom to share their bodies. Why, when I found them in the tree fort, I explained they were breaking the privacy rules, because all kids have a right to keep their bodies private. I also explained there would be no television for two days just to help them remember the rules about the importance in keeping their bodies private and terrific."

There was no need for a podium or a hunting trip with Dad. All this mom needed to do was remember that her son is little, and while she is still a reliable source of information, in his mind, she can teach him about the touching rules.

"Why, when I found them in the tree fort, I explained they were breaking the privacy rules, because all kids have a right to keep their bodies private.

Mom would have been brilliant and the FBI-type would have been moving on to her next case where parents were just available if the kids had questions.

GRANDMA KNOWS NOSES

When the kiddos started to figure out how exciting it might be to tell Grandma about the forbidden-to-talk-about body parts between their legs, the explanation for why those parts are left out of Grandma's show-and-tell exercise should relate to *pride and privacy*. And the same would be true for the missing dolly parts. Ignoring the omission of Grandma show-and-tell or missing-in-action dolly parts is dangerous, as children might find the forbidden enticing. But to use the omission to explain the logic of pride and privacy about those body parts is a great lesson in the curriculum of sexual respect.

SAVING THE SUPER SAVER SAGA

Retracing the steps of Dad in the Super Saver demonstrates a wonderful window of opportunity for the daughters watching his panic about Brunhilda getting his Tampax mixed up with the thumbtacks. In a rerun, Dad should have used the logic.

"Do you girls remember how we started planning the celebration for when your bodies will begin to change from being a girl into being a woman? Well, we began with that cool idea when you were barely able to walk, because that is such a great thing about being female. Different than boys, your body will begin to change at oh, about ten or twelve or maybe even earlier or later. And with those changes, your body will get ready to be a place where a baby could grow. It is just about the most important thing about a human body—this stuff of actually making another human."

Dad breathes, and mentally remembers the first three commandments before he goes on.

"Well girls, the funny thing about bodies is that the clock doesn't really pay much attention to what is going on in your life and how busy you are with other things, such as playing with your hamster, making hot pads in 4-H, or trying to have great jewelry bead parties with your fourth grade friends. Your body is sometimes ready to have babies even though you might be in the sixth grade, which would be dreadful. Without knowing anything about things like finishing school, going to college, or working really hard to pick the right person to share your body with when you grow up, your body makes blood each month, of course just in case you are ready for a baby. Well, since that blood doesn't have a baby that needs it, it just comes out of your terrific vagina. It has to be taken care of and that is why there are things like Kotex and Tampax. And every time we buy things like Mom's Supers, we should have lots of respect for the bodies of girls and the terrific things that will happen to those bodies when girls become women and make really, really great picks about their futures."

There it is, sweet, simple, honest logic moving Dad to his dreams and denouncing his dreads. And this lesson is a whole lot safer for Dad than dealing with his panic about Super Thumb/tam/pax.

JESSICA AND THE BATHROOM WALL

After Jessica's Mom discovered her peeping daughter's behavior with holes in the bathroom wall, and after Mom became the diva of dialogue—enhancing the conversation, she would eventually need to explain to Jessica why her behavior was wrong. And logic is the answer.

"Jessica, those boys have a right to grow up and keep their bodies private and special because, just like you, they have a right to pick someone when they are grownup with whom they can share those private parts. When you are peeking on the boys, it is a trick. It is cheating them out of feeling really great about keeping those body parts private and that is why you and I need to fix this trick. The rules say every kid has a right to feel great about those body parts, even those boys, and for sure, you have that right. So, let's figure out how to fix this mess and we will talk about it again."

And there it is—First, Second, and Third Commandments in hand, and sexual respect for Jessica in the future.

PARADES AND PROTESTS

The workers are gathered outside the smoked meat factory in New Mexico with large protest signs since the management refuses to pay minimum wage. In South Dakota, protesters scream about the proposed law making it a crime for teachers to provide any information to children about birth control. In Texas, a protest march focuses on the firing of a police officer who wears *dreadlocks* from her African-American heritage. And protest marches are held outside the White House, objecting to presidential policies about wages, abortion, civil rights, or an unwanted war. People in this country easily become vociferous and outspoken about their rights.

Why then, wouldn't it be prudent to protest and advocate for the rights of children to be protected from either sexual abuse or from becoming a sexual offender? Sadly, when protests and rallies about sexual abuse occur, they rarely focus on the logic of children's rights to sexual respect, but on battles concerning such things as whether the really bad perverts get forty-five years in prison rather than twenty-five years. The question is, why not protest in a positive way about the rights of children with an eye on sexual respect in their futures? It would be helpful if these protests were commonplace, demanding such basic things as:

Your body is sometimes ready to have babies even though you might be in the sixth grade, which would be dreadful.

When you are peeking on the boys, it is a trick. It is cheating them out of feeling really great about keeping those body parts private and that is why you and I need to fix this trick.

- Kids have a right to feel great about the private parts of their bodies.
- Kids have a right to pick someone to share the private parts of their bodies with when they grow up.
- Kids have a right to grow up and make their own sexual decisions.

Even if the family room doesn't become a protest hall similar to the White House lawn, teaching children to be indignant about not only their rights to privacy, but their *OBLIGATION* to respect the rights of others, is an important logic for raising sexually respectful children. Indignant children are very difficult to sexually abuse, and even if they are abused, they know the rules and their trauma will be minimal.

EXTERNAL LOGIC AND UNCLE HARRY

Aunt Bessie, Sister Bonnie, and Mama Bertha are washing dishes after the Fourth of July picnic in cousin Barbara's backyard. As the ladies chatter about how the scalloped potatoes were slightly burned but that the baked beans were perfect, the subject turns to a family member. Mother asks an innocent question about Uncle Harry's firing from his job at the fish egg factory, which eventually leads into a detailed discussion of Uncle Harry's moral character. They gossip about Uncle Harry's well-known *weirdness* in the family, ranging from his history of unemployment to the issue that Uncle Harry's third marriage recently ended in divorce as his wife absconded with the Fuller Brush salesman. One of the women actually proposes that perhaps Uncle Harry is *perverted*.

"He has always been weird," explains his niece, Bertha, who continues the discussion by saying, "I remember when we were kids, he seemed to always be hanging around our playhouse."

"Well, I heard at the beauty shop that Uncle Harry is always sneaking into the cigar store at the first of the month to get a peek at the girlie magazines," says Becky, the sister of Bessie.

"Oh, I heard he goes to Parkersville and has beers at the topless bar before his paycheck is gone," hoots Belinda, niece of Barbara.

These extraneous tidbits regarding Uncle Harry allow conclusions to be drawn, however unfair, about the safety of the children in the family. As the ladies tittle-tattle, they ponder whether Uncle Harry should be allowed to attend Thanksgiving dinner at Grandma's house in the upcoming months. If the women choose to protect children by keeping Uncle Harry away from family events, they may make several mistakes with this external logic.

First, the ladies are unfair to convict Uncle Harry based upon gossip tidbits. Although he may have problems in his lifestyle organization, it is not automatically clear that he is a sex offender. In spite of his weirdness, Uncle Harry deserves fairness. This external logic, focusing on who might offend, causes children and adults to look for safety through offender detection, rather than the internal logic of rule respect.

The second error in the judgment of the scandal solicitors is that by trying to identify who might offend children, there is a false feeling of safety and protection by discovering the *bad guys*. Not only is it unfair to accuse Harry, but by doing so, the real sex offenders in the family may be given free reign to abuse, especially if they don't have some of Uncle Harry's obvious problems. This is an external, rather than internal, method and it lacks the logic needed to raise sexually respectful children.

ABOUT BICYCLES

A bicycle example furthers this point, remembering Matilda's brilliance in the after-OAT/NAT-bickering, janitorial cleanup. If parents wanted to protect their children's bicycles from theft, they would not likely show children pictures of bicycle thieves. Kiddos would be taught to appreciate their bicycles and to honor the safety of their bicycles. Bicycle teaching parents would internalize the value of the bicycle for the ultimate in protection, just like the wise janitors and the food service folks suggested. The same should be true in sexual abuse prevention to not only avoid the abuse of children, but to protect the future sexual decisions of children. Although the jury is still out on Uncle Harry, the fact that the children really need an internal logic, teaching them to prize their sexual decisions just like they prize their bicycles, is the best way to protect them from Uncle Larry, Uncle Gary or Aunt Karrie, and to protect their ability to make respectful sexual decisions in their future.

This external logic, focusing on who might offend, causes children and adults to look for safety through offender detection, rather than the internal logic of rule respect.

A WONDERFUL STORY

And what a wonderful story to tell children in all the logic learning. Rather than taking a six-year-old roller-blading, perhaps taking him out for an ice cream and telling him about falling in love with his Mother and picking her out of all the ladies in the world, would be a great lesson. How about a Grandma, while teaching Granddaughter to crochet, explains that many, many years ago, she and Grandpa picked each other out of all the people in the world and they shared the private parts of their bodies only with each other, right up until Grandpa went to heaven? And revisiting Emmilou and Edward—wouldn't it have been a wonderful thing if every child sitting in the wedding audience would have had a story told to them about how hard the bride and groom had worked picking each other out of everyone else and that the whole wedding was to honor the picking by Edward and Emmilou?

How about a Grandma, while teaching Granddaughter to crochet, explains that many, many years ago, she and Grandpa picked each other out of all the people in the world and they shared the private parts of their bodies only with each other, right up until Grandpa went to heaven?

Sex Fairy Clipboard

- Accept the idea that children need logic, they need an explanation of rules, and they need guidance very early in life to make responsible sexual decisions.

- Remember that many sexual decisions have lifetime consequences and children need guidance for their entire childhood about how to make these decisions.

- Avoid trying to protect children by teaching children about who might abuse them. That is an external protection and it may unfairly accuse some people, leaving children unprotected from true abusers. Teach internal protection and always remember the power of indignation.

- Remember, we create what we fear. The *DON'T* approach has a fearful message that will probably backfire. Always resort to a positive logic about beautiful intimacy.

- Remember that children who talk to their parents about sex are very difficult to abuse, so always make sure the rescue welcome mat is out for children who are confused or concerned.

- Remember the concept of rules, robbery, and rescue. The message is simple. There are rules about touching and the rules indicate that no one should ever touch private body parts in a secret way. And the rules should also teach that if touching trouble happens, it is the same as a robbery, because everyone has a right to pick someone all on their own.

- Use any opportunity to teach children about the precious nature of *picking* a sexual partner. And even if divorce or alternative lifestyles come into play, actively teach that *EACH PICK* is very important.

- Remember the Sex Fairy goal—teach children that the sexual decisions they make will be some of the most important decisions of their lifetimes.

Chapter 7

Fourth Commandment
Thou Shalt Welcome the World

CHAPTER 7: COMMANDMENT FOUR THOU SHALT WELCOME THE WORLD

It was Christmas time. The weather made an attempt at tradition as the snow rendered outdoor travel in the outskirts of Chelsea difficult. At first, they thought it was the wind. But then, curiosity reigned and the deserted building was inspected. Two innocent men, whose lives would be changed forever with what they found on that frigid afternoon, moved toward the strange sound.

Inside the abandoned structure, half-naked Billy Paine dangled from a roof beam, wrists tied with a crude cord, stretching taut the limbs of the three-year-old, in excruciating pain. The shivering child was almost blue with cold and the red and swollen welts provided a brutal color contrast. Billy's eyes were not open and the two men feared him dead, except for the tiny cries they heard coming from his bleeding and cracked lips. The horrified men retrieved Billy and the child lived—never really being much the same, however.

Two months later, after the Christmas snows changed to mud, the citizens of Chelsea suffered an additional horror, but nothing compared to the Hayden family. After Mr. Hayden saw the condition of his son, he babbled inconsolably *how could this happen*? And why? What monster could have stuffed a dirty rag into seven-year-old Tracy's mouth, stripped him naked and beaten him with a stick? Mrs. Hayden, attending to the terrified child, numbly listened as he meekly described to the officers the horrific beating he endured being tied to a beam in another abandoned building. But that wasn't all. Tracy also told the stupefied cops of enduring threats to have his penis cut off by his wicked assailant. It was unbearable for the adults, but sadly, they were prepared, remembering that only recently they heard the same tragic tales from Billy Paine. *Two boys in two months* was staggeringly awful for all the good folks who couldn't figure out who among them could be so bad. The panic was profound for the Boston suburb of Chelsea as were the questions asked of Billy and Tracy, who could only relate a confused memory that their tormentor was a slight adult (or bigger boy) with brown hair. In the stores and on the streets, suspicions abounded and speculations about *who* simmered.

For weeks following Billy and Tracy's ordeal, parents kept their children assigned to porches and they hurried home from work, anxious about the unknown. But as the spring began to warm the community and no other crimes against children made the headlines, hope of safety for the little ones soared. That is until May, when seven-year-old Robert Maier, after being enticed by promises of seeing the circus, was abducted to a remote public restroom where he, too, was stripped naked, tied by his wrists and beaten unmercifully. Different than Billy and Tracy, Robert described a strange behavior from his abductor. He didn't understand it, but he could describe it. According to the whimpering child, the villain, after what appeared to the child as some sort of *relief,* freed Robert, suddenly unconcerned and disinterested in him.

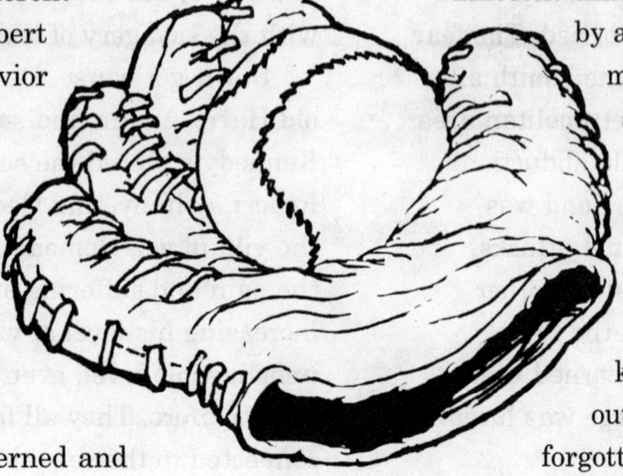

Even though Robert didn't comprehend the *relief* business, the horrified investigators did and they figured the child's innocent observations were connected to sexual relief, which made all of them sick, and made most of them wonder why they didn't work at the local fishnet factory rather than being a cop in sexual assault investigations. With Robert's revelations, the detectives noted that the offender was apparently gleeful about the torture and pain he imposed upon his captive, dancing in a frenzy, taunting the child and appearing to sexually fondle himself. After listening to Robert, the entire community of Chelsea was horrified in wonderment about what kind of soul could commit such a shocking crime? But after hearing what Robert had to say, no one wondered that these crimes of madness were obviously sexually motivated.

Uproar and panic about the suffering of three innocent children was mysteriously followed by a lull, through weeks and then months; with small hopes of safety building for the scared folks, as May turned to June and then July.

The parents of Johnny Balch were also swept up in the warmth of summer as the kiddos busied themselves with outside activities. Johnny had forgotten about the previous tales of terror and since he was enamored with "Kaptain Kidd's Kastle" in the toy store window, he was not hesitant to go with a friendly person who promised a similar wealth of playthings. It all sounded great but soon Johnny found himself like Billy, Tracy and Robert, hung naked from a ceiling beam, beaten unmercifully as his offender, dancing in wild agitation, forced him to endure torturous pain. The innocent child later described the fiend as appearing to not only delight in Johnny's misery but also in sexually touching himself while inflicting pain upon Johnny's genitalia. But the child wasn't done with the terrible tales of what happened. For the once-again-terrified cops, Johnny described the same *release* and change in demeanor that appeared to sap energy from his captor in a shudder and tremble, unknown in origin to the seven-year-old. But the adults knew. And with even more fear and anxiety, they again asked *who,* and of course, *why?*

In concert with Chelsea, all of South Boston became even more vigilant and worried. The fear was certainly warranted as only one month after Johnny's abduction, the entire metropolitan area faced not only another case of child abduction and torture, but from reports, the fiend was escalating to more dangerous sexual attacks. The story provided by George Pratt, another sweet seven-year-old, defied even the most hardened criminologists as they learned that after being promised money, George was lured to a secluded area, stripped naked and with wrists tied, beaten severely while his captor screamed and frolicked in what appeared to be sexual glee. But there was more, according to reports from the trembling child.

This time, the subjugator kicked George in the head, stomach, and groin area, which didn't seem to have occurred in the other child/torture situations. *Yes,* the investigators quietly murmured, things were getting worse. George also suffered deep fingernail scratches to much of his body which, he told investigators, brought apparent delight to his abuser. George also told everyone that the offender bit a piece of flesh from his cheek and buttocks, as well as being stabbed numerous times with a long needle, in his arm, chest, cheek and genitalia. Fishermen who found George were amazed with his ability to survive, but they were even more astonished with the savagery of the attack.

But it got worse. During September, six-year-old Harry Austin and seven-year-old Joseph Kennedy suffered the same fate as Billy, Tracy, Robert, Johnny, and George. It was clear that the villain was demonstrating sexual interest in the pain and suffering of his captives and he was increasing his level of violence to an unbelievable level, even to the most hardened investigators. They all felt that a murder connected to the sexual assaults was right around the corner—a corner none of them wanted to turn.

September was not yet over as five-year-old Robert Gould, lashed to a telegraph pole naked, was prepared for the same fate as the others. But amazingly, Robert's situation provided the proverbial corner to turn as, amazingly, three unsuspecting railroad workers happened upon the scene. Death seemed imminent for Robert had they not interrupted the savagery. An angry *young man* (or so the observers later reported) ran away from the stunned fishermen and Robert Gould's life was saved. But this five-year-old child was not terrified to the point of impairing his observations, so he had lots to say to the stressed out cops.

With clarity, Robert gave police their first real detective-type clue to identify the sexual psychopath who had, for the past nine months, terrorized the community of safety-minded folks. With Robert's descriptions and with good, old *COPS 101* investigative skills, soon Jesse Pomeroy, only twelve years old, was arrested and easily convicted for the crimes. Although everyone felt safer, no one stopped wondering how it could have happened. *Children offending children* made most good folks very uncomfortable and very, very confused—especially considering a *twelve-year-old* culprit.

But as time tends to do, eventually things began to smooth and soothe for the citizenry, once Jesse was tried and trotted off to a juvenile detention facility where he was sentenced to spend the rest of his childhood—taking him right up to the adult age of eighteen. Everyone breathed a sigh of relief with Jesse's departure from the used-to-be-safe community. Kids and parents felt safe as neighborhoods returned to normal. *Good enough*, everyone said. The problem, which few of them understood, was gone.

In kiddo lockup and in spite of the horrific nature of Jesse's crimes, he was smart about the general theme of juvenile justice that is founded on *rehabilitation* rather than the pure *punishment* focus of the adult incarceration system. So with savvy known to few his age, soon his charming demonstration of obedience, remorse and recovery influenced those in authority at the Juvenile Detention Center. Therapists, counselors and the in-charge *grand pooh bahs* all scratched their heads when they compared their expectations of the brutal child abuser to what they saw at the institution, on a day-to-day basis. Rather than behaving like most rotten teenagers who found themselves in trouble with the law, Jesse became a model example of reform and recovery. Many professionals cited Jesse's tender age as contributing to his success, but they were also pretty sure his miraculous recovery was testimony to the merits of their correctional treatment program.

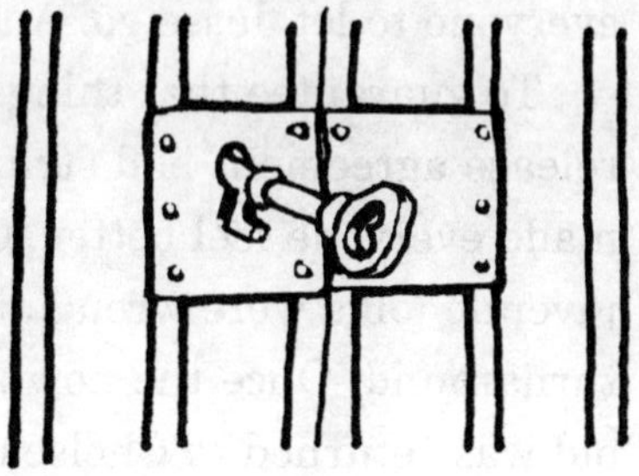

In unison, everyone at the facility viewed Jesse as a prime example of when things go well in a juvenile justice effort. It was stupendous, making many proud. And with this astounding success, they all figured there was no need for Jesse's six-year sentence to be completed. *Why*, it would be a waste of state money to keep this obviously improved kiddo in jail, the bean counters opined. So with smiles, congratulations and pats on the back, Jesse left prison after only 18 months—clearly a reformed young man who, they all suggested, just had a little slip of judgment in the past.

Besides, Jesse's mother, Ruth Pomeroy (who claimed Jesse was innocent, even though he had confessed to the crimes) organized a nasty letter-writing campaign demanding dear Jesse's release. This steadfast mother's effort had become tiresome to many officials in the state juvenile system, so it really seemed best for everyone to let Jesse go. And they did.

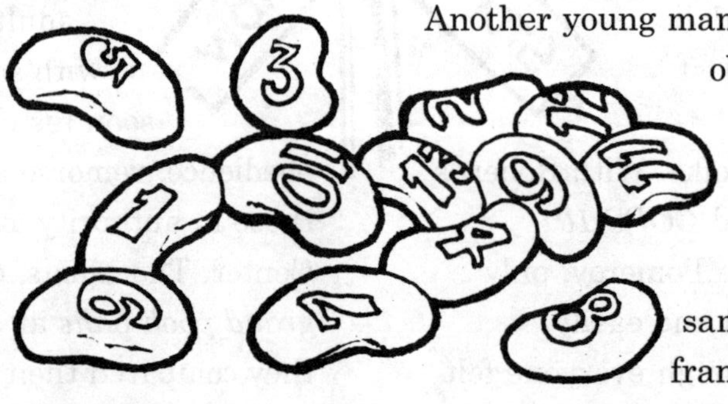

To guarantee that things were safe, Jesse's release agreement had strings attached, which made everyone feel better just in case the juvenile folks were wrong about his drastic turnaround. Once the now-almost-fourteen-year-old was returned to Chelsea and the care of his mother, he was required to get a job and continue maintaining the responsibility he had demonstrated in lock-up. Jesse seemed to have no difficulty handling these supervision obligations, showing the same proficiency he had demonstrated in the correctional facility. He took on a paper route and worked a second job in the store owned by his mother. Everything about Jesse's return to the community seemed grand.

At the same time Jesse was dazzling everyone with his continued compliance and cooperation, ten-year-old Katie Curran entered the dress shop/book store of Jesse's mother, with the mission of purchasing school supplies. Another young man being helped by Jesse observed Katie's presence, but when this man returned from a short errand, it seemed Katie was gone. That was what he told the same cops who organized a frantic search for the missing Curran kiddo. But as days and weeks passed, soon everyone began to recognize that, sadly, the effort seemed futile. Although no one made a connection to what had terrorized the community more than two years previous, an impending gloom about children's safety began to creep into the minds of many. It was like a slow-developing toothache, most good folks suggested. Only for a few fleeting moments did folks remember Jesse and his past dastardly deeds. They remembered his exemplary behavior at the juvenile detention center and his current good conduct, which seemed to put other teenagers to shame in the respect department. Jesse appeared to have changed all right, so for most, he seemed totally disconnected to the ever-increasing worry about children's safety.

Katie Curran remained missing and the

community remained gloomy. The searches revealed nothing but frustration and fear. Even more troubling was when, to the horror of everyone, four-year-old Horace Millen disappeared. The hurried investigation revealed that he was last seen sharing an afternoon treat with an older child and then the two of them easily disappeared around the corner. That was the frightening report from Mrs. Eleanor Fosdick, who was sitting near her bedroom window watching the seemingly harmless

interaction. A short time later, the body of little Horace was discovered, tied spread-eagled on the ground, beaten and murdered, genitals exposed and mutilated, eyes gouged and clear evidence of the unspeakable savagery he experienced in the last minutes of life.

The community of Chelsea felt the same panic they had years previous and with that familiar dread, the name of Jesse Pomeroy emerged at the forefront of suspicion, regardless of how much the juvenile justice folks had flaunted his recovery and rehabilitation. There were also witnesses who believed they had seen Jesse in the area where the unsuspecting men found poor Horace.

Just to be on the safe side, the cops decided to check things out with Jesse. Soon, he was interviewed and detained. And to the shock of those who believed in Jesse's turn around, all of a sudden there were nagging suspicions about his muddy clothing, scratch marks on his face, as well as a convoluted and changing story for his whereabouts at the time that little Horace was abducted and murdered. Things just weren't adding up, the detectives admitted.

When the challenging cop types asked questions, Jesse was unimpressed with their urgency. The worried investigators were stunned that the seemingly unfazed Jesse took a *nap* in his cell while they stacked up the frightening facts about Horace's demise and wondered if they would ever sleep again. Soon, Jesse Pomeroy found himself in a lot of trouble as the community was in a lot of soul searching about how this could have happened—*and happen again?*

As the investigation continued, the horrors caused by Jesse before he was sent to reform school were refreshed in not only the local area of Chelsea, but national newsmakers were also stunned AND talking. Whether it was a fancy restaurant, a group of gossiping teenagers or a coffee break at the construction company, everyone wondered if Jesse was at it again.

Eventually, the cops announced that Jesse confessed to the Horace Millen mess, but by the time of the official inquest, and after defense lawyers talked to him, he miraculously decided his previous confession

was just a mistake and that he was innocent. But in the courtroom, the defense was pitiful, as witnesses placed Jesse near the crime, his boot prints matched those found at the scene, and his knife was found to be as bloody as the unexplained scratches on his face. Although Jesse changed often his story, at times confessing but then after a nap admitting guilt, the jury and the court folks nonetheless thought he was guilty. For Jesse it was over, but for the wondering community it was not.

At the same time of Jesse's legal maneuvering, Ruth Pomeroy fell onto hard times with her business. It seems that not only were people cranky with the idea of her son getting back in trouble for horrible crimes, but Ruth had been quite vociferous with claims that her little pooper was innocent. As Ruth relentlessly rallied for Jesse, her customers rallied for going somewhere else for their books and dresses. So Ruth declared bankruptcy and moved out of the office building, determined to work from home and avoid the pesky public she so loathed.

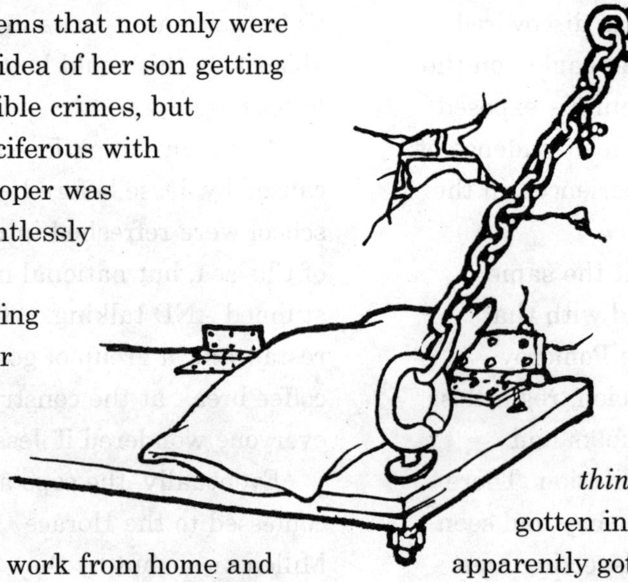

But when the new entrepreneur began to renovate Ruth's old office building, unexplained odors of a particularly obnoxious level caused concern. Nothing seemed to solve the smelly problem until a rather rude discovery in the cellar shocked everyone.

There she was, Katie Curran, brutally murdered and decomposing in the trash of Ruth Pomeroy's business. It was awful and it was clear that Jesse had something to do with Katie's demise. Eventually, Jesse admitted that was true. But it didn't seem that his confession was because of remorse or uncomfortable guilt. Jesse just seemed to be bored with all the legal fussing about Horace's murder, and after all, he had naps to take.

The good news was that the mystery of Katie was solved. The bad news was that now, the *how could this have happened?* tiptoed on the minds of everyone just as the guilt about *who let it happen?* hung in their hearts. There was fussing and fighting as well as pointing the fingers of blame in trying to understand. In the community's rage, clarity was needed so everyone speculated on the answer to the question *how could a child do these things?* especially a kiddo who had gotten in trouble before, who had apparently gotten "fixed" by some of the smartest folks in the juvenile delinquent business, and then released with so many chances for success. Some even postulated that because it was so unbelievable, maybe it wasn't true. This resistance was really pleasing to Ruth Pomeroy, who had always said the cops had the wrong guy.

But for the more realistically minded, the search was on for better answers, starting the *blame search* by studying Jesse's family. At the coffee shops and in the pubs, many gossiped about whether the family background of Jesse Pomeroy promised an answer to *why*? For all the parents in Chelsea and the greater Boston area, this avenue of blame-the-family was a bit scary but they were still interested.

The *family-done-it* pondering began with the common knowledge that Jesse's parents had a less-than-harmonious relationship, prone to much acrimony. But most folks also knew that many kiddos emerge from families with broken homes, or at best, broken promises and they didn't seem bent on becoming the neighborhood butcher. And speaking of butchering, some of the *family-did-it* folks knew that Jesse's father worked in a butcher shop and perhaps, just perhaps they speculated, Jesse gained his lust for blood by worshipping his father's vocation in the slaughterhouse. But when the children of the other butcher Dads were considered, it just didn't add up that the job of Jesse's father could be blamed for the madness.

With more pondering and searches for answers, some wondered if an errant small pox vaccination given to Jesse as just a little guy, might have driven him over the edge. But again, when it was clear that the *vaccination-did-it* folks had kiddos who had also been vaccinated, it seemed obvious there was more subtracting than adding up when it came to figuring out what went wrong with Jesse.

Other ideas were floated about, trying to identify the answer to how Jesse became a monster. One newspaper reporter suggested *Indian Spirits* might have invaded him, and some echoed with claims of evil spells and other supernatural forces that might have caused Jesse's evil. These were dramatic ideas when first speculated, flung about with great excitement. But then, as more comparisons were made, everything just seemed to fizzle.

No such luck, the soul-searching folks lamented when they tried to figure out the meaning of the madness. The eventual conclusion was that lots of kids do just fine with grumpy parents, problems with medical procedures and other common maladies. With no answer in sight, the tongue-wagging guesswork and gossip continued even though some secretly still wondered about the *Indian Spirits.*

Eventually, the mental health folks were brought in, examining Jesse for both the prosecution and the defense, hoping that maybe there was a problem between Jesse's ears, meaning a mental health diagnosis that caused all the badness. Perhaps Jesse had a brain problem rendering him mentally ill or insane, they wondered (and hoped?). Everyone knew that sometimes not-so-bad people do really bad things because they were insane and of course, if this were true, everything would make sense and everyone would feel better in the search for answers. But when all the tests were tallied and when all the interviews and professional pondering abated, the picture that emerged wasn't pretty.

Jesse seemed fine, quite comfortable and sadly, perfectly sane. They all concluded that he was reasonably smart, although not really an Einstein. They thought he knew right from wrong, but collectively they agreed he just didn't *care* about right and wrong. To most of the psych-types, Jesse seemed *unremarkable*. The most significant conclusion centered on what was missing for Jesse—such as guilt, remorse or general caring about others. In fact, how Jesse seemed to be handling his situation seemed most perplexing to the mental health folks.

His detached, if not perky attitude was not quite the condition his mental health evaluators hoped to find. In fact, they felt traumatized by listening to what Jesse had done to his innocent victims and at the same time observing how *okay* Jesse seemed to be about his deeds. His callused detachment devastated them. The professional folks were a mess but Jesse seemed *okie- dokie* with everything, even though he was going to prison for the rest of his life.

But the really good folks, who really wanted understanding about the bad kiddos, kept looking and finally the answers stepped forward with familiarity. It started with the Boston experts, and then it filtered to a country in mourning—feeling a sense of loss in the *understanding children* department.

Finally, they knew. Bringing on sighs of relief, the culprit was not only found (at last), but the culprit was comforting, because it often accounted for what was wrong with the world.

Finally, it was the ***media*** they figured, clear and simple, that spurred Jesse Pomeroy on to abduct, torture, and sexually assault numerous young children. And furthermore, the consensus concluded that the media caused, *yes caused,* him to murder at least two innocents. For sure, the media shuffled to the center of blame, a hoodlum with longevity, far beyond Jesse's short-lived crime spree.

In their conjecturing and concluding, the blamers wanted to set the record straight. Jesse was the criminal, plain and simple they clarified, but it was the media who had really *done it*—the familiar villain in line for culpability when youth wander out of control. *No,* it wasn't the parents, it wasn't some mental derangement afflicting Jesse, and *no* it wasn't a vaccination or Indian spirits. But *yes,* the offender was the media in all its power, in all its glory, and for sure, they theorized, in all its money. The media, they opined, provided the breeding ground—influencing children beyond temptation, innocently dragging them into criminal conduct they could have avoided in a time of less media influence. Such it was with Jesse—innocent really, until mesmerized by the evil media.

Interestingly, the media itself reported that *the media was the problem,* which was quite ironic. The rumors of *blame the media* wouldn't have made it past the Chowder House gossip mill if the media hadn't kindly reported themselves to be the culprit. Everyone fussed about blame and some even felt a little guilty about getting great information about the badness of the media, *from the media.* But never mind, many said, since the trial of Jesse Pomeroy was over, his lifetime sentence was secure and with the true perpetrator identified, it was time to get back to normal.

But for Jesse Pomeroy, the meddling media was somewhat different than contemporary punk rock music, Internet influences, or Beavis and Butthead on the cable channels. *No,* for the *blame the media* game in Jesse Pomeroy's time, the offenders were *Dime Novels* that served as his influencer, not Janet Jackson at the Super Bowl, MTV featuring girlies with pasties, or movies featuring Academy Award hit songs such as *It's Hard Out There To Be A Pimp.* In Jesse Pomeroy's time, it was the *Dime Novels,* and the year was 1871, not too long after the American Civil War.

The *Dime Novels* were first on the market in 1860 when a New York publishing company began to print cheap, paperbound adventure stories about fighting Indians, swashbuckling pirates, countless (but justified) murders of cowboys and cowgirls, and conflicts with all sorts of two and four-legged, wild and wooly critters. At the time, *Dime Novels* were thought to have lured Jesse into a murderous rage. Today; those novels would probably have lulled most children to sleep.

Two of the most famous and best selling *Dime Novels* were Edward L. Wheeler's *Deadwood Dick on Deck* and *Calamity Jane—The Heroine of Whoop-Up.* Absolutely obscene they were, according to the smart pundits trying to figure out the madness of Jesse Pomeroy. These literary burps were violent for sure, as they described the attack, torture and murder of various human and critter creatures with common themes describing oozing wounds and bleeding body parts. But compared to current day media, these media contributions would be categorized in the same group as Mother Goose. And even though this *media blame* was a very long time ago—the blame game is timeless, enticing each generation into not only blaming outside influences when things go wrong with children, but in doing so, cleverly abdicating responsibility for teaching children the right path to follow.

FOURTH COMMANDMENT—*THOU SHALT WELCOME THE WORLD*

Yes, times have changed since Jesse Pomeroy, but the tendency to blame the media has not. Flinging fault at the world has a soft and safe underpinning suggesting that the home and family are places where everything is *okie-dokie*, something like a Norman Rockwell painting or the image of everyone in the family being in flannel pajamas and drinking hot cocoa before 6:30 p.m. And the tailgate to that sweet, family image secures the thought that should anything go wrong, the culprit is always an outside influence with the media being a handy, dandy front-runner in the blame—just like all the good folks in Jesse Pomeroy's day.

Rather than teaching sexual respect to children ***internally,*** the idea is to attack an ***external*** influence—which allows sidestepping of parental responsibility in teaching. This outside battle ends up being quite comfy for two really reliable reasons. First, the outside world of the media is pretty raunchy, making a great target for attack in movies, music, books and the Internet. Secondly, waging war on the external smut is a whole lot easier and comfortable than internally teaching sexual respect—and having to talk to toddlers about Tinky Winky or advising teenagers about what to do in the back bedroom at the unauthorized keg party.

WORLD WAR WAGING

Waging war on the world (with the media in the managerial position) is a comfortable way for society to funnel its energy. The warmongers first blame, then they fight the media—often neglecting children in the process. But as usual in war, the various media entities fight back with grand weaponry of ratings, labels, chips, stamps and screens; claiming these concessions rescue them from responsibility for creating a sexually disrespectful climate for the sweet kiddos. For parents who care about children, and worry about the outside world, media retaliation is a seductive process—easily offering peace in ratings, labels, chips, stamps and screens. But are those cute contributions of regulations really an olive branch or just a trick to dodge the bullets of war?

WELCOME THE WORLD?

With all the war waging on the world, how can the Fourth Commandment—*Thou Shalt Welcome The World* suggest a ***welcome*** for the nasty media thought be responsible for centuries of shameful behavior? The answer lies in a call to action for first understanding how the media blame game is so seductive and easy to follow with the allure and attractiveness of the media's pretend concern about the kiddos with their ratings and such. Secondly, parents need to develop a keener eye for content of the media offerings, paying closer attention to the ***screaming subtleties*** and the ***dumbing down***

Rather than teaching sexual respect to children *internally,* the idea is to attack an *external* influence—which allows the sidestepping of the responsibility to teach sexual respect.

Parents also need to develop a keener eye for content of the media offerings, paying closer attention to the *screaming subtleties* and the *dumbing down* of sex rather than fussing about exposed nipples or poking-out-of-panties pubic hair.

of sex rather than fussing about exposed nipples or poking-out-of-panties pubic hair. And then, with all that understanding and resistance to the blame-the-media and count-on-the-media-ratings; good parents will accept the media as part of a child's world and with courage (and the first three commandments) welcome the world of the media as an antithesis, or the opposite, to teach sexual respect. But first, the blame game.

WORLD WAR ONE BLAME

Even though blaming the *Dime Novels* depicting hanky-panky in wars of the Wild West was a very long time ago, the refrain of blame seems timeless. On October 1, 1997, sixteen-year-old Luke Woodham opened fire in Pearl, Mississippi, killing two and terrorizing countless others in his school. On December 1, 1997, fourteen-year-old Michael Carneal killed three classmates and wounded eight others in West Paducah, Kentucky. On March 24, 1998, thirteen-year-old Mitchell Johnson and his eleven-year-old buddy, Andrew Golden, killed five and wounded fifteen at their school in Jonesboro, Arkansas. On May 21, 1998, Kip Kinkel, after murdering both his parents the previous night, opened fire on teachers and classmates in Springfield, Oregon. And, on April 20, 1999, eighteen-year-old Eric Harris and seventeen-year-old Dylan Klebold went on a shooting spree in Colorado's Columbine High School, eventually killing thirteen and wounding many. The murders committed by these children were senseless, everyone was sure about that, but the *why* became as familiar as the pondering in Jesse Pomeroy's days.

The search began. Snooping through the rooms, the computers, televisions, bookshelves and DVD players of the school shooters, the answer was sought. The *what caused it?* was the mission; seeking to comprehend what outside influences changed the flannel pajamas into senseless slaughter costumes. And even though the parents of the kiddo criminals were invited to the blame table, in many forms, ironically that culpability challenge was usually centered around *how could these parents have allowed the outside influences to corrupt the kiddos killers?*

BYGONE BLAME?

In concert with throwing rocks at the outside world comes a longing for the *good old days* when seemingly things were kinder and gentler, at least according to the blame game philosophers. But were things really better in the bygone, good old days or is blaming the world and longing for a nicer time just another form of denial that prevent parents from taking charge of their own children? Writing about Jesse Pomeroy, the author of *Fiend,* Harold Schechter, provides a more realistic look at the ridiculous nature of longing for bygone times.

"The longing for a bygone age—for a time when life was slower, sweeter, simpler—is such a basic human impulse that it often blinds us to the fact that the 'good old days' were a lot worse than we imagine. Living at a time of pervasive pollution, we yearn for those delightful pre-automotive days when the air was free of car exhaust—forgetting that the streets of every major nineteenth-century city reeked of horse piss, manure, and the decomposing carcasses of worked-to-death nags. Reading about the pathetic state of public education, we grow teary-eyed for the age of the 'Little Red Schoolhouse'—completely unaware of the deplorable conditions of nineteenth-century classrooms (according to one authoritative source, 'A survey of Brooklyn schools in 1893, listed eighteen classes with 80 to 100 students; one class had 158.'). Affronted by the nonstop barrage of media violence, we pine for a return to a more civilized time—conveniently forgetting that, a hundred years ago, public hangings were a popular form of family entertainment, and turn-of-the-century 'penny papers' routinely ran illustrated, front-page stories about axe-murders, sex killings, child torture, and other ghastly crimes."

The tendency is to blame influences outside the home, and in partnership, long for the good old days when Dad walked 20 miles to school (both ways uphill) and Mom had only one school dress a year. Children have been committing horrific crimes throughout history with various influences from an ever-changing outside world. But denial of responsibility, suggesting *the media done it*, coupled with longing for the good old days, is as old as Ruth Pomeroy's denial that her little pooper did anything wrong.

WORLD WAR TWO FIGHT

So, if the first avenue of abdicating responsibility for raising sexually respectful children is to blame the media and yearn for the good old days, then the only natural next step is to fight. Parents join church groups, schools, courts, organizations and political parties. With great vigor and vengeance, they organize parades, protests, and telephone canvassing campaigns in the seemingly honorable crusade of fighting the media—trying to get the disrespectful stuff censored, controlled or cancelled. And as long as the war wages *outside*, the delicate responsibility of talking to children about sex and teaching *inside* critical thinking about sex is solved—or so it is thought.

ENTER THE ENEMY

If the enemy is the media world, what exactly is this culprit ruining the lives of so many children who would, in the great parental pretend, grow up perfectly without the mean media influence? Right at the top of the enemy roll call is television, where the number crunchers know for sure that about forty percent of free time for children is spent in front of the *tuberusky* and, on the ugly average, the kiddos spend about 5.5 hours per day on some kind of electronic entertainment. And the *Boob Tube,* as some call television, leads the list. Also at the electronic media *culprit pulpit* is music, movies, and, of course, computers that not only include the Internet, but also those pesky video games that find their smutty way to laptops, PCs or the television set.

As the media cries foul for the flying fouls thrown their way, they cite their report card of being quite smut conscious and in fact, being clearly respectful to the precious little minds of the kiddos.

A somewhat slow second in the culprit designation is the non-electronic form of the media in the old-fashioned printed word, although certainly many books and other written documents are available electronically. Whether it is found on a library shelf, within a secretly printed e-mail, on the pages of Mom's magazine in the beauty shop, or on the lyrics page of the rap CD that Dad forbids, the sins of society are easily broadcast within the written word media; in partnership with the must-be-plugged-in media, making big targets for those who wage war.

FLYING FOULS, CRYING FOUL

But *whoa* say the media, retaliating in the battle and crying foul that just like in Jesse Pomeroy's day, they get unfairly blamed for everything. *Dime novels or Desperate Housewives have nothing to do with the school shootings, juvenile delinquent behavior, or the really, really big badness—juvenile sexual offending,* they collectively retort. As the media cries foul for the flying fouls thrown their way, they cite their report card of being quite smut conscious and, in fact, being clearly respectful to the precious little minds of the kiddos. And their platform comes in the form of movie, music and television *ratings*.

RATING RANTINGS

The movie industry wants no part of being blamed for the badness, since they are *Nurse-Ratchet-proud* with their efforts to make everything in movies okay with the kiddos, as long as parents also do their job in guiding the little poopers. Keeping the little ones out of things that might make them upset or expose them to something steamy is quite easy, proclaim the decency-minded movie purveyors.

Ranting about the movie ratings goes back to the 1960's when things in the movies suddenly seemed a little out of control, at least according to contemporary society at the time. *Who's Afraid of Virginia Wolf* happened to be the movie that got everything started in the rating business since right there on the screen; a foul-mouthed actor said the word *screw*. It was awful, but it wasn't all they had to worry about. The phrase *hump the hostess* in the same movie threw everyone into a big what-to-do-tizzy as they wondered where the world was headed with such smut.

So the concerned folks got together and with great pomp and circumstance they decided to axe the single "S" word, describing that little metal thing so handy in hanging pictures. *It was just too obscene* they all confirmed. But what to do with the *hostess humping* was way too complicated. So, without a clear solution, the hostess situation (however humpful) stayed in the movie. During this time, other movies with sexual innuendos also popped up and pumped up. Finally, in 1968, the United States Supreme Court took the bull by the horns (without any mention of being horny) and said *yes,* cities and states could regulate films and books to protect the kiddos from unauthorized pumpings. But how to do that was the big question.

HOSTESS HUMPING HASSLES

After planning and pondering, the movie folks got together with worried war wagers, and with the government looking over their shoulders, they came up with a movie rating system. It was magnificent, they thought, especially with the hostess humping hassle still fresh in their minds. The rating plan wasn't to suggest which movies had passing grades or were good/bad. The idea was to rate the movies so parents could be warned about what they might want the kiddos to see and what movies should be sent to the discarded screw department. And no, it wasn't that dreaded *C word* of censorship, they clarified; the ratings were simply guidelines to help the big people protect the little people from the meanness of the media.

ROLLED OUT RATINGS

Since 1968, the ratings gave the movie makers the chance to cry foul if they were blamed for corrupting the kiddos—which in reality was just passing the buck. They started with the G rating for *general,* suggesting that the movie was basically *y'all come,* generously inviting Grandma or any age gremlin kiddo to watch the flick. "Violence is at a minimum, nudity and sex scenes are not shown nor is there any drug use," touted the movie folks dodging the flying fouls of blame. But with the rather somber designation of a G rating, it soon became clear to the bean counters that there weren't enough Grandmas heading for the box office and sending folks in flannel pajamas with a cup of hot chocolate to the movies just didn't seem to be bringing in much cash. And so, even though the ratings were rolled out to protect the kiddos, the big bucks were really driving the train toward generating more beans. So the movie folks came up with a higher rating that was more box office titillating and probably more checkbook stimulating.

But what to do with the *hostess humping* was way too complicated, so without a clear solution for assuring decency, the hostess situation (however humpful) stayed in the movie.

The PG (Parental Guidance) rating advised that parents should do some guiding. *Yes,* there may be some profanity, the movie raters admit, but *no,* nudity and violence are absent, except of course, for the qualifier ***brief*** nudity and ***brief***

So the movie folks came up with a higher rating that was more box office titillating and probably more checkbook stimulating.

violence. No one is sure, however, how many *briefs* of nudity or violence could pile up to mean a lot of nudity and violence, but never mind that say the clever movie raters who just want to guarantee that the bad stuff in the flicks won't come all at once since they must guarantee the smut is only ***brief***. But the really big news is that parents can be assured with the PG rating that there is absolutely no drug use in the movie, not even one ***brief*** chemical indiscretion, which really makes everyone feel safer and ready for the flannels.

REALLY RAUNCHY R-RATINGS

Moving up on the don't-blame-us-because-we-have-ratings response to the *media done it* culpability, comes the raunchy R-rating. In order to fall into the R (for the dreaded *restricted*) category, the movie must contain "adult themes." Apparently, rape, sexual assault, and out-of-control hanky-panky are considered to be *adult,* which really questions for the kiddos what growing up is all about.

Then comes the rating of NC-17 meaning no kiddos, no way, no time. This rating is the clearest, closing the doors for anyone under the age of eighteen regardless of the amount of *guidance* parents may want to assert at the box office ticket-buying line. But, in reality, the NC-17 rating does influence what movies the kiddos watch. The seduction for parents begins when they consider this heavy hitting rating of NC-17 at the top, resulting in a great sense of security snuggled into the lower rating movies. Without really taking a look at the PG movie content or the number of *briefs* of sex and violence, Mom and Dad just know that since the kiddos were axed from going to X-rated, NC-17 rated, and R-rated, the good old PG rating starts to look pretty milk toast.

PG RATING (PARENTAL GASP)

So the movie folks and parents take great comfort in the PG rating, which in reality should stand for something like *parental gasp*. The needed critical thinking about movie influence on the kiddos will only happen if Mom and Dad really check things out and not rely on the easy way of believing the PG ratings guarantee morality for the kidlets going to the Saturday matinee.

Many PG movies make their way into the lives of children and it is true these flicks do not contain a front shot of huffing and puffing intercourse, there is no pubic hair showing, and a really good look at penises and vaginas just doesn't happen, however *brief*. But when the movie makers suggest everything is A-okay because of the rating system, good parents should avoid that seduction toward perceived safety and recognize that the *screaming subtleties* and the over sensitization of sex (*dumbing down*) is the real culprit in these supposedly-not-sexual movies.

SCREAMING SUBTLETIES & THE DUMBING DOWN OF SEX

Hostess humping ponderings and musing about whether one cheap shot at a breast nipple is going to send society into ruin, is a whole lot different than taking the Fourth Commandment challenge and resisting the allure of counting on the ratings. In reality, it is the ongoing ***screaming subtleties*** and the ***dumbing down of sex*** that teaches children sexual disrespect. A single example from hundreds of PG rated movies typifies the subtlety in a mediocre movie. About a half-decade ago, a movie entitled *Mol Flanders*, which wasn't R-rated or even PG-13 rated, was produced. In fact, it was a rather obscure, unimportant movie just trudging along in the not-Academy-Award winning category, but providing an excellent example of the true reality of sexual influence. *Good enough,* parents may have said as the pre-teen kiddos were dropped off at the Saturday matinee to see Mol Flanders, while Mom took comfort in the PG rating and in using the time to get her nails done.

The not-profound-but-classic-screaming-subtleties/dumbing-down-of-sex movie begins as a gentleman removes a six-year-old child from the orphanage where she has spent her entire life. Although he does not wear flannel pajamas, he is kind and soft as he explains the six-year-old's legacy. This back tracking in time creates the theme for the movie, which unfolds as a series of flashbacks.

First Mol (the six-year-old) is informed she was born in prison to her mother who was a prostitute. The movie depicts Mol's birth with pelvic exam-type shots of Mom, legs spread, screeching pain and the baby coming into the world to an audience of prison guards with not a single celebration cigar anywhere. Then, this not-too-bad-for-the-kiddos-movie shows Mom, with blood and guts galore, being put to death by hanging because of her sexual indiscretions that produced the illegitimate child, Mol. But of course, the movie had only a PG rating since the sexual and violent parts were *brief*. There were lots of them, but gratefully, they were all brief.

The movie progresses with Mol being raised by cranky nuns and a wayward priest who gets a little frisky with Mol in the confessional booth. Being tough like her mother, Mol retaliates by stabbing a knitting needle through his priestly and pesky hand. But never mind, the movie raters suggest, since Mol's violence against the priest was only brief.

As the years trudge forward in the movie, the six-year-old grows up with her mother's legacy and finally, *enough is enough,* and Mol follows dead Mommy into a life of prostitution. Now with this change in vocation for Mol, the little ones watching the movie won't see pubic hair shots nor will nipples be exposed. But they will see that in order to be prostitution-certified, another pelvic-exam is required of Ms. Moll, of course to an audience of leering and lecherous men quibbling over her virgin commodity.

In reality, it is the ongoing *screaming subtleties* and the *dumbing down of sex* that teaches children sexual disrespect.

When a country kid with a seductive voice was scheduled for the Sunday night *Ed Sullivan Show* in the 1950's, everyone had their underwear in a knot about the singer's tendency to wiggle his hips.

There is great question in the movie about whether Mol, in all those years in the Catholic orphanage really maintained her purity, which for the highest bidder will be auctioned off in this morally meaningful movie. The good news for the kidlets watching this *safe movie* is that everything works out for Mol as the pelvic exam conducted by men in very strange religious costumes suggests everything is intact and her virginity is rock solid—just as solid as parents thinking this kind of movie is better than the kiddos seeing hostess humpings.

And when Mom picks her kids up from the movie with still-wet fingernails, she smugly believes her still-innocent munchkins are just that—innocent, since the movie was only rated PG. But the screaming subtleties of the ordinary Mol Flanders movie include piles (but brief) snippets of nudity, the *dumbed down* message of glorifying prostitution, and the sexist normalizing of men taking advantage of women, as well as clarifying that a female's value is primarily in the sex department. And those subtle messages are a recipe for sexual disrespect with not too many folks paying attention.

Other PG (Parental Gasp) movies that look comfy but should make parents gasp, rather than guide, represent the screaming subtleties and the dumbing down of sex on a constant and ever-seducing basis. Whether it is *White Chicks*, *Mean Girls*, or even dozens of Disney-type movies, the subtlety of sex softy screams to children absolutely everything their parents usually want them to avoid. Sexual disrespect, sexual stampedes, sexual escapades and sexual *supersize-me* are sprinkled throughout these movies. True, there are no crotch shots and nary a nipple is exposed in these flicks, but for sure, sexual disrespect is saturated throughout, silently slipping past the ratings that make parents so happy and make movie makers even more happy with their paychecks.

FLYING\CRYING FOUL OF MUSIC

Even though there were no DVD or CD players in Jesse Pomeroy's time, the *music-did-it* blame game is timeless. When a country kid with a seductive voice was scheduled for the Sunday night *Ed Sullivan Show* in the 1950's, everyone had their underwear in a knot about the singer's tendency to wiggle his hips. *What could be done about the hip-wiggling smut* most wondered, fearing that if the screaming fans took one peek at an errant pelvic gyration, ruin would befall society. So Ed made a deal with the tight-lipped folks who wanted to protect the kidlets. Elvis Presley would only be shown from his waist up, and therefore the show-watching kiddos wouldn't turn their lives into sexual crime or rampant promiscuity after one Sunday evening with Ed Sullivan. Everything eventually worked out fine on that famous night and only a short time later society seemed to accept the inevitable nature of Rock and Roll, although some couldn't help longing for the days of Dean Martin and Perry Como.

LIMITS IN LYRICS?

In spite of past prohibitions on wiggling hips from the instigator of Rock and Roll, current music seems to have no limits regarding lyrics and what performers subtlety scream or suggest on stage with sex and violence as the common theme. But different than television or the movies, without seeing pubic hair poking out of someone's panties, music (sound only) seems less of a threat to the good folks wanting to raise sexually respectful children but still caught up in the media-done-it blame game. There is a world war against what is *seen* in the movies and on television, but there seems to only be a cold war against what kiddos might hear in music. Without having to worry about nudity, music just seems a little sweeter. But as the Fourth Commandment suggests, parents should carefully consider the content of music for screaming subtitles and sexual dumbing down. With this vigilance, the sad reality is that in music every conceivable sexually disrespectful message is conveyed in the lyrics and performance styles—subtle for some, and for others, not so subtle.

SEE NO EVIL

Like the movie folks, the music makers cry foul when they are blamed for the badness of American youth for a couple of reasons. First, they say, music doesn't show any sex—no pubic hair, no penises in vaginas and, for sure, no hostess humping. *No pictures means no problems* is the tune from the music troop dodging blame. They also, as a side dish, suggest that even if the music lyrics are a little risqué, maybe none of the kiddos really understand the words.

But different than television or the movies, without seeing pubic hair poking out of someone's panties, music (sound only) seems less of a threat to the good folks wanting to raise sexually respectful children but still caught up in the media-done-it blame game.

MORE FOUL CRYING

Additionally, the music folks cry foul in the blame war, touting their rating system instigated by Tipper Gore; wife to vice president, Al Gore, who raised a big fuss about music ruining the kidlets. With her hard work and the help of others, a less-than-one-inch sticker is required for record albums (CDs) telling the parents to fire up a little guidance before letting the kiddos listen to the tunes. The PA (Parental Advisory) rating ought to take care of everything, the getting-on-top-of-it Gore gang hoped.

SUPER SLEUTHING

Getting the music wholesome was also the goal of the music police in the halftime entertainment of Super Bowl 2006. Because of their sleuthing for smut, the moral music folks were ready. With great preparation and electronic maneuvering, Mick Jagger's microphone was flipped off precisely when he sang the word ***come*** in his rather dated song *Start Me Up* just to make sure the morality of American youth was *super salvaged* during the half time entertainment. Ironically, it was probably only the old-timer-baby-boomers who knew the word *come* was doing just that—

This music bleep of the word *come* sent everyone home from the Super Bowl with a really warm assurance that everything was A-okay in the music morality business.

coming in the Rolling Stone song, since it was popular so long ago. *But never mind*, many suggested, considering the awfulness of the Super Bowl two years previous, when America's youth were forced to see Janet Jackson's nipple—however pasted. This music bleep of the word *come* sent everyone home from the Super Bowl with a really warm assurance that everything was A-okay in the music morality business.

HIP HOPPING AND HOPING

Although the baby boomers were probably happy with outing the nasty word *come* in the halftime entertainment of the 2005 Super Bowl, they didn't seem to know what to do with music their kids really seem to worship called Hip-Hop or Rap—except perhaps hope the kids don't understand or pay attention to the words. In reality, the little old word *come* looks pretty peaked next to such songs as *Surrounded By Hoes*, *I Smell Pussy,* and *P.I.M.P.*, all sung by the popular star, Fifty Cent. And Eminem's versions of songs titled, *Fuck Off* and *Suck My Dick*, would have thought to cause at least a little stir for some critics of the Super Bowl ***come*** cancellation. When Limp Bizket sang, *Get Naked*, eyebrows might have been raised until he was eventually outdone by Snoop Dogg's ever-favorites *Payin' For Pussy* and *Pussy Sells*, bringing a respectful financial ring to the smut in Hip Hop and Rap music. And with all those titillating titles and lyrics it can only be imagined how the old and indignant folks could really feel better with outing the word ***come*** from the Super Bowl half time.

COUNTRY MUSIC

In the skirmish of war on the world of music, other music seems sweeter to most parents. They probably don't see much to stamp or label (Tipper wouldn't either) in Country Western music because after all, farm stuff just reeks of morality for Americans. Many conclude this kind of music is A-okay since it is usually about wholesomeness, patriotism and family values—not pussies or payment for prostitutes. But understanding the words is really easy and really scary in Country Western music, without so much as a bent dart being thrown at the lyrics in the war on the smut-pedaling music world.

COWBOY/COWGIRL CONTEMPLATIONS

There is just something sweet about cowboys and cowgirls—at least according to the country music folks—and to parents, this type of music seems generally in the *no foul* department. But if the *screaming subtleties* and the *dumbing down of sex* is examined in country music, the sexual respect category looks pretty pitiful. Generally, country music lyrics are about getting sex, getting laid, getting drunk to have sex and getting screwed to justify getting sex at the corner motel. In fact, David Allen Coe, in his old, but hot tune *You Never Even Called Me By*

My Name made it clear that certain components were required for a country song to include; pickup trucks, trains, Mama, rain, prison, getting drunk, and getting broken hearted by the babes in some form or another. And all these categories are high on the list of sexual disrespect for sure but shrouded in the country cloak of perceived wholesomeness. .

There are other country songs, not at the top of the charts, but maybe *over the top* with titles such as *Let's Get Drunk and Screw; All My Exes Live in Texas; Don't Come Home A Drinkin' With Lovin' On Yo-Mind; Feeling Single and Drinking Doubles; You Got the Money Honey, I Got the Time; If You Want Your Freedom PDQ, Divorce Me COD; It Ain't Easy Being Easy; Let's Do Something Cheap and Superficial; She Got the Goldmine, I Got the Shaft; Thank God and Greyhound She's Gone; This Good Girl's Gonna Go Bad; Tight Fittin' Jeans;* and who could forget *There Isn't Enough Room in My Fruit of the Looms, to Hold All My Lovin' For You*?

But don't worry, many of the don't-think-country-music-is-all-that-bad folks urge, there is a lot of religion included in country music demonstrated by such songs as *I Wrote a Hot Check To Jesus, Are You Drinkin' With Me Jesus*? and the ever-sanctimonious tune, *Drop Kick Me Jesus Through the Goal Posts of Life*. These titles in a pile seem awful but one-at-a-time, playing softly in the background, Country Western music seems to get a pass from blame, since hip wiggling and crotch grabbing is at a minimum and because it comes from the country heartland of America, seeming to whisper sweet morality to everyone.

There is just something sweet about cowboys and cowgirls—at least according to the country music folks—and to parents, this type of music seems generally in the *no foul* department.

BANNING THE BOOKS

Banning books is also a great way for parents to wage war on the media and in doing so, they can easily abdicate responsibility for teaching sexual respect. Book banning has a long history, probably beginning with a guy named Plato in 350 BC who told everyone that it was the purpose of the in-charge government folks to "supervise the making of fables and legends, rejecting all which are unsatisfactory." When Mr. P. was considered an expert on banning and rejecting, things were pretty simple since it took a really long time to write a book by hand, and if the hostess-humping kind of axe was needed, it wasn't very hard to build a good fire and let the only two existing copies go up in smoke. Then, in 1450 AD, the printing press was invented and after that everything about controlling written material became messy AND smoky. Consider that about 300 years later, the United States Constitution would opine about things like freedom of the press and the evils of censorship, and everything really heated up and not just in the book bonfires.

Books like J.D. Salinger's *Catcher in the Rye* have always brought the wage-war-on-the-world folks to the library meetings ever since the book was written in the 1940's. Folks have wanted it out because it describes a young man's sexual thoughts and dreams. There have been four decades of fussing about the book even though lots of young men have probably continued having sexual thoughts and dreams during that time. And it could be wondered whether waging war with the book is about not wanting boys to have sexual thoughts and dreams or just wanting everyone to pretend they don't have them. Either way, the book battle continues.

Contemporary warriors thought the Harry Potter books ought to be banned as well, spending lots of time and money fussing about whether having Harry in libraries and in the classroom would ruin the kidlets. This Harry bashing wasn't so much about sex directly, but the fussy folks worried that the stories lacked family values and, instead of mentioning God, spoke of magic and evil. The Nurse Ratchet types wanted Harry's popularity stifled because there wasn't a single scene of anyone in flannel pajamas and drinking cocoa.

The Nurse Ratchet types wanted Harry's popularity stifled because there wasn't a single scene of anyone in flannel pajamas drinking cocoa.

Ironically, these anti-evil world war wagers didn't seem to notice the evil portrayed in other favorites over time such as Batman, Spiderman, Star Trek or Star Wars; but the Harry Potter books were easily engaged in the *media done it* battle, and besides, books just make better bonfires.

CRYING CONSTITUTION FOUL

Different than the music, movies or computer entities who claim foul when they are blamed for getting bad stuff to the kids (touting their ratings, protective screens or other stop-gate stuff), the book people just claim *no foul* by using the good old Constitution of the United States. Yep, freedom of the press just about always guarantees anybody the right to express just about anything. In 2002, the United States Supreme Court said *no* to the folks who wanted virtual child pornography banned. Since the computer-generated images caused *no real victims*, the heavy-hitter legal folks said someone's right to sexual expression was clearly protected by that very old piece of paper. No matter how hard the blamers try to get things banned, over and over again it seems the expression of others finds protection in constitutional law.

Jon Stewart's book *America* caused quite a stir as it depicted naked members of the United States Supreme Court—probably from computer generated nakedness rather than from the justices agreeing to a photo shoot at a cheap motel. *Oh, it was awful* many screamed, and Wal-Mart, in prudish protest, refused to carry the pesky publication. The publishers, in crying foul in the blame game, pointed out that there was a helpful exercise in the book allowing a concerned reader to match detached clothing to the specific bodies of the justices, getting everything back in order. But that didn't stop folks from trying to get the book banned. Ironically, it will probably be members of the Supreme Court, however naked and chilly, who will be the ones upholding Mr. Stewart's right to publish their naked little bodies.

ENTER THE INTERNET

The Internet offers unlimited opportunities for children in many helpful but also scary ways. In the waging war on the world, parents may work really hard to get the movies rated, get the music controlled through an itty-bitty stamp and ban the nasty books from school. But, in reality, the Internet may make all of that fussing and fuming about the other media outlets absolutely futile. Reading lyrics is certainly boring compared to listening to rappers sing them, but with just a few clicks the kiddos can read the words of any song or find the words to any banned books on the Internet, no matter how many stickers are stuck or bonfires are built. But that's not all in the electronic dumbing down of sex.

Parents may forbid sexual web sites or certain *hotsy* words like SEX that would turn the munchkins into Jesse Pomeroy act-alikes, but that doesn't prevent e-mails with subject headings about babes and baseball bat insertion (words sanitized, of course) or tips of how to add six inches to outer genitalia in just one tasty tonic. The screaming subtitles of sex are found in advertisements, e-mail subject lines and every other imaginable electronic connection. The Internet advertises what movie star is pregnant, what celebrity has had breast augmentation, or what second grader was arrested for sexual harassment—all classic examples of the Internet dumbing down of sex and screaming sexual subtleties.

But those Internet concerns are usually second in line from the heavy-duty worry about how the Internet becomes the conduit for the really bad people—the on line sexual predators, who lure children into sexual encounters, often at significant risk. There are billboards, commercials and television documentaries about these disgusting, on-line-predators, and rightly so. Folks should be concerned about those problems. But the question more pertinent to raising sexually respectful children is what is the impact of that constant saturation about sexual predators on the sexual health of children? And where are the billboards, the commercials and the Dateline documentaries questioning why it is so easy for these offenders to lure the thought-to-be-innocent kidlets into sexual predator snares? Can the connection between the lack of sexual conversation with children and parents about sex ever enter into the concern category?

SCREEN RESCUES

But then, just like the movie and music folks, the Internet pundits cry foul with all the blaming, suggesting that whatever goes on the Internet is okay because parents can just count on the rescue of the *screens*. They suggest that just like the movie ratings or Tipper's stickers, parents can simply screen out the bad stuff. And the legal folks (naked or not) back them up, opining that with the screens, the kids are safe from smut, and the constitution guaranteeing freedom of expression is safe for the country's honor.

Ironically it will probably be members of the naked Supreme Court, however chilly or uncomfortable, who will be the ones upholding Mr. Stewart's right to publish their naked little bodies.

And where are the billboards, the commercials and the Dateline documentaries questioning why it is so easy for these offenders to lure the thought-to-be-innocent kidlets into sexual predator snares?

The electronic folks offer screens of all sizes and shapes, in a variety of filters, traps and all kinds of tricks to not only close out the Internet world that is unsavory for children, but to make Mom and Dad feel safe. Different than alphabet-soup type of movie ratings or ever-so-slight stickers, these screen contraptions are available in the stores for Mom and Dad to choose and purchase, helping them feel really in charge. These handy, dandy screens can also be downloaded from the Internet, interfaced with the server, and they also have the clever feature of *secret passwords*, really firing up feelings of security for worried Moms and Dads. Yes, the computer screen safety net is tangible, it is secure, and it a sure-fire way to avoid having to actually teach sexual respect in homes since disrespectful sex is screened out.

HOLES IN THE SCREEN

Parents from a rural, but nonetheless Internet accessible community, present their fifteen-year-old son for evaluation as he is facing five felony counts of Sexual Abuse in the First Degree. He is at risk for not only incarceration, but also sex offender registration and notification for the rest of his life. His parents are defensive and fearful as they describe their home-schooling efforts so their children could avoid *outside influences of sin*. They report the family's regular church attendance and they remark with pride that their children are not allowed to listen to rock or rap music. Most importantly, they flaunt their childproof filters and screens on the family Internet access. So *how this could have happened?* is their painful pondering with an eye on waging war outside their flannel pajama home.

But that isn't all to their child rearing opinions. These astonished parents describe the seven-year-old female victim (his cousin and their niece), as being improperly raised by her single mother, using the outside influences of the world as their weapon of criticism. *Why, the first grader is quite a vixen* they claim, obviously because she attends daycare and her mother is not married. With smug indignation, they further describe the seven-year-old *seductress* as being responsible for the sexual incidents with their fifteen-year-old son, which have occurred over the last three years. Although the parents admit the hanky-panky happened, they suggest their son should be considered the *victim* and that the inappropriate and immoral home life of the seven-year-old suggests she is equally, if not wholly, to blame. After all they clarify, their son has been protected from these sinful influences by the computer screens and other weapons they have brandished in their war on the world.

Outside the presence of his parents, the fifteen-year-old discusses his pride in being able to break through the computer screen on the family Internet access. *Yes*, he admits, he has examined many sexual sites and he has participated in sexual chat rooms with other teenagers who discuss their sexual exploits. He also explains that he felt quite secure *sex surfing*, "because my parents knew the screens were in place, so they never worried or checked anything. Besides, I helped them install the screen so I knew how to uninstall it."

As part of the complicated evaluation process over the next few days, this adolescent was asked to describe his understanding of the sexual relationship between his parents and he confidently reported, "They are no longer sexual because they don't want to have any more children." With more questioning, it becomes clear he is completely ignorant about intimacy, love, or sexual commitment. He has no idea that married adults would engage in sexual intimacy without the purpose of procreation. Sadly, he is also ignorant about the beauty of sex. Yet, through the Internet he has witnessed vaginal insertions of every imaginable household item, sexual orgies involving those numbering in baseball team size, as well as every sexual costume, apparatus, and paraphernalia known to those who traffic in such sexual treats. But he has no idea about sexual respect, and his parents have no idea about what he knows since they *screen* everything out. Or so they thought.

This adolescent, who is facing a lifetime of punishment for sexual disrespect, has been taught rigid messages banning sex outside of marriage. But sadly, the details of this lesson from his caring parents has been vague and something from the OATs curriculum of *just don't do it until marriage.* But perhaps the most heartbreaking example of his convoluted thinking comes as he justifies his three-year abuse of his cousin.

Different from his parents, this young man does not blame the seven-year-old for seducing him, but rationalizes his behavior in a sincere moral resolution that he believes his parents have taught him. He is firm in thinking that by engaging in sexual activities with a much younger child (which included oral/genital copulation, fondling, and digital penetration) he was, in fact, abiding by his parents' wishes of avoiding *premarital sex.* He has learned from Mom and Dad about the immorality of engaging in sex before marriage, but this type of learning was, in his parents' lesson, connected to teenage girls his own age. He was warned never to be alone with teenage girls at church; he was only allowed to "double date," being told he might get into trouble being alone with those hip-hugger-wearing girls; and he attended six youth group classes at church on the sins of masturbation and premarital sex just to make sure he understood never to ***do it*** before marriage. So, he minded. He didn't masturbate and he didn't get sexually involved with teenage girls. Instead, for three years, he sexually offended his innocent, female cousin because he didn't think *it would count* in the paradigm of his parent's teaching. And this loving, well-intentioned Mom and Dad blamed the world and tried to ban it, never realizing the impact of that futile effort on the son they love.

Although the parents admit the hanky-panky happened, they suggest their Son should be considered the *victim* and that the inappropriate and immoral home life of the seven-year-old suggests she is equally, if not wholly, to blame.

Instead, for three years he sexually offended his innocent, female cousin, because he didn't think *it would count* in the paradigm of his parent's teaching. And this loving, well intentioned Mom and Dad blamed the world and tried to ban it, never realizing the impact of that futile effort on the Son they love.

MORE ELECTRONIC BLAME

Also included in the mean, media roll call are electronic games of all shapes and sizes that kiddos can play on their computers. Video games topped the chart in blame about the Columbine shootings because the killers were doing lots of shooting in their own bedrooms, playing video games such as *Doom*. Another culprit in the video game world, with tons of criticism, is the famous *Grand Theft Auto* where hours of nastiness can be entertaining to the munchkins in the privacy of their bedrooms. Those who decide that video games are the true corrupters of the thought-to-be-innocent-except-for-the-world kiddos, worry because of the "first person" nature of video games where the players (personally) murder, shoot, and crash—over and over again with seemingly no consequence. Some video games feature such disrespectful delights as causing the death and demise of prostitutes and the disrobing of females for only a few bullets, but with huge increases in *scoring*.

But the video game folks cry foul when they are blamed, reminding everyone of censorship, and like the music and the movie in-charge pundits, they have their own rating system, letting parents know exactly when to do some guiding. Not to be outdone by the movie and music experts, the video game raters came up with an even more complicated but perhaps comforting *Ce* rating, suggesting everything will be great for the *early childhood* kiddos who play the game. And with all the fuss about Tinky Winky and the Teletubbies being a little over the top in toddler television, the Ce rating for the wee ones seems perfect.

Then comes the *E-rating* suggesting *everyone* in the family would love the game after, of course, they adorned their flannel pajamas and grabbed a cup of cocoa. Things start getting a little riskier, however, with the *T-13* rating, giving parents the idea that the game is okay for teenagers, but that Mom and Dad should do a little guiding for the kiddos under 13.

Adding to even more perceived helpfulness but in reality, more confusion, comes the video game *M-rating,* which means it is only for really, really mature folks, suggesting that it takes *maturity* to rape, murder and pillage innocent bystanders. A step up from the M-ratings is the *AO-rating* meaning *adults only*. Nope, the kids can't bring home the *AO rated* video game. Interestingly, for the *RP-ratings*, the kidlets can slip the games into their shopping bags regardless of the video game content and without so much as a raised eyebrow. Even though the *RP* games might be a bazillion times more sexual that those reserved for *AO* rated games—it doesn't matter. *RP* simply means the rating is pending—hasn't been done. Of course, since the whole rating process for the video games is voluntary, and if the pending-its-rating video game is making lots of money without being rated, that rating may be very slow in coming. But just thinking about the ratings and trying to list them *and remember what they mean,* makes all the video game influence on the kiddos just seem sweeter to worried Moms and Dads.

BIG, BIG BLAME BONANZA

But when all forms of media are blamed and attacked in the war on the world, there seems to be no bigger target than television. And how violence on television was handled is a good comparison to the fussing about sex and the TV tube. Different than sex, violence seems to have been more comfortable in society for a very long time. Even though in the *Dime Novels* from Jesse Pomeroy's day, the Deadwood Dicks and Calamity Janes did lots of violent things in their escapades; hanky-panky around the campfire for the cowboys and cowgirls just didn't exist in those literary masterpieces. The sexual part was forbidden while the scalping, murdering, lynching, and torturing of humans was *okie-dokie* as it has always been in the media.

CHIPPING AWAY AT TV VIOLENCE

But in recent times, with so much violence among young people, some good people said *enough was enough* and waged war on media violence. Some of the smart people like JAMA, Sissela Bok, and Ray Surette figured out that violence on television was awful, citing studies that suggest the average child witnesses 40,000 murders on television before their 18th birthday. So the concerned folks said; something had to be done about violence on television.

Taking a stab at what to do, the Federal government passed a law demanding that every single television manufactured in the United States, after the year 2000, must have a *V-Chip* installed so parents could control violence on the *telly.* And all of a sudden, the problem to the world war wagers seemed solved, since the V-Chip allowed parents to do the *guiding* on their very own televisions. Never mind that a masters degree in engineering was almost required to understand and work the V-Chip, or that the TV advertising folks wanted the whole thing kept quiet since violent shows bring in the big bucks. The war waged on the world of violence was thought to have been solved with a chip no bigger than Tipper Gore's music stamps, making everyone assured that now folks would be really sweet and nice to each other with violence on the back burner.

PEACE OFFERINGS

But when television was caught in the cross fire of the war on the world concerning sex, something beyond the V-Chip was in order. Sure, the TV folks admitted, there was a lot of sex on television, but like all the other *we-take-no-blame-media-contingencies,* they offered up a solution in two forms. First was the TV rating system with the perky little *Post It* type warnings of what could go wrong if Mom and Dad don't do some *guiding.* To coordinate with the V-chip, the TV folks first threw out the *V-rating*, warning everyone that things could get a

Adding to even more perceived helpfulness but in reality, more confusion, comes the video game *M-rating* which means it is only for really, really mature folks suggesting that it takes *maturity* to rape, murder and pillage innocent bystanders.

Never mind that a masters degree in Engineering was almost required to understand and work the V-Chip, or that the TV advertising folks wanted the whole thing kept quiet since violent shows bring in the big bucks.

little bloody with the violence level of these television shows. Then they offered the really powerful *S-rating*, which warns everyone in the sexual police department that things will be frisky on the show. Following behind is the *L-rating* warning of *strong language,* and just to make sure everyone knows the TV people are not cooking up their ratings haphazardly, there is the *D-rating* for *suggestive language*—although it may take a degree in linguistics to sort out the difference between *strong* and *suggestive* language.

But there is more from the TV folks offering the peace pipe through ratings. There is the *TV-MA rating*, which means *mature,* again suggesting it takes a lot of maturity to do the really bad things depicted on the *tube*. Next in line and making everyone feel much better, comes the *Y-rating*, which means *y'all come*, suggesting it is A-okay for everyone with flannel pajamas and cocoa to watch the show. But the raters go further in their attempt to reject blame and reassure the sex police types. They offer cute ratings about the ages of the kidlets and really complicated sticker/Tipper Gore type warnings about when the little ones will be able to tell the difference between make-believe fantasies and the real world on certain television shows. So when the television folks are blamed in the world war, they just respond by flaunting a rating system of great complication so it appears as though they are doing their job in saving the moral decay of the kiddos by just labeling the smut.

PEACE PIPE TWO

Secondly, the TV folks offer a double-decker peace pipe for assuring the wholesome nature of television in the form of bleeps, fuzzes and verbal warnings. When something frisky is about to adorn the screen, some in-charge person might say to the television audience, "we warn you that the images in this clip are graphic, so you might want to get the children out of the room." And then, in less than two seconds, a report of oral sex being performed by a pedophile on a dead child will boom from the screen, often with full-color gore. Unless Mom has bionic body parts, there is no way any child could be scooped out of the room in those quick seconds, but never mind the TV people say, because after all, they warned.

In other instances, a silent caution *Parental Discretion Advised* may silently slither across the TV screen. However, when that happens Mom might be tied up with the Tater Tots in the kitchen and fresh out of parental discretion. But the TV folks just remind everyone; they have their warnings before the smut happens—passing the proverbial buck back to parents.

TV TRICKERY

In addition to warnings, the TV people have even better tricks to help the kids get wholesome and still watch television. This peace offering comes in the form of bleeping out bad words and fuzzing out any errant peek at something smutty. The talk shows are a classic example of this denial through the bleep and fuzz business with a big *never mind* about sexual messages from the screaming subtleties and the dumbing down of sex in this programming.

Any foul words spoken by any guest, especially the one beginning with "F", are simply bleeped out, often leaving hardly any conversations left for the tawdry TV show. It is pretty clear that the bleeped-out words are known to everyone, but bleeps just make everyone assured morality is saved by the effort. And even though some audience participants crank up the risqué by ripping off their clothes—right there on national TV—the fuzzes come to the rescue. That tiny little nipple will not be allowed to tarnish the minds of innocent children, even though the fuzzed out nipple is often perched on top of a triple D-cup breast that has just been rudely ripped from an errant tube top. Regardless of all the flesh that can be seen, and regardless of the smut being discussed or the values being so ignored in the conversation, the nipple is just fuzzed by the tricky TV people who edit the show later.

NO NIPPLES

No one seems to mind the screaming subtleties or the dumbing down of sex in the topics of the talk shows, just the *no nipple* mentality. Ironically, the language and topic of each talk show is apparently given the credibility of Mother Teresa, yet the sexual content reeks of sexual disrespect. When the kings and queens of talk introduce their topic, it is not uncommon for the audience to be told something like, "Today we will be talking with couples who need to confess to their partners about having affairs with their grandchildren," or "Today we will be talking to family members who have secret sex lives with family pets," or "Today's show will bring back Tammy for her fifth time on the program as she gives DNA tests to the sixth possible father of her ten-month-old son." But with no nipples and no "F" words, everything seems fine in television land.

NUMBING NEWS

The ratings, the bleeps, and the fuzzing only happens on television programming, yet some of the most disrespectful sexual messages come to children in the form of advertising and news—not usually thought to be purveyors of smut. Some would say that children watching the news on television would be a whole lot better than watching Jerry Springer. Yet, maybe that isn't exactly true, especially since so much of the Jerry Springer show is bleeped or fuzzed.

In an adult mind, when a rapist of seven women is finally apprehended, Mom may feel better as she peels the boiled eggs for the potato salad. But her listening son may be normalizing the word rape, hearing it over and over again on the news, and even though he may not understand it completely, he is learning to be more comfortable with the term *rape* than when Mom tries to explain why he shouldn't tell Grandma what he has between his legs.

So when the television folks are blamed in the world war, they just respond by flaunting a rating system of great complication so it appears as though they are doing their job in saving the moral decay of the kiddos by just labeling the smut.

Though the TV police and waging-war-at-the-world parents get really upset with a child seeing a nipple, they apparently don't mind at all if a crime involving nipple mutilation is all over the news.

Though the TV police and waging-war-at-the-world parents get really upset with a child seeing a nipple, they apparently don't mind at all if a crime involving nipple mutilation is all over the news. Television sexual abuse prevention programs usually nix the idea of using the terms *penis* and *vagina* in the language for children, thinking those words are just too risqué. *Don't give children the names for the body parts they are supposed to protect* is the mantra in these prevention programs in spite of the fact that a lot of people have either a penis or a vagina.

Contrarily, when a suspicious person is either freed or convicted because of DNA found in a raped vagina, deposited by a criminal penis—no one seems to mind that kind of vagina language. A ripped, torn, abused and bruised vagina is a whole lot more comfortable on the numbing news than just talking about vaginas and penises that need prevention protection. When children are abducted, lurid details of rape and murder is commonplace in the news coverage but the TV experts think it would just be too nasty to tell children the names of their bodies that need protecting. And through it all, in these screaming subtleties and the dumbing down of sex, sexually disrespectful behavior is normalized, but everyone feels better with the bleeps and fuzzes of nipples and such.

NO NIPPLE NEWS

Americans really, really love the blood and guts of the courtroom and of crime, but this kind of television is rarely considered in the smut department—or even harmful to kids. After all, it is only the news and there are no nipples hanging out anywhere. Whether it is covering the Michael Jackson sexual abuse trial or other not-so-famous cases, sexual disrespect is dumbed down, over and over again, while everyone else argues about what to tell kids in high school about *doing it*. The message to kids, as the news softly plays in the background, is that sexually disrespectful stuff—crimes, sexual abuse, and rape is more common and more normal than figuring out how to value sexual decisions in a respectful way.

JACKSON JITTERS

Being such a hero to children, the Michael Jackson trial influenced many kiddos and caused lots of jitters among adults. Some suggested that the really harmful part of the legal mess was that the pesky jury acquitted the rock singer when it seemed to many that anyone with even a thimbleful of wits would have thought he was guilty. Whether Mr. Jackson was guilty or not is less confusing than what influence the trial and trial coverage may have had on children watching from the background, perhaps eating a tuna fish sandwich or riding in Mom's car on the way to ballet lessons.

Even though it would have been unlikely for any child to watch the trial gavel to gavel—probably many children, in between soccer and skateboarding, were exposed to a constant barrage of information, however disjointed or disconnected, that might have provided a complete immersing into a sexually disrespectful quagmire for more than a year. The old saying about the *devil is in the details* was probably accurate in the Michael Jackson saga.

The ongoing and detailed accounts of what the alleged victims claimed to have happened at the Neverland Ranch sexual encounters, the description of genitalia and body functioning in the alleged sexual encounters, the television *talking heads* giving their opinions about erectile functioning that may or may not have happened in the sexual scenes, suggested to children that sexually disrespectful behavior is really important and a whole lot more *normal* than what their parents try to talk to them about when they are forced to watch some silly Discovery Channel show on the miracle of birth. The Michael Jackson trial taught children little about justice but a lot about sexual disrespect being more common, more appreciated, and perhaps even more normal than a single nipple in line for a fuzz and a bleep.

NUMBING NEWS

In the numbing news about other people who are important to children, the sports folks really become the focus of sexual dumbing down and screaming subtleties toward sexual disrespect. Before the famous Kobe Bryant case, where the young and highly talented basketball star was accused of raping the concierge of a Colorado hotel, two football players made their way to court/news television.

Ray Carruth was accused of arranging the murder of his pregnant girlfriend, which caused everyone to be quite curious and saddened. In the context of not wanting children to see the nipple of a flashed breast on Jerry Springer, no one seemed to mind having wannabe child football admirers watch the salacious trial of the pigskin hero for the Carolina Panthers. And although there was no Mr. Sperm meeting up with Ms. Egg on a flip chart (which would have been highly objectionable to most parents), in proving the criminal case against the defendant, numerous Barbie Doll type ladies came to the witness stand and explained in detail, the sexual intensity needs of Mr. Carruth and how they had all been impregnated and abandoned by the star.

During breaks and in between court appearances, the kiddos were reminded of Mr. Carruth's football successes and his strong support system who said right there on TV that he was really a nice guy AND a great football player, in spite of all the criminal conduct. In the minds of the TV police or parents who want to regulate television programming, the thinking was either this kind of news teaches the kiddos about crime and punishment or that it just isn't important to the kidlets. But in the dumbing

A ripped, torn, abused and bruised vagina is a whole lot more comfortable on the numbing news than just talking about vaginas and penises that need prevention protection.

The Michael Jackson trial taught children little about justice but a lot about sexual disrespect being more common, more appreciated, and perhaps even more *normal* than a single nipple in line for a fuzz and a bleep.

down of sex in this case, the lesson learned by the watching children could have been that sexual promiscuity and murdering a pregnant girlfriend really isn't so bad, since in spite of his legal problems, Mr. C. still seemed to be wealthy, notorious, and to many of his fans, he'll always be a star and he will probably get to play on the prison football team.

PROM PERVERSION

Mark Chmura, another talented football player for the Green Bay Packers (actually, a tight end), found himself in a little hot water after a little hot tub action with teenage girls following their high school prom. *No,* the football star wasn't dating the prom girl/victim, as he was married and all squared away with a sweet and probably *flannel-pajama* family of his own. But the hanky-panky that occurred in the house where the after-prom-alcohol-party-for-teens took place was questionable, since the girl claimed she clearly said *no* to sex and that Mr. C raped her. Some future-minded parents may have thought the kids seeing this type of show on Court TV, or coverage of the trial on the nightly news might teach lessons of crime and punishment, but nothing could be further from the truth.

First, Mark Chmura was a hero of the Green Bay Packer football team that had recently won the Super Bowl. Additionally, his good (and expensive) defense attorneys vociferously attacked the victim, touting that *yes,* sex certainly happened, but *no*, nothing was forced, thus normalizing and legitimizing confusion about sexual consent when females say *no,* but males think they meant *yes*. Other sexual tidbits dumbed down through this trial included constant descriptions of such details as pubic hair distribution, vaginal tearing, and ejaculation substances, as well as the ongoing and dreadful debates about labia bruising. Over and over it went, constant exposure to the deadly combination of sexual disrespect connected to a football hero with lots of money, lots of lawyers, and lots of power who, after all the fussing, was found *not guilty*.

IRONED OUT IRONIES

But there was an irony about the Mark Chmura case. Previous to his legal mess, when the Green Bay Packers won the Super Bowl and made their traditional trip to the White House for the proverbial presidential congratulations, Mr. Chmura made a fuss and refused to attend. *Nope* was his answer, explaining his disrespect for the whole morality mess of Bill Clinton concerning his hanky-panky with a White House intern. There was no way Mark Chmura, the pillar of family and Christian values, was going to honor the dishonorable president with his presence at the Super-Bowl-win-frolic. But later, his romping in the hot tub with the after-prom-perversion made lots of folks wonder who really had the inside track on morality and who was in the fast lane of sexual disrespect.

TALK ABOUT TALK

One of the worst culprits in the dumbing down of sex on TV has to do with the mostly-thought-to-be-harmless talk shows that pedal just talk—no vaginas, penises or nipples for anyone to actually view. *No see—no harm* it is assumed. But even though no one strips naked or demonstrates various intercourse positions, the sexual content is clear, often while Mom might be distracted undoing the camping clutter while the kiddos watch AND LISTEN to a la carte sexual disrespect.

PEDALING PERVERSION

Everyone in the audience is spellbound as they anticipate announcement of Fatherhood to one of the three possible sperm donors for a three-month-old baby who belongs to the onstage, single and tearful thirteen-year-old mom. DNA testing that miraculously took place two weeks previous to the show will sort everything out after appropriate chest beating and rude accusations. The tear-dabbing teen makes it *clear* to the audience she is *unclear* about the identity of the baby's father. All three boys admit *yes,* they had sex with her at some time, but *no,* they are not the fathers.

With hoots and hollers from the audience, each testosterone-driven male waltzes to center stage and compares his tattooed-nose-ringed mug to the six-by-six foot photo of the cute baby, suggesting through the visual comparison—*he just ain't it.* At one particularly poignant moment, one of the possible Dads makes his case that he cannot be considered the baby-on-the-screen's father because of the penis comparison. *Nope*, he proclaims on national television, the baby can't be his kid because the little one has just that—a little one—nothing like the husky guy who gains the support of the cheering audience for his *not-me-as-Dad* position because of his claimed physical prowess between the legs. And, of course, the classy audience loves to tout morality by chanting *Ho, Ho, Ho*—not making reference to Santa Claus, to the status of the had-sex-with-all-three-of-them teenage girl. Then comes the also classy DNA test results where one of the resisting men will be sentenced into fatherhood for a lifetime.

Interestingly, the TV supporter folks suggest that this type of show teaches sexual responsibility, but the dumbing down of sex theorists suggest this programming teaches kids, *If you are only thirteen years old and you have three possible sperm donors for your baby, you might get to go on an airplane to a really big city and have some people clap for you on television. And even if you don't get on television, being a Mom at thirteen years old will mean you have lots of company in girls that do get to take the plane rides and enjoy the clapping.*

Over and over it went, constant exposure to the deadly combination of sexual disrespect and a football hero with lots of money, lots of lawyers and lots of power who, after all the fussing, was found not guilty.

MORE TALK TEACHING

Some parents might see a snippet of these pregnancy testing shows and somewhere between the cottage cheese salad and nut bread, figure there is sexual content. Therefore, they

Nope, he proclaims on national television, the baby can't be his kid because the little one has just that—a little one—nothing like the husky guy who gains the support of the cheering audience for his _not-me-as-Dad_ position because of his claimed physical prowess between the legs.

make a note that when these shows come on the family television, the children will be marched out of the house to watch Dad chopping wood in July. In this thinking, the rest of the non-pregnancy-test talk shows would be okay, or so it seems. But in looking at the dumbing down of sex on the talk shows, many have the content of sexual disrespect without any labels, ratings, bleeps, fuzzes or DNA testing.

GEEK TO GORGEOUS

Everyone is excited about the *Geek to Gorgeous* show where the kiddo from childhood who was teased, ridiculed and bullied because of her fifth grade cosmetic challenges, now has a burning desire to confront her tormentor on national television. With crescendo building, the eager audience finally sees what the former geek has become, quite different from the posted childhood pictures of a cute little girl who seemed developmentally in sync for fifth graders, appearing to be 90 percent teeth and eyeballs. Never mind, she is different now. Gasps and applause greet the now gorgeous diva who saunters onto the stage, hoping to stun her childhood abuser.

But she doesn't enter the stage and confront her past tormentor with a briefcase and Ph.D. from Harvard, nor does she approach the audience with brags about being a proud mother of five well-behaved and talented children. She doesn't enter the stage with certificates from beauty college or her licensure as a counselor specializing in childhood bullying. What emerges in comparison to the childhood geek is a voluptuous, sexy female who has bulging (obviously implanted) breasts (no nipples, however), a midriff-type sweater that reveals numerous belly button rings surrounded by her tight tummy, demonstrating hours of work on the abs machine. It is her *sexuality and her sexiness* that should make her childhood offender shudder.

But when the tormentor-from-the-past is challenged about his past cruelty, he justifies his childhood bullying based on the currency of sexual attractiveness—what she didn't have a long time ago. He refers to the old photos and eventually gets the audience to somewhat agree that, alas, how else could he have handled her lack of attractiveness in those fifth grade days? The bottom line of the learning is that if a child isn't attractive—*sexually* attractive, that is—ridicule and teasing are at least somewhat acceptable. And as the audience boos and hisses, the thinking is usually that without pubic hair or nipples showing, the sexual content was minimal. In reality, the sexual disrespect messages of these kind of shows was loud and clear, but it probably wouldn't get even a wiggle in the television rating system.

SITCOM SEX

And it goes on with television programming and its soft seduction, sneaking by the rating system that tends to falsely make folks feel better. The figures suggest that sitcoms present sex the most with about 84 percent of each show having graphic sexual content—not in the form of seeing the penises and vaginas *doing it,* but in the talk, the topic, and in the soft sell of sex—especially the disrespectful kind.

SOAPY SEX SELLING

The soap operas come in a close second with 80 percent of program content firing up the sexual disrespectful clipboard. In these daily shows, it would not be uncommon for Grandma, who is beautiful and gorgeous (sexy, actually), to be contacted by her illegitimate child, who was born when Grandma was 16 and having a torrid sexual relationship with her second cousin Bruce, who is now gay, but who fathered two children after being married to his formerly lesbian Aunt Lucy. It goes on and on, in scene after scene, with the sexual content sneaking in and slipping by the ratings, usually because in the Soap Operas, cucumber condom application demonstrations are forbidden.

SEVEN SEX WORDS

The pretend battle against the world of television is especially heated for the watchdog of the federal government. The FCC (Federal Communications Commission) did their part about smut on TV by banning seven specific words. And the banning was legal—making everything tidy. George Carlin, a racy comedian, developed a comedy routine around the forbidden words—bringing even more attention to the sinful seven. But still, many concluded the banning *ought to do it,* paying little attention to the fact that after the court ruling supporting the slashing of the seven words, newscasts showed children gleefully wearing T-shirts with the inscription, "I know the seven words." But it was the great pretend that smut was censored if the seven words were just axed.

SUPER SLIP

Perhaps there is no better example of the pretend posturing in the war on the world than the Super Bowl halftime entertainment show of 2004. During halftime, there were many performers, but the highlight of controversy centered on the dance and vocal routine of pop stars Janet Jackson and Justin Timberlake. Three-quarters of the way through the routine, with Janet snuggled close, all of a sudden she appeared surprised (in a Betty Boop kind of way) when Justin abruptly tore away her bustier, revealing a part of her breast. There it was, for millions to see, the one thing that had been so forbidden in the *no nipple* edicts of television rules. But there was some reprieve from total ruination. Just by chance, a wonderfully tasteful *pasty* adorned that pesky nipple, indicating Janet had her very own brand of *bleep and fuzz.*

The uproar over the halftime *foo fah* surpassed the kiddos with *Seven Word Shirts,* and probably those same kids with the shirts paid very close attention to the fussing that

If you are only thirteen years old and you have three possible sperm donors for your baby, you might get to go on an airplane to a really big city and have some people clap for you on television. And even if you don't get on television, being a Mom at thirteen years old will mean you have lots of company in girls that do get to take the plane rides and enjoy the clapping.

It goes on and on, in scene after scene with the sexual content sneaking in and slipping by the ratings, usually because the in the Soap Operas, cucumber condom application demonstrations are forbidden.

followed the Super Bowl slip. With the first outrage, Justin claimed a *wardrobe malfunction*, which was weak, but a great line. However, like the *Seven Word Shirts*, the halftime malfunction was played over and over and over, on every national and cable television network. The attention to the almost-could-see breast was also displayed to many corners of the world, of course with the saving grace of a snappy fuzz over the nipple—salvaging morality in many different cultures and languages. Thank God for the *bleeps* and *fuzzes* everyone thought, when the thing that shouldn't have been seen at the Super Bowl was played over and over.

HOOTER HEARINGS

The Super Bowl slip coverage was staggering from every network, as they fussed about what should be done with the boob boo-boo. One television channel featured the graphic *Hooter Hearings* for describing all the meetings and opinions about the controversy. A National Football League executive came forward, describing outrage with the super slip, indicating that the NFL was *extremely disappointed* with MTV, who produced the halftime show. It appeared to be a surprise to the NFL folks that MTV would have anything sexual in their show business? And a spokesperson for one of the three national networks unequivocally proclaimed that the halftime show did not conform to their broadcast *standards*. And there everyone had it. The network has *standards* and the quick flash of a breast (nipple covered, of course) is not within those *standards*. Well, what are those standards?

ERECTION OF THE STANDARDS

Most glaringly, in considering the *standards*, were other elements of the halftime entertainment and the Super Bowl commercials. The time-out advertisements sanctioned by the network (the one with *standards)* contained elements of horny chimpanzees, horses farting, boisterous men drinking alcohol while they show off for babes with really big boobs, and at least three different brands of erectile dysfunction drugs. "When a relaxing moment turns into the right moment…" begins the commercial featuring a smiling, middle-aged couple who, while holding hands, gaze into each other's eyes. But since there are standards, the almost lusting couple is nonetheless separated by two, old-fashioned bathtubs. After the gazing, it is clear the moment is right, but before the couple leaves the pastoral scene with the bathtubs perched on the mountainside, there comes a helpful disclaimer that, although rare, 36-hour erections should be immediately reported to a physician! All the chest beating about an errant boob seemed pale compared to all the *super* screaming subtleties during the advertisements that taught children a lot about sexual disrespect. And those children needing protection were also the ones who probably wondered how cold the bath water would get in 36 hours on that mountainside.

FAILURE TO FUZZ

But it wasn't over, this Super Bowl attack on the breast bumbling. Several groups and a few individuals were so upset with the slip-up mess that they filed lawsuits claiming they were tragically and emotionally damaged because their children, watching the Super Bowl, were exposed to this *failure to fuzz.* Never mind that the words to the songs sung not only by Janet and Justin, but the entire crew of halftime entertainers, glorified infidelity, described body functions, depicted domestic violence and normalized indiscriminate sex. Never mind that Super Bowl watching kiddos saw a barrage of three different and competing drug companies pushing for more competent erections. Never mind that the traumatized kiddos might have heard or seen from the other performers (Nelly, Puff Daddy, and Sean Combs) who sang sexual songs as they grabbed at their crotches (on the outside of their clothing, of course). But a lone, partially covered nipple of Janet Jackson was an unforgivable sin.

FIRED UP FEDS

With the Federal Communication Commission fired up over the Super Bowl *wardrobe malfunction* and with a number of lawsuits filed (for disrupting the serenity and sexless Super Bowl entertainment), a *get-tough* approach was taken by the federal government in the weeks following Super Bowl 2004. With numerous hearings (not Hooter Hearings) securing more outrage, decisions were made to increase the fines for those who break the rules and disrupt the pristine nature of American media. It appeared that the number of words subject to fines had not changed (still seven), but the fines were now many hundreds of thousands of dollars for the culprits and, in fact, poor CBS's slap-on-the-wrist-fine was in the millions. But most felt better with the money punishment and only a tiny number of folks wondered if any of the money collected in these fines by the fired up Feds would be used to help educate children toward sexual self-respect. And if not, where did that money go? Probably toward building better *bleeps.*

THE FOURTH COMMANDMENT & ECONOMICS 101

So with all the ratings, all the ramblings and all the sweet seduction toward believing that fighting the media is the right way to guarantee sexual respect, parents need to re-examine an old lesson in *supply and demand.*

The college professor brings her Economics 101 class to order in the not-so-large university. In order to explain the theory of supply and demand, the professor wisely uses a commodity that is important to the students such as toilet paper—just so everyone will pay attention on this Monday morning after too much fun the previous weekend. Charts and graphs on snappy PowerPoint slides easily teach that when the

The Super Bowl advertisements sanctioned by the network (the one with *standards)* contained elements of horny chimpanzees, horses farting, boisterous men drinking alcohol while they show off for babes with really big boobs and at least three different brands of erectile dysfunction drugs.

After the gazing, it is clear the moment is right, but before the couple leaves the pastoral scene with the bathtubs perched on the mountainside, there comes a helpful disclaimer that, although rare, 36-hour erections should be immediately reported to a physician!

supply of a product is restricted or limited, the price of that commodity ascends. The professor easily makes the opposing point clarifying that when there is an abundance of a product, the price plummets. The students ponder their next trip to the restroom wondering about the supply of toilet tissue while the professor has inadvertently provided a lesson on solving the war of the world (media, actually) dilemma.

WHOA BACK

As parents attempt to limit and hold back the supply of sexual information to their children, the price/value of sexual information (any kind) skyrockets. The reason the media sells sex to a voracious public is not because Jerry Springer, movie/music makers, or the Court TV ladies in designer clothes, are evil, mean-spirited folks hoping to encourage the moral decline of America's children. They do what they do because the demand for the commodity is high, making sex a big seller. And there is no mistake about who is responsible for the price hike—it is the people who, for whatever reason, righteous or just lacking in awareness, withhold healthy sexual information, making the supply so scarce.

WELCOME THE WORLD

So how do parents protect their children from a sexually disrespectful world, and also remember that banning, rating and screening may be not only futile but may make that smut more attractive, and high-priced? The right answer is to *welcome the world* (The Fourth Commandment) using all the sexually disrespectful information to build the sexual respect curriculum. This effort follows the guidance from the first three commandments of beginning early (First Commandment), using communication and dialogue (Second Commandment), and teaching a positive, respectful logic (Third Commandment). The Fourth Commandment nicely fits into that continuum, welcoming and using the world (with all its frailties) for teaching sexual respect.

MOL AND MOVIES

The Mol Flanders movie was a tiny example of those flicks that foster the screaming subtleties of disrespectful sex but it shouldn't stand alone in criticism or boycott. There are many movies that should be resisted by caring parents. But it isn't just the nixing that matters, especially in consideration of the Fourth Commandment—*Thou Shalt Welcome the World.* As Mom and Dad reject the ratings and really check out the Mol movie content, deciding that the afternoon will be spent with paper airplanes rather than seeing a flick where pelvic exams are used to determine the high-price commodity of virginity; the window for teaching opens. The key is to avoid allowing movies like Mol Flanders to become exciting because they are forbidden, but rather to use the movie, perhaps while munching on Cheerios for breakfast as the clipboard to teach the sexual respect logic of the

Third Commandment. Banning the movie from the family code of ethics isn't enough—nixing Mol AND teaching why is the answer.

LAMENTING LYRICS

With movies, Mom and Dad will find it easier to take a stand because they have the kiddos under control through transportation to the movies or through ticket purchase. But with music, the control is much more difficult since it is everywhere. So first, parents need to resist lamenting about the awful lyrics and taking on a campaign to get it all banned in favor of the forcing the kids to listen to Yankee Doodle Dandy with their friends during a sleepover. Using the ratings as a general guide is probably necessary—but just keeping music out of the family home is not enough. Keeping it out must be accompanied by the lessons of the Third Commandment logic—actively teaching why it is forbidden—and it all relates to sexual respect.

WELCOME WORLD WINDOWS

The thirteen-year-old son approaches Sunday evening in a foul mood. He has not completed his homework and he is spending a significant amount of energy avoiding his math assignment. As the time pressure mounts, he seeks a justifiable reason for his laziness. His mother appears to be a prime target.

"Whatdayathink of this, Ma?" he taunts, hoping for some kind of homework-stalling response. The record album with lyrics depicting the song of BIG BALLS is revealed to Mom with the hope of instilling a panic that will take enough time to avoid his mathematical obligations.

Mom reads the lyrics, "My balls are always bouncing to the left and to the right, and everyone comes and comes again and no one can get you higher, they say you've got great balls of fire."

Rather than a parental gasp, with this music smut, Mom sees the window of opportunity to welcome the world and bring it under her control. This smart Mother calculates that she has very little time to deliver the message to her adolescent son and she also recognizes that what her son wants is for her to become hysterical. Being wise as a scholar of *Welcome and Use the World Curriculum*, she obliges her impertinent son. If her belligerent son wants hysteria, and Mom wants sexual respect—BIG BALLS becomes the conduit.

She begins, "Oh, my God! How could these people make this kind of music?" Mom wails.

The gleeful answer from her son is, "So parents like you will get hysterical."

Mom, happy with the hysterical opening to her planned curriculum and quickly calculating that time to impart wisdom on her son is slipping away, raises her voice and yelps, "How can you listen to this? How can you play that music in this house?"

Her thinking-this-is-working son triumphantly remarks, "Mom, it's been playing in this house for two years."

But most felt better with the money punishment and only a tiny number of folks wondered if any of the money collected in these fines by the fired up Feds would be used to help educate children toward sexual self-respect. And if not, where did that money go? Probably toward building better *bleeps*.

So first, parents need to resist lamenting about the awful lyrics and taking on a campaign to get it all banned in favor of the forcing the kids to listen to Yankee Doodle Dandy with their friends during a sleepover.

Mom, happy with the way things are going so far, obliges her son by making another hysterical statement, just trying to keep the conversation going. "My goodness, how on earth can you dare play this music in our house?"

By this time, her son is completely delighted with her question and makes his final statement. "Mom, you bought this album for me last Christmas." The answer hangs in their air with the subtlety of a Whoopee Cushion.

In the silence as he walks away, her son is satisfied because Mom seems to be hysterical. He has reminded her of her failure, he has claimed a position of power and, most importantly, he has avoided his homework. Mom is also quite satisfied because she saw the window of the world open and she used it. But now, with one eye on the stopwatch, Mom wants the *coup de grace*. She turns and as she walks away, she plants the sexual respect seed with,

"How will you ever grow up and think that when you share your body or your testicles with someone, it will be terrific and respectful, if you are listening to Big Balls?"

Her son cannot resist and as most teenagers do, he must have the last word, assuring his Mother of her stupidity and his brilliance. "Do you think I'm stupid, Mom? I already know that."

There it is, lessons learned with Big Balls as a perfectly fine curriculum. The final exchange of conversation occurs non-verbally as her son wanders away, proudly reinforcing himself, "I got her." And Mom, doing the same, walks away and reminds herself, "And for another time, I got him, with my ongoing message of sexual respect." Both feel like winners and in reality, they both are just that—winners. The only loser is the neglected math homework.

TELEVISION TEACHING

Nearly every outrage parents might feel for something disrespectful on television could also be turned into a teaching moment—especially if critical thinking is the conduit. When the *Geek to Gorgeous* show is suddenly in the living room, the window of opportunity opens. Parents could turn it off, pucker their purple face and clench white knuckles, hysterically forbidding the kidlets from watching the nasty television. The message to the children will be, however, *if I want to see the exciting stuff, I must make plans to watch the Jenny Jones show at my friend's house to figure out the fuss.*

But if parents adhere to the Fourth Commandment and consider the window of opportunity through the show, critical thinking jumps to the teaching clipboard. A Mom who finds the Geek to Gorgeous show rudely in the living room, can view the disrespectful message as the teaching medium. She could explain to her wanting-to-watch-the-show son that the Geek to Gorgeous nonsense makes it sound like being sexy and beautiful is the only thing that matters. And if she continues on with her son by explaining that *after 30 years, his father adored her and thought she was sexy even if she looked nothing like the ladies looked on Jenny Jones,* then the talk show becomes the curriculum for teaching children critical thinking. Her son may scoff at the thought of Mom and Dad getting frisky, but the message will be there nonetheless, clear and respectful

MORE WINDOWS OPEN AND SHUT

While the television show of finding-the-right-DNA-Dad is playing, some teens may *need to not need* advice from their parents, just as a matter of adolescent development. So sometimes parents need to use the quick method of welcoming the world for learning sexual respect.

Mom is in the living room watching television with her sixteen-year-old and her eight-year-old. When she is just about finished snipping the tails off the green beans, she inadvertently notices two people rubbing their crotches together, simulating humping, and slapping slobbery kisses on each other in the school hallway, in this PG-13 rated movie—playing right there in the family room. Both children are watching this display of *almost sex* with different interests and with different conclusions, since they are in different stages of sexual development. Mom sees the window open (although slightly ajar), and she also sees that the same discussion for different-aged children might be precarious.

TOUCH AND GO

With her eye on the window and her beans abandoned, she rises smoothly and as she heads for the kitchen, she makes a powerful *touch-and-go* teaching statement. "How are those people going to feel good about sharing their private bodies with someone they pick and make the *sharing* of those parts a big deal if they are hanging them out here on the television in front of everyone? Do you kids want some more popcorn, because dinner won't be finished for an hour or two?"

This wise mother, versed in the different stages of development for her teenager and her eight-year-old, knew that if she attempted a discussion about the immorality of premarital sex, the older child would need to pretend he knew everything and the younger child would be either curious or embarrassed. But Mom's *touch and go* (window open and shut) approach to welcoming the world allowed her to plant the seed of sexual respect, communicate a powerful message, and then get out of the way (concentrating on popcorn) before the teen needed to be cool and show no interest. She also taught (again) the logic of being sexually respectful, as outlined in The Third Commandment. Mom's choices beyond the podium or beyond canceling the cable subscription were wise, as she used the media world to teach that important lesson of critical thinking about sexual respect.

Being wise as a scholar of *Welcome and Use the World Curriculum*, she obliges her impertinent son. If belligerent Son wants hysteria, and Mom wants sexual respect—BIG BALLS becomes the conduit.

Nearly every outrage parents might feel for something disrespectful on television could also be turned into a teaching moment—especially if critical thinking is the conduit.

Mom's choices beyond the podium or beyond canceling the cable subscription were wise, as she used the media world to teach that important lesson of critical thinking about sexual respect.

RE-ENTER THE INTERNET

In consideration of what the Internet and computers offer, ratings and itty-bitty stamps look pathetic. A good question is whether parents should put screens on the Internet, protecting the kiddos from predators, pornography and other smut? The answer is that children should not be exposed to those tawdry parts of society as they demean and degrade sexuality and intimacy. But rejecting the seductions of safety in labels, stickers, stamps and ratings doesn't mean the pornography channel wired into every room is the only other choice. Actually, doing whatever possible to keep the kiddos from the Internet filth is a good thing. But if the screen is placed on the Internet access, without any explanation of why, the window of opportunity to teach is opened and closed, and the forbidden nature of what was screened away may become the focus for children.

What a wonderful *world welcome* opportunity for a family to gather around the kitchen table and use the purchase of the computer screen for a critical discussion about *WHY* the screen will be placed on the Internet. Dad begins, "Now, kids, some people haven't learned all the right rules. Some people don't care about picking someone to share their body with when they grow up. Some people want to make lots of money and some kids don't have parents like Mom and I who explain things to them. So they put things on the Internet to try to make money and try to get kids excited about breaking all the rules. That's why we have the screen on the Internet, because in this family, everyone follows the touching rules and everyone has great respect for those rules about picking someone to share your body with and making it a terrific thing when you are older."

There it is, the lesson again—respectful of the supply and demand theory and encouraging children toward critical thinking if there is ever a hole in the computer screen.

WORLD PEACE

Good parents, bursting out of denial and re-examining the value of battling the world should become vigilant about the messages filtering in to children about sexual disrespect, but avoid being seduced into that frontline battle as a substitute for teaching sexual respect. If the school is trying to ban a certain book, a wise parent will see the window of opportunity open and teach family values of book banning issue. If the Super Bowl caused a fuss, then Mom and Dad will use the fuss for teaching. If movies have forbidden ratings, then parents can explain the really cool reasons why the movie doesn't fit the family values plan and won't be seen. If parents want to shut out the world through home schooling, they shouldn't do it unless the reason for the home schooling is an important part of the home-teaching curriculum.

Every family has a right to their own value system in teaching children about sex. But if the

SEX FAIRY DATA SHEET

NAME — The Sex Fairy

BUST — Varies   WAIST — Sure   HIPS — Very Much So

HEIGHT — Horizontal   WEIGHT — Depends

AMBITION — To have my own talk show "Fairy Flutters" and to have Dr. Phil as my first guest.

TURN ONS — The movie Moby Dick, Adams Apple Pie, visiting the Icelandic Phallological Museum in Reykjavik, lost belly buttons, Tinky-Winky and grapefruit boobs

TURN OFFS — People who are too grounded, wands that bend, birds with peckers, bees with stingers, Nurses named after a hand tool, Sex Fairies who snore, Red Fairies who wear pink lipstick and Procrastination Fairies who have short attention spans.

FAVORITE TELEVISION — Golden Girls, Sex In The City, The Flying Nun, Queer Eye for the Straight Guy and No Nipple News

FAVORITE SPORTS — Playing with Shuttlecocks in Badminton

FAVORITE AUTHORS — Slasher book writers and Dr. Ruth

FAVORITE PARTY MUSIC — Can't Get No Satisfaction and "You're Acting Single While I'm Drinking Doubles

BEST FRIENDS — Procrastination Fairy, Red Fairy and Sheena, Queen of the Jungle

FAIRY HUMOR

Why did the Sex Fairy cross the road?

Because the chicken had her wand.

◆

The Sex Fairy was conducting lessons for young children at her favorite Sex Fairy library about the miracle of reproduction. One little boy inquired, "How come there are bazillions of sperm for only one little egg." The Sex Fairy, while blushing, explained—"There must always be many more sperm than eggs probably because sperm, just like men, never stop and ask for directions."

◆

How many Sex Fairies does it take to change a light bulb?

Answer: 5...

- **One to screw in the bulb**
- **One to process the screwing teamwork**
- **One to do the billing for screwing service**
- **One to apply for a grant for more screwing**
- **One to guarantee OSHA screwing standards were met**

What do you get when you cross the Sex Fairy with a psychologist?

Answer—A wing nut.

What do you get when you cross the Sex Fairy with a Playboy?

Answer—Fairy Flings

◆

Knock Knock

Who's there?

Dewey.

Dewey Who?

Dewey really believe in a Sex Fairy?

This guy walks into a bar, his pockets bulging with golf balls. He takes a seat, as it happens, next to the Sex Fairy, who is enjoying her evening, drinking a virgin Pina Colada. Noticing the fellow's bulging pockets she can't help but stare. She tries to avert her eyes but continues her obvious glances. The fellow, noticing her gaze, explains, "It's golf balls". The Sex Fairy smiles sweetly at his explanation but continues to gawk. Finally she wonders aloud, "I wonder if it hurts as much as Tennis Elbow?"

◆

Knock, knock.

Who's there?

Cannon

Cannon Who?

Can a Nun and a Sex Fairy ever be roommates?

◆

The Sex Fairy had trouble with her wand and after working for quite some time with jumper cables, she finally got things going. Since she was exhausted, she ventured into a bar with the jumper cables inadvertently hanging from her shoulders. After she ordered, the bartender warned, "Yes you can have a drink, but don't start anything."

FAIRY HUMOR

Why did the Sex Fairy cross the road?

Because the chicken had her wand.

The Sex Fairy was conducting lessons for young children at her favorite Sex Fairy library about the miracle of reproduction. One little boy inquired, "How come there are bazillions of sperm for only one little egg." The Sex Fairy, while blushing, explained—"There must always be many more sperm than eggs probably because sperm, just like men, never stop and ask for directions."

How many Sex Fairies does it take to change a light bulb?

Answer: 5...

- **One to screw in the bulb**
- **One to process the screwing teamwork**
- **One to do the billing for screwing service**
- **One to apply for a grant for more screwing**
- **One to guarantee OSHA screwing standards were met**

What do you get when you cross the Sex Fairy with a psychologist?

Answer—A wing nut.

What do you get when you cross the Sex Fairy with a Playboy?

Answer—Fairy Flings

Knock Knock

Who's there?

Dewey.

Dewey Who?

Dewey really believe in a Sex Fairy?

This guy walks into a bar, his pockets bulging with golf balls. He takes a seat, as it happens, next to the Sex Fairy, who is enjoying her evening, drinking a virgin Pina Colada. Noticing the fellow's bulging pockets she can't help but stare. She tries to avert her eyes but continues her obvious glances. The fellow, noticing her gaze, explains, "It's golf balls". The Sex Fairy smiles sweetly at his explanation but continues to gawk. Finally she wonders aloud, "I wonder if it hurts as much as Tennis Elbow?"

Knock, knock.

Who's there?

Cannon

Cannon Who?

Can a Nun and a Sex Fairy ever be roommates?

The Sex Fairy had trouble with her wand and after working for quite some time with jumper cables, she finally got things going. Since she was exhausted, she ventured into a bar with the jumper cables inadvertently hanging from her shoulders. After she ordered, the bartender warned, "Yes you can have a drink, but don't start anything."

goal is to raise sexually respectful children, parents shouldn't seek success by blaming the media and the outside world, believing that their family value goals will be reached if the rocks are just thrown at those who sell the product that a withholding society so cleverly made into a valuable commodity. Peace with the media world is not likely to materialize, but within the confines of each private, special, and precious family, sexual respect can be taught with much of the world as the curriculum.

Peace with the media world is not likely to materialize, but within the confines of each private, special and precious family, sexual respect can be taught with the smutty world as the curriculum.

Sex Fairy Clipboard

- Don't be seduced into spending energy fighting the world—it is out there and the potential to have it become attractive to children is great.

- Don't be seduced into counting on the ratings, labels, stickers and screens to raise sexually respectful children. Pay attention to them but far more important is to examine the *dumbing down* of sex and the *screaming subtleties* of sex in these media offerings.

- Accept the fact that children are part of the world and the media is likely to reach the kiddos. Teach critical thinking by using the world and logic. Fighting the world is expended energy—taking away effort to raise individually respectful children.

- Remember the supply and demand rationale. The media sells sex because America buys it. And it is a high priced commodity with tremendous power—that is until parents take back the power by changing the supply of healthy information, encouraging sexual respect.

Chapter 8

Fifth Commandment

Thou Shalt Envision Eve and Adam

CHAPTER 8: THE FIFTH COMMANDMENT THOU SHALT ENVISION EVE AND ADAM

The smell was putrid and buzzing flies made the retrieval more difficult. But they were determined. The ten-year-old accepted the biggest burden of carefully lifting the garbage can lid while the six-year-old's job is to make the heist. The capture needs to be quick, lest the stench of family garbage cause them to succumb. So off it comes, the treasures of play successfully retrieved for these two sisters about five years apart.

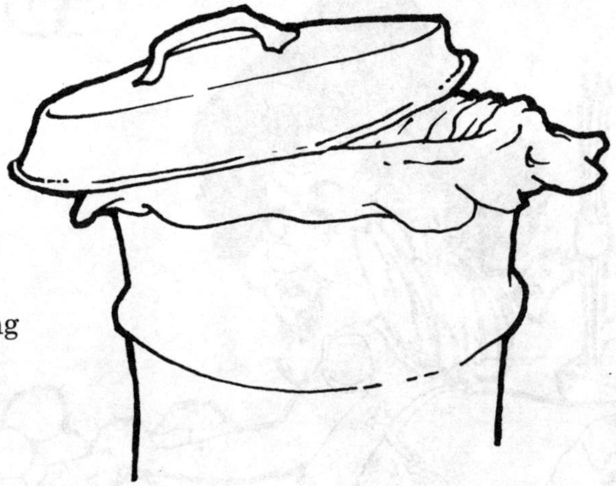

With their salvaged riches, the sisters find the garden hose needed to wash their wares before the playing can begin. Expertly, the two salvaged items are rinsed, indicating the sisters are familiar with this game-playing preparation. They have done this before. With their necessary items ready, and with only a slight odor still lingering in the air, the two pals head for the location site of their game—the playhouse. Once seated at the play table inside the outhouse-converted-into-playhouse, they begin the game of *D.D.—Dahling and Diet.*

In perfectly scripted form and with perfectly pretend spoons, the sisters feign eating the heisted food. They dine on grapefruit (actually only the now-remaining rinds) and hard-boiled eggs (actually only the egg shells). Just as they have seen their mother do in her numerous attempts to manage the Egg and Grapefruit Diet she must have read about in her Good Housekeeping magazine, the sisters mimic Mommy. The older one, after taking three imaginary bites of pretend grapefruit and two imaginary gobbles of hard-boiled eggs, coos to her younger sister in the scripted dialogue of the *Diet Dahling* game.

"Oh, Dahling, how do you think I look since I have lost 10 pounds?" she slurs to her sister.

On cue, the younger one follows script, "Oh, Dahling, I think you are so beautiful now that you are so much *thinna*. How do you think I look after being on this Egg and Grapefruit Diet for five days?" The question hangs in the air of the playhouse. Forgetting her pretend role, the younger one flourishes the conversation,

"Oh Sissy, you look so much better and *thinna* when you diet." There it was—a sister slip. The older and more-in-the-director-role sister calls for a secret conference. She leans her head down parallel to the pretend kitchen table and motions her younger sister into the same secretive posture.

As though national television cameras were somehow positioned in the playhouse peering on the two sisters, the older one reminds the little one. "Psssssssssssssst, Sissy, remember we aren't sisters on diets, we are *Dahlings* on diets!"

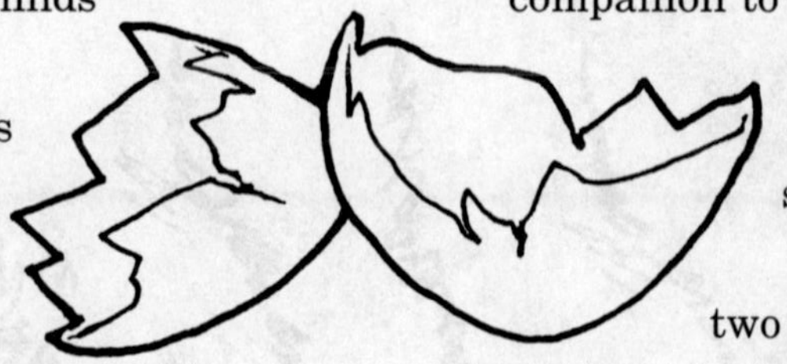

The little one gathers her lost script and coos in response, "Oh Dahling, I have been dieting for weeks and my husband says I'm so beautiful now."

There it is in the confines of the playhouse—dieting done perfectly for two little girls who know nothing of the meaning of their game, they just know how to be the *dieting dahlings.*

A few more grapefruit pretend bites, a few more nips of imagined hard boiled eggs, a few more *thinnas* and the little girls tire of the *Diets and Dahling* game. There are only so many *thinna* accolades one sister can bestow on the other sister before boredom sets in. The eggshells, now pulverized beyond recognition, are discarded but the grapefruit halves are salvaged for the next game beyond diet discussions and *thinna* thoughts.

Now the girls take another familiar path, heading for their next game site. As the woods (soon-to-become-jungle) are approached, the game-changing sisters must procure additional provisions from the donkey's pen. They add to their supply of organic material by stopping at Whimpy's quarters where, among all the donkey necessities, they find their item of interest. Gathered carefully is a comfortable color companion to the grapefruit—straw, in the finest color of yellow matching, of course, the grapefruit halves. The sisters make a second heist.

Carrying handfuls of straw and two grapefruit halves, they head for the woods in perfect color coordination, although that fashion statement is completely unknown to them at the time. They know about *Diets & Dahlings,* but nothing about style or trends. In fact, these sisters have dressed for the day with complete disregard for appearance even though the dieting game is indirectly about their appearance. The younger one is quite proud of her red pedal pushers, not because of their fine detail or designer label, but because they are *finally hers*—after being handed down from her two older sisters as they outgrew the faded, but highly treasured garb. She also chose her orange T-shirt (clashing loudly), not with any color coordination in mind, but because it just happened to be on top of the pile in her one allotted drawer in the one chest-of-drawers in the sisters' bedroom. The *fashion-playing* sisters actually care nothing about fashion—just playing out the fashion/attraction role.

The older sister's clothing is just as incongruent with appearance and high fashion standards as she adorns a pair of bib overalls, accompanied by a faded purple T-shirt that once sported a pink princess caricature. The shirt was a slightly unwelcome gift from her Aunt Adeline who tirelessly attempted to bring feminine bearing to her tomboy niece. But solutions prevailed for the determined child, so the rough and tumble tomboy simply turned the purple princess T-shirt inside out, wearing it under her bib overalls, covering the *princess* part, but failing to notice her shirt was also inside out with the label resting comfortably at her throat. But that didn't matter, since neither sister concerned herself with clothing fashion or appearance, even though they are clearly involved in feminine-type games, focusing on their future appearance. Their attention is satisfied with the perfectly color-coordinated, yellow grapefruit halves with Whimpy's heisted (also yellow) straw, adorned with only small traces of donkey poop.

They are ready. Off they go, heading for the woods that will, with great imagination, change into a vast *jungle* suitable for the new game of *Damsel in Distress*. Neither sister really understands the definition of *damsel* or the word *distress*, but just as they really didn't understand *Diet and Dahlings*, they nonetheless know how to play the new game. And they don't know these games represent their future feminine path—they are more interested in the path to their woods/jungle play site.

As if scripted, the sisters know exactly how to orchestrate the *Damsel in Distress* game. First, the older sister (now taking the role of Sheena, Queen of the Jungle) lies on the pathway, preparing to be costumed by her younger sister, who has now become (according to the game rules) *Chimp*, Sheena's chimpanzee companion. This is the proper role for the little one since older sister (Sheena) has seniority, thus the lesser role of *Chimp* goes to the younger child. It is not only clear that Chimp will be in the slightly less prestigious role in the DD (*Damsel in Distress*) game, but it is also clear that Chimp's job is to protect Sheena, which automatically turns former-dieting-younger-female-sister into a male unit. Yes, protect. From what Chimp will protect Sheena is unknown to the sisters, but it probably has to do with *distress* since Sheena has the *damsel* role and the whole game is about *Damsel in Distress*.

Without hesitation, Chimp begins his (her, actually) costuming of his beloved Sheena by arranging the yellow straw around her (Sheena's) head, covering her naturally curly brown hair with long, trying-to-be-flowing straw-yellow locks, straight as the back of their father's shovel and with only slight traces of donkey poop. According to script, Sheena is demure—lying prone on the path, pretending helplessness in pure *damsel* script. She knows that to be competent in the role, she must be helplessly *incompetent.* But the final touch in Chimp's creative costuming of Sheena calls upon the versatility of the grapefruit halves. Plop, plop, they go onto Sheena's flat chest, creating the perfect (and color-coordinated) illusion in the jungle scene. There she is, Sheena, Queen of the Jungle (*Damsel,* actually), lying prostrate on the path (probably because of previous distress) with flowing golden hair and perfectly matched golden grapefruit boobs.

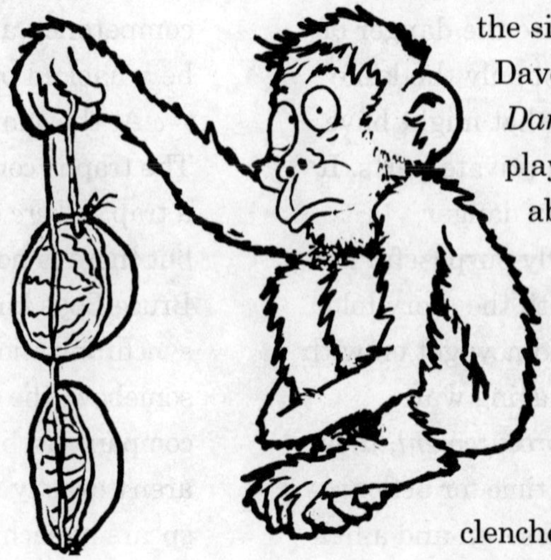

Now with his damsel in place, Chimp's job in the D.D. game is to defend his Sheena. The terms *Damsel in Distress* are about as understood as a calculus equation, but what is understood is that Sheena's golden hair and her golden grapefruit boobs are so attractive (probably because of all her dieting) that danger (distress) lurks in the woods/jungle and Chimp must be on guard.

Also playing in the woods/jungle are three little boys, close in age to the Sheena/Chimp duo and close in proximity to the game site of the sisters. For Bruce, Mike and Dave there are no diets or *Damsels in Distress* in their playbook and there is no concern about color coordination. The primary focus of the Bruce Boys' playing is whacking weapons, waging war, tricking and *trapping.* But like the girls, their game began with a heist. In clenched teeth and secret whispers (secretive from what, they do not know), Bruce pulls it out of his pants, right in front of Dave and Mike. It is so exciting and forbidden to see it. The Bruce Boys are breathless with anticipation when they finally gaze upon his prized cache.

With jaws gaping, Bruce tantalizes Mike and Dave with a story of how, with the skill of a safe cracker, he distracted (and shocked) his mother by volunteering to do the breakfast dishes thus facilitating his larceny of a single steak knife from the kitchen silverware drawer. Mike and Dave were impressed as Bruce explained the difficulty he had clearing the breakfast dishes, brushing his teeth with Mom

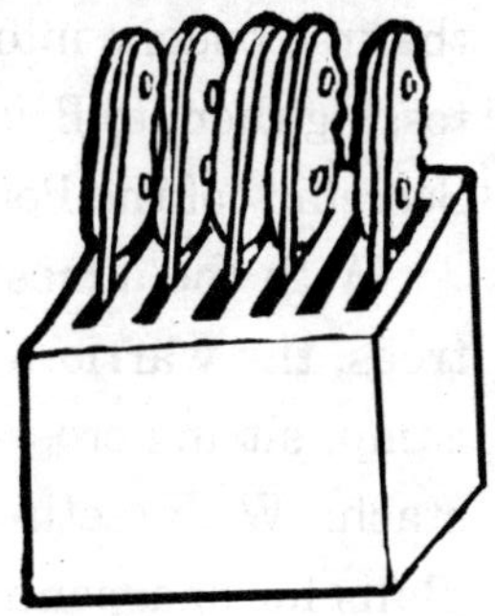

in the bathroom, and then stealthily sneaking across the patio with a steak knife secreted away in his far-too-snug Levis. As part of the play script, the boys immediately sense the danger of Bruce's past morning heist in not only the knife theft, but in the potential harm that might have come to Bruce's most precarious private parts. It was a breathtaking description of danger, sneaking and stealing, but clearly purposeful for their upcoming mission. Yes, with the story told in whispers of danger, they could now get on with the next part of their games—waging war.

Enough said about weapon procurement, they all silently agree, since it is now time for action. Mike and Dave are about six and seven-and-a-half inches too short to reach the bottom boughs of almost every tree within the chosen war zone, so Bruce, still in possession of the weapon, hoists them into position. The relay-race baton (the steak knife) is passed between the trees as they whack away at weapon making. Slice, slice, slice, they turn the young saplings from the tree boughs into weapons, tossing them to Bruce, the now appointed Secretary of the Pentagon, for safekeeping.

With the almost-weapons whacked from the trees, the warriors now move into their chosen camp, sitting cross-legged and encircling their stash. With teeth-clenched jaws, they whisper plans for sharpening their weapons into spears. Everything just seems so dangerous, exciting and secretive. Although somewhat thwarted with only one steak knife, assembly line competency and creativity allows the weapons to be whacked one by one.

At the same time, battle plans are pondered. The trap is considered, since any good war plan has a trap. *Where would they set the trap?* is a question, but there is no question that the trap is needed. The Bruce Boys know the trap must be made in synchronization with the weapon making since, somehow, the weapons and the trap are companions, but just how to do that, the Bruce Boys aren't exactly sure. Nevertheless, armed with spears in each hand, and with the secrecy of the CIA, they begin to slip through the thick undergrowth with the important war mission of *trapping*.

Breathing heavily (teeth still clenched), they prowl through the woods/jungle and finally, whispering (why, they aren't sure) as a possible spot for the trap is considered. But before a final decision is made they call a summit for the *trap talk*.

"Yes," Dave whispers, "this looks like a perfect spot."

"It's already a hole and the dirt is so soft it will be easy to dig," directs Bruce, the clear leader of the triumvirate.

"Yes! This will be a great trap," agrees Mike in clenched teeth whispers for which John Wayne would be proud.

Enthusiastically (however, stoic), the next stage in trap assembly begins. Now, with their sapling weapons, the Bruce Boys begin battling the dirt as they dig. The dual purpose of the spear-now-become-shovel is lost on them, as the hole-soon-to-become-trap grows deeper. And in this process, the trio adds to their costumes in the trapping/war game playing. Of course, getting dirty is in high demand for trap building, so the more dirt they adorn on their faces and fingers, shirts and pants, the better the trap building process seems to feel. It is so cool, all that dirt. And when one member of the triumvirate thinks the others aren't watching, an extra splash of mud or

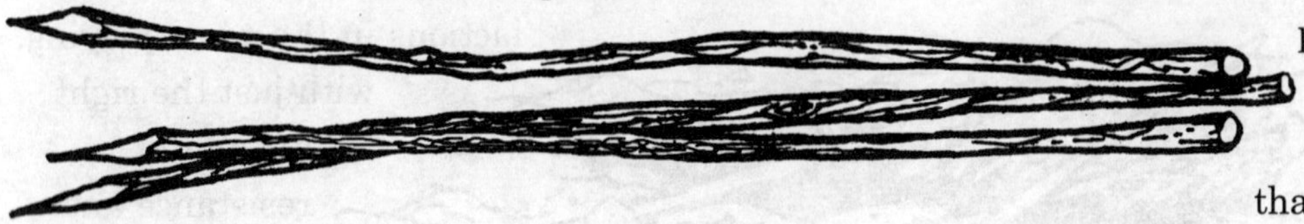

dirt is slapped to the face or rubbed on the clothing, just for extra drama.

After a while of digging and dirt adorning, another summit is required as the Bruce Boys contemplate the trap depth without suggesting they are tired or losing strength. Weakness just couldn't happen in their game playing. With hushed whispers (they still don't know hushed from what), the triumvirate try to decide whether the hole is big enough to trap the prey. In this top-secret discussion, feelings of danger hang in the air making everything flourish with a wonderful flavor of menace.

With depth of the trap confirmed, a return to the warrior's original camp/fort/compound is necessary for the last stage of trap construction. Mike and Dave carefully gather the remaining saplings and the now-slightly-soiled spears/swords. Bruce, of course, being the oldest, needs to remain and guard the trap—from what, none of the boys are sure, but they are sure guarding is necessary. Returning with the saplings, Mike and Dave carefully cover the hole-now-become-trap, creating an illusion of a solid path. It was so exciting, imagining the trickery of the trap appearing to be a path. The danger was *all* encompassing. As they admire their handiwork, they wipe dirty spears on their pants. They don't speak of it, but they feel tremendous pride in all the grunge and grime that is so *cool* and so much a part of the trick and trap game.

After all of that, on they go, the Bruce Boys armed with spears in their hands, with dirt on their faces, and with their trap ready to trick. Now, as the next scripted part of the game, they begin their sleuthing, sneaking, and stalking through the woods/jungle. Teeth clenched, breathing heavily, prowling onward, they play their game of *trap tricking* that is destined to meet up with the *Damsels in Distress.* Just like with the sisters, the game of the Bruce Boys is familiar—it seems routine, but only some parts of it are truly understood. And what both teams of the game-players know is that the glue to the destined hook-up just happens to be the *boobs*—however, grapefruited. But a careful part of the game playing is that they (the boys and the sisters) have to be *pretend* enemies while doing the dance of coming together and doing the dance of resistance. But first, the hookup rules.

With Sheena, the boobs are not only on her chest, but on her mind as well. *Yes*, the grapefruit boobs are not just important because they match her donkey-straw-only-slightly-pooped-on hair, but her boobs will justify bringing the Bruce Boys into the game on legitimate terms, since resistance is a very important rule. Somehow (she doesn't know why), she and Chimp are supposed to pretend (game rules) that she doesn't want to play with the Bruce Boys, even though she likes them and they are familiar friends. But like any damsel worth her salt, Sheena knows she must pretend to be totally ignorant about the power she has being on the other end of her grapefruit boobs.

Boob strategy is also part of the rules to the game. Sheena must have them (boobs, that is) showing, but only *accidentally* exposed (damsels will do that) while she is prostrate in the pathway (the distress factor) because something has happened—(out of her control, obviously) and the beauty of her boobs has been inadvertently revealed. *So sorry*, she non-verbally demurs in her delicate, prone posture on the path.

The boobs are also on the mind of Chimp, because they define his job description. Chimp's boob business is slightly different than Sheena's because Chimp, although less boob interested due to age-ranking, must do a delicate dance of ambassadorship in both protecting Sheena's beauty (the boobs) and not going overboard in the protection, which would prevent the *Damsels in Distress* clan from getting hooked up with the Bruce Boys. In fact, the rules dictate Chimp must establish equilibrium between the two factions in the game playing, with just the right amount of resistance and boob balancing. Chimp must pretend to protect Sheena in her precarious and prostrate position (grapefruit boobs displayed) from the pretend enemy of the Bruce Boys with whom both girls would really like to play. However, just how hard Chimp should fight the boys is delicate. Chimp knows the boobs will bring the boys and that the boobs must be protected, but Chimp also knows that fighting too hard for Sheena's honor (or her boobs) might stop the game and the Bruce Boys might give up. Of course, none of the game-playing children want that.

Now for the Bruce Boys, the boobs are also very important but somewhat confusing. They, like Sheena and Chimp, know the required bantering and balancing about the boobs. Just like Sheena and Chimp, they just *couldn't help it* if the grapefruit boobs are exposed, and the Bruce Boys also know that they are allowed to be *helpless* (rendered out of control) in their attraction toward the boobs. And there it is—the boob glue—bringing the two groups together, *helplessly.*

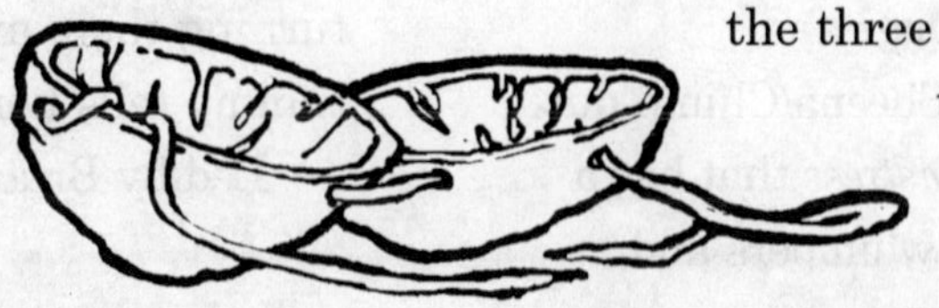

Beyond the boob justification in their helplessness, the Bruce Boys also know something about rules of engagement that, just like Chimp, require a balance without going too far. Dancing ever so softly in the back of their minds in unspoken, unwritten knowledge, is something about respecting these female units even though all morning they have been warring and whacking in preparation for hooking up with the sisters. Their invasion and their aggression can't be personal (nor mean) and that is why the raid must be all about the *boobs*—and it is.

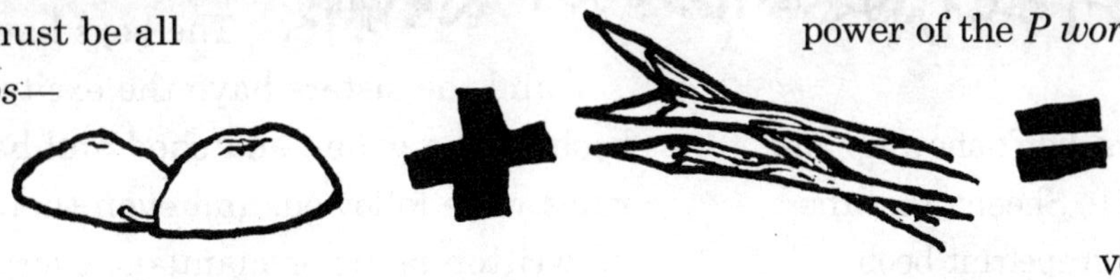

Since the DD sisters are more stationary with Sheena prone and Chimp protecting her, it will be the boys who take action for the planned convergence. So the warriors set out, armed with their spears and with only disconnected pieces of understanding the rules for resistance, codes of honor, and necessary utensils for boob balancing.

Stealthily down the paths of the woods/jungle the three warriors go, searching for their prey. Yes, they are armed—some weapons tangible, others not. In addition to their swords, now fatefully reduced to rather sorry-looking spear/sticks because of all that digging, the Bruce Boys have intangible weapons of *P words* in their mind even though not a single thesaurus can be found in the fort/camp/compound. They will (pretending, of course) practice the scripts of *prodding, poking, peeking,* and *plundering* in their morning mission. Their plan of attack is to trap the prize, winning the game and ending everything. Except of course, there is the added challenge of getting the steak knife back into the kitchen without detection. Minor problem.

Additionally, the Bruce Boys know that the power of the *P words* actually replace (and forbid) talking out loud. What is done and not done with language is very important to their play. *None needed* for the Bruce Boys, according to their woods/jungle etiquette manual concerning the spoken word. They don't know about *Diets* or

Dahlings or *Damsels in Distress*, but they know about their *P words* (not by name) and they know prodding, poking, peeking and plundering are all related to the boobs being the prize. And, most importantly, they know not to talk about it.

A different approach to language and communication comes from the Sheena/Chimp duo. They speak fluent *Damsel and Distress* that has a very unique vernacular. Sheena whimpers and sighs (true *damsel*) as she lies prostrate on the path, slightly moaning but no real words. And Chimp, running from bush to bush (looking, of course, for the peekers, pokers, prodders and plunderers) can only make Chimp sounds as his contribution to speaking pure *distress*. No words really, just Chimp sounds shrieking of the dangers that may bring distress to his damsel. Chimp remembers several DD games ago when the Bruce Boys didn't show up and she, tired of waiting, suggested to Sheena that the game be ended. Sheena, in full grapefruit boob regalia, reminded her sister, "Chimps can't talk!" And that was the end of Chimp's pursuit of language—formal anyway.

Finally, the Bruce Boys approach; peeking, poking, and prodding along the way, teeth clenched, boob focused. Sheena, speaking beautiful damsel, sensuously sighs and delicately demurs, while Chimp, *chimps* vociferously, trying to remember how far to push away the peekers, pokers, and prodders without running the risk of turning them away and missing lunch, which her tummy tells her is fast approaching.

Led by Bruce, the third heist of the morning is completed, but it is actually anticlimactic once it happens. Mike and Dave distract Chimp (probably planned because of seniority), and Bruce swoops in toward the boobs after taking an embarrassing topple, tripping on his untied shoelace and demonstrating the grace of dancing hippo. But as he recovers, Bruce squeals to his partners in crime, "I got 'em. Let's go."

In a flash, it's all over. The boys have the boobs and the sisters have the excitement of the boobs being gone—snatched and heisted. All the rules were followed, and even though there were no written plans or manuals, everything went according to the nonexistent plan. But it's not quite over. One more task, at least for the boys.

The sisters care little about the abandoned and only-slightly-pooped-on golden hair left in the path where Sheena was previously prone and pretty. It was fun, they are done, and lunch should be ready. As they leave the woods-now-really-woods, their previous feminine roles are easily abandoned as they talk excitedly about their upcoming afternoon plans to, just for fun, brush their dog's teeth or perhaps make a raft for a swamp adventure. Both afternoon play options are less sexually motivated than either *Dahling and Diets* or *Damsel in Distress*, and both afternoon selections flirt with styles much closer to what the Bruce Boys might be doing—dog teeth brushing and water escapades. It just seems easy for the girls to switch, at least for now.

But the Bruce Boys with boobs, whose stomachs are also reminding them of their awaiting lunch, remember they have one more, also anticlimactic task, for game finishing. Back to the trap they go with the coveted grapefruit boobs. There is no more peeking, prodding, poking or plundering necessary, since they have the prize and the enemy (whatever it was) seems to have dissipated. Bruce leads the way, a clear reminder of his seniority since he has them both (boobs that is) and both Mike and Dave have only their awe for Bruce. As they approach the trap, there is no hesitation. In one fell swoop (just like the original grapefruit boob snatch itself from the trash can and from Sheena's chest), the boobs are dropped in the trap and in one glorious scream, the Bruce Boys achieve game-ending satisfaction, yelling in unison the symbol of their achievement—***BOOBY TRAP!***

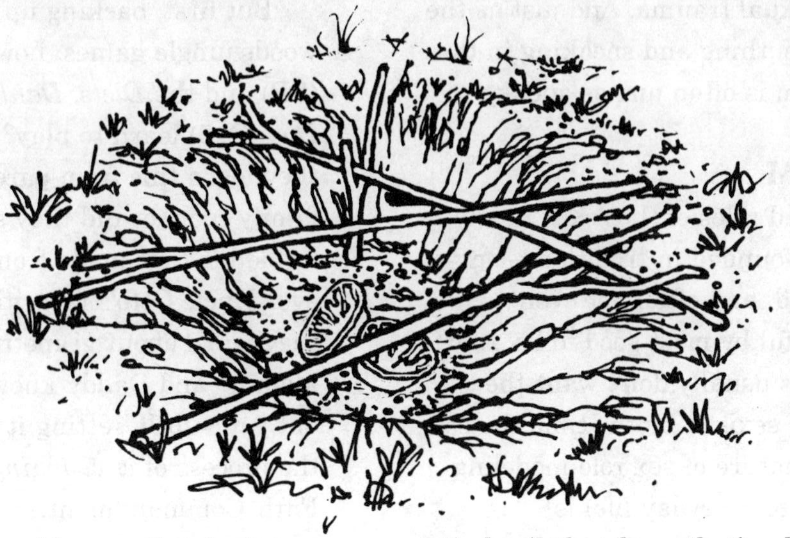

It is over. The boobs are trapped and their booby trap game was successful. They too head for their awaiting toasted cheese sandwiches. As the boys and the girls depart the woods/jungle of their play, clearly it was the grapefruit boobs that brought them together, but for totally different reasons and with totally different beliefs about each other's interest in the boobs. It may seem that, just like adult men, the Bruce Boys are attracted to breasts, and the *Damsel in Distress* duo is attracted to something else entirely. And perhaps that's where the differences dance together and that's where the dances of sexism contribute to the good and bad about sex, and eventually the *yes* or *no* about sexual offending.

And just as the Bruce Boys were sleuthing and sneaking in the woods/jungle, sexism is often just as sneaky.

THE FIFTH COMMANDMENT—Thou Shalt Envision Eve and Adam

The Fifth Commandment in raising sexually respectful children pertains to the issue of sexism—how boys and girls learn their sexual roles and how learning from childhood games, actually plays out in their eventual sexuality. Sexism is alive and well in this society and sexism is alive and well in the issue of sexual disrespect. Sexism doesn't cause sexual assault or sexual abuse, but sexual role modeling *gone wrong* can create a breeding ground for sowing the seeds of sexual thievery and often a lifetime of suffering from sexual trauma. And just as the Bruce Boys were sleuthing and sneaking in the woods/jungle, sexism is often just as sneaky.

SNEAKY SEXISM

Clear and defined roles of the sexes in any society are usually founded in tradition—long-standing, hard-wired, and often not even recognized as harmful by most good folks. And even though parents usually don't want the negative outcome of sexism, by the time the soft, subtle and sneaky nature of sex role modeling (so tightly woven into everyday life) is recognized, it is often too late. The Fifth Commandment *Thou Shalt Envision Eve and Adam* suggests a need for examining how sexist teaching creeps into the lives of children. And the word *envision* is the key, suggesting that sexism must first be understood (envisioned) and then perhaps rerouted with a more sexually respectful *vision* for children's futures. But in considering how sexism creeps along—so powerful and so easily accepted, envisioning is a difficult task because of the word *NORMAL.* Parents want their children to grow up *sexually normal* and sex role modeling just seems overwhelmingly *normal.* To challenge that ***norm*** can be a difficult step. To *envision* sexual roles for children against the norm of society is about as precarious as the grapefruit boobs perched carefully on Sheena's chest.

BOOB BLUEPRINTS

But first, backing up the boob business of the woods/jungle games, how did the Bruce Boys (BB) and the *Diets, Dahling, Damsel, Distress Duo* (Dx5) learn to play? Who taught them? Did they learn this from parents with podiums in the family room or did they sneak away to a forbidden tent made from hanging a blanket over Uncle Otto's favorite blackberry bush? Did they learn about grapefruit boobery without Mommy and Daddy knowing anything about it but yet, subtly setting it up? The answers begin the process of *envisioning*—so important in this Fifth Commandment.

The Dx5 faction focused on the boobs being the attraction for the Bruce Boys to play with them—that is the Bruce Boys *playing with the sisters,* not the boobs. And even though the sisters' morning games involved dieting, glamour and attractiveness, at this time in their sexual role training, they know nothing about bra sizes, breast stimulation, breast augmentation, or sexual foreplay involving breasts or nipples. In fact, they know nothing about sex, even though they are playing sexual games and even though they are involved with a *boob blueprint* that will influence their sexual lives forever.

MOMMY MODELING AND THE *PROBABLIES*

The *Diet, Dahling, Damsel, Distress Duo* are ***probably*** playing out a reflection of what they believe will be their adult female futures because of what they have probably witnessed (modeling) from their mother, who probably also has the biggest and most important boobs in the family—but not grapefruit ones. And teaching dangerous sexism is usually about the *probablies*—nothing really certain or intended—just probably the result of the way children learn as they sponge up sexual information.

Sheena, Chimp, and the dieting damsels probably live with a mother who is concerned about her appearance, and they have probably witnessed Mommy discussing her diets with her *dahling* friends and probably her excitement about being *thinna*. With more Mommy modeling, they probably learned a demonstrative form of communication quite different than the teeth clenching of the Bruce Boys. And probably with more modeling, they have learned that brown hair just doesn't cut it and that blondes are much preferred; even with a little donkey poop in those pretend yellow, flowing locks. And most important in the Mommy modeling is about the boobs and the boys.

The sisters probably made the connection between the Bruce Boys and the boob attraction in lessons from their father or other male role models when they made comments about breasts, probably most innocently. And through their observations of the sexual roles around them, they learned and then modeled that as female units they need to diet, they need to be dramatic (*dahlings*) in communication, and they need to be beautiful, but also distressed. The damsel modeling teaches the female units they must be demure, sweet, innocent, and most importantly, *distressed* in order to get the boys to be interested in the boobs which, in turn, bring the boys to play. The female modeling isn't about sex (yet), but it is about sexual role training providing the boob blueprint for the future.

The female modeling isn't about sex (yet), but it is about sexual role training providing the boob blueprint for the future.

MALE BOOB PROBABLIES

The Bruce Boys were clearly interested in the boobs, ***probably*** from what they learned from their male role models about attractiveness toward female bodies—especially the boobs. This learning was probably not organized by uncaring or mean-spirited men; but instead, it probably unfolded in convoluted and accidental exposure. This sex role modeling wasn't the kind of modeling found in a Victoria's Secret catalog, but a different kind of modeling where early in life,

They probably got other bits and pieces about boobs being very important by such things as seeing a two-year-old girl cover her boobs with a bikini top even though her four-year-old brother has exactly the same boobs—but uncovered.

the Bruce Boys picked up bits and pieces of sexual role learning to form a blueprint for their sexual future, however booberized.

MALE MODELING PROBABLIES

Just like the girls, the Bruce Boys collect pieces and piles of information about sex (and boobs) from their male role models that were disconnected and disjointed. *No,* they weren't interested in Sheena's grapefruit boobs because she spoke *damsel* or because Chimp protected her from *distress*—whatever that was. They didn't notice or care anything about Sheena's trying-to-be-flowing golden hair. But probably from something like Dad's girlie calendar in the garage they learned that boobs are important to male units since after all, it seemed that their Dad and uncles really acted silly (and loud) talking about *honkers, hooters, and high balls* when they were looking at the calendar. They probably got other bits and pieces about boobs being very important by such things as seeing a two-year-old girl cover her boobs with a bikini top even though her four-year-old brother has exactly the same boobs—but uncovered.

But that's not all the Bruce Boys learned about the boob concentration as they sponged and soaked up their sexual world. Probably in another piece of learning, they began to figure out about the *P words* they used in the woods/jungle. Probably they learned that their male heroes (when not hooting about hooters) were very powerful in *plundering, prodding, peeking,* and *poking* in movies, war stories, or just Thanksgiving Day football conquests on television. This learning/modeling probably came from a variety of sources, depicting men conquering things, trapping things, or destroying things, thus the *P words* and their *powerful* action of the woods/jungle play. For the boys, the male model (at least half of it) was one of power and a special kind of *powerlessness,* related to the boobs and what they represent, far beyond two grapefruit halves perched on Sheena's flat, but real boobs.

HOOTER HOOKUPS

For the male modeling to unfold, there had to be a couple of *probablies* after the hooters were hooked up to the *P words* in order for the Bruce Boys to get to the booby-trapping idea. Probably, something happened quite accidentally—perhaps overhearing a conversation. It probably (who knows for sure?) happened when the Bruce Boys, in their sexual role modeling education, combined a powerful male hero, such as a John Wayne type of image (clenched teeth and no talking), with Dad's girlie calendar (something about those hooters), and probably, just maybe, by chance something happened about the trapping of those hooters. Maybe it was something as simple as while attending Easter dinner at Grandma's, hearing a conversation of older, respected cousins making secretive plans against another team of cousins in a game of Scavenger Hunt. Maybe the Bruce

Boys were too little to play the complicated game with their older cousins, but maybe they overheard some *booby-trapping* language from these important male role models, making everything ripe for the hooter hookups later in the woods/jungle.

"Yes, we can trick 'em with a booby trap in the hayloft and then we will win," was probably something similar to what the Bruce Boys might have heard from an admired older cousin as another trap was envisioned. And with all of this mix and match of sexual snippets, they commit the heist from the *Damsels in Distress,* and gleefully trap the boobs in their very own ***Booby Trap***.

BOOBY TRAPS TO BOOBY BOY BRINGING

The sisters and the boys play together, glued by the boobs. But in their separate games they are miles apart in truly understanding the sex role modeling in which they are engaging. It is precarious, and most of the time parents never see it happen until it is too late because they didn't *envision* the outcome. Yet, these sexual roles will converge on a path, at a later time, becoming as tightly connected as hang-up handles on a crocheted hot pad with no wiggle room out. Early in childhood the kiddos participate in the developmental dance that will eventually bring them together as partners in either positive or destructive ways—sometimes as either sexual takers or sexual victims. Trying to raise sexually respectful children without envisioning sexual role training makes the process about as reliable as a Sex Fairy crapshoot.

Yet, these sexual roles will converge on a path, at a later time, becoming as tightly connected as hang-up handles on a crocheted hot pad with no wiggle room out.

THE ROAD TO THE ROLES

Backing up even further from the families of the Bruce Boys and Dx5, questions could be raised about where did the roles of sexism begin and why are the roles are so ingrained in society? What is the history of the modeling learned and adorned by the Bruce Boys and the distressed damsels?

A historical (hysterical) perspective of sexual role development offers no doubt that in very early organization of human folks, there were edicts about when boobs needed heisting and when steak knives needed procuring. Some of the first resources in Eastern philosophy, the Koran and Christian Bible, not only make the rules about how the sexes should be different but those long-time-ago scholars also (and often with vengeance) spelled out the punishment for breaking the sexual role rules. So, if the rule breaking of sex role stereotypes was in all the early writings, it can be assumed that following the patterns of how society thinks boys and girls should respond differently hasn't been easy for a very long time. The gruesome nature of some of the punishments for breaking the sexual role rules suggests that worrying about the kiddos in the woods/jungle action is a big improvement over time. This is especially true when considering that only a short century ago, a pair of folks from two different countries made a huge (and not-so-nice) impact on the whole business of *okay* and *not okay* sex role training.

VICKY AND TONY

VICKY and TONY (Queen Victoria and Anthony Comstock) held a tight reign on sexual expression in the late nineteenth century. In the times of Victorian England (Vicky's rule), sexuality was considered a necessary evil and all efforts were made to avoid those pesky feelings, especially for women. High necklines, long skirts and other efforts to tuck women into their clothing, without any chance for escape, was the accepted dress code. No accidental grapefruit boob exposure for Queen Vicky's gang.

Sexual feelings were thought to be problematic and *good women* should do everything to avoid stirring up those sexual feelings that only men were prone to have.

During this time, the only sanctioned fantasies for women were toward such things as proper diaper removal or tips for preparing a ham. Sexual feelings were thought to be problematic and *good women* should do everything possible to avoid stirring up those sexual feelings that only men were supposed to have. Queen Vicky and her efforts in keeping the men under control brought about the furniture trend to cover the legs of chairs (Victorian style) and other helpful warnings such as women should be cautious serving dinner to a male suitor on a white tablecloth lest he be reminded of the bed sheet. And who knows what might happen then, right next to the carefully prepared ham?

SEXUAL POLICE PARTNERS

Now Tony, Vicky's *sexual police partner* and America's compatriot, was Anthony Comstock—a grumpy little fellow who didn't look to some as being much fun sexually. His campaign in the United States was to squelch smut with the bottom line of influence connected to disseminating sexual material. Anthony was obsessed with anyone who wanted to publish or propagate nasty stuff, so he campaigned and was eventually successful in getting the Comstock Act passed. This federal law prohibited distribution of pornographic material through the mail and Anthony, in his zeal, even viewed birth control information as *pornographic.*

CRACKING DOWN COMSTOCK

The Comstock Act cracked down on shuffling smut through the federal post office, but it also had a definite persuasion between the sexes. Anthony was mostly concerned about women receiving birth control information and apparently wasn't too upset if men found access to the birth control directions. The idea was that sex should be for procreation ONLY, and of course, across the Atlantic Ocean in England, Queen Vicky concurred. The smut fighters questioned the *need* for birth control methods if babies were the only sanctioned outcome of sexual get-togethers. The bottom line was that if birth control was needed, then someone was having sex for some other reason, which was just too much to bear for the sexual police partners of Tony and Vicky.

Neither of them would have approved of the golden hair, golden grapefruit boob business in the woods/jungle, yet traces of their influence from years previous, obviously tiptoed ever-so-quietly in the games of the Dx5 and the Bruce Boys. Actually, the damsel and distress part was really *pure Vicky*, especially the accidental part of Sheena's boob exposure. Tony and Vicky wouldn't condone the sisters having sexual feelings at all, but when calculating and considering that society would soon perish without some sexual activity, they could concede the damsel/distress part—which, of course, would be related to the Bruce Boys and their need to procreate, thus, the accidental boob exposure that Sheena *just couldn't help*. Vicky would rationalize some of Sheena's slips only for baby production, and she was sometimes quoted as advising British women, when faced with the necessity of becoming pregnant, to simply *lie on their backs and think of England.*

TONY, VICKY & JUNGLE GIGOLOING

Tony would have had no sympathy for the sisters, suggesting sternly that Sheena and Chimp were *fallen women* (for boob exposure), probably reminding them of the need for higher necklines and long skirts in their game playing. But true to sex role stereotyping, a more lenient assessment might have been given by Tony to the male game-playing units of the woods/jungle. The Vicky/Tony duo would probably have accepted that the Bruce Boys *just couldn't help it*, once exposed to the boobs of the *fallen women*. In theory, both Tony and Vicky would have considered the damsels only to be repositories for the necessary sperm deposits of the Bruce Boys, even though the kids in the woods/jungle were far removed from any of that business.

It could probably be assumed that Vicky never played golden hair/golden grapefruit boobs, nor was she ever Sheena, Queen of the Jungle, which, in reality, might have been good for her. But remarkably, Queen Victoria also had eight children, suggesting she and her royal hubby, Al (Alfred) must have at least fooled around eight times. And Tony C. probably never would have made it stealing steak knives with the Bruce Boys, although that too, might have helped him with his frowny feelings about sex. But have the clutches of the sexual suppression from Vicky Q. and Tony C. really ended?

COMSTOCK CLUTCHES

The Comstock Act and its tight reign on dissemination of sexual information was not completely extinguished by the U.S. Supreme Court until 1965 and although the ban was lifted, this didn't mean that equal sexual expression among men and women leaped forward with the government routinely passing out spoiled grapefruit halves and stolen steak knives to children. The sexual revolution of the 60s was supposed to free things up, and perhaps it did somewhat. But perhaps the freedom to sexually abuse or to take sexual advantage of others was also set free with the same indiscretion.

The bottom line was that if birth control was needed, then someone was having sex for some other reason, which was just too much to bear for the sexual police partners of Tony and Vicky.

They say unless Sheena and Chimp play differently than the Bruce Boys, families will fall into disarray, heterosexual couples will fall into divorce, and same sex folks will fall into bed with each other.

ANALYZING ANDROGYNY

Even though the reigning rigidity of Queen Victoria and Anthony Comstock faded, there remains a big argument about changing their influence on the current sex-role development of American children. Many suggest that sexual role rigidity offered from the sexual policing of the past is not only acceptable, but necessary. And those same folks rudely resist *androgyny*, which is the equaling of sexual traits and tendencies for the two sexes. Card-carrying androgynous activists and supporters suggest that rather than the Sheena/Chimp girls playing Damsel in Distress and the Bruce Boys seeking and stalking, there should be a homogeneous human unit, with both male and female traits and only a tiny bit of difference between the gender's roles.

This equal male/female unit through androgyny would only be distinguishable by a few inches of secreted away body parts found under their underwear, which by the way, would need to be purple, since baby boy blue would need to be mixed with pretty girl pink to make the unisex color of purple. With androgyny, some folks say things would be so simple because there would be total similarity between the boy and girl units. A one-size-fits-all approach to the woods/jungle sex role modeling would occur under this plan where damsels might be getting dirty with their plundering and the Bruce Boys might have grapefruit boobs—all they wanted, in fact. But that approach to sexual role training doesn't tend to be popular, and Tony and Vicky Q. certainly would have resisted it. Think of the confusion about who should lie on their backs and who should think of England?

WHOA WAIT

But wait! Critics of androgyny suggest that without clear sexual roles, peaceful society (and an organized society) would become a thing of the past, at least in the way of the sexes. They say unless Sheena and Chimp play differently than the Bruce Boys, families will fall into disarray, heterosexual couples will fall into divorce, and same sex folks will fall into bed with each other. Androgyny, it is viewed, must be rejected since sexual roles are needed to make little boys strong because little girls need to be protected so they can have babies and keep the population going. And that is why, they say, the Bruce Boys need to practice *protecting* and little girls need to practice *attracting for the protection*, which is a lot about the accidental grapefruit boob exposure. No, the efforts at androgyny are strongly rejected by many and, in fact, sexism fostering the differences and at times, the inequality between genders seems to reign, and reign, and reign—and that same process sometimes reeks with disrespect.

THE ROLL OF THE ROLES

If sexual roles are here to stay, what roles are good, bad or contributing to the problem of sexual disrespect? And how should parents who want to raise sexually respectful children first *envision* and then handle sexual role training? The answer lies in first understanding the precarious nature of sex role training and secondly, appreciating its power and connection to sexual problems. In the simple game playing of the woods/jungle are answers for how sexual roles can roll toward disrespect and how parents can think differently (envisioning *Eve and Adam*, rather than the traditional Adam and Eve) for rerouting children toward sexual respect.

THE FINE FOUR

There are four issues of sexism (THE FINE FOUR) playing out in the woods/jungle that can have a direct relationship to sexual offending. First, roles of Dx5 and BB are established with certain blueprints being created about who is *sexy* and who is *sexual*, who is *attractive* and who is *attracted*, and there's a big difference. This learning designates the difference between one group being aroused and one woods/jungle group being *arousing*. Secondly, there is a clear pattern of *helplessness* being practiced by both groups, with the Dx5 being helpless in their attractiveness (boobs and such) and the boys being helpless in their attraction, thus forgiving their crime (however innocent) of the grapefruit boob heist.

Third, Sheena/Chimp and the Bruce Boys are *clearly* learning how to be *unclear* about their sexual intentions. This confused communication, even for these young children, breeds a ***pretend intentions*** idea to sexual consent issues about when folks are really saying *yes*—especially relating to sexual criminal conduct. And finally, the two gender groups of the woods/jungle are practicing their roles of one being an *offender type* and one being a *victim type* as clearly as the stolen steak knives in Bruce's pants and donkey poop on Sheena's golden hair. These role trainings ignore the possibility of female sex offenders and ignore the needs of male victims.

Tackling these four powerful sexist issues from the woods/jungle games can help parents understand how just one step out of the woods/jungle innocence can bring sexual disrespect, often ruining family hopes for something else. So, with a peek back to the woods, the fine four emerge for envisioning.

ROLE OUT ONE—ATTRACTIVE/ATTRACTED/SEXY/SEXUAL

For the damsels, they are learning to be *attractive* while the Bruce Boys are learning something slightly different, which is to be *attracted*. As the boys are learning about the *P words* of peeking, poking, and prodding, the little girls are concentrating (yes, building sexual interest) on how they will look, feel and smell when they are peeked, poked and prodded upon. When both groups tire of the woods/jungle, moving forward in years into more sophisticated sexual roles, they will take the boob blueprints and add what society teaches, and just as children do, they will mix and match, sometimes with hysterical but often serious results.

As the boys are learning about the *P words* of peeking, poking, and prodding, the little girls are concentrating (yes, building sexual interest) on how they will look, feel and smell when they are peeked, poked and prodded upon.

THE KEY COMBINATIONS—FOR BOYS AND GIRLS

As for the boys, they will fashion (poor choice of words for the warriors of the woods) their sexual roles by combining with the *P words of power* to develop into some image of John Wayne and a German shepherd. The combination is key with this analogy of roles describing the sexual future of the Bruce Boys and their business of being *attracted* rather than *attractive*. There is no harm meant to either the late, great actor or canines of German descent in this male role combination of John Wayne and a German shepherd. But like it or not, that combination is typical in the sexual role playing of young men and clearly relates to the issue of being strong and powerful (*P words)*, yet having only one legitimate emotion, which is sexual attraction. And balancing the power with attraction is the key combination.

RAMBO/WAYNE

Of course, John Wayne or another cowboy-type conjures a familiar image in the woods/jungle role modeling for the rural Bruce Boys. For more urban male units (without a woods/jungle), perhaps the Rambo character substitutes nicely if the cowboy image in the city is too big of a stretch. But in combination with the Rambo/Wayne image, whether boys find themselves in an apartment in downtown Manhattan or on an isolated farm in Montana, the German shepherd part of the combination remains the same—a tongue wagging, slobbering, perspiring, sexual responsive machine, with eyes darting in constant surveillance for sexual stimuli on which to pounce. *Attracted* is the canine image. Just one single sight of the golden hair and grapefruit boobs will render the German shepherd component of the male role model, out of control.

BARBIE/JUNE

And if the sexual future of boys is being aroused/attracted (as opposed to girls being arousing/attractive) what would be the sexual role model of the Diets, Dahlings, Damsel in Distress Duo? Comparatively, the Damsel Duo will fashion their golden, color-coordinated donkey hair and golden grapefruit boobs toward being arousing, but not too far. Whispers of Tony and his *fallen woman* idea still could be heard in the woods/jungle when the Dx5 girls play, even though they wouldn't know Anthony Comstock from famed pornographer, Larry Flint.

Just as the boys create a combination of John Wayne and a German Shepherd, little girls end up developing a role model combining the Barbie doll image and June Cleaver—thus *Barbie/June*. The Barbie side of the sex role image is pure beauty and clearly a graduation from grapefruit boobs and slightly-pooped-on golden hair. And yes, Barbie has real boobs and other really perfect body parts, clearly setting the stage for the role of *sexy*. And just like the donkey straw matching Sheena's grapefruit boobs, for Barbie everything will match and match perfectly. Barbie has matching scarves, purses, earrings, belts and shoes to help her be absolutely gorgeous and *arousing*. But there is need for not going too far in the arousing business as the balanced part of the combination brings to bear, and as the spirits of Tony and Vicky smile contentedly.

Just as the boys balance John Wayne/Rambo to the German shepherd, the girls have a counterbalance to Barbie (keeping her attractiveness in line), which would be something akin to the June Cleaver image taken from the television show, *Leave It To Beaver*. The June part of the image would seem at first blush (and by the way, blushing looks very good on June) to have been a distant second or third cousin to Vicky and Tony, as she would seem to have fit nicely into Victorian England sexual roles. Thinking of June Cleaver with grapefruit boobs really seems like a stretch, but seeing her mop her floors wearing pearls makes the transition or balance with Barbie, easy.

PERFECT TO POTLUCKS

Contrasted to Rambo/Wayne and the German shepherd image for the boys, the June Cleaver part of the Dx5 sex role image is one of female perfection, different than Barbie perfect matching for attractiveness. June is a perfect Mom, perfect wife and just plain perfect. Anger, power or hate are not emotions usually ascribed to the June Cleaver type, although an acceptable fussiness would seem appropriate if one of her children was overlooked in being chosen for a distinguished part in the school Christmas Pageant or if she erred and brought a dessert to the potluck rather than her designated Three Bean Salad. However, what June has in the combination with Barbie, is a deep dedication and commitment to fixing creative school lunches, making a great pot roast and being pathologically addicted to toilet bowl cleaning. She will find joy in changing poopy diapers or concentrating on the careful consistency of oatmeal. No one will ever know for sure how June captured Ward, her husband, since there isn't a single grapefruit boob to be found in the perfect house in the cul-de-sac. And no one will ever know how Beaver and his brother were conceived, because the sexual image doesn't really fit for June. But never mind, for her side of Barbie/June, she is just the picture of maternal and wifery perfection. There it is—Barbie, beauty and boobs, combined with June and her model of majestic motherhood and mopping floors (joyously) with pearls.

ROLES ROLLING WRONG

In the beginning, the *attractive/attracted* mantra between the sexes should work out reasonably well without too many problems. At first, Rambo/Wayne will powerfully roar in place, climbing cliffs, forging rivers, attacking enemies, and conquering thousands. Of course, rescuing his damsel, at least in the fantasy

The Barbie side of the sex role image is pure beauty and clearly a graduation from grapefruit boobs and slightly-pooped-on golden hair.

The Barbie/Junes of the world will forge forward being attractive, demure and pure damsel, accidentally exposing a grapefruit boob just to interest Rambo/Wayne, which in reality may only be wearing hip-hugger jeans that reveal her unauthorized-by-Dad, thong panties.

which in reality, may only be finally getting a date to the senior keg party. The Barbie/Junes of the world will forge forward being attractive, demure and pure damsel, accidentally exposing a grapefruit boob just to interest Rambo/Wayne, which in reality may only be wearing hip-hugger jeans that reveal her unauthorized-by-Dad, thong panties. And once their male counterparts with the powerful P words have rescued Barbie/June, the female units will demurely begin to raise babies and consider their pearls for mopping. It would all work out fine if things didn't change, but often they do.

Once RW (Rambo/Wayne) rescues BJ (Barbie/June) from evil (distress, actually), what does he do with his learned skills in peeking, poking and prodding? Between steady work at the furniture factory and a bowling score that steadily remains the same, where is RW going to put his energy for feeling like an honorable masculine unit? After all, how many cliffs are there to climb or rivers to forge in the cul-de-sac on Maple Place? And for Barbie/June, the same disappointment may befall the former Sheena, since her grapefruited boobs were once the focus of her femininity and now between babies and the sack lunches, she has no time to be demure, and being prone and pretty on a path just doesn't seem possible with soccer practice and her weekend job at the Pig N'Poke Pancake House. But the real problem in roles rolling wrong with the *attractive and attracted* dilemma comes in the sex department for RW and BJ.

MISSING MANUALS

If the sexual role training of the woods/jungle goes unchecked and males only learn to be attracted and females only learn to be attractive, for most couples the missing manuals on how to adjust in marriage is a huge problem and often a breeding ground for sexual disrespect. For females, marriage often requires the June side and her floor mopping talent to take center stage most of the time, except of course, when Barbie might be needed for getting frisky in the Motel 8 with RW hubby after the bowling tournament. The June side may have little interest in sexual pleasure or sexual fulfillment. No, the *sexy* part for June is often missing-in-action, and the *sexual* (and there is a difference) part of June is about as remote as Anthony Comstock and Queen Victoria teaching a film production class on pornography.

And RW seems to be missing a manual on what to do with his attraction skills that were so exciting in the woods/jungle and watching his father and uncles hooting and hollering about hooters. He is to conquer sex, but how can he do that with June so tired, and the alarm is set for 5:30 in the morning? How can he get a single *fort feeling* of danger and war, falling asleep in the hammock after mowing the lawn and when stumbling to bed he finds his Sheena-now-become-June wearing curlers?

TELL US THOMAS

Thomas looks in the mirror with disappointment. Pimples abound on his fourteen-year-old face, camouflaging any hope for someone to really notice his three facial hairs. There is absolutely nothing about Thomas resembling (even remotely) John Wayne or Rambo. But Thomas has been learning the *P words*. He knows he should be poking, peeking and prodding, and that he should be powerful.

But Thomas doesn't feel powerful, and he does feel something else. Thomas recognizes his sister-cousin-neighbor (doesn't matter as long as the focus is female) has things that cause him a German shepherd-type of *stirring* never before experienced. *Yes*, the seven-year-old has blond hair just like the ladies in the Victoria Secret catalog he has been peeking into. *Yes*, she wears shorts just like the ladies wear on Thomas' favorite television show, *Baywatch*. And *yes*, she likely has boobs that he thinks he would enjoy touching. To Thomas, she is sexy and he is sexual.

In Thomas' contemplation about what to do with his teeth-sweating-German shepherd desire and his need to peek, poke and prod, he considers sexual interactions with a Victoria Secret model or with one of the babes on *Baywatch*. But these fantasies flop. Then he tries more realistic thoughts of getting frisky with cheerleaders or popular girls in his school. Those images also fail. Looking in the mirror, Thomas concludes there is no chance for him with those potential partners. He doesn't look one bit like John Wayne or Rambo, yet his German shepherd side is working just fine and that's a problem. With few options and with no guidance for Thomas to understand something beyond the attractive/attracted differences in the genders, Thomas reaches for smaller, but nonetheless good replicas of the Baywatch babes, which could happen to be female children and which could send Thomas into the world of sexual offending.

FURTHER FAILINGS

Shannon was beautiful—absolutely gorgeous. At fourteen years old, she could have been on the cover of a fashion magazine. Mom looks just fine as well, after three children and twenty-two years of matrimonial commitment. Sure, she has gained three quarters of a pound each year of marriage, and sure, she gets her clothes from a catalog, but it is a rather upscale catalog, she assures herself. Mom wears makeup, but usually only on Sundays. She busies herself with kids, casseroles, and kitchen cleaning, but she lost her pearls for mopping a long time ago.

Now Dad (RW Gone Wrong) finds himself bored. He is still longing for his old Sheena days, because now it seems he has nothing to fulfill his peeking, poking, and prodding needs working at Ted's Tackle Shop. Mom, his long-ago Sheena, is pretty busy and not like she used to be. He loves her, especially when he has the flu or when he needs those ribs cooked just right for his bowling team anniversary parties. But considering RW's

No, the *sexy* part for June is often missing-in-action, and the *sexual* (and there is a difference) part of June is about as remote as Anthony Comstock and Queen Victoria teaching a film-production class on pornography.

But never mind, he convinces himself. *Attractiveness* has never been important to Dad types, but being *attracted* has always been a top priority.

rather rusty poking, peeking and prodding desires, Mom just doesn't *melt his butter*, he says to himself, especially when he thinks of Shannon. Without knowing it, Dad recognizes shades of Sheena in his teenage daughter.

Paradoxically, Dad has gained 1.5 pounds for each year of marriage, resulting in a rotund potbelly resting precariously on his belt. And Dad's hairline seems to have slipped to a remote destination somewhere inside his ears and nose. But never mind, he convinces himself. *Attractiveness* has never been important to Dad types, but being *attracted* has always been a top priority. Without rerouting the role modeling, Dad may rationalize Shannon to become his Sheena, because his Bruce Boys training has never been envisioned and adjusted. Mom's role is diminished as she has moved from Barbie to June and long ago retired her grapefruit boobs. Tragically, Dad can't find anything to do with his German shepherdhood.

CAUTION FLAG

The breeding ground is there, precarious and unsafe—at least in some families. But it is important to be cautious—flying a flag of ***whoa*** in the blame game. Preventing any Dad or Thomas from rationalizations that the *attractive/attracted* or the *sexy/sexual* mess of sexism causes sexual abuse is important. Sexual responsibility is paramount to sexual respect and sexism is not an excuse for offending. But for parents who want to raise sexually respectful children, it is also important that this type of sexism be recognized as creating an environment ripe for sexual promiscuity or thinking in ways that normalize breaking the rules of sexual commitment, some which could eventually result in sexual perpetration.

ROLL OUT TWO—HARMLESS HELPLESSNESS

Back in the woods/jungle, a precarious and often dangerous issue of *helplessness* provides a number two worry about how sexism can contribute to roles rolling wrong. The scripting of *just can't help it* seemed harmless in the innocent games of the Dieting Damsels and the Bruce Boys if it only stopped there. But it doesn't. This *just can't help it* thinking can impact efforts to raise sexually respectful children and it heavily influences the serious problem of sexual offending.

WHOOPS—PAYCHECKS TO PRISON

Now for the helpless Sheena—she and her grapefruit boob exposure must be accidental (whoops). After all, what would June think? It was probably the *distress* that caused the accident because Sheena (heading for pearl-floor-mopping) would never have exposed herself on purpose or unless financial compensation were on the woods/jungle horizon, which is not likely. In the light of sexism, exposing oneself has extremely different consequences for males and females. When males expose themselves, they are likely to get arrested or receive other rude responses. But when females expose themselves, they tend to get paychecks. But beyond employment opportunities at Larry's Lap Dance Lounge, Sheena must be helpless (absolutely) in her grapefruit boob exposure.

DUAL HELPLESSNESS

In the rule of engagement for Sheena, she must adapt the *just couldn't help it* posture in order to avoid the wrath of folks like Anthony and Vicky, and of course, to get approval from the June *innocent image* later on when pearl-floor-mopping is on the horizon. The sad part about this sex role training is that the Sheena types are supposed to be sexy, but only accidentally. And problems about sexual offending may take this further, especially considering the dual helplessness connected to the Bruce Boys.

The unspoken rule for the Bruce Boys is they are helpless once exposed to Sheena's grapefruit boobs. Comparatively, in the normal life of most male units there is a demand for politeness, manners and certainly no stealing, with *responsibility* being the operative theme. But in the sexual role game playing, the boobs are heisted (against all stealing rules), so the urge to do the heist must resolve the dilemma by suggesting the Bruce Boys had to be helplessly unable to resist. *They just couldn't help it* reigns for both the Damsels in Distress and the boob heisting Bruce Boys, setting the stage for possible sexual disrespect in the future.

STUD HORSE THEORY

If the helplessness issue learned so innocently in the woods/jungle never really went beyond the boob heist, things should be okay for these game-playing children. But society seems to hang on to the boobery/robbery lessons as sexual assault and rape are explained or justified. It is as though in this thinking, males become stud horses, unable to control themselves in sexual situations, and therefore, accountability and responsibility is a moot point. After all, the stud horse in a field of mares *can't help it* either, once exposed to a frisky mare with very attractive mane and matching tail.

When males expose themselves, they are likely to get arrested or receive other rude responses. But when females expose themselves, they tend to get paychecks.

STUD HORSES IN THE COURTROOM

The judge concluded at the sentencing of a sex offender and in response to the prosecutor's request for a prison term, "What we have here is a provocative and seductive six-year-old, suggesting to this court that the victim must accept some responsibility for what happened. And with that understanding, I believe a period of supervision rather than prison is in order." (Six-year-old grapefruit boobs gone wrong.)

In the rape of an adult, the jury foreman was interviewed following the not guilty verdict of the defendant. She lamented, sadly, *"We believed that the sexual activities probably happened, but the fact that she was breast-feeding her baby without closing the blinds made us believe it was possible that she was at least reckless, or maybe even consented. Why else would she tempt him like that?"* (Open window grapefruit boobery slip.)

"We believed that the sexual activities probably happened, but the fact that she was breast-feeding her baby without closing the blinds made us believe it was possible that she was at least reckless, or maybe even consented. Why else would she tempt him like that?"

STUD HORSES AND SEX OFFENDERS

When the father was asked to explain his sexual abuse of his three-year-old daughter, he clarified, "She always seemed to flaunt her body in those Snoopy pajamas. What's a man to do?" (Three-year-old grapefruit boobs.)

When the uncle was asked why he offended his ten-year-old niece, he explained, "My wife has gained so much weight since our children were born (egg and grapefruit shortage), and I just couldn't control myself once my niece started to sexually develop."

The idea is that males (like stud horses) are helpless when exposed to sexual stimulus (boobs and such) and therefore, no one is really responsible for sexual transgressions. This thinking sets the tone for not only rationalizing sexual indiscretion, but for encouraging the behavior in the first place. And it all began with the way the kiddos learned their sexual role games with both males and females being *helpless* in either their attractiveness or in being attracted. This *just couldn't help it* denies sexual responsibility, which is so important in raising sexually respectful children.

ROLE OUT THREE—PRETEND INTENTIONS

Lots of pretending punctuated the game playing of the kiddos in the woods/jungle, as it should be in childhood. But the third issue of sexism that contributes to sexual disrespect has to do with the confusion (pretending or not) of sexual intentions. ***Who really wanted what*** easily tiptoes into the heart of sexual disrespect relating to the issue of *consent*. Not only is consent important in establishing laws against unwanted sexual contact (age of consent statutes), but the issue of consent is often the foundation for making decisions when sexual stuff is okay or not okay, or when someone should go to prison or back to the woods/jungle for retraining.

In order for consent to be assured in sexual situations, communication—the verbal type—must occur to avoid confusion about intent. Many problems in sexual abuse cases wouldn't materialize if clear language made the sexual tryst on the pantry table or under the picnic table agreeable to everyone. But in the games of the woods/jungle, the intentions are purposely confusing (pretended), and in very different communication styles and abilities between the boys and the girls—laying a breeding ground for consent problems in the future.

CHITS AND CHATS

The Bruce Boys are learning the fine art of teeth clenching, which doesn't contribute much to healthy communication. They are learning the power of *not talking,* which results in lots of ***action*** in substitution for language.
Whispering, secrecy, and blunt , one syllable words is part of the chosen communication style for the boys. Silence is strong and *no need for talking* is the mantra for the Bruce Boys, sadly continuing into their sexual trysts as teenagers.

But the sister duo is learning something very different (but nonetheless confusing) about their communication styles. The Dx5 girls seem to have two languages in the woods/jungle vernacular, and the options tend to be designated by the present company. In the *Diets and Dahling* game, the language is rich with demonstrative flare. *"Oh, Dahling"* rings true, dripping with emotion for the dieting duo. But during *Damsel in Distress*, things changed. Not only was Chimp forbidden from talking (Chimps can't), but also Sheena spoke pure *damsel*, which was wordless—only sighs and helplessness.

The result of these confusing communication styles for children playing sexual games has a critical impact on sexual decision making later on. When men and women come together for a sexual relationship, they will bring to the table (back seat, bedroom, or bowling alley parking lot) different communication needs and styles, which is likely to cause confusion at best, criminal problems at the worst.

CLARIFY FOR US KOBE

The famous National Basketball Association star, Kobe Bryant, was accused of sexual assault in the State of Colorado. Shades of grapefruit boobery were clearly contained in initial reports suggesting there were *pretended intentions.* It seemed true that she (the *perhaps* victim) had flirted with the famous star through her role as hotel concierge and it seemed she had agreed to venture into his hotel room to solve a maintenance problem. And yes, it seemed that an autograph and a kiss were agreed upon, however unspoken. But then things really got confusing with claims of sexual assault. The bruises and physical damage of the victim seemed to communicate one story while Kobe maintained he thought their agreement of cooperation was clearly in another direction. But then, with lawyers, reporters and newscasters trying to sort out the *pretend intentions*, things got even worse.

Adding to the confusion, it seems the victim (if she was) had several sexual partners around the time of the Kobe get-together where, according to her, terms of the unwritten consent contracts, however unspoken, were clear. This one (with Kobe) was different for her, she claimed, and the intentions of her "no" to Kobe were obvious. *Not so,* said Kobe. *Too confusing,* he and his million-dollar attorney proclaimed. And so it was for many (sport fans, especially) who agreed that the confusion was just that—*confusing.* Who was responsible for the confusion was an even bigger question.

For Kobe it seemed to be another version of *I couldn't help it*—not in controlling himself once exposed to her grapefruit boobs, but the *I couldn't help it if I was confused about her intentions* rationalization. And after all, the jock types opined after the legal charges were dropped, Kobe wasn't a rapist, *he was just confused.* And Kobe's wife, who received a four million dollar apology ring, also concluded that

When men and women come together for a sexual relationship, they will bring to the table (back seat, bedroom, or bowling alley parking lot) different communication needs and styles, which is likely to cause confusion at best, criminal problems at the worst.

And so it was for the majority of onlookers (sport fans especially) who agreed that the confusion was the responsibility of the damsel, and Kobe was actually a *victim* of sorts because of the confusion.

Kobe was probably just bewildered and baffled about the pretend intentions of the damsel. And when the victim, being persecuted by a critical public, refused to testify, the prosecutor agreed there was no case—primarily because the *confusion* was so clear.

SUPER SEXISM

More issues of sexism relating to the pretending of intentions when something goes wrong in sex could be found in how Americans responded to the now infamous Super Bowl halftime show, concluding the 2003 National Football League season. In the war on the world, especially the media (Fourth Commandment), the posturing was about the evils that would befall the children who were exposed to a boob and not a grapefruit one. But in considering the Fifth Commandment of sexism, the farce about whom to blame was planted in the woods/jungle long before Janet Jackson and Justin Timberlake got into so much trouble.

FOCUS FARCE

With the Super Bowl super slip, everyone fussed and the focus adopted by most was a farce—especially in envisioning the problems of sexism and how the genders are treated differently in their intentions. Poor Justin appeared quite stressed in his apology, suggesting he never intended any harm but was simply a victim of *wardrobe malfunction*. After all, he nonverbally remembered from his woods/jungle training, that males are supposed to be in charge of fixing things (spears and such). So with his confusion about not knowing what to do, everyone seemed to give Justin a responsibility pass.

But Janet Jackson didn't fare so well in the sexism super slip and found herself in a lot of trouble. Immediately (once Justin slipped away quiet and confused), she became the focus of rage from an indignant public. Those who weighed in were most upset with Janet, primarily because her *intentions* didn't seem confusing since she was obviously on the other end of her exposed boob. Too much Barbie and not enough June, it seemed. She was asked not to attend the upcoming Grammy Music Awards, a punishment to which she agreed. Justin (probably still suffering from the confusion about intentions) just trotted himself off to the awards without even a sniggle of outrage.

RUDE ROLE REALITY

In reality, however, and in an effort to raise sexually respectful children, the blame for the Super Bowl debacle should have been reversed, because it was Justin who simulated a *sexual assault* in the musical concert's wardrobe malfunction. Justin, as a teen hero and sexual role model, ripped the bustier of his dancing partner right there on American television. That ripping, however pretended, was the most disrespectful of actions in the entire Super Bowl debacle—at least for people who care about out-of-control sexism. Yet in the scheme of things and with the *pretend intentions* of sexism loud and clear, it was Janet who received most of the national criticism—just grapefruit boobery gone too far with Justin seemingly being confused about everything.

PREPPY PRETEND PROBLEMS

Before the Kobe Bryant confusion and the pretend intentions Super Bowl boob business, the preppy murder case in Central Park stunned those who knew the victim. Robert Chambers found himself in a bit of a mess with his own woods/jungle business gone too far in New York City. Described as the *Preppy Murder Case*, Robert (the preppy person) was charged with the rape and murder of Jennifer Levin, who was found beaten, broken and raped—or so it seemed, at least to the cops and to her grieving family.

Not so, said Robert and his attorneys to a stunned courtroom filled with Jennifer's friends and loved ones. *Why, she really wanted it rough* proclaimed Robert, outlining his frustrated efforts to decipher her pretended intentions. And in fact, Robert suggested, he was actually a victim himself (confused with her pretend intentions) as evidenced by scratches on his hands and face that were initially blamed on his cat. Robert tried to convince everyone how hard he worked trying to decipher Jennifer's unspoken signals that she demanded rough sex. Somehow, Jennifer Levin ended up dead in all that confusion about who wanted what, and what kind of ***what*** she really wanted.

Most thought Robert's claims of confusion were preposterous. *No way* was Jennifer the type of girl who wanted rough sex, they countered. But when the jury also seemed confused about the confusion, deliberating for longer than it should, the confusion of the intentions seemed pervasive in the decision-making process about what to do with Robert.

Fearing that the jury was just too mixed up about the pretend intentions and really fearing a hung jury or worse, an acquittal, the prosecutor offered a softer deal to Robert. And before the jury returned, Robert and his attorneys accepted and it was done. Off to prison Robert went for a rather short period of time considering the fact that he had brutally murdered Jennifer. His shortened prison term, the prosecutor's panic, and the jury's *confusions about the confusion* all rested on the issue of pretend intentions that can be rooted in the games of BB and Dx5 many years and woods/jungles ago.

If part of children's sex education does not include the need for clear, precise communication about who wants what, where, when and how in a sexual relationship, then the breeding ground for sexual disrespect is laid with a lifetime of consequences based on the outcome. And wouldn't it be wonderful if envisioning parents always taught the message *if you can't talk about your sexual intentions with a partner, then you are not ready for sexual activities.*

In reality, however, and in an effort to raise sexually respectful children, the blame for the Super Bowl debacle should have been reversed, because it was Justin who simulated a *sexual assault* in the musical concert's *wardrobe malfunction.*

If part of children's sex education does not include the need for clear, precise communication about who wants what, where, when and how in a sexual relationship, then the breeding ground for sexual disrespect is laid with a lifetime of consequences based on the outcome.

ROLL OUT FOUR—VICTIM AND OFFENDER ROLES REALIZED

And finally, the fourth sexist issue emerging from the woods/jungle games of BB and Dx5 that needs envisioning in raising sexually respectful children pertains to the clear, defined and accepted roles of who, between the two genders, is the sexual offender and who is the expected victim. In the woods/jungle, so harmless and sweet (seemingly), roles of aggressor and the victim are assigned and sadly accepted, which is a powder keg of potential problems in the sexual futures of children.

DEALING WITH DANGER

In the woods/jungle games of the children, the identification of the male as offender with the Bruce Boys making the boob heist is clearly and sadly designated. Contrarily, the damsels in dealing with distress, seems to be a dress rehearsal for the role of victimhood. Noticing how both the damsels and the boob snatchers deal with danger provides insight into this offender/victim identification process of the sexist games. This role definition makes two contributions to the problem of sexual assault by first, ignoring the idea and possibility that females could actually be sexual offenders (damsels just couldn't), and secondly, ignoring the possibility and plight of male victims.

NOT MOMMIES, GRANDMAS, SISTERS, AUNTIES!

Karla was furious. Her parents were considering postponing what was thought to be Toronto's wedding of the year. *How could they,* she complained to her fiancé, Paul Bernardo. Never mind that the disrupted wedding plans were connected to the death of Karla's twelve-year-old sister, Tammy. And never mind (unknown to Karla's parents) that Karla and Paul had actually murdered her. But, they confided to each other, the wedding must go on.

And it did. When Karla and Paul walked down the aisle on schedule (no wedding postponement for them), they were aware that they not only raped and murdered sister Tammy, but by the time they exchanged wedding nuptials, Leslie Mahaffey, an innocent teenager, was sexually assaulted and murdered at their hands as well. After all, Paul had been disappointed with Karla when they first met, because she wasn't a virgin. It was an insignificant over-exposure of grapefruit boobs, but Paul felt cheated, nonetheless. So what else could Karla do for her disappointed lover but agree to drug her twelve-year-old sister, Tammy, on Christmas Eve, then sexually assault her while the video camera captured memories of the *family* event? But there was a little *whoops* in the plan, since the drugs Karla had stolen (yes, Karla stole them) from her job as a veterinarian assistant weren't the right mix with the alcohol also furnished to the twelve-year-old, and Tammy died. But never mind, the evidence was hidden and the wedding had to go on.

But before the *wedding of the year* took place in Toronto, and after Tammy's death, Paul's disappointment returned. Leslie Mahaffey, an innocent teenage girl, was kidnapped, tortured and sexually abused by both Karla and Paul for more than a week before she was finally murdered, dismembered and discarded. The videotapes later confiscated by authorities confirmed Karla's sexual abuse of Leslie and her complete disregard for the teenager's unbelievable terror.

After the couple had been married a year or so, Paul continued to be plagued with boredom, so what could the sometimes cranky couple do? Kristen French, another innocent teenager, met the same fate as Leslie. But this time, it was Karla who lured Kristen to the car and it was Karla who took an active role in the abduction. The videos also revealed that Karla participated in the raping as well. Sadly, there were other young girls, drugged and raped over the years, although not murdered, by both members of the creative couple.

When the legal folks in Scarborough finally got around to testing Paul Bernardo's DNA in connection to seventeen or so rapes occurring five years previous, Karla felt as though the proverbial *other shoe* was going to drop. She smartly left the love nest she shared with Paul, hired herself a lawyer, changed into a distressed damsel, and cut a deal with the Canadian Crown. *Karla was a victim herself* it was suggested by her really smart and really expensive legal team. After all, she had bruises and she was surely *distressed* once the Crown was brought in to investigate. And their immediate diagnosis was that she was more damsel and certainly more *distressed damsel* (victim) than she could ever be offender.

So, Karla copped a plea and trotted off to prison where she got a little sentence. Yes, the legal folks figured Karla had just experienced a few little slips of *damsel* and wasn't really a sexual deviant. That is what everyone thought until, especially to the horror of the parents of Leslie and Kristen, the confiscated videos revealed Karla's clear sexual assault and cruelty to the victims. *Egg on the face* for the Canadian Crown who gave Karla such a sweet deal was more powerful than any Egg and Grapefruit Diet since clearly, she really was a sexual offender. But probably because of too many boob heists in their own backgrounds, the government folks just couldn't break free of boys being offenders and girls being, well, something else.

But there was a little *whoops* in the plan, since the drugs Karla had stolen (yes, Karla stole them) from her job as a veterinarian assistant weren't the right mix with the alcohol also furnished to the twelve-year-old, and Tammy died.

NO FEMALE FOUL

And neither was Janice—a sex offender, that is. After seven years of Colleen Stams being forcefully kept in a wooden box underneath the bed of Janice and her husband, Cameron, she still wasn't considered to be any kind of criminal. After seven years of being right next to the sexual abuse and torture of a young woman, Janice claimed to have *found God*, and reported the gruesome story of unimaginable sexual

***Egg on the face* for the Canadian Crown who gave Karla such a sweet deal was more powerful than any egg and grapefruit diet, since she really was a sexual offender.**

torture and imprisonment to her pastor, who called the cops. In spite of Janice Hooker's complicity in taking no action (doing damsel perfectly), she was never even considered for criminal charges, which clearly designated her as part of the damsel group (victim identity) and not having membership in the Bruce Boys group (offenders).

Never mind that seven years previous, Janice sat in the front seat of the family automobile holding her baby when hubby Cameron picked up the innocent and trusting hitchhiker, Colleen Stams. And Janice was right there in the front seat when Cameron snapped his homemade wooden box (padlocked) over Colleen's head. And never mind that Janice knew Colleen would be hung, tortured, and sexually assaulted by Cameron Hooker in the family basement for seven years. Never mind that Janice, in the comfort of her own bed, knew her husband's sex slave was trapped in a wooden coffin (box) underneath and never mind that at times, Janice herself, brought Colleen out of the box for help with the housework and to baby-sit Janice's two girls, doing absolutely nothing to protect or rescue the obvious victim. When everything unfolded with the cop types, Colleen was rescued, Cameron was charged and convicted, but Janice was considered pure damsel—not responsible for anything.

BORED BABES? DISTRESSED DAMSELS?

What about Michelle—damsel? distressed? or sex offender? It was true that Michelle Michaud went a little beyond the grapefruit boobery business since, after all, she was a prostitute of sorts. But Michelle wasn't an ordinary street hooker, destitute and under the control of a mean-spirited pimp with drug problems. *No*, she lived in a comfortable home in a cul-de-sac with her parents close by to help care for Michelle's children. *No*, Michelle's prostitution was selective with several high-paying older gentlemen, often referred to as *sugar daddies*. Life was pretty good for Michelle, except that she was bored.

James Devaggio was also bored, desiring lusts beyond the imagination—except for someone like Michelle. Together they not only had great sex, but they shared their fantasies of unfulfilled and deviant desires. And therefore, what could they do? Bringing together their boredom cures, they kidnapped, raped, and murdered innocent teenage girls. Michelle was the *gofer* of the two, fetching teenage girls from shopping malls to the back of the van for James to rape and murder. One victim eventually included her own twelve-year-old daughter and her daughter's friend who were sexually assaulted but not murdered.

Never mind that Michelle masturbated while James was raping the girls or that evidence concerning their last victim clearly indicated that Michelle purchased the tools of torture and participated in the assaults. *But no.* The authorities, holding to the scripts of which gender is a sex offender and which gender is always a victim, designated the roles between Michelle and James, in spite of what the evidence suggested. When it all came down in court and James headed for death row, Michelle trotted off for a little time in prison. Just a little grapefruit boobery gone too far again, they said. Michelle was damsel all right, just a little distressed with her clearly offender male partner.

Interestingly, when a reporter interviewed Michelle in prison, she was obviously back in the woods/jungle business with her chief complaint relating to her troublesome weight gain from the starchy prison food (egg and grapefruit shortage), and she was fussy about how awful she looked in the orange prison uniforms. Her primary concern was her appearance, which of course, would be pertinent in her role of damsel, not a sexual offender.

BOOBERY GONE BAD

And it goes on and on. Mary Kay Letourneau, in the state of Washington, sexually abused her sixth grade student and became pregnant with the twelve-year-old's child. She didn't fare as well as Karla, Janice, and Michelle, however, and she was charged with a sexual crime in the state of Washington, even though she was released on her own recognizance while awaiting sentencing. But Mary Kay was just smitten with the lad and violated the terms of her release agreement, finding herself jailed and pregnant for a second time. But in spite of the sexual charges, the diagnosis for Mary Kay ranged from *Erotomania* (psychotic belief that one is loved by another) to *Bi-Polar Disorder*. Hardly anyone used the term *sex offender*. But had Mary Kay sported a penis or had she been one of the Bruce Boys, it is doubtful that a hint of *dancing with the diagnosis* would have occurred. But the gender gyrations continued, suggesting poor Mary Kay had other problems. And although the criminal records said so, most did not consider her to be a sexual offender since she eventually married her victim—just again, a little grapefruit boobery gone too far.

BRUISED BRUCE BOYS

Sadly, sexists' thoughts also discourage males from being considered as sexual victims, even though female offenders are alive and well and have carefully honed skills in not only abusing males, but in convincing a sexist society that female units aren't sex offenders. The result is a silent secrecy suggesting that boys cannot be *true victims*. And this thinking begins with the woods/jungle games of children.

When everything unfolded with the cop types, Colleen was rescued, Cameron was charged and convicted, but Janice was considered pure damsel—not responsible for anything.

Because Ryan apparently hurt his mother so badly with his three-year-old penis (according to her damsel gyrations), Ryan is required to put medicine on her vaginal area all through the night.

GENDER GYRATIONS

When Ryan remembers some of his first sexual experiences, he recalls his *offender* status from the eyes that the sexist world encourages, robbing him of the *victim* vindication he so desperately needs. At age 16, Ryan remembers being three years old, sitting naked on top of his large, naked mother. As she brings him to erection she plays pure damsel by saying, "No, no, no, Ryan. Mommy doesn't want to do this." She continues to demure, as she places his three-year-old erect penis in her forty-something-year-old vagina. And in true damsel form, she moans and groans; pretending Ryan is hurting her, which will justify, of course, even more damsel behavior during the upcoming evening. Because Ryan hurt his Mother so badly with his three-year-old penis (according to her damsel gyrations), Ryan is required to put medicine on her vaginal area all through the night. And *poor Mommy* and *bad Ryan* is the same status for many male victims, robbed of the vindication they need to recover.

But for Ryan, it got worse in the gender gyrations of sexism. Even though Mommy confessed (tearfully damsel) and even though the church forgave her, the prosecutor was so impacted with Mommy's damsel dialogue, her punishment for sixteen years of sexual abuse against Ryan was only termination of her parental rights.

And when Ryan's therapists pleaded for a more criminal approach to Mommy, citing sixteen years of horrific sexual abuse of Ryan, the prosecutor momentarily returned to his woods/jungle training and stated, "There is no greater punishment for a woman than to have her parental rights terminated. There is no need for further review; she has suffered enough."

End of story and end of Ryan's abuse by Mommy but the beginning of Ryan's abuse by a sexist system. And if Mommy had a penis and Ryan a vagina, things would have been different.

GOD FORBID

As the tragedy of the Catholic Church scandal unfolded, many folded up their tent of concern and figuratively *went home.* When adult males came forward reporting sexual abuse suffered from priests decades previous, the sympathy cards were in short supply as were the believability barometers. No one wanted to believe that priests would do such a thing, but the real problem in the whole mess was about male victims. Many suggested that it probably didn't happen, primarily because boys are strong and after all, they had their spears and their trap tricks. But an additional problem was related to the *if it did happen—so what?* And this tragic thinking was related to sexism, straight from the woods/jungle learning—*boys want all the sex they can get, so where is the foul?*

And as dozens of men tearfully and tragically came forward, the sexist thinking about who is really a victim, did not provide a soft place to land, and in fact, many of those male victims related that the response from society was more traumatic than the actions of their abusing priests.

BRUCE BOYS BRUISING BUSINESS

When data is examined pertaining to the prevalence of male sexual victims to female victims, the usual path (not to be confused with woods/jungle paths) is to count the known number of male victims. The rates of boys and men coming forth for exoneration and treatment is astonishingly low—somewhere between five and seven percent. *Not common at all,* or so it would appear. But if a different approach is implemented, one that is sensitive to sexist attitudes that likely discourage consideration of females as offenders and males as victims, a different prevalence emerges.

When sexual victims, of both genders and of all ages, are asked to discuss their histories of abuse with females, the numbers approach a snuggly second to male offenders—about forty percent. In other words, victims report being abused by females nearly as often as they report being abused by males. Yet, those girls and ladies (still considered damsels) do not represent half of the offenders in treatment centers or prisons throughout the country.

And when sex offenders, both male and female, are required to provide an actual sexual history to be verified by polygraph examination, it appears that they are abusing males nearly as often as females. But because of society's sexist attitude, begun long ago in many woods/jungle games, those male victims do not tend to come forward, and those female offenders seem to be forgiven (damsel diagnosis) and not brought to justice, just like Karla, Janice, Michelle, and Mary Kay.

THE BOTTOM LINE

So, the bottom line is that sexism is a major part of raising children in the culture even though it contributes to sexual disrespect. And it all starts so early. In the womb, parental plans are made for fluffy pink for girl units, while the stronger and less-fluffy blue await the boy units. In fact, the reason most parents desire to know the gender of the new little bundle of joy before birth is to prevent an over-supply of the wrong stuff, suggesting sexual scripting of the little ones begins even before birth.

And this tragic thinking was related to sexism, straight from the woods/ jungle learning—*boys want all the sex they can get, so where is the foul.*

Upon birth, infants are adorned with different preparation for the *Damsel in Distress* games or the *Bruce Boy business,* even though in reality, the only true difference between the pink and blue dressed babies is about one and one-half inches of apparatus between their legs. Infant girls will be adorned with lace, bows and buttons. Inscription on her infant clothing will

In fact, the reason most parents desire to know the gender of the new little bundle of joy before birth is to prevent an over-supply of the wrong stuff, suggesting sexual scripting of the little ones begins even before birth.

And within these innocent, sweet, and ever-so-subtle preparations are the sexist blueprints that will not be the cause of sexual abuse, but which will create a breeding ground for the ease with which children could cross over the line and become sexual offenders.

relate to designations of sexual roles, such as *angel* or *princess*, clearly in preparation for damsel doings. Blue baby boys will be adorned with trappings of power and strength, not so far removed from the Bruce Boys and their booby-trapping tools. Boy babies, although typically weighing less than ten pounds, will begin to sport baseball or football jerseys, and if the blue baby clothing has any inscription, it won't be angel or princess, but rather something like *slugger* or *bowling baby*. And if that isn't enough preparation for the woods/jungle business, an embroidered tool belt with an imaginary array of swords, spears and steak knives may do the job for these male units. It is so cute (and so powerful), and it is contributing to sexist thinking, which will continue into later childhood training.

BEYOND BABY BUSINESS

Beyond the nursery there are more damsel doings and booby-trapping preparations. When babies are old enough for toys, the scripting toward grapefruit boobery and the stealing of steak knives continues—harmlessly perhaps. Little girls will play games about their appearances with Barbie dolls, Polly Pockets, and jewelry craft kits, with a not-so-subtle invitation to consider their grapefruit boobs early on. Little boys will play with Power Rangers (preschool training for peeking, poking, and prodding), Lincoln Logs, and Bob the Builder equipment. Later, little girls improve their communication by getting play telephones, preparing them to become fluent in speaking *Dahlings, Dieting*, and *Damsel,* while little boys learn to curb their communication by studying teeth-clenching techniques of John Wayne during play with the G.I. Joe set, planning for war and power, and just possibly booby-trapping.

And within these innocent, sweet, and ever-so-subtle preparations are the sexist blueprints that will not be the cause of sexual abuse, but which will create a breeding ground for the ease with which children could cross over the line and become sexual offenders. These four issues of designating *sexy* from *sexual,* encouraging helplessness, being confused about sexual intentions, and designating the clear roles of males being aggressors and females being victims should be on the Sex Fairy clipboard for raising sexually respectful children.

Sex Fairy Clipboard

- Rather than demand complete androgyny and absolutely no differences between boys and girls, *envision* moderation. It doesn't seem to be the differences in the genders that causes the wheels to fall off the sexual respect wagon, but rather *inequality*.

- In the area of sexist learning about who is *sexy* and who is *sexual*, parents should envision whether they really want their little girls to grow up discounting their sexuality and whether they want their little boys to grow up and not understand female sexual functioning. If parents want the future sexual relations for their children to be equal—they must teach that both boys and girls are both *sexy and sexual.*

- Envision the sexist world around children that teaches about helplessness and the Stud Horse Theory. Use lessons in the Sixth Commandments to teach how humans are responsible for their sexual actions—quite different than animals. Parents who want to raise sexually respectful children will actively teach that absolutely no one (boob exposers or steak knife stealers) are helpless in their sexual actions. Arousal may be another matter; but control of actions is just that—controllable.

Sex Fairy Clipboard

- Envision the damage, heartbreak and sometime criminal conduct that occurs because of *pretend intentions* and *confused communication.* Males and females will probably continue to have varying degrees of language competency but boys and girls should be taught about consent messages needing to be clear, precise and unchallengeable. Do not tolerate the consideration of non-verbal cues in making sexual decisions—and if the logic of the Third Commandment is the blueprint—this will be an easy task.

- Parents need to encourage their children to understand that sexual spontaneity may be good for Mom and Dad on a Farm Bureau convention trip in a motel with the soap wrapped up and cowboys on the lamp shade, but sexual spontaneity should rarely be considered in most circumstances. The envisioning needs to remember that children will be constantly exposed to brief sexual encounters through the media that usually don't include communication, but can happen even before the third commercial break—making it seem that their heroes do just fine with the confusion of pretend intentions. Envision this dangerous message and combat it.

- Although children could be raised to be sexually respectful and still dress differently, play differently and communicate differently among the sexes, the suggestion that males and females are somehow different in the offender/victim roles is unthinkable. The term ANYONE should always be used when those people are described as sexual offenders and sexual abusers. Nothing will be accomplished by suggesting to children that only males abuse and only females are abusable.

Sex Fairy Clipboard

- Probably most important on the Sex Fairy Clipboard for envisioning Eve and Adam is for parents to be intolerant of sexist lesson planning for their very own teaching team. Parents should never consider that only Moms should teach girl things and only Dads should be in charge of male kinds of teaching. Fight this kind of sexism with great power—no matter how uncomfortable.

- Finally, envision the sexist world—don't disband it. It is sneaky, but it is manageable—as long as equality is the key to teaching sexual respect.

Chapter 9

Sixth Commandment
Thou Shalt Channel Cats, Carrots and Cows

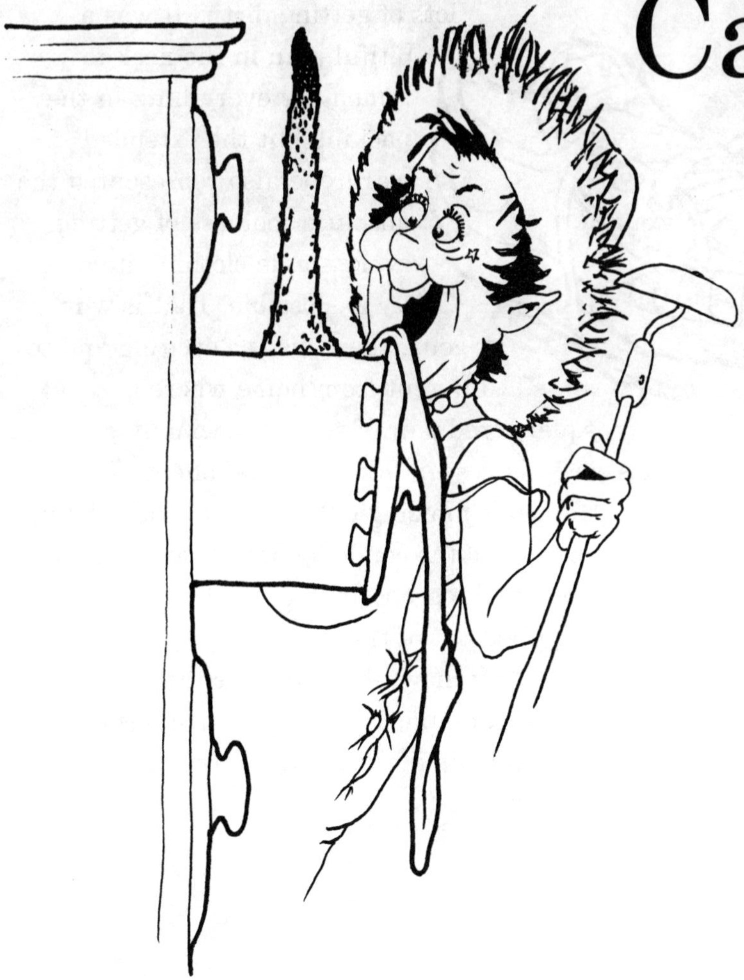

CHAPTER 9: THE SIXTH COMMANDMENT THOU SHALT CHANNEL CATS, CARROTS, AND COWS

It was a mixed bag—the final departure procedure. On one hand it was thrilling because the agonizing wait was almost over and what seemed like decades of lingering in the driveway at least had the potential of being over. But on the other hand, as his perky Mother looked in the back seat of the station wagon, announcing she was *doing the double check,* even more delay was about as possible as a fogged in airport. That is, especially if he had messed up. What if Mom's darn *double-check* revealed that he really wasn't properly packed and that in his anxious anticipation, he had forgotten something?

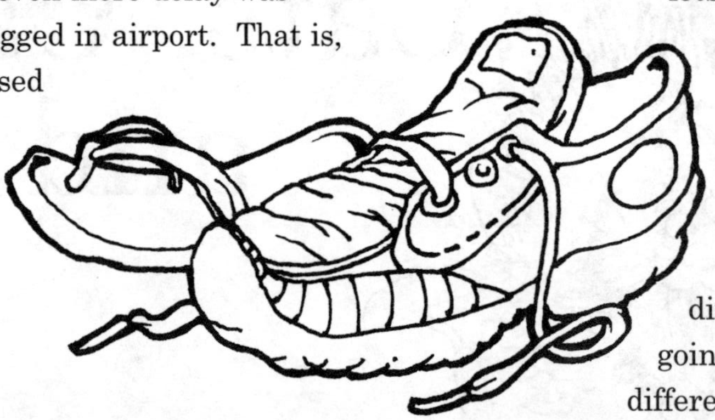

As Brandon answered himself in the dreadful pondering, he realized that his left behind items would require the departure process to stop, seat belts to be unbuckled, the condo key to be retrieved from underneath the patio potted plant, the front door unlocked and then, he would be trotted off to retrieve whatever represented his packing failure. In this doom and gloom knowledge, he also figured his Mother probably knew for sure what he had forgotten, but she insisted that he show responsibility and pack for himself. She also knew how anxious he was to leave, so with that window of opportunity for teaching, she just figured that if his longed-for departure was delayed because of his lack of organizational skills, it would help Brandon learn the hard way. She was like that—super Mom with super teaching.

With her mental clipboard in tow, she boomed to the back seat, "Brandon, did you bring your sneakers, your sandals, your sliders and six pairs of socks?" Lots and lots of clothes were always required because there would be lots and lots of getting dirty. It was a pitiful pain in the neck to remember everything in the packing but the extended wardrobe also represented the absolute coolness of getting every single clothing item as dirty as possible. That is why going there was so exciting and so different from home where a squandered pair of socks at swimming lessons might seem like a capital offense.

After an agonizing delay and several trotting trips back into the condo by both Brandon and his brother, the properly packed station wagon finally pulled out of the driveway. Several agonizing, but inevitable stops for the 60-mile-seems-like-600-mile trip will delay things even more. At the top of the agony, is the stop for gas which is Mom's favorite since it involves stuffing the *snack basket.* Being super Mom, she sports a terror that one of her babies might dehydrate before arriving and so it must be bottled water for both of them as the challenge of the journey is plotted. Mom knows the trek isn't exactly through a sweltering desert and she is aware the auto air conditioner could stave off most of those dire problems. But, nonetheless, as she does with all parenting issues—she wants to be prepared.

Also fearing malnourishment for her poopers on the less-than-one-hour-trip, Mom makes sure the car snack basket is filled with organic AND high-fiber snacks that must be low in sugar and fat content. Brandon knows she will read the labels thoroughly, right there in the gas station, just to make sure everything is healthy and nourishing for her bumpkins. Only after all the shenanigans demanding perfect nutrition, will the fuel finally find it's way into the gas tank and the station wagon finally find it's way to the freeway entrance. Eventually, Mom will do her final *double check* on what could be forgotten, even though to the waiting Brandon, it seems like a *quadruple check.*

Off they finally go, heading for their destination where all Mom's perfection, care and concern will miraculously change, at least on the surface. But for now, the agonizing one-hour drive.

Mom is not only worried that her kiddos will perish from either thirst or malnutrition, but she also worries about boredom for her kidlets which is always related to the pesky *pit stop* business. She understands the temptation for bored kids to wield the familiar "I have to go to the bathroom," just to break up the trip and that is exactly what she wants to prevent.

To Brandon and his brother, the rest areas along the way are much more exciting than the ones at the Kiwanis camp or in the city park—making the temptation even greater. These rural rest areas, displaying rotting substances, assortments of bugs and critters, but most importantly to the kids, (and most objectionably to Mom), these Port-A-Potties provide a full view of everything that has been deposited by humans in the past week before they are emptied by the road department. For Brandon, peering down the potty hole was an unequaled thrill, but for Brandon's Mother it was quite disgusting. So that is why Mom does everything to remind her boys that pit stops would really, really, really delay their arrival, which usually worked. But she had other plans to combat the excitement of pit stops.

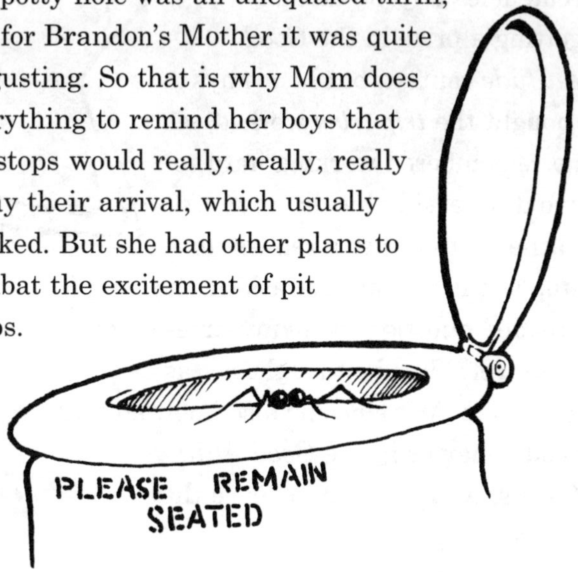

Being a good Mom, she always planned for the one-hour drive carefully, not only with bottled water and healthy snacks, but with *trip tricks,* as she called them. First she would announce there would be a *Good Attitude Contest* during the drive and that the person in the four-person family having the best attitude when they arrived would win a prize. It was quite exciting and quite typical of this Mother who always wanted the brother kiddos to concentrate on their good manners, at least before they arrived. Being a brat would never be tolerated by this Mom and even the slightest hint of *brat* took someone right out of the *Good Attitude Contest* running. Both children understood her tight reign on good and bad behavior—at least before they got there and everything changed.

Brandon could never remember anyone actually getting a prize in the *Good Attitude* contest, but he always thought the *trip trick* worked, since he remembered working hard to avoid harassing his driving Father with either a request to stop at the rest area or asking the dreaded question too many times, "Are we there yet?" But he thought it was easy to be good in the car since he also knew all that good behavior in the *Good Attitude Contest* would be scarce, once they arrived.

Mom would also help the kiddos endure the trip with songs, all very appropriate for their destination. First would come the traditional *She'll Be Coming Round the Mountain* and all the special sound effects such as *hee haw,* and *whoa back*, in both tone and volume not usually allowed at home. To Brandon, the lively singing of the song was just a small preparation for all the rules that would be slightly—no, greatly, bent once when they arrived.

Then there would be singing of the favorite, *Little Bunny Foo Foo* and how the good fairy does her *bopping on the heads* of the rather unlucky field mice. And as they sang, they all did their own pretend *bopping on the heads* in the station wagon, something that would never be tolerated 30 miles back at home. In the condo where Brandon lived there would be no bopping, hitting or smacking of any kind, as even the slightest act of violence—good fairy or bunny foo foo—would be totally banned. But as Brandon smashed his formerly-not-allowed-to-smash fists into one another in the station wagon during the Bunny Foo Foo song, he knew that the bending of this rule was only the beginning to what lay ahead in the rule-bending once they arrived.

As the small country town is approached, it is clear to Brandon that only a few more agonizing minutes must pass before he will be free. And that is exactly what his Auntie's farm is really all about—freedom. Brandon certainly appreciates his parents taking care of everything in the condo and usually he has few complaints about his situation. But those pesky rules about *what he can do* and *what he can't do*—what *is allowed* and what *isn't allowed*—are constant irritations for any child parented by vigilant Moms and Dads. But once the station wagon pulls into that driveway, once he and his brother meet up with their cousins and head for the barnyard and surrounding farm accommodations, everything about the rules changes. Brandon doesn't know why that happens; he just knows that no matter what, on the farm everything he knows about *what to do* and *what not to do* is left in the back seat of the station wagon, right next to the snack basket.

The first order of business was to feel the freedom of danger—sometimes *double-danger* as he and his cousins have learned from their Grandfather. While at home he was always reminded to be careful and avoid danger, which was always so boring compared to *double-danger*. "Brandon, that is just too dangerous," rang familiar in his memory.

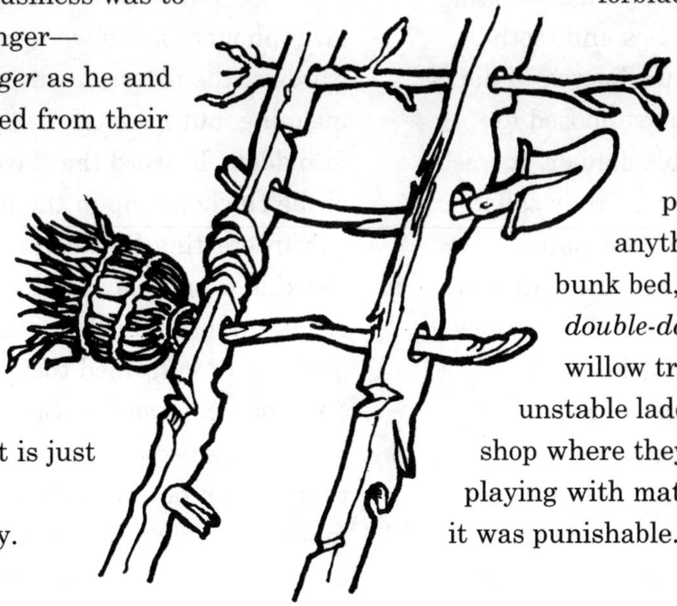

But once he and his playmates were out of sight of his usually-must-be-careful-parents, danger was just part of the exciting allure.

At home, Brandon had to be careful crossing the street, yet on the farm he not only didn't have to be careful crossing the log over the creek, but letting danger take over and falling into the muddy water made it even more exciting, especially using one of the war whoops he amplified in the station wagon singing *She'll Be Coming Round the Mountain*.

At home, there was no running (too dangerous) at the swimming pool, with infractions resulting in an embarrassing whistle from a cranky lifeguard. But on the farm, running was not only allowed, but it was dangerously encouraged, especially when running through something forbidden like sheep poop or the flock of chickens that were just trying to eat their lunch and relax.

At home there was a strict prohibition on climbing anything higher than his brother's bunk bed, but on the farm there was *double-danger* in climbing haystacks, willow trees and even the very unstable ladder to the attic in Uncle Mac's shop where they were not allowed. At home, playing with matches was not only forbidden, it was punishable. But to Brandon and his playmates, stealing matches from the outside barbecue was easy and then pretending to smoke was not only fun, it was *so dangerous.*

Sure, the brothers had learned from the special television show Mom made them watch that smoking cigarettes was pretty disgusting (and dangerous), but on the farm, it seemed A-okay. With trembling fingers and promises of *double-danger*, they would light little twigs and with delight, yell loudly to the nearby ducks, "Tiparillo!" which caused them to break out in a burst of giggles, causing the ducks to make a panicked departure. They didn't exactly know what a Tiparillo was, but they knew it had to be dangerous. And of course, carrying their *smokes* (as they called them with tight lips and teeth clenched) in their pants like Clint Eastwood did in the prison movie they weren't supposed to watch was also part of the double danger. It was really cool to be *pretend hackers,* as they called themselves, with the smokes in their pants, sauntering about boldly. But when they tried to moon the unsuspecting horses from the confines of their tree fort, they lost the smokes and matches in a rather clumsy debacle. But never mind, even the loss of smokes could be considered *double dangerous*—on the farm.

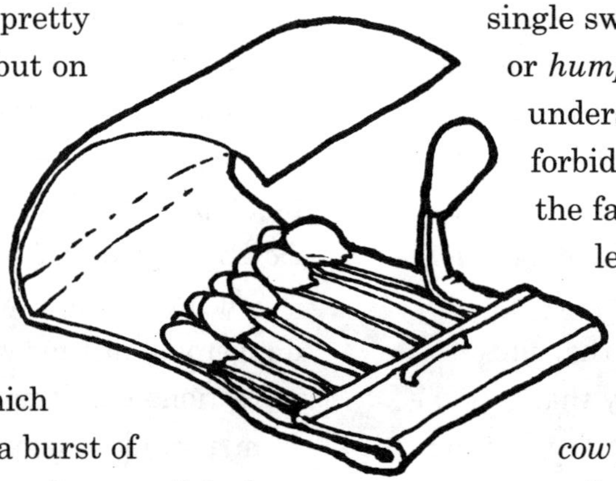

And speaking of broken rules compared to living in the city, one of the coolest farm things for Brandon was about breaking the cussing rules. His mother always made her kiddos say *please* and *thank you,* as well as other polite necessities. But that was the easy part. She had absolutely no tolerance in the condo for a single swear or slang word, such as a *hell* or *hump*. Although Brandon didn't understand half of the words he was forbidden to say, he did know that, on the farm, he not only said them, but he learned new and more forbidden ones at every visit.

As an example, he was so delighted when his exciting-to-say *cow poop* of one visit was given the vernacular upgrade to *cow turd* the next time he spent a day at the farm. He was also delighted to add *pissing* to his rather boring word of *peeing,* but he was totally thrilled to add to his farm phonetics, the word *whizzing*. Some of the words of the older cousins escaped him in meaning, but he was very familiar with the forbidden "F" word that he could say in the safety of the chicken coop in the barnyard. And what was interesting Brandon noticed, was that when the kids would play some sort of war game or sneak-up-in-the-bushes game, peeking in on the grown-ups, it seemed they too, used those forbidden cuss words. Brandon never, ever heard his parents use that language until they all came to the farm, but he resolved that there were many *not-allowed* things that just seemed to be allowed, for both grown-ups and kids.

One of Brandon's favorite forbidden farm things that was not permitted at home had to do with everything connected to body functions. Not only could the kids carelessly fart on the farm, but they could make farts purposely (really loud, of course) and most delightfully shout the word *fart* anytime they wanted. But there was more about the forbidden farting.

One of Brandon's favorite fart activities happened when he and the other kids would feed cheese to the farm dog, *Tuna,* who seemed to the kids to have special gastronomical abilities, especially with farting. It seemed that once Tuna gobbled down the cheese, she became what the boys delightfully called *Tuna the Terrible Fart Machine.* And it was so cool, Brandon thought, to make sure Tuna took a nap under the picnic table at the barbecue later in the day with all the boys barely able to eat because of all their giggling about Tuna's farts. Brandon recognized that although the grown-ups pretended to fuss at the barbecue regarding references to *Tuna the Terrible Fart Machine*, there seemed to be an overall fart tolerance on the farm.

It was the same tolerance regarding other body functions on the farm. *Why* at home he would never be allowed to spit, yet he was quite sure his parents knew the kids had contests about who could spit the farthest from the hayloft. While at home, he was forced to lift the toilet lid and pee carefully, watching for the *splitter splatters,* as his mother termed the errant urine path. But on the farm, outside peeing was not only allowed, but when they ran out of spit they had peeing contests from the hayloft. What freedom he felt to just *pee free,* as the boys called it while scattering the chickens in frantic flight.

At home, while Brandon learned about the importance of fighting germs by washing his hands with disinfectant soap from the nifty, aqua colored pump bottles, at the farm the kiddos had wars and battles throwing cow-turds, with absolutely no regard for cleanliness. While at home, Brandon learned that body functions needed to be combatted and controlled with bleach, Pine Sol, and Handi Wipes. But at the farm, he learned that the dirtier and the more filth he could accumulate, the more status he had among his farm friends. A creative collection of sheep manure, horse turds and pack rat droppings really raised one's status among the farm boys who cared nothing about germs or soap.

There was also something about critter care that Brandon noticed being very different at the condo compared to when he visited the farm. His

Mother was very, very much of an animal lover, so she ran a tight ship on animal respect. He was often trotted off to Green Peace meetings and taught to feel sadness when harp seals were slaughtered so some hussy lady could have a fur coat. Brandon was well aware of the importance of saving the whales, too, and even though he knew these special critters needed concern and protection, on the farm, things seemed a little different in critter care.

As an example, Brandon knew the tadpoles they captured in the swamp looked a little bit like small whales,

only black. He worried about getting in trouble since by the time the journey had been made from the swamp to his Aunties kitchen counter for prideful display, the tadpoles didn't look too good. But his whale-loving Mother, gazing at the still-gasping tadpoles, just didn't seem to get hysterical like she did at a Green Peace meeting talking about the plight of real whales. When she lectured at home about *every living creature being just as important as any other living creature,* Brandon worried she might be mad about the tadpoles that were squished and dripped as he opened his fruit jar next to the potato salad. But on the farm, everything seemed fine as she smiled at his prize and didn't seem to have the same rules or the same worries about critter care as she did at home. This change of attitude was perfectly fine for Brandon, but probably not okay for the on-the-counter-and-slightly-smashed tadpoles.

Critter care comparisons between the condo and farm were observed in other areas as well. At home, Brandon and his brother were marched off to the animal shelter when a dog was in the *finally allowed* category, but not without a lengthy lecture about how selfish it was to buy a dog when there were so many orphaned puppies needing homes. And the brothers, after picking out a scrawny little pup from the bottom of the pile they named *Bogie,* had to make fierce promises to help pay for Bogie's *operation* so he would be exempt from doggie Dad designation. Brandon didn't understand how their cute little puppy named after his father's golf game would have anything to do with being a Dad dog, but he learned from his Mother that pet parenting was a big *no no*, and not just for dogs.

In Brandon's family, there was a small controversy around Pumpkin the cat, and her pregnancy. Months before, Pumpkin apparently found

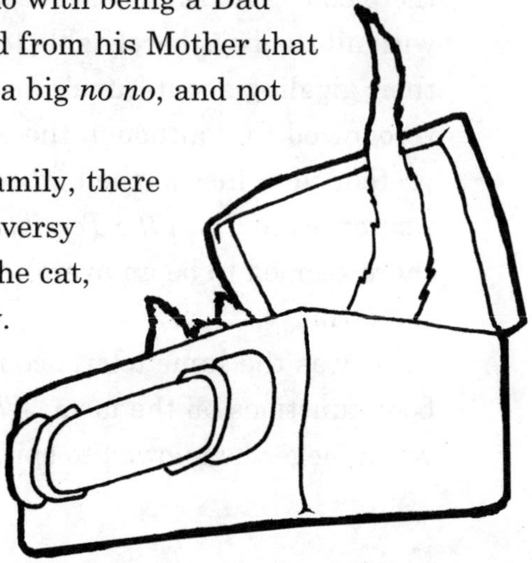

herself in the garden raspberry bushes with the neighbor's tomcat, Brandon had originally presented her to his mother with a story that, "She just followed me home, Mom," innocently shrugging his shoulders with feigned confusion about the eight-week-old kitten's need to trail the first grader to the condo. Later, Brandon's Mother told everyone that she saw her son walking home from school and carrying the soon-to-be-family-cat in his lunch pail. But she thought the "Mom, she just followed me," was just too cute to challenge.

So Pumpkin not only became part of the family, but she also became pregnant, which resulted in more required testimonies from Brandon and his brother about their responsibility to start an adoption agency for Pumpkin's kittens and eventually getting Pumpkin *fixed*. Brandon didn't exactly know what *fixed* meant, but he knew the neighbor's tomcat wasn't *fixed*, because his Father fumed and fussed when the neighbors didn't seem to understand the need to get all the critters *fixed*. But the *fixing* part for the critters was really, really different on the farm.

Whether it was the chickens, pigs, sheep, horses, or cows, having more critters was just what everyone seemed to want. Not only was every kind of critter being born, but on the farm, more babies of any kind seemed to be a good thing. *Strange*, he thought as he watched everyone delight in the number of baby chicks, baby rabbits, baby ducks, baby sheep, baby goats and for sure, baby cows that just seemed to be popping up everywhere. Brandon knew that fixing critters on the farm just didn't happen and more critter babies seemed to be what everyone really wanted. His only reference for *not fixed* pets was Pumpkin's escapades in the raspberry bushes with the also-not-fixed neighbor cat. But on the farm, no one seemed to want any *critter-fixing* and Brandon couldn't figure out how so many critter babies showed up without a single raspberry bush anywhere.

Brandon also remembered the lessons and lecturing about not just taking care of the critters and fixing them, but *respecting* them was also a very, very big deal in the condo. When it came to the family pets, he was taught to respect Bogie and Pumpkin, pregnant or not. Because they were critters, Pumpkin and Bogie couldn't get their own Friskies and therefore, the brothers always had to respect them by remembering the feeding and watering chores.

But on the farm, it seemed like those weren't exactly the same respect rules. One of their favorite games to play was *Animal Kingdom*, just like Brandon and his brother saw on television. All kinds of critter contraptions from the TV show were put together by Brandon and his buddies to replicate trapping, ambushing, snaring, caging and noosing wild animals. But lacking a good supply of tigers and elephants, the farm family pets and other critters were put into action for the Animal Kingdom games. Tuna and Bogie often had to double in the pretend play as a wounded grouse or a trapped turkey, which didn't seem to Brandon as respectful—however exciting and fun. Sometimes the canines were squeezed in backpacks when the boys pretended they were secret agent men and they had to smuggle their *secret* police dogs through the enemy's border. Brandon also wondered if Bogie or Tuna really liked being trapped in the 18-inch culvert, hidden under feed sacks with the boys who were surrounded by fierce fighters, or if the pooches appreciated having to wear sunglasses and hats on their pirate raft rides in the swamp. When Brandon wondered if his Mother would object to this seemingly disrespectful treatment of the critters, he could only remind himself that on the farm, things just seemed different.

More respect-out-the-window happened when the chickens were chased and the sheep were rounded up from their naps and ridden as bucking broncos, which Brandon thought would be completely forbidden by his parents at the condo. But with all the farm stuff about cowboys and spitting, peeing and farting, a little *mutton rodeo* didn't seem out of place. In fact, a couple of times Brandon's parents actually took pictures of the cheesy critter stunts involving seemingly disrespectful things that would never have been allowed at home in the condo.

Brandon sometimes wondered if the grasshoppers were treated respectfully when they were brought into war game playing. The boys would catch the bugs, and with just a little pinching, force them to spit their *tobaccy* juice (as their grandfather called it) on the delighted and filthy boys. They called it the *whacky tobaccy war* and it was quite exciting (and messy). Since his mother had taught him to respectfully remove spiders from the house and turn them loose on the condo patio, Brandon thought she probably wouldn't have approved of the grasshopper squeezing, especially since some of them didn't look too spry after the *whacky tobaccy war* had ended. But then again, lots of not-okay-for-home things were all right on the farm.

As Brandon and his buddies played, farted, spitted, cussed, and did all kinds of other forbidden farms things, they would usually get hungry. But even with eating, Brandon knew that the farm food protocol was very different than the one at home. In the confines of Brandon's condo, there was always a preoccupation with whole grain foods, eating from the seven basic food groups and only consuming snacks that were low in fat and sugar free. Brandon would be patient while his mom painstakingly read the labels of nearly everything purchased for her family, even snacks at the condo pool vending machine area, which was sometimes embarrassing to his hungry friends. At home, everything in the eating department was charted and calculated. But not so on the farm.

Brandon knew that at home he would be forbidden such treats as uncooked hot dogs (wieners they called them really, really loud in the smelly outhouse), unsweetened Kool Aid (sprinkled on the tongue and not mixed with water) or marshmallows right out of the package and mixed with pine needles and Spit Bugs from the swamp pirate fort. But on the farm, those gastronomical nightmares were okay. Brandon was pretty sure that when he got raging diarrhea from eating too many green grapes as a result of playing *pills,* his Mother had to know he was eating all kinds of unripened things from bushes and trees. And *sure*, there was a small murmur of a warning—"Remember Brandon, how you get the poops on the way home if you eat too many of those green apples," but it just

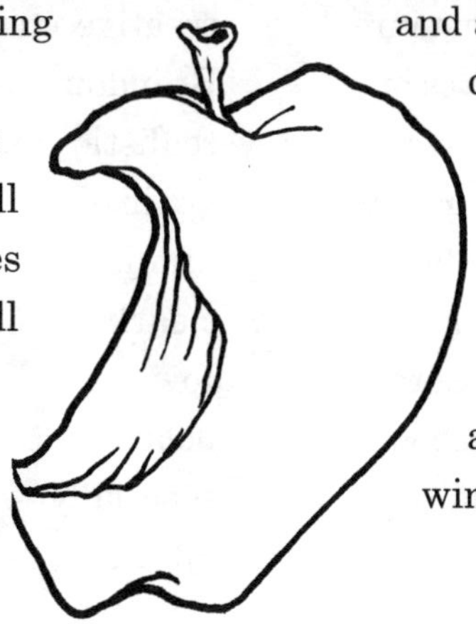

wasn't that same hysterical caution about his tummy as he got in the condo. And besides, pooping was pretty cool on the farm.

As the day wore on, nothing about the discrepancy between home rules and farm rules changed. The adults, having fun with the barbecue and an occasional Budweiser, were tolerant of things on the farm that at home would have sent them into apoplexy. Whether the kids were going way, way too high on the tire swing, building far, far too dangerous of tunnels in the hay stack, or whether they were doing way too much fooling around with the hydraulic gears on Uncle Mac's tractor, the grown-ups just didn't seem to mind. And as the day began to end, so did the supply of clean clothes, and his Mother was right; he needed all the shirts, shoes, and for sure the socks. It was so cool to have been so dangerous, so crude with things like farting, so outrageous in the things he ate, so vulgar in his language and so rude and disrespectful to Tuna and Bogie in all their Animal Kingdom pranks. But this was the farm and although he didn't know why it was different, he just knew it was.

And on the way home, sipping remnants of his Very Berry (not sugar-free) Kool Aid, Brandon inquires, "Mom, how come Henry the bull comes to visit in the spring, but he doesn't live at Auntie's farm in the summer or winter?"

The question hits the car with the subtlety of Uncle Mac's backhoe. Brandon's Mother internally panics with the question about Henry the bull's harem, but then, as she always does, she moves into educational mode and with her internal computer search, she finds the lesson of past education for Brandon as a point of reference for her teaching response.

Mom remembers that since he was just a little guy, she has been providing the *Birds and the Bees* lesson, just as she has taught him about the whales and whole grain bread. In doing so, Brandon had been taught to care for the teeny, weenie (not to be confused with wiener) carrot seeds and taught to witness the magic of watermelon production, which was much more exciting with their rather large seeds compared to the scrawny carrot ones. Just as she did in every other category, Mom taught everything about the miracle of reproduction, mostly in the garden, which was much more comfortable for her than Kotex pamphlets or what to do about possible sperm in the Scooby Doo sheets.

Brandon has been taught how to put cow manure on the compost pile, how to use the rotting leaves of fall for the flower beds of spring, and how to water the seeds so that cucumbers or carrots find their way to the top of the dirt, and later to the top of the family dinner table. Oh, Mom has been so proud of her efforts to teach about the miracle of Mother Nature for Brandon's sex education. And now, the question about cow sex and Henry the bull was on the table/dashboard from her most precocious son.

Finding her curriculum reference, she quietly calmed herself and mentally organized her agricultural answer to Brandon's Henry-the- bull question. After clearing her throat, the query began, "Brandon, do you remember last year when we planted the cucumbers in the garden and we put fertilizer on the cucumber piles with the cucumber seeds?" Her question as an answer to his question, hung in the air hopefully.

"Yep," Brandon affirms as he takes his last drink of warm Very Berry. Mom's garden goodness reminder continues to find reference.

"And remember honey, when we were planting the garden and we put the fertilizer on the cucumber seeds and soon, baby cucumbers grew out of the ground?" Mom, sweating now, gazes at her pondering son as she sees the wheels of his brain turning and churning. "Well, that is how it works with Henry and the cows. You see, the Mother cows on the farm have the seeds, Brandon, and Henry-the-bull has the fertilizer, and that's how baby calves are born in the springtime."

And while Mom is basking in her creative cucumber curriculum, Brandon has a much more realistic understanding of fertilizer, which to him is clearly cow poop, especially after a

wild day of poop extravaganza on the farm. Brandon ponders her answer of cucumber seeds and fertilizer and asks,

"Well, then how does Henry the bull get up that high to poop on her?"

While Mom gave her explanation with the hope that Brandon would understand Henry's visit to the farm by conjuring an image of a peaceful walk through the cucumber garden, Brandon got an image of the bull (fertilizer carrier in his mind) carefully approaching the awaiting cow, dumping a pile of cow poop on her, and then miraculously, cucumbers, vine and all, growing out of the poor heifer's back. His image may be a victory for the pickle industry, but Mom has no victory if she truly wants to raise Brandon to be a sexually respectful human—very different from Henry and his harem.

Parents have always found discussions about geese, gophers and guppies easier than talking about halter-tops, tube tops or what is in the top drawer of Mom's private closet in the master bedroom.

THE SIXTH COMMANDMENT—Thou Shalt Channel Carrots, Cats And Cows

The Sixth Commandment, calling for the *channeling* of cats, carrots and cows speaks to the issue in sex education that is usually (and usually very comfortably) focused on the *Birds and Bees* curriculum, eventually implementing other critters whether two-legged or those with four appendages. Good folks with good intentions like Brandon's Mom, focus their sex education with the hope that bits and pieces of seed packages and frequent trips to the aquarium or the zoo will enrich and wholesomely nourish everything in the sex department. Not surprisingly, the critter curriculum is much more comfortable than Nurse Ratchet and her flip charts or podiums in the living room.

The Sixth Commandment—*Thou Shalt Channel Carrots, Cats and Cows* first challenges whether critters make a good curriculum for teaching sex education and sexual respect with the outcome answer actually *fertilizing futility*—especially if sexual respect is the desired goal. But rather than giving up critter curriculum, banning trips to the zoo and telling Brandon types that Pumpkin was visited by the kitty stork—(thus bringing the kittens), the key word to this commandment is *channel.* That means bringing the barnyard, jungle or zoo into the curriculum, but being very careful in the comparison of animals to humans.

Even though the Third Commandment about logic is very important, gathering children around the table (in flannel pajamas, and drinking cocoa) while spinning a tale about tadpoles picking another tadpole (out of all the other tadpoles in the pond) and making a lifetime commitment to only share (whatever private parts tadpoles share) with that one special (and picked) tadpole is absurd. Showing children a critter soap opera *As the Tadpole Turns* is also not likely to be helpful, even for toddlers. But within that tadpole nonsensical comparison lays the importance of *channeling,* and that is using the critters to point out the differences in people and tadpoles. But first, a look at the ridiculous nature of the critter curriculum.

GEESE, GOPHERS AND GUPPIES

Parents have always found discussions about geese, gophers and guppies easier than talking about halter-tops, tube tops or what is in the top drawer of Mom's private closet in the master bedroom. Planting gardens or learning about the miracle of finding the kittens in brother's sleeping bag is a whole lot more comfortable and safer than discussing the hanky-panky that happened in Grandma Eleanor's broom closet.

FROM A SUBURBAN MOM

"We had a hard decision to make about getting a family pet since this road out front has so much traffic. But when we weighed everything out, we just felt that letting the children watch Katie Cat have her kittens was worth everything. Even though it was sometimes messy and a lot of hard work, we thought the whole process taught them a lot about the facts of life."

FROM A RANCHER

"Well, we use artificial insemination out here on the ranch and really, it can get rather scientific. The kids have to keep journals about the heifers and they chart which bull to use and when. And then of course, there is the sperm collection and the depositing business, so I just figure they get a whole lot more sex education right here on the ranch than they will ever get in any health class."

FROM A CITY DWELLING DAD

"Well, we planted a little garden on the balcony of the apartment and the kids were so inquisitive about growing their pumpkins in the flower boxes. This project taught them a lot about responsibility for sure, but the most important message was about the miracle of reproduction. It was a great lesson for them about the *facts of life*, even though the pumpkins weren't anything to brag about and sure couldn't be used for Halloween."

FROM A GRANDMA IN A CONDO

"Well, the best thing I ever did for my grandkids was get an aquarium. I got them involved with the pet store guy to help them pick a Mommy guppy and a Daddy guppy even though he had to do a little guesswork. Then, when the baby guppies came, the grandkids were delighted. This successful type of sex education was worth the finances, the filters, and the failure of the aquarium pump. I'd do it all again if I had a chance."

DOING DOWN ON THE FARM

So, whether it is carrots, cats, or cows, the focus of nature is the preferred sex education curriculum for many, especially those in the *Not Now* groups of the First Commandment, or parents who just have no confidence in the battle between the school teaching factions of the OATs and the NOTs. So, the at-home-take-charge parents decide to forge ahead on their own. The focus for these forging-ahead-without-help parents is usually the reproduction issue, since that seems to be where the *facts of life* come into play. This approach seems to be just a rural or critter version of the fallopian tube traffic jam, and of course, coming from the farm makes it even more soft and sweet. There are four reasons why the whole nature approach for teaching about sex is so easy and seemingly safer than geography maps pinpointing abortion clinic distribution.

It was a great lesson for them about the *facts of life*, even though the pumpkins weren't anything to brag about and sure couldn't be used for Halloween."

Smart politicians who want to pass mean-spirited laws that discriminate against someone or encourage other rudeness such as war, will find a way to spin the action as somehow being *for the family.*

FATHER NATURE?

The lesson plans of using nature to teach the kids about the *facts of life* finds its first line of defense in the *unisex* component, meaning only half of the sex equation needs to be present in class. Mother Nature is the only entity on the roll call list—being maternal, wholesome and certainly not needing any male unit to help her with her job description. Kiddos partaking of the Mother Nature curriculum are taught with dramatic fanfare that ***she*** embodies the earth, moon, sun, and of course, all the universe critters. But most importantly, she does it all by herself. It is doubtful that Mom and Dad overtly teach the kiddos that there is no Father Nature, but the unisex magic message is obvious—and comfortable. The *female only* image provides the foundation for the *down on the farm* religion that sits right at the top of the nature-teaching pyramid. But it gets even more profound, this love affair with the nature/farm stuff.

THE WHOLESOME HARVEST

Second in curriculum influence of old Mom Nature being at the top with her magic (and *partnerless*) ability to make guppies and geese get their babies on time, comes two specific influences shoring up the family farm religion Brandon so admired. Agriculture seems to have a monopoly on morality, seemingly connected to the *wholesome harvest* idea, spurring images of fresh picked corn and gathering eggs from chickens that aren't cooped up but allowed to roam free. But it isn't only the *no preservatives* produce or the absence of fruit flies making up the gospel of farm religion—it also includes one of the most powerful "F" words in the English language—***FAMILY.***

THE FAMILY FANTASY

Just as Mother Nature commands an aura of majesty, the whole concept of *family* has its own mystic morality shroud. Just about anything can be made soft and sweet with the word *family* as a tailgate. *The Family Restaurant* conjures an image of a safe place where children can throw up without anyone caring and these establishments also seem to imply there will be no wine with dinner. When the supermarket sports the sign: *We Sell Family Food,* no one would consider that preservatives were used and it is automatically assumed the fat and sugar content is low, just like Brandon's mother would have wanted. Smart politicians who want to pass mean-spirited laws that discriminate against someone or encourage other rudeness such as war, will find a way to spin the action as somehow being *for the family,* making everyone feel better..

The word *family* can be attached to anything, even not-so-nice-things, such as funeral parlors or liquor stores. *The Family Mortuary* results in a vision of everyone sitting around a fireplace singing Christmas carols—failing to appreciate that, in reality, the folks inside are dead and cold, and usually someone is sad about the loss.

The Family Liquor Store overlooks the devastating results of alcohol abuse in families yet implies a nurturing slogan that the family that drinks together, stays together. Not to be outdone by others who wield the unchallengeable power of *family*, consider the million-dollar-making National Basketball League star attempting to renegotiate his contract with the bean counters that controlled his team's checkbook. When they balked at giving the already-earning-millions star another 20 or so million dollars, the stressed athlete could only lament, "You know I have to feed my family."

FAMILY FARM FANTASY

Just like Brandon knew he could get away with just about anything on the farm, there is a general idea that morality and goodness is automatic on the farm. Since most of the population live in urban areas, the fantasies of life on the farm abound, suggesting the majority of city folks believe that what happens with the farm folks must be more natural, nourishing and healthy. Without much question, decency and honor are believed a natural partner with driving the John Deere tractor or gathering the fresh eggs before breakfast—and daylight. Cow poop, hay fever and three-fourths inch of field dust on the deviled egg sandwiches rarely finds a place in the family farm fantasy nor do images of crabby and cranky families with sexual respect issues.

America's love affair with the magic of the farm fantasy was never more evident than when the plight of the family farm in the late 1990s emerged on the media scene. Whether it was Oprah, Donahue or Hollywood, the hot topic was that the morally magnified family farm was a tragic victim of a seemingly unspoken villain. Tear-jerking pictures of the dusty tractor in the background and the devastated farm family in the foreground made great press. In the photo, Mom would hold her canned peaches, the kids would have holes in the bib overalls that were, on the average, three inches above the tops of their tattered shoes (with worn toe holes), and Dad would sport his wrinkled (but sparkling clean) flannel shirt, with a terrified look of "how will I hang onto the family farm?" With Kleenex for tears and checkbooks for help, Americans gathered around their televisions and trotted off to movies to experience the sadness of the family farm demise.

America's love affair with the magic of the farm fantasy was never more evident than when the plight of the family farm in the late 1990s emerged on the media scene.

CARROTS AND CONCERTS

Willie Nelson, famed country music singer, as well as other cowboy-type swooners conducted Farm Aid concerts all over the country to raise money for the sad farm folks. Oh, it was wonderful—all those country songs about working fingers to the bone while harvesting organically pure carrots. The concerts also made sure everyone knew how terrible the villains were—namely banks who had to foreclose on farm loans and food companies who

Comparatively, no one really seemed to care about the family tailoring business in Toledo, handed down through generation after generation, that went out of business because stacks of wonderfully tailored suits could be made cheaper and better at K-Mart and Wal Mart.

could make the carrots cheaper and better. Ironically, no one considered the reality that the vendors providing refreshments at the concerts probably got loans from the same banks so they could sell wonderfully cheap and deliciously processed food to the upset and check-writing fans.

Comparatively, no one really seemed to care about the family tailoring business in Toledo, handed down through generation after generation, that went out of business because stacks of wonderfully tailored suits could be made cheaper and better at K-Mart and Wal Mart. Not a single talk show generated even a half-box of Kleenex for the plight of the family-owned restaurant that would be closed because the left-hand lane of the new super duper interstate would be running right through the salad bar in the corner of the establishment. Those family businesses were thought to be just signs of progress earning only a rather rude response from most in society of *get over it—move on*. But not the family farm. To Americans, the family farm needed to be saved because it provided the symbol of morality and goodness leading the way for the seduction of using the family farm critter curriculum for educating children about sex.

PROBLEM FREE FARMING

The third reason that the critter curriculum seems so comfy in teaching children about sex relates to limited options and choices in making baby carrots, kittens and calves. When Mom and Dad think about sex in terms of sexual affairs, sexual dysfunction, switching sexual partners, or switching sexual genders, it becomes overwhelming. There are no options with the critters—they cuddle up for only one reason and that is just to reproduce. And *no other sexual option* brings the relief *of no sexual problems.* There are no talk shows for girl cows that really want to be bulls, for chickens that complain about the rooster's lack of foreplay or for Mrs. Goat who is suspicious about the time Mr. Goat is spending with a group of teenage male goats. Viagra-erection problems for Mr. Sheep, or divorce rates among the rabbits never become an issue, so it seems that the critter curriculum is problem free and that is one reason why it seems so painless and perfect.

CRITTER CATASTROPHE

Some challenges could be made to the idea that critter sexual problems regarding sex are nonexistent since throughout history there have been mentions and worries about sexual critter catastrophes. The Christian Bible has at least four references telling folks that doing the flippy-flop with the critters is not only forbidden, but some nasty consequences such as death (even for the innocent critter) are the result. Thirty-three states ban (by law) sexual contact with animals and, of course, groups like PETA try to police the ethical care of the critters which not only includes forbidden frisky stuff, but going so far as to protest the popping of poor Mr. Weasel in the popular song, *Pop Goes the Weasel*.

For sure then, sexual problems have been connected to animals, but the difference is that the fussiness has not been *between* the critters themselves, but *because* of humans. Additional and dreary reminders of sexual critter catastrophes includes how nervous everyone becomes when the heavy-hitter sex researchers explain the elevated rate of farm males (human types) involved with barnyard business of critter hanky panky. So it's not that sexual problems aren't connected to cats and cows (carrots excluded), but the problems are always from the two-legged critters, leaving the critter-to-critter sex curriculum rather pristine AND wholesome—or so it seems.

PRIVACY PLEASE?

The fourth and final reason why animals seem to be high on the sex education preferred list is the practical reality that the kidlets will be exposed to critter friskiness whether parents want that to happen or not. Although Mom and Dad may be able to ignore how carrots do their farm frolicking in order to get the baby carrots to show up, when Henry the bull gets a little frisky with the heifers, there is no pretending and for sure, there is no privacy. And beyond the farm, not a single parental permission slip can be found giving Mom and Dad the choice about whether the kiddos might easily get a glimpse of Fido doing the flippy-flop with Mrs. Fido in the city park during the pancake breakfast. Just as everyone knew the teenagers were *doing it* in high school, the kiddos are going to learn about the critters *doing* it. So Mom and Dad are prone to whip out the critter curriculum since privacy isn't an option.

CARROT CURRICULUM—NO TWO TO TANGO

So when the unisex of Mom Nature is combined with the fluffy farm fantasy of morality; and when the problem-free aspect of critter "facts of life" is combined with the reality of no hiding from the Henry the bull and his harem, the calculations begin. Carrots, cats and cows take over lesson planning.

The game plan usually starts out with the safest and most comfortable syllabus of the *goodness of gardening*. Just like there is no Father Nature, the unisex issues in this horticultural tutorial come in handy for kids like Brandon, learning about the miracle combination of dirt, water and carrot seeds. There are no pink and blue carrot seed packages, no *innies* or *outies* with body parts, and carrot seed hanky-panky is not even remotely evident. In fact, total segregation in the carrot seed lesson plan is demanded, since the carrots stay in the carrot row and the cucumbers have their own row—no ***twos to tango.*** The kiddos don't have to know anything about germination or cross-pollination, as that will come much, much

There are no talk shows for girl cows that really want to be bulls, for chickens that complain about the rooster's lack of foreplay or for Mrs. Goat who is suspicious about the time Mr. Goat is spending with a group of teenage male goats.

The *cat curriculum* avoids any suggestion of how Mr. and Mrs. Hamster do their magic to make little hamsters, but it does demand the kiddos learn it takes two turtles to tango in the tank.

later, most Moms and Dads comfortably muse. Yes, the carrot curriculum is safe as Mom gets the kids thrilled about picking out their carrots seeds and dreams that they will get just as excited about eating their carrots.

CAT CURRICULUM—ALMOST TWO TO TANGO

The second step in developing the critter curriculum usually happens about the time Mom and Dad notice the kiddos are bored with separate parsnip and pumpkin seed packages, compared to watching the humping cats in the shrubbery, followed by a surprise batch of kittens showing up. Other stirrings that suggest the carrot curriculum has become obsolete may be the result of overheard conversations where Aunt Zelda fusses because cousin Karen *didn't have a daddy for her baby,* or infuriated neighbors complain when their female dog ended up on an unauthorized date with the dog Dad jokingly called *Lucky.* Like Brandon, the graduates of carrot curriculum need to move on, since they have already figured out there is some mixing and matching of boys and girls, in the critter lessons.

ONE REASON ONE SEASON

The cat curriculum requires subtle mixing of the sexes—but subtle is the operative word. The educational goal is that the kiddos learn it really does take two of whatever critter, but that is as far as it goes. The cat curriculum admits that yes, the cats have some *doing* going on, but the *hows* of feline friskiness is skipped over in favor of the *whys*, which is reproduction. The power and comfort for *one season for one reason* teaches that kiddie critters just somehow materialize either in eggs, pouches or the secret stuff of birth found in the apple box underneath Dad's workbench. The cat curriculum avoids any suggestion of how Mr. and Mrs. Hamster do their magic to make little hamsters, but it does demand the kiddos learn it takes two turtles to tango in the tank. Little turtles just show up one morning and it is thrilling because the kids knew there was a Mommy and Daddy turtle purchased at the pet store. And that stage of cat curriculum usually lasts until the questions of Henry the bull's job description with the heifers, comes up.

COW CURRICULUM—THE TWO TANGO

By the time adults are faced with the reality of the kids going beyond the carrots and cat curriculum, it becomes time to introduce the teaching about HOW the turtles did the tango in the tank to get the baby turtles. Until now there was not a single lesson about cow ovulation cycles or porcupine private parts—but with this step in the critter curriculum, those comforts are gone. Now, there are too many questions and too many critters without privacy, doing strange things in the park. So the cow curriculum must come to the rescue. And sometimes the suggestions of how to organize it are absurd—especially considering the goal of raising sexually respectful children—which has little bearing on carrots and cats.

A confident kindergarten teacher testified loudly, outlining her objections to a sex education program in the school. *No way,* was her stand. The PTA audience listened to her vociferous reasoning.

"With Mother Nature at our side we don't need sex education. Our classroom is next to the pasture where the stallion and the mares sometimes mate. The kindergarten kids can view sexuality in its natural form without textbooks or uncomfortable topics about condoms and Kotex pads. I'm against it because we don't need it out here in the country where the kids can see nature take its course."

Right there it is—the equine substitution for Henry and his heifers. Although it is certainly nature at its finest—is this the lesson that the critter curriculum parents believe will help raise sexually respectful children? Although the grown-ups may prefer the mating horses to wife-swapping suggestions on the soap operas, the pasture reality may not be so wholesome—(or respectful.)

From a child's viewpoint it can only be imagined how one of those female kindergarten kiddos might anticipate her wedding night as she watches the biting, kicking, and fighting of the mare, with the stallion wielding a seventeen-inch penis between them. But this kind of teaching is common for adults who want to graduate to the cow critter curriculum, because once the miracles of the carrot seed magic is in tow, and the subtle *twos* of the cat curriculum are acknowledged, then the kiddos need to know how it all happens. Even though the stallion and the mare, in all their humping and huffing, don't have anything to offer in the sexual respect department, they are usually the favorite laboratory type of experiment in this teaching—because they are REPRODUCING. And the ***how*** of critter sex is all related to making little critters.

"With Mother Nature at our side we don't need sex education. Our classroom is next to the pasture where the stallion and the mares sometimes mate. The kindergarten kids can view sexuality in its natural form without textbooks or uncomfortable topics about condoms and Kotex pads."

RUDE REPRODUCTION REALITY

When the horse huffing and puffing is about as subtle as a circus parade, reproduction becomes the cornerstone of explanation to children—thus the nonsensical ***facts of life*** idea that makes it feel reliable in purpose. But the rude reality is that alligators, antelope and anteaters generally don't make *responsible* sexual decisions in their baby-making production. Mr. Bull, munching away in the lower forty pasture doesn't look at Ms. Heifer and think to himself, "Gee, she has nice hooves. Maybe I should get to know her and see if calves are in our future." And that stallion next to the kindergarten class didn't contemplate respectful dating techniques once he completed college and after noticing the attractive withers of Ms. Mare. No, that isn't how it works and in fact, respect and responsibility don't seem to be in the critter way of doing things—even though these critters are chosen for examples in teaching sexual respect to children.

In reality, the critters teach exactly the opposite of what parents want children to learn about sex and perhaps there is no greater absurdity to the critter curriculum than the *birds and the bees.*

In rude reality, nature has a basket full of techniques to bring the sexes together and none of it involves much of the things that parents usually want for their Edwards and Emmilous when they walk down the wedding aisle. Whether it is a female fish laying her eggs that will smell in a way that makes male fish have an uncontrollable urge to deposit sperm in the area, or whether it is the barn owl doing a little secret pecking in the daylight (their nighttime), critters generally don't do anything to make good sexual decisions and there is no responsibility and respect in their logic as recommended in the Third Commandment.

Snapping turtles have a rather rude and rough (highly disrespectful) mating scene trying to maneuver their clunky and cumbersome shells so that conception can take place. No Sex Fairy arrives after the magic moment of fertilization, so Dad turtle is off to the ocean, probably trying to find another waiting, not-yet-mama turtle for more hanky panky, never giving one rip about his eventually hatched turtles. In nature's planning, Mrs. T. doesn't show much more respect as she lays her eggs and then poof—she has had it. No motherly instinct keeps her around as she probably has places to go and new turtles to meet. The lesson from most critters is to reproduce because of biological instincts—nothing about respect for either sexual commitment or family life. In reality, the critters teach exactly the opposite of what parents want children to learn about sex and perhaps there is no greater absurdity to the critter curriculum than the *birds and the bees.*

BIRD/BEE ABSURDITEE

How seemingly intelligent adults began to attach the cute phrase *Birds and Bees* to human sexuality makes about as much sense as Henry's heifer harem organizing a woman's liberation protest march through the barnyard. First, bees have stingers and not very much is appreciated about bees, at least from the general population, especially children. In fact, bees are extremely low on the positive priority list for children and rarely are bees featured in the petting zoos. And then, to teach children that somehow their sexual future is even remotely related to the behavior of rude bees at the bowling team's annual picnic is beyond absurd. Respectful sex should have at least some component of being nice, tender, loving, gentle, compassionate and caring, something bees don't seem too good at mastering under any circumstances.

Actually, in the rude reality of the *Birds and Bees* critter curriculum, the queen bee isn't very queenly and in fact, she is quite a bitch, something most parents would not want their daughters to emulate. Right out of the chute, disrespect is clear. As soon as the new queen is hatched, she immediately murders her Mom and then sprinkles magic hormones in the hive to make all the other girl bees forget about mating and get to work. The queen bee doesn't care about coffee with friends or being the godmother for the babies of other lady bees. *No,* she wants everything to herself, so she tricks all the girl bees into not only doing all the work, but also forgetting about babies of their own. But it is even worse for the boy bees under the old girl's reign.

The boy bees don't fare too well in the hive either, and in fact, they actually represent nothing that parents usually want for their human boy units. Of thousands of boy bees born in the hive, only one hits the jackpot and actually mates with her majesty. But there is no honey bee honeymoon or cuddling, however. Once the lucky boy bee deposits his sperm through a quick and not-so-respectful hive hanky-panky, his abdomen bursts open and he promptly perishes. But the queen has exactly what she wants so she stores his sperm in her own body, allowing her to make bee babies in rapid time over the next two years without all the fuss of having a relationship with a king bee, who doesn't exist.

After that one mating moment, she has no use for any more boy bees except for about a dozen or so that she keeps around to make sure she has snacks after she lays about 1,500 eggs a day. She doesn't care one bit about boy bees and she just wants her sisters (called worker bees) to do all the hive housework. These worker bees do all the buzzing around and making of hive honey and they too, have absolutely no use for the males—keeping most of them out of the hive as they starve to death. The females run everything and they care nothing about tenderness, sensitivity or sexual responsibility—only the business of making honey. With all this rude reality, why would bees compose half of the critter curriculum focusing on the proverbial *Birds and the Bees* since they have nothing to do with the goals of raising sexually respectful children?

PECKER PONDERING

Not only are bees the opposite of what parents really want for their children in the sexual department, but also the bird end of the proverbial *Birds & Bees* critter curriculum doesn't fare much better. As a crude example, Birds have *peckers*, which is a common slang phrase used to demean the male sexual organ that for sure should be respected. Additionally, the *peckers* of birds have really nothing to do with lovemaking, sexual tenderness or a cuddle-up next to the campfire when Mom and Dad go hiking instead of attending his fifteen-year class reunion barbecue. Birds certainly use their *peckers* for the very important task of eating, but they don't use them for foreplay or getting frisky in the nest or on a power line.

The mother bird secures and dangles a worm in her pecker and holds up this tasty bite for her screeching and screaming offspring, who are also offering up their own version of *peckers* in ordering lunch. For most species, the mother bird shows no desire to nurture, parent or be tender with her babies or with her baby's daddy. Comparatively, for what parents really want their children to learn about sexual respect, it is doubtful that mother birds and their peckers

Not only are bees the opposite of what parents really want for their children in the sexual respect department, but also the bird end of the proverbial *Birds & Bees* critter curriculum doesn't fare much better.

There is no sexual responsibility among the buzzing or feathered critters, honoring a lifetime commitment to partner and love , which is usually what most parents want for their kiddos.

have ever been involved in Lamaze birthing classes with Mr. Bird, nor was their any speculation on the part of Daddy Bird to choose Mommy Bird because of her bird morality.

In using the bird curriculum, the kiddos learn nothing about sexual responsibility. They only learn that somehow the baby birds find themselves inside the bird eggs, and depending upon the different types of birds, Mother and/or Father Bird will sit on the eggs, only taking breaks for the potty or perhaps bird pizza which is certainly an improvement over the queen bee business. Rather than an anticipated birth at the hospital that involves both parents (what parents would hope for their children) at bird birth, the eggs crack and some combination of Mr. and Mrs. Bird, seek food for the offspring, dangling worms by their *peckers* into the *peckers* of the baby birds. And finally, these same *peckers*, that are hoped to be a good example of human sex education for those who use the critter curriculum chapter of the *Birds and the Bees,* push the baby birds out of the nest, getting Mommy and Daddy Bird ready for a new pecker period. There is no sexual responsibility among the buzzing or feathered critters, honoring a lifetime commitment to partner and love , which is usually what most parents want for their kiddos. With all the choices of critters for the sex education curriculum, it is amazing that *Birds and Bees* have been chosen as representatives of sexual respect.

MATHEMATICAL MADNESS

Why the birds and bees became the mantra for sex education probably had to do with their familiarity to children and because they were small and far away enough that their reproducing could remain aloof. They probably also won the title because their names sounded cuter than *ostriches and oysters.* But whether it is a hippopotamus, a hamster or a harp seal, whatever critter set is chosen for the curriculum, reproduction is the focus providing a mathematical madness of absurdity, at least when they are used to represent human reproduction examples.

If, like their critter counterparts, reproduction was the only purpose for sex in humans, how many babies would Mommy and Daddy have in a lifetime? If Mom and Dad were in biological *synch* they would get pregnant about every nine to ten months, and once Mom was confirmed to be pregnant, everything sexual would be in hibernation. Just like with the critters, sexual desire and sexual romance wouldn't exist—only baby-making concentration. Once baby pooper was pooped (born), Dad would frantically chase Mom's ovulation cycle, followed by another pooper, followed by a nine month sex stoppage program—baby after baby after baby.

If people were like animals, neither parent would mind the prescribed discontinuation of sex for nine months since, like nature's critters, once babies were conceived, sexual interest would be replaced in favor of critter care. Dad would happily work four different jobs as the *flock* or the *litter* or baby batch grew. Dad would never have an affair with a strange, raccoon-type female who would be eager to hear his tales of woe about not having enough sex in his marriage, while drinking a cold beer and listening to *Muskrat Love* on the raccoon radio. That just wouldn't happen because Dad would always be thinking about more babies and getting ready for when Mom was ready—AGAIN. And on the female side of this ridiculous critter comparison, Mom wouldn't turn away from her babies and become consumed with romance novels, feeling lonely and unattractive with her permanent and pregnant 48-inch waistline.

If human Moms were like bear or beaver Moms, they would happily wear their fingers to the bone washing dishes and drying diapers. Human moms, cloned like critters, would have no interest in Victoria's Secret underwear or a candlelight dinner with Dad when the kids are away at the outdoor adventure sleepover. College tuition or remodeling the back bedroom to accommodate the 27 children wouldn't be considered—just churning out more babies. If humans had sex like nature's critters, if the average man and woman were married somewhere around the age of 25, and 25 childbearing years were to be expected, the number of kids in the cloned critter households would be staggering. That is until Mommy and Daddy ran out of eggs and swimming sperm, then it would all be over.

CRITTER CLONING

Not only would sexual love, intimacy, and heated passion in the hot tub be nonexistent for critter cloned humans, but the entire world would be different in media, music, movies, and advertising. Rather than selling soaps, deodorant and stylish clothing—all with a sexual flare; products of media interest would focus on the joys of breast feeding, how to carefully purchase pacifiers and the importance of diaper bag packing for a mom with six preschoolers. Talk shows would feature subject matter about stroller studies and formula fraud. Breast attractiveness would be replaced by breast feeding strategies. Secret sexual fantasy discussions would be replaced by the secrets to reliable conception guarantees. And yet, even with this absurdity, the critters continue to form the sex curriculum—and sometimes beyond.

If humans had sex like nature's critters, if the average man and woman were married somewhere around the age of 25, and 25 childbearing years were to be expected, the number of kids in the cloned critter households would be staggering.

RUDE REALITY AND REPRODUCTION

Animals don't make responsible sexual decisions because their reproduction is driven biologically, making it absurd to consider the critter curriculum as a good way to teach children about sexual respect among people. But there is more absurdity, if not harm, with the critter curriculum. As far as carrots, cats and cows are concerned, the carrot part of the curriculum may not do too much damage, but when it comes to the four-legged critters like cats—things become risky. Just as Brandon had bits and pieces of the carrot/cat lessons resulting

Animals don't make responsible sexual decisions because their reproduction is driven biologically, making it absurd to consider the critter curriculum as a good way to teach children about sexual respect among people.

in his image of cucumbers growing out of the heifer backs, children may start to put things together in their own learning and apply what they see in animals for their own sexual plans. As an example, even though initially parents may feel better about cats compared to condoms, the reality is that cat sex is rather rude.

HERE KITTY KITTY

Rejecting the nonsense of *Birds and Bees* examples in the critter curriculum, some parents may believe they are adopting a more sophisticated approach by having the kiddos watch Mama Kitty have kittens. But in reality, and although sweet, Mama Kitty may provide an even worse example of people sex than *Birds and Bees.* At least birds and bees are observed by children from a distance and they are clearly of a different species—even to a toddler. But Mama Kitty is usually a family member and often humanized as much as possible. That's all fine in the pet respect department but her irresponsible sexual activities can be closely scrutinized by the kiddos in the unintended critter lesson.

One of the dreads of parents for their children is sexual promiscuity and Mama Kitty becomes the unintended teacher of that sin. Certainly the male kitty or the *tomcat* that impregnated Mama Kitty is not likely to take any responsibility for the pregnancy and he is nowhere to be found in the pre-birth process. To the observing children, Mama Kitty returns from a wild day or two in the shrubbery and then her biggest decision is whether she will have her babies in the camping gear or Mom's panty hose drawer. That's not much contribution to challenging sexual promiscuity.

Parents also fear for children regarding divorce and ruined relationships—often perpetuated by sexual problems resulting in lack of commitment to family. Mama Kitty becomes the unintended teacher in the critter curriculum about this issue. The observing kiddo/students note that once the kittens are competently peeing in the litter box and actively climbing the curtains, Mama Kitty changes. For some reason known only to Mother Nature (Father Nature apparently isn't involved), Mama Kitty has had it! Her *biological cat clock* is in snooze position and she begins to plan her getaway. The kiddos see Mama Kitty deposit her sweet little kittens in her cat food dish or some other convenient place and then she slips away—perhaps looking for more action in the shrubs? There are no Oprah or Jenny Jones talk shows for abandoned cats, but the difference in people and Mama Kitty, rarely make it to the critter curriculum, allowing the kids to observe, in the let-them-watch-the-kittens-be-born lesson, lots of information about normalizing sexual promiscuity and lack of family values.

CANCELING CRITTERS?

Even though everything in the cat curriculum wasn't so great—the answer isn't calling Nurse Ratchet or gathering the podiums into the family room. The answer isn't to keep the critters away from the kiddos—flushing the guppies down the toilet, canceling the school trip to the zoo and putting blinds up in the car for Sunday drives through the country cow pastures. And there is no need to hysterically scoop up the kiddo getting a view of Mama Kitty's cat humping followed by a rush to a sex therapist specializing in eight-year-old trauma patients. Teaching children about nature is very important for overall life appreciation and exposure to animals can usually be a very positive thing. In fact, using critters can be an excellent sex education curriculum as long as the differences between humans and hamsters are ***channeled***—and that is what the Sixth Commandment is all about.

ABANDON OR CHANNEL?

So, if birds and bees with their peckers and stingers, if cats in their hissing and humping and Henry the bull with his cucumber-growing heifers are bad examples, how can the critters be channeled in sex education if the primary goal is to raise sexually respectful children? The answer lies with lessons focusing on the differences between animals and humans as the cornerstone of the sexual respect curriculum.

CHANNEL SURF CRITTERS

Certainly there is something inherently wonderful about nature, especially considering the fast-paced world of freeways, fast food and *Super Size Me* sex everywhere. Nature, animals and respect for the environment and all living things should be welcomed to the teaching clipboard. In that effort, the differences in humans and critters should form the lesson—in accompaniment with the first five commandments.

Bringing in the critters should begin early (First Commandment) and since critters tend to be everywhere, the Second Commandment should encourage parents to just wait and watch for the windows of opportunity, to teach the Third Commandment's logic of sexual respect. *Welcoming the world* of Mr. and Mrs. Fido frolicking in the city park (Fourth Commandment) will be a smart thing for parents, and of course, making sure that the needed respect and differences between papa pig and mama pig need to be taught through the Fifth Commandment lessons on sexism. Whatever the children see from Mother Nature, in all of its rude reality becomes the window of opportunity to teach, as long as the critter curriculum is carefully *channeled,* pointing out the differences between people and ponies.

In fact, using critters can be an excellent sex education curriculum as long as the differences between humans and hamsters are *channeled*—and that is what the Sixth Commandment is all about.

Nature, in all of its rude reality becomes the window of opportunity to teach, as long as the critter curriculum is carefully *channeled,* pointing out the differences between people and ponies.

KITTY, KITTY CHANNEL

Consider a wise father using exactly the same Mama Kitty situation but combining the first five commandments into an effort to channel the Sixth Commandment into a wonderful critter curriculum.

"Now you kids gather around here. I want to tell you all about Mama Kitty because she is a good Mama kitty, but she is very, different from human Mommies. See, when Mama Kitty runs off for a few days and fights with Truman the tomcat in the bushes, she comes back and she sometimes looks like she has had a bad hair day. Even though we can't really see her fat tummy and even though she's not wearing kitty smocks like your Mom did, Mama Kitty is pregnant, and that means kittens are growing inside of her.

"Now, different than *people Moms* who get to decide who they want to pick for a partner, long after they have grown up—Mama Kitty doesn't do any picking. People Moms also get to decide when they want to have babies and since it is a very important decision—people Moms usually think very hard about when is just the right time for babies. Not so with our Mama kitty.

"Nature has a way of knowing when there needs to be a certain number of new kittens born, so every now and then Mama Kitty's body starts to act up—almost like when you kids get a bellyache. The private parts of her start to itch and smell funny. She gets cranky but her Mother Nature cat brain tells her she needs some seeds for babies to grow in her tummy."

Gaining strength, he goes on. "Mama Kitty wanders around outside where Truman, the neighbor's tomcat also has a Mother Nature cat brain reminding him that he has the seeds. Truman can smell Mama Kitty's new scent and right away he knows to plant those seeds in her tummy and he does. There isn't much special between Mama Kitty and Truman in the seed planting business—just some hissing and fighting and then its over and Mama Kitty is pregnant.

"Mama Kitty doesn't even care about the father of her babies who gave her the seeds in order to have baby kitties. She doesn't think about whether he goes to church or if he is the kind of tomcat who would help her with groceries. The only thing that Mama Kitty knows for sure is that once those kitties are growing in her tummy, she needs to take lots of naps, which is really her way of being a good Mom to her babies inside. She's not like your Mom who did lots and lots of things to get ready for you kids to be born, and Truman isn't anything like me when you kiddos arrived."

Dad keeps going, trying even harder to point out the differences between the beloved family cat and sexually respectful people. "Your Mom ate lots of vegetables, she went to very smart doctors, she took lots of walks to exercise, and she took classes so she would know exactly what to do when you were born. I bet you kids know there will be no ultrasounds, kitty showers, or plans for kitten birth pictures on the Internet—

for Mama Kitty. She doesn't pick out names for her babies or dream of her kitties growing up to be good Mama kitties. She just knows to rest and let those babies grow inside her."

Dad continues, "When Mama Kitty is so fat she can hardly stand it, her babies will come out of her uterus and slip right through her vagina and then usually right on top of Mom's panty hose. Plop! They are born. At first, she will be a very good mother, and we know this because of the way she finds a nice warm nest for her kitties and because of how she tries to hide her babies so they will be safe from Delbert, the neighbor's dog. Mama Kitty will fuss and worry about whether she has the right number of faucets for her babies and whether each of her kitties can get breakfast on time. She gives the kitties a bath in the way that only Mama kitties can give and after bath time, she gives them little tongue baths all day long. She doesn't go bowling and she doesn't watch cat TV. She only cares for her babies and she is a very good Mother, at least for a while. At times, Mama Kitty will leave her nest to get something to eat or to use the kitty restroom, but she is not interested in anything but her babies, and she has absolutely no idea about getting a kitty sitter so she can go shopping or visit her friends. She wants to be with her babies every single minute.

"But then, different from your Mom and me, things begin to change. There is something inside of Mama Kitty that tells her being a Mother to her kitties is over. It's not because the kittens didn't pick up their toys and it's not because she doesn't like them anymore. It is part of Mother Nature's plan and it is what makes kitties and people very, very different. When her babies are maybe two months old, Mama Kitty will bring all of them to her dish so that they can start to eat on their own, they are getting far too big to line up for her faucets. She will drop them off and she is done. Mama Kitty isn't mad at them, but she is done with them. Mama Kitty doesn't think about next Thanksgiving when all her babies will come back for dinner in the panty hose drawer. Nope. She has been a good Mom, but she is finished. It is just that way with animals and there is nothing wrong with it. There is only something wrong with people who don't understand that animals and people are very different."

Mama Kitty doesn't think about next Thanksgiving when all her babies will come back for dinner in the panty hose drawer.

Dad continues to his kiddos, "You see, your Mom and I are very different. We wanted to have babies together. We thought about it and we waited for the right time. We picked each other out of all the people in the world to share the private parts of our bodies with, and there came a time when we wanted to have babies. Picking someone to share your body with is a very big deal, but an even bigger deal is deciding to have babies with that person.

"Your Mom and I didn't get pregnant in the shrubbery like Mama Kitty. We made plans for when it was just the right time to bring you into the world. We even went to special classes so that when you kids were born, we knew exactly what to do. Your Mom and I promised each other that we would stay together forever, which is very different than Mama Kitty and Truman. We painted the nursery and picked out special wallpaper. The whole family gave us gifts so that we had everything you needed when you were born. We took lots of pictures and we made lots of plans about soccer practice and college. We thought about tucking you in at night when you were two, twelve, and eighteen. And most important, we even thought that someday you kids might grow up to be a Mama or a Daddy too. Always remember that Mama Kitty is a very good Mama, but she is a cat, not a person, and people are different than cats or cows or carrots."

CLOSING CRITTER DOORS-NOT!

What a wonderful lesson from Dad, channeling Mama Kitty as part of the lesson plan. But as the other commandments teach, sometimes educating children about sexual respect needs to happen quickly, on the spot, when the window of opportunity arrives. And sometimes it is the critters or learning about the critters that provides the open window that shouldn't be closed just because Dad doesn't have the luxury of thirty minutes for a peaceful discussion in the family room about the absence of kitty Dr. Spock books or cat casseroles brought by the neighbors in the cul-de-sac.

KOALA BEAR CARE

She is so excited about the Valentine present from her Aunt Ethyl, a cuddly and quite stuffed Koala bear. She hugs the toy already named "Honey" to her chest and actually calls it "my baby." A quick-on-her-feet-critter-curriculum-*channeler,* Mom sees the window open and makes a tiny contribution to the child's sexual respect education.

"Oh, isn't she just so cute that Honey Bear of yours. You know what I know about Koala bears? Well, they come from Australia and they are so different. They just hang around in trees all the time and they sleep more than twenty hours a day. They eat the leaves from the trees and about the only thing they need to teach their baby Koala bears, is how to eat and sleep. They just hang on to the trees so that their tummies will be able to digest their food from the old leaves they eat. They don't know too much about cuddling. The poor little Koala bears don't know about being held or carried, like I cuddle you and your brother. And that is why we make stuffed Koala bears, so that they get their cuddling from people, especially when they are named Honey." This critter lesson isn't much, but just an open window to pointing out the differences in critters and humans and, of course, encouraging good touching,

MIDWIFE MR. TOAD

It seems that little boys have a particular fondness for frogs, and in the critter curriculum it might be easy to just let the frog-inspired boys recognize that there are tons of frogs in the pond who lay frog eggs that eventually turn into tadpoles, that eventually turn into frogs. The *hows* of getting Mr. and Mrs. Frog together is left out of most Reproduction 101 lessons, but what if an alert parent seized the window of opportunity when their son was already fascinated with toads and channeled the croakers into a sexual respect lesson?

Dad takes advantage of the open window "You know, it is great that you are doing a science project on frogs and toads. I once read something so interesting about this certain kind of toad. Remember, toads don't date, they don't think about whom they want to pick to share their toad bodies with, and they don't think about getting married like humans. Something in nature just makes a girl toad and boy toad [illegible]ck of their brains that they need [illegible]oads. Now most of the time in [illegible]appens, like maybe a girl lizard [illegible]er eggs and a boy lizard may do [illegible] to make the eggs hatch into [illegible]ut every now and then there [illegible] interesting critter that, according [illegible]ure, does things a little differently. [illegible]sn't like people, but it isn't like [illegible]ither."

Dad continues. "I know there is a special kind of toad that they call the Midwife Toad. Nature somehow hooks up the female and the male toad to be partners in the baby toad making business but they are really different from other toads and for sure a whole lot different than your Mom and me. Well, for some reason these two toads know to cooperate and so the girl lays the eggs kind of in a string which sounds like it was a hard thing to do. Then, the male toad carries the string of eggs around his neck wherever the two toads tend to go. The eggs are kept safe until they hatch and that is why they call it the Midwife Toad. In nature, often the male isn't much involved in the baby making—once the new critters have been born or hatched or whatever. But when male critters are part of the baby business, I think it is cool."

But Dad isn't quite finished. "You know son, for people, the best thing that a male or a boy could ever do is remember how important the baby making business can be. The best boys and men in the whole world always understand that being involved in anything that would make another human being is a very, very large responsibility. The Midwife Toad is not like humans and not like most animals, but it is kind of cool to think about having babies around the boy's neck just to remind him of what a big deal people or toad babies tend to be."

"You know son, for people, the best thing that a male or a boy could ever do is remember how important the baby making business can be. The best boys and men in the whole world always understand that being involved in anything that would make another human being is a very, very large responsibility.

No matter how rude the sexual romping for animals seems to be, the critters, when channeled, can provide a wonderful lesson in sexual respect without a single cucumber appearing on a single heifer's back.

CUCKOO AND KANGAROOS

And the lessons could go on and on in almost any type of sexual respect education—even the not-so-nice ones. The cuckoo bird, fun for children and often holding their interest, could be used to point out the lesson of family respect. Although cute, cuckoo birds are lazy parents, never building their own nests but finding another weaker and smaller bird's nest in which to drop their eggs. Then, off they go, only leaving behind for their offspring, the rudeness of the cuckoo genes. Apparently, when the eggs hatch, the cuckoo babies survive by pushing the other baby birdies out of the nest and then munching on the food provided by the confused bird parents of the now departed and probably plopped birdies. What a great clipboard lesson for teaching kiddos about respect for families and commitment to responsible baby bird making by using cuckoos.

And certainly children are fond of the cute little kangaroos, hiding out in Mrs. Kangaroo's pouch. This animal, if channeled correctly, could provide another wonderful comparison of critters and humans. The *Joey,* born only the size of a bumblebee, is able to climb immediately into its Mom's pouch where it will mature for months. This provides a great lesson in mothering, but not fathering since after a romp in the kangaroo substitution for shrubbery, Mr. K. is long gone, having no desire to be a part of the family. Children could be taught to compare how the Mother kangaroo knows to prepare her pouch before Joey is born, but like Mama Kitty she makes no plans for college or commitment to Christmas dinner when Joey himself is a daddy. No matter how rude the sexual romping for animals seems to be, the critters, when channeled, can provide a wonderful lesson in sexual respect without a single cucumber appearing on a single heifer's back.

FAMILY ROOM MOMMY'S TURN

Back in the family room, Mom joins Dad's wonderful window of opportunity for the kiddos in an effort to channel cats, carrots, and cows. Mom tells her children that Daddy is right about Mama Kitty, but she also wants to teach them about two very special critters in the animal world, such as the Canadian geese and wolves. Mom wants to teach her kids that these critters pick a partner and they stay with that partner forever.

Mom joins in, "Just like I picked your Dad out of all the men in the whole world, Canadian geese and wolves do the same thing with their picks for partners. We don't know why wolves and Canadian geese are different than Mama Kitty, but they are. Once they make that partner pick, the lady geese don't pick another Daddy goose just because the old one squawks too loud or Daddy Wolf doesn't decide to pick another lady wolf that has a different color of tail just because he might have been bored with her old tail. It is true that Mama and Daddy Goose hatch lots of baby geese, and once they fly away, they don't invite the kid geese back for a Christmas visit. They don't keep track of their babies like your Dad and I will keep track of you forever, but when they pick a partner, it is forever."

Mom continues, "And it is kind of like that in wolf families. Mama and Daddy wolf take very good care of their little wolves while they live in the wolf den where they sometimes live with the aunt and uncle wolves that have also picked each other forever. But once the little wolves are grown up enough to catch their own dinner, they leave their parents and start to figure out whom they will pick for a wolf partner. The baby wolves that grow up don't come back to their families and visit their grandparents. Nope! They just have their wolf babies, teach them everything they need to know about making good picks, and poof, they are gone. But no matter what, the Mama and Daddy wolves stay together because they understand the importance of picking a partner forever, just like your dad and me."

Like a grand storyteller, Mom goes on, "I often wonder how Dad Goose, year after year, and after batches and batches of goose babies can remember just exactly what Mom Goose looks like, since all the mama geese look the same to me. But I imagine that he fell in love with her a long time ago and that he picked her out of the other geese, and I bet he knows every little feather on her head. I bet he can hear her special quack a very long way across the lake or the swamp. I bet if he had to take a quick trip across the pond (maybe with some of the other goose Dads, checking for a good place to build nests and find bugs), he would probably miss her. He probably thinks about how her little feathers fluff perfectly for him and he probably remembers how he thinks she is the most beautiful goose in the whole world, even though he knows some of the other goose girls can fly higher. And you know what kids? That is exactly how your Dad and I feel about each other, and we will feel this way forever."

Sex Fairy Clipboard

- Very important for this commandment is giving up any thinking or language referring to teaching sexual respect to children by phrases *The Facts of Life* or *The Birds and the Bees*. These old ideas about what children really need to know are not only meaningless and absurd—but they can be harmful.

- Consider that nature, animals, and all other non-human livings things are important parts of learning respect for children. Teaching children about healthy food, respect for their environment and such things as the tragedy of unwanted pets or animal cruelty are valuable educational endeavors. But just because animals don't use pornography does not necessarily make this curriculum automatically contribute to sexual respect, so caution about the critter curriculum is important.

- Challenge the *family farm religion* that suggests everything rural is peachy perfect and everything urban reeks of rudeness. Geography, neighborhoods, apartment buildings, ranches or acreage do not make children grow up with sexual respect.

Don't rationalize working harder and sacrificing more, so children can just live in the country. This thinking usually results in parents not taking the time to teach sexual respect because they believe everything will be okay when the farm mortgage papers are just signed. Nothing could be further from the truth because sexual respect can only be taught by lesson—not by topography.

Sex Fairy Clipboard

- Don't throw out the carrots, cats and cow curriculum of teaching children about sex. But it is important to remember they are a *continuum* providing a good way to start with children, then moving along as development occurs and the kiddos are ready to hear stories about how Mama Kitty is different than Canadian geese. Watermelon seeds will do nothing to help teenagers make responsible sexual decisions at the unauthorized sleepover on the beach.

- When using the critter curriculum—don't strive for perfection as a biologist or horticulturist before the lessons begin. Maybe the exact way cuckoo birds handle the birdies won't be perfect and maybe there are a few wayward wolves who don't mate for life. It is the overall message, *that animals are wonderful and an important part of the world—but different that human in sexual respect* that needs to be taught—rather than worrying about the exact timing in Fruit Fly conception.

- Always teach that animals reproduce because of biological instincts and the companion to that lesson is that the critters don't—*just don't* make responsible sexual decisions like humans need to make. And of course, that lesson opens the door for the required teaching that people should decide about sex because of love, intimacy and commitment to respect—rather than the mating habits of mares in the pasture next to the kindergarten class.

Chapter 10

Seventh Commandment
Thou Shalt Abandon 'Bad Equals Bad'

CHAPTER 10: THE SEVENTH COMMANDMENT—THOU SHALT ABANDON 'BAD EQUALS BAD'

Winona's Jiffy Pop inadvertently left in the microwave for thirty extra seconds emerged as charred mush. This was a problem since Winona was already late for the weekly staff meeting at the local mental health clinic. The quandary regarding whether she should risk another 3.5 minutes of tardiness in order to pop a new batch was quickly resolved in her mind as she remembered that, after all, she was the Executive Secretary and commencing the *Super Staff* meeting was impossible without her. In quick contemplation, she recognized that Vern, the Director of the *Super Staff,* was absolutely helpless without her handling everything, thus her decision to replace the pulverized looking pulp was a snap.

Four minutes later, Winona and the agonizing aroma of Jiffy Pop, entered the meeting room, which was a relief to Vern, yet excruciatingly painful to those among the staff who had neglected breakfast nourishment. Her spiral staff (and super) notebook with fine-tipped calligraphy pen were easily slipped into position without a single regard for *getting into someone else's space* or *violating boundaries,* common problems to mental health and social work types.

Winona distributed minutes to the *Super Staff* containing case histories of folks who need *staffing* from the *Super Staff* made up of therapists, counselors, psychologists, social workers and others. They were to make mental health decisions about patients drawn to the clinic during the previous week for a variety of problems. They were the *Walking Wounded,* according to Vern, but only in a moment of irreverence. Wisdom was a pre-requisite for the next ninety minutes, as the trials and tribulations of the troubled *customers* would become the focus of discussion and, of course, decision-making about what to do with their wounds.

Irv had the first case, introducing by proxy, twelve-year-old Danielle, who was referred, Irv explained, by the Division of Children's Services, where everyone knew Irv's wife was employed. Even though Irv pretended the referral of Danielle was *official,* all those in attendance had a picture of the referral really occurring during pillow talk or in the Smith family hot tub. But never mind, Irv had respect and he had the floor, so he continued.

"Danielle was found in the neighbor children's fort on Farley Place engaging three small females in a game of *Titty Twister*."

Irv tried not to laugh, so he intently busied himself with his file papers. He further explained that the twisting by Danielle just didn't appear to be reciprocated by four-year-old Jasmine, five-year-old Judy, or six-year-old Jennifer. And, Irv worried, the fact that the little girls showed bruising in the *Titty Twisting* suggested a less-than-playing atmosphere for the kiddos. That comment just hung in the air and made every member of the *Super Staff* wince with the thoughts of *girls-getting-frisky-in-the-fort,* going too far.

Not only was Irv concerned about the bruising, but apparently Danielle's younger brother, Devon, told interviewers that he liked to play *Titty Twister* as well, although the seven-year-old could not provide specific details about the forbidden fun. *That was curious*, many *Super Staffers* murmured to each other with unauthorized side-talk conversations. Irv brought them back to order when he remarked,

"The family history indicates that an older sister, Debra, became pregnant at age sixteen and the fourteen-year-old brother, Donald, is attending an alternative school due to behavioral problems. *Interesting,* the staff non-verbally calculated as they tried to fire up their mental health brains for understanding. But the *Super Staff* was intent on *staffing* so they peppered Irv with questions about typical mental health issues, such as the work history of Danielle's father, her mother's ability to keep a clean house and if the family was Baptist, Catholic, Mormon, or NOT. The conversation of questions among the *Super Staff* was chaotic, but determined to examine every possible explanation for the mental health mess, until Barbara spoke.

Bringing the group to attention, Barbara peered over her half glasses while sipping from her full glass of whey protein shake. Barbara was one of the few who had no interest in Winona's Jiffy Pop. With great drama and flair, she asked Irv to describe the ***abuse history*** of Danielle. The clarity of the question, familiar to all mental health-type folks, ceased the chatter among them. Not surprisingly, this was a pensive moment for the *Super Staff,* because a familiar road or pattern merged into focus with Barbara's brilliant question—*Danielle's abuse history.* As Barbara's question of clarity hung in the air, Irv fumbled through

the intake paperwork, frantically trying to find the *abuse history*—wherever and whatever it was. But before he could find the sought-after details, Barbara addressed the *Super Staff*.

"We know kids couldn't come up with this type of *Titty Twister* behavior on their own. Let's find out what kind of abuse Danielle has suffered in order to resolve her case."

"And maybe question the other children in the family as well," chimed in Charles, looking up from his Diet Coke jerked from the vending machine on a feigned *potty break,* obviously trying to look interested and helpful to Irv's case, which he knew nothing about.

The *Super Staffers* were only quiet for a moment as the question sank in—*abuse history of the other children*. Then the unauthorized side-chatter really began to percolate as everyone expanded the search for the ever-fleeting abuse histories. The chattering seemed out of control until Vern, clearing his throat, brought them back to order with his monotone, "Staff, staff!"

Bart, who was the quiet, silent type in meetings (probably because Vern wouldn't let him wear his cowboy hat) opined with power.

"This young girl is only repeating or reenacting what has probably happened to her, because *Titty Twister* types of games are just not normal behavior among children." It was just a different version of Barbara's suggestion so it seemed a congenial comment. *Yes*, the staff affirmed in their side-talk murmuring, especially about the *not normal* part. And the chatter, although audibly confusing, had a straight-arrow theme that was very clear. They would find the answer to what abnormal things had happened; so on they went, churning and turning through bits, pieces and tidbits about the family; actually doing their own version of *twisting*, but without the titties.

Questions were raised (and twisted) to Irv about Debra, the pregnant sister of Danielle and whether anyone knew about the father end of things for either the sperm donor of Debra's baby or whether there was any hanky-panky suspected with Debra's very own Father. Several at the meeting swooned with the thought of possible incest. although Barbara did note that Danielle's Father was noticed at the bank after losing a lot of weight. With her comment, there seemed to be a momentary pause as everyone tried to make the mental health connection between incest and shedding a few pounds.

But it wasn't a long silence as others jumped on the thought-thread, bringing up the mental health favorite of *family dysfunction.* Everyone's memory of the jolly and rotund bank manager turning svelte and sleek for no apparent reason strained for a connection to the family pathology. *Curious and suspicious,* several suggested it was, especially considering about half of the *Super Staffers* were dieting—most of them, unsuccessfully.

But they went on in their abuse-history-family-dysfunction sleuthing as they turned their attention to Danielle's brother. It seems that Devon had been placed in an alternative school, which took him off campus; *separated from normal kids,* one of them opined out of turn. The suspense about the reasons for such action frustrated the high school liaison, Mrs. Lotlearn, who thought she knew why Devon had been transferred but since she wasn't a full-time member of the *Super Staff*, no one listened. In the chatter, there were accusations and assumptions of drug use, juvenile delinquency and worries about Devon's mother either having a problem with housework or having an affair with the manager at the Credit Union. Several queried if the Father had been previously married, whether he had pornography in his toolbox or where on earth he had gotten the diet helping him to lose so much of his tummy. Even though Mrs. Lotlearn said quietly to Irv that

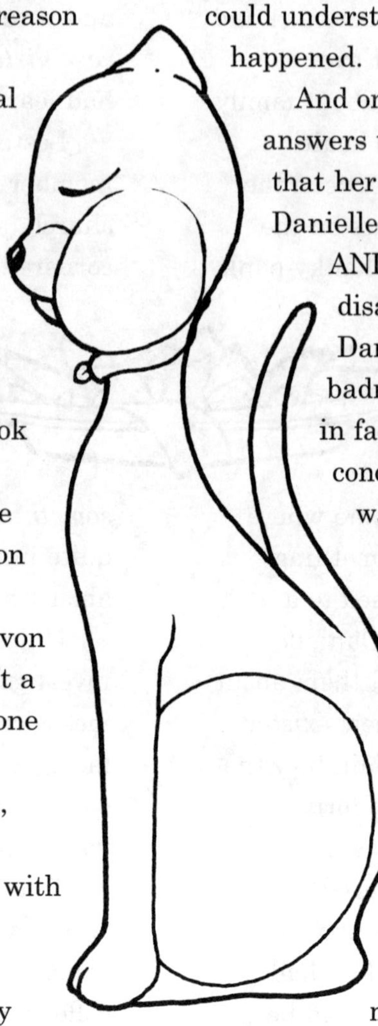

Devon was placed in the alternative school because he was gifted and would receive private tutoring, no one was interested. After all, they had to find the *abuse history* of Danielle so they could understand why the Titty Twisting happened.

And on they went, searching for the answers to the already accepted premise that her *abuse history* would explain why Danielle would do such a thing to the poor AND bruised kiddos. Much to their disappointment, Irv explained that Daniel had nothing to say about any badness happening in her family and, in fact, Irv made the very unpopular conclusion that maybe her family wasn't abusive and maybe, just maybe, there was no *abuse history*. With that obviously anti-mental-health-wisdom statement, resistance from the Super Staff was about the same as when Bart wanted to wear his cowboy hat to the meetings.

Everyone (except Mrs. Lotlearn) chimed in loudly, making it clear to Irv that his idea just didn't make sense in the mental health business. Until Danielle's *abuse history* was discovered they felt there was no need to pursue legal charges against her and there was no need to initiate any type of mental health treatment. Pending discovery of what happened to her (*abuse history*), nothing could be accomplished they concluded. And to do that—to get to the bottom of things, they had a plan.

Firm and together against Mrs. Lotlearn and Irv, the *Super Staff* pointed out that even though Danielle had nothing to say about family dysfunction, they just knew (mental health training) that somewhere lurking between the couch slip covers and the ceramic cats on the mantel, there must be some kind of hanky-panky going on—that is, in order to explain the twisting of titties. So with the power and seriousness of the Supreme Court, they decided it was best to remove Danielle from her home where obviously she was suffering from something. That was the only way, they explained to a baffled Irv and Mrs. Lotlearn, that Danielle could feel comfortable enough to tell them about her *abuse history*, which they all knew existed and which they all knew would explain how the titties had gotten twisted in the tree fort.

Most *Super Staffers* figured it was a wonderful resolution as they murmured congratulatory comments. As Irv pensively closed his Danielle file, he worried if he had enough Rolaids for his upset tummy, and he worried how he would tell his wife to line up foster care for the queen of *titty twisting*.

Barbara had wisdom, Irv had a stomachache, Winona had no more popcorn, and Karen had the next case. Lester, it seems, had been arrested for sexually abusing three of his five children, ranging in age from seventeen to seven months old. With precise mental health protocol and three sips of her latte, Karen provided the *case history* and *presenting problem* just as she had learned in state training.

Lester, she explained, was a community member of long standing and active in her church, as was Lester's defense attorney, who cornered Karen after Sunday Sacrament.

According to Lester's lawyer, Marvin Meddling, something had to be done and he was hoping a mental health intervention could be the *something*. The *Super Staffers* listened—feeling quite important with the lawyer's pontification about their professionalism and importance.

Unless someone could persuade the investigators differently, Lester was facing a messy criminal trial and if found guilty, he was facing an even messier prison term. So the solution of a *mental health evaluation* was offered with diplomacy known only to lawyer types.

"There is no expense too great for the psycho-social evaluation," Marvin Meddling had explained to Karen, somewhere between the collection plate and the after-service cookies at the church they both attended. "We want to pull out all the stops to help this family," Marvin (Meddling) implored, according to Karen, as she related to the *Super Staff*.

"So," cooed Karen, "I am wanting all of us to develop strategies for a complete no-expense-too-extravagant evaluation of Lester to see what we can discover in order to sort all of this out. Something is just not right in the accusations against Lester and I have some ideas."

But then, with the same regularity of Jiffy Pop accompanying Winona to the staff meeting, Karen was interrupted with familiar side-talks and across-table murmuring commonly associated with mental health folks in meetings. It seems their tendency for interrupting just can't be helped, probably because the *Super Staffers* tend to have so much wisdom that their brilliant ideas are difficult to stifle while another person is speaking. The butting-in began.

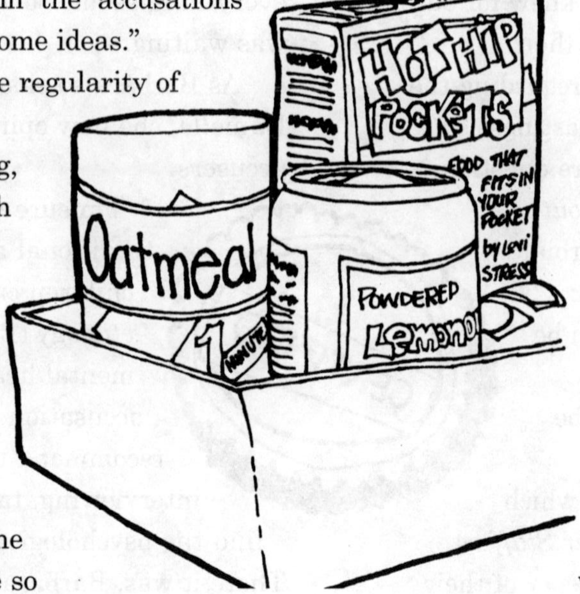

"Well, I know this family and I can tell you, Lester and the Mrs. never miss a soccer practice for those kids who are making accusations," chimed in Joe, who coaches soccer for his own three kiddos.

"Well," ranted Ruth, "I served on a Spring Sing committee at the Junior High School with Lester's wife, and I certainly didn't notice any problems in the marriage. She is very attractive and she keeps herself up with those aerobic classes, so what could have gone wrong in the couple's relationship is beyond me."

Charlene chimed in, "My daughter is in choir with Susan, the youngest girl in the family, and she seems so settled down. She's a very sweet girl. Are you sure this is a valid case of sexual abuse, Karen? All of those children seem so well-adjusted. Maybe this is one of those *false memory thingamajigs*," queried Charlene, above the voices of other *Super Staffers* who were barging in with their theories about what wasn't wrong in Lester's family. Different than their sleuthing with Danielle about what had gone wrong, with Lester, they wanted to find what was right.

The questions came in rapid-fire about this and that, as the image of perverted weirdos hanging around park bushes haunted their minds since Lester didn't seem to fit the profile. And of course, *diagnosing* was what mental health folks were all about so they had to resolve the image problem. Rather than Lester being featured on post office mug shots, they had visions of his Eagle Scout badges, his 4-H Club leadership skills (including some of the *Super Staffer's* kids) and his ability to organize *Paint the Town* projects for the elderly. Some commented that Lester was the type to guarantee the proper amount of insulation in the attic for his family's home, that he paid his taxes on time and some even commented that he was likely to be the type of person to make sure the mattress tags were intact, just like the directions required—although none of them knew for sure about that. There was a theme to their bantering. Nothing seemed to fit regarding the nasty allegations about Lester's nastiness so they flooded Karen with even more questions. *What about, what about, what about?* were the challenges for the proverbial answer to the proverbial question: "How could the alleged perversion be true for the Lester they knew?"

Not only did nothing seem to be wrong in Lester's family, but everything seemed to be RIGHT, which was quite perplexing for the *Super Staffers.* And since Marvin Meddling's whisper of their brilliance in finding the answer was still in the air—they wanted a resolution to maintain their own belief that Mr. M was brilliant in his belief about them. They reminded themselves of the importance of not only the task, but the importance of *being given the task*—especially by the important lawyer types.

The *Super Staffers* weren't the average group of folks at a coffee klatch in the cul-de-sac nor were they like a group of construction workers having a beer with burgers. This was a group of highly trained professionals in the field of psychology and the study of humankind. The *Super Staffers* attended conferences, studied diagnostic manuals and followed federal guidelines for all kinds of things to guarantee their paychecks. Yes, wisdom on how to resolve the everything-is-right-with-Lester against the everything-seems-so-wrong-with-the-allegations, was waiting.

As Barbara so eloquently suggested about Danielle, she now opined about poor Lester's accusers.

"I'm sure under hypnosis or traditional age-regression work, those children can be interviewed and the *etiology* (Barbara liked using those mental health words) of the accusation will be discovered. I recommend that someone trained in interviewing, talk to these children and find the psychological root of the accusations." There it was, Barbara's wisdom waving the familiar flag of deep-dish understanding.

Dr. Olson, not always prone to agree with Barbara, interrupted her, which he was also prone to do.

"The *Neurological Psychiatric Resolution Institute of Higher Functioning* provides day-long trainings on such things. I am certified and I could conduct the interview known as ***SIMPLE*** (*Structured Interview Method of Perpetrator Lying Efforts*), which is likely to uncover whether Lester is lying. It would seem

better that Lester be examined rather than the children," Dr. O. offered, knowing Barbara would be offended with his suggestion of switching the test subject.

Before Barbara could express her objection to the idea that Lester might be telling a few fibs, Helen, who usually brought her own Jiffy Pop and was still wistfully yearning for Winona's, was startled out of her trance at Dr. Olson's comments and offered her own.

"Well, the Crooksville Mental Health Center had a training by Dr. Terry Trumpet, and he didn't have anything positive to say about the Neurological Psychiatric Resolution Institute of Higher Functioning. He suggested rather than using the ***SIMPLE***, an assessment called ***RESCUE*** (*Resolving Effects of Sequenced Childhood Uncomfortable Events*) would be better. I am ***RESCUE*** certified and I would be willing to evaluate Lester. I would be very interested in this new assessment, especially if it prevents use of the ***SIMPLE***, which I am sure is outdated and wouldn't tell us anything about poor Lester's suffering from past child abuse." With that, Dr. Olson fumed.

With comments from Barbara about her hypnosis interviews of the accusers, Dr. Olson with his snide quips about Lester's lying and then Helen challenging ***SIMPLE*** certification with ***RESCUE*** expertise, the real divergence of the Super Staff's discussion factions weren't likely to make Marvin Meddling happy.

Winona, who usually just took notes coughed loudly so that her boss, Vern, would stop snoozing, and stop the chatter. After regaining his attention, Winona smartly suggested to Vern that considering the seriousness of the situation, perhaps he should *facilitate* the discussion, which was another mental health word for just running the show. And as he always did—Vern pontificated.

"It seems to me we have two approaches, with the first pertaining to whether Lester is guilty as accused. I realize for many of us, these accusations are hard to believe because he just doesn't seem the type. But being the forensic professionals we are—an objective approach is our trademark. So some of you need to offer suggestions to Karen that would address the propensity or probability that Lester is indeed, guilty as charged."

Although many Super Staffers wanted to jump right in, a small moment of silence enthralled the meeting—just hearing their boss say those inspiring mental health words about propensities, probabilities and especially the word, *forensic*. But Vern wasn't finished, especially since he hadn't explained the other side, so important in forensic fundamentals. He went on.

"But there is another approach, since some of you will use your expertise in diagnosing the psychiatric conditions that may have affected Lester—rendering him basically not *psychologically guilty* of molesting the children."

With that, no one said a word, remembering the awe they always felt toward their leader when he used those mental health concepts. He was basically telling them that ***all*** their ideas would help Lester, even if he had molested his children. They didn't really have to figure out why Lester didn't look like a post office pervert picture since even if Lester was a molester—he really might not be guilty because he just might have psychiatric conditions! Oh, the compromise was magnificent—and so *mental health* like.

Magnificently, they now had their paths ahead—contemplating if Lester was a molester or if he was only a *sort of* molester, which meant *not guilty* because of mental health problems. Dr. Olson now felt better about his ***SIMPLE*** test since it related to whether Lester was lying and he was ready to jump in, but Lilly cut him off. She offered another idea to get to the bottom of the Lester mess.

"You know, I am ***CHAT*** certified, which is a great assessment for these mysterious things in a person's past. Why, administering the ***CHAT*** just might help us understand about Lester's situation."

"What does ***CHAT*** stand for?" asked Winona, trying to take careful notes with buttery fingers.

Lilly leveled with them. "***CHAT*** stands for *Conversations Hoping to Address Trauma,* and I am certified in its administration. And I really believe that with this instrument, any psychiatric problems Lester might have could be addressed, helping us determine either what trauma happened to Lester or whether these are false charges."

"***CHAT,*** indeed," scoffed Scarlet, who offered her own contribution of another testing instrument which was helpful, but also making everyone get confused about all the letters.

"TRIC (*Trauma Repression Investigation in Childhood)* is an assessment that would be much better than the ***CHAT***," she explained. But before Scarlet could elaborate on her preference for this assessment, Thomas offered the **DENYE** assessment tool (*Denying Existence of Normal Youth Environments*). *Yes,* Thomas was sure the **DENYE** assessment could help everyone figure out exactly what had, and what had not happened in Lester's situation. But before he could explain his certification in the **DENYE**, Benjamin butted in.

"But there is another test that may also work in helping Lester," offered Benjamin, who had been reading the newest *Therapist for a Day Journal,* but was now hoping to contribute to the conversation.

"Here it is," offered Ben, quoting out loud from the magazine. "For answers about repressed memories of childhood sexual abuse or

for false claims of sexual abuse, therapists can find answers never before revealed, and some not even known by the mental health patient." There it was for Benjamin to offer, right from the *Therapist for a Day Journal*. Ben continued, "It is called the *Repressed Images of Perpetrator & Offender Family Fighting—**RIPOFF**.*"

Only for a moment did silence envelope the meeting as they tried to consider ***CHATs, TRICs, RESCUEs, SIMPLEs, DENYEs*** and now ***RIPOFFs***. Not to be outdone with all these fancy test offerings, Doris Downpour, a graduate student completing an internship under Irv, could no longer contain herself. Recognizing her newness to the *Super Staff,* but also being the one (and perhaps the only one) who had direct knowledge of the latest, newest, and most-up-to-date techniques in discovering the human soul, Doris decided to speak. She was nervous, but prepared. She checked her body language and eye contact skills (so important to mental health types) before beginning.

"There are two new tests with strong validity of research," Doris Downpour suggested, "that probably would help Lester and Mr. Meddling," quietly hoping that the *Super Staff* would give her some credibility, even though she was still technically a student. Surely, Doris cared about Lester and Marvin, but she cared even more about her trustworthiness with the *Super Staff*. Carefully, she went on.

"There is a new test called, ***GITS,*** which stands for *Getting in Touch With Self* and the ***TILT**, Trust in Lying Test*, and both have good citations in the literature."

In the silence following her presentation of the ***GITS*** and the ***TILT***, Irv, Doris Downpour's supervisor, felt the pressure to respond with brilliance and typical of mental health types, he began with astute mathematical questioning.

"Does the ***GITS*** and the ***TILT*** have cross-reference validity and peer review?" Irv quizzed, remembering a few important terms from his twenty-five-year-old statistics class. "And," Irv interrupted, before giving Doris a chance to respond, "does the data support replication studies?"

Doris, feeling the edge in her favor since she was aware Irv hadn't taken a college class for almost a quarter of a century, expertly closed the discussion with the utmost respect for her supervisor, who would actually determine if she could truly become a certified and official *Super Staffer* at some point in the future.

"The answer to your question is affirmative. And, Mr. Smith," Doris ventured far away from her status as a student, "the proper term is '*these data*' since the term *data* refers to the plural." There, it was done. Doris prevailed, Irv was corrected, and Lester was long ago lost in the discussion.

But Karen quickly jumped in for *debriefing*—she called it, another mental health term although she quipped about things becoming so brief with all the letters and acronyms, her head was spinning. Karen explained her frustration with trying to keep track of the ***CHATS, TRICS, RESCUES, RIPOFFS, GITS*** and ***TILTS*** and she was ready to synthesize all the helpful suggestions so no matter which of Vern's paths were taken, the judge could understand this was all a mistake for Lester. But Karen's debriefing was interrupted when Betty butted in.

"For my graduate degree, I became trained on ***FUN***, *Fugue states Uncovered Now*," Betty furthered. "This would be so helpful to Lester because I think the answer lies in understanding fugue states."

Before Betty could finish, Dr. Olson quipped, "Is there a governor of the Fugue State?" Betty was burned and the rest of the staff concurred that jokes at this time of crisis for Lester were not in order. But as typical, Dr. Olson was unfazed.

"No" Betty balanced, "a fugue state is when stressors, psychiatric conditions or neurological tensions accumulate in the brain's neurotransmitters, causing blockage for a short period of time and then the fugue state is a time period when no memory is recorded."

Dr. Olson, never one to give up the fight, bantered at Barbara, who was nodding agreement with Betty, and stated, "That is a very fine dissertation on neuropsychiatry, but what the hell does a fugue state have to do with charges of sexual abuse against Mr. Meddling's poor Lester?" *Good question, Dr. Olson*, some of the Super Staffers thought.

Betty began, "Understanding fugue states will be helpful because if the ***CHAT***, the ***TRIC***, the ***RESCUE***, the ***SIMPLE***, or the ***RIPOFF*** don't reveal sexual abuse in Lester's history, the ***FUN*** will tell us if Lester was traumatized or abused but he has forgotten about it, because he was in a fugue state when it happened. But there is more to it Jerry," she opined, taking pleasure in forgetting to remember he preferred *Dr. Olson*. "Finding out about fugue states would tell us if this is a false memory of the children as well and maybe Lester is innocent. I think this forensic assessment would be the answer to determining if Lester is *guilty* or if he has so many traumas that he is also *innocent*. I haven't gotten my certification in the instrument yet,' she offered helpfully, "but by the time all the other assessments have been administered I think I could be ready for ***FUN***." Betty, being bent to the limit with Dr. Olson's flip comments, waited for retaliation, but none came.

And somewhere between Winona's calligraphy pens, Barbara's lattes, and Dr. Olson's bad jokes, the *Super Staff* solved the situation of Danielle and Lester. For the titty twisting Danielle, the *Super Staffer*s would isolate the child in order to find out what abuse she had suffered in their quest to explain her abuse to the others.

And for Lester, there were two possible solutions. First, maybe there were just too many good things in Lester's current situation to render the accusations from his children making sense. So the *Super Staffers* had the first option of proving the claims of Lester's badness were unfounded because of all the good he had going for him. And the second option was that just like Danielle, the *Super Staffers* wondered if there was something in Lester's history—something bad—to explain his seemingly bad behavior. All the potential mental health problems, found in books, manuals and conferences probably could explain the psychiatric conditions that as Vern so eloquently stated would render Lester (even if a molester) *not really guilty.* But the very best part of all the posturing was that, even if Lester couldn't remember something bad happening, it could be explained in *a fugue state*—which, by the way, has no governor.

Mostly good people, have a hard time thinking anything other than *when people are bad, something bad must have happened,* and in that hope, everyone stops thinking.

THE SEVENTH COMMANDMENT—Thou Shalt Abandon 'Bad Equals Bad'

Vern's *Super Staff* seems to be a reflection of society—generally a good group of folks who believe (and hope) that when people act badly, it is because something bad happened to them. A choke hold on this belief is that a good person could never do bad things. The same tightly held belief in humankind assures that when good things happen—folks will always be good. Unfortunately, parents who rationalize what to teach and what not to teach children, based on those ideas, may find the wheels coming off the sexual respect wagon.

The Seventh Commandment *Thou Shalt Abandon Bad Equals Bad* challenges the safety net of thinking by parents that if everything good happens to the kidlets—if they have the best of all childhoods; and if all bad is avoided—the munchkins will evolve into good people. Not only are Vern's *Super Staffer's* enmeshed in this sacred cow of thinking, but humankind wants it to be true. It is so sweet and so honorable.

But a hop, skip and a peek to the Eighth and Ninth Commandments that spell out the known characteristics of sex offenders, reveals those hopes to be quite hazardous. In fact, believing that avoiding bad and nourishing children in nothing but good, may spell out the keys to becoming a sex offender. But first—the *Thou Shalt Abandon Bad Equals Bad* Commandment and it's contribution to raising sexually respectful children.

ABOUT GOOD AND BAD

Tacky and simplistic terminology about *bad people* doing *bad things* seems disrespectful to human worth and spirit. Using terms such as ***good*** and ***bad*** to describe people is probably about as insensitive as having Henry the bull and his heifers become poster critters for sexual respect. Although those terms seem brash and rude, so is the single-minded thinking of people who tout *bad equals bad.* Sadly, the simplicity of the terms are the rationalization parents use to avoid talking to their children about sexual respect. *No bad sexual things happening—no need to talk to them about bad sexual things* is the mantra. So tacky or not, brash or rude—the terms ***GOOD*** and ***BAD*** are needed to undo that deadly thinking. And that is because the Seventh Commandment is not about doing something, but it is about undoing something—the hazardous hope that *bad begets bad.*

MISGUIDED MYTHS, HONORABLE HOPES, AND SACRED COWS

As the thinking goes, it is a *bad equals bad* mentality that constitutes the hazardous hopes and the misguided myths that support the Lester type conflicts in people's mind. Mostly, good people have a hard time thinking anything other than *when people are bad, something bad must have happened,* and in that hope, everyone stops thinking. Although society in general may not have the tools of ***GITS, TRICS, RIPOFFS, SIMPLE, RESCUE*** and ***FUN*** as the *Super*

Staffers had at their disposal, most folks still search for the badness to explain the badness. It is the sacred cow of society, represented by leaders such as the talk show hosts, defense attorneys, religious leaders, college professors, news commentators or crime writers who do their own, less complicated search for the badness. And sadly, everyone eagerly follows in lockstep even though the sacred cow of that misguided myth may actually be out to pasture.

THE BASIC BUSINESS OF BADNESS

To begin the abandoning of the Seventh Commandment, the sacred cow thinking that no one would become bad unless bad things happened, must be validated which would make Vern with his forensic mind very pleased. The *bad equals bad* principal is unquestionably strong, but more questions also surface regarding the concept of good and evil. Questions abound.

- ✓ Are we born good, and only if something bad happens to us will we become bad?
- ✓ Are we born bad, and only if someone teaches us how to be good will we maintain human goodness and respect?
- ✓ Are we born without either, and becoming bad or becoming good is nothing more than the luck of the draw?

The questions are easy, but the answers are not. At the core of this debate are some of the most sacred and fundamental beliefs known to humans. It is a religious question, a sociological question, a psychological question, and for some, a medical and legal question. The *Super Staffers* were trained professionals in the business of badness—analyzing it, understanding it, explaining it, and most importantly, finding it. But in the normal, everyday business of badness, most folks on the street, in the bowling alley, at the fish food factory, or even watching Little League seem automatically drawn to such conclusions as, "That's sick behavior,"—suggesting that the conduct is abnormal (sick) because normal conduct would be the opposite (not sick). Or, "No one in their right mind would do such a thing," is from the same honorable hopes of good people, who somehow believe that right-minded folks would never be so bad. It is easy to ride on the badness bandwagon, especially when good folks are forced to try and explain the bad folks—way beyond the Danielles and Lesters of the *Super Staff.*

It is easy to ride on the badness bandwagon, especially when good folks are forced to try and explain the bad folks...

WHAT WENT WRONG WITH THE WORST?

The media is a reasonable reflection of society and when the media wails and mourns the loss of goodness as it unveils really good examples of badness, everyone begins to frantically search for answers. And from this media journey to explain atrocities of society's

As Mom and Dad look upon their six-year-old little pooper sleeping in his *Bob the Builder* pajamas, they see nothing that resembles someone such as Jeffrey Dahmer.

most bad—everyone is supported in the thinking that the answer (badness, actually) must be found. Even though the majority of society will trot after the media's search for *what went wrong with the worst*, the target population of the bad folks is hardly representative or valid. And even though Vern prided himself in probabilities, statistics, propensities and such—he and his *Super Staff* were obviously students of national teaching about the *wrong of the worst*.

A FEW BAD MEN

Sexual offenders making the headlines and supporting the *bad equals bad* contention such as Jeffrey Dahmer, Ted Bundy and Westley Alan Dodd only represent a tiny, tiny proportion of those who sexually offend. Yet sadly, folks like Jeff, Ted and Westley will comprise more than 90 percent of the coverage, loudly screaming the absolute truth about how someone becomes a sex offender. Rarely do the headlines flaunt cases where children are sexually abused by someone who comes to Thanksgiving dinner or those situations where the sexual disrespect starts early between children getting frisky in the camping tent. No, those are the boring cases of sexual disrespect and they won't sell many newspapers. But it is the titillations of sexual murderers or raging pedophiles that brings everyone to their knees and the mostly good folks search for answers about the bad folks, giving parents a great permission slip for not talking to their children about sexual disrespect. As Mom and Dad look upon their six-year-old little pooper sleeping in his *Bob the Builder* pajamas, they see nothing that resembles someone such as Jeffrey Dahmer. And they also figure nothing bad is going to happen to their little Bob bumpkin, so there won't ever, ever be a need to worry about him becoming bad.

SACRED COW MILKING

Parents are taught by spiritual leaders, teachers, philosophers, researchers and crime writers to adopt the conclusion that something bad must have happened to the bad folks, which is actually an easy tutorial. The inquiry begins especially in cases such as Jeffrey Dahmer, who did really bad things and represented the desperate search for society to understand. *JEFFREY DAHMER—A Bizarre Journey Into the Mind of America's Most Tormented Serial Killer* provides an excellent example of the misguided myths, honorable hopes, and scared cows of the well-intended attempts to understand his mind-boggling badness. One of the first books regarding this sex killer came onto center stage at the news stands and the attempt to explain the badness was obviously previewed in the title. The author does not use the word *tormenting* on the book cover, which may have been respectful to the dozens of young men tortured, sexually assaulted, and murdered by the book's subject, Jeffrey Dahmer. But the term *tormented* is used to describe the famous killer; hinting there just must have been some badness (some tormenting badness) bugging Jeffrey. The title made it clear, he was *tormented*, not *tormenting*. And the difference was profound and typical.

LISTENING LOUDER

The *tormented* gist of the title seemed to reveal the general thesis of the publication, which was to explain Jeffrey Dahmer's torment that caused him to engage in the uncivilized behavior of drugging, assaulting, murdering, and eating (yes, eating) at least seventeen young men. There seemed no other way to explain how this could happen in a highly civilized society.

And what was the torment? Two tormented things seem to have emerged, at least according to the author; the divorce of Jeffrey's parents, and the fact that he was the firstborn son, bringing a difficult pregnancy to Mom Dahmer. Of course, *Super Staffers* throughout the country would be really busy if those were the two keys to criminality, since every single problem brought into the mental health clinic could be explained by divorcing parents or the kiddos who were first out of the birth chute. But this thinking was comfortable for everyone, suggesting that if nothing bad had happened to Mr. Dahmer, surely he would have developed into an altar boy or at least a Boy Scout.

The desperateness of those interviewing Mr. Dahmer was clear, since his crimes defied logic and so many good folks wanted—no, they *needed*, answers. And Jeffrey obliged. Even though he admitted to the assaults and murders, he wanted a trial, which really delighted the *bad finders*. Expert witnesses filed in from both the prosecution and the defense, debating if it was badness or madness. The defense, not surprisingly, appealed to the good people of the jury, asking the question about whether someone could be sane and commit such terrible deeds. The strategy asked if another human could behave in such a *sick* manner without being *sick*. "This is not sane behavior," became the battle cry (or hope) of the defense.

The strategy asked good people if they believed that another human could behave in such a *sick* manner without being *sick* himself. "This is not sane behavior," became the battle cry (or hope) of the defense.

BADNESS AND MADNESS

The prosecution had another idea and focused on the sanity of the defendant, as evidenced by Mr. Dahmer's ability to lure and manipulate his victims into his apartment, as well as his skill in hiding evidence to avoid detection. They also raised the same sanity flag for Jeffrey about his abilities and competencies—reminding everyone that while he was supposed to be *nuttier than a mashed cat,* he was able to convince legal authorities that he was a compliant parolee, working faithfully at his job and making the Department of Corrections very convinced of his Boy Scout status. Clearly, the prosecution contended, Mr. Dahmer was extremely competent, which spoke to his lack of mental illness. *No insanity here,* cried (or hoped) the punishing types.

Even though the jury eventually agreed with the prosecution, the overall effort of good people trying to understand the badness of Mr. Dahmer was perplexing and interesting. As television cameras from across the country covered the sensational hearing, a desperate society honorably hoped that badness could be explained, perhaps by madness. The madness or the badness of Mr. Dahmer's life was contemplated, studied, argued and postulated, because, of course, for good people, the alternative (that some people are just bad) was just too painful.

BAD FINDING BANDWAGON

After the hearing and after Mr. Dahmer sauntered off to prison, came lightning bolts of "ah-ha's" as authors jumped aboard the bad finding-bandwagon. The divorce of Jeffrey's parents started the list. Never mind that more than half of American children experience the divorce of their parents, the *bad finders,* in their honorable hope, suggested that the divorce of Lionel and Joyce Dahmer *could* have caused him to rape, torture, and murder at least seventeen young, innocent men. Many of the divorce descriptions of Jeffrey's parents were prefaced with such hopeful statements as, "He may have felt..." or, "It is likely he..." since nothing else was there in the history of Jeffrey in the form of really good badness (abuse, torture, brain damage). Without much else in the wagon of the band, the ordinary, divorce issue had to be relied upon. There were more questions than answers, and the divorce issue seemed (however dim) to be the shining light of understanding. What else could it be?

LISTENING IN

One author opined, "The problem for Jeffrey Dahmer was that all during the period up until he was eighteen, he was asked to choose the parent he intended to live with. When he reached eighteen, however, he was considered an emancipated child by the court and was excluded from any court settlements. Therefore, although his brother was provided for, Jeffrey was summarily dropped from consideration by the court, beyond the legal custody of either his father or mother. It was as if he had been officially removed from the family. At age eighteen, he was actually a legal adult and no longer a child. It's not farfetched to say, however, that Jeffrey might well have considered himself a child emotionally, because in his mind, he had been deprived. His brother was provided for, and he wasn't. The whole conclusion to his parents' divorce was quite possibly, for him, an emotional replay of what happened when he perceived that his mother had withdrawn from him during her pregnancy. He was angry then, but there was precious little he could have done about it. For a child who had claimed to have been neglected when he was younger, what happened during this divorce might have been his worst nightmare."

The Dahmer family history provided by the author is less interesting than the desperate effort in bad-finding. "It's not farfetched to say…" or, "Jeffrey might have considered himself a child," were the phrases of the author who, with honorable hopes, took ordinary family events and postulated whether these events might explain Mr. Dahmer's horrific behavior. These speculations were sprinkled throughout most books on the subject by most of the well-intended and honorable (hopeful) bad-finders who just wanted to make sense of the badness. Honorable it was, but right, it was not.

SAY IT AIN'T SO, JOE

The parents of Jeffrey Dahmer were interviewed extensively and they described to the rather disappointed bad-finders, a rather mediocre childhood for Jeffrey. In fact, Jeffrey's father, Lionel Dahmer, wrote his 1994 publication, *A Father's Story* to provide another perspective. The book was clearly a less flamboyant perspective of Jeffrey's childhood than the other bad-finders had portrayed. Different from those who postulated and speculated on the deep trauma Jeffrey experienced in the womb, Lionel Dahmer admitted to a somewhat difficult pregnancy for his wife, but he also described his firstborn son as happy, loved, and a delight to his parents and extended family. The obviously grieving father described different perspectives of the same incidents where the bad finders focused their *maybe* or *likely* opinions about what caused Mr. Dahmer to be filled with such hate that he could not resist the temptation to sexually assault and murder. Lionel Dahmer's perspective of Jeffrey's childhood was rather normal and predictable, making everyone, especially the bad-finders, quite nervous and unfulfilled.

To demonstrate the strength of the bad-finding business, against what was perhaps more reliable testimony from a father who was present during the days of Jeffrey's parents' final divorce arrangements, the same event unfolds differently. An author described Jeffrey living alone in the family home with no money and (God forbid) a refrigerator that was dysfunctional. Because of the perilous situation of an empty house and a not-working fridge, Jeffrey, according to one author, fell into deep depression, obviously (and understandably) building an arsenal of hate that would later navigate him into a campaign of killing. There it was, the building of the badness for bandwagon freight.

Lionel Dahmer, however, described the same situation with a bit less excitement. He indicated in his publication that it was true when the couple divorced that Joyce Dahmer was allowed to live in the family home with Jeffrey and his twelve-year-old brother while Lionel had weekend visitation rights. Although arrangements had been made for a transfer of residence from Joyce to Lionel, there were a few days before the father visited the home and

These speculations were sprinkled throughout most books on the subject by most of the well-intentioned and honorable (hopeful) bad finders who just wanted to make sense of the badness. Honorable it was, but right, it was not.

discovered that his wife and youngest son had departed early and Jeffrey was alone. But this whole *bad-finding trauma* of being alone in the family home for a few days happened when Jeffrey was *eighteen-years-old!*

Apparently, teenage Jeffrey faced the tremendous trauma (according to the bad finders) of being a teenager, alone in his family home, with no adult supervision. The moaning and groaning about abandonment (and the fridge) were profound in the bad finder's books. But Father Dahmer added in his book that when, a few days after the departure of his mother, Jeffrey was discovered, he was far from alone. In fact, Lionel was dismayed to find the house full of teenagers who seemed to be having far too much fun without chaperones. Ice chests replaced the defunct fridge quite nicely—chilling the alcoholic beverages perfectly.

Additionally, the abandonment issues seemed quite pitiful compared to Lionel Dahmer's descriptions of how he and his wife put forth exhaustive efforts to get Jeffrey into jobs, into college, and eventually into the military. But these dedicated efforts on the part of Jeffrey's parents did not fit the business of bad-finding, so they were ignored in most publications under the flag of abandonment. *Deep dish depression* and *deep-seated trauma* seemed more comfortable than perhaps describing a disrespectful and spoiled young man who had no interest in being responsible.

***Deep dish depression* and *deep-seated trauma* seemed more comfortable than perhaps describing a disrespectful and spoiled young man who had no interest in being responsible.**

It was not mentioned in the bad-finding books that Jeffrey's parents paid for college, but that Jeffrey chose not to attend class. The love Jeffrey's grandmother had for him, eventually allowing him to live with her as a young adult, requiring no payment or work obligation, was also ignored. And it was never mentioned that Jeffrey successfully completed three years in the Army, receiving an honorable discharge, and that this success occurred *after* he had already killed twice.

THE RAGING DEBATE

And so the debate rages with honorable intentions, mixed with the business of bad-finding, trying to understand and find an answer to the absolutely unanswerable horror Jeffrey Dahmer inflicted on innocent young men and their families. Perhaps there will always be a debate about who is really right and wrong in these cases and in these publications. But there is no debate about the existence of the debate. And it wasn't just about Jeffrey. Ruthlessly pursued in nearly every murderous sexual offender is a quest from the good people for understanding about why someone could turn out so badly.

ABOUT BEING BAD

Those good folks, who courageously navigate the waters of wisdom, hoping for validation of *bad equals bad*, may have fared better with a different view of the badness. Is it possible that what didn't happen (the focus of the Eighth and Ninth Commandments) in the face of developing badness, that may have caused the problem for Jeffrey? Although ignored by most authors, other than Lionel Dahmer, it seems that Jeffrey was *being bad* very early in life. He seemed to develop a keen interest in torturing animals, which might be explained by the bad finders as simply evidence of the deep-dish trauma he suffered in the womb, or from being forced to use ice chests for his beer in the shadows of the dysfunctional fridge. The pattern of preoccupation with hurting other living things was evidenced early on, regardless of the reason for the pattern. And why wasn't something done? When children are showing signs of badness, it seems easy to discount the pattern—after all, everything good is happening to the child, so bad behavior doesn't often seem important.

TELL US, TED

Just the same as with Jeffrey Dahmer, several books were written about the infamous serial sex killer, Theodore Robert Bundy. Although different viewpoints emerged, the basic search for badness in the history of Ted was generally the same with all the well-intended authors. Crime writer, Ann Rule, had a personal relationship with Ted Bundy, but she admitted that like many others who knew him, she was completely surprised with the unveiling of the real Ted.

"Ted has been described as the perfect son, the perfect student, the Boy Scout who grew to adulthood, a genius, as handsome as a movie idol, a bright light in the future of the Republican Party, a sensitive psychiatric social worker, a budding lawyer, a trusted friend, a young man for whom the future could surely hold only success."

Could this shining star be responsible for the brutal sexual murders of somewhere between twenty and forty young women? was the question many, including his friend Ann Rule, asked.

And then there were others with wisdom about the business of finding the bad in Ted. Authors Stephen G. Michaud and Hugh Aynesworth wrote about Ted Bundy with a personal involvement of a different kind. Ted, while awaiting execution, agreed to exhaustive interviews with the pair —not confessing and describing his crimes, but *speculating* his opinion about the crimes. And in his hypothetical musings, he offered helpful tips about someone else who *probably* committed the murders. Ted and his telling, offered *speculation* about what might have been done in the dormitory, side street, or cold mountain terrain where innocent girls were brutally raped and murdered. For the Ted Bundy case, there were different authors, different perspectives, different exposures, yet a consistent effort of riding the bad-finding bandwagon in search for understanding.

When children are showing signs of badness, it seems easy to discount the pattern—after all, everything good is happening to the child, so bad behavior doesn't seem like a big deal.

For the Ted Bundy case there were different authors, different perspectives, different exposures, yet a consistent effort of riding the bad-finding bandwagon in search for understanding.

"No one noticed that he was different, not like other children. He looked and acted like them. He believed in Santa Claus, hated vegetables, and sometimes imagined ogres and scaly things crouching in his closet waiting for night to fall. But he was haunted by something else: a fear, a doubt—sometimes only a vague uneasiness—that inhabited his mind with the subtlety of a cat. He felt it for years and years, but didn't recognize it for what it was until much later. By then, this flaw, the rip in his psyche, had become the locus of a cold homicidal rage."

TRAGIC TED TELLING

In extensive interviews by the same authors, there was rampant, tragic, *Ted telling.* He reported being a shy boy, embarrassed about his stepfather's *sensible Ramblers*, which Johnny Bundy drove for efficiency. Quite traumatic for Ted, he explained, being embarrassed by his father's other thrifty choices. For the spectators of Ted's *speculations*, he described how upset he was when his mother, who gave birth to him while living with her parents in Philadelphia, decided to relocate to the home of relatives in Tacoma, Washington, lest her son's parentage be questioned.

He described his (four-year-old, actually) impressions of the move to the west, suggesting he considered the sister city of Seattle to be "raw and impermanent to him; just a jumble of ugly brown and gray buildings on a hillside surrounded by water and mountains." Four-year-olds are like that, it could be assumed, since these were direct quotes from Ted as he described his tragic childhood. He made further suggestions to his rapt audience, who later concluded the trouble with Ted: "He would outgrow this initial distaste for his new home, but he never got over an innate, arrogant disdain for anything he regarded as common. This attitude was linked to how he felt about himself, his self-doubt, and also to his later conviction that life had wronged him."

The spectators in Ted's speculations honorably believed in the badness that befell poor Ted, but they also learned other things that were subtle and may have been more pertinent to the real Ted and the focus of the *keys to criminality* outlined in the Eighth and Ninth Commandments. Did Ted really know that as a four-year-old, he resented the move to Washington State, especially the *ugly brown and gray buildings,* which undoubtedly would be the entire focus of any four-year-old? It was true Ted hated mediocrity, he resented the fact that his stepfather drove sensible Ramblers because he wanted brighter and shinier cars, he hated Boy Scouts because of the sweating, and he detested his family's modest lifestyle. But did he really feel that way as a child, or was that a comfortable rationalization for an on-death-row serial murderer trying to rationalize his deeds to bad-finders urgently seeking answers?

The authors learned, but didn't focus upon, that as a child, Ted was a lady charmer, an excellent student, vice president of the Methodist church youth group, a smart dresser and a competent skier. He was an especially smart dresser because he was very competent at shoplifting and burglary in order to get his classy clothes. Ted was careful to point out to his spectators in his speculations, that he never stole to *fence* items for money, but that he had the *honor* of a high-class thief, only heisting what he personally desired to have in his possession. *Yes*, Ted was quite a moralist when it came to discussing some of his bad deeds, and he was really, really good at pointing out bad things that happened to him—conveniently overlooking the bad he was doing as a child.

Ted's interest in skiing showed a different reflection other than a downtrodden boy embarrassed to ride in the family Rambler. *Yes,* Ted really liked the high-class nature of skiing because he was designing, with his friend from the Methodist youth group, a ski forgery pass system. No matter how many competencies about Ted ("Teddy" actually, as he liked to be called when reminiscing about childhood) were discovered, to the bad-finders there had to be some internal problem. It was the *flaw,* they hoped. And when the bad-finders bandwagon stalled, the authors wondered if Ted might not have known the bad that may have happened to him—perhaps calling on the fugue business for rescue.

NATURALLY NICE

It may not be what these sadistic and horrifying criminals such as Jeffrey Dahmer and Ted Bundy relate about their childhood that is most profound, but rather the ruthless search for what happened to them by good folks who aren't so sadistic and horrifying. The search to understand errant human nature has at its foundation, an understanding about normal human nature. In order to embark on the mission of finding out what went wrong, there has to be a belief of what *going right* is all about. Questions as to whether humans are born good and will only become bad if bad things happen opens the door for debate about whether humans are naturally nice, or are they born with only a *potential* to be nice.

Researchers who study the brains of developing children believe there is a connection to certain brain patterns for those people who become extremely violent and inhuman. But what questions are raised about the brain patterns of someone who becomes extremely compassionate and good? Is the same cause and effect true if exceptionally good people are considered for examination? Why weren't the childhood experiences of Mother Teresa extensively perused to discover what event or what experience made her become such a saint—literally? Why isn't it just as interesting to study the brain of a philanthropist who gives millions to humanity as it is to study someone who trespassed into the lives of so many with total

It was the *flaw,* they hoped. And when the bad-finders bandwagon stalled, the authors wondered if Ted might not have known the bad that may have happened to him—perhaps calling on the fugue business for rescue.

Why isn't it just as interesting to study the brain of a philanthropist who gives millions to humanity as it is to study someone who trespassed into the lives of so many with total destruction?

destruction? The answer is two-fold. First, being bad is always more interesting than being good, but secondly, it is assumed that being nice is normal and therefore being *not nice* is abnormal. But sadly, being really, really nice just peters out without much excitement.

GOOD GRANDPA?

When standing at the gravesite of Grandpa, tears blinding family members with the joyous understanding of a positive and tender life now ended, is the niceness of dear, sweet Grandpa accepted as normal or was he off the charts in the nice ratings? Should it be asked, "How did Grandpa learn to be so tender?" Or is it more exciting to ask why Jeffrey Dahmer murdered? Why not search for what significant event happened in Grandpa's childhood to make him love all seven of his children, work unselfishly at the railroad supporting his family, and shed tender tears for an old and smelly family cat who succumbed to death after seventeen years of companionship? What happened to make Grandpa, at age 83, still unequivocally call Grandma "his honey" and have no problem admitting at Thanksgiving dinner that to him, she was still "drop-dead gorgeous?" Is being nice natural and automatic, helping the bad-finders figure that to venture off the goodness path, something had to have gone wrong with the natural flow of niceness? If not, then shouldn't the reason Grandpa was nice be the subject for research providing the keys to raising sexually respectful children?

STUDIES OF THOSE WHO STUDY

Those concerned with protecting children from becoming sexual offenders feverishly look to researchers and professionals for answers. But who looks for possible bias among those folks, which could affect the outcome of their conclusions? Rarely are there studies of the childhood experiences of the bad finders who study badness. And, in fact, there are few government grants or teaching institutes throughout that support the *study of those who study*.

It is automatically believed (or hoped) that someone who has a Ph.D. in psychology, who is a licensed social worker or perhaps a professional counselor, has an objective view in the search for understanding the badness of bad people. But inquiry may be helpful to determine whether evaluators and examiners of bad people are predisposed to a specific mindset about badness. Does this group of professionals have the same contention as society, harboring the honorable hope that bad begets bad?

STUDYING THE STUDIERS

In Las Vegas, Nevada, 1992, approximately 197 professionals attending a conference on Juvenile Sexual Offending answered a survey designed to determine how much child sexual abuse was in their history. Among other questions, this group was asked whether they had been sexually abused in childhood and more importantly, whether they had been involved in criminal conduct *for any reason,* with special questions about sexual crime convictions. It was a reverse of the bad finding—asking good people about the badness in their own histories.

BACKWARD BAD FINDING

This *backward bad-finding* related to the *sacred cow* of belief (or hope) that sexual offenders became antisocial, cruel or criminal because they were offended in childhood. Of course, the ultimate bad-finding discovery for someone who was sexually bad focused on the hopeful conclusion that they had been sexually abused themselves. It was all so tidy—*being abused makes one become abusive.* So a comparison was sought between those folks who may have been sexually offended in childhood, but instead of becoming an offender, embarked on a career in the socially helping field. Therefore, asking professionals attending a sexual abuse conference whether they were victims of abuse and additionally, whether they had committed criminal acts, was at the top of the inquiry clipboard and a huge challenge to the sacred cow of belief that *bad begets bad.*

PONDERING THE PATTERN

And somewhere between the conference high-fiber muffins and fruit plates, the surveys were completed and handed in by the good folks coming to a conference on kiddos who were not doing so *good.* Long after the conference ended and the surveys were tallied, a history of childhood sexual abuse, but an avoidance of sexual criminal conduct, emerged as a clear pattern for the 197 good people. The bean counting revealed curious comparisons, since it seemed that people who were in the helping profession had a significant history of suffering from sexual abuse, but not sexual offending. Bad didn't seem to beget bad, at least for these good folks. And the pattern pondering also suggested that children who were sexually abused in childhood aren't likely to grow up and become sex offenders, but rather therapists, social workers, psychologists and other tenderhearted folks in the helping professions.

Of those professionals surveyed in 1992 in Las Vegas, 62% reported being sexually abused in childhood, while only 7% reported any involvement in the criminal justice system as a child or as an adult. The result was a big *yikes,* throwing rocks at the carved-in-stone mantra of *bad begets bad.* The curious results also inspired a need to repeat the survey and figure out what has gone wrong with the thinking about how folks go wrong.

In Portland, Oregon, (1995); in Honolulu, Hawaii, (1995); in Farmington, Maine, (1996); in Fort Worth, Texas, (1997); and in Atlanta, Georgia, (1998); similar surveys were administered, tallied and pondered, asking good folks in the helping field about bad things happening to them, and whether they had been bad on their own through criminal conduct. The result of surveying nearly 1,000 professionals

And the pattern pondering also suggested that children who were sexually abused in childhood aren't likely to grow up and become sex offenders, but rather therapists, social workers, psychologists and other tenderhearted folks in the helping professions.

...but rarely is there a squeak of consideration that someone on death row might have a bit of motivation for embellishing about the bad things needed to explain their badness. More cows needing sacred pasture, it seems.

over a time span of nearly six years, asking important questions regarding sexual abuse in childhood and sexual criminal conduct, revealed the same story, year after year, city after city, conference after conference. The bad-finding bandwagon's wheels seemed to be coming off.

BEANS AND BADNESS

At percentages ranging from 32 percent to 75 percent, the professional population in attendance at sexual abuse conferences reported being victims of sexual abuse in their childhoods. With lining up the beans and doing some fancy bean counting, it appeared that on the average, slightly more than half the good folks who came to study what to do with the bad folks, had bad things happen to them. But the bean counting also pointed out that less than 9 percent reported any type of involvement with the criminal justice system for any kind of conduct. The conclusion seems to be that abused folks become involved in the helping professions, but abused folks do not necessarily become involved in the criminal justice system.

And some critics or deep dish researchers might claim foul, wondering how a self-report survey could ever be meaningful in the big picture of badness bean counting. But when the bad-finders write the books about folks like Ted and Jeffrey, self-report not only seems to be the gospel and an unquestionable source of reliable information, but rarely is there a squeak of consideration that someone on death row might have motivation for embellishing about the bad things needed to explain their badness. More cows needing sacred pasture, it seems.

THE MEANING OF THE MESSAGE

"So what?" is the response regarding the meaning of the message. What does it matter that professional people were sexually abused in childhood at extremely high rates, but did not become sexual criminals? The answer is the bias. The professional people (usually the bad-finders) who are attempting to provide answers about bad people may not represent a balanced cross section of society, having a much higher rate of childhood abuse than the population at large. Like the *Super Staffers,* this group may be biased in understanding and in eventually influencing society on the important issue concerning the etiology of sexual offending. And it's not a mean-spirited bad-intentioned bias, but a bias nonetheless.

BACKWARD BIAS

Interestingly, if those folks in the helping field have a bias because they were abused in childhood but didn't become sexual offenders, then it would seem their strong conviction to the misguided myths, honorable hopes and sacred cows, is backwards. Bad things happened to them, but they didn't become bad, so it would seem more natural for them to be intolerant of the bad-finders' mission in explaining the badness of criminals.

But that doesn't seem to be the situation and the puzzlement can only be explained as testimony of the ingrained and hardwired belief (hope) that *bad begets bad*, especially in the childhood department. And this backward bias, however sweet, should be part of the arsenal in helping parents understand that if they have trouble objecting to the natural and easy *bad begets bad* ideology, they are not alone. Even really good folks in the helping field, who had really bad things happen to them, have the *buy-in* to the belief. And that means using the Seventh Commandment to undo that thinking isn't always an easy way to put the cows in the proper pasture.

WHAT WENT WRONG WITH WESTLEY

Westley was frustrated. Sadly for him, when he accosted the Neer brothers in the public park, he was distracted with fear of detection, unfairly cheating him from enjoying the molesting, stabbing, and murdering of the innocent young boys. With scientific detachment, he noted in his journal, not only his annoyance with the hurried atmosphere of murdering two young boys in a public place, but jotting down a sincere promise to do better next time. And he did.

Next time came with Lee Joseph Isili. With the four-year-old, there was ample opportunity to follow through on his scientific promise, since the child was abducted and taken to Westley's apartment for uninterrupted sexual assault and torture. But, like many scientific experiments, things were less-than-perfect, forcing Westley into further irritation. With meticulous notes, long after Lee's torture and death, he complained that because he had resorted to manual strangulation of the child (which, according to his notes was clumsy and cumbersome), the result was a certain level of distraction from his keen interest in the careful process of molesting and murdering an innocent child. *Next time*, Westley wrote, he would use duct tape on the child's mouth, allowing strangulation to occur by simply pinching the victim's nose with a clothespin, cutting off the air supply *and* giving Westley full benefit of observing the slow and intermittent strangulation. *Why*, to Westley, it would be the Wal-Mart of torture and sexual assault—easy access, easy process, low price, and no hassle. *Such satisfaction and such hope for next time,* Westley's journals promised.

It was all set. Success should have been assured. But with the combination of an alert stepfather and a non-firing Pinto piston, Westley's plans to kidnap his next victim were foiled. After abducting Steve Hall from a movie theatre restroom, Westley experienced an unplanned mechanical failure of his aging auto. While bent over the hood to examine the engine, Steve Hall's stepfather distracted Westley with feigned assistance, and authorities were called. Westley was apprehended; Steve Hall was rescued.

With scientific detachment, he noted in his journal, not only his annoyance with the hurried atmosphere of murdering two young boys in a public place, but jotting down a sincere promise to do better next time. And he did.

***What went wrong with Westley*, many pondered, especially the bad finders who were ready to charge into action.**

Appearing unfazed, Westley Alan Dodd not only admitted to sexually assaulting and murdering three little boys in 1989, but as Washington State investigators probed further, Westley cooperated. His journals, scrapbooks, and photos, capturing his treasured moments of his horrendous crimes, were shared with the same detachment he had when murdering innocent children. Westley not only admitted to his crimes, but he resisted typical rationalizations, blaming, and denial so desperately needed by good people who examined his bad crimes. *What went wrong with Westley*, many pondered, especially the bad finders who were ready to charge into action.

Never really asking if something really did go wrong and wanting no part in considering that Westley was just a bad apple, the bad-finding band wagon fired it's engine. The search was on and as time went on, Westley didn't seem to give the psychologists, prosecutors, investigators, historians, and criminologists the proverbial pot of gold (answer) that seemed so easily swooned by the Ted types.

Although Westley seemed cooperative and helpful, he really wasn't. They wanted the bad to be found and Westley just didn't come through. Just like Winona and Vern's *Super Staff*, the bad finders were sure there was an answer to Westley's badness, and they weren't about to accept his description of a rather boring, uneventful childhood. After all, what did he know about a childhood gone badly and what did he really (they hoped) know about his own childhood? And then some remembered the ace in the hole. If nothing else worked, maybe Westley was in one of the fugue states without governors when all the badness happened?

BUSY BAD FINDING

After digging and digging for *what went wrong with Westley*, some things emerged on the bad-finding horizon. Just like with Jeffrey and Ted, the bad finders got busy and discovered that in 1973, at age nine, Westley and some of his same-age friends examined and touched each other's penises. It wasn't much, but it was something. And with the same milk-toast enthusiasm, they learned that during the next year, a female child and Westley examined the differences in their bodies. No arrests were made, which was disappointing for those with bandwagon tickets, and the minor incident was only revealed after a long bout of suggesting things to Westley in the bad-finding sessions. But again, it was something, perhaps. Also, when Westley was really, really pressed by the hopeful studiers and searchers, he finally admitted that his sister looked (yes, looked) at his penis on one occasion. She didn't touch, but she looked, Westley clarified to the disappointed *What Went Wrong With Westley* group.

One member of the Wx5 studiers concluded an "*Ah-ha*" to the mediocre childhood tragedies by suggesting that these appearing-to-be-harmless events were not, actually innocent. He went on to postulate that to Westley, having his sister take a quick peek at his penis probably contributed to why he would have an uncontrollable, lustful need to rape and murder little boys. The connection just had to be there, the bad-finder opined.

And there was more, the good doctor thought. During the years of age ten through fourteen, Westley had five or six lustful peeks at National Geographic magazines, which just might explain everything, some of the bad finders hoped. It was weak, but it was hopeful. And even though Westley (obviously a good historian) described reasonably normal sexual-acting-out in childhood, the naysayers refused to budge. *Fugue states* were never really suggested by the Wx5 group, but clearly, the *Fugue Folks'* position tiptoed ever so slightly around the hopes of an answer to Westley's badness.

TWO THINGS

The Westley Alan Dodd case emphasized two major points in trying to understand the badness dynamic and its relation to raising sexually respectful children. First, although less exciting, the few bad men of Ted, Jeffrey and Westley were *acting out* badness very early on, but that wasn't as exciting for the bad finders as the contemplations of the badness that happened to the bad guys. And Westley Alan Dodd is a good example of this switch in the bad business.

BAD IN REVERSE

There is no doubt that beginning at age fifteen, Westley was doing bad things, just like Jeffrey and Ted. His first attempted sexual offense of an eight-year-old was serious enough to result in criminal charges, but he was later acquitted. At age fifteen, therefore, Westley learned the criminal justice system was clumsy and vulnerable, which may have meant he learned badness just might slip by authorities if cleverness was adopted. He probably also learned that with cunning, his badness would be overlooked. And for sure, Westley continued his badness.

At age fifteen, therefore, Westley learned the criminal justice system was clumsy and vulnerable, which may have meant that at that age, he learned badness just might slip by authorities if cleverness was adopted.

Soon after his acquittal, Westley found it interesting to expose himself to young children, either in the front window of his home or by riding his bicycle through streets or areas where vulnerable kiddos congregated. It was there in the history but it was overlooked. As an older teenager, Westley was prone to grabbing girls, trying to get them to reciprocate genital touching, and making advances on younger and innocent children. Yes, Westley was bad all right, as he was a groper, a grabber, and a molester early on. The irony may have been that Westley's parents probably disregarded the bad behavior because they believed in the sacred cow, that if nothing bad was happening to him, he would remain (operative word *remain*) good.

LOOKING AT THE OVERLOOKING

Even though Westley was reporting to the bad-finders that he was *being bad* in childhood, they just weren't happy. He admitted that by age fifteen he was seriously offending, yet he still reported he "had no sex education." Perhaps Westley had a Nurse Ratchet with podiums in mind when he gave the answer. Yet in reality, with all his offending it seemed he had plenty of sex education—however deviant.

But there was more overlooking in the deep-dish therapy department. Throughout his childhood, Westley was discovered, investigated, and even given therapy for sexual misconduct, by many professionals who were a bit shy about the TV cameras in the *what went wrong with Westley* campaign that awakened the state of Washington with Westley's capture. *Yes*, many good therapy folks *cured* him several times, obviously without much luck, which should also have been considered a *red flag* by many. But after everything was discovered, the bad finders didn't want to consider the chances upon chances that Westley had to get better and stop his bad behavior. Just like with Jeffrey and Ted, the finding was selective, overlooking those factors that might suggest challenges to the sacred cow and honorable hope of *bad begets bad*.

NUMBER TWO

The second lesson Westley Alan Dodd teaches about the bad-finders or the *Super Staffer's* search for understanding bad folks, has to do with the reliability of the data. When the bad finders asked Westley about his understanding of *what went wrong*, Westley was happy to oblige, just like Jeffrey and Ted. Ted Bundy never really admitted to his crimes and in fact, he made the state of Florida *prove* his guilt in the murder of Lisa Levy and Margaret Bowman (two Chi Omega sorority sisters at Florida State University), as well as seventh grader, Kimberly Diane Leach. In spite of overwhelming evidence for the innocent females who were all raped, mutilated, and bludgeoned to death, Ted still wanted an audience. And, when it was all over and Ted was awaiting the death penalty, he had yet another audience—a mourning nation, waiting with baited breath to understand. And the lined-up bad finders hoped to oblige. With all the anxiety and apprehension to make sense of the senseless, everything Ted fed the folks was accepted as gospel without a shred of question concerning his veracity.

Even though Ted had the ability to escape from two incarceration situations, was able to sneak around in the states of Washington, Utah, Colorado, and Florida, undetected by authorities, was able to lie and cheat his way into coveted positions in the crisis hot line for victims of sexual assault, he was still considered to have the veracity of Mother Teresa when he described his childhood and gave answers to the eager bad-finders. Everyone knew Ted was a liar, a cheat and a con. But in spite of all that, when he gave the answers folks wanted, nary a single Bible was brought forth for truth swearing and his story was never really challenged.

BACK TO WESTLEY BUTS

Like *Teddy*, Westley reported his childhood history with few questions about his truthfulness or motive to give a slanted story. He said his parents (just like Jeffrey) had a divorce situation that made him cranky. Good enough, said the bad-finders. Upon further questioning, he also said he was double cranky about the birth of his younger brother and sister, allowing the bad finders to do deep-dish contemplations that these feelings of ill just probably provided the root to becoming a murderer and sexual sadist of young, innocent children. But two *buts* emerge, with the siblings of Westley providing the first *but*. The other Dodd kiddos claimed to the-trying-not-to-listen bad finders that Westley's conclusions about a deprived childhood were just not true. They took collective issue with Westley's claim of badness. He was cranky all right, they opined, but that was his choice and none of them were deprived or abused. And the second *but* in Westley's campaign to explain his badness should have occurred, but never seemed to materialize.

If Ted Bundy was on Death Row, if Jeffrey was awaiting life in prison (housed with not-so-friendly folks who frown on murdering young men), and if Westley Alan Dodd was waiting and wondering about his precarious future with the state of Washington, should there be questions or *buts* about the motive for these criminals to help bad finders *find* the badness? Why would Westley and Ted and Jeffrey be believed or considered reliable in consideration of their situations? Who would be better believed, a criminal who needs to explain his badness, or siblings, parents or others involved in their childhoods who may have no motivation to make claims of childhood abuse?

And with everything sorted and fussed about, the bottom line is that it just feels better to believe that someone wouldn't become bad unless something bad happened to them and that is why so many parents adopt the same feel-good position. The result of this acceptance also puts the proverbial damper on that pesky task of overtly teaching sexual respect, because if nothing disrespectful is happening between T-ball practices and swimming lessons, then everything will be fine.

DANIELLE, DENNIS AND LESTER

Whether considering the *Super Staffers* or choosing a gymnastic coach, another issue relating the strength of the *bad- begets-bad* hope pertains to the pride good folks have in knowing about the bad folks. People want to believe they have the ability to know who is bad—because it

Everyone knew Ted was a liar, a cheat and a con. But in spite of all that, when he gave the answers folks wanted, nary a single Bible was brought forth for truth swearing and he was never challenged.

And with everything sorted and fussed about, the bottom line is that it just feels better to believe that someone wouldn't become bad unless something bad happened to them and that is why so many parents adopt the same feel-good position.

makes them feel smart AND safe. Tremendous vulnerability comes with not being aware of bad business. And this happens in everyday life, not just for the authors of books about really bad people.

Moms often convince their kiddos that they have the ability to know when the little ones aren't telling the truth and some ladies even go so far as to claim X-ray vision just so the kidlets think Mom actually knows everything they do. Partners often take pride in believing they would know if their wife had an affair or if hubby spent way too much money gambling. When the *Super Staffers* were faced with Danielle, they did the traditional bad finding business just as was done with Jeffrey, Ted and Westley. *Find the bad to explain the bad* was the approach and for sure they didn't want to feel fooled about missing the signs in Titty Twisting precursors.

But things got a little messier with Lester when he was accused of being bad and when his lawyer was asking the *Super Staffers* to examine all the good, to prove Lester wasn't—bad, that is. People have pride in believing that they know who is good and who is bad, so the *Super Staffers* got fired up to help Lester. They lined up lots of fancy tests and processes, but the bottom line was that none of them thought Lester was a bad person and they wanted no part of being fooled. And so it was with Dennis.

BTK BADNESS

Wichita, Kansas is considered the all-American city and when horrific killings began in the late 1970's the good folks were stunned about the bad business going on. Families were bound, tortured, some sexually assaulted and all murdered. But that wasn't all. This killer toyed with police, sending notes and taking pride in his status as a single-handed tormentor of an all-American and all-terrified city. Everyone was baffled and the tallying began. Over shopping carts in the grocery stores or over burgers on the barbecue, everyone speculated who it could be—this killer who proudly called himself BTK, standing for bind, torture and kill. It was awful and it went on—both the killing and the speculating. Everyone had an idea of who this monster was and who he wasn't.

But then in 2005, Mr. Dennis Rader was brought to the attention of authorities. It seemed that new technology brought new suspicions about a highly unlikely fellow. More shocking than the crimes he committed was who he really was and his identity was especially hard on those around him who, for decades, had done their own bad finding and *good calculations* with no one pointing the finger at Mr. D. He was in the Air Force in Vietnam, eventually receiving an honorable discharge. He was happily married to a wonderful sweet woman, as well as having two terrific kiddos of his own. He was a security expert with ADT Company, actually helping people install equipment in their homes for protection against the BTK killer. He had a degree in criminal justice at a Kansas college, he attended church regularly, and he was a Cub Scout leader. Nothing computed.

GAUGING GOOD

As the evidence piled up against Mr. Rader, many good folks had a pile of embarrassment and dismay about their good-gauging in order to separate the good from the bad. Most Wichita folks had used the good-gauge to weed out suspicion of who might have been the BTK killer. And of course, Dennis Rader had too many good things going for him to ever be considered to be the bad one. And perhaps this good-gauge—this thinking that as long as someone does really good things, they could never be guilty of really bad things—is another spin on the *bad equals bad* thinking. It is another example of the honorable hope, the misguided myth, and the sacred cow of thinking that is not helpful for parents who wish to raise sexually respectful children.

HISTORICAL HISTORIES

In the early years of understanding and treating sexual offending, professional protocol required sex offenders to report their histories—not necessarily to authors or criminologists, but to those in charge of managing and treating them. The results were staggering, but not unpredictable and most importantly, not unwelcome, in the 70's, 80's, and 90's. These were the decades of bad-finding at its finest and the sex offender histories only furthered the cause.

When reports were taken, sex offenders reported extremely high rates of childhood sexual abuse in their histories, some programs suggesting as high as 95-100% of them were sexually abused as little poopers. From Oprah to Donohue to Jenny Jones, the question was asked, the statements were made, and the comfortable conclusions lined up. Some didn't even take the first step of inquiry and ask ***if*** childhood sexual abuse occurred, instead asking, "What type of abuse? How long did it happen? And what kind of trauma have you suffered?" Few thoughts were ever given to the idea that perhaps no abuse existed. And in some cases, for those offenders who seemed confused about their history of sexual abuse, hypnosis was suggested, or amnesia solutions were brought in for the rescue. And yes, fugue state rationalizations were waiting in the wings.

HELP US HARRY

Question: "Harry, why did you sexually abuse your three-year-old daughter?"

Answer: "Her Strawberry Shortcake pajamas drove me wild. What's a man to do?"

Question: "Harry, were you sexually abused in childhood?"

Answer: "Yes."

It is another example of the honorable hope, the misguided myth, and the sacred cow of thinking that is not helpful for parents who wish to raise sexually respectful children.

Yet when he is asked about his own childhood sexual abuse, he is given a get-out-jail-free card with no consideration that he might be lying.

Those working in the field of sexual offending found this type of questioning tidy since everything fit nicely into previous beliefs about how someone could become bad. Harry's response to the first question about why he offended was considered predictable. Blaming the Strawberry Shortcake pajamas as the reason for deviancy was expected, and although most fathers would find the explanation absurd, the professional community (in spite of the fact that many of them were dads) found Harry's answer conventional. They figured that if Harry thought differently, he probably wouldn't have offended his daughter and for sure, he wouldn't need treatment. But what about the second question concerning Harry's childhood sexual abuse and what about how the two questions are handled differently?

One answer from Harry is viewed as ridiculous but expected (*Strawberry Shortcake Arousal Out of Control*), and yet he is given absolute acceptance of his veracity (truthfulness) in the other question about his childhood sexual abuse. In other words, Harry is expected to provide a dishonest and irresponsible answer to explain why he offended his daughter, yet when he is asked about his own childhood sexual abuse, he is given a get-out-of-jail-free card with no consideration that he might be lying.

HARRY WAS HEARD

But then things began to change—at least for some. In 1983, a rural Eastern Oregon program had some suspicious folks who had lost their seat on the bad-finding bandwagon. The obvious predicament in Harry's interview of believing him in one answer and accepting his dishonesty in another answer made these folks itch. And so the program began to use polygraph examinations (lie detectors) to verify the sexual history provided by offenders. In 1988, the study compared sexual histories of offenders with verified sexual histories to offenders in the same rural area who were allowed to make self-reports about their past history with no verification or test of accuracy. And thus, a significant first challenge to the scared cow about why some people do bad things.

WHOOPS AND WAILING

The research was not conducted with the influence of a large universities statistics department but to check to make sure everything was as it seemed in a program of sex offenders. Later, it was published as an afterthought, but soon the word was out and it wasn't pretty. The overall message was that things might not be so tidy and sweet in the bad finding business since a big *whoops* caused a lot of wailing. There was a huge difference in what sex offenders shared in the tearful interviews about their childhoods and what they shared with a lie detector test checking things out. In fact, it appeared these folks were lying in the self-report interviews—wailing loudly about the bad things that had happened to them and discounting any bad things they might have done as kidlets. *No,* they weren't juvenile sex offenders (about 30 percent) but *yes*, they were victims of sexual abuse (about 70 percent), they tearfully explained in self-report interviews. But when the lie detector or polygraph became part of the program in the next five years, those numbers basically reversed, suggesting *yes,* just like Westley, Ted and Jeffrey, they were being bad in childhood and *no*, nothing much bad happened to them. And this was for sure taking those sacred cows out of their pristine pasture—upsetting everything in the peacefulness of *bad begets bad.*

HAIL HATE MAIL

But the results of the *accidental research* was not as interesting as the significant volume of *hate mail* directed at the overall notion that the sacred cow of *bad-equals-bad* was challenged and attacked. Volumes of grumpy critiques poured in with the superficial focus of scorn (after a few delightful hysterics) relating to how the polygraphs were administered, whether the polygraphs were ethical and, of course, when the *60 Minutes* television show would arrive at the office front door. Fussing and fuming was the response to the hazardous hopes that no one would really become bad unless something bad happened. And many questioned where the fugue state literature was when everyone so desperately needed it.

And this was for sure taking those sacred cows out of their pristine pasture—upsetting everything in the peacefulness of *bad begets bad.*

BALANCING THE BADNESS

Not only did the research (however accidental) throw the bad finders into being out of balance in 1988, but it kept going. The hate mail from bad-finder faithfuls encouraged more study and in 1994, and again in 2001, more offenders, more polygraphs, and more Harrys were counted and calculated. Junior Harrys were also included in the new data. The charts and graphs were perhaps more sophisticated in the next study, the sample was a bit more varied, and the slides for presentations at national conferences looked snappier. But all in all, the results were just about the same. When held to accountability of a polygraph examination, sex offenders report that they were offending (the badness) in childhood, and that they were not sexually abused in childhood any more than the population at large.

BLAMING AND ABANDONING BAD BUSINESS

Challenging the tradition of *bad-equals-bad* sacred cows is difficult and sometimes rocks are thrown because something comfortable is taken away with the thought. Blame only sidesteps the responsibility, and besides, it is difficult to know where blame really lies in the bad finding

When held to accountability of a polygraph examination, sex offenders report that they were offending (the badness) in childhood, and that they were not sexually abused in childhood any more than the population at large.

business. Is it with sex offenders who, like Harry, lie about their histories? It didn't seem to take a rocket scientist to conclude that Harry and Harry proxies knew how badly the bad finders wanted them to reflect the badness of their childhood. Just as the authors of books about bad people desperately search for *what went wrong*, normal *Harry-type* sex offenders know how desperately it is hoped they will answer "yes" to the simple question of whether they were sexually abused in childhood. These same everyday sex offenders watch the talk shows, they read the books written by the bad-finders, and they know what is expected. And they deliver. So maybe it's not the sex offenders to blame but the people who buy into the myth and encourage sex offenders to give certain answers.

Maybe the blame is in the bad finders themselves, who just want to sell books or find themselves on talk shows. Maybe it is the court expert witnesses who want to make the big bucks in testifying about the *bad equals bad* scenarios so they can pay for their hot tubs. Maybe the blame should be given to the professionals who bring their own bias to the field because of their own abuse. But all the blame rocks in the world thrown in frustration will only postpone the inevitable issue that sexually disrespectful people don't always do bad things because something bad happened to them and for parents, giving up the blame and accepting responsibility for sexual respect is the only way to go.

Sex Fairy Clipboard

- Different than other commandments, the Seventh Commandment of abandoning *bad equals bad* is an attitude adjustment process. Beginning with the sacred cow of belief, stop believing and hoping that if the little poopers have everything good happen to them, everything will turn out okay. Give it up and put that sacred cow in the pasture of the Eighth and Ninth Commandments concerning the true keys to becoming sexually respectful.

- Do not accept the misguided myth that being nice is automatic, because in this world of take-what-you-can-get mentality, being *not nice* may be the more natural outcome. Accept the cold reality that growing up in this kind of world to become a taker, a user, a manipulator or any other category of selfish person may be easy. And with that in mind, get very busy in actively teaching NICE.

- Remember that people who do bad things may have begun those behaviors in childhood rather than suffer from abuse in childhood. But also remember that some people really do reenact childhood trauma in abusive ways. So always maintain a spirit of dignity for each person on an individual basis—throwing out contentions that there is one answer for why things can go wrong.

- Remember the lessons of many hardened criminals in the overlooking categories. Many of them were acting badly as children and, sadly, no one paid attention.

- When questions are raised about abuse to children, always remember the power of resiliency. Humans can endure many things and remain good. Remember, there are hundreds and thousands of people who endure horrific abuse, and yet remain tenderhearted and good. Always honor that hope in humankind and avoid the self-fulfilling prophecy that suggests everyone who is abused will become an abuser.

Sex Fairy Clipboard

- Always remember that responsibility for actions is the key to respectful behavior. Challenge excuses provided by anyone about bad behavior, but also remember that abuse of children can contribute to causality.
- And finally, collect the first six commandments and give up the myth of the Seventh Commandment that children will automatically be good if nothing happens to them. And then, with the ammunition and skills of the other commandments move into the Eighth and Ninth Commandments of what really happens to create a sexually disrespectful person.

Chapter 11

Eighth Commandment Thou Shalt Demand Delayed Gratification

CHAPTER 11: EIGHTH COMMANDMENT— THOU SHALT DEMAND DELAYED GRATIFICATION

The airplane is full. Stuffy. Weary warriors of travel are approaching the last stages of shuffling lattes and luggage into place. The early afternoon air outside is clear and crisp, while inside an emphysema nightmare is nurtured. Many finding their way to assigned seats sport a look of dread, considering the number of children on board. Although most passengers trudge past the munchkins and make attempts at pleasantries, all of them harbor secret trepidation about the potential screamers, as well as hopes for finding their seats far away from the little people.

Oddly, the mother sits in the middle. She is large and would obviously fare better in the roomier aisle seat which strangely, she relinquishes to her perhaps, eight-year-old son. The seat selection of the mother is even more puzzling since not only is the roomy aisle seat given to the seemingly second grader, but in the cramped quarters of the middle seat, the mother holds a toddler. But then it happens and her purpose unfolds.

The airplane begins to move and the engine growls in direct proportion to the toddler's developing terror. And just at the precise moment when bellowing from the two-year-old seems imminent, Middle-Seat-Mom expertly moves into action, distracts the tot and deposits the little one on the bigger one's lap. The toddler's terror toward the engine howling is easily forgotten as the new surroundings on brother's lap are curiously considered. But with the seating change, terror engulfs a watchful group of high-level executives across the aisle, clutching briefcases and lukewarm lattes, as they contemplate the dreaded screaming. The situation of *a child tending a child* shatters any hope for a peaceful flight, or so they think.

As the airplane taxis, Middle-Seat-Mom does not reclaim the toddler, even though the engine racket and the taxi process of the plane is frightening. Wide eyes and a quivering bottom lip tell Middle-Seat-Mom that her game plan needs altering or the little one will provide the across-the-aisle business folks what they most fear. First, drawing the tot's attention to her hand, she makes a two-finger walking parade, beginning at the toe of toddler, expertly walking up the leg, onto the tummy, out the extended arm, and finally into her rather unstylish coat pocket where her two fingers momentarily hide. The little one beams with recognition that this game has been played before and with keen anticipation, watches for the escape of whatever Mom is hiding. The anticipation can be smelled in the air, regardless of the roaring of the ready-for-takeoff airplane.

Just about the time it seems that the toddler might be wavering on whether Mom's pocket treasure is more exciting than the screaming engines, Middle-Seat-Mom claims from her pocket, a single Cheerio, perching it in the air with flare and triumph. Oh, the excitement seemed grand. If the toddler had a tail, it would surely wag with gleeful anticipation at the Cheerio. But not yet—that is clear from the calm and confident Mom holding the priced morsel.

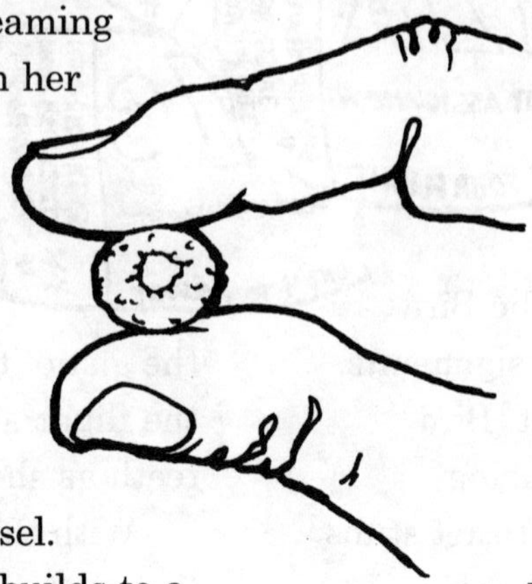

As the frightening takeoff process builds to a crescendo, the pilot attempts to reassure passengers with scratchy announcements on the loud speaker that no one can really decipher. In spite of all the noise and ruckus, the single Cheerio remains perfectly perched, matching the gaze and anticipation of the toddler with an *on-looking* attention from the eight-year-old caretaker, still in the coveted aisle seat.

"We are ready for takeoff. Flight attendants prepare the cabin," roars the captain from the cockpit. The sound of the engine is deafening as the plane approaches shattering, lifting itself into the air. But in spite of the racket, the lone Cheerio remains poised in position by Middle-Seat-Mom, solid as the left-behind tarmac of the runway. And just as the rattling is at its worst, and just when the toddler looks closest to screaming, the Cheerio at last begins to move.

The swelling of excitement among the family of three over this culinary contribution of a single Cheerio (no bigger, by the way, than the hearing aid of Grandpa Guy in the window seat next to Middle-Seat-Mom) is equal to the anticipation of most American Thanksgiving dinners (at least for the toddler). As the apex of anticipation is reached, Middle-Seat-Mom does not make the final deposit of the culinary treat, but with the toddler thrilled and with mouth wide open, Middle-Seat-Mom diverts her descent by plopping the Cheerio—not into the mouth of the little one, but into the fingers of the eight-year-old, who delights in making the final drop off into the toddler's grateful and grinning mouth. Smiles and contented sighs abound between the three of them. That tiny, long awaited Cheerio brings complete family fulfillment to the brood of Middle-Seat-Mom with such anticipation and such build-up for such a tiny, but valuable sense of satisfaction. Oh, it was grand! But not all was as peaceful on this 97 minute flight to Anywhere, USA.

The Bird Babies are on the other side of the airplane from the contented scene of Middle-Seat-Mom and her now-satisfied kiddos. In the boarding process, Bird Mom herded her flock of Bird Babies (one appearing age three and one perhaps, age five) onto the airplane as she navigated her bird supplies, which was no small task. Her Bird provisions included taking full advantage of the allotted two carry-ons for each passenger, which meant Bird Mom had six luggage items to maneuver into position. That task might not have been so difficult had the Bird Babies cooperated with the seating assignments. Always looking for a teaching moment, Bird Mom wanted the kiddos to try recognizing numbers and letters by reading their ticket stubs to understand who was designated for the coveted window seat. She had it all planned ahead of time, but with the rush of juggling the carry-ons, and with temper tantrums from both Bird Babies about who got to sit next to Mom and who got to look out the window, the ticket stubs were lost somewhere between the Scooby Doo backpack and the Barbie Doll staircase, which had been already removed without authorization from Bird Mom.

Arranging the bird provisions for the flight had also been difficult for Bird Mom, since the fancy flight attendant made it clear that the Bird Babies must put at least half of their carry-ons in the overhead bins. *Yes,* she confirmed they could have some of the Bird Backpacks underneath the seat in front of them, but they really needed to be *under* the seats and not open on the floor, as the debacle with the now-broken Barbie Doll staircase demonstrated. She was firm on that.

But the trouble started when the Bird Babies figured out right away that some of their backpacks in the overhead bins would be inaccessible to them during takeoff and that caused very loud protestations. *How could they possibly manage?* was the gist of their hysterical AND loud fussing to the flight attendant, who had notably clenched teeth as she tried to explain the takeoff rules.

With the Bird Babies squawking, the fancy flight attendant tried to be helpful by explaining that once the airplane was high, high in the air, Bird Mom could retrieve whatever they wanted from the overhead bins. But that did nothing to persuade the Bird Babies in their agony about what would happen if, in the takeoff process, they really, really needed something in the secreted away bags. Bird Mom tried to do her "everyone has to make choices" speech she had learned on a parenting talk show, but the Bird Babies were screaming so loud they didn't hear the *choices are our friend* singsong. In desperation, and with passengers around them clearly annoyed, Bird Mom tried distraction with the now-available-

and-underneath-the-seat-in-front bird supplies.

Knowing her kiddos always appreciated lots and lots of choices as the singsong suggested, Bird Mom decided to display their takeoff options of snacks and toys. Just as Middle-Seat-Mom got the attention of the toddler with a single Cheerio, Bird Mom got the attention of her kiddos as she flaunted her carefully packed Bird Provisions. With grand fanfare she exhibited a full Tupperware tub of Cheerios (no single stuff for her Bird Babies), but also accompanying (and of course, carefully labeled) were tiny zip-lock bags of Fruit Loops, Crispy Critters, Rice Krispies, Cocoa Puffs and Apple Jacks. Yes, five cereals. Bird Mom also proudly displayed for the choosy Bird Babies, Snack & Quack Crackers, Juicy Fruit Rolls, miniature Baby Ruths, ham roll-ups, Juice-In-A-Box (several boxes), Lip Smacker Lemonade and, of course, what appeared to be five quarts of designer drinking water, divided into miniature and quite cute, six-ounce bottles.

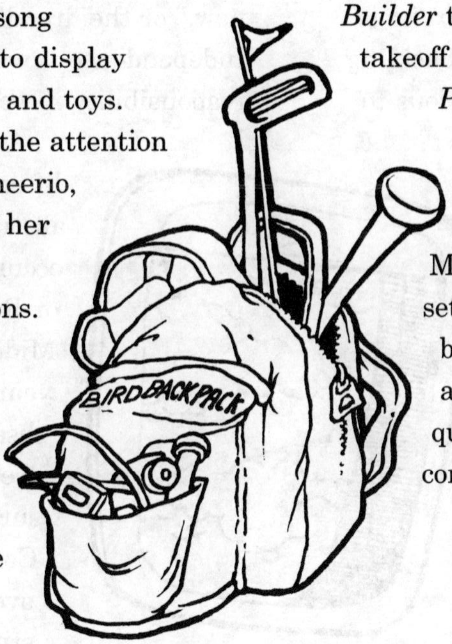

But Bird Mom had only begun to impress the Bird Babies with their choices for takeoff stimulation as she unloaded non-edible items for Bird maintenance. From the underneath and in-front-of-them carry-on luggage came *Power Rangers*, an *Etch-A-Sketch, Ken and Barbie dolls, Magic Markers* (both pastel and primary colors), *SpongeBob* coloring books, *Bob the Builder* tool kit, and of course, what airplane takeoff process would be complete without a *Polly Pockets Rock Band Stage?*

Before Middle-Seat-Mom has even contemplated reaching in her pocket for a single Cheerio during takeoff, Bird Mom supplied the Bird Babies with one set-out-to-be-shared *Pop Tart*, one-half of a banana, one eventually spilled box of apple juice, one zip bag of Doritos, one quarter of an apple, AND she settled the controversy over why there are not 2 (two) separate zip-lock bags of granola (the agony of forced sharing) by promising ice cream from TCYB upon landing at the airport. The Bird Babies begrudgingly accepted the peace offering.

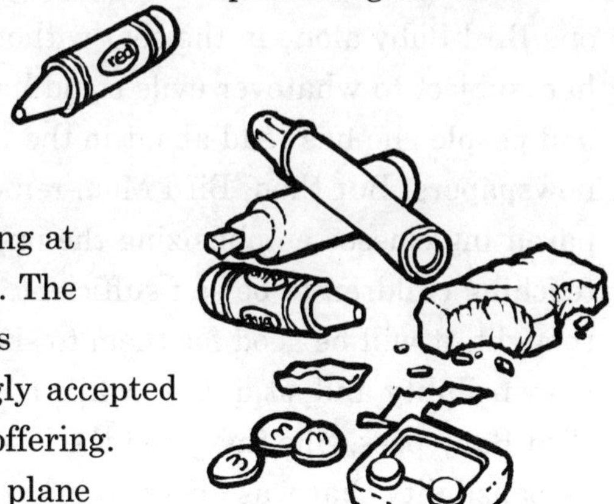

And as the plane engine shattered the sound, the Bird Babies weren't interested in being frightened—only making sure Bird Mom could hear their request for a desperately-needed-at-that-precise-minute item for takeoff.

As the pilot tells everyone that the *cruising altitude* has been reached and as the perky flight attendant announces that the *in-flight service* is about to begin, the sound of seat belt unbuckling from other passengers becomes quite curious to the Bird Babies. Of course, seeing others released from the bonds of seat belt confinement results in both of them loudly claiming uncontrollable urges to urinate. *Yes*, they desperately need to use the restroom, they whine to Bird Mom, and *yes,* they want Bird Mom to take them *"all by myself"*—meaning Bird Mom must make separate trips for each Bird Baby.

At first, she worries about leaving one Bird Baby alone in the seat without her, subject to whatever evils could happen from bad people she has read about in the newspapers. But then, Bird Mom remembers the parenting classes emphasizing the importance of teaching children to be self-sufficient. Sure, she thought, it will be good for them to show responsibility and sit quietly while the other Bird Baby pees. She imagined the lessons in responsibility that was about to infiltrate her little poopers with the independence process. As she left one child and took the other to pee, she imagined a wonderful teaching moment, while all the other passengers saw each abandoned Bird Baby have total *independence* in rifling through the Bird provisions, unencumbered by Bird Mom's constant reminders of "share with your sister," "that's too much," "only one for now," or the dreadful "let's not spoil dinner." Independence it was, for the Bird Babies, but responsibility it wasn't, for teaching.

Across the aisle, another very different handling of the cruising altitude and the flight service occurs. There are no Polly Pockets or Rocket Rangers for excitement. Middle-Seat-Mom and her eight-year-old encourage the toddler to observe his or her (gender just doesn't seem to matter) airplane surroundings for excitement. Compared to Tootsie Roll overload and apple juice stimulation in the Bird Baby nest, Middle-Seat-Mom and eight-year-old son are encouraging the toddler to concentrate on the blue-sky outside the airplane window, pointing and whispering how the sky blue color matches big brother's blue shirt. And then, both of them substitute Tonka Toys for a delightful *mouthing together* with the toddler in the way to pronounce the ***B*** in blue just perfectly, followed by quiet applause among the family of three, for ***B*** word pronouncement competency.

Then comes other concentrations of the surroundings by engaging the little one in the thrill of counting his/her (still doesn't matter) fingers, in opposition to the *Count the Peanuts* and *Count the Chipmunks* math games in the

Bird Baby's books that are now crumpled underneath the seat of the passengers in back of them. And of course, the fingers of Middle-Seat-Mom and brother can also be highly stimulating two-leg walkers, designed to bring delight from ever-so-slight tickling for the toddler.

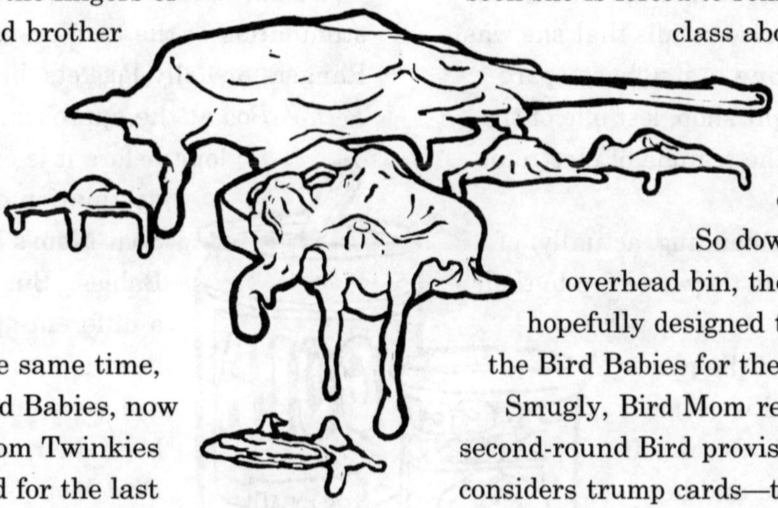

Meanwhile, at the same time, the fingers of the Bird Babies, now sticky and stained from Twinkies (supposed to be saved for the last treat), M & M candies that really did melt in their hands, and sloshed about melted yogurt bars will not engage anyone in a game, but will be the reason for two more trips to the airplane lavatory, much to the Bird Babies' delight.

But even after all the tromping down the aisle and after unauthorized rifling through the Bird provisions in Bird Mom's absence, the Bird Babies make it quite clear they have had it. It is time to shift. Although it may not yet be halfway through the 97-minute flight, the underneath-the-seat-in-front-of-you Bird Backpacks are now boring and they want the in-the-overhead-bin supplies and they want them right now. They explain to Bird Mom, they aren't interested in helping repack the Bird Backpacks with the discarded toys and half-eaten treats. Bird Mom does her best at insistence, reminding them of their at-home chores regarding toy pick-up but they do some effective Bird Baby bantering and soon she is forced to remember the parenting class about *Choose Your Battles.* Mom decides this is a Bird battle that she should give up. And she does.

So down they come from the overhead bin, the new provisions, hopefully designed to occupy and entertain the Bird Babies for the rest of the flight.

Smugly, Bird Mom remembers how these second-round Bird provisions are what she considers trump cards—toys that always seem to do the trick in occupying the Bird Babies, whether they are flying on airplanes, in the SUV on the way to Grandma's house, or even driving to the shopping mall across town. The ace in the hole for Bird Mom always comes electronically. Not surprisingly, the Bird Babies are immediately enthralled with Bird Mom's cleverness, as she crowns them with their headphones for CD players, unpacks one *Palm Pocket* to share (likely?) between them, as well as various *Game Boys*, *Phonics Game*, and the latest audiotapes of *Scooby Doo Adventures* and *Dora the Explorer*. As Bird Mom repacks the first round of Bird provisions

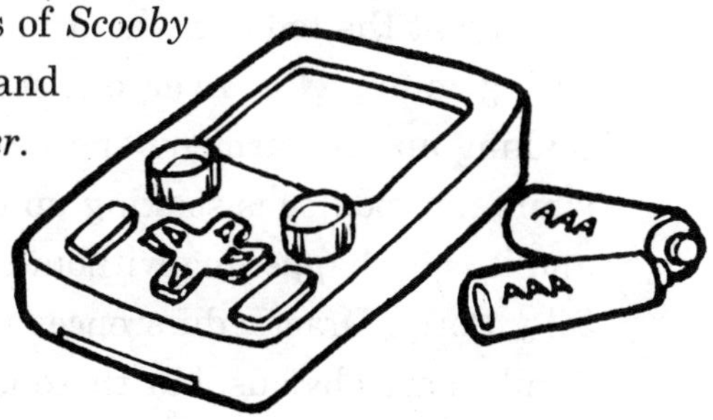

strewn about by the bored Bird Babies, she laments the fact that in Bird navigation onto the airplane, she left her latte in the boarding area. But in that memory she also recalls that she was on her toes in remembering to purchase spare batteries in the airport gift shop, lest one of the Bird Babies experience the trauma of electronic toy failure.

With the chirping (demanding, actually) of the Bird Babies quieted as they hook up to their electronic stimulation/entertainment, the rest of the plane experiences a unique and welcome hush. Most listen intently to the soft voice of Middle-Seat-Mom and her older son gently cooing the toddler into self-entertainment, mostly focusing on the airplane surroundings. The formerly-terrified-now-relaxed elderly man in the window seat smiles sweetly to the little one, every now and then thrilling the kiddo with a wink, a smile, or a simple, "Hi there." With these tiny acknowledgments, the little one appears so thrilled that a tail again can be imagined as wagging. Across the aisle, the also-formerly-terrified business folks smile broadly at the toddler who facially reciprocates with grinning glee. Everyone seems to be soaking up the harmony and peace of the toddler while the toddler is soaking up the environment, and it is all happening without a single jar of Silly Putty. Drastic differences in the two families are obvious, but there is no difference in the two families about interest in the arrival of the beloved beverage cart.

Middle-Seat-Mom and her son enhance the stimulation of the toddler, not with Power Rangers or Polly Pockets, but with the game of *Peek-A-Boo* at the approaching beverage cart long before it is even halfway to its destination of serving Middle-Seat-Mom's kiddos or the Bird Babies. But the Bird Babies have a different approach to the beverage cart arrival. Nearly everyone on the airplane can hear their rapid-fire questions to Bird Mom, demanding of course, to know how many minutes it will be before the cart arrives. Mom does her best at quieting them by reading on learning the numbers on her watch. They aren't interested. She also tries a more familiar time frame game by suggesting, "Maybe it will take as long as it would to cook six Pop Tarts in the toaster." That is the best Bird Mom could do, but the Bird Babies want more specific answers—and just like with the beverage cart—they want to know *now.*

The agony of waiting for the beverage cart is shared with every passenger within earshot as the Bird Babies continue with their relentless questions. *No,* they aren't satisfied with "Wait until it's our turn," from Bird Mom and besides, they have other questions. They want to know NOW what the beverage cart has to offer and they aren't interested in waiting for the flight attendants to read the menus. Bird Mom perks herself up by considering that this beverage-cart-option-inquisition is really another teaching moment, so she turns to the Airplane Flight Magazine just as the perky flight attendants had recommended when they announced the in-flight service was about to happen. Retrieving the magazine from the front seat pocket, Bird Mom turns to page 99 where the beverage selection is printed. She does her best to interest the Bird Babies in listening as she reads the drink options reminding them again that *choices are our friends,* and hoping to engage them in the singsong to divert their agony of waiting. But without visual stimulation of red ones, green ones, or the forbidden brown ones, it was almost impossible for them to pick out their drink selections ahead of the cart arrival. And *no,* they inform Bird Mom, they aren't interested in any of the unopened drinks of Gator Aid, Fruit Punch or Cherry Choke Kool Aid she carefully packed in their Bird Provisions. Surely, they hope, the beverage cart will have something more exciting.

As the beverage cart gets closer to Middle-Seat-Mom and her troop, the getting-excited-about-the-beverage-cart games are very different. Sure, her kiddos are concentrating on what will be available, but this parent seems intent on also getting the kiddos excited about what other passengers are selecting. If an orange one goes to someone a few seats back, Middle-Seat-Mom and her kiddos practice saying "orange" together and the same is true for a green drink or a brown drink—a hot one or a cold one with ice. There is more peek-a-booing and more enthusiasm, but few demands from the toddler and the kid caretaker. And when it finally arrives, the toddler gazes with amazement and satisfaction, just as though a huge obstacle had been conquered. The older child shares the glee of the little one. It has finally arrived and Middle-Seat-Mom's troop is thrilled.

Beverages from the beloved beverage cart are dispensed to both sides of the aisle, but with entirely different approaches. The toddler and brother seem excited AND impressed with the beverage cart and the smiling flight attendants. They order something rather shyly, much to the delight of the flight attendants who appear desirous of lingering with Middle-Seat-Mom's kiddos, since they are reluctant to approach the Bird Babies. Several seats back, the Bird Babies ventured into the aisle and began tugging on the pant legs of a frustrated male flight attendant attempting to place their beverage order prematurely. They wanted no part of waiting as Bird Mom was urging. She was able to steer them back to their seats explaining that it won't be their turns for six more seat sets, but they were unimpressed and began shouting their requests for drinks just so they could get a head start on refreshments. Meanwhile, Middle-Seat-Mom's kids find themselves in possession of a red drink and a gold drink—absolutely thrilled with whatever they are. They take turns sipping from each other's plastic glasses never really minding the content or flavor, since whatever the red or gold concoctions are, they seem to be quite satisfying, especially compared to the anticipation of just getting them.

The Bird Babies however, are quite perturbed with the wait, but there is no doubt they are ready. And, they are not easily dismissed with reminders from Bird Mom about how she had read the choices from the silly magazine. *No*, they not only want a complete menu selection/option explained to them from the two exasperated flight attendants, but *yes,* they also want Bird Mom to provide a menu-cross-reference-listing, just to make sure what they order from the stalled beverage cart is something that Bird Mom does not have in her Bird backpack. And while the thirsty passengers ahead recognize the unlikelihood of ever getting their beverage, the Bird Babies are unfazed to their surroundings, taking whatever time necessary to guarantee that their choices (not their *friends,* but their privileges) are perfect—for them, at least.

Following the turmoil of bantering with beverage cart and restroom romps, approximately 15 minutes before descent, the Bird Babies settle. On the other side of the

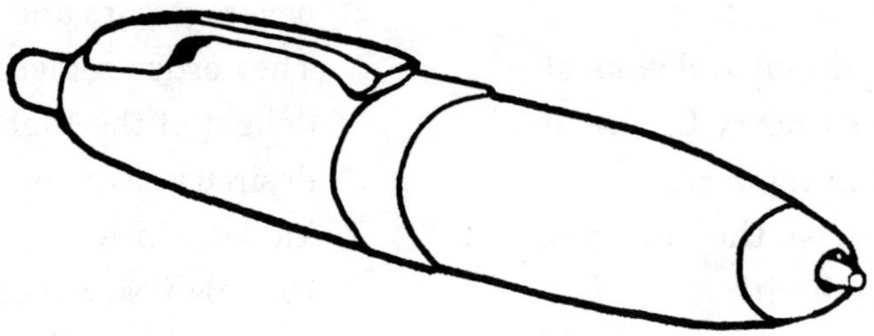

airplane, the toddler also begins to sleep, cuddled in brother's arms, elbows extended into passage aisles to a point that only a skilled flight attendant could navigate past. But they don't mind moving carefully by, the scene is so sweet.

The Bird Babies too, are quiet, outstretched arms carefully clutching the plastic cups from the beverage cart, one quarter filled with Diet Coke (not allowed at the Bird home and not in the Bird Backpacks), and each fist tightly treasuring the remains of the pretzels supplied by a tight-lipped flight attendant and chosen by the Bird Babies because, of course, Mom forgot the pretzels. Middle-Seat-Mom contents herself with smiles of encouragement to her eight-year-old for a job well done, while Bird Mom contents herself by noting in her Day Planner that she will never, ever again, forget the pretzels. No way will Bird Mom ever let her Bird Babies ever, ever be without. No boredom and no Bird business of waiting. Gratification will be ongoing and immediate. Bird Mom will guarantee that.

EIGHTH COMMANDMENT—Thou Shalt Teach Delayed Gratification

On the simple 97-minute flight to USA Anywhere, a lesson of paramount importance in raising sexually respectful children unfolded for two Mommies —hidden inconspicuously somewhere between the Rocket Rangers, the smashed Twinkies and the single Cheerio. Both Mothers, in their harmless and seemingly insignificant parenting patterns, are shuffling their children down an educational path for how they will learn to either control their impulses or demand immediate gratification for their wants and needs. The Eighth Commandment—*Thou Shalt Teach Delayed Gratification,* requires an examination of the connection between becoming a sexual abuser and lessons learned from well-intended, but misguided parents such as Bird Mom.

BIRD BABIES, BORING, AND BECOMING A SEX OFFENDER

Mommy comparisons between the two mothers shed understanding on how the kiddos are learning a powerful lesson in gratification of needs. Bird Mom is terrified of her kidlets spending even a second in *need* of something. She isn't mean-spirited or selfish, but she has read books, studied parenting techniques or somehow learned to equate being a good Mommy with protecting her kidlets from wanting something she can't immediately satisfy. And there she is on the flight to Anywhere, waiting and watching for the Bird Babies to open their beaks and let her know what they need so she can do her good Mommy Bird plopping. And her panic about being unsuccessful comes in two packages—both highly connected to how sexual impulses will be controlled or not controlled later in life.

First comes Bird Mom's uncontrollable fear of food and drink deprivation for her bumpkins. Her piles of Fruit Loops, Juicy Fruits and Baby Ruths are all part of her need to supply the Bird Babies with nourishment lest they perish from dehydration or malnutrition before the plane lands. It started when the Bird Babies were born and when it was absolutely necessary to supply them with nourishment upon demand. Her infant's survival depended upon her to be there with her beak whenever the Bird Babies peeped and that is exactly how it should have been. But as they grew older, their brains began to develop and change, as they became part (not the focus) of their world and saw that food and drink are distributed and controlled with different barometers. But even though the Bird Babies changed—Bird Mom didn't and she still feels that vigilance for their food-and-water-chirping beaks.

But there is another issue for Bird Mom beyond making sure the kiddos don't die from malnutrition on the way to Wal Mart and that additional ingredient is also connected to raising sexually respectful or disrespectful children. And it all has to do with another B word—having nothing to do with birds and their beaks—but rather, BOREDOM. It is not likely that educational talk shows or parenting seminars provide workshops for Bird Moms titled, *Anti-Boredom Strategies*, but indirectly that tends to be the focus of contemporary Mommyhood. Even though no one in the parenting classes or magazines would use the term *boredom*, Bird Mom packs her Bird Provisions with the intent of protecting the kiddos from the times when their bird brains aren't fired up and stimulated. She will probably provide some kind of distraction for the Bird Babies even on the 15-minute trip to Wal Mart lest they have nothing to buzz, read, bang or undo. Just as Bird Mom plops with those things to keep the munchkins from ever experiencing a millisecond of thirst or an iota-sized pang of hunger—she will make sure that never a moment goes by when their minds are not stimulated—lest boredom set in. Had Bird Mom known that her well-intended (and exhaustive) effort had a direct influence in delaying gratification—a key to becoming a sexual abuser—she might have cut back on the Gummy Bears a bit.

PARENTING GRATIFICATION

In reality, Bird Mom wants her own brand of immediate gratification in her determination to adopt a high-tech parenting paradigm. When she plops supplies into the beaks of the Bird Babies, *she* gets immediate gratification. They smile, they gulp, and they ask her for more. Right there, without delay, Bird Mom gets reinforcement for not only a Mommy-feel-good-moment, but also she is protected from the agony of saying *no* to the Bird Babies, which would seem to her as a negative. She enjoys having the Bird Babies contented. The Bird provisions make her feel like a good Bird Mom, so she is immediately gratified, just like the Bird Babies.

And there is nothing wrong with parents who want their children satisfied and who enjoy the pleasure of being a good parent. And besides, thinking about the extra Polly Pockets videos or Quack-N-Snack being connected to the kiddos being criminals in the future is just too much for her, as it is for most parents. Ironically, how she *gratifies* herself and her Bird Babies is the key to the Eighth Commandment and understanding how handling gratification contributes to raising sexually respectful or sexually disrespectful children.

Had Bird Mom known that her well-intended (and exhaustive) effort had a direct influence in delaying gratification—a key to becoming a sexual abuser—she might have cut back on the Gummy Bears a bit.

ACROSS THE AISLE

Middle-Seat-Mom represents the other side of boredom, and in fact, that *B* word may describe her approach to parenting. Bells, whistles and heavily packed Bird Backpacks aren't important to her. In her parenting lessons she looks ahead into the future of her kiddos and recognizes they will have a lifetime of challenges in balancing their desires for gratification. Whether she has the finances to bring six carry-on bags wouldn't matter, since the desired lesson

She wants them to learn how to delay their gratification *now* for planning in the future, whether they grow up to be airline pilots or airport restroom janitors.

for her kidlets is to teach them how to have their needs fulfilled by their surroundings—by what is available. She wants them to learn how to delay their gratification *now* for planning in the future, whether they grow up to be airline pilots or airport restroom cleaners. And this style of parenting is surely less exciting and more *boring* than the frenzied flying (literally) of Bird Mom between the wants and desires of her Bird Babies. But for Middle-Seat-Mom, her brand of teaching about managing gratification is money in the proverbial bank of sexual respect.

WISDOM WANTED

A return to USA Flight Anywhere furthers the hypothetical situation of Middle-Seat-Mom and Bird Mom who have both reached their destination. Perhaps they are traveling to attend a conference on sexual offenders. In the hypothetical, maybe they shuffle off to the same hotel where a training seminar will commence the following day—of course after babysitters have been lined up for both families of kiddos (with the sitters for the Bird Babies probably needing twice as much financial compensation). Both Moms are excited to receive pearls of wisdom about those horrible perverts in the park that they have been reading about in the newspapers. They are both good Moms and they both want their children protected from perversion. And they are waiting for wisdom about those who offend children.

WIMPY WISDOM

In the conference hall hypothetical, shared by hundreds of concerned parents, and with most attendees on the edges of their seats, the guest lecturer begins. They pay close attention to the *grand pooh bah* who is about to announce one of the key ingredients for becoming a sex offender. With note pads and pens poised in readiness, the two Moms hear the highly anticipated announcement that *sex offenders don't control their urges!*

Now if that was it, if that was the wisdom offered by the slick-high-priced expert, the two ladies might have asked for a refund since it probably wouldn't seem like a grand revelation and in fact, the explanation seems rather wimpy. Of course, everyone knows that uncontrolled urges are a problem for sexually disrespectful people. And ironically, probably both of them would have thought the conference's big proclamation was actually quite BORING. But would either Mom see that the way they taught their children on the airplane to the conference was really a significant key to exactly that issue—*sex offenders don't control their urges?*

BIG BORING

But Middle-Seat-Mom and Bird Mom wouldn't be alone in being bored or disappointed in the revelation that impulse control is related to becoming a sex offender. Therapists, doctors, lawyers, butchers, bakers and candlestick makers would all mutter "big deal, we knew that," to the rather mundane idea that sex offenders can't control themselves. And that is because no one doubts that arousal control, or control of any impulse, is a major problem facing those who sexually offend. In fact, controlling arousal is on the minds of lots of people who pontificate about protecting children from sex offenders through legislative actions, community protection efforts or other grand plans.

ROUND UP AROUSAL

So, if impulse control is out of whack for offenders, then anything that can whack them back into control is looked upon with eager and welcome eyes from the folks who think they have an inside track on what to do about the perverts in the park. Many examples abound in this effort—most having a serious purpose, but some having the potential outcome of the ridiculous. As an example, in 2006, the State of Virginia had an interesting idea in response to getting everything under control for sex offenders. Their proposal was a little surgical castration and they thought the suggestion was actually being kind to those pesky perverted folks in Virginia prisons. The American Civil Liberties Unions and other *private-rights-police* types weren't so sure.

The idea was that after a term in prison, Virginia sex offenders would be trotted off to a facility for evaluation. The heavy-hitter folks in the facility would do all kinds of fancy testing and checking to determine if the sex offender should be held longer in prison or be released, depending upon whether the potential parolees could control themselves. And no matter how fancy and complicated everything seems, the bottom line is about controlling those pesky impulses that got the offender in trouble in the first place.

But the new castration proposal was designed to take the guesswork out of determining who was in control and who wasn't. The lawmakers proposed that the sex offenders should be given options and one of those offerings was that if they agreed to surgical castration, they could then get the green light to be released, since control of impulses would be taken care of by the surgeon's knife. Oh, it was wonderful, everyone thought, that a little operation would get everything under control. In spite of the enthusiasm, most people in the business recognized that the effects of castration are controversial about whether it really does control those pesky urges, and those battles are often fought between the courts and the cattle ranchers. But for sure, the castration suggestion made everyone feel better about getting everything under control. But did anyone wonder how these folks ended up having no control in the first place? And is there a connection to Bird Mom and her tendencies to make sure the Bird Babies have everything they want (and right now) to growing up to be those sex offenders with the options of castration?

In spite of the enthusiasm, most people in the business recognized that the effects of castration are controversial about whether it really does control those pesky urges and those battles are often fought between the courts and the cattle ranchers.

There should always be caution in ever suggesting that a single factor is an absolute guarantee of a certain outcome. Humans are just too complicated for that single-minded thinking.

CRIMINAL KEYS

The Seventh Commandment of *abandoning bad equals bad* challenges the heart-held hopes that good people have about bad people. In reality, not all bad people had something bad happen to them, sometimes really good people do really bad things, and sometimes when bad things happen to people—they turn out quite nice. With the knee-jerk beliefs aside, that there is one cause—the door opens to suggest that there are many keys to becoming a criminal, and the Bird Babies may have more of a navigation plan for taking that path than those children who are abused in childhood and grow up to become therapists.

So, if sex offenders weren't sexually abused in childhood any more than the population at large, then questions can be raised about how they did develop. How does one become a sex offender? What are the keys to becoming a sexual criminal and do those keys have anything to do with the differences between Middle-Seat-Mom and Bird Mom? Well, it seems that the two prevalent characteristics or patterns in sex offenders—the keys to becoming a criminal, aren't very exciting, profound, and earth shattering. But these factors are unmistakable. And the first key to becoming a sex offender is the focus of the Eighth Commandment—*delaying gratification*.

CRIMINAL KEY CAUTIONS

Realistically, there is no guarantee that the Bird Babies are automatically heading for prison as sexual offenders just because Bird Mom overdid the Fruit Loops. And there is no guarantee that Middle-Seat-Mom is going to raise a perfect child who grows up to run the homeless center, feeding Cheerios to the downtrodden. There should always be caution in ever suggesting that a single factor is an absolute guarantee of a certain outcome. Humans are just too complicated for that single-minded thinking. But the reality of what sex offenders are and are not is important to understand in the effort to raise sexually respectful children. Rather than just picking up a newspaper and reading about the pedophile who abused 400 children, smart parents will realize that the person in the headlines, however perverted, represents only a tiny, tiny portion of those who offend. The *normal* sex offender is not as interesting as the ones who make the Oprah show, but they provide a wealth of information about how to raise sexually respectful children. And just as Bird Mom didn't want her babies bored, the true data about what sex offenders are and are not is also rather boring.

BRINGING IN THE BOLTS

In the late 1980's the sacred cow of beliefs about why someone sexually offends were really put out to pasture. Nope, it just didn't seem like sex offenders, once held to polygraph examinations, were overwhelmingly victims of childhood abuse—no matter how comforting the idea seemed to be for nice folks who had nice hopes about bad folks. But that prompted further inquiry. If sex offenders weren't victims, then what did happen to them to contribute to a lifetime of sexual disrespect? What were the lightning bolts that caused the problem if being sexually abused wasn't it? The search was on.

Over a 25-year period, more than 900 sex offenders were charted, graphed, stacked and studied in a rural community program that was bursting at the seams with sex offenders, their victims, their families and a group of professionals wanting to bring in the lightning bolts of understanding. Tests were administered, sexual histories were taken and interviews were conducted on all kinds of sexually disrespectful folks, including juveniles.

Some of these offenders were in prison, seeking a chance at treatment and some offenders were luckier and had probation/ therapy status in a community program. Some of the sex offenders emerged from disastrous households where physical, emotional and psychological abuse was commonplace. Some offenders described despicable scenarios of childhood where survival of the children in the family was a flat-out miracle. When the numbers of the sample size were low, there seemed to be some glimmers of light. Maybe the bolts could be found and maybe there was something tragic in childhood that could explain the tragedies they had caused. But as the numbers grew, the data sample enlarged as the years tumbled on and the piles of information stacked up, the rates of childhood abuse in the 900-plus sex offenders averaged out to be about the same as for society at large. But the biggest (and boring) part of the dimming bolts of lighting was that with such a large number of folks, pretty soon the group didn't look much different than the rest of the folks in the community. And park bush occupation remained about the same.

But the biggest (and boring) part of the dimming bolts of lighting was that with such a large number of folks, pretty soon the group didn't look much different than the rest of the folks in the community.

NO LIGHTNING BOLTS

The honorable quest to discover what happened to these offending folks began to reveal that there really was no *lightning bolt* of understanding for an event, a disease, a characteristic, or a math test score. Instead, regular old childhood stories emerged from the studied sex offenders, flirting with and evading any attempt to find clear threads of understanding of what the heck happened to these sexually disrespectful folks. The conclusions were elusive. Just as soon as the record of one offender painted a picture of a true lightning bolt, another record emerged that would rival the childhood of Beaver Cleaver.

Every rock was overturned looking for the answers to *what happened.*

Many of the sex offenders appeared more normal than not, and so many of them came from just ordinary families. Most had wives or husbands, many had jobs, and yet many were unemployed. Some had children, some were dedicated to children, some hated children, and some acted like children. They were male and female, but primarily male. They were short and tall, thin and fat, fun and grumpy, just like the society from which they emerged. No lightning bolts of understanding lighted the inquiry to help with the puzzle. But the work went on. Offenders were convicted, evaluated, treated, and processed. But the piles only collected in size, not in strength of brilliance in finding the one or two *ah-ha's* in understanding about what happened to these folks to break the path toward sexual disrespect.

REINING IN THE RAINBOW

Questions were asked about everything under the rainbow, and in fact, a *Rainbow Data Collection* form was used to cover all bases of inquiry by a diligent and impatient group of folks who really wanted to know what happened to sexually disrespectful folks. Each color of the rainbow packet represented a section of life examining birth order, family structure, family contacts, questions about marriage and relationships of parents, family mobility, vocational history of parents, domestic violence, substance abuse of parents, holiday celebrations, parent affections or promiscuity, criminal behavior among family members, discipline styles, and on and on. Every rock was overturned looking for the answers to *what happened.*

PENCIL/PAPER PRODDING

Now the evaluation folks not only asked lots and lots of questions about the childhood experiences in their rainbow reining, but they decided to increase the extent of their prodding by administering tests, still attempting to find the lightning bolt of *what happened.* Pencils and pens increased the flow of information in all areas of human functioning. The piles and files stacked up, as did the mounting concern that maybe the pencil and paper process wasn't going to be any more successful. But they trudged on with the spirit of Vern and Winona's *Super Staffers* with their testing. Some were psychological tests designed to determine all kinds of heavy duty problems like mental illness, examining afflictions such as depression, criminal thinking, anger, delusions, empathy for others, and on and on. Some tests were about hostility levels, the ability to care for others and about relationships that were fulfilling and those relationships that filled everyone with fear. But the pencil/paper prodding didn't produce the lightning bolt about what had *happened* to these offenders.

SEX SLEUTHING

And in all the studying, and in all the boring results, a new approach garnered favor—sex sleuthing. Some thought maybe the answer was in the sex stuff, so with purple faces exiled to the proverbial back burner, the sex sleuthing began. The sexual offenders were lined up and their sexual histories were taken with the hope that surely, this sex sleuthing would not only reveal juicy tidbits of information, but perhaps find out what sexual things happened to cause sex offenders to be disrespectful. Questions were asked regarding just about everything sexual under the sun (or under the sheets) such as pornography in the home, sexuality of the parents, sexual language in the home, codes of modesty, swear language, and of course, issues about where the Kotex could be found in the family home. Every attempt was made to understand how the sexual atmosphere of the sexual offender unfolded from everything to knowing that sister put Kleenex in her bra, to whether the Sheena types in the family had a bra for her grapefruit boobs. But even with all the salacious details about sex, and with numerous sexual tests being administered, the lightning bolts continued to dim because these folks looked just about as perverted and puritanical as the rest of the world. Where was the answer to the question about how these 900 folks became sex offenders?

BIRD BABY BLUEPRINT

After all the sleuthing and shuffling and after fondling the facts, something else seemed to emerge—but just in the realization of the staff. That is because it had always been there so it was not *emerging*. Suddenly it was observed by the folks who had blinders for what didn't happen—only telescopes for what had happened. They saw *Bird Baby blueprints*. They saw spoiled and indulged children who never had to wait for anything. They saw early patterns of thievery, they saw parents being controlled by *out of control* children, and they saw things like a strong sense of entitlement on the part of the kiddos, beginning with Gummy Bears and Polly Pockets, but later in life, moving into bigger items they just felt they couldn't do without, such as affairs with the juice-bar attendant at the country club or embezzling $300 from the Nature Hike Fourth Grade Field Trip Fund.

ADDITIONAL AFFIRMATION

And since most of the 900-plus sex offenders were from a small geographical area, there seemed to be plenty of confirmation about the histories of these folks, the number of people they still seemed to control, and their continued, seemingly selfish lifestyle. Some were very powerful people and others were not. They came from all walks of life with some being mailmen and some being ministers. There were cops and some ran the local co-op. There were teachers and there were people who mowed lawns for the

Some thought maybe the answer was in the sex stuff, so with purple faces exiled to the proverbial back burner, the sex sleuthing began.

And although the sex offenders had different demands as adults compared to the Bird Baby demands of the flight attendants operating the beverage carts, they still demanded and usually received the same dedicated brand of support so entrenched in Bird Mom.

teachers. There were truck drivers and people who wrecked trucks. And many of them had families waiting in the wings to support them, almost blindly and often at the expense of the victim. And traces of the Bird Baby business, screaming that their needs needed precedence, were very loud.

A FAMILY AFFAIR

The number-crunchers and statisticians about sexual abuse and sexual assault know for sure that most folks will be victimized by someone known to them, someone important to them, and usually someone who will help hide the Easter eggs at the family picnic. And when these 900 sex offenders were processed through evaluation over many, many years, with all of their differences, there was nonetheless a common thread of family members or other support system folks, hanging around and looking very similar to Bird Mom. Whether it was a wife, a brother, a minister or a parent—the continued (and sometimes blind) support for the offender was often evident. Considering the way the family responded to the sex offenders, there was not-so-subtle evidence that they were *bird-babied* very early, because the patterns were still there in adulthood. And although the sex offenders had different demands as adults, compared to the Bird Baby demands of the flight attendants operating the beverage carts, they still demanded and usually received the same dedicated brand of support so entrenched in Bird Mom. This discounting of responsibility and obvious (dimly lit) support was often illustrated:

"Well, he has always been a good father and those girls just went a little too far in the way they dressed and acted. He is a sexual person and like most men, he just couldn't resist. I think it's understandable the way things turned out."

"I worked with this guy in Kiwanis Camp. I don't know anyone who did more for children and, considering his wife's death, I think we know why this happened. Frankly, I think the restrictions on him are bunk and when he is off probation I want him back as camp director."

"I think this young man knew what he was doing and when my husband was faced with the temptation in all his difficult coaching activities, we all know what happened."

"She has always struggled with her marriage. Her husband is just a jerk. I think she was just trying to find love through this relationship with those children. It's not criminal; it's just a need for love."

"My son has always been a good person and he has been following our rules about premarital sex being forbidden. This is just a little slip and just a little *boys will be boys*. There is no need to destroy his family by charging him with crimes."

"My husband is a good provider and my daughter is quite seductive. I think they are both equally to blame."

"Our minister has done so much for the community. He has been forgiven by God and I don't know why the treatment center can't do the same. Under the Lord's guidance he will find the help to control himself. Those children have problems of their own, you know."

This family/friend/congregation/community influence—this sometimes blind maintenance, suggesting the sex offenders just couldn't resist the temptation to offend, was more profound in the findings than any pencil/paper test, any interview, or any juicy tidbit revealed in a sexual history about what happened parked in the Volkswagen bus at the gravel pit. To the sleuthing staff, it seemed Bird Baby business continued into adulthood with everyone making sure that the sex offender was not responsible for controlling sexual desires or there was just some other explanation why the sex offender's needs really should have been fulfilled upon demand. And even though this Bird Mom type of support on the part of the sex offender's support system was particularly traumatic to their victims, it was nonetheless obvious.

THE ENVELOPE PLEASE

These grown-up Bird Babies (sex offenders) and the information they and their families provided, caused the bean counters looking for an answer to WHAT HAPPENED, to pause. The obvious Bird Baby issue of *don't make me wait for anything* in the histories of these offenders seemed to suggest that it wasn't *what happened* (such as abuse or other bad things), but maybe something else. Perhaps, they wondered, it wasn't *what happened* in childhood to the sex offenders, but more importantly, *what didn't happen*. Maybe, they wondered, it was the failure of undoing the Bird Baby business of childhood that contributed to the sexually disrespectful adulthoods of these sex offenders.

EVIL OCCURS WHEN ...

One of the most powerful thoughts about how the wheels come off in the race of raising respectful children is what *didn't happen.* Martin Luther King Jr.'s powerful phrase, *Evil Occurs When Good People Do Nothing* is fitting to that thinking. When a society or a community or a family fails to take action when badness is obvious, the inaction becomes the breeding ground for flourishing sexual disrespect. Whether it is lawmakers in Virginia or psychiatrists in a sex offender evaluation center, there seems to be no doubt that sex offenders *fail*

When a society or a community or a family fails to take action when badness is obvious, the inaction becomes the breeding ground for flourishing sexual disrespect.

to delay gratification. The operative word is *fail,* which presupposes that the desire for gratification is a normal condition, and that controlling it or delaying it is where the troubles begin. And that brings questions about when humans learn to demand gratification.

Infants show absolutely no remorse for their actions, they tend to be self-centered, they concentrate only on their needs, and they have no connection or interest in the needs of others.

THE ANTISOCIAL INFANT—A CALLUSED BEGINNING

Whether it is a child development professor at a large university or the proud parents of a first-born son, infants are generally viewed as the epitome of sweetness and innocence. And those same experts on the really, really little kidlets would also view sex offenders as the opposite—not sweet, not innocent. Yet in reality, the infant and the sex offender share a very clear characteristic, and that relates to how they delay gratification. Even though infants are precious, they also begin life in complete and total self-centeredness—actually (by diagnosis) sociopaths or psychopaths. Infants are born entirely dependent on others, and therefore infants have no qualms about making their needs known, regardless of surrounding circumstances. And for sure, the infant wants no part of waiting for anything.

Although no psychologist would provide a "psycho" mental health diagnosis for an infant, clearly these little ones have many of the same sociopathic/psychopathic features that experts study, describe and contemplate in folks like Jeffrey Dahmer, Ted Bundy and Westley Alan Dodd. Infants show absolutely no remorse for their actions, they tend to be self-centered, they concentrate only on their needs, and they have no connection or interest in the needs of others. Infants cry and scream in the middle of Mom's Tupperware party or they easily poop their pants in the grocery store checkout line without so much as a single thought for the other shoppers. Infants do not care if they wake up the entire family with shrieks of indignation, even if Grandma is staying over for Thanksgiving dinner. They don't care about the needs of others and they refuse any negotiation about their needs being delayed. Of course no one would even consider that infants are psychopaths, but in raising sexually respectful children, and in consideration of the Eighth Commandment, it is important to understand how people begin their selfishness.

PEEK-A-BOO IN THE NURSERY

Peeking into the bassinets of the cute little poopers and suggesting they share characteristics with sex offenders may be a stretch for most. But with all the staff sleuthing of more than 900 sex offenders, the clarity that it wasn't what happened (abuse and such), but perhaps *what didn't happen* helps accept the connection to similarities. If life begins with a tendency to demand gratification, then maybe the problem with sex offenders, smelling slightly of being Bird Babies, provides even more answers. If evil occurs when good people do nothing, then perhaps people don't BECOME selfish people, refusing to delay gratification. Just maybe, the selfishness and refusal to delay gratification is just never UNDONE from the psychopathic beginning of life. And just maybe that was the biggest difference between Middle-Seat-Mom and Bird Mom. One parent is continuing the *my needs come first* attitude of infanthood, and one parent is trying to undo infanthood.

DOING AND UNDOING

However shocking it is to think of infants sharing the same characteristics as sex offenders, having the courage to take that step can provide a valuable contribution for the parents wanting to raise sexually respectful children. And it all has to do with the *undoing*. The first thing on the clipboard should be a recognition that little folks start out life with many criminal characteristics—however sweet and innocent they tend to be. That does not mean the flight attendants should try negotiation with a three-month old, screeching loudly before take off. Nor does it mean parents should treat infants any different than normal—and in fact, every single desire of an infant or even young children should be met. The key is in understanding the beginning of life and how delaying gratification needs to be taught as children begin to need to learn other things.

And then, if proactive and taking-charge-of-kid's-sexual-respect lesson, parents figure out where their kiddos are heading if they do nothing, they can figure out what to UNDO from infanthood as childhood moves along. So, if a peek in the nursery says the kiddos have many selfish and *give me what I want* approaches to life, then what is the approach to life lessons for sexual offenders? Are sex offenders surly kinds of folks, seething with rage and carrying pornography in their backpacks? Or are most sex offenders (not just the ones who make the headlines) really just Bird Babies continuing to bake in the gratification ovens of selfishness? And how does Middle-Seat-Mom have the inside track on sexual respect?

The first thing on the clipboard should be a recognition that little folks start out life with many criminal characteristics—however sweet and innocent they tend to be.

BETWEEN THE EARS, BETWEEN THE LEGS

To help parents who want to raise sexually respectful children, a distinction needs to be made that sex offenders are more like other people than they are different. This requires dispelling certain myths about the sex offenders who end up in the newspaper headlines and those who end up causing a mess in the family room. An irreverent rhetoric can classify sex offenders into typology by their body parts. Some offenders have a problem *between their ears,* and some have a problem *between their legs*. And for the purpose of understanding these folks, to help parents protect their children from becoming them, this means that some sex offenders have true *deviant* arousal or sexual problems (thus between the legs business), but the majority do not. The sex offenders (both child molesters and rapists) with problems

These thinking-problem child molesters have *arousal capacity* to do sexual things to kiddos that would make most good folks either throw up or throw themselves off a very high cliff.

between the legs are very different from those who have problems between their ears, and the Bird Babies have a potential for falling into the last category.

BETWEEN THE LEGS

Those sex offenders who molest children and who seem to have a problem between their legs, have true deviant arousal to little people. These disturbing folks are often called pedophiles, which is a fancy name that unfortunately is thrown around to describe all of those folks who offend children, which is regrettable and wrong. True pedophiles have a leg problem, because they have limited interest in grown-ups or partners who have secondary sexual characteristics. The undeveloped body of a child is much more interesting and arousing to these child molesters—compared to an adult partner with pubic hair, muscle buildup, or breast development. These leg-problemed sex offenders often have many, many victims. Since children grow up and develop the body parts (sexual characteristics) pedophiles don't find very interesting, the pedophile discards them at puberty and moves on to other, undeveloped children. Pedophiles are much more dangerous than the most common kind of child molester. And yes, as far as numbers are concerned, pedophiles—those child abusers who have clear problems with arousal deviancy (between their legs)—are much, much smaller in numbers than the other kind of child molester.

But most importantly, when good parents organize the sexual respect curriculum, it must be recognized that even though the pedophiles are smaller in numbers, they are the most common child abuser that Mom and Dad read about in the newspapers found behind park bushes. And if the parents don't understand that most of the time sexual disrespect problems are between the ears, not between the legs, the kiddos may be abandoned in teaching the lessons they desperately need.

BETWEEN THE EARS

Mom and Dad need to know that the majority of child molesters don't have arousal difficulties between their legs, but tend to have a problem between the ears, which pertains to the way they think, especially about their needs being met. These thinking-problem child molesters have *arousal capacity* to do sexual things to kiddos that would make most good folks either throw up or throw themselves off a very high cliff. These ear-problem folks also have arousal to grown-ups with secondary sexual characteristics, but because of the way they *think*, doing something to children to fulfill their own needs is possible and sometimes preferred, since it is exciting and *not boring*. And their capacity to have sex with children is not a sexual deviance problem, but a thinking problem, usually because of the way they were taught to handle their needs in comparison to the needs of others in the world—Bird Babies personified.

DEBIT AND CREDIT THINKING

A very important issue in child molesters with ear problems is that they view their wants and needs in terms of *entitlement.* They believe the world owes them, and just like the Bird Babies, they do not want to wait, to withhold, or to postpone gratification—and sexual gratification is included. Debits and credits are the thinking pattern—*what I can get, what it will cost me?* allows this kind of offender to navigate the world in a certain way and may easily include using a child for sexual needs. It isn't the chubby thighs of the child, the tousled towhead hair or the dimples in the knees that is arousing; it is the thinking process of *I have needs now—why should I have to wait for anything?* and that learning began early and perhaps was just never UNDONE because their Bird Moms and Dads just loved them so much, they gave them everything.

AND ABOUT RAPISTS

Rapists tend to fall in the same two categories of offenders with problems between the legs and between the ears but with a difference in the arousal focus of the smaller group, often referred to as *arousal rapists,* or the folks who have a problem between their legs. Arousal rapists have an erotic preference for violence, for aggression, and for hurting someone in a sexual way. And that is about all they have in the arousal department. Cuddling up in front of the fireplace with a Budweiser after bowling with a wife of 24 years just doesn't get things going for an arousal rapist. Something has happened in the arousal development of this offender so that just like the pedophile who has no arousal to developed adults, this rapist has no arousal to consenting sex with a loving partner. And the something-gone-wrong means these folks are in bad shape and very, very dangerous. But they are small in number, especially compared to their counterpart, the problem-between-the-ears rapists who are really grownup Bird Babies.

SITUATIONAL RAPIST

Different than an arousal rapist is a sex offender who rapes during a certain situation, under certain circumstances, and who has a problem between the ears. Just like the child molester who is not a pedophile but one who has a thinking problem, the situational rapist usually has healthy arousal *capacities*, but when certain thinking conditions exist, this person has the ability to achieve sexual pleasure while someone is being hurt. They tend to be quite versatile—probably preferring sexual cooperation, but they can have their sexual needs fulfilled regardless of the partner/victim's consent and cooperation. Their actions are a robbery or a theft and just like traditional robbers or thieves, the motivation for the crime is to just get the goodies. Not too many people ponder deeply about why someone steals stereos. They either want the stereo or they want the

Their actions are a robbery or a theft and just like traditional robbers or thieves, the motivation for the crime is to just get the goodies.

Although sometimes difficult to consider, perhaps there is little, if any, difference between infants, sex offenders with thinking problems, and people like Enron executives.

money the stereo will bring at the pawnshop. No one muses about whether the thief had some kind of deviant attraction toward music, which resulted in the heist. The same is true for between-the-ears rapists and their thefts of sex. This rapist seizes upon situations where their needs can be met and a rape occurs. It is in the thinking of, "My needs come first," "I shouldn't have to wait," "I should always have beautiful partners," and, "I should never, ever, ever have to postpone my gratification." Again, it is Bird Babies personified.

INFANTS, SEX OFFENDERS AND ENRON EXECUTIVES

When parents who wish to raise sexually respectful children organize their curriculum—questions will surface on where to focus the teaching. Without other references or understanding, the morning newspaper or a titillating talk show may provide the scoop and Mom and Dad may move forward with that profile in mind. Unfortunately, the folks who make the news are usually those offenders with leg problems—highly deviant, very dangerous and not so normal in the perversion department. Media information will flirt with parents—seducing them into thinking that the focus of education should on deviant arousal. Easily, parents buy-in to the idea because it takes them out of the pesky task of dealing with arousal and the kidlets. So the game plan is to do everything to stop, stifle and subdue even the slightest sign of arousal, which not only won't pertain to the problem, but could have a negative impact for children who need to be learning positive and healthy lessons as outlined in the Third Commandment.

Understanding the antisocial nature of an infant and accepting the fact that the majority of sex offenders have ear problems, then the focus for raising sexually respectful children should be on how they are taught to think—how they grow up to delay or not delay their wants and needs. A curriculum-philosophy check suggests a comparison of other criminals or folks who may not sexually offend but who were probably Bird Babies who grew up to be adult birds doing other selfish things. It is an attitude, a way in which they easily put their needs first, which all boils down to how they deal with gratification.

Although sometimes difficult to consider, perhaps there is little, if any, difference between infants, sex offenders with thinking problems, and people like Enron executives, who suggest to themselves that their needs must be met—and *no,* they aren't interested in waiting in line like everyone else. Although the jury is still out on the Enron case, that example assists in understanding how sometimes those in power, appear to be just grownup versions of Bird Babies. For some people, it would be just as impossible to sexually abuse a child as it would be to stand before hundreds of employees and cheat them out of their hard earned retirements. And perhaps there is only a thin line between politicians, insurances executives, or even someone on a city council in a tiny little city somewhere, who lies and deceives others for their own gratification—usually in the form of bank accounts—but not always. And perhaps these are just people who never had the selfishness of infanthood undone. So the bottom line is that rather than looking at *what happened to sex offenders,* it would be more helpful to examine what *didn't happen* and maybe undoing the psychopathic nature of infanthood is the key.

CREATE OR UNCREATE

The Bird Babies certainly wanted no part of postponing their needs. They could (operative word could) grow into demanding children, not only demanding things, but also perhaps demanding to have constant stimulation because boredom is so repulsive. Therefore, an excellent question is whether sex offenders are *created,* because parents do not *uncreate* the natural tendencies of selfishness normally found in early childhood. The Bird Babies were older than infants, but their behavior was similar to families with an infant, concentrating on every burp and responding to the demands of every cry or every desire.

LOVE, LUST, AND LONG TIMES

If the selfishness of an infant is interesting, what about delaying gratification in other areas of life for either the kiddos of Middle-Seat-Mom or the Bird Babies when they grow up? Most people recognize that sex feels good. People like sex—it is pleasurable and for many it is something of value. Some people steal sex and some people steal stereos. And if the majority of sex offenders have ear problems and difficulty delaying their gratification, then comparative questions could be asked about how some folks end up different. Perhaps looking at those who *are successful* in delaying gratification can provide answers.

Some people steal sex and some people steal stereos.

How do normally good people, handle the burning desire to be selfish and have constant sexual gratification? For most folks, there is an event or an experience where at first they fall in love and the feelings of attraction toward another person are breathlessly exciting and intense. Some describe those first experiences of falling in love as *teeth-sweating*. Some experts on the physiological aspects of love, suggest that perhaps the emotion should be listed in the DSM-IV (Diagnostic and Statistics Manual of Mental Disorders). Those who become smitten with another person report being unable to eat, sleep or breathe without salivating over thoughts of the lover. And *yes,* by all physical accounts, the condition borders on mental illness.

What makes this couple tolerate life's changes, the predictable boredom in life that does not bring the intensity of first love? Why are they willing to tolerate boredom, bulging, and burgeoning bellies if the original thrill of lust/love and excitement is still remembered?

And then for most, the relationship putters along and things fall into place and sometimes fall into bed, as well. Perhaps they get married and have sex or that order might be reversed in some situations. But nonetheless, the lovers follow their lusts and eventually make a commitment. As time goes on, they begin to concentrate on saving money, matching their couch pillows and making sure the toast doesn't burn. They begin to acquire furniture payments and house mortgages, and often babies.

The little ones bring burps, sleepless nights, and eventually a sister or two. The used-to-be-mentally-ill-with-lust lovers remember to cuddle up in the swing porch on a summer night after the children are in bed, and with the assistance of their day planners, they remember their anniversary. They also remember to sometimes hold hands in church, but mostly to offer spiritual support rather than in anticipation of a *hot roll in the hay* after the church buffet and bingo. The lust has turned to love and the passion turns to life, over time.

After many years, they look at each other and they recognize that she has suffered some slippage in various parts of her body but if she works hard she can remember to put on her makeup before firing up the car pool. And he has the same little backside buns that he had when he drove his 1962 Chevy to his wife's house for their first date. But over time his chest has somehow slipped and his belt seems to be in hibernation. However, his bulging belly may be his wife's favorite place to rest her weary head after too many 4-H meetings and too many country fair baked food sales. It is a life of less intensity and excitement, lust and passion adjusted over time. But most of the time, the couple trudges on through a somewhat boring lifestyle, at least compared to when they were both mentally ill with lust/love.

TIME AND TOLERATION

What makes this couple tolerate life's changes, the predictable boredom in life that does not bring the intensity of first love? Why are they willing to tolerate boredom, bulging, and burgeoning bellies if the original thrill of lust/love and excitement is still remembered? Likely, the lust-lovers, now lost to time, have both had opportunities for affairs; they both could have fooled around with someone more exciting, and perhaps, again found that thrill of romance they experienced so long ago. But somehow they remember their commitment, they remember their promise, and they tenderly tolerate the inevitable, less-than-passionate lifestyle. But who taught this toleration and why do sex offenders seem to be so deficit in this thinking?

Thieves steal because they want things and they don't want to follow rules. Most sex offender want sex and they steal it. They rob childhood and they rob older victims of sexual safety. Sex offenders are not often the kind of people who will settle into a long commitment to boredom and accept a life that is not exciting and stimulating. They are seekers of intensity and personal gratification, and these patterns began early in life. Perhaps they were once Bird Babies whose mother simply could not tolerate her children wanting for anything, and in this subtle and unintended lesson, a failure to uncreate from infanthood, they were learning one of the most important lessons of becoming a sex offender.

HELP US UNDERSTAND RANDY

Randy is a sixteen-year-old young man finishing his juvenile sex offender treatment. He is a straight-A student who aspires to attend medical school on his almost guaranteed football scholarship. He is attractive, articulate, and popular. He has always excelled and he has rarely been forced to wait for anything. Randy has had numerous girlfriends and peer sexual partners, but he has also engaged in intercourse with his eight-year-old sister for two years previous to his arrest. He dazzled the juvenile court officials with his "good kid" image and was sentenced to two years of treatment, which for him was easy considering his excellent *people skills.* This good-looking and competent young man will quarterback the high school football team following his last appointment with the therapist who has managed his treatment. And he will probably have an attractive date for the Homecoming Dance after the game. In this closing session, Randy is asked if he has any questions of his treatment specialist.

"Do other boys think about having sex with their sisters?" asks this teenager of his therapist.

The therapist remarks that this is an excellent question, and proposes a hypothetical situation for Randy's contemplation.

"What if four teenage boys are riding around in a car on Saturday night and all of them are feeling a little aroused," she suggests in the question posed to the teenager. "Maybe they are just thinking about girls and breasts, perhaps thinking about which girls have big ones, and which ones have little ones, so they are all just a little bit aroused. Do you think, Randy, that it would be normal or abnormal for all four of the teenage boys to be aroused with these thoughts of girls' breasts?"

"Normal," replies Randy, as he explains that he believes all four of the young men would normally experience arousal with this type of buddy conversation on a Saturday night.

The therapist continues the hypothetical dialog. "But why, Randy, will three of these aroused teenage boys go home and dream about the high school cheerleaders and maybe even masturbate, while you will go home and rape your sister?"

Without any hesitation, and with obvious bluntness, Randy replies, "They are fools, if they have sisters. It takes time and effort to date a cheerleader. You have to buy them Big Macs, and sometimes they turn you down. Why endure the hassle if you have a sister?"

"They are fools, if they have sisters. It takes time and effort to date a cheerleader. You have to buy them Big Macs and sometimes they turn you down. Why endure the hassle if you have a sister?"

The subtleties of Randy's statement are shocking, but understandable if Randy began life as a Bird Baby and never changed. Randy is saying, "If I have a sister and if I can get away with rape, I will take the easiest route to sexual pleasure, because I should not have to delay my gratification." Being sexual with girls his own age is work for Randy because it involves the agony of purchasing Big Macs, as well as other *waiting* obligations. The question is, what makes one child willing to wait, willing to tolerate rejection, and willing to play by the rules, while another child absolutely demands to have his gratification be immediate? Perhaps Bird Mom might have an answer.

In contemplation for how Randy could have developed such thinking, the therapist remembers noticing Randy's mother, always bringing him to treatment, waiting for him, reinforcing his treatment success, and figuratively *wagging her tail* at just the sight of her favorite child. The therapist also remembered how difficult it was for Randy's Mom to avoid blaming the eight-year-old sister for at least half of the responsibility for the sexual abuse. *After all*, she shared with the therapist, Randy has been such a good kid, quite different than her daughter who has caused her nothing but problems.

The problem of sexual assault of teenagers and woman has staggering proportions in this country, shocking the bean counters and statisticians. Dr. David Lisak, famed researcher, has studied what he calls the *Undetected Rapist*—referring to men who are just like Randy—seemingly normal in most ways and often in positions where "acquaintance rape" can easily occur. These folks don't have to hang around the park bushes nor could someone easily spot them at the dry cleaners and know for sure they could rape young women. They look like everyone else and act like everyone else—thus the term "undetected." Yet these men have a core belief system that suggests the rules of sexual engagement are for everyone else and they should not have to withhold their quest for needs being met. They don't froth at the mouth and their underwear looks like everyone else's. But when the opportunity arises—when the stealing of sex is possible just like Randy, it is considered the easiest route and a viable conduit for their needs being met—and besides the buying of Big Macs seems to be just so cumbersome.

SELF-ESTEEM, SELF-CENTERED

In the parenting library Bird Mom visited while she was pregnant, there were probably other things she learned in addition to making sure her babies didn't dehydrate or die from malnutrition. Probably right at the top of the good parent list was the importance of raising her children to have high self-esteem. Whether it was clapping if they peed perfectly in the airplane restroom or when the Barbie Doll staircase was erected perfectly before takeoff, the important thing was that the kiddos have constant reminders of their excellence. Bird Mom, like most good parents, learned wonderful things about the art of building self-esteem in children and the horrors of children who didn't have a chance to believe the world would stop without their contribution.

But in those resources was there ever any help for Bird Mom to know the difference between self-esteem and self-centeredness? Did anyone ever suggest to Bird Mom that there is only a thin line between the two, and that many criminals have incredibly high self-esteem—in fact self-esteem gone out of control? As the Seventh Commandment warns, good people make a mistake in thinking that no one would ever become bad unless something bad happened to them. But in reality, many people do very bad things because of self-esteem gone out of control into self-centeredness with the approach to life that *my needs come first and I should never have to wait for anything because my parents have taught me I am so wonderful.*

In raising sexually respectful children, the issue is balance. Building self-esteem is a wonderful contribution to parenting, but there should also be awareness that self-centeredness is right around the corner, waiting to engulf children into a belief that the world owes them (of course, because they are so wonderful) immediate and constant gratification.

But in those resources was there ever any help for Bird Mom to know the difference between self-esteem and self-centeredness? Did anyone ever suggest to Bird Mom that there is only a thin line between the two, and that many criminals have incredibly high self-esteem—in fact self-esteem gone out of control?

MORE IS BETTER—THE PATH TO PERVERSION

And in the ongoing battle of being good parents and wanting to build self-esteem, many parents rush to the shopping mall to purchase educational toys, video games, and, of course, the best sneakers, lest their children do without. Just like Bird Mom, the hope is that their children will have advanced skills, automatically bringing about high self-esteem. Rationalizations are that children who feel good about themselves and who have a positive self-image will be headed down a productive avenue. Unfortunately, sex offenders, the ones with ear problems, often have the same thinking. It is an unbridled self-esteem that actually results in self-centeredness, suggesting their sexual acting-out was unstoppable and justified by their needs being unmet in other more boring situations in life.

MORE AND MORE IS BETTER

But there is more than just self-esteem in the equation of what to buy for the Bird Babies. Of course good parents want their children to do well in school, to have advanced skills and to know everything about the science fair workshop for five-year-olds. The infant isn't just given a mobile to hang above the crib, but an *education mobile* with vowel sounds, just to get the six-week-old prepared for kindergarten. And there is a rush for the toddlers to learn about farm animals and what sound each of them makes.

It is not mean-spirited; it is just dangerous if unbridled and unbalanced in the effort to raise sexually respectful children.

Why, parents even want high stimulation and educational training when the Bird Babies are in the womb—taking steps to hold the symphony-playing cassette tape to Mommy's tummy and honing classical music skills pre-birth. Many of these well-intentioned efforts to get the kiddos skilled early, becomes the Olympics of high stimulation that should help the babies get a head start on all the other less-stimulated kiddos in the car pool. It is not mean-spirited; it is just dangerous, if unbridled and unbalanced in the effort to raise sexually respectful children.

In Bird Mom's panic about the Bird Babies not having constant stimulation with their Rocket Rangers, their Polly Pockets and their A, B, and C Flash Cards, she is really teaching there should never be a *lack of stimulation.* And it seems that is what Middle-Seat-Mom is doing so perfectly. Rather than throwing one stimulating thing after another at her children, she is teaching both of them a beautiful lesson of finding stimulation in their surroundings—in making their own excitement according to what is available. Anticipating the arrival of the beverage cart is teaching the toddler and the eight-year-old something wonderful about life and that is to find *internal contentment*, which will really help them when they realize that the natural progression of life is not always immediately gratifying.

And sadly, Bird Mom is teaching her children that if they are not constantly stimulated, life is boring and they should do something about it. And if at the same hypothetical conference on sexual offenders, Middle-Seat-Mom and Bird Mom learned that sexually disrespectful folks not only can't control themselves, but they have high needs for constant stimulation—they probably wouldn't be surprised. But do Moms really think about how constant stimulation to their own children contributes to that problem?

A GREAT GIFT FOR CHRISTMAS

Three little girls sit in their *Sunday best* dresses with stiff and uncomfortable petticoats in the back seat of the 1949 Plymouth. Their arms are outstretched, holding various cookies, candies, and Christmas concoctions to be delivered in the neighborhood. The three little girls have named the vehicle the *Torture Mobile*, because they feel they are being ritualistically tortured on this Christmas Eve day. The family ritual, year after year, requires that everyone participate in giving Christmas gifts to others before (yes, *before)* they are allowed to open their *one present* (yes, one present) on Christmas Eve night. And it gets worse, because they want to hurry with the boring gift-giving process so that they can go home and get to their gift. And each Christmas Eve day, it always seems like their parents enjoy the agony of waiting.

If it was any other day of the year, the little girls know exactly what to do in order to hurry along their parents and get the polite neighbor visiting over with. From past experience, they know a little fuss here and there would usually non-verbally persuade their parents to end their visiting and take the kids home. But not on this day. If they fuss or if they show even a slight tendency towards boredom or not being in the true Christmas spirit of gift giving, the wise father and mother who are evaluating their daughters' ability to delay gratification will simply sit back down and visit longer. The waiting for the three of them is agony—thus the *Torture Mobile.*

The little girls believe they are tortured with this waiting process. They want their present *now*, but their parents not only force them to wait, but force them to achieve the goal of delaying gratification. Finally, at home with the waiting hopefully finished, they anxiously gather around the kitchen table, watching their Father and Mother who seem to be agonizingly slow. The Father begins to puff on his pipe, saying to his wife, "Do you think there is someone else out there in the neighborhood that needs some cookies that we may have forgotten?" The little girls' hearts sink and they nearly pass out from panic of another anticipated and quite agonizing *wait*. How could this torture continue outside the *Torture Mobile*, they wonder? The mother wisely recognizes that her children are far too anxious to open their only present, and she counters her husband's question by stating, "Well, I don't know about someone needing cookies, but perhaps there's someone out there who needs fudge."

Now the fudge suggestion is devastating, because the little girls know that fudge takes twice as long as cookies. They writhe with agony, believing that there will be even more hours of delay before their single present is to be opened. And probably, the presents ended up being quite anticlimactic compared to the lesson learned about waiting. This tiny bit of parenting teaches the girls that delayed gratification is an expectation for reaping something desired. But the real gift to the girls is what their parents are teaching them about delayed gratification and postponing their desire for high stimulation encased in the wonderful lesson of thinking about the needs of others who might be without cookies or the dreaded fudge.

But the real gift to the girls is what their parents are teaching them about delayed gratification and postponing their desire for high stimulation encased in the wonderful lesson of thinking about the needs of others who might be without cookies or the dreaded fudge.

FAST FOOD, FAST TRACKS, FAST WAITING LINES

But it's not just Bird Mom with a problem. American society simply isn't interested in waiting for anything, and in fact, high stimulation and making sure there is never a wasted minute, seems vogue for the time. Adults want to eat a *Fast Track Breakfast Bagel* in the car, driving on the freeway's *car pool only* lane (with a blow-up doll figure, feigning occupancy), and they take pride in hurrying to work for a parking spot *extra close* to the elevator so they don't have to walk very far. Adults want *preferred customer* privileges to avoid standing in line at rental car counters, the cleaners, or

There is something about Americans and the prices they will pay to avoid waiting or for sure, standing in line.

even Disneyland. Advertising makes claims of hand-held computer games for the kids to use in school, "So he will never be without his Play Station." I-Pod advertising suggests that no one should ever be without access to 10,000 songs in times when they might be in the car pool or driving to the gym. And of course, waiting to get e-mail until connected to the home computer is totally out of the question and thus the need for everyone to have a Blackberry to bring every single thing into constant efficiency. It is a fast-paced, highly stimulated world where no one should ever have to delay gratification.

WAITING WEARINESS

There is something about Americans and the prices they will pay to avoid waiting or for sure, standing in line. Different from years past, amusement parks have solved the problem of waiting in line, which to Bird Baby families is ideal. Family registration for the ride can occur with a payment and a computer check-in so the family can do something else with the time other than waiting. This process is interesting since, just like the Bird Babies, while the family is waiting for a ride on the roller coaster, they will not likely follow Middle-Seat-Mom's teaching and have a picnic together, enjoying the process of anticipating the excitement of the ride, but they will probably engage in some other activity, another ride or game, or another level of high stimulation so that not a moment is wasted and there is not a moment of limited stimulation.

Eating at McDonald's or other fast food restaurants does not even require waiting, since eating establishments all over the country provide either coloring utensils, special games and toys, or at McDonald's, a complete playground so that children don't even have to sit at a table and eat their meals. No waiting for orders, no waiting to eat. The kiddos can grab a Big Mac and hit the Silly Swing without ever experiencing any kind of stagnant, boredom of lowered stimulation.

SUPER SIZE ME

As the twenty-first century rolled around, obesity of American children became a stark reality. From the Big Gulp to the Big Mac, it just seems that filling a tummy just to contentment was not the desired outcome. *Bigger is better* is noticed in a society that super-sizes everything from French fries to fried chicken buffets. Never in the history of America has there been a society so indulgent in the gratification of their stomachs. And maybe that is just a concern for the health clubs, the health care systems, or the food industry. But it would seem that the same demand for constant food gratification might be considered a partner to others who are intolerant of postponing sexual gratification.

TIME OUT

American families also seem to feel terrified if their children aren't spending all of their time *in action*. Bird Mom learned the importance of her day planner, taking pride in keeping track of all the activities of the Bird Babies, never once wanting them to be without something to do. She prides herself with her coordinated efforts at soccer practice, the art institute, 4-H club meetings, gymnastics and swimming lessons. Of course she also had to balance library reading time with aikido and Karate car-pooling, since she just couldn't be in two places at once. *Keep them busy and they will stay out of trouble* is what she believes is good for them, never making the connection between failure to delay gratification, constant stimulation, avoiding boredom and people who will later demand that the world owes them constant intensity.

TO GRANDMA'S HOUSE WE GO

"But Grandma's house is boring," screech the Bird Babies in protest when they learn that on Sunday, the two-hour trip to Grandma's will occur. Not only does the two-hour drive pose problems for Bird Mom who is in charge of constant stimulation and avoiding boredom at all costs, but the kiddos really complain of the boredom once they arrive and are faced with the reality of Grandma's array of 1963 childhood toys. It is the ride, the toys, and Grandma that is boring, they implore on Bird Mom.

But they aren't finished with their protesting about being without their laptops or their Power Rangers and Polly Pockets. In addition, it is difficult to schedule the trip to see Grandma for the Bird Baby parents in the first place, because visiting her might interfere with a variety of activities such as soccer, tap dancing, or a slumber party with friends. But most importantly, every Born Again Bird Baby thinks Grandma is just flat out boring. Without seeing this as a window of opportunity to raise sexually respectful children, Bird Mom and Dad will probably do everything they can to avoid the boring business—getting DVD players for the kids to watch movies in the back seat, allowing them to take their laptops and other toys, and begging them to be polite for the 27-minute dinner that boring old Grandma will prepare. Window of opportunity to teach delayed gratification opened—and slammed shut.

Without seeing this as a window of opportunity to raise sexually respectful children, Bird Mom and Dad will probably do everything they can to avoid the boring business...

BODY BIRD BABY BUSINESS

"But Mom, my boobs are flat. Who will ever want to date me or vote for me on the rally squad looking like this?" the daughter complained. And this protest came shortly after another quandary presented to Mom (probably Bird Mom's sister) about her son who wasn't really taking steroids for football, even though his football coach confronted him about the nasty rumor. After all, his friends only *visited* the sport health food store and asked for an *athletic consultation* to see what each of them might need in the way of body enhancement. *Yes*, the coach had made the suggestion (off the record, of course) primarily since another bigger boy was challenging the child's position on the football team. Something must be done, he had implored

Daughter relented her demanding, but as she departed the kitchen she made a mental note to nonetheless check the Internet about breast augmentation for twelve-year-olds, and to search the family photo album for a refresher peek at Aunt Thelma.

to Mom, as he was threatened with not being the best. Surely Mom would understand and help him get the edge on the advantage he was quickly appearing to lose. After all, she had always suggested he was just a notch above the rest. His pictures on the refrigerator had told him so, for 13 years, so why should it all stop now?

The second onslaught of the morning by daughter was temporarily won by Bird Mom's sister, who encouraged her daughter to postpone saving her allowance in preparation for breast augmentation since she was only 12 years old and breasts have been known to have massive growth spurts beyond the sixth grade. This clear fact of biology was only somewhat reassuring to discouraged daughter, especially when Mom reminded, "You could end up being just like Aunt Thelma. Remember, she ended up with TOO MUCH in the *T* department, if you know what I mean?"

Daughter relented her demanding, but as she departed the kitchen she made a mental note to nonetheless check the Internet about breast augmentation for twelve-year-olds, and to search the family photo album for a refresher peek at Aunt Thelma.

For Son, Mom didn't fare so well. He was absolutely intolerant of *tolerating* his *average-*sized body. Why, who would consider waiting until his senior year for full physical maturity? *Not me*, Son non-verbally committed. The terrain is not unfamiliar and Son is ready for his retaliation against Mom and her detouring suggestions. "Remember," he reminded, "you and Dad agreed to not just get me braces, but the invisible kind of braces, because I didn't want a birdcage mouth?" Mom remembered. Mostly she recalled canceling the new couch she had ordered, since to protect Son from the agony of brace discovery by his friends would have been too much to bear, even though the old couch was quite bare itself.

Son continued reminding Mom of other advantages he had enjoyed as Mom and Dad had indulged him and surely they couldn't stop now. He reminded her of his extra early tennis lessons (designed to escape mediocrity) when he was in the 7th grade. Teeth whitening, he reminded her, had also been her previous commitment, which was a natural tailgate to braces, since the other boys, who only had the slower kind of braces, were obviously behind him in the race for the straight teeth department. And of course, he knew how much pleasure his parents got from all of his medals, honors and awards, so certainly they weren't going to stop giving him the edge now. He seems to be just a Bird Baby who is a little bigger, with bigger demands and even smaller tolerance for delaying gratification.

Sex Fairy Clipboard

- Most important concerning the issue of delayed gratification is to remember the key of balance. Teaching children to delay gratification does not mean a diet of bread and water, absent of a single toy. It means avoiding a constant onslaught of stimulation (that includes nourishment) for children, without times in between to help develop an appreciation for those needs being met.

- Remember the strong connection between failure to delay gratification and fear of boredom. When children complain of boredom, the window of opportunity opens for parents who want to encourage delayed gratification. When children scream about being bored, and Bird Moms rush to stimulate—a dangerous message is being taught about gratification needs.

- Remember the balance. Battling boredom should include everything from riding in the car to Wal Mart without a Game Boy in sight or learning to be content (and respectful) at Grandma's with her outdated toy collection. But the key is to follow the deprivation with things like the excitement of playing with the Game Boy after Wal Mart (and after homework), and on the way home from Grandma's having a huge celebration of expensive ice cream for such respectful behavior in the face of severe toy deficit.

- Remember that self-esteem is very important to teach children. Low self-esteem can be highly destructive and dangerous as children grow up. But the key is to build self-esteem around those things that teach children they are a part of the world—not the entire focus.

- Avoid building self-esteem only toward tangible accomplishments, but rather provide the highest rewards for children when they put their needs in synch, or secondary to the needs of others.

Sex Fairy Clipboard

- Have courage when children demand things. Being a good parent requires children to wait for things, to earn things, and to appreciate things. Fight the urge to have constantly happy children with high stimulation/constant gratification. Treasure parenting processes when children are the proud owners of fulfilling their owns needs through creativity and valuing the balance of their needs with the needs of the world.

- Understand how sex offenders really develop, and reject the 30-second sound bite on the evening news suggesting the featured criminal is a normal sample. Remember that sexual offenders most commonly offend because of what is between their ears, which relates to their thinking. How children think about their needs being met or being balanced with the world is a key to either sexual respect or disrespect.

Chapter 12
Ninth Commandment
Thou Shalt Teach Vulnerability Appreciation

CHAPTER 12: NINTH COMMANDMENT—THOU SHALT TEACH VULNERABILITY APPRECIATION

Snow, fog, and freezing rain turned the Atlanta airport into chaos. Bulging backpacks, battery-dead computers, and silenced cell phones adorn bleary-eyed passengers who file off the planes—signs of bravado completely banished. The overflow of stranded folks missing a cruise to the Caribbean or a meeting in Minneapolis stretched everything to the limit. They all seem to be moving, but clearly, no one is going anywhere, at least on airplanes.

Although the destitute passengers were diverse in destination, they were simultaneously hurried in their hunger. Eating establishments were plentiful but tiny, in this ever-so-large and frantically busy airport. Businessmen with rumpled suits, Hawaiian vacationers with crushed leis and shivering elbows, as well as parents with disgruntled and *when will we be there?* questioning children, all begin the process of dietary decision-making. Most ponder the coveted possibility of sitting down to eat, since the waiting lines for hamburgers, hot dogs, or hardly-fresh sandwiches are immense. They all navigate toward eating opportunities with their tummies and their complaining children at the helm of deciding whether to stand in line or partake of the luxury of sitting down at a restaurant table. And for most, the extra price of a sit-down dinner is well worth the sacrifice, since even the burger-grabbing folks find securing any type of sit-down situation nearly impossible as the airport swells with the standing-stranded.

Ahead, a small Chili's Mexican restaurant boasts perhaps 20 small tables with each eating opportunity entirely exposed to not only the airport corridors, but also to the weary, waiting-in-line travelers. Reservations on a color-coded chart marked by cute, college-looking kids, are out of the question, since waiting is the name of the game and serving folks on a next-in-line basis is the only way to handle the airport-stranded crisis.

Those who have made the decision to wait in line for a table rather than standing in a telephone booth and balancing hot dogs in styrofoam containers, form an orderly procession, understanding that table availability will be the determining factor for when their posteriors will find relief in a chair and when their tummies will find relief in something other than a day-old doughnut.

Inside Chili's, and close to the airport corridor, a middle-aged woman is perched on a tall stool at an even taller round table, adorned with an unused table setting for three, the remnants of the sandwich and fries she consumed long ago, and a glass of water she occasionally fondles. Her check for the meal lies obvious and neglected on her table. She is in a strategic position of observation for those who long for her table. Although hungry eyes constantly scan the scene, she is apparently unfazed to others around her, perfectly perched on her throne. Initially, she shows not the slightest awareness of how her perching is so distinctly different from the weary waiting who long for the perching privilege she covets.

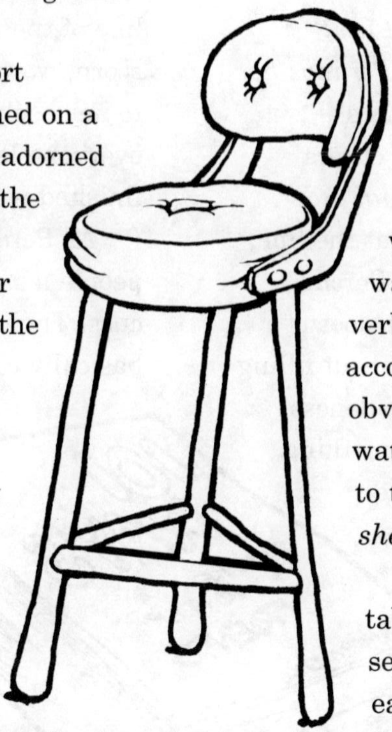

Directly across from Perch Woman, at a distant of only twenty feet, tired travelers with growling tummies stand in line. She perches, they watch. Hungry eyes notice how the waiting-in-line folks seem to naturally influence other customers in the restaurant. It seems those who gain custody of tables and are finally rewarded the opportunity to sit and eat, constantly glance to those in line, apparently finishing their food quickly, then respectfully departing their tables so that another tired traveler can be admitted to the crowded-to-capacity small restaurant. Over and over courtesy is silently demonstrated among most of the throng, as an orderly and cooperative atmosphere seems to float among them—unspoken, but obvious. But for Perch Woman, this doesn't seem to be the case. The weary waiting-in-line notice that when waiters visit her table, she non-verbally motions to her glass of water, accomplishing two things: first, it is obvious she wants another glass of water, and secondly, her gesture signals to the waiter that there is no confusion, *she is not finished.*

And the agony goes on. Table after table is set, traveler after traveler is seated, meal after meal is provided, eaten, then cleared away, making way for the next individual, couple, or family. As sandwich after sandwich is shuffled, Perch Woman remains perched on her throne. And most important for all to see as they wait in line, is her attitude. There is no mistaking her intentions, she is not influenced by the waiting weary and clearly, *she is not finished.*

In spite of their differences, the weary travelers are thrown together in an unwelcome, but common goal. Everyone seems

together in feeling the rhythm in the agony of waiting, thus the balanced cooperation. Good folks who don't believe they could perch, take a stab at understanding. *Maybe she just isn't aware of us waiting,* some speculate. *Perhaps her view of the waiting line is blocked,* others murmur with hope. *But maybe,* some others suggest, *she is waiting for an additional order.* But then, a yawn, a stretch, a glance at the line, a shedding of a jacket, all signal that Perch Woman knows of their plight, but just doesn't care. Then, as the fatigued fantasize about filling their bellies and grumble about her rudeness, they notice that Perch Woman has something else that makes her detachment to their needs take away any hope she is innocent. Right there they see it—*her book!*

As they agonize about her disinterest in their plight, the book she is reading really makes everything unbearable. Right there it is—huge, open and the subject of her attention and distraction. They just can't believe it. At first, some hope maybe the book explains why she is so detached. *Maybe,* they surmise, *she is engrossed in a world-altering book of such significance that in order to save humanity, her attention can't be distracted. Maybe she is reading about the key to world peace or the answer to getting the planes up and flying again?* they non-verbally hope. Those who know they couldn't perch with so many waiting, try to make sense of her perching. But then, every now and again, she glances at the on-lookers, moves her eyes up and down the line of the weary waiting, and for all to see and scorn, *she yawns.* That is, right before returning to her book. And again, she makes it clear to everyone looking at her perch, that she is not finished with her table.

As Perch Woman is reading at her table, the people *waiting* for her table contemplate and cuss. Their hope for her innocence is gone—basically turned to rude reality. The subject matter of her book becomes the only possible focus of their rage and frustration. One rumpled-suit man suggests to his rumpled-suit companion, "I bet she's not reading *How to Win Friends & Influence People.*"

His companion snorts, "Maybe she's reading *101 Ways to Make People Hate You.*"

They further indulge in loud sarcasm, hoping she will notice. And she seems to. But her response is not to rush hurriedly from the table, prostrating herself humbly in front of her rumpled-suit critics, begging forgiveness. With the deliberateness of a surgeon, Perch Woman, after direct eye contact to the rumpled-suit-guys, makes it quite clear that she heard their remarks and then, expertly motions for the waiter. They are at first hopeful, but only for a minute. When the also-hopeful-that-she-will-leave waiter arrives at her table, she doesn't pay the check as the hungry hoped, but instead, deliberately orders another glass of water and after looking back at her rude remarkers, places the unpaid restaurant check in her book as a marker. Obviously unfazed and content, smugly she just continues reading. She reads and she perches, after smiling sweetly at the waiter for her refreshed glass of water.

Hearing the rumpled-suit conversation, and seeing Perch Woman's obvious rebuke, others of the weary waiting chime in. "I bet she's reading *All About Me and My Inner Idiot*," scoffs what appears to be a person from the hippy-dippy-do-days, backpack bulging with organic snack wrappers, long ago consumed. A Mom with three tired kiddos gives her two cents on Perch Woman's book by loudly suggesting, "I bet she's reading *Coming in First: Screwing 101.*"

Not to be outdone, a dad holding a toddler while Mom is standing in the restroom potty line purports, "I bet she's not reading *The Kindness Handbook*, or *Taming My Inner Brat*. Instead, I'll bet the title of her book is something like *I Am Me and You Are Toast."*

And it went on and on, subtle insults about her selfishness. But Perch Woman just perched. Another bleary-eyed cowboy type speculated her book title to be "*I'm Constipated, and Therefore I Don't Give a Crap*," while his female companion carrying her way-too-tight cowboy boots on one arm suggested she was reading *"Jesus Loves You, But I'm His Favorite."* And every now and then when someone spoke directly at her, suggesting she hurry it up or take a hike, she just ordered more water, making it quite clear she was *not finished and she is not hiking anywhere.*

A family of four, longing for the four coveted place settings at Perch Woman's table, hears the rude talk from the passengers about her ever-so-important reading material. The seemingly four-year-old son inquires of his father, "Daddy, is that lady being selfish?"

Daddy is caught between his rage at Perch Woman and the morality training of his son. "I just don't know, son," Daddy laments, and thanks the little one for waiting. But then Daddy's older son inquires, with all the spirit of a teenager,

"Dad, are you allowed to sit as long as you want in a restaurant?"

The slightly older sister notes to Dad, "I see the sign *We Reserve the Right to Refuse Service to Anyone*, but once they serve her, can they refuse to let someone just suck service?"

Dad isn't sure how to answer the inquires of his alert children. Even though he doesn't know what to say, he wonders himself about the situation. Running through his mind is also the question, where are the signs, *No Perching*, or *Perchers Will Be Prosecuted*, or *Perching For 7 Minutes Only—Others Will Be Towed At Percher's Expense*? *No,* Dad realizes, there are no signs or rules about perching. And Dad is struck with his inability to know how to talk to his children about handling someone who is demonstrating the exact opposite of how everyone else is taught—or, Dad wonders, have they been taught?

He is so angry at her behavior that he contemplates acts that would send him to jail, but reality and thoughts of being arrested quell his actions. But inside, Dad wonders. The questions of his children make him consider why she is so different than everyone else? He also ponders whether he had really taught his children better behavior and will they be future perch people?

In another part of the travel world, they are heading for the coast in their four-wheel-drive Bronco (not yet bucking) pickup, towing a Rancho Rambler camper that is also towing a six-foot travel trailer, that is also towing another almost-trailer loaded with three small motorcycles. Attached to the backs and tops of the Bronco/Rancho Rambler assortment, is an interesting hodgepodge of toys, such as bicycles, surfboards, camping gear, and of course, the TV antenna. A weekend at the beach is on the front burner for this entourage sporting a front bumper sticker: *Beach or Bust.*

But the Rancho Rambler troop isn't alone on the highway heading west on the narrow, two-lane road, filled with beach-bound buggies of all shapes and makes. Vehicles follow, filled with families that are also filled with the same hope of a frolic in the sand. The 58 miles that must be traversed west is mostly a conglomerate of autos and such, all anxious to hurry the journey for enjoying the ocean. The winding road is a challenge, since everyone is in a hurry to escape the city and yet, because of the mountainous terrain and narrow access, passing the vehicle ahead to increase speed is often impossible. Although there are occasional spots where the road slightly widens to the right for slower vehicles to pull over, there are no passing lanes on the left for this Saturday morning crowd.

Not surprisingly, the anticipation of relaxing romps on the beach is in conflict with white-knuckled drivers, who must follow, however slowly, the Rancho Rambler in front of them. There is no passing, but there is bunching up—

big bunch-up bands of cars all prey to Rancho Rambler's speed. Even though all of the vehicles piled with their own version of Rancho Rambler's toys have the same hopes of a great weekend, and even though the vehicles all have different speed capacities, everyone will travel at Rancho Rambler's speed, like it or not—unless, of course, he realizes the band is bunching up behind him. Even though all the vehicles in the Bunch-Up Band started out somewhat the same, eventually the bunches begin and Rancho Rambler is the ruler of the pace.

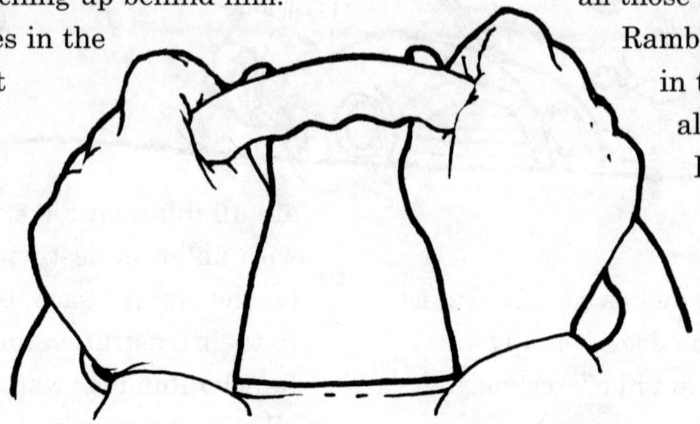

Soon, Rancho Rambler has collected a bunch behind—a very big bunch. Even though the Chevrolets, the Fords, the Oldsmobiles, and even the Corvettes are capable of driving much faster and even passing Rancho Rambler, the two-lane highway forbids it. On they go, around and around, up and down the beautiful coast road, at the speed, the slow speed, designated by the leader of the bunch, Rancho Rambler. Those in the bunch do not enjoy the beautiful scenery on this beautiful Saturday, noses seemingly pressed on windshields with the American frustration of being in line. The helplessness is profound, at least from the behind bunch, who no matter what the capabilities of their vehicles, must follow behind the road hog of Rancho Rambler.

The tension builds with the Bunch-Up Band as white knuckles grip and fathers grump out loud, "Road Hog." But Rancho Rambler just rumbles along while the band bunches up. Then a sign of hope emerges with a promise to dismantle the Bunch-Up Band. The obvious sign, *"Slow Vehicle Turnout Ahead"* brings comfort for all those in line. Surely Rancho Rambler will pull to the right in the slow vehicle turnout, allowing the faster of the Bunch-Up Band to pass.

At last, or so it seems, with the promise of the slow vehicle turnout approaching, the Bunch-Up Band begins to race their engines in anticipation. Here it comes.

But it is all for naught. Shocking as it is, Rancho Rambler turns down the turnout. And to some, he (assumed to be of the male gender) even seems to slow down, passing on the left those other more courteous conglomerates of campers and motor homes that had pulled into the turnout. He passes them all, and the disappointment of the Bunch-Up Band is profound as they now know it will be many more miles of up and down, over and around the beautiful scenery of the coastal range before another opportunity to pass the ever-so-slowly moving Rancho Rambler. *How could he do it?* they all wail and wonder?

Those who believe ***they*** would have pulled over in the turnout begin to ponder why Rancho Rambler isn't following the rules of the road.

"How could he do that?" they wonder. And in the wondering, they begin the hoping.

Maybe Rancho Rambler is from a foreign country and doesn't understand the meaning of *Slow Vehicle Turnout? Yes*, maybe that is it?

Others consider maybe he has so many items packed in his trailer that he doesn't really know the Bunch-Up Band is behind him? *Yes*, maybe that is it, they hope.

Several wonder if maybe his side mirrors are fogged in the morning dew, prohibiting him from seeing the Bunch-Up Gang? *Yes*, maybe that is it.

But some ponder why the contemplation centers around males and that maybe it is a female driver, too short perhaps, to see into the mirrors or see the *Slow Moving Vehicle Turnout* sign? But the females in the Bunch Up Band vehicles, hearing those sexist comments, wonder out loud if maybe it is a rude husband, back seat-driving his wife into passive-aggressive behavior? But then they realize there is no back seat in the Rancho Rambler for the wondered-about back seat driver, so that idea is abandoned just like the turnout was abandoned by R.R.

Not only are there speculations from the Bunch-Up Band about why Rancho Rambler refused to pull over, but they are also beginning their own bickering. The tension is tedious. The adults rage about Rancho Rambler and the children ask the tried and true, "Are we there yet?" They are all different folks, with different vehicles, with different destinations and different plans for the sunny beach, but they are fused together in their frustration and wonderment about Rancho Rambler who, with the slow pace, makes all of them exactly the same.

After a few more miles, a ray of hope emerges again. The sign reads, "*Slow Moving Vehicle Turnout—One Mile Ahead.*" Engines race and optimism is rekindled. The Bunch-Up Band expects to finally (and legally) squeeze by Rancho Rambler, hopefully allowing them to stop their bunching up and spread out more fairly—according to speed and power. *Surely this turnout will be the trick*? they hope.

But it is not to be. With the slow vehicle turnout on the right, Rancho Rambler turns it down, slowly lumbering on past the other campers and cooperative slow moving vehicles that took advantage of the turnout. Clearly, there was plenty of space for RR to pull over among the other obviously more courteous drivers, but he just putted along. The Bunch-Up Band is devastated, unable to pass on either side. The turnout is turned down and the Bunch-Up Band, bunches up even more. Rancho Rambler rules, without any apparent consideration for the bands of bunched-up cars behind.

Who is behind the wheel of Rancho Rambler is unknown to the Bunch-Up Band, but the *following folks* continue to try to figure out why Rancho Rambler doesn't behave as they believe they would behave. "Doesn't he (maybe it's a she) understand the obligation to pull over?" the bunch-ups ponder. "Perhaps he's a terrorist," is suggested by a few of the more political. But whatever or whoever is driving Rancho Rambler, the Bunch-Up Band has no reprieve, except for every now and then, a faster car takes a risk, pulling out in the left hand lane, trying to speed around RR. Everyone in the Bunch-Up Band hopes for the courageous one to make it. But curiously, everyone notices that when a car attempts to pass on the left, Rancho Ramble seems to muster previously unavailable speed making the pass impossible. And when a oncoming car approaches in the other direction, all the Bunch-Up Band can do is let the once-courageous-now-humbled car back in the dreaded line that putters along at the speed and rule of Rancho Rambler.

And then, finally after nearly two and one half hours of traveling under Rancho Rambler's reign, for a trip that should have taken about an hour, the beach town is approaching. About two miles from the ocean, the friendly road signs tell everyone that double lanes are approaching and there are other signs explaining how to maneuver the increased capacity. After about a mile, the sign states clearly: *Keep Right Except to Pass* and every single vehicle in the Bunch-Up Band gets ready to pass—finally. Some particularly frustrated members of the Bunch-Up Band contemplate the joy they will feel pulling up on the left side of Rancho Rambler, shaking their fist for the discourtesy displayed on the agonizing trip, but also getting a good look at the person who made their beach drive so miserable. Some began to make bets whether Rancho Rambler was a man or woman, young or old, short or tall. Some wager whether the vehicle has a single driver or whether it is filled with tons of not-paying-attention folks. And even though they all had different ideas among the vehicles for the left-hand pass, they were all equally frustrated and equally wanting to get a first-hand look at the rotten road hog. So up it comes, the moment of revenge and resolution.

With the arrival of the two lanes, the sad reality hits for the Bunch-Up Band. *Why should they have thought differently,* some consider as they watch Rancho Rambler slide easily into the left-hand passing lane, perching there as the road travels on, slowing down with no regard for the chirpy sign that suggested since he was a slow-moving vehicle, he should be in the right lane. Rancho Rambler can no longer hold the Bunch-Up Band back, but those who were lined up to pass him on the left are denied.

Those who not only wanted to settle their wagered bets on the particulars of who was driving Rancho Rambler, but who also wanted to wave a middle finger, are also denied. Once they figure out he is staying in the left hand lane they are disappointed, but they also realize they can finally pass—however, it is anticlimactic. Just as he had done on the mountain road, he is still in control, and they are forced to pass him under *his conditions*. So they do, and the passing on the right begins with a *kissing-your-sister* level of excitement.

But it seems Rancho Rambler isn't really finished with his control. Like pouring salt into their wounds, as they pass the conglomerate of towing contraptions, they read the bumper stickers pasted to Rancho Rambler's entourage. As the Corvette finally sweeps by, the seething driver reads, *"It Matters Not If You Win or Lose, It Only Matters That I Win."* Another fumes reading the bumper sticker, *"Oh, Look, Just 2,852,677 More Days Till I Start Caring What You Think."* The Ford (finally) is able to pass, but not until the driver rages and reads, *"Sorry, It's Not Your Day and Gee, I'd Like to Care, But I Don't Possess That Gene."* And then the Chevrolets all pass (still on the right, since Rancho Rambler enjoys left-lane perching), reading other bumper stickers such as, *"I'm Trying to See Things Your Way, But I Can't Get My Head Up My Butt,"* and, *"I'm Not Good at Empathy, Will You Settle For Sarcasm?"*

They trudge on by, torn with their need to retaliate, but with their hopes of a beach weekend waiting. They can't see the driver, but the bumper stickers make them realize Rancho Rambler was not ignorant, not from a foreign country, and not a terrorist. As they drive by, infuriated by the bumper stickers, they realize two things. First, the driver knew and didn't care about their bunch-up frustration, and secondly, that their middle fingers would remain pocketed because of Rancho Rambler's final cleverness.

They all pass and Rancho Rambler eventually pulls over at a large truck stop/gas station with one of his favorite gift shops to buy bumper stickers. For him, the trip is realized as a success, since he puttered along at his own speed and had a certain enjoyment in the scenery and showing off his carefully chosen bumper stickers. As he breathes in a final sigh of satisfaction, his cell phone, that had been out of commission during the mountainous drive, rings. It is his wife, stranded in the Atlanta airport for most of the evening. He is sad to hear about her calamity, but heartened when she tells him the night wasn't too stressful. After all, she related, she was able to finish her novel and yes, she will arrive at the beach, in a rental car, to join him and the kids for the weekend.

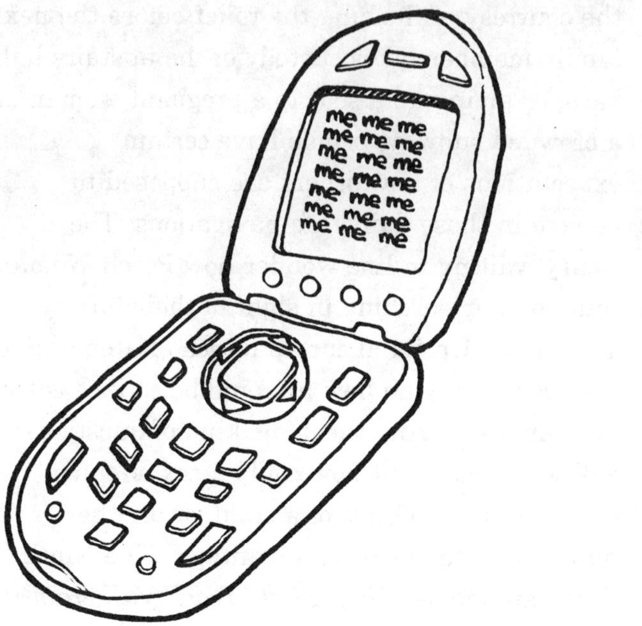

What makes some people follow the rules of courtesy? Is it guilt or goodness?

THE NINTH COMMANDMENT—THOU SHALT TEACH VULNERABILITY APPRECIATION

Different than the days of covered wagons and open prairies, for the most part, life bunches people up, just as happened on the trip to the coast and in the Atlanta airport. In these close proximities, there is a human demand for connection and cooperation that cannot be denied, however uncomfortable. The waiters, the weary travelers, the drivers and most people in daily life activities are constantly enjoined in the human connection/cooperation process as they move about in the world.

Most of the time there is no choice—everyone is married to the madness of how humans navigate around each other. Whether it involves the courtesy of flushing the toilet before the next family member takes custody of the upstairs half bath, or giving up a seat to a pregnant woman on a crowded subway, people have certain expectations of how others are supposed to behave in those daily, life navigations. The weary-waiting in line wonder how Perch Woman could do her perching in sight of their misery. The Bunch Up Band curses Rancho Rambler and they can't imagine how he could be so insensitive to their needs. And the same kind of questions are pondered about how could a sex offender disregard the feelings of a child, or another human and take sexual advantage. The Ninth Commandment—*Thou Shalt Teach Vulnerability Appreciation* provides lessons about how people like Perch Woman/Rancho Rambler can easily emerge from normal American families—probably without too many serious problems with sexual offending. But raising children to be those who discount the feelings of others, in airports, on highways, in courtrooms, in boardrooms or in bedrooms is a precarious crapshoot, leaving a breeding ground for sexual disrespect.

REVERSE RAMBLINGS AND PERCHINGS

To reverse the situation in the busy airport or on the busy coastal highway, it is important to ask why other people would behave differently than Perch Woman or Rancho Rambler and who taught them? Why did some courteous folks gobble down their turkey sandwiches, feeling the hunger pangs of the weary waiting in line? Why would most of the Bunch-Up Band, had they been in Rancho Rambler's ruling position, felt relief when the slow vehicle turnout finally arrived, because pangs of guilt for holding everyone up would have made them uncomfortable? What makes some people follow the rules of courtesy? Is it guilt or goodness?

GUILT OR GOODNESS

Some people do the right thing because it is just that—the right thing to do. For these folks there is a universal or spiritual need to follow the order of *goodness*, sometimes on a devout or divine plane. Some of these people are religious, but many are not. For these folks, being good is important for no other reason than because of a belief in a universal plan for cooperation among humans. They believe in a general design about goodness—that it is just the right thing to do. Most importantly, these people wouldn't care if anyone else knew about their kindness, courtesy or contribution to the big picture of goodness.

GUILT TRIP

And then there are the guilt folks, who also do what is right, not necessarily because of any universal goodness belief, but because they want to *avoid feeling guilty*. They would give up their seats in the restaurant and they would pull over for the Bunch-Up Band. But mostly, because they can't bear feeling like the inconsiderate slobs of Rancho Rambler and Perch Woman. An overall sense of guilt governs the lives of these people and that operative level of *avoiding guilt* isn't a bad thing or a trait that will send them into therapy or a tragic talk show featuring topics such as *The Ghosts of Guilt*. The people who feel guilty when they don't do the right thing are very important in keeping the world sweet and safe.

GOOD TRIP

And then there are the good folks who do their pulling over and their seat-sacrificing because they want *everyone to know* they did the right thing. It's not about feeling guilty for not doing the courteous thing. They behave properly for their own personal reinforcement that comes from knowing everyone in line saw them graciously give the table to the Mom with three screaming preschoolers, or they do it for the pleasure that comes from the friendly wave from the Corvette driver who is grateful for the chance to pass. This effort may not be a bad thing, just something that makes these people feel good, so they do it. These people are particularly good at making big scenes out of their goodness and often they do lots of really, really good things as long as really, really lots of people know about it. And like the guilt-driven folks, these people also help the world function harmoniously.

TIPPING THE SCALE OF GUILT

The way in which people tip for services provides a good example of the *guilt to goodness* spectrum of who does what and why—especially since tipping is an unwritten rule. Just about all the folks on the *guilt to goodness* spectrum tip in restaurants—after all, people are watching. Unless a James Bond type of escape occurs after dessert, there is direct knowledge of the tip or lack thereof, from the waiter, the cashier and the two business partners joining for the power lunch. With the unavoidable audience in restaurants, most people tip.

But when it comes to tipping a bellman or a skycap luggage handler, pressure about whether someone notices the financial exchange (guilt) diminishes. After all, readings on the goodness barometer, drastically drop standing in the

The people who feel guilty when they don't do the right thing are very important in keeping the world sweet and safe.

So perhaps the reasons people feel guilty or do the right thing has to do with who is watching.

The issue of how one person navigates life in consideration of how others feel, seems to be the second most powerful key (in addition to delaying gratification) in becoming a criminal, especially a sexual criminal.

hallway of a large hotel, late at night, with luggage tucked safely in the room. If only a pleasant smile is given to the sweating bellman and the door quickly closed, who will know the tip was withheld? Or standing on a snow-covered airport entrance with luggage safely sent down the conveyor belt, it is easy to just smile and walk away—*no one of importance* being aware of the slight cheat, except the disgruntled suitcase skycaps. Rationalizations conclude that in this faraway airport, at this time of day, with this weather, there is likely never to be another encounter with the person—reducing the guilt possibilities. Only two people will know of the slight and probably only one of them cares.

And then there are the least tipped and perhaps the hardest working of the depending-on-tips employees—the hotel housekeepers. It is true they leave the cute little notes on the desk with a breath mint saying, *Clara Cleaned Your Room*, which is meant to remind you about the need for tipping those who keep the toilets tidy. But these poor folks rarely get the tips probably because of the out-of-sight-out-of-guilty-mind operating as it is recognized that Clara won't even show up to know she was neglected for several hours after checkout. So perhaps the reasons people feel guilty or do the right thing has to do with who is watching.

BUT MORE

But there is more about why people do good things and it relates to the Ninth Commandment and raising sexually respectful children. This critically important issue goes way beyond tipping bellmen or perching on a Chili's restaurant stool. There are people who do the right thing because they are tuned into the feelings of those around them and they can actually experience the feelings (frustration, hunger, fear, etc.) of others. In other words, it is the *vulnerability* of other people that seems to guide the really good people, and sex offenders lack that quality. So the Ninth Commandment is about understanding the issue of vulnerability, and the key it holds in sexual respect or sexual disrespect.

TO CRIMINALITY TWO

The issue of how one person navigates life in consideration of how others feel, seems to be the second key (in addition to delaying gratification) in becoming a criminal, especially a sexual offender. That doesn't mean that Rancho Rambler and every other road hog or table percher is destined for, or just escaped from, sex offender prison. Nor does it mean that every person who forgets to leave Clara a tip is automatically the proud owner of deviant sexual arousal. For sure, there are lots of very, very successful people who have a callused concern for others and they make it just fine in the world, and they sometimes make lots of fine money.

But in the big basket of 900 sex offenders, studied and studied, there was no doubt that stalking in their backgrounds were subtle tendencies to place their needs before the needs of others, which has a prerequisite of discounting the feelings of others. In those findings, there was clear evidence of such things as taking advantage of a younger sister or brother, whether playing a game or engaging the more vulnerable one in a simple trick. There were constant examples of rule breaking, cheating, and *fudging* the advantage to their favor, sometimes ever-so-slight.

WRONG ROUND-UP

It was also clear that many had an attitude that breaking the rules was only wrong if they were caught. These offenders were often competitive folks, usually trying to edge out others in the workplace, the baseball dugout, the backyard, the video arcade, or the family room. Many of them were in do-good positions—leaders of groups, coaches, religious mentors, community icons, or esteemed and powerful family members. And their mantra was often talking about the wrong of others. But even though they often did helpful things, their good deeds had a subtle, self-centered motive, often bringing something powerful to them rather than being because of the needs of others.

These lacking-in-connection-with-others sex offenders were loved folks, having scores of supportive cheerleaders such as partners, parents, friends, and sometimes even their victim-children. But under careful scrutiny, those relationships were less than reciprocal, with the offender enjoying support from others, without much return. The ability to connect with the feelings of others seemed to be missing in most sex offenders. And that lack of concern was not always guided by meanness, cruelty, or anger, fostered in a hatred of others. The ability to connect with the feelings of others just seemed *undeveloped.*

These lacking-in-connection-with-others sex offenders were some of the most loved folks, having scores of supportive cheerleaders such as partners, parents, friends, and sometimes even their own victim-children.

EMPATHY ENVELOPE

So along with a failure to delay gratification as emphasized in the Eighth Commandment, the second key to becoming a sexual criminal seems to be a failure to appreciate vulnerability. And a fancy term for that failure has to do with *empathy*. Whether it is a newscaster irate about sex offender legislation, a psychiatrist testifying at a sex offender sentencing, or an educator at the Sex Offender 101 conference attended by Bird Mom and Middle-Seat-Mom, the idea that those who are sexually disrespectful *don't have empathy* for others would not be a shocking revelation. Sex offender treatment centers throughout the world focus on empathy training as a cornerstone of therapy. And so if treatment for sex offenders focuses on how to train them to feel for others, then it doesn't take much to figure out it is exactly what is missing in the first place.

But with sexual crimes, there is an up close and personal issue that requires the offender to completely disregard the feelings of the victim—detaching from the tears, the sadness, and the panic.

CLOSE UP AND PERSONAL

Just like denying Clara her hard-earned tip is easy because no one has to see her disappointment, many crimes are also faceless. Those who embezzle from the co-worker's picnic fund can commit the crime with a felt tip pen in the privacy of the staff lounge and still get a great big thanks from those co-worker victims for bringing the doughnuts to the Monday morning staff meeting. The crime is faceless. A neighbor can burglarize a house without ever having to hear about the family's sadness in losing the family heirloom brooch that belonged to sweet Aunt Sadie. But with sexual crimes, there is an up- close and personal issue that requires the offender to completely disregard the feelings of the victim—detaching from the tears, the sadness, and the panic. But that isn't all in the differences of person-to-person crimes.

When sex offenders are face-to-face (or what ever other body part is pertinent) with their victim, they must maintain enough control to manage sexual arousal while someone is crying, hurting or even bleeding. That kind of detachment is necessary to be successful and that kind of ability is usually amazing to those who feel for others and could not handle the disturbance in arousal maintenance.

For most people engaging in a sexual experience, distraction must be managed. An irritating telephone call from mother-in-law in the middle of a Sunday afternoon sexual tryst, might send everything back to the starting gate—sometimes getting the couple so out of "the mood" that nothing materializes until next Sunday. For offenders to be able to concentrate and not be distracted by the victim's trauma is very different than the shoplifter committing the heist, but then having no problem wearing the illegal (and expensive) skirt later, while enjoying a vacation in the Bahamas. In the moment of the offense, using the traumatized victim for sexual pleasure, the sex offender must have the ability to detach and that can only happen if they have been taught to discount—either the hungry waiting-in-line, the cars bunching up behind, or the tears of the child being sexually disrespected.

RAINBOW NOT RANCHO RAMBLINGS

Returning to the 900-plus sex offender evaluations conducted for the honorable search of *what happened* to make someone become a sexually disrespectful person, it is clear that encased in their histories was a failure to develop vulnerability appreciation. But the research and the rainbow ramblings probably weren't really needed for that conclusion. Just as most folks know that sex offenders didn't develop (especially if they grew up with Bird Moms) the ability to delay gratification, it is also pretty evident that sex offenders also have difficulty appreciating the vulnerability of others, which is a fancy way of saying, they lack empathy.

SIBLING STUFF

One of the best categories for figuring out how children learn or don't learn about vulnerability appreciation has to do with relationships between brothers and sisters. Unless there is a constant supply of twins, triplets or quadruplets, a natural state of vulnerability between brothers and sisters unfolds in families, with a guarantee that some will always be older and younger, littler and bigger. Sibling rivalry was not only clear with most of the studied sex offenders, but the parents of these offenders also seemed to condone this conflict as a natural outcome of family life. And maybe most families, sex offender or not, do the same.

Are children naturally in conflict with one another and will most children be expected to hate their brothers and sisters? Could sibling rivalry be prevented if parents, undoing infanthood's lack of empathy, began teaching the vulnerability of the youngest child right from the beginning, just like teaching how to look both ways before crossing the street? Could teaching about the vulnerability between children in families be a lesson plan for raising sexually respectful children?

As sternly instructed, the fidgety six-year-old approaches her father as he sits in the old rocking chair. She climbs onto one knee, while he hands her the baby sister that was held on his other knee. This eight-pound blob of flesh, with absolutely no hair, is quite perplexing to the six-year-old sister, and besides, this little bundle of nonsense doesn't even smell very good. The older one is curious, however, as the baby's blanket is gently pulled aside to reveal a prune-like skin condition and a bagging and sagging body tone, nothing at all like her own Sparkle Plenty doll. What the fuss seems to be about this tiny, wrinkled-up thing, escapes her, but she is six years old and she is well versed in recognizing her father's serious tone. So she listens and tries to figure out the big deal of this baby business.

At first, Dad asks incomprehensible questions such as, "Isn't she cute?" which has absolutely no meaning to the six-year-old. Inside her, however, is an understanding that this is probably one of those times when it is best not to give an honest response to a question, remembering what happened at Thanksgiving dinner last year when she announced that her Aunt Bertha needed to brush her teeth because she had *buzzard breath.* With Dad's question about cuteness, the older child smiles and nods. It was the best she could do under the circumstances.

Then the lesson comes. As Father tenderly holds the six-year-old, who tenderly holds the infant, he teaches. "Mary is your little sister. She isn't even one month old and you are already six-years-old. She will always be littler than you. Don't ever hurt her, because no matter what happens, for the rest of her life, she will always be littler. Don't you ever let me see you cheat or trick her, because you will always be bigger." Lesson learned and lesson ended.

"Mary is your little sister. She isn't even one month old and you are already six years old. She will always be littler than you. Don't ever hurt her, because no matter what happens, for the rest of her life, she will always be littler."

A lifetime later, the two sisters lament. One gets misty-eyed when she remembers that *yes,* she hit her sister once and *yes,* the other regrets that she committed an act of betrayal and tattled— but only once. The miracle is that it was a lesson in vulnerability from one child to the other (perhaps undoing the self-centeredness of infancy) and the two times of transgression from Dad's teaching still makes both sisters shed a tear and feel a loss. Vulnerability appreciation at its finest, but sadly so often missed by parents who expect sibling rivalry as a natural outcome of raising children because they never stop it early, before it even developed.

GOOD GUILT

Also in the scheme of parenting lessons that are rarely challenged—but just accepted, are the edicts espousing that guilt is always a bad thing for the kidlets. Just as many parents reached for high self-esteem but actually created self-centeredness in their precious little poopers, sometimes fears of guilt and the effort to avoid guilt at all costs, can foster the same errors. That tendency is founded on the belief that guilt is always a bad thing. "My mother is a guilt goddess," or "My wife is a travel agent specializing in guilt trips," are the common ideas of those suggesting guilt equates with a negative. Ironically, sometimes in the effort to teach vulnerability and empathy to children, a little guilt can go a long way. Like anything, however, too much guilt can be disastrous and even destructive, but in revisiting the same two sisters who learned not to hurt each other, a beautiful lesson in guilt emerges.

FROSTING FUN

They walk a mile home from school every day. No, this wasn't the proverbial walk home from school Dad proclaims to have had, walking to and from school, five miles each way, *both routes uphill.* These little girls really did walk one mile home (neither up nor down hill) on a comfortable country road, and the excursion made them hungry. When they reached home, their choices of snacks usually included what Mom called *healthy choices*, which from the viewpoint of the sisters were *chump choices*. Quite boring were the sliced apples, cheese strips, and whole grain crackers left by Mom. The hungry sisters really wanted a Hershey bar or Hostess Twinkies, but none were available. Mom would not be available either, at least for an hour or two, until she returned from work. With Mom absent and both the digestive and creative juices flowing, the sisters decide to create their own snack, partly to quell their hunger, but also to avoid the boredom of the *healthy choice* layout from Mom.

They both recalled their 4-H lessons in baked foods for the county fair. A little bit of butter, a little bit of water, and a big bit of powdered sugar would result in a medium-sized bowl of frosting. Usually, the sisters delighted in licking the bowl of frosting when Mom helped them with their cupcakes for the fair, but now they were at the forefront of having their own entire bowl of frosting. Unimaginable culinary genius it was, and salivating, they moved forward with the project. But after the frosting was whipped, the tummies were filled, and the bowls were washed and put away to hide the evidence, trouble began. The problem was that the sisters began to think, and with that thinking came guilt.

Somehow, very unlike Perch Woman and Rancho Rambler, the little girls began to feel badly about what they had done. And why? Did they think Mom would return home and with the expertise of a crime lab technician, discover the missing butter, sugar, and water from the kitchen supplies? Did they wonder if, after they flushed the *healthy choices* down the toilet to hide the evidence, Dad might come home, call the Roto-Rooter man to dig up the septic tank, and actually discover the apples, cheese, and whole grain crackers? Or did these little girls just feel guilty about doing the wrong thing, even though they would likely never get caught?

Or did these little girls just feel guilty about doing the wrong thing, even though they would likely never get caught?

FROSTING FELONIES

Good guilt, however uncomfortable, wandered on between the sisters. The older child made a suggestion to which the younger one agreed, wholeheartedly. "Let's take money from our piggy bank and put it in Mom's purse for groceries," was the idea of the guilt moment.

The little one responded with her own suggestion of, "Let's look in the newspaper and see how much it costs and put a little extra in Mom's purse to make up for the trick." And they did it. They put money in Mom's purse and they felt somewhat guilt-relieved, at least for the moment, happy that Mom's crime lab kit never emerged and the Roto-Rooter man worked elsewhere.

However, in the rest of their childhoods, other frosting escapades occurred for the sisters when hungry tummies and the *healthy choices* became unbearable. And every time they indulged in the frosting venture, they slipped some money into Mom's purse. A lifetime later, when the now-fifty-something-year-old sisters sit by the pool in their swimming suits, they each wonder if the *thunder thighs* they complain about just might have something to do with the frosting felonies they committed as children. Their dimpled and jiggling thighs look like most other women's in the aging process, but for them whispers of memories makes an ever-so-slight difference. The guilt doesn't mean they weep at the grave of their Mother, begging forgiveness for the healthy choice flushing. Nor does it mean they become an aerobics instructor for the sole purpose of ridding themselves of their *guilt endowed thunder thighs*. It just means that someone taught them about guilt—about thinking of personal responsibility—which indirectly made a contribution to their vulnerability appreciation lessons.

Starting with the obvious, it does not take rocket science to figure out those who abuse and torture animals would at least have the tolerance to abuse humans as well.

CRITTERS AND CARING

In checking out sex offenders and where they land on the guilt to goodness spectrum, caring for critters provides interesting information. How parents organize critter care can be an important issue in raising sexually respectful children, especially considering the number of households that have pets, and the number of studied sex offenders who demonstrated a consistent thread in animal involvement from their childhoods.

Starting with the obvious, it does not take rocket science to figure out those who abuse and torture animals would at least have the tolerance to abuse humans, as well. Animal cruelty, as an example, is especially high in families with domestic violence, so few questions should be asked about the crossover rates of animal abusers and those who could take advantage of the vulnerability of humans in sexual and non-sexual ways. But that is only one linear connection from critter cruelty to people cruelty, not including what happens in the other direction.

CAUTION CRITTER CROSSING

In studying the 900-plus sex offenders, something interesting emerged that may seem different in thinking from other studies—probably because the sample was so big. Sure, the researchers would say, if several dozen wife batterers were evaluated, they would probably show high levels of animal cruelty and child sexual abuse. But the heavy-hitters in the number crunching would also say that with 900 sex offenders, studied over nearly a quarter of a century, someone should really pay attention to those findings and for sure, what the findings didn't find.

Animal cruelty at high rates, or even elevated rates, among the 900-plus offenders just didn't seem to materialize. However, a significant number of the offender folks seemed to like their dogs and cats better than they liked some of the people who came to the family reunion on Labor Day weekend. Some offender families were really, really proud of their Fido and Flopsy, and liked to show them off. But just being good to the critters didn't mean there was a free ride to being good to human critters.

CRITTER ALLOWANCES

But the one thing that seemed prevalent was the studied sex offenders seemed to share a lack of *appreciation for the vulnerability* of the critters in the family. As children, most of them took care of the critters, but they did this *for an allowance*, not because the animals were incapable of caring for themselves. They had animals for show or for drudgery in many cases, but little understanding about vulnerability and the critters was ever taught.. *No,* there didn't seem to be evidence of torture chambers for the critters in the big picture of things and *no*, most of the offenders didn't have a history of even animal neglect. But *yes*, the window of opportunity to teach vulnerability appreciation in critter care was slammed shut—opportunity missed by their parents.

Trying to find a balance between his love of trout fishing and his desire to have his girls appreciate vulnerability, Dad does what he must—he lies.

GUILT AND FISH GUTS

She knows that punishment is imminent as she is solemnly trotted to the garage—her father's domain. He has a quart jar of water and with her in hand, he scowls, and pours the water into the cat dish. His demeanor is stern as a clear indication she has done something or she hasn't done something dreadfully wrong. Either way, she knows she is in big trouble. Peg, the three-legged cat, runs (hops) to the cat dish, eagerly lapping the water poured by the Father. Now it comes—the lesson.

Father scolds, "How would you like to be that thirsty and have someone forget to do their chores and bring you water?" Guilt is in the air. Father is teaching his daughter about vulnerability. It is not that she will receive, or because of her indiscretion *not* receive, an allowance for feeding the garage cat. It is that she will be punished for not respecting the vulnerability of the old cat that cannot pour the water on her own. It is vulnerability appreciation that Father is teaching, and in reality, this Dad didn't even like this three-legged cat, Peg. She pooped in his toolbox on one occasion, which is apparently just about the limit for any reasonable Dad. Nonetheless, in the lessons of the Father, this old, not-so-popular-with-Dad cat, Peg, deserved to have her vulnerability respected, which is *anti-sex offender education* at it's most subtle and finest.

OOPS

This same father, who has religiously taught his daughters to care for Peg the cat, in spite of her transgressions with his toolbox, later finds himself in an *oops* situation with other lessons about vulnerability of the critters. Although Dad is not particularly fond of Peg the cat, he is very fond of trout fishing. On one particular day, as his little girls gather around, watching his feat with a rather feisty trout, Dad ends the fishing victory by pulling out the hook. With his tool of conquest comes a rather rude collection of guts and intestines, much to the horror of the little girls.

"Daddy! Daddy! You're hurting the fish!" screamed the female munchkins, who were quite familiar with their father's instructions about vulnerability of critters. Like this rather unlucky fish, Dad is caught. But because he enjoys trout fishing and since he does not want to stop fishing because of hypocrisy, Dad must find a solution. Trying to find a balance between his love of trout fishing and his desire to have his girls appreciate vulnerability, Dad does what he must—he lies. Clearing his throat, he weakly searches for a rationalization that will protect his integrity with his daughters *and* allow him to continue trout fishing. He testifies falsely to his gullible daughters.

"It doesn't hurt the fish," he reassures the three little ones, eyes fixed on the dangling intestines.

Child protection workers are often amazed that the critters in an abusive home may be fed and sheltered better than the children.

"But Daddy, why doesn't it hurt them?" is the desperate question from three girls competent in vulnerability and critter care.

He lies, falsely proclaiming, "It doesn't hurt fish because they have no arms and legs." There! The little girls will absent-mindedly accept this explanation, at least for a few more years, and Dad will continue to trout fish. His effort is admirable, even though his biology knowledge and honesty is questionable.

LOVING LIABILITIES

It is true that some people who love the critters may not always be good at appreciating the vulnerability of humans. It doesn't seem automatic. It is likely that Rancho Rambler may even have a dog or two inside the camper who will be cuddled up when Perch Woman arrives in her rental car. And it is also true that some people may even care for their animals more than they care for people. The criminal character in the movie *Silence of the Lambs,* who brutally murdered young women, absolutely loved his little poodle, *Precious*—obviously more than he cared for other humans. Child protection workers are often amazed that the critters in an abusive home may be fed and sheltered better than the children. As the headlines scream, "Neglected Children Had Nothing To Eat Except Dog Food," the priorities of the parents are clear and often more common than not. But in these situations, no one really wonders or considers that animal attachment or appreciation has anything to do with the critter's vulnerability but more likely what the animal provided the owners from a selfish perspective. The debate continues about whether the care of critters in the backgrounds of sex offenders is any more unusual than it is in other families, but there is no debate about the value in teaching children to appreciate vulnerability—to protect them from becoming sex offenders—through the teaching avenue of animals. Yes, even an old, three-legged cat and a gutless-and-unlucky trout can be teaching opportunities.

RULE REALITY

The sex offender studies also revealed what seemed to be significant styles of subtle rule breaking and that issue seems directly connected to vulnerability appreciation—or lack thereof. Whether it was tricking a younger sister in a game of Tiddily Winks, outsmarting school officials by forging absent excuses, or stealing small change from Grandma's purse, the sex offenders seemed to feel that the rules were for others to follow. That was especially true if the rules infraction went unnoticed. It was a different spin on the old question about trees, forests and sound. "*If a tree falls in the woods and no one hears it, does sound exist?*" is the age-old question for philosophers and think-tank graduate students. Sex offenders (and the Perch Woman, Rancho Rambler types) spin the idea of *if you break the rules and no one finds out, was there any foul?* What seemed to be clear with these offenders was not only a rule-breaking reality and lifetime pattern, but also a disdain for people who either weren't smart enough to call foul, or for people who followed the rules when easier paths were available.

CAUGHT OR NOT

Yes, Perch Woman probably would have relinquished her restaurant seat if the manager had spoken to her and demanded she pay her bill and depart. And yes, if the state police did some red and blue light flashing following Rancho Rambler, he certainly would have pulled over and with a little discussion, he might have taken the next slow moving vehicle turnout. But it seems, ever-so-subtly, that PW and RR probably have character flaws similar to sex offenders, and both would have not only challenged the demands that were attempting to be reined upon them from a cranky Chili's manager or a sassy state police officer, but both probably would have enjoyed the discord. "Where are the signs outlining table time limits?" may have been the claimed outrage of Perch Woman, or she may have really enjoyed demanding to know if the CEO of the restaurant chain could be contacted (at midnight) from the Atlanta airport. Of course, that ploy would have really been exciting for her—gaining attention from others in her claimed outrage.

Rancho Rambler may have also enjoyed quibbling with the state police about whether the sign *Slow Vehicle Turnout* was a law, or just a *suggestion*. "What exactly does the sign say that defines the word ***slow***" might have been his pleasurable posturing with the cop. But neither Perch Woman nor Rancho Rambler would have had a single consideration for the vulnerability of the hungry passengers or the other vehicles in the Bunch-Up Band—just whether or not they got caught or whether they could win the argument. Truly it would have been about them—not the others influenced by their behavior.

GUILT, GOODNESS AND GRANDMA

In addition to sibling conflicts being accepted, if not encouraged, it seemed the studied sex offenders grew up in households with no concept of vulnerability for the elderly. When sex offenders abuse children, they do not appreciate or feel the vulnerability of the child, whereas those empathic feelings seem to exist for those who don't offend. In other words, people who couldn't use an innocent child for sexual pleasure usually have a connection to the child's vulnerability. When crimes are committed against the elderly, the handicapped, or others so vulnerable, judges, juries, and society become outraged. "How could they take advantage of someone so vulnerable?" is whined concerning the rape of an elderly woman. "They violated the most sacred of trusts," some opine when sexual abuse in a nursing home is discovered. Yet do parents teach the vulnerability of Grandmas and Grandpas as a lesson in raising sexually respectful children or is the teaching window ignored?

In addition to sibling conflicts being accepted, if not encouraged, it seemed these studied sex offenders grew up in households with no concept of vulnerability for the elderly.

Mom exhibits her dangerously demanding quiet, clears her throat, and at eye level says to the now trembling son, "I never, ever, want to see your butt on any piece of furniture when your grandmother walks into the room. Do you hear me, young man?"

GOOD GRANDMA GUILT

He moans and groans, clearly feeling sorry for himself. "But there are thirteen grandkids in the room and there is a chair for everyone. Why do we have to stand up and give Grandmother all our chairs? It's stupid. She can only use one!" complains the eight-year-old to his glaring mother, the queen of reprimand. The silence and cold-eye stare from his mother signals trouble. The child knows that when Mom is pensive and quiet, danger lurks. He prefers a nice, hysterical answer from Mom that would traditionally signal to him that he had the upper hand. Not this time.

Mom exhibits her dangerously demanding quiet, clears her throat, and at eye level says to the now trembling son, "I never, ever, want to see your butt on any piece of furniture when your grandmother walks into the room. Do you hear me, young man?" There it was, not a question, not an issue for debate, and not subject to any discourse. Son is clear and as he slips away, grateful for no further punishment for disrespecting his elders, he makes a mental note to just give it up, give her his chair, and to stop—yes, stop—contemplating the true capacities of Grandma's posterior.

NURSERIES TO NURSING HOMES

Whether nature intended it or not, it seems that the way in which humans begin life shares many characteristics with the way humans end their lives. Chubby cheeks, balding heads and sagging skin were there in the nursery when the wee one came into the world and as Grandma and Grandpa consider the nursing home, those traits seems to return. Not surprisingly, the vulnerability issues are also similar in the very young and the very old. Caring for the elderly, actively teaching (demanding) vulnerability appreciation for those in the later stages of life seems to have been absent from sex offender backgrounds. Teaching children to respect the vulnerability of their baby siblings should be in concert with teaching children to respect the vulnerability of their elders.

THE SPORT OF VULNERABILITY

America seems to be a sport driven society—loving the challenge of competition. Mothers and Fathers commonly consider soccer, volleyball, football and other ball bouncing competitions as an automatic demand in the parenting paradigm. It is difficult to determine if this love affair with athletics is because Mom and Dad really think the kiddos will benefit from running up and down the field, the court, or the ice rink, or if it is Mom and Dad who love the competition and the fact that through their very own little ones, they can fulfill their dreams of competitive success. But regardless of the reason, most kiddos are at least given the chance at athletic involvement and it was no different for the studied sex offenders.

There were high levels of sports competition among the sex offenders, but that is also true of most American families. When competition is extracted from the sports equation, the glaring reality of vulnerability in athletic competition is difficult to discount. That certainly doesn't mean every Little Leaguer who destroys the other team in the state championship game is likely to set up his own adult bookstore chain or seek residence in the Playboy mansion. But if vulnerability appreciation is lacking in sex offenders, then those parents who wish to raise sexually respectful children should carefully examine the vulnerability issue in athletics.

BALANCING BOUNCING BALLS

The acrimonious marriage of sports and vulnerability is important to understand for parents who strive for balance, but it may be an unwelcome consideration for fanatical parents who live for the competition of Saturday afternoon and who, in their own comfort paradigm, believe it is always good for the kidlets to win, win, win. Horror stories abound regarding parents resorting to violence at T-Ball games about whether the four-year-old really touched the second base bag. Tales of parents bribing the soccer coach with free bowling passes if their clumsy seven-year-old daughter will get to play the entire game on her birthday may simply cause some to smile at the fanaticism of ball bouncing parents. More seriously, Moms and Dads have been known to commit crimes of violence over the issue of sports competition.

FOUL BALLS CALLED

Suggestions that athletics may be harmful to children are rudely resisted (crying foul) with counter arguments about sports teaching such honorable skills as teamwork, cooperation and physical strength. Those gains may exist in some sport situations, but like it or not, athletics clearly teaches taking advantage of vulnerability. This understanding is sometimes an uncomfortable reality for fanatical sports parents, crying foul and resisting the idea that anything but wholesomeness comes from sweat-smelling locker rooms and $150.00, must-have Speedos. But truly understanding the issue of vulnerability in sports allows a focus of wisdom for parents who want their children to play sports, but also want their children to become sexually respectful adults.

THE BALANCE

The softball coach gathers the Fighting Phantoms around in the proverbial huddle before the Little League game. It is time for last minute pointers. The boys eagerly await the advice of the coach since, after all, he has promised pizza and root beer with a win in this, the last of their season games. The Phantoms want all the tips their beloved coach can offer to secure the win (as well as pizza and root beer), and the anticipation is also high for the parents of the Little Leaguers, bearing the heat and stale hot dogs in this grand finale. The coach tells the team, with the authority of a state-of-

That certainly doesn't mean every Little Leaguer who destroys the other team in the state championship game is likely to set up his own adult bookstore chain or seek residence in the Playboy mansion.

This doesn't mean following the Little League dog pile of celebration, Son is required to seek out chubby boy and apologize to the right fielder, promising never to do it again.

the-union presidential address, "Hit the ball into right field. He is real chubby and can't run very fast." There it was. The boys understand the instructions, and as they complete the multiple, stack-up, hand shake, so familiar to jock types, the last word they chant is, "Right field!"

The coach was right, that was the spot. The game stays close with Little Leaguers catching and dropping flies, striking out and running out of the base lines, and yet showing baseball competency more often than not. With competencies ranging from stolen bases to forgetting the order of bases, the score bounces back and forth. Mom and Dad of one Fighting Phantom watch with agony as their son comes to bat in the last inning. The tension mounts with this last opportunity to win the root beer, and the Fighting Phantom dugout occupants begin to chant, "Right field! Right field!" Son sweats, but eventually bats exactly as he was told, six inches above the huffing and puffing (and chubby) right fielder, winning the game and the prize of pizza and root beer.

Son took advantage of the vulnerability of the right fielder, as he should if he is to excel in Little League and at least fantasize about a baseball scholarship to the State University. But clearly, Son spotted vulnerability, aimed for it, and took advantage. Will he become a sex offender because he took advantage of vulnerability through athletics? Once the home run was registered, should his parents have begun screaming, "You're going to become a pervert!" Should Mom and Dad register Son as a sex offender, right after pizza and root beer, just to expedite the process, since that is Son's destination?

Perhaps the answer lies in the issue of *balance* between taking advantage of vulnerability and teaching children to appreciate vulnerability. Just as unbridled self-centeredness of infancy can result in failures to teach delayed gratification, perhaps athletics, with its focus on taking advantage of vulnerability, if left unbalanced, could result in the kidlets missing out on those very important vulnerability appreciation lessons.

OUT OF BALANCE WISDOM

As proud Mom and Dad watched Son hit the ball over the huffing and puffing (and chubby) right fielder, they have options, considering their desire to prevent Son from becoming a sex offender. They can stop the athletics and get Son interested in bug collecting or they can just try to balance things out. What Mom and Dad may need to do is recognize they are now out of balance in the scheme of vulnerability appreciation education.

This doesn't mean following the Little League dog pile of celebration, Son is required to seek out chubby boy and apologize to the right fielder, promising never to do it again. But it does mean that Son is in the debit column of the vulnerability ledger. And Mom and Dad should celebrate and glow with Son about his win. But smart parents will remember the deficit in vulnerability appreciation and make it a point to organize something in Son's life pertaining to the opposite. Something perhaps, like arranging for Son to play checkers with Grandma Gertrude at the nursing home for three hours on Saturday, just to keep her company. Teaching Son about Grandma's vulnerability and balancing the vulnerability advantage ledger is a priceless gift to children. But it shouldn't be something Son begrudges and it shouldn't be something felt as punishment. Son must get the same accolades and celebration for these acts of appreciating vulnerability with Grandma Gertrude as he did for winning the Little League game.

THE BASEBALL MOM

The little girls understand the ritual. While doing housework with Mom, the family radio will broadcast major league baseball games, and Mom listens to them with a vengeance. She is not a nice baseball fan, taking her job of rooting for her favorite team, very seriously. With a blue bandana wrapped around her curlers, and with a broom and dustpan in each hand, she shouts obscenities. "Dammit!" she yells, looking at her three daughters sitting apprehensively on the couch, anxious about her next move.

She raves on, "He struck out when you girls were sitting on that couch. Now get over here on these chairs and he will have better luck. Hurry now! It's the second pitch. Dammit!" It was a wild scene with cursing and cussing as Mom urgently wills her team to victory. Yes, she was a baseball fan of the highest caliber, and on the surface it could seem that Mom's vociferous rooting and her less-than-sportsmanship-like conduct might teach the girls something about vulnerability disrespect. But that isn't the whole story.

RERUNNING THE ROOTING

That vulnerability disrespect is not the way it was for this baseball Mom. The radio broadcast, complete with her cussing and cursing, was preceded by Mom's lesson to the girls with the morning newspaper. The breakfast ritual required the little girls to read the baseball box scores in the win and loss columns, and with this wise Mom's guidance (and mathematical skills), she taught her daughters to calculate *which team needed to win next*. Yes, that was the balance. Baseball Mom never had a consistent team in all her years of cussing. She always rooted for the underdog and she always wanted the most vulnerable team to win. And that was the lesson of a beautiful balance with athletics and sports not being the lone culprit, but rather how parents use the process in the vulnerability appreciation.

And that was the lesson and that was a beautiful balance with athletics and sports not being the lone culprit, but rather how parents use the process in the vulnerability appreciation.

THE COMPETITION CATCH

Many believe it is a disservice to children to set up situations where competition is avoided. Some advocate that without competition in schools, the process of *dumbing down* of education occurs where no child excels and no child fails. Those folks argue that competition builds character and is needed as a life skill. Their opponents claim that the playing field must be leveled so that children live in a fair world, free of competition and differences. The concept of diversity spills over into the idea that there should be fewer differences in people in order to assure a peaceful human race.

The answer to the debate may lie somewhere in between, somewhere in the balance. Competition may be valuable in building character and strengthening a child's self-esteem, but left out of balance, competition may teach that taking advantage of vulnerability is not only acceptable, but also honorable, without any exceptions. Teaching children that the world is entirely fair and that they will never have to compete, may also work in a negative direction, creating spineless kiddos who will never excel for fear of competition. The answer is in the balance—teaching children to appreciate vulnerability and teaching them to compete, building their self-esteem and teaching them to appreciate the self worth of others. And teaching them that their needs only extend as far as the needs of other people is the solution, and the lesson should always consider the vulnerability of others. This lesson was obviously something missing from the childhood education of Perch Woman and Rancho Rambler.

MOB MADNESS

The power of groups is well documented in history as a raging force against vulnerability. Many people do unimaginable things to vulnerable people or groups if others tag along. But in a one-on-one situation, those abilities toward cruelty easily diminish—or it is hoped. Lynching, as an example, was viewed as technically against the law but easily condoned throughout the country since, after all, there were a whole lot of folks involved in the terrible madness. Executions (lynchings) were thought to be public entertainment, often where tickets were issued, refreshments were served, and the kidlets got the coveted front row seats. And those unspeakable acts of violence against the vulnerable continued until the 1930s and 1940s, even though few of those people could have committed those murders by themselves. It seems that the vulnerability of the victim can be easily forgotten within the group spirit.

As society put the clamps on such horrible hate crimes as lynching and other mob violence in the 1950s and 1960s, the group mentality of caring-nothing-about-vulnerability of others just seemed to change costumes. In recent history, official street gangs have commanded more sophisticated violence against the vulnerable as they sport their names, logos, colors, etc., and enjoy movies being made about their codes of honor in murdering and raping, as long as it is all done within the confines of the gang *family*—making the rudeness seemingly sweet.

As the lynching ropes and the bed sheets used for terror-wielding costumes of the last century were put in the closet, out came different costumes of hate and vulnerability disregard with shaved heads, fancy slogans, and perverted pride in one's race or sexual orientation. And when folks whine about such hatred toward anyone who is not the same, it is usually in the context of race relations or historical issues rather than a worry that these crimes represent the ultimate in vulnerability forgetfulness. And then, in the same category of forgetting about vulnerability, there is the issue of bullying, which doesn't take costumes and fancy slogans, but seems to impact nearly every type of family and every type of child.

BIG BUSINESS BULLYING

The numbers are staggering—not just from the victims of bullying—sometimes shattered for a lifetime, but from society's apparent acceptance of the bullying problem as *normal.* The library shelves and the teacher conferences are filled with *what-to-do-about-it* bullying business considering the prevalence of the problem all across the country. It is so prevalent that the number crunchers wonder if, statistically, the bullying problem approaches the norm.

Mostly it happens in groups of children who seize upon another vulnerable child with unimaginable viciousness. Gossiping, teasing, forming cliques, and constant coercion sometimes result in violence that seems to be without conscience. These terrors aren't just wielded by high school seniors with gang-colored and very expensive costumes. Some of these bullying behaviors are used by kiddos as young as first and second graders. The talk shows are filled with sad stories about the lives of children ruined by a group (however small) of kidlets making life miserable for other, more vulnerable kidlets. Many wonder how it could happen and what can be done?

It's interesting that the solution to bullying in most of the books and guidelines from the think tanks and fancy conferences focuses on helping the picked-on munchkins avoid *appearing vulnerable* because, so the experts say, the bullying kiddos won't lust for the opportunity for making those lives miserable if they don't *smell* vulnerability.. But no one seems to ask about whether this absolutely-no-conscience-attitude by the bullying children was a natural outgrowth of society's competitive ways or was it something like a failure in the parenting department of vulnerability education. Just like the acceptance and expectation in sibling rivalry—it seems parents do the same with the viciousness of one kidlet to another—especially in the form of bullying.

But no one seems to ask about whether this absolutely-no-conscience-attitude by the bullying children was a natural outgrowth of society's competitive ways or was it something like a failure in the parenting department of vulnerability education.

It seems that the old days of dipping a braid of the student in front into the ink well, have been replaced by drawing nipples on Cinderella or passing notes about the culinary delights of the fourth-grader's crotch.

SEXUAL BULLYING

As expected, the studied sex offenders had staggeringly high numbers of those who participated in bullying—mostly from the dishing-it-out side and, perhaps later they just graduated into sexual bullying. Sometimes however, the sex offenders were on the receiving end of things, using the unsavory experience to pile up hatred until it could be used in retaliation against someone else more vulnerable. And just as the studied sex offenders seemed unlike Bushes Bob in the park shrubbery and very much like the folks next door in the cul-de-sac, bullying children across the nation don't seem to be the kids who are abused, neglected and abandoned. Nope, they appear to be the kids with lots and lots of stuff, and without a clue about the feelings of others.

BULLYING BADNESS BEYOND

In the effort to raise sexually respectful children, the issue of sexual disrespect in bullying is hard to ignore. It seems that a significant weapon in the bullying arsenal for the best of the bullies, is sex stuff. It is as though the most humiliating, terrible torments to use in the bullying of others has a sexual connotation, such as the name calling of "slut," "whore," "fag," or "lesbian." Sometimes the behaviors of bullying include sexual behaviors such as snapping an embarrassed eighth-grader's bra, drawing sexually provocative pictures of the victim to be distributed during the Pilgrim parade or on the Internet, writing sexual stories, or producing sexually compromising, but nonetheless edited, sexual pictures of the victim. It seems that the old days of dipping a braid of the student in front into the ink well, have been replaced by drawing nipples on Cinderella or passing notes about the culinary delights of the fourth-grader's crotch. There is a huge piece of sex in bullying and the blueprint has its author in parents who failed to teach vulnerability appreciation—very, very early.

SNEAK UP SEXUAL DISRESPECT

Just as the problem of bullying and its disregard for vulnerability appreciation seems to have crept into the norms of school battlegrounds, other examples of ever-so-subtle vulnerability disregard occurs on a regular basis—similar to the *screaming subtleties* and *dumbing down* of sex in the Fourth Commandment. The talk shows seem to be at the top of the television vulnerability viciousness, sneaking up on parents without them ever seeing the connection. Most of the time the Jerry Springer, Montel, or Maury shows might be banned by tight-lipped Mom and Dad because of their sexual content. *Nope, the kids aren't going to watch the show on birth control or date rape* say the parents who are worried about the kiddos learning something about sex. But those parents who worry about raising sexually respectful children might want to look at what the talk shows indirectly teach about vulnerability appreciation rather than what they teach about homosexuality or hormone hoedowns.

As a daily dose of talk, the topic matter is usually some situation of vulnerability where someone is taking advantage of another. Lining up in the vulnerability check-out line, the subjects include the aerobics teacher who couldn't resist installing a two-way mirror to peek on the dancing seniors when changing their Speedos, the affair Grandma is having with her grandson's girlfriend, the bus boy who thought it was fun to leave spermicidal gifts in the salad bar, or the jealous friend who contaminated the home pregnancy test of her roommate in order to exact revenge. They are usually sexual topics ranging from sexual attractiveness, to sexual escapes, to sexual incompetencies. But in the vulnerability appreciation barometer of parent worry, there should be more concern about the *audience response* on these shows concerning vulnerability, rather than the hole in the condom or whether there is nutritional value in the salad bar debacle.

Often, when a controversial participant walks onto the stage, the hooting, the booing, and the hissing seems to normalize brutal attacks on just about anyone, regardless of their vulnerable position. When the twelve-year-old confesses to having sex with her sister's boyfriend, the audience is ruthless after chanting to the barely-pubescent kiddo, "ho, ho, ho!" not having a single reference to Santa Claus. When the sad woman complains that the Father of her three children won't attend to hygiene while they live in the homeless center, the audience chants "piggy, piggy, piggy," without a single concern with the plight of homelessness. There are chants, catcalls, and absolutely no regard for the vulnerability of the person, with everyone seeming to enjoy the mob-like, emotional lynching. If the guests are fat, missing teeth, or bald, the chants and hisses are personal and cruel without a single regard for the vulnerability. The audience seems to have no concept of caring for the show's guests, even for babies.

But those parents who worry about raising sexually respectful children might want to look at what the talk shows indirectly teach about vulnerability appreciation rather than what they teach about homosexuality or hormone hoedowns.

PATERNITY PARADES

On the paternity parades in many talk shows, few think of the true vulnerability issue of the supposed "victim." Babies without the true identity of their male heritage are shown on national television with their smiling mug on a six-foot screen so that each one of the suspected and possible sperm donors can stand next to the photo for audience-applause-meter-response to determine which young man most resembles the baby. The hooting and hollering is overwhelming with the audience pretending to have DNA testing ability just through picture-glancing. Did any of the talk shows hosts ever think about the future vulnerability of that baby in preparing for the show? Does anyone consider what it might be like for that baby, at age twelve, to watch the rerun of the talk show when her mother was

Does anyone consider what it might be like for that baby, at age twelve, to watch the rerun of the talk show when her mother was hooted as a whore, her father-sperm-donor is revealed after he proclaimed he wanted nothing to do with the kiddo?

hooted as a whore, her father-sperm-donor is revealed after he proclaimed he wanted nothing to do with the kiddo even if he was announced the winner (loser, actually), and where the two other possible sperm donors receive standing ovations from the audience since they escaped parental responsibility and are crowned the winners of *not having to accept the child* prize? How can the contestants, the audiences, and the talk show hosts fail to recognize the vulnerability disregard of the show process, suggesting it is the national norm? Do the patrolling-for-smut parents ever believe that Grandpa's sexual escapades with the family cocker spaniel may be less destructive in their effort to raise sexually disrespectful children than the audiences of the talk shows and their sanctioned and complete disregard for vulnerability?

AND IT WAS THE CHILDREN

There are other subtle ways that children learn from their parents about rule stretching, taking advantage, and putting their needs first without any regard for vulnerability appreciation. Sometimes it is a harmless misstep that parents fail to see as the development of self-centeredness rather than self-esteem. But often it is a tragedy—a missed window of opportunity for teaching vulnerability appreciation that can have disastrous consequences.

The lines were established, there were two of them, and for the most part, they each had a different focus. The lines began to form two hours before the museum opened and the long line and the short line varied completely. Order permeated the long-liners who had a peculiar method of sorting each other calmly. New arrivals to the long-line group checked in with each other, politely comparing ticket stubs and eventually, finding their proper place. It was obvious their tickets had been issued the previous day in chronological and timed order, which allowed the long-liners to be precise and calm in their organization. The attitude of the long-liners seemed to be one of respect, mirrored by the museum's clear recommendation that tickets be purchased the day before so that no energy would be spent on the hassles of standing in line, thus allowing only deep concentration for the subject and purpose of the museum.

But for the short-liners, it was different. They had arrived early, but it was the old *first come, first serve* process, which resulted in some shoving, scrambling, and spilling of lattes, even though signs at the entrance clearly indicated NO FOOD OR DRINK ALLOWED. Different than the long-liners, the short-liners demonstrated an aura of chaos, wondering out loud if they would be admitted, yelling to children who were out of line, and generally making complaints about the coolness of the morning air and the fact that someone had forgotten a sweater.

When it finally happened, the long-liners first, and eventually the short-liners, journeyed to the elevators where they received a mock passport before traveling to the top floor of the museum where they would begin their passage downward. The passport represented someone, a real person, who years ago perished under unimaginable cruelty. That trauma was displayed within the walls of the building. This was the Holocaust Museum.

The top floor represented the beginning of the end. First came the propaganda, then the war/conflict, then the imprisonment, and then the death of over six million vulnerable humans. The final floors were dedicated to the children and the aftermath of the Holocaust. There were obvious survivors of the Holocaust present on this day, watching with familiar horror and terror. These past victims were often in wheelchairs or tenderly held by family members, who were witnessing and enduring memories of old.

One particularly impacted family of five had finished. As they came away from the purposely-darkened museum (to impact that darkened time in history), the outside light, even from the cloudy day, seemed blindingly bright. Shaking fingers dabbed away tears and tender embraces traveled through what was possibly three generations. A white-haired, elderly woman in a wheelchair accompanied by what appeared to be a Jewish husband, seemed to garner the most attention from the family. What appeared to be married children and adult grandchildren continued to console her, kneeling down, eye-level with her wheelchair view, whispering softly. To observers it was obvious that the two elders had been victims of the Holocaust—at least in some capacity. But consolation could not quell her tears as she trembled with memory grief. As the family attempted to soothe, a member from the third generation asked, "Grandma, tell us what part was most heartbreaking for you. Tell us, Grammy. Get it out so we can help you."

With encouragement, Grandma spoke. But it was difficult. Choking back tears and trembling, she said, "It was the children. It was the children. I will never forget today's children." What did Grandma mean, *today's children*? Did that statement relate to Grandma's misery from 60 years previous when she was a child victim of unspeakable disregard for vulnerability? Of course, that would be true. But specifically, Grandma was referring to the children of her day—the children who shared the aisles with her, traveling through the Holocaust Museum.

What Grandma and both the long-liners and short-liners saw before their entrance into the museum were clear directions. First, everyone entering the museum received instructions that children under the age of 12 should not attend. It wasn't a NO, but a *strong* suggestion, complete with an explanation that because of the subject content of the museum, children would not likely benefit. There it was, respectful but very clear.

With encouragement, Grandma spoke. But it was difficult. Choking back tears and trembling, she said, "It was the children. It was the children. I will never forget today's children."

And in the spirit of this disrespect, Grandma saw Mom (and her apparent partner, Dad) non-verbally respond to their children, silently agreeing that *this was boring*.

But there were other directions that were not suggestions, but demands, such as NO CAMERAS or PHOTOGRAPHS, and NO FOOD OR DRINK ALLOWED IN ANY PART OF THE MUSEUM. The *No's* were clear, at least to those with respect.

Grandma, in double ordeal, watched several families of children, many under the age of 12, behave as though they were at the playground of the state fair's carnival. Running up and down, they were eating candy bars, drinking sodas, and at times (when boredom set in), playing games of touch-tag. As the museum displays depicted the horror of the time, they were not shy about complaining that it was taking too much time. The children of Grandma's misery continually harassed their parents, loudly announcing, "Mom, this is stupid. Let's hurry." And in the spirit of this disrespect, Grandma saw Mom (and her apparent partner, Dad) non-verbally respond to their children, silently agreeing that *this was boring*. And there wasn't just one family, but several, seemingly on each floor of the several-story museum, with irreverent, disrespectful, and bored children accompanied by parents who tolerated the behavior.

When Grandma cried, "It was the children," she was referring to the entire collection of children throughout the museum on that day. But one particular family broke her heart with unbearable pain. It happened on the leveled and tiered depiction of Holocaust victims being unloaded from rail cars, shuffled through long lines, separated from families, forced to strip naked, and then funneled into fake showers which were actually gas chambers. The huge display in various layers also depicted the naked, dead bodies of victims being removed from the chambers and then destroyed in human bonfires. Varying tiers depicting various stages of human disregard provided a powerful impact to anyone observing. Well, almost anyone.

The family most troubling to Grandma was comprised of a Mom, Dad, and five children, only one appearing older than age 12. While Grandma and her group, with their tears falling, were taking in the massive layered scene, the Mom and Dad, with kids in tow, also crowded around, pushing, shoving, calling each other names, and establishing a clear pecking order among the less-than-respectful-to-each-other kids. Grandma watched as Dad adorned his camera (not allowed) and began to snap pictures, complete with flash, rudely stunning the purposely-darkened atmosphere. What appeared to be a middle child, protested loudly between bites of her Skittles candy (which was also not allowed), "Daddy, the sign says you're not supposed to take pictures. You're breaking the rules."

Dad doesn't miss a beat (or a flash) as he continues taking pictures, only remarking, "Oh, it's okay. It doesn't matter, no one is going to throw us out."

"*It doesn't matter*," Grandma repeats to herself in between her tears.

Grandma also witnessed this particular family viewing and commenting on the display. With broken heart, she saw the seemingly ten-year-old and a twelve-year-old, giggling incessantly at the naked bodies being piled for burning. She watched them roar and laugh, drawing attention from the two middle children to the number of breasts and penises that were exposed, using language appropriate for a bachelor party and a red-faced groom. Dad continued to snap pictures in Grandma's grief, and Mom continued to complain (loudly) because there were no changing tables in the way-too-small restrooms and, after all, the toddler was wet. And Grandma's tears were drowned out because the next-to-the-toddler kiddo spilled the entire contents of his grape Slurpee and his older sister (the one who complained about Dad's Kodak) teased him. They went on and on with their disregard, as did Grandma's tears.

MISSED WINDOWS

The parents with the slurping kidlets didn't intend to break Grandma's heart and their behavior wasn't purposefully mean-spirited. Likely, the family was on vacation and perhaps planned several *cultural experiences* for the kiddos while visiting the nation's capital, Washington D.C. But here was a window of opportunity open to teach vulnerability appreciation and it was not only missed, but defiled. Sadly these parents probably see no connection to their kiddos making Grandma cry—if they even noticed.

VULNERABILITY VIBRATIONS

As the Fourth Commandment, *Thou Shalt Welcome The World* suggested, forbidden things stifled by crusading parents can sometimes become very attractive to children just as a matter of human nature—especially in fashion or other trendy things. Wanting what others have, seems to be part of human nature as well as bad for household checkbooks, but good for Wall Street. Since in the sexual department, grown-ups want to do a lot of withholding from kids, then sexual searching often becomes the quest of curious kiddos, which is usually the opposite of what Mom and Dad had in mind. Dangerously, sometimes there are vulnerability sexual vibrations toward the forbidden and when that happens, sexual disrespect is right around the corner with potentially disastrous possibilities. And being able to discern normal or harmless sexual acting out from those behaviors that are worrisome is important in raising sexually respectful children—and the key is vulnerability.

DIALING DEVIANCY

Making sexually obscene telephone calls can be considered a crime, but in some situations, the act can be considered a normal (but deviant) part of a child's sexual development—based on curiosity and game playing. The differences between the behavior being concerning and perhaps just normal snooping, has less to do with the *dialing deviancy* and more to do with

But the target of their arousal is the key to understanding whether this is a deviant act, or whether this is normal, sexual game playing among children.

the possible focus on vulnerability.

The batch of kiddos—cousins, brothers, and some sisters—have attended Sunday school and now they are instructed to walk to Grandma's house, six blocks from the church, and wait for their parents who are attending the adult church service. Grandma's house is familiar and comfortable with her various games and oatmeal cookies that should have been featured in *Good Housekeeping* magazine. But more important than the treats, the children are excited about the unrestricted use of Grandma's telephone. Munching on cookies, they decide to make an obscene telephone call—not because they are deviant psychopaths or because they even understand the word *obscene.* They want to do this because they are attracted toward the forbidden sexual words they heard in the dressing room during swimming lessons.

Forgetting everything they learned in Sunday school, they gather in a circle. A random number is dialed and the telephone receiver is held in the middle of the circle. When they hear a person answer, they yell in unison, "TITS!" and then quickly hang up. Oh, it is exciting just to say the word, and yes, they are aroused with the whole process. But the target of their arousal is the key to understanding whether this is a deviant act, or whether this is normal, sexual game playing among children.

The answer lies in the focus of their arousal and the issue of vulnerability. The naughty children are aroused to themselves and the excitement they feel by saying, in unison, "TITS!" It is thrilling just to say the word out loud—in front of each other—especially since both boys and girls are doing the *tits talking*. Although the unlucky recipient of the *tits* call should be their consideration, he/she is not. Quite differently, in consideration of vulnerability, another situation of dialing deviance occurs.

REAL DIALING DEVIANCY

She returns home from school and begins her ritual. First, she changes her clothes and eats the snack her mother has left. She changes from her Catholic school uniform into her much more comfortable Charlie Brown sweatpants. She checks to make sure her older brother is busy washing his car and then dials. The number is memorized in her mind—one of an elderly woman she knows from church, but who does not know she is calling. Anonymity is guaranteed. When the call is answered, the female child spews sexual words, describing obscenities (probably few that she really understands), and then (different from the *tits talking* kiddos) *listens intently* to the woman's horror. There is no unison yelling for excitement, but instead, the focus of her arousal is the elderly woman's response of horror. She is focusing on the vulnerability of the woman, the terror she is creating, and the control she has over the upset victim. Different from the kiddos with the *TITS* titillation, this little girl, unchecked, is heading for escalation of arousal toward vulnerability, which is not only a key to becoming a sex offender—but becoming a very dangerous one.

PEEKING PERVERSION

The behavior of *peeping* is also debated about whether it falls within the category of *normal deviancy,* or if the behavior is clear evidence of reservations being needed for a park bush. Is it normal or abnormal for children to want to peep on someone in order to snoop and sneak a look at something sexually curious? Two examples may provide insight to the debate, especially in how differing situations relate to the issue of vulnerability.

There is giggling and snorting, with the two brothers finding themselves safely outside, not being noticed by the adults who continue to play Pinochle inside the house. Earlier, they have realized that Aunt Agatha has interesting evening behaviors inside her motor home parked in the driveway. The boys remember how, the night before, they could see from their bedroom that she disrobes without closing the gingham curtains, and they are very interested in getting a closer look, or peep. The two culprits sneak through the bushes, position themselves under the motor home window, and then one boy bends over while the other kneels on his back to get a better shot. Each takes a turn as they accomplish their mission, getting a full peep at Aunt Agatha's very, very full boobs while she is changing into her pajamas. As they relish their achievement with giggles, the question is whether they are truly deviant and heading for a career of perversion, or whether this is normal behavior among curious children.

As they relish their achievement with giggles, the question is whether they are truly deviant and heading for a career at perversion, or whether this is normal behavior among curious children.

The key to understanding if a potential problem exists for the two boob-shot burglars is in considering *how* their mischief occurs and whether Aunt Agnes was really the source of their attraction. Just as the Bruce Boys concentrated on Sheena's boobs (not really Sheena), these boys may be interested in who was on the end of the boobs, or just the boobs?

Obviously, the hardest part for the villains is controlling their laughter while they peek, until they return to the sanctuary of the bushes and burst out with raucous merriment. The last thing they wanted was to be apprehended or to have Aunt Agatha *know* about their peeping and the only thing they wanted was a peek, nothing more. They just wanted to see them. In fact, the boys would feel quite badly if they were caught, since they wouldn't want to hurt (vulnerability issue) Aunt Agatha. After all, she was quite nice to them and she makes the very best blueberry cobbler.

PERVERSION PEEPING

But further down the road, another pair is also peeking, and they, like the boys, begin in the bushes. The difference is these girls are giggling in the bushes outside the home of

There is it, the same sexual behavior of peeking, same aged children, and two very different approaches toward sexual disrespect.

someone they know and someone they personally dislike. This is not like Aunt Agatha and her best blueberry cobbler peeping. These girls are outside the home of a teacher from their school whom they despise and whom they want to personally embarrass—(vulnerability issue). And just like the boys, neither girl is big enough to peek inside the bedroom window without one kneeling down and the other kneeling on the back of the kneeler. And yes, they get a peek at this teacher disrobing, just like Aunt Agatha. But the real difference is that after the peeking, these girls want the teacher to know she is being watched.

Different than the boys, the girls are focusing their excitement toward their victim's humiliation and fear when they tap on the window to startle her and then leave her a note tied to a rock saying, "You have fat tits." Different than the boys who really want to see Aunt Agatha's breasts, these girls care little about the boobs (not because they are female) and they care a lot about the teacher knowing they are looking at her breasts. Their focus of arousal is toward their target's humiliation—her vulnerability. There is it, the same sexual behavior of peeking, same aged children, and two very different approaches toward sexual disrespect.

FANTASIES AND FLASHING

The same type of distinguishing could occur for children who engage in *flashing* or more professionally, *exhibitionism.* How common is it for children to streak through the house naked, *moon* their friends by pulling down their britches, or flash a penis at female cousins who have wandered into the barn? Could flashing or exhibitionism be a sure sign of sexual problems for children, or is it just a sign of normal deviant behavior? Is the issue of attraction toward vulnerability the line of demarcation for this type of sexual behavior just as vulnerability separated the telephone callers and the peepers into two groups of concern?

The boys are making their plans. The female cousins on the other side of the barn are also plotting. Uncle Frank who is preparing to milk Frankie the cow can hear the giggling of both factions, who are too excited to notice his close proximity to their game-playing. Nonetheless, the two groups of children continue with their fantasies and fun about the upcoming *flashers.* And with the synchronized expertise of an ice follies show, the girls and boys run toward each other, breasts bared for the female units and penises wagging for their male counterparts. They race by each other in absolute glee, clearly aroused and interested in the flashing.

Interestingly, probably most of the boys briefly glanced at the girls and their breasts, but it was probably different for the girls. They were likely aroused and excited about the *boys looking at their breasts.* But considering the girls looking at the flashing boys—it is likely they have more interest in math problems than getting a good gander at the boys' penises. The excitement was toward their own arousal and excitement for doing the deed of exposing themselves to members of the opposite sex. Thrilling it was for both groups flashing; but short it was in the vulnerability barometer.

In another place, two boys also make plans. They have intentions of flashing and exposing, but their target is carefully selected and different from the barn flashing business. One of the girls visiting their sister is particularly clumsy, both socially and physically, and she is the intended target of the boys. Their older sister's birthday party is occurring in the backyard, complete with a barbecue and swimming in the family pool. The boys have chosen for their flashing, the one party attendant that seems the most hesitant, the most uncomfortable, and the one who will most likely be shocked and terrorized by their flashing plans. They notice she is shy in her bathing suit, she is apprehensive about eating her hamburger, and she is, in their view, *cosmetically challenged.*

After the festivities have been concluded, as she walks down the shrub walkway to her mother's awaiting car, they jump from the bushes, exposing their penises to her. She is shocked and horrified (just as they hoped), and they are focused on her response. Different than the boys and girls in the barn who are aroused to their own arousal, these boys are clearly focused on the victim's shock, couched carefully in her vulnerability. Two sets of children, same set of behaviors, and two different paths toward sexual disrespect.

For all the curious children dialing, peeping and flashing, the key was how they learned about vulnerability and how they attach vulnerability to sexual arousal. Some of the most dangerous sex offenders are aroused primary to vulnerability—to the hurting of others. Those folks are dreadfully dangerous but also few in number. But there are also huge numbers of sex offenders who may not have clear, sexual arousal to vulnerability but simply cannot connect to the feelings of others and, therefore, they can easily take sexual advantage. But before offenses are committed, long before Aunt Agatha's big boobs are contemplated, the kiddos were taught or not taught about vulnerability issues—setting the blueprint for sexual respect or disrespect.

As is true with nearly every commandment, balance-gone-bad is a problem in raising sexually respectful children, and teaching vulnerability appreciation is no different. What a world it would be if no one ever acted without considering the needs of others. Streets wouldn't be crossed, lest someone else needed a turn; intersections would be blocked for miles as courtesy stopped everyone from moving ahead; restaurants would be empty because no one

They were likely aroused and excited about the *boys looking at their breasts.* But considering the girls looking at the flashing boys—it is likely they have more interest in math problems than getting a good gander at the boys' penises.

But before offenses are committed, long before Aunt Agatha's big boobs are contemplated, the kiddos were taught or not taught about vulnerability issues—setting the blueprint for sexual respect or disrespect.

would want to be selfish and take a table just in case someone needed a place to eat. The slow moving vehicle turnouts would have traffic jams filled with folks waiting for someone who needed to pass. Moving about in society, accomplishing lifetime dreams and even competing in the soccer tournaments require concentration on private needs—sometimes even at the expense of others. There is absolutely nothing wrong with those human interactions and protections.

But in examining sex offenders and recognizing that no one quibbles that they lack empathy skills or the appreciation to feel for others, and considering that society subtly encourages children to take advantage of vulnerability, well intentioned parents who want to raise sexually respectful children will put vulnerability on the clipboard of teaching and they will do it with balance.

Sex Fairy Clipboard

- Do not accept nor condone sibling conflict as being natural—but recognize it is likely to happen if it isn't curtailed before it is tempting to the kiddos. Begin early, actively teaching vulnerability appreciation among family children. Take just as much pride in a child winning the spelling bee as when a child helps a little sister pass a second grade spelling test.

- Do not raise guilt-free children, but show caution. When children are made to feel guilty about things that are out of their control—lifetime trauma can be the result. But when children are guided to feel guilty about being insensitive to others, that may be good guilt. Most importantly, always give children a chance at atonement or restitution for less-than-sensitive behavior. When children show a lack of empathy—allow them to feel guilty—but then, allow them to compensate and make up for the error—hopefully working toward a celebration of achieving the opposite of disregarding others.

- Raising children to care for animals can be a good thing—especially if the vulnerability issue becomes the focus. Just as the Sixth Commandment teaches—animals are not humans and that difference should always be part of the lesson planning. But considering the Ninth Commandment about vulnerability—animals should be part of the curriculum. Teaching children that no matter how well Malcolm and Angus can fetch their sticks or play dead, they are still vulnerable pooches—needing humans to care for them. Children should be involve in the care and feeding of the non-human family members—not for allowances directly, but because the critters are vulnerable.

Sex Fairy Clipboard

- Remember the importance for children to appreciate the vulnerability of the elderly. Many families have adult children who worry, fret and eventually care for those aging family members but children are rarely involved. Just as it is important for kiddos to grow up and appreciate the vulnerability of their baby brother, children must be taught to appreciate the vulnerability of their baby brother's Grandmother. Taking Grandma to Sunday breakfast should be just as important as taking children to gymnastics practice each week.

- Do not be frightened of sports in raising sexually respectful children—but be alert to the vulnerability issue. There is absolutely nothing wrong with children being competitive—even fiercely competitive, in order to win the football jamboree. Parents should allow the competitive juices to flow—especially if teamwork and sports ethics are part of the paradigm. Just remember the vulnerability ledger and, separate from athletics, help children compensate by showing vulnerability appreciation in other parts of their lives after they have annihilated the vulnerability of the opposing team in the soccer tournament.

- Not only should bullying not be tolerated, but parents should begin preparing against bullying before children can even recognize the letter ***B***. Long before the opportunities arise, children should be taught about the feelings of others as an anti-bullying campaign. When television shows, books, or media snippets capture a tragic scenario of bullying—that teaching should be on the sexual respect clipboard.

- Remember, children are sexually curious and they will act out—sometimes in embarrassing and uncomfortable ways. The key to the seriousness of the sexual acting out is vulnerability. Try to examine whether, in the hanky panky, the kiddos are concentrating on the vulnerability of the person or something else. But most importantly, use the Ten Commandments to intervene appropriately, stop the behavior in a logical way and get children excited about a more respectful sexual future.

Sex Fairy Clipboard

- Remember, sexual respect isn't limited to what happens under the sheets. Combating acts of vulnerability disregard such as hate, racism, and times in history when war or other acts of atrocities have occurred, not only contributes to a respectful society in general, but to sexual respect as well.

- Never, ever give to charities, help paint the homes of the elderly or send money to a telethon—that is, without involving children. Remember, the world in which children live does little to encourage vulnerability appreciation and, in fact, the messages children generally receive encourages a ME, ME, ME approach to life. So when parents give to charities or make other civic-minded contributions to society—make sure family children being involved is as important as the gift to those who deserve.

Chapter 13

Tenth Commandment
Thou Shalt Teach Touching

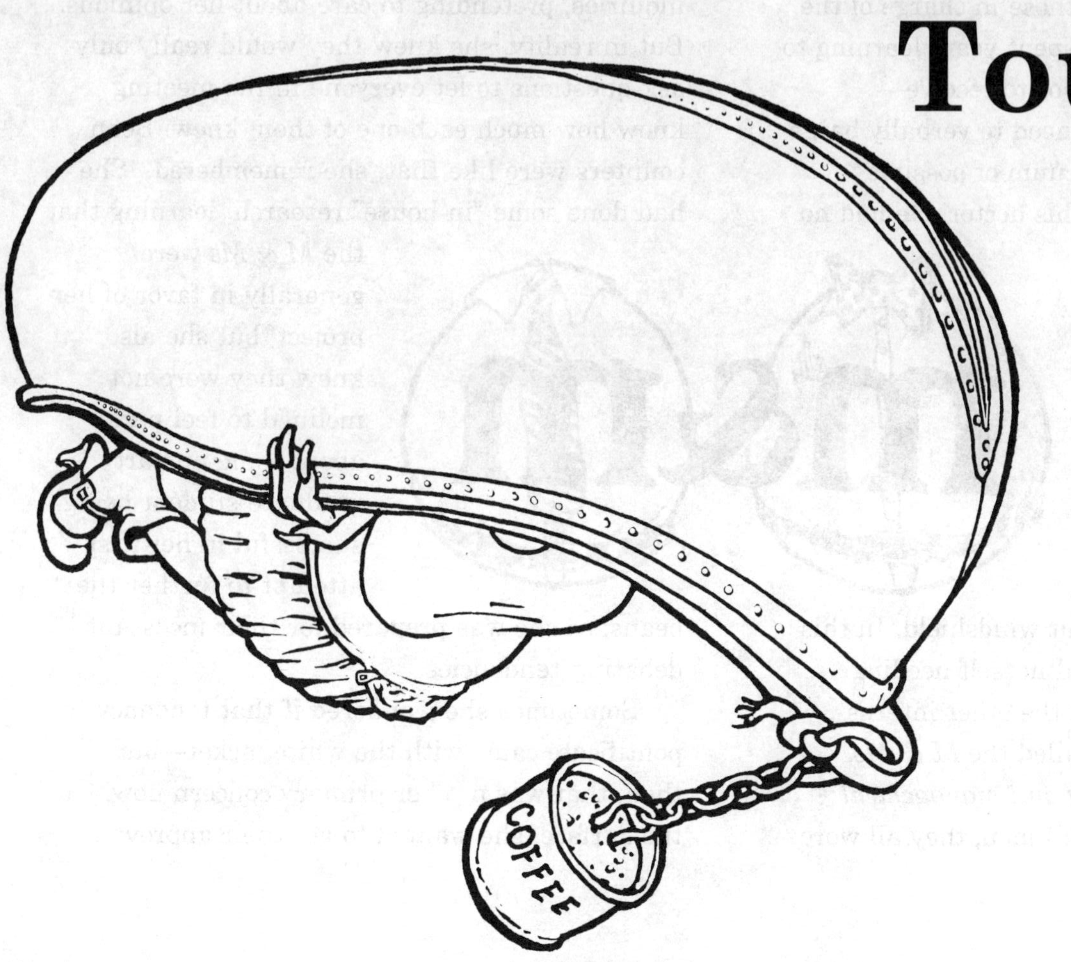

Chapter 13: TENTH COMMANDMENT—THOU SHALT TEACH TOUCHING

Different than most of the psychiatrists in the hospital, he had a wonderful skill that, for sure, he didn't learn in *shrink school*—as some called psychiatric residency. *No*, the wise doctor and mentor had the uncanny ability to *listen* rather than feeling inadequate unless his lips were moving. Contrarily, most of the docs in the psych hospital, especially those in charge of the money end of things, had spent years learning to talk, to explain, to process or to resolve—manifesting in a constant need to verbally barge forward, abhorring the vacuum of possible pensiveness. Not so with this doctor. He had no fear of catastrophe if silence enveloped the conversation.

And here she was, so excited about her *just started* career, with graduate school in the rearview mirror and an internship with her beloved mentor on the front windshield. In this conference room, she found herself needing approval for what she and the other interns sheepishly and secretly, called the ***M & Ms,*** referring to the *marketing and management* group of docs. They were all men, they all wore white jackets and they were all pretty smart about medical stuff, but none of that medicinal expertise had been important to them for a long time. Now, they were the bean counters in the psych hospital's outpatient program, and in the *marketing* rather than the medical end of things. They wanted all the beans to tally up and they would be putting in their two-cents about her proposal for an outpatient project, if it would bring in more beans.

Unlike her mentor, the docs would be talking a lot, pontificating often, and making many inquiries, pretending to care about her opinions. But in reality, she knew they would really only ask questions to let everyone in the meeting know how much each one of them knew. Bean counters were like that, she remembered. She had done some "in-house" research, learning that the *M & Ms* were generally in favor of her project, but she also knew they were not inclined to feel perky about some upstart graduate student being successful in her first attempt to further the beans, so she was prepared for their incessant debating tendencies.

Sometimes she wondered if that tendency to pontificate came with the white jacket—but then, that was not her primary concern now. On the surface, she wanted to get their approval, but deep inside she also really wanted to help the people who were signing up for her weekend retreat. *Yes*, she still had the idea that helping troubled folks was an honorable focus of her career but she often wondered if the *M & Ms* had forgotten that mission. But most importantly, she wanted his endorsement, since after all, he was the one who had taught her to think in terms of just helping people, regardless of the beans. But for now, he was quiet with no instructions, only a posture of pensiveness so different than the tittering *M & M* docs.

After pleasantries and a few excuses about being late, they all gathered around the conference table with their high-fiber muffins so superficially important to the health conscious hospital world even though most of them looked like they hit the maple bars and Twinkies whenever they got the chance. Some things just weren't as they seemed, she thought, but for now, never mind that. What was important was that she get her project approved to further her helping mission.

Her job was to propose a moneymaking weekend retreat as part of the outpatient package the *for-profit* hospital offered to the community. And *for profit* were the operative words, even though no one talked about that. The really big bean counters supervising the *M & Ms* knew it was important to offer outpatient services to garner community support and appear in a helpful light. So these weekend offerings were important to the hospital's image, making most community folks think that the hospital really wanted to do good things. But a kind of jeopardy also existed since they wanted the hospital beds full so they could make money, but they wanted to pretend as though they really wanted everyone to stay out of the hospital. So the bean counting about the weekend retreat was all very precarious, and she knew that since they were in charge of marketing, the *name business* was very important in getting people interested in signing up.

She began by explaining that she had spoken privately with more than ten couples that were interested in attending, but she anticipated twice that many couples would register, especially if she had a catchy name for the weekend retreat. She told the docs that she hoped they could be very clever with the title for advertising purposes, since that kind of accolade was right up their marketing alley. And since this was her first project, she really hoped *he* would weigh in on the name because it was so important.

She had several title choices to offer them, but she explained she wanted them to make the final decision, also feeding right into their marketing egos. But as she started to read the name options, she was interrupted by one of the *M & Ms* who said (after giggling slightly) that he just couldn't get *in the mood* for deciding on a name without knowing about the facility where the retreat would be held. His sniggling suggested he took pride in stumping her efforts, right out of the chute, but she was prepared for those interruptions.

With ease, she honored his diversion of wanting to get *in the mood* about the facility and without even a slight hesitation, she turned on the slide projector, and with great fanfare, flashed 17 vivid, color slides of the resort where it would all take place. They were stunning. The first slide showed a three-foot plaque that was unreadable, but nonetheless adorning the front of the resort, providing a history of the pristine location. The Native American motif was a nice touch, she explained, touting the rustic, natural atmosphere so important for her weekend mission. Being impressed with her visual aids skills, they paused only momentarily, thinking about Indians and the mission—actually confusing themselves, until she went on.

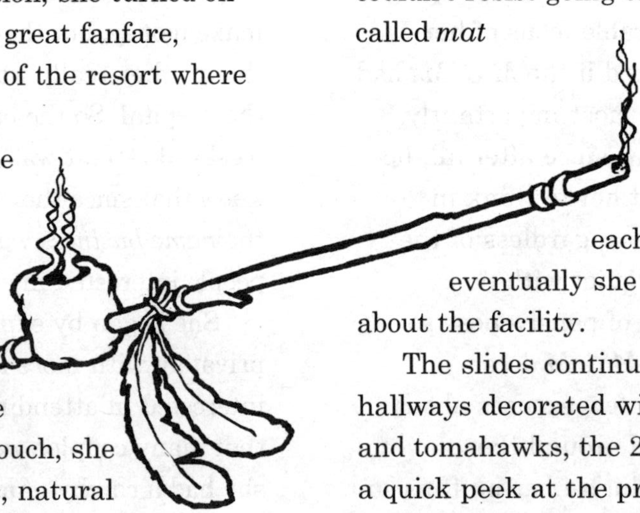

Also without hesitation, she showed a vibrant picture of the Peace Pipe Pavilion where the larger get-togethers would be held, making sure to note that in order to get everyone *in the mood,* as one of the docs had quipped, pillows and cushions would be disseminated during the large group gatherings, allowing the couples to sit close together on the floor rather than using the formality of hard chairs in classroom-style seating. Predictably, the *M & M's* jumped in with their ideas about adding all sorts of other mood enhancing things such as yoga relaxation exercises or sewing nametags on the pillows and mats for a *personal space* emphasis. They couldn't resist going on and on about what they called *mat management,* pondering how to arrange the mats, the color theme of the mats, the positioning of the mats—trying to outdo each other with ideas until eventually she got them back on track about the facility.

The slides continued, showing the resort hallways decorated with pony pictures, tepees and tomahawks, the 28-foot lobby waterfall and a quick peek at the private room decorations, causing everyone to think momentarily about what would or wouldn't happen there on Saturday night. Just as she thought, once they saw the sleeping rooms, the docs jumped in with raunchy suggestions about consideration of using a facility with vibrating beds and mirrors on the ceilings. But she was prepared for this diversion, and she explained that if she had chosen a facility with those accommodations, she would have had to sacrifice the rustic, Native American motif, so she had made her decision for the softer ambience rather than the seedier motels where those *props* (as one doc called them) also brought in the problem of

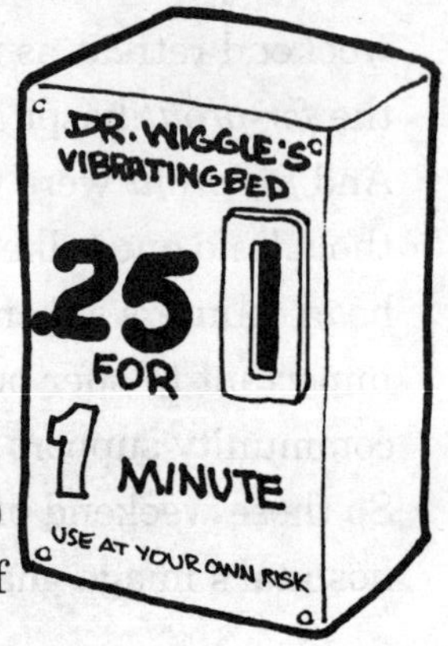

busy traffic and lots of noise. Everyone in the meeting agreed with her except one doc who made the crack about *bells and whistle noises* possibly being helpful to her Saturday night mission, but she ignored him and went on.

Still, her mentor didn't comment on the facility as she had hoped, so she returned to several name choices for the docs to finalize. She explained that she really liked the title *Marriage Matters,* but she had to admit not all the couples scheduled to attend were married and at least two couples made it quite clear they had no intention of doing the aisle walk. *No*, they were just there for the subject matter and they wanted no pressure or critical insinuations about marriage, she reported. One of the *M & Ms* suggested publishing a pre-screening quiz in the newspaper to weed out the wedding-dodgers, and another doc wondered about doing a background check on marriage licenses at the registration door. Another *M & M* suggested using lie detector tests just to make sure everyone was married, and with all of those wild ideas, she just let them titter for awhile before moving on.

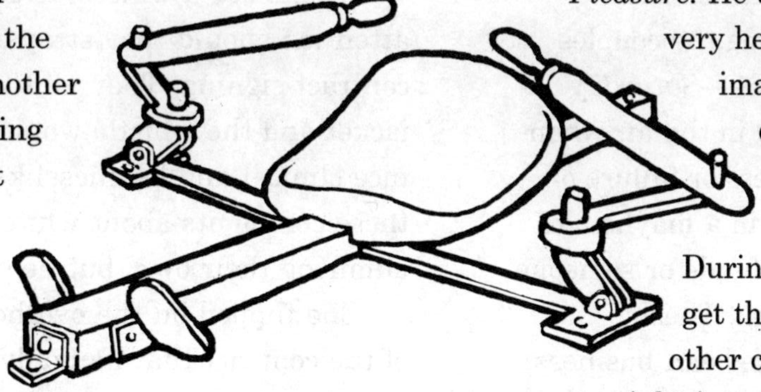

Clearing her throat and clearing off the possible title of *Marriage Matters*, she told them she also liked *Love, Lust and Longing* for a title, but she was afraid the word *lust* might be a little too strong—especially since one pastor was referring two couples. But just to keep the conversation controversial, she told them the hospital chaplain had given his permission for the *lust*-type title, knowing that would get them all fired up about the religious controversy, which was always important in bean counting. Additionally, she explained, she was counting on several churches to lend support, and since the God types weren't very comfortable with the topic in the first place, she thought the lust word might send some over the edge. They argued with each other about leaving the lust word or opting for a less racy title, but with their snickering, she went on.

Before she could give them her next option, one of the white-jacketed docs suggested his own title of *Aerobic Sex—Huffing and Puffing to Pleasure.* He thought the aerobic part was very healthy and good for the hospital image. Not to be outdone, another doc thought *The Ins and Outs of Doing Ins and Outs*, offered a nice play on words.

During this bantering, she tried to get them to pay attention to her other choices but one of them jumped right in, suggesting the title of *Getting it On—A Weekend Workout in Sex* while another one threw out his idea of *Kinks to Kinky—Exploring Your Sexuality.* With all of them tossing out silly ideas, she looked at him for input. None came. The docs were unfazed by his silence and continued their tittering, so she just went on to a different subject, suggesting they table the title until later.

Using the overhead projector, she began with the itinerary for the weekend, navigating their focus, forgetting about their title tug-of-wars. Being marketing people, they liked plans and schedules, especially when it gave them opportunities to chime in and show off their marketing expertise. She reminded everyone that the couples would be arriving at the resort on Thursday evening, giving the weekend retreat two full days of work on Friday and Saturday. Without hesitation, she reminded them that Sunday morning would be for debriefing and, hopefully, celebration—that is, if she was successful—meaning the couples had hit the jackpot on the big one—*Saturday night*. There was a little tension in the air when she brought up the idea of success or failure on Saturday night, which resulted in a mayhem of comments and worries about refunds or someone wanting part of their money back. These ponderings were really about the bean business so she quickly diverted them back to the schedule and the Thursday evening rally.

She explained that during this first meeting, the couples would be given Valentine-red three-ring binders and then, sitting together on their mats, they would learn about the ground rules for the weekend and, of course, the contract they must all sign. Now, signing contracts was very important to marketing minds, so they listened intently. She explained that it was important to have the attendees agree to the terms of the weekend, and one of the docs chimed in that the contract was important since this retreat wasn't for *lollygagging around*, especially if everything was to work out on Saturday night. *This was serious stuff*, another commented, and *the more businesslike it seemed to be,* his to-the-right-side colleague suggested, *the better chance for success*. The final comment she received about the contract signing was from two docs who suggested she not only wear a white jacket for a clinical flavor, but that she use a whistle to get everyone's attention should they stray away from the contract-signing. They all thought the white jacket and the whistle would give everything a nice clinical and businesslike touch. They made these comments about white jackets while admiring their own, but he still said nothing.

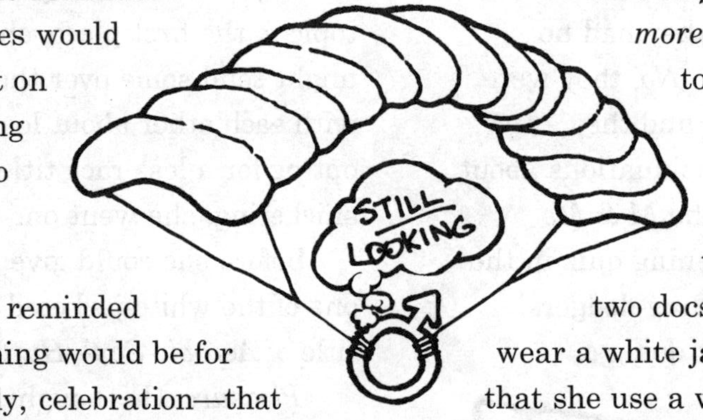

She flipped on the overhead, revealing a copy of the contract that had only three points, knowing the never-stop-talking docs would add many more items. Her contract read #1 *No Golf; #2 No Missing Meetings*; and *#3 No Sex Until Saturday Night*. But as she suspected, they had more. One offered *No Slipping Off*

Spontaneously During Meetings, since, he thought, some of the material was erotic and some of the attendees might get the urge to try out the wares before Saturday night. He giggled with his pesky suggestion, even though no one else really laughed. Another doc wanted *No Sex Toys* added to the contract, but several suggested using the term "Unauthorized" Sex Toys, since they all knew sex toys would be part of the weekend instruction on the subject of *props.* Another doc wanted the contract very clear that there would be no toleration of unauthorized aphrodisiacs and, for sure, no alcohol, which brought on a heated debate about whether alcohol was a sexual depressant or a sexual *frisky-me-up,* as one brazen doctor rudely opined. *Yes,* he knew from a physiological perspective that alcohol slowed things down, but he also explained that everyone knew that alcohol also had a way to free things up in the hanky-panky department. As they argued about the effects of alcohol, she went on to another item in the Valentine-red notebooks.

She showed them a nifty color-coded map of the premises along with an itinerary of the scheduled meetings. She showed them how the general sessions would be in the Peace Pipe Pavilion in the mornings, and then smaller sessions in the *Harmony Hatchet* and *Ten Tomahawk* enclaves with breakout rooms. She also explained that her male counterpart would be introduced at the Thursday night rally, which made all the docs speak to the importance of him also wearing a white jacket just so the clinical feeling of the retreat would be reinforced. Several made remarks about the value of looking like medical folks, but as they chattered on she noticed that he neither contributed to the conversation or wore a white jacket.

She continued, explaining that the Thursday night rally would also focus on the fantasy logs—*an absolute requirement* of the endeavor, one of the doctors chimed in. *There would be no excuses,* another interjected. Then the doctors began the discussion/debate about sexual fantasies. Some wondered if the attendees really had fantasies to report, so she tried to explain that they needed to create fantasies if they weren't having them and quite frankly, she clarified, the missing-in-action fantasies may be why the couples needed the retreat in the first place. Not really listening to that idea, another doc suggested that the fantasy logs shouldn't be haphazard and another thought there should be detailed structure about how they were to be written—leaning toward a businesslike approach. And then the discussion really got out-of-hand with several of them suggesting helpful books that could be used for fantasy study such as *Fantasies Are Our Friends*, or *Get the Fun Back in Fantasies*. Among all the resource suggestions came that same rude idea that polygraphs or lie detectors be administered every morning to verify that the folks were telling the truth about their fantasies. With everyone talking, of course except him, she could only try to help the docs feel important so she recorded their ideas and moved on with the fantasy discussion.

Several mumbled about the wretched problem of one of the attendees fantasizing about someone other than their partner, which made her pause, but only momentarily. She was vivacious in her response, reminding everyone of two things. First, the entire retreat was very regimented. It clearly focused on such things as business contracts and business deals, which made most of the marketing folks feel really good. After all, that was the way of bean counting. So, she told the docs that to combat the potential wandering fantasy problem, she would just remind all the couples that they paid good money to meet the Saturday night goal and if they wandered off the fantasy path about someone other than their partner, it would just be a waste of their money. Right away she could tell the docs loved the emphasis on the money/bean counting for getting control of things. There were a few smirks and whispers from the *M & Ms* about how some of them hadn't had a fantasy in years, and she heard someone say it would take them all week to muster up a single *hot thought* about *old what's her name*, so with all their sniggling and snide comments, she knew it was time to move on.

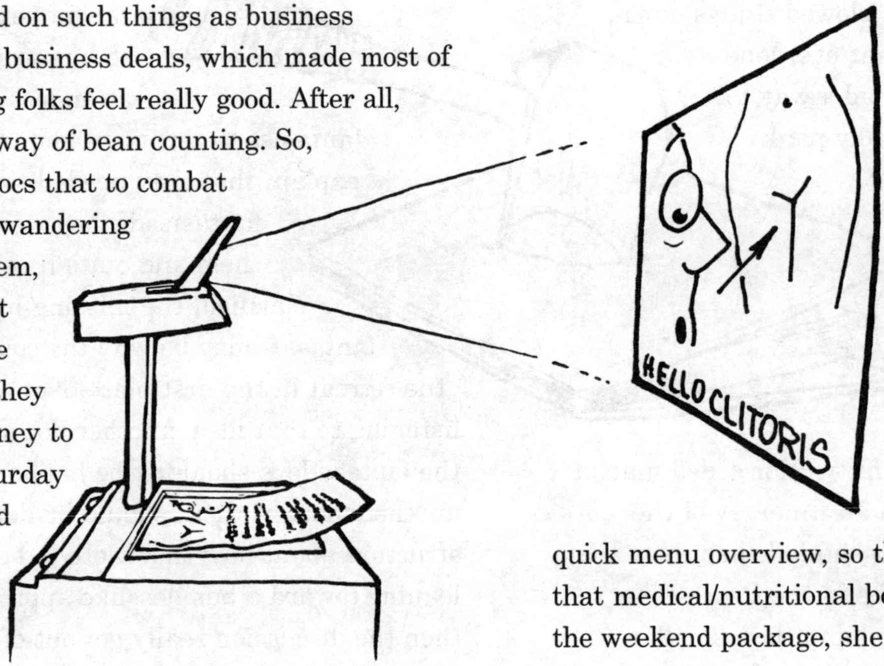

Next, she outlined the Friday morning session in the Peace Pipe Pavilion, explaining that all the refreshments for the weekend retreat would be organic and high-fiber—giving every ounce of effort to make their bodies nourished enough for the Saturday night performance. Someone snickered about the men needing twice as much protein, and perhaps the food portions needed to account for that imbalance since *performing* was really a male thing. But she tried to ignore the gender-biased suggestion in all their tittering. So with a quick menu overview, so the doctors could see that medical/nutritional boosts were included in the weekend package, she trudged forward.

On the overhead projector came the Friday morning session title: *Pleasure Particulars—The Body Blueprint.* She explained the session goal, which was to make sure everyone's sexual equipment could be understood in order for Saturday night sexual success to be possible. She talked about how everyone would receive a color-coded diagram of male and female sexual parts for their Valentine-red notebooks and then, after another protein-rich snack, they would head out to segregated sessions where obviously she would meet with the females and her co-therapist would gather with the men. That was, of course, after their fantasy logs had been turned in and critiqued with her felt-tip red pens matching the Valentine-red notebooks. They were impressed with the fact that she seemed to be covering all the bases, which made them stop talking, but only for a moment or two. But even with a slight lull in the conversation, he showed no interest in joining the conversation.

More overheads provided the late morning and separated session titles for the workshops. The female units, she explained, would attend the workshop, *Hello Clitoris,* and the men would be attending the session, *My Penis Power*. With that, the docs started throwing out snide comments. One of them asked if she didn't know that men probably already knew about their penis power because, as another one chimed in, penises tended to be *just out there*. She quickly explained that *yes,* she understood the differences between the two gender topics, and since many women didn't even know about their clitorises, saying HELLO in the session title emphasized the discovery part. With snorting and sniggling, the docs suggested that after a quick overview of their penises, the men should probably study clitorises, since that tends to be some of the problem—too much penis power and not enough clitoris appreciation. She made a note to guarantee that the men would have what she called *clitoris sensitivity training* in their penis power session as well. But even with all the tittering about clitorises and penises, her mentor still had nothing to say.

Although there was snickering from the docs about equal time for penises and clitorises, she moved on to more detail about the *Hello Clitoris* session, explaining that although she knew it was risky, she had props for the ladies. This caused the docs to pause. She showed them the earth-tone-colored mats on which the ladies would sit for self-examinations, *really saying hello to their clitorises,* one doc giggled. This would be impossible, she reminded them, without the accompanying hand-held mirrors, also provided in shades of mauve to match the mats. And when the chortling resulted in questions about whether she would say hello to her own clitoris in the session, she went on to her last prop for the clitoris session.

She asked for calm and explained that only with the doctors' approval would she consider using a Polaroid camera. They were spellbound as she explained her thinking that if the ladies took a snapshot of their clitorises then they could not only say hello for sure, but they could present the snapshot to their male partners at the luncheon following the session. She tried not to pay attention to their ensuing jokes about penis pictures, pointing out to the *M & Ms* that women were different than men and looking at penises just wasn't going to help anything for Saturday night success. She explained that she knew some women who had been sleeping next to a penis for a couple of decades and still didn't want to take a peek at it. But everything got so out of hand talking about who wanted to see what between penises and clitorises that she never really did get an answer about the Polaroid. Several times she looked directly at him for some contribution, but nothing came—only what appeared to be deep pensiveness in contrast to the raucous Polaroid pondering of the other docs.

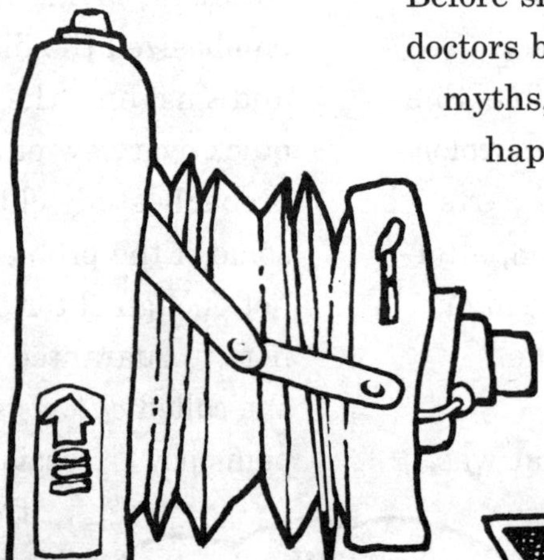

She forged on, using the overhead to display the title of the luncheon film shown after the meal was consumed and after the possible photo presentation of various clitorises. There will be two short films for lunch she explained, one titled, *"Oh, the Orgasm,"* and the second one, "*Mature & Immature Female Sexual Response*." Before she could show a clip of each movie, the doctors began a heated discussion about orgasm myths, with some saying that mature orgasms happened without clitoral stimulation (which would make the snapshots and the *Hello Clitoris* process meaningless), while two other docs said *an orgasm,was an orgasm, was an orgasm*. There seemed to be no way to get everything back on track about the orgasm maturity stuff, so on the overhead she flipped to a color photo of the high-fiber, high-protein lunch of poached salmon salad, suggesting to everyone that getting folks fired up with food might be a better focus.

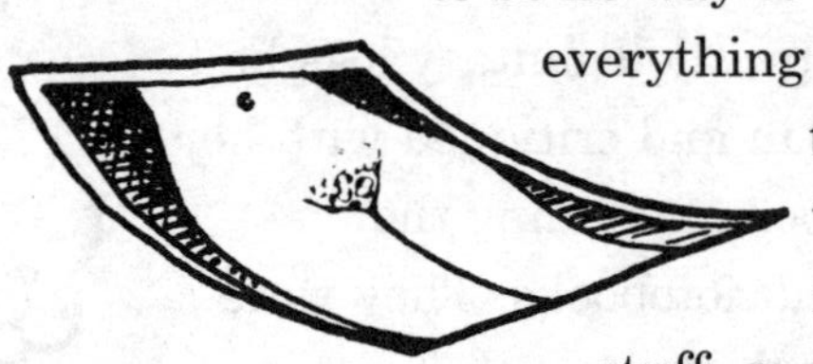

She went on to the rest of Friday's itinerary, explaining that in the afternoon and evening they would be switching gears, moving their studies from dysfunctional female parts to male parts that over-functioned—confronting the pesky problem of *premature ejaculation*. She had a little satisfaction with the glum-faced

docs in the room, noticing this was the only time they didn't have much to say. She thought the subject must have hit home, so she let it just hang in the air—providing her some relief from their incessant chattering. She also wondered if their embarrassed silence might allow her mentor to finally speak, but he remained mum.

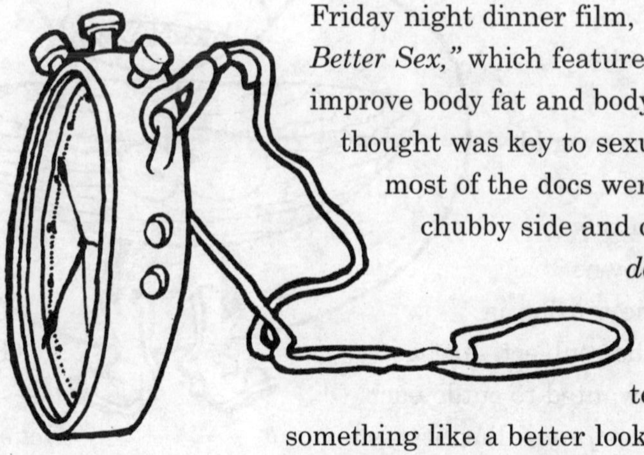

After her somewhat spiteful pause, she explained how the Friday afternoon session would focus on timing. And since she began to feel sorry for the uncomfortable docs, she took a stab at humor, pointing out that timing was everything on the road to simultaneous orgasms. Smartly, she quipped that since clitorises tend to limp along and penises tend to be in the fast lane, the couples would need a lot of help with timing. She told the docs that stopwatches would be handed out to everyone just to get the timing tools under control for Saturday night use, but it would be important to collect them at the end of the session so the timing wouldn't be tried out in their private room while preparing for Friday night dinner. One of them asked if a little homework (*so to speak*, he said) would help everything for Saturday night, but she made it clear that *no practicing* was the only way things would come together for Saturday night success. Then one of them wisecracked about the choice of words *coming together*, so she felt proud of herself that she had gotten them out of their gloomy attitude related to timing and too-fast penis power.

She forged forward with a short clip of the Friday night dinner film, *"Better Bodies for Better Sex,"* which featured various ways to improve body fat and body image, which she thought was key to sexual satisfaction. Since most of the docs were a little on the chubby side and clearly *dunkin' some donuts* when no one was looking, several of them wondered if teaching about something like a better looking body would be helpful, since not much could actually be accomplished between Friday and Saturday nights. There was a brief discussion about attractiveness, but clearly the docs didn't want to talk about body fat, so they asked to move on to the rest of the Friday evening program.

With lights and action, she showed a clip of the Friday evening film, which would be the counter-point to the lunch film *"Oh, the Orgasm."* The title *"Ten Tips to Better Orgasms"* with the subtitle, *"Oh, Yes You Can!"* caused them to pause, but only momentarily. She explained that in anticipation of the evening film getting things pumped up (*so to speak*, one doc joked), she would do a distraction exercise before they left for their rooms on Friday night, which included a multiple-choice quiz on the day's lessons and a rereading of the contract just to get everyone back in the clinical and business mode, preventing any action on Friday night that should be saved for Saturday night. The docs liked that idea and they murmured approval, but he was still silent.

Trudging forward, she flipped her overhead to Saturday's program that would begin back at the Peace Pipe Pavilion, leading up to the Saturday night showdown. Everyone could feel the tension in the air, approaching that subject. Just as she thought, the docs wanted to outdo each other since the topic was *props*. But first, she began with an introduction of the day's focus.

Right at the top, in Valentine red letters, the overhead sported the words *Super Saturday*. There were tittles among the docs, but the mood now seemed more serious. One mentioned it should be titled *Saturday Showdown* just to make everyone understand the seriousness of the situation. And another said it should be about *Super Bowl Sex Saturday,* while another thought the alliteration just seemed too much.

She told them that the day was basically planned around props that would help the couples with their goal on Saturday night. She was pretty proud of herself, since she had visual aids with the three prop topics of *Sex Toys, Pornography* and *Aphrodisiacs*. She explained that in the morning there would be a session on *The Right Vibrator For You—From Voltage to Visual Effects.* Following that, there would be a session *Oysters and Orgasms—Fact & Fiction.* Before she could move on, one of the docs suggested a short film he knew about titled, *Soft Porn for Soft Results,* which didn't seem to be very well received by the other docs.

She explained that after the coffee break there would be a presentation on *No Nonsense Nipple Knowledge, Vaginal Lubrications—Our Friend,* and finally *Tired Testicles—Tips and Technique.* The idea of tired testicles made them all a little nervous so they didn't have much to say—but only momentarily.

Regaining their enthusiasm, the *M & Ms* couldn't resist offering familiar learning tools about sexual props from their previous marketing endeavors. One suggested *Vibrators With a View.* and another thought something might be gained from the series, *Sex and the Senile,* although he agreed it might be somewhat daunting to the younger group. Then someone threw out the familiar film, *Viagra Victories,* and one of them remembered a training film on the art of pubic hair shaving, but couldn't recall the exact title. Finally, she got them to understand that the schedule was very tight and she had no way to incorporate their additional resources. But in spite of their tittering to come up with more—he still said nothing.

She went on with the Saturday schedule, explaining that after watching the videos there would be a question and answer segment and, of course, another quiz. Trying to be a team player, she told them that she needed their help for the potential problem of sending the couples back in their rooms while getting ready for dinner, but she didn't want any practicing and it worried her that some might jump the gun before the Saturday night showdown. One of them suggested that the men and women get ready for dinner in shifts to prevent any friskiness. And one doc questioned the wait, which resulted in another suggesting that spontaneous sex might be great, since he had training on that subject several years ago. But then he seemed befuddled about whether it was *spontaneous sex* or *simultaneous sex,* remembering only that the examples had to do with hanky-panky in an airplane lavatory. With all the confusion, she tried to regain control of the discussion making it clear she wanted all the couples to wait until after Saturday night dinner. With that thought, the *M & Ms* realized that the words *after dinner* meant the showdown of Super Saturday Sex. They tittered to each other and to her, wondering out loud *what would be the measure of success* to know if the bells and whistles resulted in the desired fireworks? Since she was ending her presentation to them and the success was the important part of their bean counting, she really hoped he would chime in. But he was still quiet.

The chattering was almost unbearable when they came to the Super Saturday Sex and the Sunday morning measures of success. *Would there be evaluation forms, post-event data and assessment inventories,* one of them asked? Being bean counters, they needed to know if the beans would be in their favor for the hospital marketing project, so they chattered incessantly about the money. They demanded to know how many of the couples would really be successful and how would she know the marketing conclusion? They went on to confront her with outcome studies, retrograde data, control groups, and anything else that made them seem smart about the number crunching. They demanded to know how, on Sunday morning, she would know if Saturday night was really a success. She suspected they didn't know either but the challenge was in her lap and she felt the pressure.

She felt overwhelmed, but not impotent. She told them that on Sunday morning, the couples would review their fantasy logs, they would recheck and turn in their contracts, and there would be analysis of the written expectation forms they completed in the first Peace Pipe Pavilion session on Thursday night. *Yes*, she could easily create an evaluation form for the participants to complete as they left on Sunday morning if that was what the docs wanted. That made them all feel a little better since as bean counters, they would have something to measure with the forms. But then the discussion centered on a frightening topic to the marketing folks, which related to *refunds*.

What would she do if some were not successful on Super Saturday night and wanted their money back? What was her refund policy? Was it spelled out in the beginning? the docs queried, making it clear that she must define the goal at the beginning so there would be no fear of having to give back any beans. This time the suggestion of using lie detector tests was seriously considered, but probably too late in the discussion. *How will you define Super Saturday success?* was the final question that rendered her speechless.

She knew the marketing docs were right and she knew she didn't have an answer. Fearing complete panic, she looked to him for help. None came. Finally, she risked everything. She looked him in the eye and asked of her beloved mentor, how she should define *good sex,* and finally he spoke.

"If they can ask their partners to have sex standing up in a canoe, assured that if they fall in the water, their partner won't let them drown, then that would be your measure of ***good sex***. And that should be the goal for your weekend and the goal for the couples' lifetime."

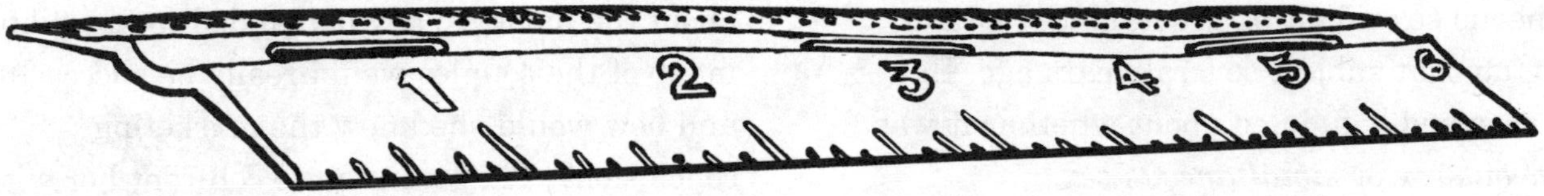

THE TENTH COMMANDMENT— Thou Shalt Teach Touching

So what is the strange lesson of canoes and rescue from drowning with the wise doctor? How does he equate *good sex* to trying to have intercourse standing up in a canoe, but making sure if one of the partners falls in the water, the other won't let them drown? How does that definition of good sex compare with the group of sex therapists and bean counter doctors with their gidgits and gadgets about everything from Viagra to vibrators, and orgasms to oysters?

The answer is that between the tittering docs and the wise mentor, one provides a representation of a lifetime commitment of love and safety while the other represents the ***Super Size Me*** hype of sex, so common in society. But both opposing ideas contribute to the doctor's canoe theory since he is suggesting that the two ingredients for healthy sex are combining ***vulnerability and safety***—thus canoes and water rescues, without a single concern for bean counting.

STANDING UP IN THE CANOE

The astute doctor believes that standing up in a canoe represents how most people really feel when they are sexual, yet constantly exposed to a barrage of sexual hype just like the marketing docs thought would be helpful with all their silly sexual props, videos, and bells/whistles for Saturday night showdown. The young therapist and the *M & Ms,* with all their toys and tired testicle technique, represent how society tells folks sex should be, which contributes to the vulnerability part of the canoe analogy. Ordinary people, just trying to figure out sexual satisfaction, are constantly bombarded by sexual messages shuffled through their brains about perfect bodies and performing perfectly.

Yet in reality, just plain, ordinary folks crawl into bed every night with other ordinary folks—hardly any of them perfect or even close to perfect, but most of them perfectly vulnerable. Unlike the way sex is represented in American society or by the weekend sex warriors of the psych hospital, good sex might really be more about untangling nightgowns or treasuring the familiar smell of Bengay and Vicks VapoRub that replaced exotic perfume years ago. According to the doctor, good sex might be about the pleasure of over thirty or forty years of *spooning* with that person's body a few hours before the alarm goes off, with a short fantasy about how in the past, they ran their fingers through each other's hair that fell out long ago. According to the doctor, that is what a sexual relationship really means—sweet, simple, and anything that makes folks feel safe in all the vulnerability of the *Super Size Me* hype of society.

Yet in reality, just plain, ordinary folks crawl into bed every night with other ordinary folks—hardly any of them perfect or even close to perfect, but most of them perfectly vulnerable.

In reality, ordinary folks who jump into bed together, look funny, smell funny, and usually have dips and dives on their bodies not thought humanly possible. It doesn't take much to figure out that most ordinary folks are not even close to

He believes that good sex isn't about simultaneous orgasms, perfect bodies, sex toys, great penis performance or just the right number of nipples.

the sexual hype forced upon them every day from society. There is probably no other human condition where folks are so vulnerable as when they attempt to be sexual—just as standing up in a canoe for intercourse would be quite precarious.

DOING DISAPPOINTMENT

The reason the doctor was so quiet and so unwilling to participate in the sexual gymnastics discussion was because he knows how tragic that sexual hype can be to just ordinary normal people, and perhaps he wanted to influence the young intern in a more positive and people-respectful way. As he watched the emphasis on the showdown of sexually saturated ordinary couples—perhaps he knew about the human failure factor, that didn't have anything to do with penis power failures. The wise and helpful doctor probably knew that with all the hype, sexual disappointment is right around the corner as those weekend retreaters listen to the world around them about how they *should be sexual*, causing them to eventually line up in a Peace Pipe Pavilion for props. But that vulnerability from disappointment is only half of the *good sex* message.

THEY WON'T LET ME DROWN

The sexual vulnerability part of the doctor's analogy is represented by the *standing up in a canoe* image of sex, while the drowning part has to do with the partner relationship and eventual rescue. If, in all that sexual vulnerability, cuddled in the armpit of that partner becomes the safest place to be, the doctor believes that is *good sex*. He believes that good sex isn't about simultaneous orgasms, perfect bodies, sex toys, great penis performance, or just the right number of nipples. It isn't about *Saturday Super Sex* or a big sexual showdown related to the Sex Fairy's arrival after the wedding reception. It is about being safe in vulnerability. When the doctor talks about a person falling into the water and the partner not letting the other partner drown, he is speaking to that safety issue. When there is so much trust, he teaches, that however one person really is under those sheets—vulnerable and imperfect—they are safe, loved and cherished, then *good sex* really materializes. But in this fast-paced world with sexual Olympics always on display, that sweet, simple canoe theory doesn't come easy. It must be taught. And it all centers on the concept of touch.

BEGIN WITH THE END

The Tenth (and last) Commandment asks parents to consider teaching touch by considering the end product for their children concerning sexuality—long into the future. Hopefully, when Mom and Dad conjure an image of Little Pooper being a sexual person, they first and foremost want a sexually respectful person who isn't a sex offender, since it is obvious sex offenders would never tolerate the canoe kind of sex—finding it disappointing and boring. Sex offenders would probably be the type of person signing up for *Saturday Night Super Sex* but they also might want those sexual showdowns several nights a week with several partners. But is just staying out of sex offender prison what parents want for their children's sexual future? If they had to think about their child's future sexuality, would they pick a cuddling partner for a canoe kind of couple, with touching and tender sex all through the stages of life? Or would they rather have their kiddos signing up for the sexual gymnastics weekend retreat because they feel they haven't yet achieved the *Super Size Me* sexual image that seems desirable?

MIRROR, MIRROR ON THE WALL

"When I really thought about it, I tried to get an image of my four-year-old son being a forty-year-old man and having sexual respect. It was difficult, of course, since sex should be private, and me thinking about his sexual *doings* under the sheets was too much of a privacy invasion. But when I really worked on the general image of sexual respect, the mirror centered on touch—my son tenderly touching the person he loved and him being touched, whether it was in bed or in the Bingo game at church. I got a picture of him not being afraid to cuddle his partner in the grocery store and I guess what stuck out for me was seeing him in love with his partner—not powerful or out of control—just sweet, in love and feeling love in return. And the only way I could find that image was with the idea of tender touching."

SUPER SEX SHOWDOWN

Without active teaching about the canoe theory—combining vulnerability and safety—most kiddos have a good chance of listening to the sexual hype world, and first, being disappointed; and secondly, falling prey to problems such as failed or dissatisfied relationships, having affairs, or being sexually promiscuous, needing higher intensity about sex through pornography use, or signing up for the weekend retreat of Showdown Super Sex. As clarified in other commandments, like it or not, the world will teach about sex—usually the gymnastic kind—rarely teaching about tender touch or canoe rides.

So, in teaching children to have healthy canoe-kind-of-sex, they have to be taught touching and what comes in partnership with that lesson is teaching about arousal. When arousal is understood, honored and controlled, a wonderful outcome occurs on the path to sexual respect and it doesn't have anything to do with sexual super sizing. When children learn from their bodies that touch sometimes brings arousal, but that their arousal is normal and natural, and most importantly, they don't have to act on it, then sexual respect can be possible. But if the kiddos don't learn that lesson about touch and arousal, things can go disastrously wrong.

When arousal is understood, honored and controlled a wonderful outcome occurs on the path to sexual respect and it doesn't have anything to do with sexual super sizing.

"I felt a feeling I had never felt before, so I just thought, this must be love." There it is—a child blind-sided by arousal, mistaken for love, and now with tragic results.

AROUSAL GONE WRONG

She had only two more weeks before she would finally be thirteen, and only two more months before she would finally deliver her child. Of course, everyone wanted her to get therapy due to the tragedy of it all. So here she was—smiling, but uncomfortable and unaware of what lies ahead for *a baby about to have a baby.* The therapist asks, "Did your parents or anyone else ever talk to you about sex?" She answers affirmatively explaining that *yes,* her mother had provided sex education. The shocked therapist inquired further, asking the child what she had learned in the lessons since it seemed the pregnancy outcome was not what would have been expected from a sexually savvy child.

"Well, my mom told me that I should never, ever have sex until I was in love—she was really firm on that. She always told me love was great and that sex was okay with love. I guess this guy and I started messing around a little, hugging and kissing in the mall and in the car. I felt a feeling I had never felt before, so I just thought, this must be love." There it is—a child blind-sided by arousal, mistaken for love, and now with tragic results.

REALITY RERUN

Rerunning the lesson in the Third Commandment of teaching logic about sex, it appears that even the little ones can be taught sexual respect for choosing a partner and sharing the private parts of their bodies as grown-ups. If parents use the logic blueprint of the Third Commandment, this lesson helps children avoid a quickie humping session underneath Grandma's quilt in the back bedroom, and hopefully, the logic gives kiddos a great start for their sexual futures and for making responsible sexual decisions. But that logic is about how the kiddos should think about *privacy, pride,* and *picking a partner* when they grow up. Those are great things to teach toward the path of sexual respect, but that logic does not address the part of sex that pertains to arousal and what to do about those feelings that may not be love, but just flat out sexual desire. How parents teach arousal directly, or how their children indirectly learn about arousal is the *key or the killer* in raising sexually respectful children, since arousal really is the fuel to firing up the sexual equipment. A precursor to tackling that uncomfortable issue is for parents to recognize that whether they send their kids to the monastery or wire them up for electricity for their cardboard boxes in the backyard, the kiddos are going to get aroused—no doubt about it.

THE SEX FAIRY AND AROUSAL

Just as most parents struggle with talking to their children about sex in general, talking about sexual arousal is really a stretch and that is because they don't want to consider the pesky subject and they, for sure, don't want arousal happening. Although arousal is the cornerstone of being sexual, it is usually not part of any curriculum—even from the seemingly most enlightened parents who may have prided themselves in going beyond Nurse Ratchet and her podium pad presentation. Yet when parents are asked to begin with the end, and imagine their children growing up to be sexually respectful, they see an image of touch and arousal being safe and sweet. But how will the kiddos get to that image without guidance—especially considering what society teaches? The answer may just be that parents believe or hope that somehow their children will grow up to have healthy arousal—perhaps with just a few wand whirls when the Sex Fairy turbo charges the arousal system into normal mode, getting it up and running right after the wedding reception.

Yet when parents are asked to begin with the end, and imagine their children growing up to be sexually respectful, they see an image of touch and arousal being safe and sweet.

TOUCHING TREPIDATION—AROUSAL FEARS

Even though it is important, it is rare that parents feel comfortable talking about arousal and they have good reason to feel that trepidation. What anthropologists, historians and sociologists learn from their bean counting about touch helps most parents do the *touch taboo*. It seems the English Americans hit the jackpot for the *no, no touch* avoidant societies of the world. Coming in second for the societies that put the brakes on touching are the Germans, the English Canadians, and just about anyone in the white Anglo-Saxon group. But it might not be just geography that makes the difference in who wants to cuddle up and who wants to freeze up. The Christian Bible seems to muster up a lot of fear of body pleasure and body function, which really means arousal. Now the Bible doesn't tell the ladies to lay on their backs and think of Jehovah, but it is pretty clear that putting the brakes on body pleasure might be just the thing to do, according to the Bible writers. This fear is probably one of the reasons why so many Americans stop touching their children. Gradually, it happens. The trepidation that somehow touching them brings the dreaded arousal—but arousal from whom?

But it might not be just geography that makes the difference in who wants to cuddle up and who wants to freeze up.

TOO BIG TOUCHING

"She's just too big to be sitting on my lap," a worried Dad says about his now turned 13-year-old who is clearly showing signs of mammillary gland growth and mascara use. But is Dad frightened of *daughter's arousal* if she sat on his lap or is Dad frightened of *his own arousal* if they cuddled up. In the deep, dark thoughts of Dad, he probably couldn't imagine himself being aroused to his daughter, but instead he just has a general fear that her development means she is becoming a sexual person, and touching her is terrifying for him because in his lessons, he has always equated touching with his arousal, followed (quickly) by his sexual action. And sadly, in the message he is teaching, as he avoids his now-developing daughter, is that no one can control arousal, which is a very dangerous message for children. But there is more in the *too big to touch* tragedy concerning the American family's response to touching.

He died later that night. I will never know if he died because it was so terrible that I forced him to touch me, or if he missed me too, after all these years and finally found peace in that special moment."

TOUCHING TRAGEDY

"Once I started to sexually develop, my Dad never got close to me again. He stopped touching me, he stopped hugging me and he seemed afraid of me. As I tried to reach out, he would pull away, sometimes making me feel so ashamed. I hated my body because I knew it pushed him away. I longed for him and I felt touch-starved as a teenager, so it was easy to turn to boys because my Dad had turned away from me. Thirty years later, he was dying in a nursing home after a massive stroke. I could finally touch him, cuddle him, kiss him and do to him what we did when I was little. One afternoon as he lay in a coma, I laid down next to him and draped his arm over my shoulder just to have that feeling of being close to him and having him hold me, just one more time. He died later that night. I will never know if he died because it was so terrible that I forced him to touch me, or if he missed me too, after all these years and finally found peace in that special moment."

FREUD FEARS

In addition to parents fearing their own arousal to children, some parents pull back on touching in fear of arousal *in their children*, and the overall conclusion is that all arousal is bad. That is until the Sex Fairy arrives right after the reception and changes everything. Dr. Sigmund Freud didn't help the kiddo arousal worries when he announced the deep-dish diagnosis for children who seemed to yearn for Mommy and Daddy. The *Oedipus Complex* was the name he gave little boys who feel sexual about their Mothers. Apparently, Dr. Freud was convinced that young male kiddos wanted a roll in the hay with Mommy more than they wanted Tootsie Pops. Interestingly, no one considered that maybe rather than a sexual yearning, it was just a little boy longing for the touching Mommy had so freely given the him during an earlier, and not-touch-phobic time. But Dr. F. went further with the pesky problem of children being aroused, deciding that the *Electra Complex* occurred when little girls yearn for a sexual romp with Dad more than they want their Polly Pockets. Dr Freud saw sex as a motivation for just about everything, and it seems as though most Americans have just followed along with their hyper-vigilance in stamping out any kind of sexual feeling—especially for the kiddos, and that means squashing the snuggling for sure.

PHOBIC FEARS OF TOUCHING

It seems that with perhaps a Bible in one hand, Dr. Freud's theory in another hand, and the Sex Fairy myth flying around somewhere, parents believe that arousal is bad for the kids and touch brings on arousal, so putting the brakes on touching is the chosen path toward morality. The final nail in the no-touch coffin is that touch brings arousal, arousal brings sex, and all of that is bad until after the wedding reception. The connection between touching leading to hanky-panky is ingrained in this society by folks who want no out-of-control sex in the playhouse or the White House.

LUSTFUL LESSONS

President Jimmy Carter, when once interviewed, was asked if he ever committed a sexual indiscretion. His answer was that in fact, he had *lusted in his heart.* Well, some thought his comment was so egregious that it was just the first wheel in the eventual *all wheels coming off* his presidency. The great pretend was that President Carter was the only man who ever had a sexual thought outside of marriage—thus the indignant outrage by many Americans. It was as though people believed a sexual thought had to lead to a sexual action and they didn't want to think about hanky-panky and their president.

PINK AND BLUE DIFFERENCES

Furthering the idea that sexual arousal must lead to sexual action is the annoying, but typical idea that boys and girls develop and act on arousal very differently, setting the stage for touch disasters later on. Very early in life, the blue boy babies get a head start in arousal acceptance. Little erections in the swimming pool locker room are easy to see, discuss and at least accept. There are numerous, sort-of-humorous books written on not only names for male genitalia but also raucous slang words for male masturbation—something never to be found for the ladies. Later, Viagra commercials monopolize television making male arousal appear to be something perfectly fine to discuss and about as normal as the nightly news.

Unfortunately in the *it ain't equal* realm, the female sexuality bean counters suggest as many as 60-70 percent of women report being unable to have orgasms through intercourse even when those Viagra-reinforced penises are working perfectly fine. Only on an obscure satellite channel, perhaps after the kidlets are in bed, will there be a commercial featuring a fatigued woman with too many kids and too many loads of laundry to feel frisky with her husband. *But there is hope,* she hopelessly offers. Holding up a Jell-O-sized box of herbs, she tells everyone that the ladies can get things fired up by just placing an order through an 800-number in Omaha. Nope, arousal acceptance is very different between the sexes and eventually those differences will be related to touch.

The final nail in the no-touch coffin is that touch brings arousal, arousal brings sex, and all of that is bad until after the wedding reception.

OUTIES AND INNIES

So blue boy babies get more credit for their signs of arousal because of many things, but for sure because their sexual parts stick out—making everything much more acceptable and easier to understand. Since girl's sexual parts stick in, their signs of arousal (vaginal lubrication and such) are more unmentionable and for most, more shameful. It would be a rare Super Bowl where commercials provide tips for females about what to do with four hours of uncontrolled vaginal lubrication as the Viagra

It would be a rare Super Bowl where commercials provide tips for females about what to do with four hours of uncontrolled, vaginal lubrication as the Viagra commercials suggest for men and their fired up penises.

Between the two genders, it seems girls *touch* while boys *tussle.*

commercials suggest for men and their fired up penises. But there is more to innies and outies in the arousal/touch issue, especially when things switch around in the *okay to touch* and the *not okay to touch* paradigm.

NURTURING NEEDS

Girls fare better than boys in the *permission-to-touch* category. Female units seem to be socialized more favorably into non-sexual touching, probably in preparation for the making-babies-business when they grow up and their nurturing needs are in demand. But it might also be that since arousal for females is more unmentionable, folks might think it is more acceptable for girls to touch since nothing would really have a chance to get out of hand considering the lack of female arousal worries. Between the two genders, it seems girls *touch* while boys *tussle.* While little girls would commonly be seen holding hands with other girls or cuddling and nurturing their dogs and dollies, little boys are taught to avoid those touching behaviors and be relegated to the fine art of hand shaking. That is, of course, unless the touching is connected to sports, which changes everything.

TOUCHING TIME OUT

Concerning touch apprehension, it seems that when balls, sticks, nets, scores and goals get fired up, the touch trepidation among boys is diminished. In the huddle, on the sidelines or near the dugout, butt pats, hugs and even emotional outbursts (such as crying) are acceptable as long as the touching males are connected to some kind of jock business. The touching taboos are batted out of the park as long as sports or some kind of competition is the mission. But that touch *permissioning* is short-lived because when the game is over, as far as touching is concerned, males must return to the properness of a handshake.

FUNCTION FEAR

Adding to the dreaded connection between touch and arousal seems to be the great American fear of body function. Switching of permission and acceptance between the genders is an unwritten law about how boys and girls handle body functioning, which, although few want to address, is a requirement for being sexual. Regardless of how disgusting it seems, bodies must function in order for sex to happen and the body works between the genders starts everything out miles apart without a canoe in sight.

DADDY DOES IT

Every morning the ritual was the same. He rose from the breakfast table, put his pipe in his mouth, his newspaper under his arm and announced to three little girls and their mother, "I'm going to go take a dump!" Down the hall he went, into the bathroom, closing the door. The pipe smoke filled the air, as did other evidence that Dad's body was working perfectly fine. As an adult, one of those little girls remembered the routine and the differences between her parents and body functions.

"My father taking dumps in the morning was just part of the plan. I thought it was all interconnected. I got up, ate breakfast, my Dad took a dump and the bus came. But I lived in that house 18 years and there was never a shred of evidence that my Mother's bowels moved. Later, I wondered how she managed to convince us all her body didn't work. She just wasn't dump material."

SHAME OR CELEBRATION

It appears that male body functions are more acceptable than female body functions and that probably leads to lots of problems in the sexual respect department. First, women spend millions of dollars on *chocolate mousses* and *strawberry flips* to put between their legs and between other body parts to pretend as though their body parts aren't working. Women operate differently in restrooms, obsessively trying to cover up signs of body function, pretending as though their bodies don't work while men have more permission to just hang things out for functioning. "Never let them see you sweat" is a common refrain for the mantra of how women should handle (or deny) their body functions. It is no wonder that when women finally enter into a sexual experience—being a happy camper about body functions (which is required) doesn't happen very easily for the ladies. Rather than feeling celebration for sexual commitment, the feelings are often a mirror of years of shame about body functions, which certainly puts the brakes on feeling positive and looking to hitch a ride on a canoe.

FUNCTION FREEDOM

The differences in male and female comfort about body function also plays into the ideas about control. Girls control and deny their bodies work, and yet boys are much freer to not only take dumps, but allow other body parts to function normally. Boys can fart—girls can't. Boys can see their arousal on the outside of their bodies, girls can't. Boy bodies work, girl bodies don't or aren't supposed to work without shame. Those differences lead to the idea that the arousal of boys (a body function) is normal, natural, and most importantly for the sexist game planners—out of control. Further ideas suggest that boys can't control their arousal and shouldn't have to control it. Thus the kind of statement when considering how much touching—kissing or cuddling so easy for girls—should be allowed for boys. "Don't let me start something I can't finish," accentuates the thinking that the functioning freedom about farts may go all the way to other functioning when exposed to sexual stimulus. In other words, if the boy body is functioning, it must be acted upon regardless of other things such as consent, which is in conflict with the sexual

Boys can fart—girls can't. Boys can see their arousal on the outside of their bodies, girls can't. Boy bodies work, girl bodies don't or aren't supposed to work without shame.

respect paradigm. Criminal case after criminal case is decided upon the idea that males can't, and shouldn't, control their arousal.

"Well, she wore skimpy clothing, what did she expect?" or "she made it clear from her body language that she wanted him, so what else could he do?" The old stud horse theory—where males are exposed to sexual stimulus and then *just can't help it* exemplifies this idea. The sad bottom line is that girls should control their body functions and for sure, not ever fire up those functions—especially in the horse pasture.

PHOBIC FUNCTION FEAR

And it goes on, the fear of body functions occurring through touch. The hot dog handler at the airport or Subway sandwich shop wears cute plastic gloves while preparing the food so the person wanting the Double Deluxe Combo feels better. Even more reassuring to the phobic-function-fear population is that the food folks put on a new pair of plastic gloves for each sandwich-ordering-customer, even though nothing changed behind that Subway counter—not one drop of snot came anywhere near. So to make everyone happy, a new set of gloves is used for each hungry person just so the touch fears are soothed in sandwich making. It makes everyone feel better and it makes everyone remember the disgusting nature of human contact.

Public restrooms do everything they can to avoid the *take a relaxing dump with a newspaper and pipe* image, and instead focus on fear of function/touch. Rather than having to touch the probably-already-totally-sanitary toilet seat cover in the cute little dispensers, a ready-to-sit-down-and-pee-person can just wave a hand over a sensor and a toilet seat cover automatically slips on the lid—with no touching required. More reinforcement that the dreadful touch/function is protected comes with sensors used to dispense water so no faucet has to be touched and the same is often true for soap and paper towel dispensers. *Touch nothing* is the tune of a successful trip to the restroom, especially for the female units.

Caution about diseases and bacteria are certainly important issues, but how much is really necessary and how much is related to the fear of body function is debatable. But little confusion exists about the constant reminders to most folks that touching and body functions are disgusting, which directly impacts the path to sexual respect and cuts off the supply of available canoe rides.

SEX FAIRY FUNCTION FEAR

Even the Sex Fairy, in all her ineptitude, knows that no matter how disgusting body functions may be portrayed in everyday life, they are nonetheless required for sex. No amount of wand waving will change the fact that bodies work and bodies must function during sex. So a prerequisite in raising sexually respectful children involves lessons on body functions that move toward canoe rides and water rescues.

DREADFUL DECLINE

Departing from sandwich shops and toilet seat covers in public places, how do parents handle the touching of their children and how does that process contribute to sexual respect or disrespect? It seems apparent that things in the touch/function department start out pretty good. In fact, life begins with absolute acceptance of body functions, as the babies are dependent on getting help with all aspects of *body works*. Changing Little Pooper's poopy diaper can easily occur on the picnic or pool table without anyone getting upset or anyone bringing out a pair of Subway Sandwich plastic gloves. And the wee ones also get lots of tender touching—usually lots and lots of it. The opposite makes the point.

Babies have been known to die in orphanages without being touched. The fancy diagnostic term is *failure to thrive*. The baby studiers know that touch is very important to infants and toddlers, but where was it studied that the teenager who doesn't get touched every morning before school would fail to thrive as well? Or is it just pretend that the teenager doesn't need touch because in the deep, dark corner of their minds, Mom and Dad are frightened with what the touch will bring to the sexteen-year-old? But beyond that question, there are no questions that the little ones get lots of touching without any fear and with lots of really good stuff.

TELL US, DOC

The conference hall was filled as professionals and parents waited for Dr. Herman Belmont to deliver his address. Expectations were high, since he was an expert, and at least for Flo, Mo, and Joe, the trip from New Hope had been long, especially since they hit the road before any of them had breakfast at their usual stop, Gracie's Grill. After the perfunctory introduction of the speaker and the initial applause, Dr. Belmont approached the podium, momentarily fumbled with his notes, and began. With a deep and powerful voice, he read:

It was dusk; the apartment was empty, save for the two of them. As they lay entwined in a warm embrace, this room, this bed, was the universe. She stroked the nape of his neck; he nuzzled her erect nipple, first gently with his nose, then licked it, tasted it, smelled and absorbed her body odor. Slowly he caressed her one breast as he softly rolled his face over the contours of the other. He pressed his body close against her, sighed, and fully spent, closed his eyes and soon fell into a deep, satisfying sleep. Ever so slowly, she slipped herself out from under him, lest she disturb him, cradled him in her arms, and moved him to his crib!

Mo, Joe, and Flo were stunned. As Dr. B. read, it felt as though they were peering into an apartment of a couple that had returned home for lunch after working the morning shift at K-Mart. The described sensuous scene was at first embarrassing as the erotic nature of the couple's

The baby studiers know that touch is very important to infants and toddlers, but where was it studied that the teenager who doesn't get touched every morning before school would fail to thrive as well?

The early years are extremely sensual and in fact, the same human-to-human contact given to babies in the first few years of life is usually the same sexual conduct desired by adults in their later sexual years—that is if they had a canoe handy.

hanky-panky was imagined in the minds of the teeth-sweating trio, as well as the rest of the audience. Until the last sentence, it was not clear that the seemingly sexual scene actually involved a breast-feeding mother and her male child, rather than a hot-and-sweaty, lunch hour sexual tryst between two K-Mart supervisors. Shockingly they wondered, how could the normal process of breast-feeding be so arousing? And what does the arousing nature of mother/infant breast-feeding have to do with contemplations about teaching touch and withholding touch in families?

What Professor Herman Belmont presented in his speech on the *sexual development of children* was not only arousing, but also demonstrative of the sensuous nature of childhood—no, infanthood. Everyone expected a professional type of lecture, perhaps on something as academic as breast development correlations between girls who attend public (not to be confused with pubic) or private schools, or perhaps studies about the onset of sperm production in males who live west of the Mississippi. But instead, they received a lesson on the sensuousness of being a child and a very, very young child at that.

SLIPPING SENSUOUSNESS

The early years are extremely sensual and, in fact, the same human-to-human contact given to babies in the first few years of life is usually the same sexual conduct desired by adults in their later sexual years—that is if they had a canoe handy. If parents *began with the end* of sex education and tried to imagine a sexually respectful future for their children into adulthood, it might be something similar to the imagined K-Mart lunch hour scene. The reason Flo, Mo, and Joe experienced uncomfortable stirrings in their bodies while listening to Dr. Belmont is that the erotic description sounded very much like something they would like to do with their own partners on Saturday night after the kids went to bed. The tenderness, the touching and the absolute comfort of body reciprocity and pleasure was not subtle, but it was between an infant and a mother. But if this beginning was so sensuous and seemingly just fine if it lasted a lifetime, what happened to make it stop and wait patiently for the arrival of the Sex Fairy? Sadly, as kiddos move forward in development, they are moved back-burner-bound in the touch department—stopping this wonderful, sensuous beginning of life—all based on fear of touching and arousal.

AIRPORT AGONY

Everyone in airports seem to have a special positive feeling for soldiers returning home safely from military duty, especially when war is involved and especially when a family is waiting. As he walked off the exit escalator, three children and a wife gleefully rush forward. Mom, of course, gets a hug with a couple of slobbery lip kisses—no problem there. But then Dad begins to touch (all differently, according to the fear factor) the three kiddos who are bursting with excitement. They exude anticipation and although they are different in age, they are just the same in the thrill of greeting the Dad they have missed for so long. Equally, they reach out.

The toddler, of course, is scooped up into Dad's arms and is immediately engaged in neck kissing, cheek pecks and even an elbow or two gets a slobbery smack from Dad. Waves of sensuousness and affection flood from Dad onto the little one, cradled in his arms. Then comes the appearing-to-be six-year-old whose head reaches to Dad's waist. Dad draws the middle one to his hip in a top-of-the-shoulder hug. It is a grand wrap-around hug, but there is no kissing. Not wanting to move away, this middle one hangs on and as Dad begins to walk down the airport corridor, the child encircles Dad's leg with her arm and keeps stride, her elbow bouncing ever so softly on Dad's testicles with each step. She just moves with him, his leg cradled by her arm, matching him step for step, much of his crotch bumped and bounced by her arm. But this hug-step is just fine with everyone and the testicles probably also fared safely.

But then there is the seemingly ten-year-old, obviously longing for Dad, who gets a *hair tousle* every now and then. For this oldest child there is no kissing, there is no touching, there is no testicle bouncing, just occasional hair tousling, as Dad moves between the kidlets, touching them according to the unwritten books on the dreadful touch decline in American families.

BABY, ME, BABY

Interestingly, in spite of the decline in that wonderful sensuous touching reserved sadly for the little ones, there still seems to be a longing for the image of babies and the touching that comes with that wonderful time (however short) in life when touching is acceptable. ***BABY*** is one of the most sensuous words in the songwriter's repertoire. Whether it is *Baby Love*, *Be My Baby Tonight*, *Baby it's All Right*, or *Baby Shake Your Thing*, the word *baby* has a sensuous image and connotation. In movies, lovemaking scenes often include the terms of *"Oh, Baby"* and all the watchers can connect to the sexual connotation, since babies start out life in a very sensuous state. What a tragedy it is that because of touching fears leading to arousal, Americans are sentenced to their own *failure to thrive*, longing for the kind of touching that began life but then was so prohibited later on. Right at the bottom (not the baby's bottom) of the fear is that touching leads to arousal and the fear of arousal is because it leads to sex. So it all must stop. And putting the brakes on something everyone started out with and everyone wants, brings a whole basketful of problems, few of which enrich the prospect of sexual respect.

SEXUAL DISRESPECT 101

Most often at the top of the worry about the touch/arousal list are those folks who become sexual offenders, perhaps the most disrespectful of all. They are often the kind of folks who

What a tragedy it is that because of touching fears leading to arousal, Americans are sentenced to their own *failure to thrive*, longing for the kind of touching that began life but then was so prohibited later on.

believe that touching means arousal and arousal means action, and coupled with their strong sense of entitlement, using children or another more vulnerable person for the source of their sexual action seems okay with them. Considering they tend to be folks who don't want to delay gratification, resulting in affairs and such, it is pretty easy to understand that the whole business of canoe sex wouldn't hold a candle to their more-than-likely-Bird-Baby upbringing or their experiences of living with parents like Rancho Rambler or Perch Woman, where caring about the feelings of others gets the *slow moving turnout*. But that is just the basic part of sexual disrespect 101. What does the touch-phobic-arousal-fear do to just ordinary folks—beyond those who sexually offend?

BIG BEDROOM DISAPPOINTMENT

If parents don't touch their children and teach about arousal, then children learn the traditional messages from society about Super Bowl Sex and head into the hotel honeymoon with high expectations. And this sexual hype message isn't always about vibrators with a view or Polaroid snapshots of clitorises. Sometimes the narrow and rigid focus of the *OATs* in their abstinence-only programs really hype the waiting with promises that postponing is really, really worth it. The obvious missing-in-action issue for those seemingly wholesome programs about touch and arousal is ***just don't***. No training, no understanding, no honor—***just don't.*** The *do nothing but let the world educate children* approach, coupled with touching taboos but longing for baby touching, adds up to a recipe for disaster and disappointment. It is as though the touching is great in the beginning, and then it is cut off with the big wedding wait. And usually the Sex Fairy can't deliver and a lifetime of disappointment is usually the result.

LANDERS LETTER

Ann Landers, famous newspaper columnist, was spurred on by a letter she received from a sexually disappointed woman. The author of the correspondence bemoaned the fact that she felt forsaken by her husband who could not offer her touching unless it turned to sex. Sadly, she longed to be held, feeling barren and abandoned in her marriage. Impacted by the woman's plight, Ann Landers conducted a non-scientific survey in 1985, just asking women about their bedroom satisfaction—especially related to touch. At first, she was shocked at the number of women who answered and even more shocked at the result to her touch inquiry. In her informal survey she asked women to express their opinion on whether they would rather be touched, cuddled and held, than engage in THE ACT—(politely meaning intercourse). The results came in and they weren't pretty.

More than 90,000 women responded and about 64,000 (72 percent) said *yes*. The ladies wanted the touching—they wanted to be held, they wanted to be treated like babies—although the survey didn't exactly capture that idea. More than 72 percent of the respondents wanted touching more than they wanted intercourse. Interestingly, the ladies who expressed these views weren't typically elderly women worn out from too many Super Saturday nights at the Peace Pipe Pavilion. They were women *under the age of 40*—lost in a sea of disappointment about how touching was taught and not taught to them and to their partners, so long ago.

ROLES AND ROADS

So if many folks are disappointed and so far apart in their sexual desires—how did this happen? How did the longing ladies get so separated from their no-touch male partners? Whether it is being an *outie*, whether it is not being touched as often as girls, or whether it is Mom and Dad worried that son will be a sissy if he learns anything but the art of handshaking, the touching phobia is very different between the genders, and for sure, those male partners of the sad lady letter writers. Boys don't fare too well in the roles of touching, which doesn't do much to help out in the bedroom, long after the honeymoon hotel visit with the Sex Fairy. And just like the intern and the *M & M* docs wanting stopwatches for the Peace Pipe Pavilion folks, many arousal/touching problems between the genders has to do with timing.

Because male units are denied non-sexual touching, they learn arousal equals sex and that they should be quick about it, bringing on another set of problems relating to timing and dissatisfaction later on. If boys masturbate in childhood, they are usually speedy because they don't want to be discovered by sister who is outside the upstairs bathroom door wearing her shower cap. They learn arousal and action need to partner up in that order, and in short order, as well. Males actually train their bodies to work efficiently and quickly from a sexual perspective, getting their timing ready for the fast lane. They rarely learn about female arousal and the importance of touching, and they often assume the ladies are just as *Jenny-on-the-spot* as they feel *Johnny-on-the-spot* with touch turning to sex. This learning is usually just the opposite of what would have been helpful in the touch training for the not-so-prone-to-be-quick females.

They rarely learn about female arousal and the importance of touching, and they often assume the ladies are just as *Jenny-on-the-spot* as they feel *Johnny-on-the-spot* with touch turning to sex.

The touch/arousal paradigm is very different for females, and when the *Super Size Me* society influences them, they expect the promised bells and whistles, but also they expect/hope for a little pacing from their male partners. Sadly, with all the fear about touching and arousal, that isn't likely to materialize from the male section of the touching continuum. While little boys are hanging out their penises in the locker room and learning about what to do with Viagra-induced four-hour erections, little girls may be learning to touch, cuddle, and coo, but nothing, usually absolutely nothing, about clitoral erection or vaginal lubrication. So if women rarely learn about their own arousal and are looking for tenderness and, at least, timing help from their male partners to get their equipment fired up through romance and tenderness, males tend to be in a hurry because they have learned that touch equals arousal and arousal needs action—and fast action. The two genders come together with different expectations about touch and timing. No wonder there is the sad (but popular) joke that, to some men, foreplay means, "Brace yourself Ethyl."

TIMING TRAGEDY

Many marriages eventually fail because touch was never taught and because sexual expectations were way off the charts before the Sex Fairy was scheduled to arrive. Before the wedding, couples traditionally do the dance of courtship that tends to lean toward the female side of touching needs. This involves romance and usually slowing down the timing of touching and arousal. Men usually know in courtship that they are expected to hold hands, talk tenderly, touch a lot, and for sure, go slow. Even though those codes of touching and timing may not have been in the lesson plans for their touch education so long ago; in courtship, males usually *walk the walk* and *talk the talk* of touching and they slow down the timing which is very, very important to the ladies.

Then things change and settle down, the wedding present toasters are counted and marriage moves into normal mode. With this calming, males tend to move back to the handshake mode of touching, worrying that if something gets fired up, he will need to act on it, right there in the Sears' toy department. He pulls away from the romantic touching, not because he doesn't love his partner, but because he isn't familiar with those touching protocols that do not result in action. Contrarily, women want the tender touching they received in courtship and they crave it somewhere between the breakfast bagels and Corn Flakes in order for them to feel frisky at bedtime. This timing of touching at breakfast or a slow sensuous kiss good bye in the morning, usually makes no sense to him since *starting something* (his fear) is silly when the car pool guys are waiting in the driveway. He sees no connection between touching at breakfast and sex after the Tuesday night church buffet, and that is why things end up falling apart when the couple finally falls into bed.

GAGGING GIFTS

The couple really thought it was over and they wanted therapy only as a last-ditch effort for a professional to confirm their marriage was toast. *Yes*, they had been married ten years; *yes,* they thought they loved each other after two years of courtship; *yes,* they cared about their two children; but *no,* they didn't think the marriage was salvageable, especially in the sexual department, which in turn related to other areas of relationship dysfunction—including gift-giving. Sensing the seriousness of the situation, the sex therapist separated the couple and spoke alone with both of them in order to learn the differing points of view regarding the marriage disaster.

She'd finally had it. For her, it was over because he didn't love her. *Yes*, he did at the beginning, she explained, but once the wedding bells quieted, he became complacent. The romance was gone as was his passion for her, even though she tearfully explained how she worked so hard to be attractive. She believed he only cared about his job, his house and his yard.

"All he wants to do is work and there is no romance or love left in him for me. I feel tricked and alone," was her heartbreaking complaint. The question from the therapist about the worst thing he had done recently brought a scathing reply. "For Christmas, he bought me this damn pad. It is this $40.00 styrofoam, vibrating pad for me to stand on when I iron," she wailed. "It was so impersonal. I thought I would just die. It ruined Christmas and we have been fighting ever since. That stupid gift just told me the romance is gone and that he doesn't love me anymore."

The therapist gently asked about what she would have wanted for Christmas, and it was only describing the black negligee she longed for that brought a sparkle to her worn and sad face.

In a private session with hubby, the complaints were different but the frustration was equal.

"She just doesn't seem to care about me anymore. I work hard and that seems to make her mad. I care about her and the family, but she wants to mess everything up, leave the dirty dishes, leave the house a mess, and go up the river for a picnic. It just seems so irresponsible. She has these strange ideas about what we should do if, according to her, we still love each other. I don't want to walk to the store and get an ice cream cone. We have perfectly fine ice cream in the freezer, so what is the point? I don't want to go on a picnic and hold hands. That is why I built the deck so we could eat outside at home."

And when he was asked about the worst, most recent rudeness from his wife, it was also the Christmas gift-giving.

"She gave me this bracelet with something silly engraved on it, which was so ridiculous. She knows I will never wear it and she knew how badly I wanted that screwdriver set. It was one of those really cool sets that are rolled up in the canvas and I showed it to her in the store. She just ignored it to spite me and bought me something she knew I didn't want."

When each of the warring couple was asked about sex, the screwdriver set and styrofoam pad nightmare was replicated, but in different forms. Sex was awful with just as much confusion about who wanted what and why. The subject of how to be touched typified the problems since each had different needs and neither had the skill or inclination to share those sacred thoughts about touching—the forbidden topic. When hubby was asked about why he didn't talk to his wife about how and where he wanted to be sexually

He sees no connection between touching at breakfast and sex after the Tuesday night church buffet, and that is why things end up falling apart when the couple finally falls into bed.

Her reply was complicated, but typical. "If I tell him how and where I want to be touched sexually, *he* will know, that *I* know."

touched, he stammered at first. Words evaded him. Finally, his answer suggested he didn't think men (at least real men) needed to discuss sex. It was just supposed to come to them and come quickly, he suggested. "If I have to talk about the sexual touching, I must not be very good at it," he whined. "Did John Wayne ever have to talk about it?" was his final and pitiful complaint.

When the wife was asked to describe the sexual touching, hesitation was also the nature of her reply. "Why don't you just talk to him and tell him how and where you want to be touched?" was the question from the therapist.

Her reply was complicated, but typical. "If I tell him how and where I want to be touched sexually, *he* will know, that *I* know."

TOUCHING TROUBLES

So here they are—a marriage on the way to ruin, children to be raised without both parents, two pretty nice folks feeling failure. Neither can talk about their touching needs, since he feels a need to be strong and perfect and she is embarrassed that she might really know about her own arousal and know what she wants from him. The expectations are as out of control as are the problems. He was blueprinted early in life to equate touch with acting on arousal and he has no concept of tender, romantic touching still being a need for his wife. She feels unloved without the spontaneity and romance of tender touching she found in courtship, and without that, she can't be sexual. Both really love each other and their family, but neither feels loved with such different lessons in childhood about arousal and touch. Sadly, it all could have been prevented had they been taught different expectations for sex and if they knew how to touch each other.

WANDERING WINDOWS

With the sexual Olympic image and little discussion about canoe-kind-of-sex, the window for touching satisfaction is rather short and unpredictable. The continuum begins with touch being A-okay for little ones, so the babies and the toddlers get the good touch. But then, once they start to walk, the kiddo touching taboo gets fired up and the window of opportunity begins to close. So life starts out with tender touching, then it is gradually withdrawn and by the time kiddos are in puberty, usually very little touching is going on just to make sure nothing is going on in the arousal department.

But then the *A-okay to touch* window frantically reopens around the time the Sex Fairy shows up at the wedding, getting things fired up at least for a short time. However, that window of touching acceptance also seems to have a short life after the wedding window, especially between the genders.

Following the wedding, the sexually-acceptable-for-touch window seems a lot shorter for women if the touchable business is only connected to sexual attractiveness. This is evidenced by advertising and other media representations such as television or magazines. No one thinks too much about a slightly plump, but not-so-slightly bald, male newscaster on television whose wisdom really matters more than his waistline. But that acceptance would be rare for the same-age lady newscaster who has begun to stack up the decades and usually get recycled to the back newsroom once they begin to show signs of aging. Advertisements of women rarely sport an attractive fifty-year-old looking sharp in panty hose, but would maybe show her in a magazine from the waist up, smiling about her creative recipe for cheese balls. The sexual attractiveness (and, therefore, touch acceptable) image is gone very quickly for female units. There is more pressure on women to be sexy looking in order to fit the okay-to-touch category. But sadly, men soon follow this direction and the result becomes this society's *untouchables.*

UNTOUCHABLES

Since the okay-to-be-touched focus is toward sexual attractiveness, then the *touchables* seem to only be those with flat tummies, a full head of hair and a 24th birthday looming in the future. Being touched seems reserved for either the very young—wee ones—or the svelte twenty-four-year-olds. Contrarily, society automatically designates its UNTOUCHABLES—usually by age, especially for women. Even though canoe rides should be available for anyone, at any age, it seems difficult for most Americans to consider Grandma and Grandpa as prone to hanky-panky, although it may seem a little more okay for Grandpa. There are sometimes references or jokes about *dirty old men* with eyes wandering away from Grandma. So males get a little longer window to still be touchable but usually not with same age females—just the younger ones which suggest Grandpa is still doing fine in the frisky department, he just isn't doing fine with Grandma. Since elderly women are not considered so touchable or lovable beyond their baked beans recipe, they have been known to trot themselves off to the beauty parlor *just to be touched,* since usually they fall short in the touch/acceptable continuum.

But there are more untouchables in society who don't fit the just-zapped-by-the-Sex-Fairy image, such as the handicapped. Some folks are uncomfortable with the thought of the mentally retarded being sexual. After all, some argue, how could developmentally delayed folks understand how to work the Polaroid for the clitoris snapshot sharing right before the poached salmon luncheon? Many believe that people with spinal cord injuries or other wheelchair confining problems should have no interest in fantasy logs or nipple knowledge. The elderly or the handicapped don't fit the image of sexual Olympics, so no one touches them and no one can understand why anyone else would touch them. But how would that all change if it was really just as the doctor said—about touch, safety and, of course, canoe rides?

Since the okay-to-be-touched focus is toward sexual attractiveness, then the *touchables* seem to only be those with flat tummies, a full head of hair and a 24th birthday looming in the future.

So in order for children to make sexually respectful decisions, they need to know about arousal and know that arousal means just one thing—that all systems are go but that nothing needs to go anywhere.

DOING DESPERATE

Another result of the touching disaster has to do with the desperateness children feel when arousal happens without any preparation from their parents. When arousal hits, some children believe it must be love, or they have learned from the world that arousal must be acted upon and the result is desperate sexual risk taking. Some children feel guilty about arousal, especially if they have been taught that nothing *should* be happening in the sex department until marriage. Other kiddos worry that they have done something wrong, often connected to fears or taboos about self-stimulation, and they also worry that something might be wrong with their bodies considering these unknown *stirrings.* Without knowledge, arousal can blindside children with disastrous (and often sexually disrespectful) consequences.

SYSTEMS GO NOWHERE

So in order for children to make sexually respectful decisions, they need to know about arousal and know that arousal means just one thing—that all systems are go but that nothing needs to go anywhere. Arousal needs to be simplified, *clinicalized,* and centered on body functions. Kiddos need to learn that arousal does not mean love, it does not mean guilt is in order, nor that anything will be damaged if no sexual action takes place. Arousal just means the body is working, and that arousal control is in order, which is really important for raising sexually respectful children. That understanding of arousal (with its celebration and control) has to be taught—not only by the OAT's and the NAT's sex education programs, but also by parents who wish to raise sexually respectful children.

DESENSITIZING DESPERATE

Especially important in the Tenth Commandment, *Thou Shalt Teach Touching,* is challenging the typical touching decline and commitment to touching children, especially when they get older. The sixteen-year-old quarterback on the football team needs fearless touching at breakfast from both gendered folks in the family. *Yep*, his body might work a little, right there underneath his pancakes, but nothing terrible will happen if his body responds to the quick cuddle. In fact, he needs to be taught that arousal isn't frightening and that it doesn't have to be acted upon. It is such an important lesson in desensitizing son—to feel a little arousal happening next to the syrup but then his body learns nothing needs to happen and he catches the bus just fine. His body will learn to welcome arousal and honor his ability to control it. So for sure, the more boys are touched at breakfast, the more touching that quarterback gets at home, the less desperate he will be in the back seat of the Chevrolet.

For girls, the same desperateness about touching often attacks with confusion about arousal being signs of love. Additionally, daughters are often more prone to higher levels of embarrassment about body functions, especially concerning menstruation and the disgusting emphasis on sex education being connected to baby-making rather than female arousal. Different than males who crack jokes and read books about arousal and masturbation, many females never learn their signs of arousal in vaginal lubrication, clitoral erection, or blood rushing to the genitalia. When arousal feelings happen for girls, the range of emotions and responses are often confusing, guilt inducing, and sometime encourage sexual risk taking. If Mom and Dad want daughter to experience sexual respect so that she can make responsible sexual decisions, they must not only teach her about her signs of arousal, but teach her she doesn't have to act on arousal—just celebrate it. And most importantly, that daughter needs her Dad to touch her and hold her and model sexual respect—demonstrating that men can touch without sexually responding. If Dad wants his pink princess to choose male partners who make responsible sexual decisions, he must role model arousal control as he holds daughter to his chest and kisses her forehead right before her date to the prom.

CANOE KIND OF SEX

If sexual teaching changed from one household to another, if the sexual gymnastic attitude of society's super sex was ignored and if touching was fearlessly taught, then Mom and Dad could see the hopeful end product for their Little Poopers, having to do with canoe kinds of sex—sweet, safe, respectful and for a lifetime. If not, then good folks are often sentenced into a lifetime of longing for touch that they are forbidden to receive.

CUDDLE, CRITTER CATASTROPHE

Even though she loves him, Grandma may not want to cuddle with Grandpa in the hammock after hoeing the jalapeno peppers in the garden. The thought may cross her mind, but she easily cancels the cuddle. Typically, she resists out of fear that the touching she so craves will get Grandpa feeling frisky and wanting to head for the upstairs bedroom, which usually makes her feel less than attractive and embarrassed. She doesn't have a flat tummy, her body sags and bags, and she has lots of unattractive (to her) features that make her feel unlovable and untouchable—at least according to what she sees in the media and the world. And Grandpa is also hesitant to cuddle, since he loves Grandma and hates to expose her to his *failures*. He can never count on things to work out, so sometimes the shame of super sex failure just isn't worth it. So two loving people just avoid touch—feeling lost and unfulfilled.

Sadly, when Brutus and Baxter, the two Pomeranians, come bounding up to the garden patio, both Grandma and Grandpa easily move into tender touch mode. *The boys* are touched just like Grandma and Grandpa wish could

If Dad wants his pink princess to choose male partners who make responsible sexual decisions, he must role model arousal control as he holds daughter to his chest and kisses her forehead right before her date to the prom.

So two loving people just avoid touch—feeling lost and unfulfilled.

happen between the two of them if long ago things would have been different. To the critters, there is petting and patting, direct eye contact, head holding, kissing and caressing, smiling, and words of encouragement, tenderness, acceptance and love. Grandma and Grandpa easily provide the critters with what they crave for themselves. It won't matter if Brutus has a little potbelly or if Baxter has zoo breath. If won't matter if they are perfect purebreds. They are loved and they are touched—and this is safe touching, because it is not likely either Grandma or Grandpa is going to bed down with *the boys* for a sexual romp in the hammock. The touching of the dogs is safe—no performance, no pretend, just very much like a sweet canoe ride that Grandma and Grandma are denied.

BLUE BABY BEGINNING

When Mom and Dad peek into the baby boy bassinette, considering their Little Pooper in the future touching department, do they want a powerful handshake kind of guy who buys a vibrating-ironing-pad-for-old-what's-her-name? Or, would they envision and hope Son to be a sweet Grandpa, a man who had been taught tender touching without fear and *yes,* after hoeing the jalapenos, he could cuddle up with Grandma and kiss, caress, and encourage her just as he does with Brutus and Baxter? When Mom and Dad think of Son, do they want someone sexually powerful with a Ph.D. in sexual props, perhaps with an affair or two on the side of his marriage, resulting in a smelly divorce that sends their grandchildren across the country? Or do they want a man, strong and powerful in whatever he chooses, but also strong enough to know and appreciate the need and the power of touch. Do they want to see their son still kissing, cuddling and holding his partner, long into life, exuding arousal control and sexual respect? If so, they must teach touching—actively teach it, because it won't happen magically from a few wand whirls of a fairy in charge of sex.

PINK PONDERING

And what about girl baby pondering and the issue of touching? Sadly, the *do nothing* approach, allowing the Super Size Me sexual teaching to unfold for Daughter in the touching department will allow Pink Princess to have a deep appreciation for touching, but it is likely to be only in the *giveth* department. The constant flow of sexism will teach her to give touching to her dollies, her doggie and even her Daddy for longer than her blue boy brother. The secret will be what Mom and Dad want for Pink Princess in the touch satisfaction department, which has to do with the *taketh* taboo touching paradigm.

When Mom and Dad peek into the bassinette and decide that canoes are in the future for Daughter, they should first conjure an image of a touch-healthy woman, who has the ability to *taketh* her sexual satisfaction. Don't Mom and Dad want her having a relationship and choosing a partner who understands her needs for touching, and who also understands her sexual arousal and satisfaction needs, not just after the wedding but also after the jalapeno hoeing? Can Mom and Dad conjure an image of their Pink Princess bringing them just as much pride for having a partner who, after the family Easter egg hunt, cuddles on the couch with her at age 42, as they have pride in her pimento-stuffed bell peppers? Don't they want her to be just as fulfilled in her touching as in any other aspect of her life? And if so, they must teach her about touching and about arousal.

Do they want to see their son still kissing, cuddling and holding his partner, long into life, exuding arousal control and sexual respect?

Sex Fairy Clipboard

- Begin with the end. Think about touch all through the lifespan of children and set goals for sexually respectful children, focused on human touch and tenderness. Imagine for children the canoe kind of sex where vulnerability and safety are the cornerstone of good sex throughout a lifetime.

- Recognize the *Super Size Me* sexual image of society and do whatever possible to teach a rejection of that thinking. Using all the other commandments about logic and communication, become hyper-vigilant about taking inventory of society's messages and combating them with the canoe kind of sex lessons.

- Don't decline in touching. Toddlers and teens need lots of touching. Make a commitment that the family will touch—everyone, all the time. Do not succumb to society's teaching that touching is only for the babies. Teach touch—and especially important is to teach older children in families to touch younger children.

- Appreciate the developmental issue of teenagers needing to pull away from the parents and reject needing Mom and Dad. Don't wait for teens to initiate touch—just do it, sometimes in the *stop and go* manner. Showing teenagers touching and affection is a good way to show love without the dreaded talking or lecturing. Just touch them. It is just an investment in their future sexuality.

- Examine past lessons in the phobic-fear-of-touch and then fight those prejudices that suggest males and females must be different in who *giveth* and *taketh* in touching. In teaching children sexual respect, it is important to establish equality in sexual desire, sexual arousal and sexual touch needs for both boys and girls.

- Accept the challenge to include males in the touching teaching since males are usually left out and/or ignored. Dads need to accept that his involvement with all the children will provide critical lessons—not because Mom isn't important, but because the females will already get lots of sanctioning about touch.

Sex Fairy Clipboard

- Accept the importance of male children needing to be touched by men. Remember, nothing bad will happen if Dad excels at touching his son and, in fact, male children who appreciate touch are the most appreciated by females. Dad should be Son's role model for the touching paradigm. Son needs to see Dad totally unafraid of touch and role modeling that touch is good, arousal need not be frightening, and no one has to act on anything except family love.

- Dad must not decline with Daughter, either. Unfortunately for girls, the sexual issue has so much to do with appearance. So she needs to be touched, even after she begins her sexual development. If she is touched when she is little and then that touching stops when she sexually develops, disastrous things can happen.

- Remember to model control. This is especially true when Dads touch daughters. Nothing is better for girls than to have trusted males touch them without sexual thought, action or interest. For her Dad or other male role models to be unafraid of touch is a wonderful message. Her choices for partners will mirror what Dad demonstrates through his tender, unafraid and, most importantly, totally-under-control touching.

- Actively teach children about arousal. It may be uncomfortable, but it will be less uncomfortable than dealing with an unwanted pregnancy, a new venereal disease, or just a child who makes sexually disrespectful decisions because they didn't understand arousal. And these lessons include respect for body functions, which will be a huge contribution to healthy sexuality. The most important lesson to teach is that arousal is normal and natural, and it doesn't have to be acted upon.

- Teach children touching of all kinds of people under all kinds of situations. A great contribution to sexual respect is to teach children the wonderful experience of touching their grandparents, touching their siblings, and touching babies. Learning to touch in nonsexual ways, to lots of different folks, is a great contribution to a lifetime of good touching and good sex.

Sex Fairy Clipboard

- Remember the lesson of touch and teach by behavior. Children who witness their parent's tender touching of each other will make better sexual decisions in their own futures. When Mom and Dad role model respectful touching, they will have a much better chance of raising sexually respectful children. When children live with sexually healthy parents who can engage in respectful touching in the kitchen, they will have the role models to send them down the same path toward safe canoe rides and water rescues.

Dear Edward and Emmilou,

Thirteen chapters ago, your wedding signified the *Myth and the Madness* of how parents do everything for their children, especially for weddings and yet, often do nothing to help them navigate their sexual journey that will last a lifetime. We giggled about the fancy wedding plans and all the fussing about the sexual showdown that everyone knew would happen in the honeymoon hotel room, but that no one really wanted to talk about. The madness had to do with good parents like yours, loving you dearly, but in spite of knowing the high price and expensive currency of sex, they just turned everything sexual over to a befuddled Sex Fairy—me!

But now, Edward and Emmilou, it is time to really give you some gifts—not toasters from the wedding reception and not a wand whirl from a fairy in charge of sex. It is time to give you the gift of goals for your sexual future—to guide you on a journey with navigation tools of canoes and sexual life jackets for each other.

Please remember that no matter how fancy or expensive the wedding was, no matter how much money you will make or how many important things you will accomplish in life, you are just two ordinary people who, if everything works out, will be sharing a sexual bed forever. Neither of you are now, or will ever be perfect, like the fancy people on television or the beautiful, flat-tummied folks in movies and magazines. You will be challenged everyday with this society's *Super Size Me* sexual message, screaming to you to be perfect and suggesting if you aren't like all the beautiful people, you should be disappointed and feel like a B+. So you must be aware of society's sinister sexual message and fight it. Remember, good sex has nothing to do with beautiful bodies, perfect waistlines, and perfect knowledge of super sex toys. It has to do with the combination of ***vulnerability and safety***—not just in the honeymoon hotel, but in your sexual lifetime together.

As you are influenced by the sexual hype of the world, give yourself a gift of remembering reality. Honor the gymnastic hyper-sex messages all around you and consider those snippets the vulnerability part of sex. Then remember, that in all the sexual screaming for perfection, you have each other for sexual safety. Treasure the fact that together, cuddling in each other's armpits, you are both safe, and together, you will remember to never let each other drown in the sea of sexual vulnerability. Cherish each other's acceptance of your imperfections, and then you can cuddle into the rest of your lives with life jackets of safety.

Trust each other and work hard at giving the gift of touch. Each night when you climb into bed, treasure touching whether you are sexual or not. Force yourselves to think about the entire world's population, and in that vastness, remember each of you has one person who absolutely adores you now, and forever. Remember the two of you share the most intimate and vulnerable experience known to humans—sexuality, in all it's imperfection.

Remember you will both change, age, wrinkle and stoop. But concentrate now, when you are young and beautiful, on how that safety and sweetness will be the same when you are old and tired from hoeing the Jalapenos. Honor your commitment in youth and dream about having that same sweet safety of touching when you are 40, 50, 60, and on and on.

As you putter through all of life's challenges, never leave each other or greet each other without touching. Fight the idea that touching normally fades away without difficulties. Cuddle carefully when you are together, make a commitment to hold hands whenever possible, and always end each day with holding each other. Never be too busy, too tired, or too important to touch. Put nothing else on the priority clipboard than concentration on your safe canoe ride with each other, forever.

Love,

The Sex Fairy

SEX FAIRY CITATIONS

Ahlmeyer, S, Heil, P., McKee, B, & English, K., *The Impact of Polygraphy on Admissions of Victims and Offenses in Adult Sexual Offenders,* Sexual Abuse: A Journal of Research and Treatment Vol. 12, No. 2, (April 2000)

Aynesworth, Hugh & Michaud, Stephen G. *The Only Living Witness* New York, New York: Linden Press/ Simon & Schuster, 1983

Berry, Jason *Lead Us Not Into Temptation* New York, New York, Doubleday Dell Publishing, 1994

Burnside, Scott, & Cairns, Alan *Deadly Innocence* New York, New York: Warner Books, Inc., 1995

Cunningham, Carolyn & MacFarlane, Kee *When Children Abuse* Safer Brandon, VT, Safer Society Press 1996

Dahmer, Lionel *A Father's Story* New York, New York: Avon Books, 1994

Davis, Phyllis K., *The Power of Touch* Carson, California, Hay House Inc., 1991

Ehrensaft, Diane *Spoiling Childhood* New York, New York: The Guilford Press, 1997

Emberley, Michael & Harris, Robbie, H. *It's Perfectly Normal* Cambridge, Massachusetts: Candlewick Press, 1994

Ewing, Charles Patrick *Kids Who Kill* New York, New York: Avon Books, 1990

Fernandez, Yolanda *In Their Shoes.* Oklahoma City, Oklahoma: Wood'N' Barnes Publishing & Distribution, 2002

Hindman, Jan & Peters, James *Polygraph Testing Leads to Better Polygraph Testing Leads to Better Understanding Adult and Juvenile Sex Offenders*
Federal Probation Journal, December, 2001

Hindman, Jan & Peters, James *Research Dispute Assumptions About Child Molesters* National District Attorneys Association Bulletin Volume 7, No. 4, July-August, 1988

Hindman, Jan *A Very Touching Book* Ontario, Oregon: AlexAndria Associates, 1983

Hindman, Jan *Just Before Dawn* Ontario, Oregon: AlexAndria Associates, 1989

Hislop, Julia *Female Sex Offenders* Ravensdale, Washington: Issues Press, 2001

Hunter, Mic *Abused Boys* Toronto, Ontario Canada: Ballantine Books, 1990

Karr-More, Robin & Wiley, Meredith S. *Ghosts From The Nursery* New York, New York: Atlantic Monthly Press, 1997

King, Gary *Angels of Death* New York, New York: St. Martin's Press, 2003

King, Gary *Driven to Kill* New York, New York: Windsor Publishing Corp., 1993

Kirwin, Barbara R., *The Mad, The Bad, and The Innocent*, New York, New York: Harper Paperbacks, 1997

Lew, Michael *Victims No Longer—Men Recovering From Incest and Other Sexual Child Abuse* New York, New York, Nevraumont Publishing, 1988

Lockwood, Randall and Ascione, Frank R., *Cruelty to Animals and Interpersonal Violence*: West Layfayette, Indiana: Purdue University Press, 1998

Masson, Jeffrey Moussaieff *When Elephants Weep* New York, New York: Bantam Doubleday Dell Publishing, 1995

McGuire, Christine & Norton, Carla *Perfect Victim* New York, New York: Dell Publishing, 1988

Molesters, National District Attorneys Association Bulletin: Volume 7, No. 4, July-August, 1988

Morrison, Blake *As If—A Crime, A Trial, A Question of Childhood* New York, New York: Picador/St. Martin's Press, 1997

Norris, Joel *Jeffrey Dahmer* New York, New York: Windsor Publishing Corp. 1992

Olsen, Jack *"I" The Creation of A Serial Killer* New York, New York: St. Martin's Press, 2002

Olsen, Jack *"Son" A Psychopath and His Victims* New York, New York: Antheneum Publishing, 1983

Pron, Nick *Lethal Marriage.* New York, New York: Ballantine Books, 1995

Rule, Ann *The Stranger Beside Me* New York, New York: W.W. Norton & Company, Inc. 1980

Salter, Anna *Predators—Pedophiles, Rapists, and Other Sex Offenders* New York, New York: Basic Books/Perseus Books, 2003

Samenow, Stanton, E. *Inside the Criminal Mind,* New York, New York: Random House, Inc., 1984

Schechter, Harold *Fiend –The Shocking True Story of America's Youngest Serial Killer* New York, New York: Simon & Schuster, Inc., 2000

Schutze, Jim *Bully—A True Story of High School Revenge* New York, New York: Avon Books, 1997

Scott, Robert *Rope Burns* New York, New York: Pinnacle Books, 2001

Simon, Robert *Bad Men Do What Good Men Dream* Washington, DC: American Psychiatric Press, Inc., 1996

Smith, Carlton *Hunting Evil* New York, New York: St. Martin's Press, 2000

Smith, David James *Fatal Innocence* New York, New York: St. Martin's Press, 1994

Spiering, Frank *Who Killed Polly?* Monterey, California: Monterey Press, 1995

Taubman, Bryna *The Preppy Murder Trial.* New York, New York: St. Martin's Press, 1988

Understanding of Adult & Juvenile Sex Offenders Federal Probation Journal, December, 2001

van Dam, Carla *Identifying Child Molesters* New York, New York: The Haworth Maltreatment and Trauma Press, 2001

Williams, Stephen *Invisible Darkness* Toronto, Ontario Canada: Bantum Books, 1996

Zimring, Franklin *An American Travesty—Legal Responses to Adolescent Sexual Offending* Chicago, Illinois: The University of Chicago Press, 2004

NOTES

NOTES

NOTES

NOTES

NOTES

NOTES